THE LEGACY OF
GREECE

THE LEGACY OF
GREECE

A NEW APPRAISAL

EDITED BY

M. I. FINLEY

Oxford   New York

OXFORD UNIVERSITY PRESS

1984

Oxford University Press, Walton Street, Oxford OX2 6DP

London Glasgow New York Toronto
Delhi Bombay Calcutta Madras Karachi
Kuala Lumpur Singapore Hong Kong Tokyo
Nairobi Dar es Salaam Cape Town
Melbourne Auckland

and associates in
Beirut Berlin Ibadan Mexico City Nicosia

Oxford is a trade mark of Oxford University Press

British Library Cataloguing in Publication Data

The legacy of Greece.—(Oxford paperbacks)
1. Civilization, Greek 2. Europe—Civilization—Greek influences
3. Greece—Civilization
I. Finley, M.I.
940 CB203
ISBN 0-19-285136-5

Library of Congress Cataloging in Publication Data

Main entry under title:
The Legacy of Greece. (Oxford paperbacks)
Includes bibliographical references and index.
1. Europe—Civilization—Greek influences—Addresses, essays, lectures.
2. Greece—Civilization—Addresses, essays, lectures.
I. Finley, M. I. (Moses I.), 1912—
CB203.L38 1984 940 83-13465
ISBN 0-19-285136-5 (pbk.)

Printed in Great Britain by
The Guernsey Press Co. Ltd.
Guernsey, Channel Islands

PREFACE

The Legacy of Greece, edited by Sir Richard Livingstone, was published in 1921 and is still deservedly popular. If a new appraisal is now being offered, that is not only, or even primarily, because the information needs to be brought up to date, but because a different approach seems desirable. Sir Richard and his ten distinguished colleagues took 'legacy' in its root-sense, a bequest, and so, after an initial paean by Gilbert Murray to the glory that was Greece, they portrayed ancient Greek culture, field by field, beginning with religion and philosophy and ending with art and architecture. This volume retains that element, on a much reduced scale, and then proceeds, in each chapter, to examine what later ages, down to our own, have made of the inheritance from the Greeks. Schematically, one could say that whereas the original *Legacy* was about Greek culture, this version is about its meaning in the history of European culture.

Each contributor had a free hand in selecting his emphases and in determining the structure of his chapter. Editorial intervention was restricted to fixing tight space limits, to a plea for the avoidance of potted history and of catalogues of names, and to elimination of excessive duplication (though a small amount was unavoidable). There was not the slightest effort to impose a consistent 'line' in any respect, other than the need to consider both aspects of the concept of legacy. Formal consistency has, however, been achieved in the method of citation (thanks to the editorial staff of the Oxford University Press), and in the weight given in the reading-lists to books in English. The latter was determined by the primary needs of readers of the volume, not by any false belief in English superiority in the study of the Greek world or of its legacy.

Seven years have elapsed since this project was begun. The patience of those contributors who met deadlines has been exemplary, and I should like to express my particular appreciation to them. One of the most prompt, Professor Marrou, died before the book went to press, and his loss is one that we all mourn.

M. I. F.

Darwin College, Cambridge
June 1979

CONTENTS

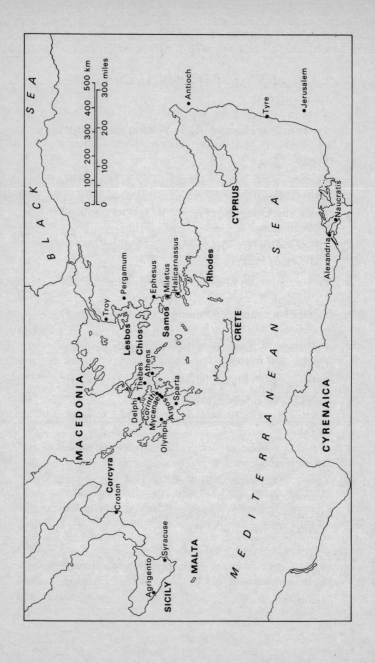

1

INTRODUCTION

M. I. FINLEY

1.

What is Greece? or Greek? Or, in the terms the Greeks themselves have always employed, what is Hellas, Hellene? Today Hellas is the name of a country, like France or Italy. In antiquity, there was nothing comparable, either geographically or politically. 'There is our Hellenism', Herodotus (8.144) has an Athenian say near the end of the Persian wars, 'our being of the same stock and the same speech, our common shrines of the gods and rituals, our similar customs.' Not only is the absence of any political content noticeable, but also the circumstance which elicited the remark, namely, a rumour that Athens might be about to turn traitor in the struggle against the Persian invader. Their common Hellenism never prevented Greeks from fighting or enslaving other Greeks, and from employing foreign mercenaries in the attempt. Nevertheless, considerable reality and ideological power lay behind the abstraction, Hellas, comparable to that of Christendom in the Middle Ages.

When Herodotus was writing, Greek communities were scattered from Phasis at the eastern end of the Black Sea all the way to Marseilles. The Greek peninsula itself was solidly Greek, as were the islands in the seas around it. The western coast of Asia Minor (modern Turkey), much of the coast of Sicily, the southern tip of Italy from Naples down were heavily Greek, though they also contained substantial non-Greek populations. Elsewhere Greek communities tended to be more or less non-contiguous tiny dots in an alien world of Scythians, Thracians, Libyans, Celts, and dozens of others. This geographical pattern was the product of continual bursts of migration, normally in small groups, that began as far back as 1000 B.C. Later, another and rather different wave of dispersions, following the conquests of Alexander the Great, introduced Greek ruling élites and a Greek life-style into hitherto largely untouched areas: central Asia Minor, Syria,

Egypt, and more sporadically, Mesopotamia and even Iran and Afghanistan.

The great creative period, at least with respect to those elements of Greek civilization which made up the bulk of the legacy, had come to an end in Alexander's day. There were later exceptions—they will become apparent in the individual chapters of this volume—but the 400 or so years between Homer and Aristotle produced nearly all the key ideas, literature, and art-forms that were transmitted to later ages and cultures. One need only enumerate the still commonly known names of the men (and one woman: Sappho) in poetry, historiography, or philosophy. The Hellenistic list, apart from scientists, is remarkably short—Polybius, Theocritus, Callimachus, Zeno, Epicurus, Plutarch—and most of them lived in the first century after Alexander.[1] 'An observer in the third century B.C.', wrote E. R. Dodds, would have been painfully surprised 'to learn that Greek civilisation was entering . . . on a period of slow intellectual decline which was to last, with some deceptive rallies and some brilliant individual rear-guard actions, down to the capture of Byzantium by the Turks; that in all the sixteen centuries of existence still awaiting it the Hellenic world would produce no poet as good as Theocritus . . . no mathematician as good as Archimedes, and that the one great name in philosophy [Plotinus] would represent a point of view believed to be extinct—transcendental Platonism.'[2]

It follows that, throughout this book, consideration of the legacy that was transmitted, and of its creators, is virtually monopolized by the archaic and classical Greeks. And the first thing that has to be said about them is that, for our purposes, place, region, is largely a matter of indifference. One need only plot on a map the main figures discussed in this book to see the point dramatically. Of course there were variations:

[1] The division of Greek history into periods is not in a happy state, partly because there are divergent practices, partly because the basis (or at least the terminology) is inconsistent. We shall employ the simplest: archaic to *c.* 500 B.C., classical to Alexander, Hellenistic and then Graeco-Roman thereafter. The Mycenaean age does not enter into consideration: the Greeks were unaware of its existence and had the vaguest notions of a pre-Greek population in what was later Greece, together with a conception of a properly Greek 'heroic age' in the past; anyway, there was no direct Mycenaean legacy. The Roman conquest of the Hellenistic world, for all its political significance, left no Latin imprint on that civilization.

[2] *The Greeks and the Irrational* (Berkeley and Los Angeles, 1951), p. 244.

one thinks of painted pottery, for example, of the property rights of women, or, above all, of political organization. Nevertheless, in any given decade, or half-century, a Greek would have found himself in a familiar physical world more or less anywhere, from Olbia on the northern shore of the Black Sea to Thessaly, Cyrenaica, and Marseilles.[3] To begin with, nearly all cities were at or near the sea—'We inhabit a small portion of the earth,' wrote Plato (*Phaedo*, 109B), 'from Phasis to the Pillars of Heracles [Straits of Gibraltar], living around the sea like ants and frogs around a pond'—and they had a common look. Although not every city had an acropolis, and no other city set aside about one third of its central plateau for a complex of over-size temples, as did Selinus in Sicily, these were obviously exceptions. No one could have had the least hesitation in identifying a Greek city as a Greek city, and nothing else. Present-day ruins are not deceptive in this respect. More notable variations occurred over longer periods of time, not according to place. And the cities, not the countryside, were where public affairs were conducted, where most major cult centres were located, where monumental architecture and sculpture were to be found, where education, military training, and cultural activities in all their forms were carried on.

This physical uniformity was a reflection and a consequence of the deeper uniformity of which Herodotus spoke. Language, both spoken and written, remained astonishingly stable for something like a thousand years, in contrast, for example, to English between Chaucer and Dryden (a mere three hundred years). There were changes, to be sure, and there were different dialects, involving pronunciation, orthography, morphology, and vocabulary; in the case of poetry, rather complicated mixtures. By and large, however, any Greek was intelligible to any other. Differences according to education, or to the town/country division, were as great as differences according to region. The occasional mockery of 'funny' dialects in Attic comedy reveals this point, as it shows that there was never a real problem of comprehension. Then, early in the Hellenistic age, a common dialect (called *koine*,

[3] The peculiar problem of Spartan exceptionalism need not concern us, though it is perhaps worth noting that there is little of it in Herodotus or Thucydides, for example, before the onset of the 'Spartan mirage' with Xenophon in the early fourth century B.C.

the feminine form of the adjective meaning 'common'),
perhaps most familiar to us as the Greek of the New
Testament, became universal, except in poetry and among
odd individuals, such as Archimedes who persisted in writing
his scientific treatises in the Doric dialect of his native
Syracuse. The alphabet tells the same story. It was appropriated by the Greeks from the Phoenicians early in the
eighth century B.C., with some essential modifications, and,
after a relatively brief period of experimentation, it became
stable and essentially unchanging. Expert epigraphists can
date inscriptions to within a few years by the letter-styles, but
anyone who knows a little Greek can read off the text of a
well-preserved stone without difficulty. Here, too, educational
differences reveal themselves, notably in 'home-carved'
tombstones, but only in mistakes in spelling or grammar and
in the obviously unprofessional carving.

Next on Herodotus' list came common shrines and rituals.
The choice of words is significant: Herodotus did not say
'beliefs' or 'creed' or 'theology', and, though books have been
written about Plato's theology (by way of example), none has,
or can be, written about (pre-Christian) Greek theology.
Greek piety, Greek religion, the subjects of countless books
and articles, appear to be a matter of rituals, festivals,
processions, games, oracles, sacrifices—actions, in sum—and
of stories, myths, about concrete instances in the working of
the deities, not of abstract dogmas. Not even the oracle of
Apollo at Delphi gave religious instructions or laid down
doctrinal tenets. Of course every Greek had certain 'religious'
notions, notably the firm conviction that the gods interfered
in the daily affairs of men, and that in large part they did so in
response to the ways in which men behaved towards them.
Hence that behaviour, expressed in a bewildering variety of
actions, was at the centre of religion. What was lacking,
except among rare individual thinkers without public influence, such as Plato and Epicurus, was a systematically
formulated set of doctrines, a dogma or creed. Hence, too,
there could be blasphemy or sacrilege—misbehaviour towards
the gods that would bring down their wrath if not punished—
but neither orthodoxy nor heresy.

All this was inherent in a polytheism that grew by accretion
and spread over many centuries, with its innumerable supernatural beings (or powers), gods, demigods, spirits, demons,

'heroes', with separate and often overlapping, even conflicting, functions and roles. No one could have named them all,
let alone describe them: there are more than 350 names in
Hesiod's *Theogony*, some three times that number in a modern
handbook of pre-Hellenistic religion (the first volume of
Nilsson's *Geschichte der griechischen Religion*). Nor could any
individual, or even community, pay homage to them all. Each
community had its patron deity or deities, about whom the
main civic cult was centred; every household acknowledged
Hestia, goddess of the hearth; nearly everyone heeded the
oracles, a branch of divine intervention in which Apollo was
pre-eminent but not alone; proper arrangements existed for
the cult of Demeter, goddess of fertility; seamen took care to
appease Poseidon; hot springs and other mysterious places had
shrines of their attendant spirits; and individual Greeks were
free to join and organize local, private cult-associations, of
which there were tens of thousands, or to develop personal
relations with individual spirits, even to claim special powers
of divination and prophecy. At one level, the result was
massive untidiness; yet there was an overarching uniformity—
in the conception and account of the Olympic pantheon; of
the 'chthonic' (underworld) deities, most notably Demeter; of
the character and behaviour of the supernatural powers; and
in the nature of the rituals—so that, details apart, Herodotus
was correct to speak of 'our common shrines of the gods and
rituals'. In this field, too, a Greek would have found himself
on familiar ground everywhere.

Much of the cult activity was conducted outdoors and was
organized directly by the state. In our eyes the temple is the
evident symbol, and it is hard to think of a parallel in other
cultures to the monotonous sameness of the column-framed
temple, century after century from one end of the Greek
world to the other, even allowing for the differences between
the Doric and Ionic orders. Certainly the communities themselves lavished their greatest effort and resources on their
stone temples. However, the temple was rather the god's
habitation, not a house of worship. In the locked interiors
were to be found the god's statue and treasures, not altars,
prayer-stools, or 'shrines' in the sense familiar in medieval or
modern churches. Religious activity as such went on outside,
necessarily so because the chief activities in which the people
participated were sacrifices and processions. The altar, not the

temple, was the most ubiquitous construction for the practice of religion. Altars were everywhere, and sacrifices were a regular feature of every serious action, private as well as public.[4]

None of this uniformity was linked with a central authority. In the sphere of religion there was, strictly speaking, no 'church'. That is to say, there was no body of men with a divine mission or sanction, as there was no revelation (oracles and other divine messages merely gave instructions about specific situations, as often as not secular ones). The Greek word *hiereus* that we translate 'priest' normally referred either to an official, a layman, whose duties happened to be the management of public cult, or, as in the cult of Demeter at Eleusis in Attica, to a member of the family or families who by ancient tradition had charge of a local shrine. Thus, in Athens the highest cult official was one of the annual archons, given, interestingly enough, the generally obsolete title of *basileus* ('king'). There were rules of behaviour imposed on him during his tenure of office, a short one (commonly one year), and anyone who interfered with him in the performance of his duties was liable to a charge of sacrilege, but he was in no sense sanctified, as our words 'priest' and 'holy orders' normally imply.[5] There were also local experts, whose knowledge of sacred rules and rituals was widely acknowledged, even officially by the state. But there was no one who could *impose* either beliefs or practices outside the particular community in which he lived and functioned; the Panhellenic centres (about which more will be said later) did not even try to do so.

Politically the absence of a central Greek authority was total. Territorial states emerged in the Hellenistic period, chiefly in the conquered east rather than in the old Greek centres. Before then, the Greek world was one of fiercely autonomous small communities, which they themselves called generically, if loosely, *poleis* (conventionally and rather misleadingly translated 'city-states'). The occasional 'league', such as the Peloponnesian, Arcadian, or Boeotian, and the more tightly controlled Athenian empire of the fifth century B.C., in one way or another reduced that autonomy, in the

---

[4] It will be evident that there could have been no 'legacy' of Greek religion as it was practised. Hence in this volume there are chapters on myth and on the influence of Greek philosophy on Christianity, but there is none on Greek religion.

[5] There were rare exceptions, which need not detain us.

freedom to make war, for example, but never to the extent of imposing cultural modes or ideas. In no way can they be credited with the kind of uniformity we have been considering.

Indeed, it has been argued that the absence of any central authority contributed to the preservation of the many common ways of behaving and thinking, precisely because there was no antinomy, empire/subject, orthodoxy/heresy, to stir up resistance and reaction. The term 'colony' customarily applied by modern historians to the new Greek settlements in the western Mediterranean and in the north-east is singularly unfortunate. With a handful of insignificant exceptions, they were in intention and in practice independent *poleis*, with ties to their respective 'mother-cities' that were psychological and sentimental, not political or economic. Those ties were strengthened, and extended to the Greek 'motherland' more widely, because so many of the dispersed communities were located within non-Greek lands and were therefore stimulated to preserve their Greek identity, in their town-planning and architecture, their language and literature, their religion. Modern art historians may speak of the 'provincialism' of, say, the pottery of the western Greeks, but that overtone was notably absent among the 'provincial Greeks' themselves in so far as we can judge from the surviving evidence. The rapidity of diffusion of new cultural practices and ideas among the far-flung Greek communities was in consequence a feature of the archaic and classical periods: the alphabet, the passion for finely engraved silver coins, the Doric temple are perhaps the clearest cases.

Diffusion was fostered by the considerable amount of steady traffic throughout the Greek world. Concentration of settlement around the Mediterranean, Aegean, and Black seas, which constituted the main highway, facilitated travel and trade. Ordinary people, migrants, merchants, travelling artisans, casual visitors were the main instruments of cultural transmission. Neither special Panhellenic occasions nor professional teachers and philosophers were necessary, though both made their contribution. The former not only brought into immediate contact relatively large numbers of men from dozens, sometimes a hundred or more, of Greek communities, on a regional scale in the more modest festivals, on a genuinely Panhellenic scale in the major ones—possibly forty to fifty thousand came to the Olympic Games, a figure larger than the total populations of all but ten or twelve city-states—but they also offered a platform (or a display-case) for poets, musicians, orators, architects, and sculptors. At the level of technical science and philosophy, the ordinary layman was of course not the bearer of new ideas. But at that level there was also a rather remarkable mobility, in part the consequence of the chronic political instability and conflict within the in-dividual *poleis*, leading to frequent exile. One thinks of Pythagoras, compelled to leave Samos and settle in Croton (in southern Italy), or of Herodotus, driven from Halicarnassus to Samos, whence he later moved to Athens and ultimately to Thurii (also in southern Italy). These two examples under-score the important point that such men were not comparable to modern refugees because they moved from one Greek community to another. Exile apart, poets, playwrights, medical men and artists, or the professional teachers known as Sophists travelled freely and widely for financial reasons. They were thus both beneficiaries of, and contributors to, the preservation of a common Hellenism.

What, finally, of Herodotus' inclusion of 'our being of the same stock' in his list of elements making up 'our Hellenism'? This is a difficult question for more than one reason. There is no problem about the biological facts: the ancient Greeks were a thoroughly mixed stock. To begin with, there were the many centuries of prehistoric intermixture, starting long before the Mycenaean period. Then, the Greeks who were the historic amalgam began fairly soon after the fall of Mycenae to migrate in small groups normally restricted to males, who married native women in their new homelands, Thracians, Carians (Herodotus himself was the scion of such ancestry), 'Libyans', Sicels, Campanians, and so on. But all this is irrelevant; what matters socially and therefore historically in the field of 'race' is not science but beliefs. From the tangled Greek mythology, ancient scholars eventually sorted out a genealogy: Deucalion, son of Prometheus, had a son called Hellen, founder of the Hellenic race, and his sons, Dorus, Xuthus (father of Ion), and Aeolus, were the ancestors of the Dorians, Ionians, and Aeolians, respectively. It is futile to ask how literally that was believed. There is no way of knowing, but there is massive evidence of widespread belief, at all levels of society, in a fundamental qualitative gulf between Greeks and all other peoples, 'barbarians'. That word, the pejorative overtones of which were always present, was applied to all non-Greeks, regardless of cultural level, regardless of the fact, which presumably no one denied, that Egyptians or Persians were more advanced than Scythians or Sicels. Herodotus went to great lengths to insist that there were important things to be learned, even in moral behaviour, from the Persians; Plato challenged the view (held by Heraclitus, later by Aristotle and probably by Epicurus) that only Greeks possessed the faculty of rational thinking. There were other intellectual disagreements on the subject. The practical consequences were never drawn logically or rigorously, either in the behaviour of Greeks to each other or in Greek–barbarian relations, individually or collectively. Yet 'our Hellenism, our being of the same stock' was surely a generally accepted, if rarely thought out, conviction, held subconsciously rather than consciously most of the time, one which was essential to the uniformity we have been considering.

The question has been bedevilled ever since antiquity by the sons of Hellen. An old classification of the Greek dialects into Ionian, Dorian, and Aeolic—no longer accepted by philologists without sharp modification—was tied at an early date to subdivisions of the Greek 'race', a confusion of categories familiar enough in our own age. Hence that section of the Asia Minor coast which was settled by Ionic-speaking migrants came to be known as Ionia; the two earliest architectural orders, in turn, were labelled Doric and Ionic; and so on. Inevitably value-judgements based on the confusion set in. A long catalogue of examples can be assembled, but perhaps it is enough to note the open dislike of Herodotus, a native of Doric-speaking Halicarnassus, for the Ionians of Asia Minor, despite his own use of the Ionic dialect in his *History*. A great additional stimulus to the confusion came from the 'Spartan mirage', with its factually false generalization from Sparta to 'Dorians' in general. Even the Doric and Ionian orders became expressions of different 'racial spirits', although the best known of Doric temples, the Parthenon, is in Athens, the mother-city of the Ionians in the accepted legend. These absurdities have been held still more virulently in modern times, among those who idolize Spartan virtues against Athenian vices.[6] They are ignored in this book.

[6] See Edouard Will, *Doriens et Ioniens* (Paris, 1956).

2.

Beneath the ramified cultural Hellenism stressed by Herodotus there were, as he and every other Greek writer testified, basic internal cleavages and conflicts. Greek *poleis* can be classified in different ways, according to the criteria selected. One we have already mentioned is environmental, so to speak, as between those *poleis* existing within a larger Greek environment and those created within an alien world. A second is economic: although agriculture remained throughout the activity that involved the majority of the population, an important distinction emerged when genuinely urban centres arose—such as Miletus, Athens, Corinth, or Syracuse—with substantial mercantile and manufacturing sectors, while other regions—Thessaly, for example, or Arcadia, or Elis—remained agricultural and pastoral. The third is political. At the dawn of Greek history, the so-called 'dark age' and the early archaic period, there was a considerable uniformity in the administration of the embryonic *poleis*, by aristocratic families acting more or less in concert according to customary rules and monopolizing all the organs of decision-making, warfare, and judicial procedures. Several centuries of development at very uneven tempos, which we perceive only dimly, led to an elementary distinction between oligarchic and democratic states, first visible about 500 B.C. and then rapidly spreading throughout Hellas.[7]

Yet the Greeks applied the label *polis* to them all, regardless of these distinctions, because, in the accepted ideology, each autonomous city-state, big or small, agrarian or more highly urbanized, oligarchic or democratic, was a *koinonia*, a 'community' in the strong sense of that word. That is reflected in the linguistic usage: in ancient Greek such statements as 'Corinth decided' or 'Athens declared war against Sparta' were *always* formulated as 'the Corinthians decided', 'the Athenians declared war on the Spartans'. Athens, Corinth, Sparta were geographical place-names, not the names of political communities. Because the Athenians held as their territory the whole of the district of Attica, we risk ambiguity by saying 'Athens did this or that', 'Anaxagoras visited Athens', whereas the Greek practice was specific and clear on this score. More important for our purposes, it was psychologically and politically precise.

[7] The place of the tyrants in this history is outside the scope of this brief account.

There are other terminological difficulties with our translations. The modern word 'citizen', for example, has a
primarily political connotation: it defines the man or woman
who has the right to vote and to hold office. In ancient Greece
a citizen could in fact lack political rights, as many did in the
oligarchies, while retaining other vital privileges of citizenship, the right to own land and houses, to intermarry, to
participate in certain public cult activities that were closed to
outsiders. As for non-citizens more or less permanently resident
in a community, what are we to call them? Or, for that
matter, transient Greeks? Modern language, George Grote
pointed out, 'is not well furnished with expressions to describe
Greek political phenomena. We may say that an Athenian
citizen was an *alien* when he arrived as a visitor in Corinth,
but we can hardly say that he was a *foreigner*.'[8] Today it is
doubtful that such a distinction exists between 'alien' and
'foreigner'. By convention we call the alien resident a metic,
borrowing the term from the Athenians (even though its
meaning is not crystal clear for Athens and the extent of its
use elsewhere is largely unknown), and we require at least an
adjective to distinguish a Greek alien from a non-Greek.
There is no good way out of the difficulty. To proliferate
words like 'metic' would lead to an arcane jargon requiring
an extensive glossary. One can do no better than to continue
with state, citizen, community, and to remain alert to the
differences in nuance.

A necessary condition for the strong community sense of
polis was smallness of size, both of territory and of population.
Aristotle expressed the common view, though explained
in terms of his own philosophy, when he wrote (*Politics*,
1326a35-b24):

A *polis* has its proper scale like all things, animals, plants, inanimate
instruments. ... A state composed of too many ... will not be a true
polis because it can hardly have a true constitution. Who can be the
general of a mass so excessively large? And who can be herald,
except Stentor? ... The optimum size of a *polis* occurs when the
numbers are the greatest possible for self-sufficiency, while living
within sight of each other.

The overwhelming number of *poleis* in fact met Aristotle's
norm, or fell below his optimum. All population figures are at

[8] *A History of Greece*, vol. ii (London, 1862), p. 40.

best educated guesses, for the pre-Hellenistic Greek states took
no censuses and kept no central lists, except such obviously
necessary, and partial, ones as the 'catalogue' of hoplites
(heavy-armed infantry). At the outbreak of the
Peloponnesian War in 431, the Athenian population, then at
its peak, was of the order of 250–275,000, including the free
and the slave, men, women, and children. With the possible
exception of Syracuse, which is not properly comparable for
various reasons, no other Greek *polis* approached that total
before the Roman period. Corinth may have reached 90,000,
Thebes, Argos, Corcyra, and Acragas (in Sicily) 40–60,000
each, and the rest tailed off sharply, many to 5,000 and even
fewer. It was therefore more than a metaphor to say that most
Greeks were 'living within sight of each other' in what
modern political scientists have called a 'face-to-face society'.
Two behaviour patterns helped: the preference among the
rural sector of the population to live in villages (or, if their
holdings were near enough, in the city itself) rather than in
single homestead-farms, and the custom of conducting not
only their social life but even public business out of doors. In
the few large *poleis* with more extensive territory, many could
not 'live within sight of each other' on the city-state level, but
the community aspect was saved by the existence of smaller
groupings within the *polis*, the village, for instance, or the
deme in Athens and elsewhere.

Deep-rooted though the community notion was, it never
included or aspired to egalitarianism. At most, some *poleis*—
classical Athens and Sparta, for example, each in very
different ways—introduced devices creating a measure of
equality of opportunity among the citizens in access to
political office and in the exercise of political rights; still more
took emergency steps to protect the weakest sector during a
famine or a siege. But it was universally the case, and
universally accepted as 'natural', that the members of the
community were unequal in resources, skills, and style of life.
In characteristic Greek paralance, the main division was
between *hoi oligoi* and *hoi polloi*, literally 'the few' and 'the
many', otherwise the rich and the poor. In the oligarchic
communities this was a formalized division separating the
citizens with active political rights from those without them,
or with what may be called passive political rights. In the
democratic communities, too, there was a formal line at least

with respect to military service: the cavalrymen and the hoplites were required to equip and arm themselves, and normally a fixed property qualification determined whether a citizen fell in or out of these categories. Roughly speaking, furthermore, though there was no neat one-for-one relationship, 'the many' worked for their livelihood, in the overwhelming majority as independent farmers, craftsmen, and shopkeepers, while 'the few' lived off the labour of others, in most cases as rentiers free from even managerial cares.

With a negligible number of exceptions, a *polis* was an urban centre and its rural hinterland together. In small, essentially agrarian communities, the citizens were numerically predominant, unless, as in Sparta or Thessaly, the rural labour-force consisted of a subject population, helots, *penestae*, or whatever they were called. Elsewhere, as the size of the population and the extent of urbanization increased, the balance changed, so that in the most highly urbanized, richest, and most powerful *poleis*, Athens above all perhaps, the citizens were very much a minority.[9] Below them in the hierarchy were many metics and the still more numerous chattel slaves. The complex differences between the latter and the helot-type of compulsory labour need not concern us. The ubiquity and, for the élites at least, indispensability of one or another form of servile labour were taken for granted, and they were built into every cultural activity, from burlesque scenes in comedy to formal philosophy. In our legacy context, however, slavery had little direct impact, save in the peculiar instance of its deployment as an historical defence when slavery was revived in the New World in modern times.

The prevailing standard of living was low: the flamboyant conspicuous consumption of an Alcibiades highlighted that in its excessive over-expenditure. The Greeks inherited from their Mycenaean predecessors, and from the older civilizations of the Near East, the basic technologies in agriculture, stone, clay, and metal-working. They themselves made few qualitative advances, the most notable exception being perhaps in the construction and operation of ships. That is not

[9] The proportion of citizens is even smaller when only males are included in the calculation. Throughout this brief account of social structure, the status of women is not considered. Politically excluded everywhere, their 'citizenship' or 'noncitizenship' was nevertheless essential in the transmission of status and property to the succeeding generations.

said to underestimate Greek craftsmanship, whether in fine painted pottery or in stone temples or in sculpture; aesthetically satisfying though they may be, they did not increase the productivity of the society. Until the invention of machines that could be powered by energy-sources other than human or animal, what scope was there for technological growth, after all, given the inherited level the Greeks started with? Significantly, they never thought of the windmill; and the water-mill—an invention probably of the first century B.C.— received little application.

One social (and political) consequence was the permanent threat of insufficiencies, above all in food supplies. Aristotle, as we have seen, and other social theorists laid great stress on the virtue of self-sufficiency (*autarkeia*), a norm that was for all practical purposes unattainable, in particular by the larger urban *poleis*. Before the beginning of the classical period, the latter had outgrown the productive possibilities of their hinterlands and were compelled to import foodstuffs year in and year out.[10] Even the Peloponnese, self-sufficient in this respect in peacetime, had to seek grain abroad during major wars. Grain was the staple of the diet. Hence genuine famines were not infrequent, because of crop failures in any given year or disruption of imports, compounded by the limited technical possibilities of food preservation. And no *polis* could treat famine as a matter of indifference. 'The many' would not tolerate that; the idea of community was felt to be compatible with inequality, but not with starvation. Stated differently, 'the many' felt themselves entitled to direct benefits, not merely abstract rights, by virtue of their membership in a community. That entitlement was a privileged one, without any element of broad humanitarianism. Thus, a public distribution of grain in Athens in 445 B.C., the gift of an African prince, led to a purge of the citizen roster following an outcry that some non-citizens were sharing in the windfall of free corn by having been falsely inscribed as citizens.[11]

The frequency of civil strife, *stasis*, within the *poleis* is expressly attributed by Aristotle (*Politics*, 1302a32) to the desire for *kerdos*, profit, gain, material advantage, and for

[10] Even the theorists of course acknowledged that self-sufficiency was absolutely impossible for certain necessities, metals above all, but also leather and slaves.

[11] The sources are inconsistent in the details; see A. W. Gomme, *The Population of Athens in the Fifth and Fourth Centuries* B.C. (Oxford, 1933), pp. 16–17.

more *time*, honour. Obviously 'the many' sought the former, 'the few' the two together, and both sides were quick to turn to violence in order to achieve their aims. *Stasis* is a very broad word, ranging over the gamut from 'normal' political methods to open civil war—always within the limited enclave of the citizen-body (who did not hesitate to seek other allies, even slaves, when *stasis* reached its extreme form). The relative freedom of classical Athens and Sparta from civil war, each for its own peculiar reasons, should not blind us to its frequency throughout the rest of Hellas. War was a regular feature of Greek life, not only in the perspective of centuries or half-centuries but every few years in many, perhaps most *poleis*, and, though people were less quick to go to war internally, the barriers proved weak and ineffectual over and over again. The paradox of the strong community sense was that, in a world with a weak and inflexible economy and with substantial inequality, it was precisely the community-notion that led to the kind of demand which at times brought about the breakdown of the community, at least temporarily.

3.

In this society of unequals, the élite who dominated all activities, political, military, athletic, and cultural, constituted a single group. That is not to say that the same individuals played leading roles in several fields, though a few did, but to stress that they all came from the same minority of wealthier families, barring the inevitable exceptions. The acceptance by 'the many' of this perpetual domination by 'the few' is a significant fact in classical Greek history, even in Athens during its most democratic period, from the time of Pericles to the time of Alexander the Great. Whatever the political implications of that fact, the more opaque (and often neglected) cultural implications are no less important, and they are our present concern, not politics. Legacy is essentially a matter of high culture, the impact and manipulation of ideas and values in philosophy and science, social and political theory, literature and art, all of them propounded and developed within the élite circle. The survival of rituals and ceremonies, of rustic dances, costumes, language and vocabulary, is an interesting subject in its own right, when it can be traced, but it is something different from the legacy of high culture.

'High culture' is perhaps an unfortunate phrase, and it can be misleading because of the tendency to project contemporary judgements and values back in time. The opposition between high culture and popular (or mass) culture is rarely a neat and simple one, and it is never identical in different historical eras. A sufficient warning-signal is raised by Greek tragedy, uniformly solemn in theme, tone, and language, difficult even for contemporary audiences to follow very closely. Today it is impossible to think of anything comparable that would draw into the theatre up to 14,000 spectators, for whom only the most primitive facilities were available, and many of whom attended on several successive days. Plutarch reports (*Life of Nicias*, 29.2)—and the story is no less revealing if it is *ben trovato* rather than true—that of the thousands of Athenian soldiers taken prisoner after the defeat at Syracuse in 413 B.C., a few were set free because they could recite some of the choruses of Euripides. 'The Sicilian Greeks', Plutarch explains, 'had a passion for his poetry greater than that of any others. They were constantly learning by heart the little examples and morsels that visitors brought them from time to time.'

Plays were of course available in writing, and by the time of the Sicilian disaster there was something of a book market. The scattered evidence also suggests that a considerable (though unquantifiable) proportion of the free population could read and write, especially in the urban sector. The professional scribe, a feature of all ancient Near Eastern societies and also of the eastern Hellenistic monarchies, was missing from the Greek *poleis*. Athens from about the mid-fifth century adopted the practice of inscribing on stone and publicly displaying a considerable variety and a large number of official texts—treaties, laws and decrees, lists of tribute payments and of men fallen in battle, and so on. A few other cities did likewise, though it is necessary to stress Athenian exceptionalism in this respect.

All this, coupled with the unavoidable fact that our knowledge of Greek culture depends on the written word and the material object, creates an illusion. The reality, as Plutarch's Syracusan tale implies, is that classical Greek culture was essentially an oral one, in which ideas as well as their literary expression were transmitted and debated primarily by word of mouth, publicly and privately. Plato was not being merely eccentric when he expressed distrust of books (*Phaedrus*, 274–8) or when he cast his philosophical treatises in the form of dialogues. His reasons were his own, the logical consequence of his conception of the nature of philosophical inquiry, but he would have met little disagreement among his contemporaries. In his own day, oratory was a fully developed literary genre, the most important form of literary prose, and rhetoric became, under the influence of Isocrates, the centre of higher education. Historians rarely cited documents, preferring eye-witness accounts; Thucydides notoriously failed even to mention documents in his statement (1.21–2) of his research methods. Perhaps more surprisingly (to us), the verbal testimony of witnesses was also preferred in business arrangements and in the law-courts; so simple a piece of paper as the receipt was uncommon until the bureaucratic demands of the Hellenistic monarchies intervened.

In part, there is a simple technical explanation, at least with respect to literature. Then, as at any time before the invention of printing, the number of copies of a work available for circulation was severely limited, each being written out by hand. The likelihood of the permanent disappearance of a work was greatly increased for the same reason: in the library established by the Ptolemies in Alexandria, the greatest in the ancient world, more than a dozen of the plays of Euripides were already missing, less than two centuries after his death. Reading aloud was therefore common, both in small private circles and on public occasions, and no doubt memories were sharpened. It is demonstrable that quotation from memory was frequent among writers, with a corresponding loss of textual accuracy. The literary field apart, the very nature of this society, with its stress on face-to-face relationships, encouraged verbal communication in its varied forms. In politics, the importance of ostracism and exile is then easily intelligible: the physical removal of an individual from the community effectively prevented him from communicating his ideas to his fellow-citizens.

All this presents difficulties of appreciation and comprehension for the modern student. How can one assess the response of 14,000 people to the plays of Aeschylus and Aristophanes, or of perhaps 6,000 to the debates in the Athenian (or any other) assembly? That they varied over a wide range of possible reactions is obvious, but not especially helpful. Nor is insistence on their lack of knowledge, a favourite complaint among Greek writers, as devastating a charge as it may seem at first glance. Living and growing up in this kind of society was itself a form of education. On the surface, at any rate, much of what we should consider élite (high) culture was public and to that extent popular—not science and philosophy, of course, but literature and the visual arts.

'Public' implies both sponsorship, financial support, and organization by the state, and public participation. In the heyday of the annual Great or City Dionysia, celebrated in Athens in the early spring, not only did up to 14,000 spectators sit in the audiences daily and a large, indeterminate number join in the procession, the dancing, and the singing that preceded the five days of performance in the theatre at the foot of the Acropolis, but some 700 men and 500 adolescents, all citizens, took part as performers, 1,000 in the competition among dithyrambic choruses, the others in the tragedies and comedies, as actors and choruses. The same phenomenon was repeated on a smaller scale and with different programmes, especially at first the absence of tragedy, throughout Hellas. With the notable and peculiar exception of the Olympic Games, music, dancing, and poetry were also included, in addition to the athletic competitions, in the great pan-Hellenic Games (a somewhat misleading label for another type of festival). In sum, a large proportion of the Greek population were in one way or another brought into direct contact with major facets of high culture, whatever the degree of appreciation. And it is necessary to add architecture and sculpture, both closely associated with the centres in which the festivals and celebrations took place. The museum and the private art collection belonged to the future, not to this world.

The close association of high culture with religion was obviously central to this behaviour pattern, and it is doubtful whether the modern student can wholly grasp so alien a phenomenon. The mood, the tone, of Greek cult practices ranged very widely, from, let us say, that of Mardi Gras and of still more ecstatic revels at one extreme to that of the austere forms of Protestantism at the other. However, we are in this context not dealing with extremes. The Olympic Games can fairly be called the major pan-Hellenic festival of all, in honour of Olympian Zeus (hence the name of the shrine, Olympia). Yet the centrepiece, against the expected background of sacrifices and prayers, and of some of the finest architecture and sculpture in existence, was a series of physical competitions, not only in foot, horse, and chariot racing but also in the tough *pankration* (a mixture of boxing and wrestling) and in boxing, which the Greeks considered to be even more brutal, with the single objective of victory over all opponents. Nothing could be more false than the cynical view that the religious background was just a pretext for an athletic event, or reference to the modern metaphor, 'the religion of sport'. No less 'peculiar' is the case of the Athenian Great Dionysia, when the god Dionysus was celebrated by theatre, again in competitive terms, that encompassed both the moral high-mindedness of an Antigone and the gross irreverence of the comedies.

The pervasiveness of competition in the cultural activities, including those most closely associated with cult and festivals, is arguably the greatest of the peculiarities. The Greek word is *agon*, and its emotional overtones are pointed to by *agonia*, whence our 'agony'. There were rules, to be sure, and cheating was not permitted, but there was nevertheless a clear divide from the notion of sportsmanship. This is how Pindar congratulated a winner in the boys' wrestling event at Delphi (*Pythian*, 8.81–7):

> And now four times you came down with bodies beneath you
> (You meant them harm),
> To whom the Pythian feast has given
> No glad homecoming like yours.
> They, when they meet their mothers,
> Have no sweet laughter around them moving delight.
> In back streets out of their enemies' way
> They cower; disaster has bitten them.[12]

Pindar was the greatest of the poetic celebrants of athletic victors. His victory odes reveal main facets of the spirit of the *agon* and of its tenacity. Although his career spanned the first half of the fifth century B.C., his values were those of the

[12] Translated C. M. Bowra in Penguin Classics.

archaic age and its aristocratic élite. It may be argued that his
victory odes, unlike his hymns or paeans, are no test because
they were not part of the public side of high culture; they
were commissioned by the rich winners, the men who considered themselves to be the élite, for their private celebrations. That is true, but the spirit of the *agon* was already
fully present, and indeed pervasive, in the Homeric poems,
especially the *Iliad*, and the unique status of Homer, 'the
poet', helped preserve an aristocratic leaven in classical Greek
culture, even in the most democratic communities. Plato
protested (*Republic*, 606E) that there were Greeks who believed that Homer 'educated Hellas and that he deserves to be
taken up as an instructor in the management and culture of
human affairs, and that a man ought to regulate the whole of
his life by following this poet'. This is not to be understood
simple-mindedly, but it can scarcely be denied that the values
on which many Greeks were nurtured through Homer stressed
this element of the *agon*, the desire to surpass all others, not
merely in athletic or dramatic competitions but in the
greatest *agon* of all, in war.

Pindar, finally, was a professional poet even in our sense:
he composed on commission for fees, presumably good fees.
However, the question of payment is a relatively unimportant
side-issue, despite Plato's incessant hammering of the Sophists
for accepting pay, a mark of moral debasement for him.
There is no ancient Greek equivalent for our word 'amateur';
the nearest is *idiotes*, which meant someone untrained, incompetent, ignorant (hence our 'idiot') or, in different contexts,
civilian or private citizen. As against *idiotai*, the creators of
Greek high culture, in every field, were fully professional;
they had the necessary training and they devoted themselves
more or less full-time to poetry or science or philosophy or the
writing of history. And often enough they were financially
remunerated, if not by fees then by gifts, rewards, state
pensions.

4.

It has already been said that most of the culture that formed
the legacy of Greece was created in the archaic and classical
periods. The corollary is that the history of transmission
begins with the world Alexander left at his death, not at some

later date, such as the Roman conquest of Hellas or the end of the Roman Empire (the conventional date for the end of antiquity). The persistence of the Greek language is irrelevant. In the first place, words may change their meanings radically: the office of *strategos*, still common in Roman Greece, bore no more resemblance to the *strategia* of fifth-century B.C. *poleis* than do the baronetcies of twentieth-century England to those of Magna Carta. Second, for a very long time the legacy was transmitted in Latin by and from Latin writers; even after the revival of Greek in the Renaissance, Roman authors remained prominent in the story—one need cite only Ovid and Greek myths.

The diffusion of ideas and institutions—legacy is one form of diffusion, in time rather than in space—is never a mechanical copying merely for the sake of copying. Legacy implies values; it is always selective, that is to say, there is also rejection, non-legacy, and there is unending adaptation, modification, distortion. Much of this volume consists of an account of these transformations and rejections. The institutional and social framework of European civilization changed fundamentally, not once but several times, in the more than two thousand years since the end of classical Hellas. Hence there was no institutional legacy in any meaningful sense, despite occasional futile pleas for turning back the clock, and even more common illegitimate claims of ancient authority for institutions and institutional changes. The French Revolution, it has been noted with pardonable exaggeration, 'draped itself alternately as the Roman Republic and the Roman Empire'. It was of course neither, an excellent example of the ideological use (or abuse) of the past for present purposes. But there was a very substantial, genuine cultural legacy—that is a commonplace—and the complexity of fitting that into a succession of different environments is perhaps the most interesting, and most difficult, aspect of all.

2

POLITICS AND POLITICAL THEORY

I. *Politics*

M. I. FINLEY

In Athens, explained the Sophist Protagoras, 'when the subject of their deliberation involves political wisdom ... they listen to every man, for they think that everyone must share in this virtue; otherwise there could be no *poleis*' (Plato, *Protagoras*, 322E–323A). Euripides made the same point in his *Suppliant Women* (ll. 438–41), produced in the 420s: quoting the words of the herald at a meeting of the Assembly, 'What man has good advice to give the city (*polis*) and wishes to make it known?', Theseus comments, 'This is freedom. He who wishes is illustrious; who is unwilling remains silent. For the city, what is more fair than that?'

The judgements of Protagoras and Euripides were possible only because of a fundamental Greek innovation—politics. Government is another matter: every society of any complexity requires a machinery for laying down rules and administering them, for performing community services, military and civil, and for settling disputes. Every society also requires a sanction for both the rules and the machinery, and a notion of justice. But the Greeks took a radical step, a double one: they located the source of authority in the *polis*, in the community itself, and they decided on policy in open discussion, eventually by voting, by counting heads. That is politics, and fifth-century Greek drama and historiography reveal how far politics had come to dominate Greek culture.

Of course there was discussion about policy in neighbouring and earlier societies, in the court circles of the kings of Egypt, Assyria, and Persia, or, on lower levels, in the courts of the Persian satraps and the circles of the Homeric 'heroes'. Such discussions did not constitute politics, however, for they were neither open nor binding. The king or satrap received advice, but he was not obligated to heed it or even to request it.

Those with access to him planned, manoeuvred, and some-times conspired to direct his decisions, in a procedure that has been called government by antechamber (rather than govern-ment by 'chamber'). The same was true of Greek tyrants, whose existence was therefore a denial of the *polis*-idea, and in whose regimes politics ceased to exist.

It must be acknowledged that there were also some early non-Greek political communities, among the Phoenicians and the Etruscans at any rate. Nevertheless, it remains correct to say that, effectively, the Greeks 'invented' politics. In the western tradition, the history of politics has always started from the Greeks; that is symbolized by the word 'politics' itself, with its root in *polis*. In no Near Eastern society, furthermore, was the culture politicized as it was among the Greeks.

Nor did any previous society secularize government in all its aspects, the ideological as well as the practical, as did the Greeks. Nothing could be further removed from, for example, Hammurabi's code. The lengthy preamble says in its opening paragraph: 'Anum and Illil for the prosperity of the people called me by name Hammurabi, the reverend God-fearing prince, to make justice to appear in the land, to destroy the evil and the wicked that the strong might not oppress the weak.' Solon of Athens, in contrast, was assigned the task of codification by mutual agreement among the contending factions; he claimed neither divine guidance nor revelation nor 'royal blood'.

This insistence on the secular quality of public life appears to overlook the ubiquitous piety of the Greeks. Altars were everywhere; no public actions (and not many serious private ones) were taken without a preliminary sacrifice; the oath was the standard sanction in public agreements; the gods were consulted through oracles and other media; successes were shared with the gods; the management of major religious festivals was the state's responsibility, as was the punishment of impiety and blasphemy. Yet in neither the classical nor the Hellenistic period did this vast amount of ritual activity normally or seriously impinge on, or divert, political deci-sions. A battle might be delayed for a few days, a conviction for impiety might damage an individual's career, but there is no known case when the Delphic oracle, for example, de-termined a state's course of action (as distinct from providing a retrospective explanation of a failure). In the Hellenistic east after Alexander, perhaps even more significantly, kings of Egypt and Syria became gods, stressed their divinity in cult, on their coins, occasionally in their epithets (Epiphanes = God Manifest), but their laws and edicts were invariably issued in the name of men, not gods, and violation was never treated as a sacrilege.

Likewise in the courts: witnesses continued to testify under oath, but the oath had become a ceremony, not a formal proof as it had once been (Homer, *Iliad*, 23.581–5). It was now necessary to persuade the judges and jurymen; the threat that perjury would bring down the wrath of the gods was no longer of itself persuasive. How, then, were justice and injustice to be defined and determined? That is, of course, the problem that runs through both archaic and classical Greek literature, more sharply among the philosphers beginning with the Sophists. But it was equally a problem at the level of practical affairs, not in abstract or general terms but in the day-to-day decisions of assemblies, magistrates, and courts. Since Greek religion as far back as we can trace it lacked the component of revelation—oracles and other forms of communication from the supernatural powers referred to specific actions, not to principles—or even of what may be called the 'quasi-revelation' of a Hammurabi, man had to fall back on himself and his ancestors (tradition or custom) for the answers. At critical moments, the Greeks may have turned to a 'lawgiver' to codify the right answers, but that step was no departure from the rule of human self-reliance.

For such a society to function, not to tear itself apart, a broad consensus was essential, a sense of community and a genuine willingness on the part of its members to live according to certain traditional rules, to accept the decisions of legitimate authorities, to make changes only by open debate and further consensus; in a word, to accept the 'rule of law' so frequently proclaimed by Greek writers. The process thus produced both new rules and their sanction simultaneously, and, as has already been said, that is politics. In a world, furthermore, in which inequalities were sharp even among the members of the community (quite apart from those, such as slaves, who were wholly excluded), and in which communities were small in both territory and population, issues were relatively clear and obvious, and conflict was often acute. The Greek word for political conflict was *stasis*, a very awkward term with a gamut of connotations ranging from day-to-day 'party conflict' (to use an anachronistic modern phrase) to open civil war, which marks the final breakdown of consensus and the abandonment of politics. Civil wars, with their attendant bloodshed, exiles, and property dislocations, were frequent in the classical city-states, with such notable exceptions as Athens and Sparta. They were the subject of much concern among the great surviving political writers—Thucydides, Plato, and Aristotle—and we therefore tend to misjudge the situation. Only in Utopia can there be a society without dissent over important issues; in a political society, 'party conflict' is essential for its continued existence and well-being, and it is as wrong to regard all instances in the Greek *poleis* pejoratively as it would be to denigrate contemporary party politics in the same way.

Understandably, our main sources concentrate on constitutional *stasis*, on conflict between oligarchy and democracy, the chief stimulus to outright civil war. But they also offer enough examples of *stasis* among oligarchic factions to remind us that politics was not restricted to democracies. Oligarchies also accepted the rule of law and also lacked an external authority or sanction; hence they, too, were political societies. The range of participants and the instruments of political activity differed, but not the underlying role of politics.

Today the right to vote is widely believed to be the most essential privilege (and a duty) of a citizen, and that was also the case, within limits, in the Roman Republic. In the Greek *polis*, however, though it was an important right, it was only one of several equally exclusive rights—the right to own real property, the right to contract a legal marriage with another citizen, the right to participate in various major cult activities—and it was available to all citizens only in the democracies, whereas the other rights were universal, normally even under tyrannies. Hence membership in the body of 'active citizens' and membership in the 'community (*koinonia*) of all citizens' were often not coterminous; hence, too, the frequency with which *stasis* for access to political rights erupted into civil war.

The political rights over which they contended included but transcended the right to select officials and legislative bodies. At issue was the direct share, by voice and vote, in the

decision-making process and in the judicial process (understood broadly enough to include evaluation of the performance, and if necessary punishment, of civil and military
officials). The right to vote, in other words, meant above all
the right to vote in a legislative or judicial body, not merely at
an election. That is why classical Greek governments, whether
oligarchic or democratic, are classified as 'direct', in contrast
to 'representative'.[1] When, as in Athens and other democracies, every citizen became a member, barring a few
excluded for specified personal offences, 'rule by the people'
eventually acquired a literal connotation never approached
before or since in western history.

No one, however, not even the most 'radical' democrat,
wished to break the traditional 'community' of male citizens,
a closed body of families whose members succeeded each
other in the orderly progress of the generations. In Greek
usage, the Athenians (never 'Athens') declared war on the
Spartans (not 'Sparta'). If one were not an indigenous
Athenian, only a formal act of the sovereign body could admit
one to the community. Not only were women, children, and
slaves excluded, which is no surprise, but so were freed slaves
(unlike the Roman practice), or free men who migrated from
other Greek states or from the 'barbarian' world, or even their
children, born and raised in the cities that labelled them
aliens. In the classical period, grants of citizenship to outsiders
were rare and were always the consequence of exceptional
actions or circumstances. Aristotle, writing at the end of the
classical era, observed that a more open-handed policy was a
temporary measure in times of severe manpower shortage,
abandoned as soon as the crisis was over (*Politics*, 1278a26–
34). Democracies, it is worth adding, appear to have been
particularly jealous of citizenship.

In political terms, the power possessed by the community

---

[1] There is confusion in some modern works on this point, when they call the
Athenian *boule* (Council), for example, a representative body. No community as
complex as Athens could function without assigning much of the daily work of
government and administration to individuals or small groups. The real question is
one of power. In a representative democracy popular 'control' is restricted to the
selection of officials and legislative bodies, followed by the right to reject at a
subsequent election; in a direct democracy, there is not merely indirect control but
immediate popular sovereignty. The difference will be readily apparent in the
decision to declare war.

was total. That is to say, within the limits imposed by 'rule of law', however that was understood, and by certain taboos in the fields of cult and sexual relations, the sovereign body was unrestrictedly free in its decision-making. There were areas or facets of human behaviour in which it normally did not interfere, but that was only because it chose not to, or did not think to do so. There were no natural rights of the individual to inhibit action by the state, no inalienable rights granted or sanctioned by a higher authority. There was no higher authority.

Ideally, of course, a full share in the decision-making process meant the full right to influence decisions by speaking in the sovereign body as well as by voting, whether in an oligarchy or in a democracy. And, still from the ideal point of view, a full right meant both equality with every other member in this respect and the right to speak freely. Assemblies of Greek citizens were not restricted to democracies: they are already found in the Homeric poems, but there the ordinary people were mere auditors; in Crete and Sparta, according to Aristotle (*Politics*, 1272a10–12), they were limited to voting on proposals put before them by Elders and officials. In the final form of the Athenian democracy, however, and presumably in other Greek democracies, every citizen present had the right in principle to make or amend proposals, to speak for or against the motions presented by others. That was implicit in the herald's call, 'What man has good advice to give to the *polis* and wishes to make it known?'

In practice things were different. The Athenian Assembly normally met in a natural amphitheatre on the hill called the Pnyx, and it is incredible that at such an open-air congregation of thousands of men, unequipped with modern amplification devices, with an often crowded agenda that had to be completed in a single day's sitting, the ordinary citizen would have wished, or dared, to take the floor, or that he would have been listened to if he had. We need not force ourselves to believe the unbelievable: the literary and epigraphical evidence leaves no doubt that the speech-making and the actual formulation of policies and proposals were a monopoly of what we may call a 'small political class', those whom Thucydides had in mind when he complained (8.1.1) that, once the news of the Sicilian disaster had been confirmed, the people 'turned against the public speakers (*rhetores*) who had

favoured the expedition, as though they themselves had not
voted for it'.[2]

Any account of politics in the *polis* therefore requires a
careful balance between the ideal and reality, between
ideology and practice. That this can be attempted only for
Athens, given the state of our evidence, is no great handicap,
as Athens was the quintessentially political *polis*. What follows
thus refers specifically to Athens alone, though it was presumably true of the other democracies in important respects,
but not in all.

The most obvious limit to the realization of the ideal, with
its stress on equality, stemmed from the considerable inequality among the citizen population. It is sufficient to single
out differences in wealth. Without the means and the leisure
to obtain an appropriate education and to keep constantly
abreast of finances, foreign affairs, and the other matters of
public concern, a citizen could hardly be expected to speak
out and be heard during the deliberations. He could even find
it too costly and burdensome to attend the Assembly meetings
regularly, forty days a year spread throughout the year,
especially if he were a peasant living in the more outlying
villages of Attica. This was all so self-evident that steps were
taken, mostly in the middle decades of the fifth century, to
equalize the citizens artificially. Nearly all public offices,
including the 500 members of the Council, were chosen by lot
and were rotated, thus not only opening them to people who
might otherwise have little or no chance of selection but also
ensuring that direct experience in the day-to-day affairs of the
state was spread among an uncommonly large proportion of
the citizen-body. The principle was also introduced that men
serving in the administrative and judicial bodies should be
compensated with a modest daily allowance.

Paradoxically, attendance at Assembly meetings was the
last of the duties to be compensated with a daily allowance, at
the beginning of the fourth century after the overthrow of the
Thirty Tyrants. Just how high the average attendance was
remains a controversial question. Archaeological excavation
has revealed that in the fifth century the Pnyx could not
accommodate more than 6,000 men, that some enlargement

[2] Thucydides' remark also raises pointedly the question of political responsibility,
to which we shall return.

was made early in the fourth century, and that the capacity was perhaps doubled *c*. 330 B.C. It has been plausibly suggested that the introduction of pay for attendance necessitated these changes, and that in the fourth century 6,000 was a normal figure, increased at meetings devoted to major items of public business.[3] Whether more or less regular attendance by 15–20 per cent of the eligible men should be considered high or low is a subjective matter not susceptible to satisfactory resolution. The more objective question, how representative a sample was this 15–20 per cent?, is unanswerable from our evidence, though repeated attempts have been made to guess from odd remarks in the sources. The one undeniable fact is that there were times when either the richer or the poorer sector of the population was unavoidably under-represented for military reasons; the former, for example, in 462 B.C. when Cimon took 4,000 hoplites to help Sparta subdue the helot revolt in Messenia, the latter in 411 when the Athenian fleet was stationed at Samos. It is plausible to believe that the absence of 4,000 hoplites facilitated the democratic advances initiated by Ephialtes; it is certain that the absence of thousands of *thetes* was vital for the oligarchic coup of 411.

It is equally certain that the active politicians appreciated the significance of such fluctuations in attendance, and included them in their tactical calculations. This integral aspect of Athenian politics, the planning, organizing, and manoeuvring that went on day in and day out, is largely missing from the available sources, which lack anything comparable to Cicero's letters. Attention is concentrated on the debates in the Assembly, summarized by Thucydides, caricatured by Aristophanes and Plato, or exemplified in the surviving speeches of Demosthenes and Aeschines. Certainly they mattered, far more than parliamentary debates today. Just as certainly, political leaders were not so foolish as to gamble their policies and their careers solely on their oratorical skill.

The game of politics was a rough one. The speeches of Aeschines and Demosthenes, no matter how much edited prior to publication, are a surer guide to its harsh tone than the austere version of Thucydides (all 'reported' in his own

---

[3] This is a higher figure than appears in most modern accounts; I follow the detailed analysis of the evidence by M. H. Hansen, 'How Many Athenians Attended the Ecclesia?', *Greek, Roman, and Byzantine Studies*, xvii (1976), 115–34.

language). They tell us how politicians spoke in public and what arguments they deployed, but unfortunately little beyond hints about the day-to-day political activity outside the meetings of Assembly and Council or in diplomatic negotiations. The one piece of concrete evidence about canvassing, for example, comes from a batch of chance archaeological finds in the potters' quarter, more than 11,000 ostraca of the fifth century B.C., with names inscribed on them. These were the ceramic voting tokens employed in an ostracism, a procedure by which a political figure was sent into exile for ten years if at least 6,000 votes were cast altogether. In this collection, a few men are named on many ostraca, Themistocles on more than 300, obviously inscribed by a small number of hands. In other words, large numbers of ostraca were prepared in advance and distributed, in an elementary form of canvassing.

Formal machinery was lacking for such activity, of which the distribution of ostraca is only a minor example. In particular there were no political parties, for the simple reason that the indispensable patronage was unavailable. The governmental system did not provide jobs, as there were neither elective posts nor an administrative bureaucracy; the economy offered scant opportunity for public contracts, monopolies, licences, or grants. Instead, politicians had to rely on family connections and on small informal groups or coteries, identified in the language of the time as 'those with (or about) so-and-so', a phrase recurring in both private and political contexts, in oligarchies and in democracies.[4] The terminology reflects the personal and fluid character of the groupings, which were none the less effective, and indeed essential, despite their informality and their transient nature.

The two common Greek words for such a group are *hetaireia* and *synomosia*, sometimes rendered in English by the pale word 'club', which at least has the merit of accenting their social aspect, as does the Greek. For they were not political organizations in essence or origin (except for the conspiratorial groups that sprang up to prepare the oligarchic coup of 411). Often, if not always, they were dining-clubs of men who had done their initial military service together, as 18 and 19

---

[4] A good illustration from Thebes is given by the anonymous historical work known as the *Hellenica Oxyrhynchia*, ch. 12, in a passage in which the author expressly notes the inseparability of policy and personal concerns among the political class.

year olds, and that restricted their membership by definition to the wealthier half of the population, those liable for infantry duty as hoplites, the same social sector which monopolized political leadership and, more or less, professional political activity throughout the history of Athens. The change in leadership which came about during the Peloponnesian War occurred within that limited circle: 'new politicians' such as Cleon, hated and derided by playwrights and philosophers, were as wealthy as the traditional landowning aristocracy with whom they competed for political authority but whom they never wholly displaced. Scarcely a single important politician is known to have come from a background of poverty. Nor were there lower-class 'clubs' of this kind.

Assessment is not easy of this willingness by the mass of the population to leave active politics to a small number of wealthier citizens backed by their upper-class friends and associates. In particular, the temptation should be resisted to fall back on popular political apathy. Then, as now, politics was instrumental for most people, not an interest or an end in itself. On the one hand, political gossip and jokes were enjoyed by everyone, politics was a constant subject of conversation; on the other hand, the hard, more or less full-time work of formulating policies and steering their acceptance through the machinery of government was left to a small number of men, who had not only the knowledge and the leisure but also the confidence of large sections of the citizenry.

One pragmatic test of the system is the extent to which there was continuity of policy over a longer period of time. Consideration of the history of the Athenian empire in the fifth century, again of the second Athenian League and the complicated struggle with Philip of Macedon in the fourth, reveals that the Athenian achievement, on that test, was a notable one. There were disagreements and failures—which society has not had them?—but they were outweighed by a skilful pursuit of major objectives for long periods. Whether modern historians and moralists approve the policies or, following the lead of hostile ancient critics, disapprove, is irrelevant to the question at hand, as is the familiar condemnation of the 'demagogues'. 'As for the Athenian system of government,' wrote an oligarchic pamphleteer of the latter part of the fifth century (Ps.-Xenophon, *Constitution of Athens*, 3.1), 'I do not like it. However, since they decided to become a democracy, it seems to me that they are preserving the democracy well.'

Continuity of policy implies more than able leadership; in the kind of society we are considering, it would have been impossible without widespread political responsibility among the mass of the citizenry. Responsibility, not an easily defined concept, has several elements in this context. One is clearly 'obedience to the law' in the sense not merely of general law-abidance but also of acceptance of all specific decisions taken by the sovereign bodies through lawful procedures, no matter how painful or objectionable they may be personally. Plato's *Crito* argues the position beautifully. A second element of responsibility is manifest in the relationship between the 'active political class', the political leaders, and the rest of the citizenry. Civic responsibility may thus be said to consist of responsible selection of leaders who are in turn accountable for their actions and policies.

The 'orators' against whom the Athenians turned were not officials, not what the Romans called 'magistrates', and it is significant that officials as such play little role in Greek discussions of politics and political responsibility. Cicero was certainly conscious of the contrast when, in the opening pages of the third book of his *Laws* he insisted that *imperium* is essential by nature for justice and orderly existence, whether in the household or in the state. The root sense of *imperium* is 'order', 'command', and, though the Romans spoke of the *imperium populi Romani*, the sovereignty of the Roman people, they normally had in mind the official power of the higher magistrates, and that is what Cicero was extolling: 'it can truly be said that the magistrate is articulate law (*lex loquens*), the law a silent magistrate.' Hence obedience to the magistrates is a necessary condition of a just society. The line between obedience to the law and obedience to a magistrate (or monarch) may appear to be a blurred one, but the gap between the two emphases, the classical Greek and the Roman, is unbridgeable. And the latter, not the former, was to provide the main political legacy for most of subsequent European history.

A severe breakdown of political responsibility could lead to anarchy, but in classical Greece it commonly led to civil war. It has already been noted that Athenian immunity was exceptional, though not unique—Sparta provided another exception for a long period, though for different reasons. Why was that? Specifically, why did the Greek *polis* so often fail to resolve its internal differences by political means? That question must be linked to another. Why did the Greek *poleis* war with each other incessantly? No simple answer is available. In the present context, the suggestion may suffice that Greek *poleis* lacked the resources in men, land, and materials with which to provide for their citizens the 'good life' that was the avowed purpose of the state. They could overcome chronic scarcities only at the expense either of a sector of their own citizenry or of other states. It is useless to speculate on the possible outcome of the endless *stasis* of the fourth century had the Greeks been left to themselves to sort things out, for superior power from outside gave the answer, beginning with Philip of Macedon and his son Alexander.

Alexander died in 323 B.C., Aristotle in the following year. The Hellenistic world which followed was monarchical in government. Some independent *poleis*, such as Rhodes, survived as genuinely political communities until the Roman conquest drew down the curtain. They were the exception, however, and they were under constant pressure from the kings. Although the word *polis* continued in regular use everywhere, the reality became much closer to 'city' in the narrow sense than to *polis* in its classical meaning. Cities grew larger in the Hellenistic period and their number increased, thanks to new foundations in the eastern territories conquered by Alexander: Alexandria and Antioch are major examples. In these cities, there was still the appearance of continuous political activity: public offices were sharply contended for, there were disagreements over policy, and there were factional troubles. But in most cities, those within the territories ruled by monarchs, the *subject-matter* of politics was reduced to a shadow. Foreign and military affairs were taken from them completely, and the kings intervened in purely domestic questions when it suited them. At the end of the fourth century B.C., for example, Antigonus I of Macedon ordered the merger of two Asia Minor cities, Teos and Lebedos, and he laid down in detail not only the conditions but also the legal system.[5]

Not surprisingly, in many cities the highest municipal offices became those connected with cult and games, replacing the archons and *strategoi*, the political and military posts of the classical city-state. Paradoxically, the word 'democracy' acquired a radically new sense, and a halo—among Hellenistic Greeks it meant 'republic', among the Greeks under the Roman emperors it could even be applied, as a term of praise, to the autocratic emperor: 'a common democracy of the earth has been set up, under one man, the best, ruler and director, and all come together, as in a common civic centre, each to receive his due' (Aelius Aristides, *To Rome*, 60).

The Hellenistic monarchs, unlike the earlier Greek tyrants, sought to institutionalize and legitimize their position, but they were not 'constitutional' monarchs. Institutionally they relied on bureaucracies, a new phenomenon in Greek history; for policy-making they relied on the advice of 'friends' and, in the last resort, on their own unrestricted right to make decisions. It was government by ante-chamber. 'Public opinion' no doubt expressed itself, but never through the open discussion of the past, for which the forums were now lacking. Politics had died; there was no legacy of the city-state as a political organism in the Greek world after Alexander.

Nor was there such a legacy in later periods of history. That is to say, the long and complex story of the cultural legacy of Greece was precisely that; it was not accompanied by an institutional legacy. Sparta provides a sufficient illustration: among all the many admirers of Sparta over the centuries, most recently in Nazi Germany, no trace can be seen of the idea of holding up as a model or imitating Spartan institutions, as distinct from Spartan 'values' or 'ethos'. The same is true of Athens, with one minor though interesting exception to which we shall return briefly. Politics as such is a way of public behaviour that can exist within a variety of radically different societies. The notion of 'legacy' is meaningful only with respect to the framework within which politics occurs, not to politics itself. In principle, it is possible to borrow a machinery of government or a system of law, in whole or in part, as occurred widely in Latin America. That nothing remotely comparable was ever tried with Greek institutions, Athenian or Spartan, democratic or oligarchic (though they borrowed freely from each other), is not difficult to understand. Much of the explanation follows immediately from the fact that Greek politics presupposed small, face-to-face communities; all their main institutions derived from that basis, and they were not transferable to larger territorial units. In the latter, some form of representation was unavoidable if there was to be decision-making based on discussion and consent. Representation, in turn, required different mechanisms from the Greek *polis* forms (though the old labels were sometimes retained), and a different relationship between the citizen-body, however defined, and the 'active political class'.

None of this applies to republican Rome, of course, which was a city-state in origin and which maintained the fiction of being a city-state long after it had in fact become a large territorial state. That republican Rome was a thoroughly political society needs no argument; our sole concern is with the presence or absence of a Greek legacy on the institutional side, a different matter from the impact of Greek political philosophy. The relative chronology throws up an immediate warning: Roman interest in Greek writers and theorists cannot be found much before 200 B.C., a century or so after the demise of the classical Greek *polis*, and also well after the Roman institutional system had been fashioned. This does not of itself rule out the possibility of Greek influence on early Rome: men do not have to turn to books to learn from their neighbours. Although we may ignore as obvious fiction the reference to Solon, for example, which the learned Dionysius of Halicarnassus, writing under Augustus, gave to a fifth-century B.C. senator (*Roman Antiquities*, 5.65.1), Greek communities existed in southern Italy when Rome was still no more than a rude village under Etruscan domination. A possible source from which to learn and borrow was therefore at hand. We must judge from the institutions themselves; there is no other guide-line. Parallel developments can be discovered, but were they any more than independent responses to similar problems in small communities living and growing under comparable ecological and technological conditions, with common roots in still more distant, prehistoric times? Thus, when monarchy was overthrown, others had to take charge of the community, and they were, as a matter of course, those with the power, namely, the heads of the aristocratic families who controlled the land, the basic resource. When we turn to the details, and indeed to the

structure, of the governmental machinery, the framework of
political behaviour, the differences are so fundamental that
we must conclude against there being any significant Greek
legacy in Rome in this area. With the establishment of the
Empire by Augustus, all doubts disappear.

Thereafter, down to our own day, there was little scope for
any influence. Only the communes of the later Middle Ages
and the Renaissance, notably in Italy, were small enough in
scale. They, however, came into being in too different a
context, economically and politically, with a different relationship between town and country at all levels, whether
that of the peasantry or that of the feudal nobility, to have
permitted institutional borrowing, even had they known
much about the classical Greek city-state, which in fact they
did not. A further deterrent was the long hostility to democracy, with which classical Athens was integrally linked.
When Wordsworth wrote in a private letter in 1794, 'I am of
that odious class of men called democrats',[6] he was being
defiant, not satirical. One need only read the first modern
histories of Greece, written in that era, by Gillies, Mitford, or
Thirlwall. When Grote replied, so to speak, he reflected the
philosophy of the Utilitarians: they were the exception to
which reference has already been made, and the value they
found in the Athenian political experience was educational in
a rather narrow sense. 'Notwithstanding the defects', wrote
John Stuart Mill, 'of the social system and moral ideas of
antiquity, the practice of the dicastery and the ecclesia raised
the intellectual standard of an average Athenian citizen far
beyond anything of which there is as yet an example in any
other mass of men, ancient or modern.'[7] The shadow of the
Funeral Oration in Thucydides is evident: it is in the field of
political theory, not of institutions, that one must look for a
possible legacy.

[6] Quoted from R. R. Palmer, 'Notes on the Use of the Word "Democracy" 1789–
1799', *Political Science Quarterly*, lxviii (1953), 203–26.
[7] *Considerations on Representative Government* (Everyman Library edn.), p. 216.

II. *Political Theory*

R. I. WINTON and PETER GARNSEY

The Greeks created politics; they also created political theory, and there is an obvious relation between these two elements of their creativity. The *polis* was, ideally, a community of equals, the *politai*, who determined policy in open and organized discussion. Such debate was likely to generate within itself comment and reflection upon the terms on which it occurred: for example, the observations on the character of the Athenian Assembly made by Cleon and Diodotus in the 'Mytilenian Debate' (Thucydides, 3.36–49). Greek political theory may be seen as an abstraction of this inherent reflective tendency: the political theory of the Greeks was, centrally, reflection upon the nature of the *polis*, conducted as a self-conscious intellectual enterprise distinct from, and at a more general level than that of, discussion on specific political issues. Political theory was thus a second-order activity in respect of the *level* at which it handled its material; though to say this is not to suggest that it lacked the element of political commitment characteristic of the first-order activity out of which it developed.

In terms of extant works, Greek political theory is that of Plato and Aristotle. It is clear, however, that political theory in the sense we have suggested had emerged earlier. Given the nature of our evidence, and that of the issue itself, it is impossible to offer any precise date, but if one discounts the dubious evidence for early Pythagorean political theory, the first attempts to analyse the *polis* seem to have been made in the fifth century.

There had been earlier precursors: the verses of Solon are an obvious instance. But Solon was essentially concerned with a particular crisis in an individual *polis*, and his political verse constitutes a contribution to a specific political debate. Analysis of the *polis* conducted outside the context of individual political debates first appears as a distinct mode of intellectual activity during the period between the Persian and Peloponnesian wars. It was in this period that tragedy achieved its acme; reflection on the character of the plays extant from this period may help to define the contemporary emergence of political theory. These plays are themselves centrally concerned with political issues such as the nature of justice and the relation between the individual *polites* and his fellow-*politai*; but it would be absurd to characterize Aeschylus' *Oresteian Trilogy*, for example, as a work of political theory: Aeschylus is not concerned to offer an argued analysis of the concept of justice of the kind presented in Plato's *Republic*. The works of the tragedians can be seen as an intermediate stage between the two levels of political argument we have distinguished: themselves an element of the formal institutional life of the Athenian *polis*, they present their audience (who, in another role, constituted the Athenian Assembly) with the spectacle of men seeking to understand their experience. Their endeavours generate reflection that reaches the most abstract level; but the focus of such reflection remains the particular issues and individuals in each case. There is a clear distinction between the tragedians' mode of engagement with political themes and the more rigorously analytic approach that developed around the middle of the fifth century. The emergence of the latter marks the beginning of Greek political theory as such.

The first genuine theorists of the *polis* were the Sophists and Socrates. Their careers symbolize the new relation that they created to the *polis*: while seeking to understand the *polis* in the abstract, neither the Sophists nor Socrates lived as ordinary *politai*. The Sophists spent much of their lives away from their native cities, travelling throughout Greece as a whole; Socrates remained in Athens, but took as little part in its ordinary political life as he could. This self-distancing from the politics of their individual cities may indeed have been a necessary condition of their analysis of the *polis*.

Any attempt to assess the political thought of these men must begin with an emphatic caveat concerning the evidence. The Sophists were prolific writers, but with the exception of two brief rhetorical exercises by Gorgias, their works survive directly only in fragments, for the most part consisting of a single sentence, sometimes of a single word. To attempt reconstruction of their ideas, one has to turn to secondary evidence, above all that provided by Plato, especially in his earlier dialogues. This evidence is, unfortunately, extremely unstraightforward. Plato attributes various views and arguments to the Sophists, individually and as a class, and the question always needs to be asked whether such attributions are historically accurate, since, other considerations apart, Plato was radically hostile to them. In the case of Socrates, Plato is again our most important source, supplemented by Xenophon and Aristotle. Socrates, who himself wrote nothing, figures in almost all of Plato's dialogues, so that the question of authenticity is far larger than in the case of the Sophists. Again, the matter is complicated by Plato's attitude: hostility towards the Sophists is paralleled by reverence of Socrates.

The Sophists were primarily teachers who offered formal instruction of a wholly new kind. The fact that Protagoras, for example, offered to teach *politike techne*, the art of being a *polites*, itself suggests an analytic attitude to the *polis*; and the relation seems clear between the Sophists' activity as teachers and their attempts to provide a theoretical account of the nature of the *polis*. If they were to attract students willing to pay to study with them, they had to offer something not already available, systematized and articulated expertise in political affairs. Hitherto young men had relied on informal and unconceptualized association with older members of their *polis*, usually relatives or family friends. Sophistic education constituted a twofold innovation: formal, theory-based instruction by someone not a member of his pupil's *polis*. The hostility that the Sophists encountered can be understood as reaction to both departures from tradition.

One fundamental aspect of the Sophists' theorizing was their creation of rhetoric—analysis of the modes of argument to be used in the assembly and law-court—and its location at the core of their education.[8] Beyond that, they were concerned to provide accounts of the concepts embodied in the *polis*, and, in the case of Protagoras at least, an understanding of the *polis* as a whole. Such attempts not surprisingly exposed incoherence or inadequacy in prevailing attitudes, for example in the conversation on the concept of law between Alcibiades and Pericles (Xenophon, *Memorabilia*, 1.2.40 ff.). Not surprisingly, too, the enterprise generated opprobrium: members of communities that operated on the basis of reasoned debate would hardly have welcomed demonstration of illogicality in the conceptual framework within which they

[8] Protagoras' famous statement that 'on every issue there are arguments on both sides' *may* have occurred in a treatise on rhetoric; it can certainly be seen as an articulation of political and legal practice.

acted. Protagoras, for one, appears to have been well aware of this hostile reaction (Plato, *Protagoras*, 316C–D), further compounded by the financial element in the relationship between Sophist and pupil, and, possibly, by the feeling that this relationship was redolent of homosexual prostitution. In Xenophon's *Memorabilia* (1.6.13), Socrates is quoted as saying: 'With us ... the same view is taken as to what is honourable and what is not with regard to the bestowal both of physical beauty and of wisdom. A man who sells his favours for a price to anyone who desires them is called a pimp. ... In just the same way those who sell wisdom at a price to anyone who wants it are called sophists; but if anyone, by imparting any edifying knowledge that he possesses, makes a friend of one whom he knows to be naturally gifted, we consider that he is behaving as a good and honourable citizen should behave.'

None of this implies that reaction to the Sophists was one of straightforward antipathy and outright rejection: they did, in fact, achieve considerable success, and this must mean that what they offered was regarded as worthwhile—as Socrates points out in rebutting Anytus' condemnation of them (Plato, *Meno*, 91C–92A). One has to conclude that Sophists were regarded with radical ambivalence: if they constituted a threatening innovation in their role as teachers, their effectiveness was also recognized and made use of; if their analysis of the concepts in terms of which the *polis* operated revealed intellectual inadequacy among ordinary *politai*, this could also—given the character of the *polis*—be accepted as a stimulating challenge, rather than rejected as subversive, or merely ignored.

Although the precise character, or even the intellectual calibre, of the Sophists' activity as political theorists cannot be determined, one can establish the issue with which it concerned itself. The focus was the *polis* considered as an abstraction from the very large number of individual *poleis* spread throughout the Greek world. These *poleis* manifested an enormous variety in their institutions, within the basic framework that distinguished them as a class from other societies. One might characterize the political theory of the Sophists as an attempt to define and analyse what the many *poleis* of Greece had in common, and to make sense of the remarkable diversity apparent among them.

One of the clearest ways in which *poleis* differed was in respect of which members possessed citizenship in the fullest sense. The emergence of democracy put in question the nature of citizenship, the qualities and abilities demanded, and the way in which these were acquired. When the *demos*, in the narrow sense, began to claim a right to full citizenship, the traditional, élitist ideology of political competence became problematic: assumptions became issues. The issue whether *arete*, the ability required for successful participation in running the *polis*, could be taught, as opposed to its being inherited, and if so, how, and to what extent, was at the heart of fifth-century political argument. In his 'Great Speech' in Plato's *Protagoras* (321C–328D), the Sophist argues that it is reasonable for the Athenians to allow any citizen to contribute to debates on matters of policy, because all citizens have the necessary expertise; that is the result of a process of socialization that begins in earliest childhood and continues throughout the citizen's entire life. Just as all citizens necessarily practise *politike arete*, so all are teachers of it; the Sophist simply does better what the ordinary *polites* is doing all the time. Protagoras thus offers a rationale both of democracy and of sophistic education, and the issues he raised became central to the political theory of both Plato and Aristotle.

Much as the Greek *poleis* differed with regard to the proportion of their *politai* exercising full citizenship, they shared the belief that the defining characteristic of the relationship among those who were full *politai* was that it was based on *nomos*: a code providing equal participation in the *polis* for all. This form of relationship among *politai* the Greeks termed *isonomia*; its antithesis was tyranny, violation of the code by an individual *polites* who successfully set himself above his fellow-*politai*. The Greeks' attitude to tyranny was ambivalent: the tyrant was at once the most fortunate and the most unrighteous of men. It seems clear that the Sophists' endeavour to analyse the *polis* articulated this ambivalence, raising the fundamental issues of why *politai* should observe *nomos*, in what sense tyranny was unrighteous or unjust, what the nature of *nomos* was. The existing ideology could provide no coherent answers. Crucially, the assumption that *nomos* had divine sanction faced the difficulty that religion existed institutionally as an element of the *polis* itself, and thus could not be used as the basis of an intellectually adequate account of the *polis*. Given the character of Greek religion, belief in the traditional gods became problematic together with, and as an aspect of, the *polis*.

In engaging with these issues, some Sophists originated a conceptual distinction that has been fundamental in subsequent political theory: the distinction between what is necessary and what is contingent in human societies. One form this contrast took was that between *nomos* and *phusis*, 'convention' and 'nature': between what men could decide upon for themselves, and ineluctable circumstance. Both concepts had developed during the archaic age, but their use together as an analytic tool appears first in the fifth century. One should be clear, however, that this particular dichotomy was only one of the tools with which analysis of necessary and contingent in human society was conducted: it is absent in Protagoras' argument that the *polis* is a necessary mode of society, which is based instead on a theory of how the *polis* originated.

It is traditional to draw a sharp distinction between the Sophists and Socrates. In the present context, however, what strikes one is the close relation between them. Socrates, it is true, explicitly rejected the role of teacher, and, of course, he did not require those with whom he conversed to pay him fees. But he shared with the Sophists a concern to elucidate the concepts in terms of which the *polis* operated. Unlike the Sophists, Socrates seems not to have offered any substantive analysis of these concepts; he limited himself to drawing attention to the inability of ordinary Athenians to give a coherent account of the concepts they used in their political activity. Socrates' substantive contribution was rather a theory as to how the analysis of political concepts was to be conducted. He believed that genuine understanding of a concept could be achieved only by means of argument that could justify itself at every stage. To ensure this, analysis should take the form of discussion with others, nothing being taken for granted and agreement being secured at each step in the argument. The demands Socrates made of an account of a concept were such that he found the theories put forward by the Sophists themselves inadequate; they lacked the essential analytic rigour. He thus made greater intellectual demands on himself and on others than did the Sophists. Yet the ordinary Athenian was right to regard Socrates and the

Sophists as being engaged in the same kind of activity: both were considering the *polis* in a new way.

The emergence of political theory is sometimes characterized as a movement of 'Enlightenment' analogous to that of the eighteenth century. The parallel seems to us unfruitful because of the absence in fifth-century Greece of the kind of systematic and articulated body of doctrine confronted by the thinkers in the eighteenth-century Enlightenment. Religion was profoundly important for the Greeks, the *polis* was a community of men and gods—but matters concerning the gods were subject to debate in precisely the same way as were all other affairs. Hence in this field, too, the Sophists were 'subversive' not in relation to an established system of ideas but by their attempts to make sense of, to systematize, the assumptions implicit in society. The same was true of Socrates.

And the experience of Socrates was fundamental to Plato's intellectual career. Socrates is presented by Plato as the model of the good man, antithesis of the archetypically evil man, the tyrant, and his significance for Plato is symbolized by his role as the protagonist in all the early and middle dialogues. Indeed, Socrates figures in all Plato's writings, with the single exception of his last work, the *Laws*. Socrates had been concerned with analysis of moral and political concepts, designed to produce the understanding that Socrates believed essential to 'living well'. Socrates operated on the individual level; eschewing, so far as he could, political involvement, he sought moral improvement for himself and his interlocutors by means of personal conversation. Plato elaborated the Socratic commitment to moral understanding in two ways: first, he developed the Theory of Forms; secondly, he extended the scope of analysis from the individual to the *polis*—he came to believe that virtue requires an institutional framework, which could be worked out in theory if not realized in practice. This extension was itself institutionally embodied in the Academy, founded by Plato probably in the 380s, and designed at least in part to provide an intellectually rigorous education for (rather than in) statesmanship.

In the early and middle dialogues, political themes tend to be enmeshed in a complex set of issues; the late dialogues are more readily classifiable as to subject-matter, the *Statesman* and *Laws* being clearly 'political'. The development that

characterizes Plato's work as a whole is strikingly apparent in
his political thought, but one continuing feature merits
emphasis at the outset. Apart from the *Apology*, Plato's version
of Socrates' speech at his trial, the writings all take the form of
dialogues in which Plato himself never figures as a participant. It is a noteworthy paradox that a thinker who has
become notorious for his authoritarian political views should
throughout his career have used a mode of writing that,
strictly speaking, commits him to not a single proposition on
politics, or any other subject. This self-effacing device can be
variously interpreted; in a consideration of Plato's political
thought, it may be seen as an expression of Plato's relation to
the *polis*. The essence of the *polis* as a political community lay
in its institutionalization of debate; Plato, believing the
polis as currently instantiated—all existing political
arrangements—to be radically corrupt, its leading politicians
using rhetoric as at once a means of pursuing, and a mask for
concealing, self-interest, argued for a reform that replaced
political debate by disinterested philosophical dialectic of the
kind his writings exemplify. The relation between these two
types of discussion constitutes a central theme in Plato's
political thought throughout.

Two superb early dialogues, the *Protagoras* and the *Gorgias*,
express Plato's critique of the theory and practice of contemporary politics. In the former, Protagoras is given an early
opportunity of setting forth at considerable length his theory
of the *polis* as a community all of whose members possess at
least minimal competence in *arete*, and of the role of the
Sophist as a particularly talented teacher of *arete*; Socrates'
subsequent questioning reveals that Protagoras can in fact
give no coherent account of what *arete* actually is. The
contrast between rhetorical speech-making and Socratic dialectic is again central in the considerably longer *Gorgias*.
Socrates, taking up the claim Gorgias had just advanced at
the end of a splendid oration, of being able to answer any
question on any subject, engages him in a discussion on the
nature of his own subject, rhetoric. Gorgias soon finds himself
out of his intellectual depth and retires graciously from the
argument. His pupil Polus takes his place as champion of
rhetoric and is eventually obliged to agree that though
rhetoric is a means to power, the common view that supreme
power brings supreme happiness is radically false—the tyrant
is in fact the most miserable of men.

At this point their Athenian host Callicles bursts out with a brilliantly forceful statement of the thesis that might is right. He in turn undergoes Socrates' questioning, and he too is ultimately forced to agree that his position is intellectually untenable. Callicles is presented as an aspiring Athenian politician: Socrates is in love with philosophy, Callicles with the Athenian *demos* (481D). Callicles' thesis is hardly that of a sincere democrat; Plato's intention, one may surmise, is to suggest that the true dynamic of Athenian politics is that glorified by Callicles—ruthlessly egoistic ambition (one notes Socrates' praise of Callicles for his willingness to state openly what others shrink from admitting). Further, Socrates argues that Callicles' view of the politician as master of his fellow-citizens is the reverse of the truth: as things stand, the politician can succeed only by becoming the servant of the *demos*, subjecting himself to its every whim. True statesmanship consists not in pandering to the desires of the *demos* but in making the *demos* as good as possible; the one genuine statesman in Athens is Socrates, whom Callicles has scorned for pursuing philosophy, 'whispering with three or four lads in a corner' (485D).

The conclusion reached in the *Gorgias*, that only the apparently useless philosopher is equipped for political activity, forms the central thesis of Plato's first major constructive work of political theory, the *Republic*, a dialogue in which Plato brings together a wide range of topics—politics, morality, aesthetics, education, psychology, epistemology—treated in his previous works. The crucial thesis of the *Republic*, that 'unless either philosophers become kings in our cities or those whom we now call kings and rulers take to the pursuit of philosophy seriously and adequately, and there is a conjunction of these two things, political power and philosophical intelligence ... there can be no cessation of troubles ... for our cities, nor, I fancy, for the human race', emerges towards the end of Book 5, nearly half-way through the work. Socrates propounds this view in reply to the question as to how the ideal *polis* elaborated in Books 2–5 might be brought into being. The articulation of the ideal *polis* had been undertaken on Socrates' earlier suggestion that this may facilitate the enterprise of justifying his claim that *dikaiosune*, conventionally but inadequately translated as 'righteousness', is a good *per se*, and that its nature may be more easily discernible if one considers *dikaiosune* not in the individual but in the *polis*, where it may be assumed to be, as it were, writ larger. He then constructs an ideal *polis*, comprising three elements: rulers, soldiers, and labourers. Since the *polis* is *ex hypothesi* good, it will possess what are agreed to be the four virtues: wisdom, courage, moderation (an again inadequate translation, of the term *sophrosune*), and *dikaiosune*. The first three are identified as proper to, respectively, the rulers, the soldiers, and the labourers; *dikaiosune* remains to be accounted for. Reflection suggests to Socrates that *dikaiosune* consists in one's doing that for which nature has equipped one: the ideal *polis* exhibits *dikaiosune* in that each class performs its proper function.

Does this analysis work in respect of individual *dikaiosune*? Socrates argues that it does: the individual soul (*psyche*) comprises three elements analogous to the three elements of the *polis*, reason, temper, and appetite; *dikaiosune* again consists in each element performing its proper function. Since the function of reason is clearly to rule, this definition entails that *dikaiosune* in the soul exists only when reason rules the other two elements; similarly in the *polis*, *dikaiosune* exists only when the class possessing wisdom rules the two other classes. But, crucially, the relation between rulers and ruled is one of loving harmony; in contrast with all existing *poleis*, in which there are in fact at least two *poleis*, that of the rich and that of the poor, at enmity with one another, the ideal *polis* is characterized by willing subordination on the part of the two lower classes, and altruistic exercise of authority by the rulers, whose concern is for the good not of their own class but of the *polis* as a whole. This commitment is reinforced by abolition of the two main forces that occasion abuse of power: the rulers are forbidden private possessions and families of their own.

The analogy between *polis* and soul is central to the thesis of the dialogue as a whole. The difficulties it involves cannot be discussed here; they arise above all from the fact that one element of the analogy, the soul, is itself essential to the other, the *polis*. The problems that result are perhaps most acute in the case of the third class; one reason why these may not have impinged forcibly on Plato is that his interest is clearly focused on the two higher classes, and more particularly on the highest, now defined as that of philosopher-kings. Plato's discussion of this class centres on the question of their education. The *Republic* has nothing to say about political institutions in the narrow sense; Plato refers casually to the laws that the rulers may find it necessary to introduce, but he is clearly not concerned with the elaboration of a constitutional framework. This is understandable, since in the ideal *polis* politics in the ordinary sense will not exist: no conflicts of interest or opinion can arise between its constituent elements. The conflict between rhetoric and philosophy is resolved by the creation of a society whose basis is philosophy, in which rhetoric can have no role.

As remarked earlier, Plato's later dialogues are characterized by greater specialization as to subject-matter; the two that engage with political themes are the *Statesman* and the *Laws*. The former is on the whole one of Plato's most arid works, though enlivened by a marvellously sardonic analysis of politics as currently practised. Exploiting an analogy that recurs continually in his political writings, Plato depicts a *polis* whose citizens refuse to recognize the authoritative knowledge of those who possess technical skills, and insist on subjecting the latter to laws that are no more than embodiments of popular ignorance. Such is the fate of the true statesman in the contemporary *polis*; no particular city is specified, but there can be no doubt that Plato has Athens in view. This critique occurs in the section of the dialogue that argues that the ideal ruler can dispense with written law, and the main interest of the *Statesman* in a study of Plato's political thought lies in its making clear that Plato still retains his belief in the ideal of an absolute philosopher-king.

Plato is reported to have expended great care on the opening sentence of the *Republic*. No such anecdote exists concerning the *Laws*, but it is surely not by chance that the opening word of this massive work (the longest of all by far) is *theos*, 'God'. Three old men, a Cretan, a Spartan, and an Athenian, are walking from Cnossos to the shrine of Zeus on Mount Dicte and carrying on an appropriately rambling conversation. At the end of Book 3 it emerges that the Cretan is a member of a commission charged with establishing the laws for a new city to be founded. He proposes that his companions join him in constructing such a body of laws as they continue their journey. The remainder of the work is devoted to this enterprise.

Discussion is led by the Athenian, and even the pretence of dialogue is in places totally dropped. The Athenian in particular expatiates on the distribution of land (to be divided into 5,040 lots in perpetuity), citizenship, the family, education, political and juridical institutions, and above all the law-code for the new city. The contrast with the *Republic* is obvious. Whereas the latter ignored constitutional detail, the *Laws* expounds these with an exhaustive minuteness (though it is uncharacteristically inexplicit on the crucial issue as to whether all citizens have the right to address the Assembly). Above all, Plato has now given up the ideal of rule by philosopher-kings. He acknowledges that no human being can safely be entrusted with absolute power; law as embodied in the constitution and law-code of the *polis* replaces philosophy as the basis of society; rhetoric is reinstated, as an essential element of the law-code—each law is to be prefaced by a preamble whose purpose is to *persuade* the citizens to obey it. The central thesis of the *Laws* is that law instantiates reason; law is the human embodiment of the divine Reason that governs the universe. Traditional Greek religion provided no intellectually adequate legitimation of such a thesis; Plato offers this in Book 10, arguing against those who maintain that human laws are simply human creations. 'God is the measure of all things, not, as they say, man' (716C).

The *Laws* is *prima facie* a severely pessimistic work; not simply in that it expresses Plato's renunciation of the philosopher-king as an unrealistic ideal, but in the view of human life in general that permeates it. Men are no more than playthings of the gods; human affairs are of no great consequence—though it is necessary for us to treat them as if they were (803B). However, it would be a mistake to regard Plato's attitude in the *Laws* as one of contempt for this world. Plato's recognition of the inadequacy of his earlier political ideal generates not resignation but a gigantic work offering a more viable alternative. Philosophy is no longer to rule; but human reason remains necessary and competent in political affairs: the task of the legislator is to ordain 'what is good and expedient for the whole *polis* amid the corruptions of human souls, opposing the mightiest lusts, and having no man his helper but himself standing alone and following reason only' (835C).

Aristotle's political philosophy is closely related to and strongly influenced by his moral philosophy and philosophy of nature. However, the very fact that he composed the *Politics*, with its often very detailed and specialized examination of political themes, indicates that he thought political philosophy to be worthy of extensive treatment in its own right. The *Politics* is Aristotle's only work of systematic political philosophy. Yet his preparation for it involved the composition of no fewer than 158 studies of individual constitutions. This should discourage us from underestimating the importance Aristotle attributed to politics and political philosophy. The 'theoretical sciences' were a more central concern of his, but it is noteworthy that he characterized politics as the *architectonike techne*, that art among the 'practical sciences' which presides over and controls all others, ethics included.

A comparison between the *Politics* and Plato's more political works, especially the *Republic*, will necessarily dominate the discussion that follows. Aristotle is often critical of Platonic arguments in the *Politics* as in his ethical writings, and this reflects some significant differences between the two philosophers in both doctrine and approach. But Aristotle, who worked at the Academy for twenty years, was Plato's heir as well as critic. For example, in Aristotle there is a decided and pervasive emphasis on teleology: both the *Nicomachean Ethics* and the *Politics* begin with a statement of the doctrine of ends. But the teleological assumption is also fundamental in Platonic doctrine. The end of man is variously described by the two philosophers as the good for man, living well, and happiness, *eudaimonia*.[9] *Eudaimonia* is Aristotle's preferred word, and in the *Ethics* he provides the first systematic analysis of what it is to be *eudaimon*. The concept is also a central one for Plato—*eudaimonia* is a necessary ingredient of the ideal state of the *Republic*—and nothing in Aristotle's discussion or his eventual definition of *eudaimonia*, as the activity of the soul in accordance with virtue, would have offended or surprised him.

Man's search for the good or happiness is necessarily set in the context of the *polis*. It is stated in the *Ethics* and reiterated in the *Politics* that the individual and the *polis* have similar ends. In *Politics* Book 1 this is elaborated in the setting of a discussion of the growth of the *polis*, which finds that man is by nature a *zoön politikon*, a being naturally fitted for and needing to live in a *polis*. The epigram is Aristotle's, but its

[9] *Eudaimonia* unlike 'happiness' embraces both 'faring well' and 'doing well'.

content was the common property of all Greeks of the classical age, as was the corollary, the superiority of Greek society because it had the *polis*. Plato, for whom good man and good citizen were identical, was in full agreement.

It follows from Aristotle's teleological account of the *polis* that the life of the *polis* is a more complete goal than that of any one individual. This is already implied in the *Ethics* in the characterization of politics as the *architectonike techne*; which is glossed with the following assertion: 'Even if the good of the community coincides with that of the individual, the good of the community is clearly a greater and more perfect good both to get and to keep. This is not to deny that the good of the individual is worthwhile. But what is good for a nation or a city has a higher, a diviner, quality' (1094b6ff.). In the *Politics* there is further development of the thesis through the demonstration by an evolutionist argument that the *polis* is the summit of man's achievement. The *polis* grew out of the village, the village grew out of the household, the household had its roots in the association of men with women and with slaves. The evolutionary process reaches its end and goal in the *polis*, which, unlike the other forms of association, is self-sufficient. The *polis* is therefore the highest form of natural association. The inference that the individual is subservient to the state is then drawn, with the aid of the doctrine of the whole and parts. This doctrine, which has a biological model, often appears in the *Politics* in conjunction with an explicit analogy with the body, and so it does here:

Furthermore, the city or state has priority over the household and over any individual among us. For the whole must be prior to the parts. Separate hand or foot from the whole body and they will no longer be hand or foot, except in name. ... It will have been ruined by such treatment, having no longer the power and the function to make it what it is. ... It is clear then that the state is both natural and prior to the individual. For as an individual is not fully self-sufficient after separation, he will stand in the same relationship to the whole as the other parts. (1253a19ff.)

The organic conception of the *polis* and the doctrine of the supremacy of state over individual are both present in the *Republic*. This doctrine, with its totalitarian overtones, may offend the modern mind but it would have been accepted as entirely natural by the Greeks. The authority of the classical

Greek state was in principle unlimited; it extended even to the field of morality. And this was recognized by democrats and oligarchs alike. Moreover, the doctrine invariably occurred in Greek political theory in association with positive ideas about the character and aims of the state.

These ideas are set out in detail in the context of discussion on the ideal state, its defining characteristics and underlying principles. Books 7 and 8 of the *Politics* are wholly devoted to this subject, and there is some brief, anticipatory discussion in early books. There was fundamental agreement between Plato and Aristotle over basic principles of the ideal state. (For present purposes it matters little that Aristotle generally allows these principles to be relatively independent of one another, whereas Plato's tendency is to unify them.) First, in the good *polis* the citizens flourish, they lead the good life. This for Aristotle was the actual aim of the *polis*. Second, the good *polis* is a 'just' *polis*. *Dikaiosune* was a central concept for both philosophers, even if their analysis did not coincide. Third, in a good *polis* the political arrangements are expedient and advantageous, serving both the common interest and the interest of individuals or groups.

The difference in the approach of the two philosophers to *dikaiosune* (to be discussed shortly) is in marked contrast not only to their shared assumptions about ends, but also to the very similar role of interest, *sumpheron*, in their theories—as it figures in the conditions for constitutional stability, in their preoccupation (characteristic of the whole tradition of Greek political thinking) with the causes of instability, and in the consequences of this concern with stability on their views of who should govern. In the *Republic* the only rulers capable of governing in the interests of all sections of the community, capable therefore of maintaining a stable state, were philosophers. By the time the *Laws* was composed, Plato had come to recognize that the qualities required were not to be found in mere men—'We are talking of men now, not gods (732F)'— and fell back onto a small group of guardians of the laws elected by a citizen-roll of 5,040. Aristotle at the end of Book 3 says that the best state will be ruled by a single person of supreme virtue or a body of such people. Some have thought that he had his former pupil Alexander the Great in mind when he wrote of the man who deserved to be sovereign 'not in turn but absolutely' (1288a28). This is improbable, not only because Aristotle is almost completely silent about the Macedonian monarchy (and one might think defiantly so), but also because he seems to think of the 'superman' as only a theoretical possibility. Aristotle does not welcome the superman. In Book 1 he was classed as unfit for the *polis* (*apolis*), and in Book 3 Aristotle shows himself almost as reluctant to admit him. Aristotle, we suspect, was at heart a believer in constitutional government and the rule of law. Be that as it may, he gives much more space to polity, his best constitution, which is controlled by a 'middle class', consisting of men of moderate wealth and unusual virtue, who will not favour either the extremely poor or the extremely rich.

Aristotle's flirtation with the idea of the superman is one of many occasions where an *a priori* and even deductive method of argument is allowed to coexist, here in the self-same discussion, with a more inductive or common-sense approach. Aristotle is often contrasted with Plato for his commitment to properly empirical scientific method and for his abandonment of a view of reality as consisting in eternal, absolute Forms, apprehensible by the intellect alone. But Aristotle was no sceptic or relativist in theory of knowledge or in his theorizing about society and politics. He thought he had found an objective basis for political theory in nature. But Aristotle's observations concerning nature and what is in accordance with nature are not purely descriptive: they are as impregnated with *a priori* assumptions as any of Plato's more evidently metaphysical views. This is because they are often statements about ends. The definition of 'natural' as the *final* rather than the *first* state of something is crucial. Speaking of the *polis*, Aristotle says:

This association is the end of the others and its nature is itself an end; for whatever is the end-product of the perfecting process of any object, that we may call its nature, that which man, horse, household, or anything else aims at being. Moreover, the aim and the end can only be that which is best, perfection; and self-sufficiency is both end and perfection. (1252b31ff.)

Nature thus defined is invoked to confirm all Aristotle's own conservative views on social, economic, and political life. For example, in the section on the household in Book 1 we encounter arguments asserting the inferiority of women, justifying the subjection of slaves, and opposing property acquisition above what is required for self-sufficiency—all based on an appeal to nature. Also in Book 1 the supremacy of the *polis* over other associations and over individuals is established, and in Book 3 the problem of how to achieve *dikaiosune* among unequal men is resolved, by means of arguments from nature. In the latter case it is decided that the distribution of goods and honours should be made in accordance with virtue. This is consistent with the end of the state, which exists to further the good life.

Another rule laid down by nature which makes frequent appearance in the *Politics* is 'nothing in excess', the doctrine of the mean. The doctrine is introduced to provide support for the idea of distributive *dikaiosune* (with not altogether happy results) and to justify Aristotle's preference for a middle-of-the-road polity.

Given that Aristotle is apparently so wedded to *a priori*, theory-laden political analysis, it might be wondered how much room is left for a more empirical method of argument. Aristotle is severely critical of Plato for failing to relate his doctrines to the experience of men. If the ideal state was so superior, says Aristotle (in Book 2), it would have been discovered by now. All good things have been discovered by now, even if they have not necessarily been given systematic trial. Besides, Plato's city is quite incapable of being instituted—and here Aristotle brings forward a number of considerations mainly of a practical nature. Similarly pragmatic arguments are employed against Plato's measures to secure unity in his city—through the common ownership of property, the elimination of the family, and the transfer of children between the classes.

In his own study of constitutions he places strong emphasis at the outset on the actual, the practical realities of Greek politics: 'But it is necessary to say at a little greater length what each of these constitutions *is*' (1279b11–12). Even tyranny, which was commonly held to be the negation of constitutional government, receives analysis, and remarkably dispassionate analysis at that. In a somewhat similar spirit he insists on a reduction of the oligarchy/democracy dichotomy in class terms (1279b34ff.).[10] The discussion of oligarchy and

---

[10] 'The argument seems to show that the number of the governing body, whether small in an oligarchy or large in a democracy, is an accident due to the fact that the rich everywhere are few, and the poor many. Therefore . . . the real difference between democracy and oligarchy is poverty and wealth. Wherever men rule by reason of their wealth, whether they be few or many, that is an oligarchy, and where the poor rule, that is a democracy.'

democracy furnishes a vivid illustration of his fondness for classification and sub-classification, explicable in terms of his scientific background and interests. Aristotle will not accept a simple dichotomy: rather, there are five main kinds of democracy and four of oligarchy. This conclusion is preceded by the general observation that there is a plurality of constitutions. Each city has a plurality of 'parts', that is, social classes or groups, which differ in kind among themselves, and also within themselves from state to state. 'It follows therefore that there are as many forms of constitution as there are modes of arrangement according to the superiorities and the differences of the parts' (1290a12–13).

Aristotle was the closest approximation to a political scientist—where political science refers to the descriptive account of the functioning of government—that the ancient world produced.[11] Aristotle however would have preferred the title 'political philosopher': 'But is is necessary to say at a little greater length what each of these constitutions is; for the question involves certain difficulties, and it is the special mark of one who studies any subject philosophically, and not solely with regard to its practical aspect, that he does not overlook or omit any point, but brings to light the truth about each' (1279b11–16). Aristotle here provides a rudimentary definition of the 'aporetic' method, which involves the raising of difficulties (*aporiai*) relating to the main concepts of political theory. The procedure is set out clearly in Book 7 of the *Ethics*. The first step is to set out the appearances, or what seems to be the case (*ta phainomena*), the second is to raise the *aporiai*, the third is to resolve them, if possible by confirming all the received opinions (*ta endoxa*), or at least most of them and the most authoritative of them. 'For if we both refute the objections and leave the common opinions undisturbed, we shall have proved the case sufficiently' (1145b1–7). The method is immediately employed to undermine the Socratic (and Platonic) explanation of errors in human behaviour in terms of intellectual ignorance rather than moral weakness. This, Aristotle claims, is conspicuously at odds with 'what seems to be the case' (1145b28).

The same method is on display in the account of *dikaiosune*

---

[11] Note in this connection the study of 158 constitutions carried out by Aristotle and his school. The only surviving work of this large and unusual research project is the *Constitution of Athens*.

in the *Politics*. Plato is not openly criticised, but his radical redefinition of *dikaiosune* for both *polis* and soul in terms of the proper co-ordination of their constituent parts is implicitly rejected, as only loosely related to ordinary linguistic usage and the opinions of men. Aristotle in contrast begins with the commonsensical idea of *dikaiosune* as equality and fairness (1280a12). The crucial question is how equality is to be judged. Aristotle gives the main competing claims a hearing, even if not always a sympathetic one. The democratic belief in equal shares for all free citizens is quickly dismissed, because it clashes with Aristotle's firm conviction that men are morally unequal. The oligarchic argument that those who make the larger contribution should receive the larger share of the benefits is accepted. But when it comes to a consideration of the kind of contribution it is to be, Aristotle rejects financial investment, noble birth, and free birth (the basis of the claims of oligarchs, aristocrats, and democrats, respectively) in favour of noble deeds. Aristotle's 'polity'[12] is more *dikaios* than the alternatives because those within it who benefit from the distribution of goods and honours are men of superior virtue whose lives are attuned to the correct aim of the state.

Although the teleological principle has been invoked here and also the doctrine of the mean to support both his choice of polity and his definition of *dikaiosune*, this is not one of those occasions on which he uses it in a heavy-handed way. In case neither an individual of transcendent goodness nor a considerable body of virtuous men is available, he is ready with some second-best (or third-best) solutions. The precise form of constitution should reflect the way virtue, wealth, noble birth, and free birth—all necessary attributes of the *polis*—are distributed among the members of the community. No one constitution is everywhere appropriate. Moreover, *dikaiosune* may characterize any of several constitutions, provided the ruling authority governs in the common interest. There is a sense, then, in which the aporetic method has ended in something less than a cut-and-dried solution, if not strictly in total *aporia* in the Socratic sense of bafflement.

---

[12] 'Polity' is introduced as one of three 'correct constitutions', kingship, aristocracy, and polity, of which tyranny, oligarchy, and democracy are the degenerate forms. Aristotle nowhere discusses what a 'polity' is or how it operates. See e.g. 1293b32–94a25 (mixture of democracy and oligarchy), 1295a25–96a22 (rule by a 'middle class').

What deserves to be stressed is the pluralism of Aristotle's methods and assumptions about the proper subject-matter and function of political theory. For example, he combines a concern with the ideal state with an interest in analysing actual types of constitution and providing practical political advice; his own theory of nature is pervasive, yet he regularly appeals to received opinion; he has a liking for highly theoretical frameworks of explanation, and yet relies heavily on common sense; he has a clear and unqualified commitment to certain values and assumptions about the *polis*, yet is quite prepared to leave difficulties unresolved; finally, to point to a distinction which he himself would not have recognized, he employs moral criteria, such as *dikaiosune*, virtue, the good life, while admitting also the more pragmatic criterion of interest, *sumpheron*. These kinds of contrasts help to define the special character of the *Politics*.

The early Hellenistic age[13] was a period of lively philo-sophical activity, particularly at Athens, which retained its role as the meeting-ground and institutional centre for philos-ophers from all over the Greek-speaking world. For political philosophy, however, it was a lean period. Our knowledge is severely limited by the fragmentary state of the evidence; but it seems true that not one of the thousands of philosophical treatises produced in the period from Aristotle to Cicero (the Stoic Chrysippus alone is credited with the authorship of 750 books) can be described as a substantial account of the nature of the *polis* and the concepts associated with it. Zeno's *Republic* and Chrysippus' work of the same name, which might seem from their titles to have been serious and systematic political treatises, were nothing of the kind (see below). The *Politics* of Aristotle had no successor. Meanwhile, that work disappeared from sight and mind, playing virtually no part in philo-sophical discussion until it was rediscovered in thirteenth-century Italy and France.

Moral philosophy by contrast flourished. But that which was produced by Cynics, Sceptics, Epicureans, and Stoics, the most characteristic philosophical movements of the age, diverged sharply from the classical tradition, in that it was not

[13] Our interest is mainly in the period from the death of Alexander the Great in 323 to the middle of the second century B.C. Thereafter Greek philosophers operated increasingly under the shadow of Rome, with a consequent loss of independence and vitality.

centred on the *polis*. Already in the lifetime of Plato and Aristotle, Diogenes the Cynic (from Sinope), 'a Socrates gone mad', according to Plato,[14] had preached the irrelevance of the *polis* and all political systems, holding that the virtue of the wise man is self-sufficient. Cynicism had a profound impact on early Stoicism. For us the main interest of Scepticism, which from the middle of the third century was unexpectedly installed in the Academy, is that its unrelenting negative criticism forced the Stoics into revision and development of their doctrines.

Early or 'classical' Stoicism is very elusive. This is largely explicable in terms of the factors just alluded to—the poor state of the evidence and the apparent doctrinal instability of Stoic political theory. It is reasonable to attribute to both Zeno and Chrysippus a youthful iconoclastic phase. This is well established at least for Zeno, who studied under the Cynic Crates (among others) before passing on to the greater respectability of the Academy under the direction of Polemo. Zeno's *Politeia* is clearly an early work. His ideal state is a Cynic paradise. It is a *polis*, but one stripped of all the characteristic features of a *polis*. Social, economic, and political institutions are all absent, no distinctions based on sex, birth, ethnic background, and property are recognized. Life is lived according to nature, and the implications of this Cynic adage are drawn out with an insensitivity to conventional opinion that would have pleased Diogenes. In Chrysippus' state cannibalism, living with and living off a prostitute, and leaving the dead unburied are all acceptable practices (*SVF*, iii. 746, 751, 755).[15] Doubtless these works contained some traces of positive doctrine: the self-sufficiency of the wise man, the value of friendship, the harmony and equality of the community—not however the brotherhood of man, for the ideal state was composed only of the wise. Of substantial political theory there was apparently none.

Zeno's mature position with regard to the *polis* was probably that it provided a suitable background for human life. Chrysippus explicitly accepted the Aristotelian dogma that man was by nature fitted for *polis*-living (*SVF*, iii. 314). But neither man regarded the *polis* as the summit of human

[14] M. I. Finley, *Aspects of Antiquity* (2nd edn., Penguin, 1977), ch. 7 at p. 91.
[15] *SVF* = *Stoicorum Veterum Fragmenta*, ed. H. von Arnim (4 vols., reprint Stuttgart, 1964).

achievement or the fulfilment of man's potential. For the Stoic the ultimate goal was the harmony of the individual soul with the universe: 'The virtue of the happy man and a smooth-flowing life consist of this, that all actions are based on the principle of harmony between his own spirit and the will of the director of the universe' (Diogenes Laërtius, 7. 88). Life in the *polis* was classed—along with wealth, good health, and other 'things to be preferred'—as 'indifferent' (neither good nor bad), without significance for the development of a virtuous disposition. Participation in politics received from the Stoics a similar kind of limited positive evaluation. Later Stoic thought, in the same spirit, taught that one's fellow-citizens were the object of one's natural *oikeiosis*—an un-translatable word meaning approximately 'concern for', 'being well disposed to'—but only after one's inner family, other relations, and above all, oneself.

No Stoic concept, as far as we can tell, had an overtly political content. *Oikeiosis* may be said to have had political implications, but no more, in classical Stoic thought. Later Stoics actually derived *dikaiosune* from *oikeiosis*. There is no sign that classical Stoicism treated *dikaiosune* as anything other than an aspect of personal virtue (cf. *SVF*, iii. 264). Its component parts, piety, kindness, fellow-feeling, and fair-dealing govern human relationships (except in the case of piety), but are not set peculiarly or primarily in the political context. Concepts such as 'natural justice' and 'natural law' are implied in some fragments of Chrysippus: in one it is insisted that 'the just' (*to dikaion*, probably here indistinguishable from *dikaiosune*), law, and right reason exist by nature not convention (*SVF*, iii. 308); in another, all existing laws and constitutions are rejected as having 'missed the mark' (*SVF*, iii. 324). The notions of a 'universal justice' and 'common law' for all men are likely to have been little stressed until the Roman period. It was Cicero who popularized them, drawing on philosophers of the 'middle period' of the Stoa, and particularly Panaetius. Similarly, the purely moral conception of *to kathekon* (to be translated not 'duty' in the modern sense but 'what is appropriate') did not acquire an unambiguous political colouring until it was adopted by Roman aristocrats, again through the agency of Panaetius. The effect of *kathekon* (translated into Latin as *officium*) and of the attendant idea of *constantia*, which taken together entail holding consistently to one's predetermined station in life and to the conduct it requires, can be measured in the careers of famous figures in Roman political life such as the younger Cato, Thrasea Paetus, Helvidius Priscus, and Marcus Aurelius.[16]

Epicurus' main formative influences were Ionian natural philosophy, which he studied under Nausiphanes the Democritean, and the Scepticism of Pyrrho, a personal acquaintance of Nausiphanes. From the former he learned that man is the product of the accidental combination of atoms moving in empty space, from the latter the desirability of withdrawal from the world and the pursuit of *ataraxia*, freedom from disturbance.[17] The result was a doctrinal system which contrasted radically with the basic presuppositions of Plato, Aristotle, and the Stoics alike.

With regard to the *polis*, Epicurus took up a negative stance. In contrast to the Stoics he rejected the Aristotelian dictum that man is naturally fitted for *polis*-life (fr. 523 U.). For Epicurus, the state's *raison d'être* is merely to enable the philosopher to attain peace of mind. Positive law, similarly, has the function of protecting the wise from injury, not of preventing the wise from injuring others (fr. 530 U.).

Epicurus' thinking on *dikaiosune* bears a striking resemblance to the argument of Sophistic origin which Glaucon uses against Socrates in *Republic*, Book 2.

'What they say is that our natural instinct is to inflict wrong or injury, and to avoid suffering it, but that the disadvantages of suffering it exceed the advantages of inflicting it; after a taste of both, therefore, men decide that ... they had better make a compact with each other and avoid both. They proceed to make laws and mutual agreements, and what the law lays down they call lawful and right. This is the origin and nature of *dikaiosune*'. (*Republic*, 358e3–359a5.)

The Epicurean version of this social-contract theory is summarized in the following maxim: 'There never was an absolute *dikaiosune*, but only a compact made in dealings between men in whatever places and times, providing against

---

[16] See P. A. Brunt, 'Stoicism and the Principate', *Papers of the British School at Rome*, xliii (1975), 7–35.

[17] D. L. Sedley argues for the positive influence of Pyrrho; *Etudes sur l'épicurisme antique*, ed. J. Bollack and A. Laks (*Cahiers de philologie*, i, 1976).

the infliction or the suffering of injury' (Diogenes Laërtius, 10. 150, no. 33). The theory receives a distinctive Epicurean twist in the maxim that follows, which asserts that although *adikia* is not in itself bad (any more than *dikaiosune* is in itself good), its consequence is, because of the fear of being discovered by the forces of law and order. This amounts to a refutation of the saying of Antiphon the Sophist (fr. 44 Diels-Kranz) that it is unnecessary to behave *dikaios* when there are no witnesses to one's conduct.

It would however be a mistake to attribute to Epicurus (or for that matter to Antiphon) a comprehensive account of *dikaiosune*. In general, while it is legitimate to characterize Epicurean philosophy as a reassertion of the values of fifth-century philosophical theory against the massive weight of Platonic and Aristotelian doctrine, this should not be taken to imply that the Epicureans produced anything that could be called systematic political theory.

The poverty of Hellenistic political theory is an inescapable fact. Any explanation must begin with the political context. The retreat to self-centred philosophies stressing the happiness of the individual and the sufficiency of virtue, independent of external circumstances, was primarily a reaction to the arrival of the large-scale state and the demise of the free *polis*. A very different but equally predictable response to these changes was a proliferation of treatises on kingship, works of adulation, not serious analysis—not therefore composed in the spirit of Aristotle. The most accessible kingship theory is that emanating from the Neo-Pythagoreans—if we can assume that the basic content of the works of Diotogenes, Ecphantus, and Sthenidas (writing during the Roman Empire), of which we have substantial fragments, derives from earlier works written in the Hellenistic period; it is also the most extravagant, arriving at the doctrine of the king as law itself (*nomos empsuchos*, or *lex animata*) by means of an analogy between the cosmos and political society. At least three of the early Stoics, Cleanthes, Persaeus, and Sphaerus, wrote treatises on kingship, of which nothing survives. The tone of these works is unlikely to have been negative. Persaeus and Sphaerus served as advisers to kings, the latter in lieu of his teacher Cleanthes and his fellow-pupil Chrysippus, both of whom declined the invitation of the king of Egypt. But Chrysippus recommended that the wise man should become king or advise a king (*SVF*,

iii. 691), and elsewhere refers to the rule of a king as unaccountable (Diogenes Laërtius, 7. 122), having apparently abandoned the Aristotelian distinction between constitutional and absolute monarchs. Epicurus, who also wrote a treatise on kingship (of which next to nothing is known), may have adopted a slightly more critical stance. At any rate, he is said to have advised against seeking 'symbiosis' with a monarch (fr. 6 U.). On the other hand he could also advocate paying court to a monarch when the occasion required it (fr. 577 U.) He himself, in the words of Momigliano, 'steered cleverly among Hellenistic kings'.[18]

·The decline of classical political theory was also predictable. The analysis of the *polis* may have been in part a casualty of a reaction against Plato's deductive moral system and Aristotelian teleology—for both philosophers it was axiomatic that virtue was embedded in the *polis*. A more pragmatic consideration was the unrealistic and anachronistic character of much central Platonic and Aristotelian doctrine. Plato's *polis* was never intended to resemble reality, but Aristotle's civic ideal may have seemed hardly more practical and just as remote from the contemporary world. What deserves comment is the absence of any attempt to interpret classical political theory in Hellenistic terms. Aristotle's own pupils and heirs had no higher ambition than to fill out the theories of the master.

There is no sign that the Macedonian kings deliberately accelerated the decline of classical political theory. The questions that it had raised—centrally, in what social or political framework can *dikaiosune* be located and the end for man achieved?—and the answers it had provided in terms of the *polis* would not have appealed to them. But that is not to say that the classical doctrines were held to be politically subversive. Aristotle's doctrine that the *polis* is a necessary condition of achieving happiness might perhaps be taken as a covert attack on alternative political structures. Against this, however, must be set the essentially quietistic doctrine of Book 10 of the *Ethics* that the highest good for man is philosophical contemplation. If the élites of the Greek cities had subscribed to this view, absolute monarchy would have been assured of a long life. Be that as it may, only the hostility of Athenian

[18] A. Momigliano, in a review in *Journal of Roman Studies*, xxxi (1941), 156.

democrats to Aristotle is well documented. After his death his ideas were carried on by his successor Theophrastus, tolerated by the Macedonians (who entrusted Athens in the first instance to a pupil of Aristotle's, Demetrius of Phalerum). Strato, who succeeded Theophrastus in *c.* 287 B.C., did not share his interests. Aristotelian political theory may be said to have died a natural death during his presidency of the school.

The Greeks had created a new discipline, political philosophy, equipped it with an appropriate vocabulary, range of concepts, and subject-matter, and engaged in it systematically by means of debate, instruction, and literary composition. Moreover, the formidable body of literature that they produced contains at least two works which are recognized as classics, the *Republic* of Plato and the *Politics* of Aristotle.

The impact of these works and of Greek political theory as a whole through the ages can easily be exaggerated. In the history of European philosophical and religious thought, Platonism has practically approximated to Platonic metaphysics and the various systems derived from and inspired by the original. After late antiquity, the political themes of the *Republic* have been influential among philosophers and political thinkers largely in two periods, in the Renaissance— where they left their mark on the writings of humanists such as Erasmus, Bodin, and More—and in our own day in the context of the contemporary conflict between democratic and totalitarian ideologies and systems. The curious importance attached in this controversy to Plato's personal attitudes, in so far as they can be isolated in a work which is after all of strongly utopian character, is itself testimony to the authority of the man and the central place attributed to his work in university curricula.

The interest aroused by Aristotelian political theory in the late medieval period was altogether more appropriate. The newly rediscovered *Politics* was an important weapon in the hands of North Italian republicans in their struggle to defend the autonomy of their cities against ecclesiastical encroachment. More generally, the re-emergence of the *Politics* among other lost works of Aristotle led to the development of a secular conception of society to compete with and gradually erode the dominant Christian theory. After the Renaissance the *Politics*, like the *Republic*, can be assumed to have been widely read among the educated, but to have had little direct influence on the development of modern political philosophy—it is of historical interest only that Marx admired Aristotle (and Luther reviled him). In any case, Aristotle has traditionally won respect or attracted criticism for his contributions to science and logic rather than for his political philosophy.

Whereas topics such as justice, law, the nature of man, the origins and ends of the state, or constitutions and their decline have always been part of the subject matter of political philosophy, others of central concern to modern philosophers were not surveyed by the Greeks. For example, the notions of liberty and the active rights of the individual are absent in Greek thought. Conversely, those of political obligation and duty are present only in embryonic form. In general, the prescriptive element in Greek political philosophy is very weak. Plato's definition of *dikaiosune* as soul-health makes any exhortation to pursue it otiose; Aristotle likewise assumes that we will want to fulfil the ends laid down by nature because to do so is in our interest; while Stoic philosophy through the concept of *kathekon* merely enjoins us to walk in step with nature, to fill the role given us by Providence. The relative neglect of Greek political theory to which we have referred reflects the distance that later thinkers have moved away from the preoccupations (and methods) of their ancient counterparts, which in turn reflects the differences between ancient and modern society.

Further Reading

Sources: Recommended Translations

Aristotle and Xenophon on Democracy and Oligarchy, trans. with commentary by J. M. Moore (London, 1975).
Plato—*Gorgias*: W. Hamilton (Penguin).
    Republic: F. M. Cornford (Oxford).
    Protagoras: W. K. C. Guthrie (Penguin).
    Statesman: J. B. Skemp (Routledge).
    Laws: T. H. Saunders (Penguin).
Aristotle—*Politics*: E. Barker (Oxford).
    Ethics: J. Warrington (Everyman).
E. Barker, *From Alexander to Constantine, Passages and Documents Illustrating the History of Social and Political Ideas 336 B.C.–A.D. 337* (Oxford, 1956), an anthology with detailed running commentary.

Politics

V. Ehrenberg, *The Greek State* (Oxford, 1960), with excellent bibliographies, has long been the standard introduction to the subject. The latest edition is the French translation prepared under the supervision of Ed. Will (Paris, 1976).

On special topics:

W. R. Connor, *The New Politicians of Fifth-Century Athens* (Princeton, 1971).
M. I. Finley, *Democracy Ancient and Modern* (London, 1973), and *Politics in the Ancient World* (Cambridge, 1983).
Y. Garlan, *War in the Ancient World: A Social History*, trans. J. Lloyd (London, 1975).
A. H. M. Jones, *Athenian Democracy* (Oxford, 1957).
Claude Mossé, *La Fin de la démocratie athénienne* (Paris, 1962).
E. S. Staveley, *Greek and Roman Voting and Elections* (London, 1972).
R. Thomsen, *The Origin of Ostracism* (Copenhagen, 1972).
The fundamental synthesis of Hellenistic political history is Ed. Will, *Histoire politique du monde hellénistique* (323–30 av. J.-C.), 2 vols. (vol. i in 2nd edn., 1979; vol. ii, 1967, Nancy). Briefly see W. W. Tarn and G. T. Griffith, *Hellenistic Civilisation* (3rd edn., London, 1952), chs. i–ii.

Political Theory

W. K. C. Guthrie, *A History of Greek Philosophy*, vol. iii (Cambridge, 1969), pt. 1 (also available separately in paperback) on the Sophists; I. M. Crombie, *An Examination of Plato's Doctrines*, 2 vols. (London, 1962–3); G. E. R. Lloyd, *Aristotle* (Cambridge, 1968); J. H. Randall, Jr., *Aristotle* (New York, 1960); A. A. Long, *Hellenistic Philosophy* (London, 1973); F. H. Sandbach, *The Stoics* (London, 1975).

The more general studies just mentioned all discuss political philosophy. The following specialized inquiries may also be recommended: G. Vlastos, 'The Theory of Social Justice in the *Polis* in Plato's *Republic*', in *Interpretations of Plato*, ed. H. F. North (Leiden, 1977), pp. 1–40; B. Williams, 'The Analogy of City and Soul in Plato's Republic', *Phronesis* Supp. i (1973), pp. 196–206; M. Defourny, *Aristote, Etudes sur la 'Politique'* (Paris, 1932); the relevant chapters in *Articles on Aristotle*, ed. J. Barnes *et al.*, vol. ii (London, 1977), with detailed bibliographies; two chapters in *Problems in Stoicism*, ed. A. A. Long (London, 1971): ch. vi, 'Oikeiosis', by S. G. Pembroke, and ch. x, 'The Natural Law and Stoicism', by G. Watson; G. J. D. Aalders, *Political Thought in Hellenistic Times* (Amsterdam, 1975).

On the later impact, the following books deserve special mention among those that may be profitably consulted: A. MacIntyre, *A Short History of Ethics* (London, 1967); M. Wilks, *The Problem of Sovereignty in the Later Middle Ages* (Cambridge, 1967); Q. Skinner, *The Foundations of Modern Political Thought*, 2 vols. (Cambridge, 1978); R. Tuck, *Natural Rights Theories: Their Origin and Development* (Cambridge, 1979); K. R. Popper, *The Open Society and Its Enemies*, vol i (5th edn., London, 1966); R. Bambrough, ed., *Plato, Popper, and Politics* (Cambridge, 1967); F. Novotny, *The Posthumous Life of Plato* (Prague, 1977), a compilation.

3

HOMER AND THE EPIC

K. W. GRANSDEN

The *Iliad* and the *Odyssey* are by general consent the beginning
of European literature. It might be expected that the oldest
surviving works of a culture would be fragmentary, shapeless,
or primitive. The *Iliad* and the *Odyssey*, however, are fully
achieved masterpieces, narrative poems of enormous length
and sophistication. They represent the Greek heroic age with
extraordinary vividness and clarity and have consequently
been widely regarded as in some way authentic or 'true'.
Their attribution to an Iron Age poet of outstanding genius of
whom we know virtually nothing except his name, Homer,
was generally accepted in classical Greece. The poems
became at an early date the foundation of Greek culture and
education, as well as setting the highest standard of poetic
excellence. Plato in his *Republic* attacked them because he
considered that poetry should be banned for telling 'lies'.
Greek did not distinguish between fiction and falsehood, but
what chiefly disturbed Plato, as it had disturbed earlier
moralists, was not Homer's heroes, who on the whole act
rationally and with dignity under the psychological stress of
extreme situations, but his stories of the outrageous behaviour
of the gods, who engage in deceptions, quarrels, adultery, and
violence. In attacking Homer Plato was really paying him a
compliment. He was the most dangerous influence because he
was the best poet; his 'lies' had become canonical and
consequently harder to resist. In another dialogue of Plato,
the *Ion*, the rhapsode Ion (a rhapsode was a professional
reciter of, and commentator on, epic poetry) says that
Homer's are the only poems in his repertoire discussion of
which never bores him.

The primary age of Greek heroic epic begins, and ends,
with the emergence as written texts of the so-called 'monumental' *Iliad* and *Odyssey* in the eighth century B.C., when the
invention of an alphabetic script made it possible to set down,
perhaps by dictation, and perhaps before it was lost for ever,
the heritage of Greek heroic song. For these gigantic works,

some 16,000 and 12,000 lines long respectively, did not spring
from the mind even of 'many-minded Homer' like Athene
fully armed from Zeus' head. Homer is an Ionian poet
standing at the dawn of Greek history, but his poems depend
upon a long, composite, and uniquely rich oral tradition
whose origins may go back to the twelfth century B.C. For an
indeterminable period of time the legends of Greek prehistory had been treated orally in poetic narratives by
illiterate bards composing from memory for illiterate audiences. Oral epic is not peculiar to ancient Greece, but no
other oral tradition is known to have produced poems
comparable in scale and quality to Homer's.

In Plato's time, and beyond, there survived other traditional epics about the heroic age. They seem always to have
been regarded as inferior, and it is doubtful how long any of
them remained in general circulation. All are lost, known
only from fragments, summaries, references, and imitations.
The only other poems still extant from Homer's time are the
shorter didactic and mythological poems of Hesiod (who was
probably composing around the end of the eighth century).
These also exhibit features of an oral tradition, but they are
not sustained narratives and they do not depict a heroic
society.[1]

The lost heroic epics seem to have been written down in the
three centuries after Homer by poets who followed in his
footsteps. Some of them were composed to cover those parts of
the story of Troy not treated by Homer. The *Cypria*, a prelude
to the *Iliad*, told of the judgement of Paris in favour of the
goddess Aphrodite, of the subsequent hostility of Hera, one of
the unsuccessful candidates in that celebrated divine beauty
contest, and of Paris' elopement with Helen which caused the
war. Other poems carried the story on from the point where
the *Iliad* ends, down to the death of Achilles and the sack of
Troy, both of which are referred to in the *Odyssey*. The poem
about the sack of Troy was used by Virgil in *Aeneid*, 2. There
were also 'Odyssean' epics about the return journeys (*nostoi*)
of other heroes from Troy, and about Odysseus' own adventures after the killing of the suitors with which the *Odyssey*
ends. Of the non-Trojan epics the most popular was a poem
about the legends of Thebes, used by many later writers,

---

[1] See further pp. 86–91, below.

including the Greek tragic dramatists and the Roman epic poet Statius (who also wrote a poem about Achilles).

Many of these stories, and many other traditional tales about the gods, giants, and earlier heroes, are referred to by Homer *en passant* and were as familiar to him as those he selected for his principal treatments. Thus the story of the murder of Agamemnon and of the revenge later taken by his son Orestes, mentioned in the *Odyssey*, was used in a number of plays by the Athenian tragedians and was refashioned in our own century by von Hofmannsthal in his libretto for Strauss's opera *Elektra*. The Trojan war provided many stories for dramatists from Aeschylus and Sophocles to Giraudoux, whose *La Guerre de Troie n'aura pas lieu* is an ironic study of historical necessity. Aeschylus wrote a trilogy about Achilles which must have been based on the *Iliad*, but only fragments of this survive.

None of the lost traditional epics seems to have approached the length of Homer's or to have possessed anything comparable to their artistic design and structural and thematic unity, qualities which are particularly remarkable in the *Iliad*. The poem opens with a quarrel between Achilles and Agamemnon over Achilles' refusal to give up (*luein*) a girl, a prize of war: in itself an echo of the motif of Paris' refusal to give up Helen. Angrily, Achilles withdraws from the fighting, to which he only returns towards the end of the poem in order to avenge the death of his friend Patroclus by killing the Trojan champion Hector. The poem ends when Achilles, his wrath spent, agrees to give up (*luein*) the body of Hector which he has deliberately dishonoured. During Achilles' long absence from the action of the poem, Homer is able to tell of the prowess of other heroes. This pattern of absence, return, and revenge also occurs in the *Odyssey*, and forms an argument in favour of the traditional view of a common authorship, as does the fact that the action of both poems is largely determined by the psychology of the two principal characters.

Although the Homeric epics are dependent on oral tradition, they were not composed in any ordinary spoken language but in a highly stylized and elaborate professional diction evolved for the specific purpose of heroic song in a quantitative metre, the dactylic hexameter, at once formal and flexible, which was the first great achievement of classical prosody. The chief characteristic of Homeric diction, as of all oral poetry, is that it contains a very large number of repeated phrases or formulas, metrical units of two words or more (sometimes a complete line of verse): 'swift-footed Achilles', 'Agamemnon lord of men', 'the strengthless heads of the dead', 'when early dawn appeared, the rosy-fingered'. The oral bards drew on these formulas to build up their narrative, with its constantly recurring characters, actions, objects, and phenomena, memorizing the existing formulas and creating new ones in the same traditional style until a very late stage in the poems' oral evolution. Stock set-pieces, like the arming of a hero, are almost entirely built up of formulas: the descriptions of the arming of Paris and of Agamemnon begin identically, diverging when the poet wishes to describe one of the *Iliad*'s unique artefacts, Agamemnon's shield. A favourite simile may crop up several times, with varying degrees of appropriateness. Up to one third of the Homeric epics consists of formulas which occur more than once, yet there is at the same time a large variety of formulas, especially of the commonest two-word formulas consisting of a proper name and a variable adjective. The poet's decision whether to call Achilles, for example, 'swift-footed' or 'son of Peleus' at a given point is not governed by sense or context but by metrical requirements. Each formula has a different metrical value, and the 'right' formula is one which will slot in to the metrical space available, the poet's task being to have this ready when composing aloud. Thus in order to help and not to strain the bard's memory, unnecessary metrical duplication of formulas tended to be avoided, though so rich a tradition could sometimes accommodate the luxury of metrically interchangeable alternatives; it may also be assumed that Homer, at the point when the 'monumental' *Iliad* and *Odyssey* were achieving written form, operated more freely and personally within the formular tradition.

Oral transmission may also have continued even after writing became established. Nor does the fact that a poet goes on using traditional language prove he was illiterate. Homer mentions writing only once, in *Iliad*, 6, where signs engraved on a tablet are sent as a secret message. Homer does not seem to have regarded writing as a part of the heroic age, although in the Gilgamesh epic, which was committed to writing at roughly the same time as the *Iliad* but whose oral origins go back much further, the hero 'returning from his adventures engraved on a stone the whole story'. Here the act of recording confers authenticity, but Homer's authenticity depends entirely on the 'song in the ears of men' and on the reliability of the bardic tradition. In a famous passage in *Odyssey*, 8, Odysseus is being entertained at the court of king Alcinous. The blind minstrel Demodocus, who has been specially brought in for the evening, is asked by Odysseus, who has not yet identified himself, to sing the stratagem of the wooden horse by which he himself had captured Troy: 'for you sing of the fates and sufferings of the Achaeans as if you had been there yourself or had heard them from someone who was.' Demodocus has already performed one 'number', the tale (another stratagem) of how the god Hephaestus caught his wife Aphrodite and her lover Ares in a golden net, and that has been followed by a display of dancing and juggling. He now takes up the tale of Troy 'at the point where the Achaeans sailed away, leaving the horse in the market place, while the Trojans wondered what to do'. The picture is of an accomplished professional bard with an established reputation for 'telling it as it was', drawing on a large and popular traditional repertoire.

The passage seems to reflect the kind of performances with which Homer was familiar, and which he here imagines had already started in the heroic age itself. It suggests that the intense air of authenticity in his own poetry is probably not the result of fidelity to an actual historical past but of fidelity to a poetic tradition. The reliability rests in the continuity of an established technique. Homer's appeals to the Muses for an authentic remembering are a convention, but not, as they later became, a literary convention. They guarantee certain traditional tales which the bard might have felt free to elaborate but not radically to alter. In the *Odyssey*, the hero himself tells some of his adventures to king Alcinous in the first person, using the narrative device of the 'flashback', still popular today, especially in the cinema. But the parts of the poem thus told are the least realistic, the tales most obviously drawn from folk-lore and fairy-tale. The most famous literary imitations of Odysseus' narrative are Aeneas' account of the fall of Troy and his subsequent wanderings in Virgil's *Aeneid*, and Dante's narrative of his visit to the underworld, in which the poet is not only the shaping, invisible bard but also the experiencing hero: his repeated 'I saw' is echoed from *Odyssey*,

11. Both are authorial devices to create the necessary suspension of disbelief in the hearer or reader.

So conspicuous are the formular lines and phrases in Homer that it may seem strange that the evidence they offer of the poems' oral origin should for so long have been ignored or misunderstood. This is partly because ancients critics lacked the techniques and motivation for research on texts of uniquely classic status. It was not until our own century that Milman Parry, 'the Darwin of Homeric studies', compared the Homeric poems with modern oral epics and worked out in detail the metrical values of the formulas. Repetition is the hallmark of oral poetry, just as the avoidance of it is the hallmark of written poetry. But the elaborate metre of Homeric epic, and the fact that Greek is a highly inflected language, demanded of the oral bards a repertoire of formulas, and a skill in handling them, beyond anything we know from other cultures.

The discovery of the significance of the repeated formulas does not create special criteria for appreciating Homeric verse nor make it a solecism to speak of Homer's style. Indeed, the sheer amount of repetition in Homer, especially of such 'conventional' epithets as 'deep-soiled', 'rich', 'godlike', helps to build up a reassuringly grand and solid heroic world. We judge the poems by what is in them, not how it got there. Homer's impersonal style seems the only possible stance for a poet looking back on the legendary past, and no less impressive because its origins are traditional. Nor does the fact that the oral process has left inconsistencies worry the modern reader, partly because of the vast scale of the poems and partly because we do not expect the *Iliad* to read like a series of dispatches from a war-correspondent. The main impression the poems give is of a quite remarkable cohesiveness and harmoniousness which the various anachronisms and contradictions do comparatively little to disturb.

Homer's genius lies in his multitudinousness, his power to create a world in which many things are possible. Some of these things—the burning river, the automatic tripods and robots in Hephaestus' house, gods who can assume the forms of living people—anticipate the most extravagant fantasies of science-fiction. Others—Nestor's advice on how to win a horse race, the conduct of Patroclus and Hector in the face of catastrophe and death—continue to surprise and gratify our sense of human reality.

No poetry is richer than Homer's in the various 'figures' of the 'high style' subsequently codified by literary critics and copied throughout the ages by imaginative writers of every class. Dramatic irony, to give a single example, has been universally exploited, but never more effectively than by Homer in the passage in *Iliad*, 22, where we, the audience, knowing Hector to be dead, hear how his wife Andromache, 'for she had not yet heard the news', set about preparing her husband's warm bath against his return from the field, 'unaware that he lay slain, far from warm baths, by Athene at the hand of Achilles'. Although Homer wrote before the emergence of other genres, his range is such that he offers anticipations of these. The beginnings of drama may be detected in the last book of the *Iliad*, which falls naturally into scenes, with a central confrontation between Achilles and Hector's father, King Priam, and a formal triple lament over the dead Hector to close the poem.

Homer's similes are perhaps the most widely imitated of his poetic skills. Like the famous descriptive set-pieces, Achilles' shield or his spectacular fight with the river-god, they serve to enrich and vary the narrative. There are many two-word similes—'he fought like a lion'—simple descriptive formulas of a type common in all primary compositions. But it is the extended, independently developed similes which are most characteristic of Homer. For example, Ajax's stubborn refusal to leave the field until ready to do so is compared to the behaviour of a lazy donkey whom boys cannot drive from a field until he has eaten all he wants to. The common factor on both sides of the equation, so to speak, is stubbornness: Ajax is in no other way like a donkey.

There are three times as many similes in the *Iliad* as in the *Odyssey*. The texture of a tragic war-poem needed especially to be interwoven with nostalgic images of ordinary life, which take us away from the horror of the battlefield. The *Iliad*, said Goethe, teaches us that men in this life are condemned to enact hell. We are offered refreshment and relief from violence and slaughter by glimpses of the poet's own, non-heroic world, in which a woman bears the pains of labour, a child builds sandcastles or pesters its mother to be picked up, tired woodcutters come home to supper, shepherds watch the weather, gardeners irrigate crops, men argue about a boundary. Milton in particular imitated Homer's pastoral similes and also followed him in introducing the contemporary and

non-heroic into epic narrative, as when he compares Satan, in
Paradise Lost, 4, first to a wolf entering a sheepfold, then to a
seventeenth-century thief 'bent to unhoard the cash of some
rich burgher'.

Homer's similes are a good illustration of Erich Auerbach's
perception that 'what Homer narrates is for the time being
the only present.' When Homer is describing a donkey we do
not worry whether or not it is appropriate to compare him
with Ajax. We see only the donkey, the boys, and the field.
Literary imitators of Homeric epic, in contrast, sought to give
their similes some symbolic relationship to the main action,
expecting the reader to hold two things in his mind simultaneously. Homer's art is consecutive, reflecting a world of
action. Every object, gesture, action is seen as an end in itself
and has no other significance.

Homer's world is a world of heroes, an aristocratic warrior-
class whose objects of luxury and weapons of war were made
of bronze. They had gold, too, but it was their bronze which
especially captured the imagination of the Iron Age poet and
lends a peculiar magnificence to his descriptions of heroic
warfare:

> As destructive fire burns up a vast forest
> On a mountain peak, and from far off the blaze is seen,
> So as they marched the gleam of marvellous bronze
> Went dazzling through the air to the heavens.

Homer continually reminds us that he is looking back to a
glamorous past, when men had abundant material wealth,
fifty-roomed palaces, patriarchally large families, and enormous physical strength. When Diomedes picks up a stone the
poet says, 'even two men, of the sort now living, could not lift
it, but he lifted it easily on his own.' (The impotence of
Turnus to perform this traditional act of heroic prowess at the
end of Virgil's *Aeneid* perhaps represents the closing of the
'Homeric' chapter in Rome's prehistory.) The aged Nestor's
four-handled cup with its golden doves (another of the *Iliad*'s
unique, richly described artefacts) could scarcely be lifted
even by his younger contemporaries at Troy, which implies
that the heroic age was by then already past its zenith and in
decline, and Homer refers to myths about earlier, even
mightier heroes, notably Heracles, the Roman Hercules.
There is a nostalgic tone in Homer's celebration of the Greek

heroic past which goes beyond the convention of primary epic, and indeed beyond the 'once upon a time' of all primitive story-telling. The Near Eastern *Gilgamesh* is a primary epic looking back to a much more remote age, the dawn of prehistory rather than its evening: in this work, too, the convention of the hero's enormous strength occurs (Gilgamesh 'donned a breastplate weighing thirty shekels as if it had been a light garment'), but there is little trace of the tone of nostalgia, of wonder at a lost, treasure-laden past, which pervades the Homeric epics, as for example when Telemachus and Peisistratus in *Odyssey*, 4, wonder at the richness of bronze, gold, amber, silver, and ivory in Menelaus' palace and compare it to Zeus' palace on Olympus.

Homer's picture of the heroic age is primarily a poet's imaginative reconstruction of the past, in which are preserved many details of the world he knew. In that world there may have survived, if only in the confused form of legend and folk-memory, elements from the Mycenaean Age itself, a late Bronze Age civilization of great wealth and complexity which flourished in Crete and mainland Greece until the end of the thirteenth century B.C. Archaeologists have found writing from this age preserved on tablets: it consists solely of bureaucratic documents, is in a syllabic script not an alphabetical one, and is in a language which, though Greek, is far removed from Homer's. Its decipherment has, at best, suggested the possibility that the Ionian tradition of hexameter verse which emerged in the eighth century with Homer may include a few formular phrases of Mycenaean origin.

The Mycenaean civilization was destroyed by the end of the thirteenth century and succeeded by a much poorer, simpler society which had lost, along with much else, the art of writing, and whose greatest artistic achievement was the oral tradition of heroic song, preserved in the Homeric epics.

It seems unlikely that for four centuries generations of oral bards could have maintained an accurate and uncontaminated record of the Mycenaean Age. Indeed, the longer an oral tradition continues, the less likely it is to be 'authentic'. The social and political background of the *Odyssey* seems to reflect a time nearer to that of Homer himself than to anything that archaeology has enabled scholars to reconstruct of the Mycenaean Age. Troy existed, and Homer's heroes may be based on characters who once lived, but it is as products of the poetic imagination that they have taken root in the mythology and legends of Europe—Odysseus, whom the Romans called Ulysses and whose later metamorphoses from wise to evil counsellor, hero to cuckold, explorer to exile may be followed from Virgil through Dante to James Joyce; Helen, of whom the old men on the ramparts of Troy say in *Iliad*, 3, 'No one can blame the Trojans and Achaeans for suffering so much for her sake, for she is wonderfully like the immortal goddesses to look upon.'

> No marvel though the angry Greeks pursued
> With ten years' war the rape of such a queen,
> Whose heavenly beauty passeth all compare.

Homer himself emphasizes the importance of the bard's role as the unverifiable voice and memory of the people, when he makes Helen say in *Iliad*, 6: 'Surely Zeus brings an evil doom on Paris and me, that even in the days to come we may be a song in the ears of men hereafter.' The poet alone has the power to preserve the past. As Horace said, there were many heroes before Agamemnon, but—in the words of Pope's version—'they had no poet and are dead.'

It is Homer's Troy and no other, certainly not the Troys of the archaeologists, which has passed into history. This process starts in the *Odyssey*, in which the war is a recent memory to the heroes, both those who survived and those who did not but whose shades look back on it (in *Odyssey*, 11 and 24) from Hades. The 'diaspora' (dispersion) of heroes from both sides which followed the war was the source of widespread colonization-legends throughout the ancient world. Odysseus was said to have visited Italy and to have founded, by a local nymph, the Italian race. In another Greek legend, taken up by Roman antiquaries and ultimately by Virgil, Homer's Aeneas, of whom it is said in *Iliad*, 20 that he was 'destined to escape, so that the race of Dardanus might not perish', settled in Latium and laid the foundations of what was to become the Roman nation. In medieval Britain, Geoffrey of Monmouth, a successful writer of historical romance, invented an analogous genealogy for the British, who, he said, were descended from the Trojan hero Brutus, a non-character whose name is not merely unhomeric but, absurdly, not even Greek. This eponymy was revived in Tudor times, along with the far more potent myth of Arthur, developed by Geoffrey from hints in earlier tradition. Arthur is the hero of Spenser's national epic *The Faerie Queene*: in him we have, perhaps, our nearest equivalent to a heroic past, but without a Homer. Arthur has been zealously pursued by archaeologists as in the nineteenth century Schliemann had pursued Agamemnon.

Homer's influence pervades the whole cultural tradition of Europe, going far beyond the comparatively few deliberate imitations. The *Odyssey*, in particular, is the ancestor of a whole range of fictional genres. It is a comedy of manners, in which conversation is as important as action, and has been called Europe's first novel. Its largely domestic setting allows portraits of people from other social classes besides the heroes—a swineherd and a nurse play central roles in the story; it is also notable for its portraits of women—again the *Iliad*, a war-poem, offers the poet little scope for this aspect of his art, though there is a moving portrait of Hector's wife, Andromache, and a realistic one of Priam's wife, Hecuba. Odysseus' encounters with women include, besides the highly affecting reunion with his faithful wife, Penelope, the touching, undeclared love of the fairy-tale princess Nausicaa for the handsome stranger cast up on her father's shore. Samuel Butler argued that the *Odyssey* was actually written by a woman.

But the *Odyssey* is also a sequence of adventures, unified by the fact that they all happen to a single hero, whose reputation for resourcefulness and toughness, established in the *Iliad*, makes him an appropriate central figure. But many of the adventures are common to the folk-lore of other cultures—the theft of a god's cattle, the visit to the underworld, the fights with monsters and enchanters are all popular motifs. Odysseus is a hero in the modern as well as the Homeric sense: cool, rational, versatile, keeping his nerve in tight corners like Richard Hannay in John Buchan's *Thirty-nine Steps*, unlike Achilles and Agamemnon who, though they fight bravely, are petulant, unstable, easily angered and discouraged.

The *Odyssey* is also the first of the far-fetched travellers' tales, a genre which is developed in the *True History* of Lucian, with its tongue-in-cheek title, and continues through the medieval and Renaissance wonder-voyages, down to *Gulliver's Travels*. The poem also has a sub-plot; the hero's son, Telemachus, despairing of his father's return which, unknown to him, is even then being brought about by the gods, sets out in search of him. This double narrative is imitated by Joyce in *Ulysses*, in which Stephen Dedalus plays Telemachus' role, Leopold Bloom Odysseus', his wife Molly Penelope's, with 'Blazes' Boylan and others as her 'suitors'.

Homer's Odysseus is guided home by the goddess Athene. Her tricks and subterfuges, so admired by her protégé, seem less admirable in the *Iliad*. It is she who deceives Hector by assuming the form of a comrade-in-arms, only to vanish, leaving him alone on the field to face Achilles and death. But the moral structure of the *Odyssey* is simpler and less ambiguous than that of the *Iliad*. We expect Odysseus to triumph like any fairy-story hero. The suitors are obviously wicked and deserve to die. The poem thus offers the first happy ending in story-telling. In the *Iliad*, with its darker and more complex psychology, there are no villains, with the possible exception of Paris and Helen, whose elopement is a *fait accompli* nearly ten years before the action of the poem begins. Indeed, the lovers' act, though not glossed over, is not dwelt on. The idea that a whole city must be punished for the blood-guilt of one of its heroes is not emphasized as it is later by Aeschylus and Sophocles. Indeed, Zeus sympathizes with the Trojans. The intensely idealized patriotism which fills Pericles' praise of Athens in his funeral oration in Thucydides three centuries later is not present in the *Iliad*. Loyalties are local and personal. It is not the fate of Troy but the thought of his wife's unhappiness in captivity which most affects Hector in his parting from her in *Iliad*, 6, a scene of great pathos in which may be detected the beginnings of that 'literature of sensibility' which was to dominate Europe. Homer, a Greek poet, not only shows no racial bias in depicting the Trojans, who share the same code, culture, and gods as the Achaeans, but arguably makes Hector a more sympathetic character than any of his opponents, not because he is 'right' and Achilles 'wrong', but perhaps because he conforms to the Geneva convention of the day while Achilles flouts it. And when the poet, referring to Achilles' dishonouring of Hector's body by dragging it round the city behind his chariot, says that 'Achilles devised foul deeds for noble Hector', this seems as much moral condemnation as a comment on a grim tradition. Pope, in his preface to his translation of the *Iliad*, reminds his eighteenth-century readers that the poem was conceived in a barbarous era, 'when a spirit of revenge and cruelty, joined with the practice of rapine and robbery, reigned throughout the world'. Our own age, which has known wars of unprecedented horror and grown used to violence in life and art, will not be likely to recoil at Homer's battle-scenes and his 'anatomical' descriptions of wounds.

The heroes of the *Iliad* are not always 'heroic' in the modern sense of the word. Helen's lover Paris is depicted as a playboy and frequenter of the dance-hall, 'woman-crazy', sneered at by foe and kinsman alike, but he is none the less a hero in the Homeric sense, not least because of his conspicuous physical beauty. When Homer's heroes fight, it is not for the chivalric motives of their medieval successors, but to preserve their status and to win glory, an abstraction (and as such rare in Homer), but quantifiable in terms of material possessions. And even glory involves calculated risks. Agamemnon is ready at times to counsel retreat—'There is no shame in running away from disaster, even at night'—while on another occasion he reckons that 'of those who shun dishonour more survive than are killed, but those who run away get neither safety nor glory.' Homer's heroes say what they feel at the time. 'I hate the man who says one thing and hides another in his heart', says Achilles: Odysseus' role-playing was clearly felt by Homer to be exceptional.

It is their mortality which confers on the heroes of the *Iliad* their tragic stature and dignity. Gilgamesh went in search of immortality but failed to secure it; the same myth is preserved in Genesis in the story of the garden of Eden, and perhaps also in the *Odyssey*; but there is no sense in the *Iliad* that man, even heroic, semi-divine man, ever had or expected immortality: one immortal parent was not enough to confer exemption from the human condition. (An exception is made in the *Odyssey*, though not in the *Iliad*, for Heracles: the beginning of the concept of the 'deified hero' which was to play so important a part in Greek, and even more in Roman, religion.)

In contrast, the gods live for ever and can therefore behave irresponsibly. They have no sense of reality since their actions are not bound by natural laws. 'You had no vengeance to fear in the hereafter', cries Achilles to Apollo, who has snatched from him the glory of taking Troy single-handed, beyond what was fated. When Ajax cries aloud to Zeus, who has shrouded the field in mist, 'If we must die, let us die in the light', it is the reproach of a morally superior being. Zeus' famous comment on mankind—'There is nothing more wretched than a man among all things which breathe and creep on the earth'—gains its poignancy from the fact that it is addressed to the immortal horses of Achilles, who stand transfixed by grief for the fallen Patroclus. Unlike the horses, unlike the gods, the heroes are trapped in time, in the knowledge of their mortality. It is this awareness of 'ten thousand forms of death' which gives the *Iliad* its tragic intensity and sublimity.

Successive ages have seen in Homer's poems what they wanted to see. This has sometimes meant seeing in them what is not there, and not seeing what is there. The Alexandrian editors of the Hellenistic age edited the texts with much literary learning but no historical sense. The best-known Greek literary imitation of a traditional epic dates from this time. The *Argonautica* by Apollonius of Rhodes,[2] who wrote in the third century B.C., is short by Homeric standards, in accordance with the literary fashion of the age, but its four books, amounting to about 5,000 lines, span a subject of Odyssean dimensions and possibilities, Jason's quest for the golden fleece. Apollonius had access to traditional epic material on this theme, now lost but known to Homer, who alludes to the story in the *Odyssey*. Apollonius' poem, which is still read and has even been filmed, is the first in the catalogue of European secondary epics composed over a period of two thousand years and deriving ultimately from the example and inspiration of Homer. It is a genre with a long history but one which, unlike the lyric and the drama, has become obsolete with the rise of the novel as the dominant narrative mode. Apollonius took over the epic hexameter, by this time appropriated also to less exalted genres, along with some of the stylistic features and linguistic forms of primary epic, now as self-conscious archaisms. His technique reflects the cleverness as well as the sensibility of his own age. His highly romantic treatment of love, in marked contrast to Homer's matter-of-fact and reticent narrative of Odysseus' encounter with Nausicaa, provided Virgil with the model for his treatment of Dido's violent and self-destructive passion for Aeneas

[2] See further Chapter 4.

in *Aeneid*, 4, which ends in suicide, again in marked contrast to Homer's account of Helen in the *Odyssey*, safely back at home with her husband.

Roman writers, who largely depended on Greek culture, sought to emulate the Greek achievement in the various genres. It needed a poet of genius to accomplish in Latin a heroic epic of comparable scale and grandeur to Homer's. Virgil, who had triumphantly naturalized Theocritean pastoral in his *Eclogues* and Hesiodic didactic epic in his *Georgics*, crowned his career with the *Aeneid*, in which he interwove the themes of the *Iliad* and the *Odyssey* into a single epic. His poem differed in one all-important way from Homer's. It was 'teleological', that is, it had a purpose and meaning outside that of its immediate narrative. This underlying significance was seen from earliest times to be the founding of Rome and the coming of Augustus, events whose fulfilment lay far beyond the time of the Trojan hero Aeneas, who is thus in the poem a prefiguration or 'type' of Augustus.

As the first great 'imitation' of Homer in a language other than Greek, the *Aeneid* became the inspiration for Statius (as he explains to Virgil and Dante in *Purgatorio*, 21–2), and for the vernacular epics of the Renaissance. Not only was it regarded as the only poem fit to stand comparison with Homer's; it also, for centuries, virtually displaced them. Latin was the dominant language of European culture from late antiquity till the Middle Ages, and Virgil was the most influential and revered Latin poet. St. Augustine in his *Confessions* movingly records his love for Virgil. He also admits to disliking Homer because he was forced to learn Greek which he found difficult. For Dante, Virgil, not Homer, is 'l'altissimo poeta'. Even Petrarch, the father of the Italian Renaissance, could not read Homer in Greek. Thus for perhaps a millenium and a half, despite a revival of Greek learning in the twelfth century, Homer's epics were like distant monuments, venerated but seldom visited, known chiefly by repute or hearsay, their true nature and stature debased and trivialized in late antique Latin summaries and paraphrases. It was on these that the popular twelfth-century French *Roman de Troie* was based, and it is from the *Roman* that the 'Homeric' tales of Boccaccio, Chaucer, and Lydgate derive. Medieval authors rewrote Homer in the spirit of an age of chivalry and courtly love.

Even in the Renaissance Greek texts were only beginning to

be properly edited. Homeric Greek, moreover, which differs considerably from classical Greek, was still a strange and difficult dialect whose philology and prosody were imperfectly understood and remained so until the emergence at the beginning of the eighteenth century of the scientific study of historical and comparative philology. Nor did Renaissance criticism of Homer break with the long tradition of allegory which began in antiquity (originally as a means of explaining the poems' moral inadequacies), and flourished throughout the Middle Ages, when allegory was the dominant mode of reading and of writing. The allegorical tradition reached its zenith in the sixteenth century. The first English vernacular epic, Spenser's *Faerie Queene*, was proclaimed by its author to be an allegory or 'dark conceit' intended to 'fashion a gentleman . . . in virtuous and gentle discipline'. The Renaissance theory of poetry was that it should be 'delightful teaching': delightful, because it shared with music qualities of rhyme, rhythm, and harmony, but didactic because Renaissance writers believed, under the influence of Plato, that art ought to have a moral function and that, despite Plato, it could and did discharge that function provided it was not taken literally. Thus the *Odyssey* was 'explained' allegorically as the triumph of wisdom over adversity and vice.

In allegory nothing is what it appears, but must be interpreted as meaning something else and, indeed, as having been intended by the writer to mean something else. The allegorizing process tends to generalize every character or action into an abstraction. No poetry is less susceptible to this process than Homer's. It was composed to be heard, not read; for entertainment, not instruction. It has no hidden meanings. Everything described in it is intensely and uniquely itself.

The practice of allegorizing worked much better for the *Aeneid*. It is not merely that Aeneas prefigures Augustus, but that the poem itself is concerned with man's evolution towards virtue, the recurring conflict throughout history between *furor* and *pietas*, barbarism and civilization, darkness and light. The humanistic ideals of the Renaissance were largely based on the Latin classics: Rome itself represented the earthly embodiment of the ideal of order and civilization. The stoical Aeneas exemplified the ideal prince more consistently than the much more egocentric Achilles or Agamemnon. The neoclassical exaltation of Virgil finds its most extreme statement in the *Poetics* of the French classical scholar, J. C. Scaliger (1561), but most Renaissance critics agreed that, although Homer, coming first, excelled in 'invention', that is, was more original, Virgil was the more polished artist and reflected the values of a more civilized age. Homer's poetry seemed in comparison alien and remote, and remained throughout the sixteenth century inaccessible to all but a very few. A poet's greatness will not be seen if he cannot easily be read, either in the original or in a good translation.

The first complete English translation of Homer, using the Greek text, was made by Chapman. His *Iliads* began to appear at the end of the sixteenth century. It was a literary event—Francis Meres refers in 1598 to 'Chapman's inchoate Homer'. Chapman still saw the poems allegorically, the *Iliad* as the personification in Achilles' wrath of 'the body's fervour and fashion of outward fortitude, to all possible height of heroical action'; the *Odyssey* as the personification in Odysseus of 'the mind's inward, constant, and unconquered empire, unbroken, unaltered with any most insolent and tyrannous infliction'. His aim as a translator was to restore Homer to his proper place as a greater and no less morally schematic poet than Virgil: 'the majesty he enthrones and the spirit he infuseth into the scope of his work so far outshining Virgil ... not only all learning, government and wisdom being deduced as from a bottomless fountain from him, but all wit, elegancy, disposition and judgement'. Shakespeare's *Troilus and Cressida* may have been prompted by Chapman's *Iliad*, but its sour and cynical tone ('nothing but wars and lechery') seems at times deliberately reductive of Chapman's lofty grandeur. It is also largely indebted, as its title shows, to medieval Troy-tales. Pandarus' role as go-between is not Homeric, while Cressida, the medieval type of the 'light woman', is a distorted form of the name Chryseis, a minor character at the bottom of the cast-list of the *Iliad*.

By the end of the seventeenth century, changes in literary taste had made Chapman's style seem old-fashioned. Dryden translated the whole of Virgil into the 'reformed numbers' of the age, but only completed the first book of the *Iliad*, 'albeit', he said, 'with greater pleasure than any part of Virgil'. If Dryden's expressed preference did not yet dislodge Virgil, his example inspired Pope to do for Homer what his predecessor had done for Virgil. Pope's *Iliad*, with its profusion of polished antitheses and exalted sentiments, has been seen as a grand allusion to the original, as Homer refined and civilized according to Augustan neo-classical ideals, but it was none the less an influential contribution to Homeric studies by a poet of international prestige (especially in Germany). Pope follows Renaissance critical tradition in comparing Homer with Virgil—'Homer was the greater genius, Virgil the better artist'—but there is a significant shift of emphasis. Pope compares Homer's 'pure and noble simplicity'—a quality his translation can hardly be said to reproduce conspicuously— with the Scriptures; he also emphasizes Homer's primitiveness and his historical authenticity. 'Homer is the most ancient author in the heathen world', and must be prized because he is 'the only true mirror of that ancient world'.

Thus in place of the old 'literary' Homer of antique and Renaissance tradition a new 'historical' Homer arose. Robert Wood, in his essay *On the Original Genius of Homer*, 1769, followed Pope and the Italian philosopher Vico in emphasizing Homer's naturalism and his veracity to a remote culture. Wood actually went to Greece, an undertaking pregnant with significance, for it presupposed that the 'truth' about Homer was not to be found in allegorical commentaries or comparisons with Virgil but in the real world. Virgil himself, according to Pope in his *Essay on Criticism*, had found that 'Nature and Homer were the same.' Wood also suggested that the relation between the written text of Homer and his originals might be like that between Macpherson and Ossian, then newly published and widely read. The analogy was unfortunate, for 'Ossian' proved to be a literary counterfeit, but the suggestion itself was far-reaching, forcing upon scholars the so-called 'Homeric question' from which all modern readings of Homer have begun.

This new emphasis on Homer's naturalism, primitivism, and simplicity came when the long tyranny of Roman classicism over the European sensibility was being undermined. Homer played a major part in this process, especially in Germany, then experiencing a delayed cultural renaissance. Winckelmann, Lessing, and Herder glorified Greek art for its 'Apollonian' qualities of calm and noble simplicity. Goethe and Schiller saw in Homer not the crude 'primitive' neglected by neo-classical taste, but rather the supreme example of the kind of poetry defined by Schiller as 'naïve', in which the artist does not intrude his own personality but which draws its power from nature and expresses the culture of a whole people.

The romanticism towards which the poets of this period were moving might seem to, and indeed ultimately did, point away from Homer; but in a seminal essay the German critic Wolf, taking his cue from Wood, argued that there never had been a personal Homer at all, only a late editor or compiler (as late as the sixth century B.C., he supposed) who collected up primitive folk-lays. The Homeric epics were therefore a different *kind* of poetry from anything written by the Romans. This idea caught the imagination of Goethe, who saw in this new 'impersonal' Homer the very spirit and reflection of a young untarnished world in which nature's intentions came nearest to finding perfect expression and fulfilment. It was a radical commonplace of the age that modern man was diseased, living in an artificial civilization. The 'nature-worship' of the late eighteenth century merely emphasized the alienation of man from his environment. Homer saw no need to worship nature or to admire shepherds, swineherds, or leech-gatherers. For Goethe and Schiller, Homer is free from the teleological curse, the desire to reach some goal. He is equally content with whatever object, event, or character he is describing. He lives in each moment. His world is uninfected and whole.

Schiller summed up in an epigram this view of Homer as the archetypal 'child of nature':

Tear to shreds the garland of Homer, and count the fathers
  Of the perfect eternal work!
Yet it has but one mother, and the features of the mother,
  Thy undying features, Nature.

It was at this time that Voss translated Homer into sonorous, unwieldy German hexameters—an achievement comparable to Chapman's in England two centuries earlier. As Chapman was to open up 'the realms of gold' to Keats, so Voss opened them up to Goethe, who made experiments in 'impersonal' Homeric epic, including an unfinished *Achilleid*.

In the nineteenth century, the view that Homer offered a true picture of primitive Greece was subjected to the scrutiny of the Higher Criticism along with traditional beliefs in the historicity of the Bible. German scholars produced new theories about the poems' evolution: the 'analytical', according to which the poems were composed of independent lays stitched together, and the 'nucleus' theory, which won wider acceptance, and according to which the poems as we have them consist of Homer's original compositions with accretions by later poets. Archaeologists tried to test Homer's veracity by digging for Priam's Troy and Agamemnon's Mycenae, but poets and literary critics re-emphasized Homer's qualities as an imaginative artist. Browning, in a late poem, *Development*, looking back on the controversy which had started with Wolf, concludes that even if there was, after all,

> No actual Homer, no authentic text,
> No warrant for the fiction I as fact
> Had treasured in my heart and soul so long,

it need make no difference to Homer's value for humanity. In perhaps a similar way the Darwinians contended that the theory of evolution strengthened rather than destroyed the value of the Scriptures. Gladstone continued to believe in a personal Homer who lived at a time closer to that of Troy than to that of Herodotus and who was thus 'in the highest degree historical'. To him, as to Goethe, Homer was a noble primitive of genius, both realist and idealist, in whose poems is captured the youth of the world. He illustrated his belief by translating some passages of Homer into the literary ballad form popularized by Scott.

Francis Newman (brother of J. H. Newman) went much further in an attempt to reflect Homer's primitivism, using an absurdly archaic and obsolete diction, which was attacked by Matthew Arnold in his lectures 'On Translating Homer'. Arnold realized that the short lines and jog-trot rhythms of the ballad are far removed from the sweep and dignity of the epic hexameter, and that the use of out-of-date words is misleading since it suggests that Homer is quaint. He reminded his age that Homer's poems are classics of the grand style, not primitive efforts whose chief merit lay in a disputed historicity or in their links with folk-culture.

Homer's art reflects an aristocratic society, a fact the eighteenth-century radicals ignored. The *reductio ad absurdum* of the 'balladmonger' view of Homer is to be found in Kipling's poem:

> When 'Omer smote 'is bloomin' lyre
>   'E 'eard men sing by land and sea
> And what 'e thought 'e might require
>   'E went an' took—the same as me ...

in which the cockney idiom provides the ultimate debasement and distortion of Homeric *Kunstsprache* and turns the poet into a kind of archaic Autolycus picking up popular songs from shepherds and fishermen. Arnold argued that the language of the ballads, and even of Chaucer, was foreign to the educated Englishman in a way Homer's Greek had never been foreign to Plato, to whom Homer had been a classic, a combination, perhaps, of the Bible and Shakespeare. Arnold applied to Homer the same touchstones of great poetry which he had applied to Shakespeare or Milton, thereby reasserting Homer's place at the fountainhead of the European cultural mainstream, 'the most important poetic monument existing'. He maintained that Homer's nobility and simplicity (criteria he took over from Pope) demanded a diction familiar to educated men and free from any taint of the common or the grotesque. The Victorian scholar Andrew Lang and his associates Butcher, Leaf, and Myers translated Homer into a pastiche of the King James Bible. Their versions are faithful to the original in a way the great poet-translators had disdained (Dryden had defined translation as 'closer than paraphrase, not so close as metaphrase'), and the analogy they imply has some validity, since the Old Testament contains much traditional poetry and describes an age of hero-kings, but they perhaps turn Homer into the equivalent of a Hollywood costume epic since we, unfortunately, are no longer as familiar with the Authorized Version as were the Victorians.

Of the twentieth century it may be said that it has reasserted Homer's primary function as a story-teller, and that the versions of Lattimore, Fitzgerald, and others have, with the help of the paperback revolution in publishing, brought the poems alive for more readers than at any previous time in their long history. In addition, new attention has been paid recently to certain aspects of Homer largely ignored by, and irrelevant to, the controversy over authorship and authenticity—his mythology, his theology, and his morality.

Scattered through the poems, as through other traditional compositions, are examples of 'wisdom', the kind of material separately assembled in certain books of the Old Testament. This wisdom represents man's earliest attempts to conceptualize about life, before the emergence of the abstract or speculative sciences. 'As are the generations of leaves, so are those of men; the wind scatters the leaves to the earth, but in spring more are put forth, and so too of the generations of men, one is put forth, another dies': this generalization, which can readily be paralleled in the Old Testament, not only reflects observed experience, but seems appropriate to a poem in which immortality remains a gift the gods conspicuously withhold from man. Zeus in the *Iliad* is at one point tempted to bestow immortality on his son, the slain hero Sarpedon, but is dissuaded by Hera on account of the dangerous precedent this would set. A more imaginative parable is that of Zeus' two jars, which stand on the floor of his house, one containing evils, one blessings. Zeus gives to mortals either a mixed lot or, to an unlucky few, only evils. No mortal ever receives only blessings. This homely image of wine-jars may have come down from an earlier mythopoeic culture to which Homer still had access, but its appearance in Achilles' great speech to Priam in the last book of the *Iliad* provides a tragic moral summary of the whole poem, the truth about human life as the *Iliad* has shown it.

Homer also includes myths about the origin of the universe and stories about the gods. Some of these resemble those preserved in Hesiod's cosmogonic poetry. But some seem to have been put in for the sake of the plot with no didactic purpose or moral justification. The story of the 'beguiling' of Zeus by Hera in *Iliad*, 14, is charming and sophisticated, with the frivolous sparkle of high comedy, and may well have been introduced at a late stage in the poem's evolution. It is the kind of story which caused Plato to condemn Homeric theology as disreputable and false, and it is indeed a disconcerting blend, in part high imaginative fantasy—for instance, the brilliant description of Poseidon's sea-journey in *Iliad*, 13, in which the sea-beasts frolic in joyous acknowledgement of their lord and the waters are parted for his chariot— but pervaded also by an emerging sense of rationality, psychology, and morality.

When Agamemnon and Helen speak of Ate as the cause of their passions they do not seek to disclaim responsibility for what they have done but to define the nature of the irrational forces which sweep over men and cloud their judgement. In the vague figures of Ate (Madness) or Eris (Strife) Homer begins the technique of externalization by personification which was to have such far-reaching effects on later literature. These abstractions exist alongside the startlingly anthropomorphic Olympian deities. Homer's most fully developed piece of allegory occurs in *Iliad*, 9, where penitential prayers are described as Zeus' daughters, lame and wrinkled, vainly trying to catch up with sin, which is strong and nimble and always keeps ahead, causing men to do wrong, 'while the prayers follow behind healing the harm'. In this passage are sketched the beginnings of a theory of general morality. In another passage in *Iliad*, 16, Patroclus' pursuit of the Trojans is compared with a storm sent by Zeus 'to punish those who violently pronounce crooked judgements in the market-place, and drive out justice, not caring for divine vengeance'. These passages resemble some lines in the more overtly moralistic Hesiod, and have been labelled interpolations, but they are not inconsistent with moral views expressed elsewhere in Homer. In the *Odyssey*, Zeus censures Aegisthus for ignoring Hermes' warning not to kill Agamemnon and make love to his wife, 'for their son Orestes would punish him when he grew up'. This is the theme of Aeschylus' *Oresteia*, in which the archaic doctrine of sin and atonement finds its fullest expression. Homer's Zeus is, of course, citing Aegisthus as a contrast to Odysseus, who heeds the gods, and one cannot pretend that the austere figure of the Aeschylean Zeus has much in common with the fretful, henpecked, philandering, uneasily self-assertive figure in the *Iliad*. Yet even the Zeus of the *Iliad* does preside over some kind of rough justice: he acknowledges, and pays, his own debt to Thetis, and protects Priam in his role as suppliant.

The *Iliad* sets out to tell how 'the design or will (*boule*) of Zeus was accomplished'. But this grand design, which is co-ordinate, but not identical, with destiny, does not absolve the heroes from responsibility for their acts nor permit these acts to take place in an existential vacuum. This is particularly clear in the last book of the *Iliad*, in which Apollo denounces Achilles to the other gods for 'destroying pity', and Achilles, obeying the gods' will, hands back for ransom the body of Hector. This is a morally acceptable resolution, but it has in no way been imposed on the story—or on Achilles, who makes it clear that he acts of his own free will.

The relationship between the supreme deity, fate, and human free will was to become an important theme in later epics, but is already adumbrated in the *Iliad*. Homer's psychological and moral vocabulary is perhaps not so simple as some critics have assumed. Zeus, like Milton's God in *Paradise Lost*, knows what is destined to happen. Both deities may deflect some immediate action whose consequences would conflict with or 're-route' destiny. Zeus sends Apollo to stop Achilles storming the walls of Troy 'beyond what is destined'. Milton's God stops Satan from challenging Gabriel. It is in the nature of epic that the 'end' is foreseen and included in the poem, though its fulfilment lies beyond the end of the narrative. This design is already present in the *Iliad*, which begins 'in the middle'—the Horatian precept, deduced from Homer, became mandatory in literary epic— but stops short of the event towards which it moves, and which is foreseen not only by Zeus but by Agamemnon and Hector, the fall of Troy. The difference is that for Homer the fall of Troy is simply another story which he did not choose to treat; the *Iliad* is complete without it. For Virgil and Milton the past is incomplete until it is fulfilled in the future. The fall of Troy and Aeneas' arrival in Italy have no significance except as prefiguring the rise of Rome and the coming of Augustus, which Virgil introduces into his epic by means of long prophetic passages. In the same way, the fall of man and Adam and Eve's expulsion from Eden cannot be fully understood except as prefiguring Christ's incarnation and redemptive death, events likewise introduced into *Paradise Lost* in prophetic speeches.

In heroic epic moral questions are subordinated to action and generalization kept to the minimum. In the didactic epic of Hesiod moral issues become central. Hesiod writes in the same metre and the same kind of Greek as Homer and uses traditional material, but his poems probably represent Europe's first purely literary compositions. Of his two chief surviving poems, the *Theogony* is a catalogue of the genealogies and functions of the gods, a kind of creation epic describing the origins of the universe over which Zeus rules. The *Works and Days* is more interesting to the modern reader. It is a 'preceptive' poem, giving advice to the poet's brother on farming and, more generally, on how to manage life. It introduces the ordinary man into literature. Hesiod was himself a farmer in Boeotia, and his poetry deals with his own time, with the harsh reality of daily life, and bears the stamp of his own personality. It is thus an important landmark in early literature. Didactic poetry requires its author to identify himself no less than heroic epic requires its author to conceal himself—one does not take advice from an anonymous source—so Hesiod uses a different technique from the 'impersonal' Homer.

Hesiod draws on traditional myths to explain why men must work so hard for so little, just as the author of Genesis does when he tells how Adam was expelled from Eden. Hesiod says that work is Zeus' will for men. He tells how Prometheus stole fire from the gods, and how Zeus then created woman: the myth of Pandora, who unloosed from a jar all the evils which afflict mankind, only hope remaining sealed in the jar, has affinities with the myths of Eve and of Zeus' two jars in the *Iliad*. Equally bleak and pessimistic is the myth of the five races of man (or 'ages' as the Latin *aetas*, the equivalent of the Greek word *genos*, is usually rendered). Only the first race, the 'golden', was blessed. Plato was the first to point out that Hesiod used 'golden' metaphorically since the golden race did not mine metals, and the term has been current ever since to describe man's first state of happiness, which we call prelapsarian. Then followed in succession and in steady deterioration the silver and bronze races, the race of heroes who fought at Troy and Thebes (the ones celebrated in heroic song), and lastly, the iron race of Hesiod's own day, whom the poet says Zeus will destroy in its turn when its babies are born with grey hair and when the wicked prosper at the expense of the righteous.

Hesiod thinks this time may be coming. Zeus has endowed all men with the ability to tell right from wrong, but only princes have the power to exercise this faculty, and Hesiod, dependent on princes for judgement and justice, warns them to eschew bribes and crooked dealing. The warning plainly reflects the poet's experience. Hesiod strikes for the first time that note of complaint and criticism of the great which was later to declare itself in satire. Hesiod's advice to work hard is based on self-interest: it is the poor who are most at the mercy of the great. Hesiod makes an important advance in moral speculation when he formulates the difference between the bad kind of Strife, which causes war, personified in Homer, and a good kind, competitiveness, which makes lazy people work, 'and neighbour vies with neighbour', the first known reference to 'keeping up with the Joneses'.

Hesiod is the father of mythological poetry and was used as source-material by many Greek and Roman poets. Ovid's *Metamorphoses* starts with a 'creation' epic in the Hesiodic tradition. As a practical and didactic writer Hesiod continued to be influential even after prose had become the medium for instruction. Later Greek poets wrote hexameter verse about philosophy and astronomy. Among Roman writers, Cicero made translations of Greek didactic epic. The most famous Latin didactic poems are Lucretius' *De rerum natura* and Virgil's *Georgics*. Lucretius sets forth a philosophy of scientific materialism. The account in his fifth book of man's evolution is an up-to-date version of Hesiod's myth of the five races of man. But the power and beauty of his poem do not derive from its didactic purpose but from its author's moral fervour, sense of mission, and desire to counteract the fears instilled by traditional religion. Like the *Works and Days*, the *De rerum natura* includes satirical and consolatory elements.

Virgil's *Georgics* owes its inspiration directly to the *Works and Days*. It gives instruction on viticulture, bee-keeping, and other aspects of farming, on which earlier Roman writers had produced treatises. Hesiod's advice on how to prune, reap, plough, keep warm in winter was not only the first of its kind committed to writing, it was also highly practical. But although Virgil himself loved the countryside, it is unlikely that any farmer in his time needed to have recourse to a composition so sophisticated and profoundly 'literary' as the *Georgics*. Much of Hesiod's advice is linked to the calendar. For Virgil the natural cycle is primarily a topic on which to lavish his art, and the poem is chiefly celebrated for its deeply felt, nostalgically idealized praise of the Italian countryside and the Italian rural virtues of hard work and simple living, contrasted with the decadent manners and corrupt morals of the city. Virgil also uses the poem as a framework for narrative display-pieces in the Alexandrian style. In England, Thomson's *The Seasons* (1730) was modelled on the *Georgics* rather than on Hesiod. Written in a Miltonic—which is to say a 'Virgilian' rather than a 'Homeric'—style, it includes scientific and technical passages and meditations on nature. Thomson, writing in a civilized and optimistic age, sees the environment as not only favourable to man provided he exploits it properly and lives prudently, but also as offering all he needs for happiness. In the peaceful fields and farms, the golden age lingers on.

But the world Hesiod lived in, and described, was an iron one. From this world Homer turned away to an imaginative retrospect of a more splendid, though far from peaceful age, which had been preserved in the traditional art of heroic song. So completely did he realize that age, and that art, in his epics that nothing like them exists. He left 'that high horse riderless'. It is perhaps fitting that the only modern work which in the breadth of its humanity and the vast scope of its conception and grandeur of its execution can truly be called 'Homeric' is Tolstoy's *War and Peace*, which expressly rejects the heroic view of history as no longer meaningful.

Further Reading

A translation of the Gilgamesh epic by N. K. Sandars is available in Penguin (1970). Among the numerous available translations of the Homeric epics, R. Lattimore's *Iliad* (Chicago, 1962) and *Odyssey* (Chicago, 1968) are strongly recommended: the former is available as a paperback (Phoenix, 1951). There is a useful *Companion to the Iliad* (based on Lattimore's translation) by M. M. Willcock (Chicago, 1970). The Victorian version of the *Iliad* by Lang, Leaf, and Myers is available as a Macmillan paperback (1947), as is the *Odyssey* of Butcher and Lang (1949). R. Fitzgerald's *Odyssey* is also recommended (Anchor paperback, 1967). Pope's *Iliad* is reprinted with his preface in the World's Classics (Oxford, 1902). Arnold's lectures on translating Homer are included in *Essays Literary and Critical* (Everyman, 1964) and *Essays, Letters, and Reviews* (Oxford, 1960).

On Greek mythology, see G. S. Kirk's *The Nature of Greek Myths* (Penguin, 1974) and his comparative study, *Myth: Its Meaning and Functions in Ancient and Other Cultures* (Cambridge, 1970). On the historical background of Homer, *History and the Homeric Iliad* by D. L. Page (Cambridge, 1963) emphasizes the Mycenaean elements in the poem; *The World of Odysseus* by M. I. Finley (new edn., Chatto and Windus, 1977) looks at the background in the light of Greek archaic society.

On the poems themselves, the basic work on the oral tradition is *The Making of Homeric Verse*, ed. A. M. Parry (Oxford, 1971), which includes the papers of Milman Parry; but it is highly technical and the reader without Greek may prefer a more general account such as *Homer*, by C. M. Bowra (Duckworth, 1972), or *Homer and the Epic*, by G. S. Kirk (Cambridge, 1965), a shorter version of his authoritative *The Songs of Homer* (Cambridge, 1962). Gilbert Murray's *Rise of the Greek Epic* (Oxford, 1960) is much less up-to-date, but it remains an exciting and stimulating work of imaginative scholarship. On Homeric religion and beliefs, see *The Greeks and the Irrational*

92   *Homer and the Epic*

by E. R. Dodds (California, 1951), chs. 1–3, and *The Justice of Zeus*, by H. Lloyd-Jones (California, 1971), chs. 1 and 2.

On the history of Homeric scholarship, the standard work is *Homer and his Critics*, by J. L. Myres (Routledge, 1958). On the lost Greek epics, see *Greek Epic Poetry*, by G. L. Huxley (Faber, 1969). On Homer's fortunes in the Middle Ages and the Renaissance see R. R. Bolgar, *The Classical Heritage and its Beneficiaries* (Cambridge and Harper Torchbook paperback, 1954); the Index, under 'Homer', in E. R. Curtius's *European Literature and the Latin Middle Ages* (Routledge, 1953); and (mainly on Chapman's *Odyssey*) *Homeric Renaissance*, by G. de F. Lord (1972). *Goethe and the Greeks*, by H. Trevelyan (Cambridge, 1941) examines Homer's importance for the German pre-romantic revival. *The Ulysses Theme*, by W. B. Stanford (Oxford, 1963) traces the fortunes of Homer's hero in post-Homeric literature down to modern times.

On Homer's style, the reader with no Greek will profit from the first chapter of Erich Auerbach's *Mimesis: the Representation of Reality in Western Art* (English transl. by Willard Trask, Anchor paperback, 1953). Those who are interested in the technique of comparative criticism of Virgil and Homer will find useful material in *Darkness Visible: A Study of Vergil's Aeneid*, by W. R. Johnson (California, 1976). A summary of the various and mainly misguided criticisms of Homer through the ages is included in *Enemies of Poetry*, by W. B. Stanford (Routledge, 1980).

4

LYRIC AND OTHER POETRY

A. M. DAVIES

Greek poetry includes almost every known kind, and has been written more or less continuously from the eighth century B.C. to the present day. The Greeks were inventors of many of these kinds, although an awareness of genre developed only gradually. This chapter will consider what remains of ancient Greek poetry, that is not epic or dramatic, as far as the fourth century A.D. and say something about its influence.

The legacy of Greek poetry has been transmitted directly to those who could read Greek, and indirectly through Latin literature and through translation into modern European languages. Like all legacies it has been differently perceived at different times; knowledge of Greek, though it has grown and spread in the past few centuries, has always been rare; but new texts have come to light from time to time, and understanding of the ancient world has grown. Lacking, as a rule, theatrical or narrative interest, shorter poems are in some ways more difficult of access in translation than epic or drama; and the intense fusion of form and content possible in such poems suffers a greater loss; but the range and variety of Greek poetry that is not epic or dramatic, and its excellence in many kinds, has enabled it, whether in the original or in translation, to exercise a powerful effect on at any rate some readers since the Renaissance—itself essentially the rebirth of art and literature under the influence of classical models, with at its heart the birth, or rebirth, of a glamorous idea of ancient Greece.

Aspects of the influence of Greek poetry will appear as we trace its history. Any account of the ways in which an influence has affected a later age or been absorbed into a national tradition is bound to be uncertain and imprecise, but with Greek poetry there is this further fact that it has often been mediated through Latin—either through classical Latin poets who have used its subjects, kinds, styles, images, and metres for writing their own, or through Renaissance scholars, who translated it into Latin from which further translations were made into the vernacular languages. Also, in education, Latin literature has played a larger part than Greek, and teaching of Greek poetry has concentrated on epic and drama. Translations of other kinds of Greek poetry have been fewer. Texts of some early Greek poets have been undiscoverd or fragmentary, and understanding of them imperfect. It cannot be said that the direct influence on European literature since the Renaissance of Greek poetry that is not epic or dramatic has been substantial, though it can be found here and there like clear light or pure colour. In an important sense the great legacy of Greek poetry consists of its own remains.

To make sense of so wide and long a subject will require a loose framework of development and change in which to place the many individual poets—some of whom, indeed, have had almost no discernible influence at all—but first a few comments may be made about Greek poetry in general. Perhaps the first thing that should be said is that Greek poetry tends to be not only beautiful but also intelligent: meaning is not sacrificed to rhetoric or sensibility; a reasonable sense always exists. It tends to be a poetry at once clear and fine, comparable in clarity of outline and refinement of detail to a Greek temple or a Greek vase. The image of a few columns standing in sunlight on a cliff above the sea, as at Sunium, may be a relevant analogy; to a modern taste the incomplete or fragmentary—as is so much of early Greek poetry—is more suggestive and satisfying than the Greek ideal of perfection; and the appeal of ruins in a Mediterranean landscape, as of a free, passionate, fulfilled life in such a climate, has been a part of romantic Hellenism in literature since the eighteenth century. Byron's Don Juan and his Haidée formed

> a group that's quite antique
> Half-naked, loving, natural, and Greek.

Greek poetry tends to be simple; which is not to say that it lacks subtlety or suggestion, but that even in work of the most impassioned or elaborate kind the meaning is expressed as simply as is consistent with nuances of truth and musical harmony. Simplicity was a value in Greek poetry from the beginning, and with modifications and exceptions remained so through the classical period into the centuries of scholarship and sophistication. Greek poetry tends to be marked by a conscious economy of means that makes for elegance and brevity. It is not surprising that much Greek poetry should show the virtues of a good theorem in a culture where mathematics was highly regarded; and not surprising that much Greek poetry should be concise as well as euphonious in a culture where, understandably, the Muses were held to be the daughters of Memory.

By and large there is a concentration in Greek poetry on what is universal and central in human beings and in life; a lack of interest in the eccentric and the odd, whether in the poet's temperament or his subject. There is a concern with truth that restrains flights of fancy and rhetorical excess. The Greek poets did not always see life steadily and see it whole, as Arnold asserted of Sophocles, but they usually tried, in another of his phrases, to see the object as in itself it really is, and having done so, to state their insights directly. Their sense of form may be reassuring, and sometimes exquisite, but it is normally in close relationship to content. Sometimes there is a satisfying tension in a poem between two forces: the modulation and flexibility of an individual speaking or singing voice, and the perfection of a few impersonal words inscribed as if for ever on a stone. Always, however, there is an awareness of what is being said. A sense of proportion, itself an ethical as well as an aesthetic concept, required an acceptable bond between form and content.

That content was centred on human life. Of course, some Greek poems were more or less religious, honouring or describing the divine principles of the universe, but for the most part Greek poems were about people living their lives here on earth—after which, it was generally believed, there was only a dark and dismal existence. Men should respect the gods and show a sense of moderation rooted in self-knowledge, but they should also live to the full the only life they would ever enjoy. The noble simplicity and calm grandeur which Winckelmann saw as characteristic of the best Greek art are certainly to be found in some Greek poetry, but they are not the only qualities and there is much else besides.

Many of the Greek lyrics of the archaic and classical periods that we now read were written for singing, and sometimes dancing also, at a performance before others to the accompaniment of music by lyre or flute or both (though of that music and dance almost nothing is now known). A poet composed words and music. The art of lyric poetry involved a technique of rhythm that was more complicated than the metres of intoned or spoken verse such as epic and iambic; and a full awareness of this poetic rhythm had been lost as early as the third century B.C. So when we read these Greek lyrics silently to ourselves, we lose in some of them the sense of participating in a visible and audible occasion, and in all of them something of their rhythmic power or subtlety.

Greek poetry, though of many kinds and metres, was all composed on a different system of scansion from that of English. The rhythms were based not on stress but on time: on the musical time (or quantity) of long and short elements (or syllables)—a 'long' was normally twice the length of a 'short', though time may have been allowed to vary with the music in sung verse, and stress may sometimes have played a part. There was also the matter of pitch. Accents to mark pitch—acute, grave, circumflex—began to be used on Greek words by the Alexandrians in the third century B.C., and it is stated that the variation in pitch between an accented and an unaccented syllable could be as much as the musical interval of a fifth. We are not sure of the relationship between pitch and stress in Greek—which itself changed over the centuries—and this is part of the reason why we are not able fully to respond to the sound of Greek poetry. There is no rhyme.

We do, however, have a fair knowledge of how the twenty-four sounds of the Greek alphabet were pronounced, and can note certain features of the Greek language that were significant for its poetry. It had a higher proportion of vowels to consonants than English, more pure vowels and a large number of short vowels; though this varied with author, dialect, and period. This vocalic quality of Greek, together with the way in which its syllables were separated—so as to end usually in a vowel rather than a consonant—tended to create a more melodious, rapid, and flowing language than either English or Latin, though perhaps it was spoken with something of the harsh beauty to be heard in modern Greek. Ancient Greek had a considerable range of grammatical forms: it was an inflected language with three persons (single, dual, plural), five cases (nominative, vocative, accusative, genitive, dative), three genders (masculine, feminine, neuter) three voices (active, middle, passive), four moods (indicative, imperative, subjunctive, optative), and a variety of past and future tenses as well as the present. It had a large vocabulary, and was especially rich in particles which subtly modify the sense at the same time as they lighten the sound. It lent itself to the creation of new words by combining prepositions with a verb or by compounding an adjective with another adjective or an adverb. Though in poetry even more than in prose rhythm was always a determinant of word order, and there were many mobile words that might be found at the beginning, middle, or end of a clause, yet despite this flexibility, Greek syntax tended to be more simple than Latin and is more like English.

As Greek poetry was composed over a long period in many places, its language varied in dialect or in mixture of dialect: Attic, Ionic, Aeolic, or Doric. In prose the dialects were gradually absorbed into a new common language, the *koine* (the language of the Greek New Testament), but in poetry a dialectical colouring remained for a long time. A traditional dialectical language was associated with some kinds of poetry, though the poet might exercise a certain degree of freedom. Epic poetry was basically Ionic in dialect, dramatic poetry essentially Attic with Doric elements, but lyric and other poetry was written in many varieties and fusions of dialect.

Early Greek poetry was composed either for one voice (monody or *melos*) or for a choir (choral poetry or *molpe*). But choral songs might involve solo singing: Homer in describing the shield of Achilles in the *Iliad* tells of a boy singing while his companions sing and dance. He also refers to various kinds of choral song—songs of celebration, triumph, thanksgiving, mourning. Choral songs were longer than monodies and written in more elaborate metres; monodies were more intimate and dealt with a wider range of themes. Both choral songs and monodies were accompanied by lyre or flute or both. The Alexandrians later made a list of the nine lyric poets, poets who had composed to the lyre (*lyros*) poems that were not in iambic or trochaic metre and were not in elegiac couplets: Alcman, Stesichorus, Sappho, Alcaeus, Ibycus, Anacreon, Simonides, Pindar, and Bacchylides.

Elegiac poetry in Greek means not poetry of a particular mood or subject, but poetry composed in elegiac couplets: a line of six feet followed by a line of five feet, both lines consisting of feet that are either dactyls or spondees or part of a spondee.[1] Originally elegiac couplets were written for the flute (*elegos*) and so got their name, and were used for songs of marching, conviviality, or love. But soon elegiac couplets were used for other kinds of poem, and from being sung at banquets came to be engraved on tombs. They continued to be written in Greek for many centuries and were to be the form of some of the finest Latin love poetry by Catullus, Propertius, and Tibullus.

We do not need to be bound by the Alexandrian list of the Greek lyric poets, and on a wider definition of lyrical poetry we may well begin with a glance at the so-called Homeric *Hymns*. Poetry was doubtless composed before Homer, but we have none that is earlier than his epics because it was then, probably in the eighth century B.C., that Greek poetry began to be written down. Some of the thirty-three Homeric *Hymns* seem to be as old as Homer himself, though they are no longer thought to have been written by Homer (if, indeed, there was one person, Homer, who 'wrote' one or both of the poems ascribed to him), and many date from later epochs. Probably recited by an individual poet, they are literary rather than devotional in character, and apply an epic manner to themes that are romantic rather than heroic. They vary in length from the long (500–600 lines) *Hymns* to Apollo, Dionysus, and Demeter to short prayers of a few lines. Some may have been preludes to the recitation by a rhapsode of an epic poem, and one of them, the brief (sixth) *Hymn to Aphrodite*, although not of the scale or power of the longer (fifth) *Hymn* to the same goddess, may serve as a prelude to a consideration of Greek lyric poetry:

I shall sing of holy Aphrodite, beautiful with her crown of gold, who is mistress of all the high battlements of sea-girt Cyprus, where the moist West Wind brought her over waves of sounding sea on soft foam; and the Hours in hairbands of gold received her gladly, dressed her in divine raiment, and set on her undying head a beautiful, well-made crown of gold, and in her pierced ears jewels of orichalcum and gold; around her neck and dazzling breasts they hung such golden chains as the Hours are adorned with when they go in hairbands of gold to the lovely dance of the gods in their father's house. When they had finished adorning her body, they led her to the immortals who, when they saw her, welcomed and

[1] An iambus is a short followed by a long ˘¯; a trochee is a long followed by a short ¯˘; a spondee is two longs ¯¯; and a dactyl is a long followed by two shorts ¯˘˘

embraced her, and longed every one to take her home as his wedded wife, marvelling at the beauty of Cytherea garlanded with violets.

Greetings, with your darting eyes and gentle sweetness; grant me victory in this contest; inspire my song. And I shall remember you in another song.

This celebration of beauty and sexual love, of art and nature, gold and flowers, with its prayer for inspiration, hope of victory, and promise to remember, strikes a recognizably Greek note.

The Homeric *Hymns* were translated into English by Chapman, not as effectively as he rendered the two epic poems, and seven of them by Shelley, well and more or less faithfully. Shelley's delight in Greek literature may have expressed itself obliquely and selectively in his own writing, with its transcendental and ethereal tendencies, but it was firmly rooted in a knowledge of Greek. Goethe included the *Hymns* in his immense admiration for Homer, which was only a part—if the chief part—of his strong feeling for all Greek poetry: a feeling which, though not always based on precise knowledge, was sustained and inspiring. His vision of Helen of Troy in *Faust* (Part II, Act III) has a multiple resonance that brings together his own deep and complicated responses to Greek poetry and art and suggests much about the intense and difficult relationship between Germany and the idea of Greece that has been so fruitful and sometimes disturbing over the past two centuries.

A contrast to the *Hymns* comes in the poetry of Archilochus, perhaps the first great personal poet of European literature, writing in the seventh century B.C. Again, he is not strictly a lyric poet as he wrote mainly in elegiac and iambic verse. We have nearly 300 fragments that may have been written by him, some no more than a word or two on papyrus strips, others longer, including a recent discovery of about thirty lines. The fragments are as varied in subject and tone as in metre and diction—love-poems, hate-poems, elegies, marching songs, fables—closer to speech than song. A vivid personality is expressing itself freely and forcefully, it may be in his own voice or dramatically. Meleager, the poet and anthologist of the late second and early first century B.C., was to call him 'a thistle with graceful leaves', and Longinus, to whom is ascribed the critical treatise *On the Sublime*, probably written in the first century A.D., was to praise his divine spirit that made up for a lack of control. (Here from the start is a challenge to any simple view of the distinction between 'classical' and 'romantic' poetry.) Horace proclaimed that he had imitated the metre—and moods—of Archilochus, but that he had made modifications, as Sappho and Alcaeus had done: a reminder that the legacy of Greek poetry was dynamic and cumulative throughout antiquity.

Archilochus was poet and soldier:

I am servant of the God of War and the Muses—their lovely gift is known to me.

But he admits that he has thrown away his shield on the battlefield, as Alcaeus and Anacreon were to admit later:

Some Saian glories in a shield—it was not to blame—which I left by a bush—against my will, but I saved myself from death. Let that shield go. I shall get another as good.

In a few words he paints a picture or records an emotion, freshly and sharply:

She was delighted to hold a spray of myrtle and a beautiful rose-blossom: her hair shaded her shoulders and back.

Unhappy with desire, I lie lifeless, my bones—by the grace of god— pierced with sharp pains.

O that I might touch Neoboule's hand.

He can be gnomic:

The fox knows many things, the hedgehog one big one.

And in these fragments of Archilochus are to be found some of the moral attitudes that will resound through Greek poetry: courage in the face of suffering; efforts to moderate the violence of sorrow and joy; reverence, mixed with fear, for the gods. He is an unforgettable voice.

Other writers of elegiac couplets in the seventh century were Callinus and Tyrtaeus, who both wrote of war and urged the military virtues of bravery and honour in defence of one's country. The elegiac couplets of Mimnermus, on the other hand, were about love, youth, and pleasure. Mimnermus was a poet and musician of importance, and may be seen as an early ancestor of the Latin writers of love-elegies: Propertius pays tribute to his smoothness. Mimnermus hated old age and death:

> O Golden Love, what life, what joy but thine?
>   Come death when thou art gone and make an end!
> When gifts and tokens are no longer mine,
>   Nor the sweet intimacies of a friend.
> These are the flowers of youth. But painful age,
>   The bane of beauty, following swiftly on,
> Wearies the heart of man with sad presage
>   And takes away his pleasure in the sin.
> Hateful is he to maiden and to boy
>   And fashioned by the gods for our annoy.
>
>   (Translated by G. Lowes Dickinson.)

At about the same time, Semonides was writing iambic poetry of a satirical kind on the vanity of human wishes and the nature of women. The iambic metre was associated with satire. He compared various female types with animals in a tradition of invective that had its roots in folklore. 'Woman is the worst of all evils', but there is one good type of woman, sprung from the bee, who brings joy and happiness. It is not poetry of a high order but has its own kind of interest. An imitator in the sixth century, Hipponax, wrote on a wider range of themes with a fierce realism that endeared him to many readers throughout antiquity, especially the Alexandrians. His bleak vision and sharp language remind us of the variety of Greek poetry and of many features of ordinary Greek life.

The poets of the seventh century wrote in Ionic Greek under the more or less strong influence of Homer. They lived in Ionia (Asia Minor) or the islands, except for Tyrtaeus, who wrote in Sparta in the southern part of the Greek mainland, the Peloponnesus. Sparta was not yet the military state it later became but a home of music and poetry. Spartan literature began in the seventh century with Terpander, who is said to have invented the seven-stringed lyre, and the treatise 'On Music' ascribed to Plutarch speaks of two 'schools' of music there at that time. We have only a few fragments which may be Terpander's but his name was associated with the development of the ritual song or hymn in honour of Apollo, the *nomos*. It was the counterpart of the dithyramb, or hymn in honour of Dionysus, which, perhaps beginning as a simple melody, was made into an elaborate form by Arion of Lesbos at Corinth in about 600 B.C. The dithyramb, in combination with other elements, was to develop into Greek tragedy. Later the *nomos* and the dithyramb were to converge.

It is from Sparta that we have our earliest substantial fragments of choral lyric, which are the work of Alcman.[2] The form was doubtless more ancient: in the Homeric *Hymn to Apollo*, on Olympus Artemis and the Muses sing as Aphrodite dances with the Graces and Hours while Apollo plays the lyre; and similar scenes take place on earth in the *Iliad*. On the shield of Achilles Homer shows young men and marriageable girls dancing with their hands on one another's wrists, as a minstrel sings divinely to the lyre, and a couple of acrobats keeping time with the music throw cartwheels in and out among the crowd of people enjoying the spectacle; and elsewhere on the shield there is singing and dancing to pipes and lyres in a wedding procession; and at the vintage, young men and women dance while a young boy plays the lyre and sings the lovely Linus song.

The longest fragment of Alcman consists of the hundred or so lines, complete or partial, of his *Parthenion* or Maiden Song. It seems to have been sung by a choir of girls at a religious festival before dawn, competing in music and beauty with another choir. The poem has the three traditional elements of a choral ode: myth, maxims, and personalities. It tells the story of the sons of Hippocöon, who were slain by Heracles or Castor and Polydeuces; it warns against *hybris*, violent pride; it makes remarks about individual girls. The structure may be one of recurring strophes; rhythm is mainly trochaic or dactylic. Its swift simplicity, brilliant images, and melodic beauty convey the grace and gaiety of an archaic world.

> There is vengeance from the gods;
> but blessed is he who blithely
> winds out all his day of life
> without tears. But I must sing the
> light of Agido. I see

---

[2] Of Stesichorus, the first great poet of the Greek west, who lived in Sicily, and whose fame and influence in the ancient world were considerable, we have almost nothing. He wrote long and complex choral lyrics in which he told stories from the heroic cycles. His poetry seems to have represented a significant stage in the movement from epic to tragedy.

> her like the sun, whose shining
> on us is witnessed through Agido.
> But our lovely choir leader
> will not let me praise her, nor
> say she is not fair.
> She knows well that she herself is
> something dazzling,
> just as if among a herd of
> cattle one should set a racehorse,
> sinewy, swift, and with feet full of thunder,
> creature out of a dream with wings.
>> (Translated by Richmond Lattimore.)

Of the other fragments of Alcman that survive, in quotation or on papyrus, out of the several books of his poems published by the Alexandrians, two at least are worth quoting. The first (if it is his) is an early example (though there are even earlier examples in Homer) of the evocation of nature by Greek poets. They often wrote of it. They did not, however, ascribe human feelings to natural objects and phenomena, for all their personification of features of nature as divine or semi-divine entities, and this is perhaps why it used to be said that the Greeks lacked a poetry of nature.

> The far peaks sleep, the great ravines,
> The foot-hills, and the streams.
> Asleep are trees, and hived bees,
> The mountain beasts, and all that dark earth teems,
> The glooming seas, the monsters in their deeps:
> And every bird, its wide wings folded, sleeps.
>> (Translated by H. T. Wade-Gery.)

In the second fragment, Alcman, weak from old age and unable to dance, alludes to the myth that, when the male halcyons grow old and are no longer able to fly, they are carried by their females.

No longer, maidens with honey tones and voices of desire, can my limbs carry me. Would, ah, would that I were a king-fisher, who flies with the halcyons over the flower of the wave, having a fearless heart, the sea-blue, sprightly bird.
>> (Translated by C. M. Bowra.)

The story now moves to the island of Lesbos, where in the seventh century a culture had developed that was favourable to poetry. It is an island rich in water and grass, olive and plane trees; in the spring covered with anemones, orchids, and wild tulips. Terpander and Arion were said to have come from Lesbos, and its association with music and poetry is marked by the later story that after Orpheus had been torn to pieces by Thracian women, his head and lyre were carried, in Milton's words in *Lycidas*, 'down the swift Hebrus to the Lesbian shore' where they were buried. Here it was that about the year 600 lyrical monody reached its zenith in the poetry of Sappho and Alcaeus.

With characteristic simplicity Sappho once wrote:

> I say that someone will remember us afterwards

and the prophecy has been fulfilled. She became and has remained the most famous of women poets, the composer of a clear, intense, and melodious poetry that expresses what she has to say sharply and directly, but also delicately. Of her many poems in various metres, choral and narrative as well as personal, we possess only fragments, but some may be almost complete. She wrote in the Lesbian variant of the Aeolic dialect. Most of her poetry that survives is about girls: her own passionate feelings were fused with the Lesbian cult of feminine beauty. One of her poems states firmly her own preference as opposed to the military values of male society, from whom the women may have lived largely apart:

> Some say that a host of horsemen is the fairest thing on the black earth, others of foot-soldiers, but I say that it is what one loves. It is very easy to make this understood by everyone. For she, who surpassed all human beings in beauty, Helen, left her most noble husband and went sailing to Troy with not a thought for her daughter or her dear parents.
>
> (Translated by C. M. Bowra.)

Longinus, quoting the verses translated below, praises her skill in selecting realistic details and making a unity of them so as to create a complex of extreme emotions. He also stresses her detachment in treating such a violent disorder of the senses. It is this control and objectivity, neither over- nor under-stating, that makes her at once essentially Greek and difficult to translate.

To me he seems like a god
as he sits facing you and
hears you now as you speak
softly and laugh

in a sweet echo that jolts
the heart in my ribs. For now
as I look at you my voice
it empty and

can say nothing as my tongue
cracks and slender fire is quick
under my skin. My eyes are dead
to light, my ears

pound, and sweat pours over me.
I convulse, paler than grass,
and feel my mind slip as I
go close to death
(Translated by Willis Barnstone.)

Her work touches, sometimes lightly, on many aspects of love, its aesthetic and social delights, its bitter sweetness, its longings and regrets, and appropriately there are several invocations of Aphrodite, who appears as the goddess of many kinds of beauty. A keen observation of nature shows itself from time to time:

Now she shines among Lydian women as
into dark when the sun has set
the moon, pale-handed, at last appeareth

making dim all the rest of the stars, and light
spreads afar on the deep, salt sea,
spreading likewise across the flowering cornfields.
(Translated by Richmond Lattimore.)

But above all she was devoted to her art, of which the variety is much greater than a brief account can indicate, and which she thought, rightly, would save her from the oblivion that awaits those who are ignorant of the Muses.

When you have died, you shall lie there, and there will never be memory of you or longing hereafter; for you have no share in the roses from Pieria; but in the House of Death also you shall walk unseen with the insubstantial dead, when you have flown from here.
(Translated by C. M. Bowra.)

Sappho has survived, though most of her work has not: as an ideal and a personality rather than an influence. Catullus translated into Latin the same poem, or part of a poem, the second ode (which was later to be quoted by Longinus) characteristically making use of literary tradition to express his own emotions. Ovid linked legends about her—her love for Phaon, her leap into the sea from a Leucadian cliff—in one of his heroic epistles; of which Pope produced a sparkling version in his *Sappho to Phaon*. (In the poems of Ovid and Pope passion coexists with wit, a quality almost entirely absent in most senses from Greek love poetry of the archaic and classical periods.) In ancient and modern times she has often been represented by artists: she has an honoured place, for example, in Raphael's *Parnassus*.

During the Renaissance, versions of her poetry were done in Latin. In French literature there have been Sapphic echoes and references since the Pléiade in the sixteenth century. Ronsard translated the same ode as Catullus, and Racine incorporated some lines of it into *Phèdre*, commenting that he had seen nothing more vivid and beautiful in the whole of antiquity. In the nineteenth century, Chénier was among those who imitated the same ode. Leopardi made her a symbol of despair (love must end in death), and there have been many Italian renderings. Kleist and Grillparzer wrote tragedies called by her name.

In England imitations of the Sapphic metre occur as early as the sixteenth century, though Sidney, in adapting her second ode in *The Old Arcadia* ('My muse, what ails this ardour'), interestingly uses an anacreontic metre making patterns of stress and quantity coincide. Tennyson paraphrased the ode in *Eleänore*, and Swinburne paid tribute in a virtuoso display of her own metre ('Ah, the singing, the delight, the passion'). In this century the Imagist poets tried to reproduce the clarity of suggestive images in early Greek poetry, and Pound aimed to create fragments which Sappho might have written. He twice uses the name of Gongula, one of her pupils. Eliot went further and used the evocative power of fragments to build a great poem of disintegration, *The Waste Land*, a poem under Greek influence in more ways than one.

Alcaeus, who was her friend and contemporary, wrote, as an aristocrat and soldier, of love, drink, myths, war, and politics (he may have invented the image of the ship of state, but here as often he may well have been using or adapting a traditional idea or phrase). His poetry is of limited value, but at its best has an immediacy and force that appear all the more strongly by contrast with the polish and intricacy of the Latin poems which Horace wrote in imitation of his. The achievement of Horace in adapting Greek metres, notably those of Sappho and Alcaeus, to Latin poetry shows him, in this respect as in others, a gifted and appreciative heir of the legacy of Greek poetry.

With Anacreon, writing more than fifty years later than Alcaeus at the courts of tyrants, in Samos and Athens, we are in another world, where pleasure is all. Born in Ionia, and so using that dialect, he fled westward before the Persian advance, and represents a new kind of migratory poet who found patronage where he could. His pleasures are those of love and conviviality. He was not concerned with war and politics; and when asked why he wrote hymns not to the gods but to boys, is said to have replied: 'they are our gods.' Anacreon's is a poetry of charm. His lyrics are elegant, light, fanciful. They strike a new note in Greek literature, and if they are sometimes shallow they are always skilful. He has an eye for an image and a notable sense of colour. In his way he strikes a Greek balance between excess of indulgence and deficiency; and he is clear-sighted—resigned to old age and death. He is never gross or feeble in the manner of some, but by no means all, of the later poetry that goes under his name: the *Anacreontea*, those many imitations of his work which went on being written in Alexandria and Byzantium over several centuries, and which have had such an influence on lyrical poetry in England, France, and Germany since the Renaissance. The following translation, although it blurs the final point that the girl is more interested in another girl, conveys something of that tone in Anacreon and his followers which was to attract such Cavalier poets as Herrick and Lovelace.

> Once more the Lad with golden hair
> His purple ball across the air
>   Flings at me, true to aim;
> And light her broidered slippers go,
> That Lesbian lass—my playfellow
>   As Love would set the game.

> O Lesbos isle is tight and trim.
> She's not the breed to pleasure him,
>   Another game she plays;
> My hair mislikes her, grown so white;
> There's someone lovelier in her sight
>   Who draws that callow gaze.
>   (Translated by T. F. Higham.)

Anacreon was the last of his line in the writing of monody, though we should not forget the name of Ibycus, his near-contemporary at the court of Polycrates in Samos, where he moved after an earlier career as a narrative poet in southern Italy. Although probably a solo song, this part of a love poem by Ibycus employs the gorgeous style of choral poetry with a use of metaphor that makes it one of the most evocative symbolist fragments in Greek poetry:

> In the spring the Cydonian quinces bloom, watered from the flowing rivers where is the maidens' inviolate garden, and the vine blossoms swell to strength under the shady sprays of the vine; but for me Love sleeps at no season. But like the North Wind from Thrace, aflame with the lightning, it comes with a rush from the Cyprian, dark and shameless with shrivelling madness, and masterfully shakes my heart from the roots.
>   (Translated by C. M. Bowra.)

Meanwhile elegiac couplets were being written on the mainland of Greece, as in the islands. The metre was used by Theognis to express an aristocratic distaste at the rise of democracy and its values, or to offer advice to his squire Cyrnus (one poem on the theme, so frequent in Greek poetry, of the immortality that the poet can confer ends oddly, though not ineffectively, with a note of complaint at the deceitfulness of the loved one, in a way that recalls some of Shakespeare's sonnets). Solon, the Athenian reformer, used the metre to express his moral views and political principles; Xenophanes for explicating his theology.

None of these writers can be regarded as poets of a high order, but they have interesting and sometimes important things to say and all belong to the extensive realm of Greek poetry that is not epic or dramatic. So do the short drinking songs, anonymous or ascribed, on political, moral, or mythological subjects, sung in chorus or by individuals at male dinner-parties, especially at Athens, to traditional tunes. So also do the archaic inscriptions in verse, hexameters or an elegiac couplet, that were written on vases, stone, and even gold-leaf from as early as the eighth century. This bleak epitaph is an example:

Whether you are a citizen or a stranger coming from elsewhere, take pity on Tettichos as you pass by: a brave man killed in battle, who there lost the pride of his fresh youth. Mourn for him awhile, and go on. May your fortune be good.

(Translated by Richmond Lattimore.)

We may think of the lines written for his own tomb by Yeats, who in the ethical values and severe power of his later poetry has more than a little in common with some of these early Greek poets.

> Under bare Ben Bulben's head
> In Drumcliff churchyard Yeats is laid.
> An ancestor was rector there
> Long years ago, a church stands near,
> By the road an ancient cross.
> No marble, as conventional phrase;
> On limestone quarried near the spot
> By his command these words are cut:
>> *Cast a cold eye*
>> *On life, on death,*
>> *Horseman, pass by!*

Simonides, writing in the late sixth and early fifth century, took this simple form, objective manner, and restrained tone for his epigrams, at which the Greeks thought he excelled. By an epigram they meant originally anything written on a surface capable of receiving it, perhaps in prose to record laws or titles, but more usually in verse—as being more memorable—to inscribe an offering, celebrate a hero, lament a death. It acquired a wide meaning to cover many kinds of short poem. Simonides concentrates and selects what is to be remembered, stating it musically but with a minimum of imagery. To Simonides were ascribed many of the best epigrams, including perhaps the most famous: an epitaph on the Spartans who died at Thermopylae. Employing the fiction that the dead speak, the author reduces their message to one of fidelity even unto death. But the elegiac couplet in which he does so derives its amplitude from a fusion of straightforward syntax with poetic diction and metrical virtuosity. Music has become language carved on stone. The pressure of feeling has been controlled and transformed into two lines that contain an order to report what is neither a boast nor a fancy because it is a fact. The Greek lines can hardly fail to be inadequate in English, but a reader may catch their appeal even in translation.

> Tell them in Lakedaimon, passer-by
> That here obedient to their words we lie.
>> (Translated by various hands.)

Some of the other epigrams are more obviously beautiful, though always clear and simple and with a marked sense of structure. They may be about an old spear or a dead dog. They may be about the difficulty of achieving virtue, the fragility of monuments, the brevity of happiness. In a longer poem, which may be complete or part of a longer whole, he shows poignantly the grief of Danae as with her child she is swept out to sea in her wooden chest, the child sleeping as the wind and waves rage in the darkness. It ends with a prayer to Zeus to forgive her boldness in asking him to change her fortune for the better. Pathetic but enchanting, the poem makes explicit the human feeling that lies behind his bare epitaphs.

Simonides wrote poems of many sorts as he had to, being one of the new professional kind of poet who wrote for a living and travelled widely in order to do so. They included choral poems—dithyrambs, dirges, and epinician odes to honour victory at the games (he was perhaps the first to write such odes), as well as narrative poems and epigrams. He also reflected on the nature of his art if two famous sayings are justly attributed to him:

> Painting is silent poetry; poetry painting that speaks.

and

> The word is the image of the thing.

These statements raise difficulties too large to explore here, but they certainly have an application to Simonides' own work, for example to the Danae fragment, and, it would seem, to a lost poem praised by Longinus for its power of visualization. Altogether, in the humanity of his poetry, its wisdom, and its qualities of restraint, clarity, and simplicity, Simonides represents a quintessential aspect of Greek literature.

So does Pindar, whom many Greeks regarded as their greatest lyric poet, and who differs from Simonides as much as he resembles him. The same is true of Pindar's other rival, Bacchylides, the nephrew of Simonides; various remains of his poems have been found in the past hundred years, and they reveal a poet of talent and charm, with a gift for narrative. Of Pindar's seventeen books of mostly choral poetry—hymns, paeans, dithyrambs, songs for girls, songs for dancing, songs for processions, threnes, and encomia—only four books of epinician odes and a number of fragments survive. But they are enough for us to form an impression of his excellence—or *arete*, to use a favourite word. He believed that excellence, of whatever kind, was partly inborn, and a gift of the gods. He was a deeply religious poet who was also interested in worldly success and its meaning. His epinician odes celebrate victories in various events at four Greek festivals of games. The Games were important to the Greeks as sacred festivals where individuals won fame and honour and where people came together from all over Greece with a consciousness of all being Hellenes. The important thing was to win—breaking records was of little interest—and to achieve the ideal of life expressed by Homer: always to excel and to be distinguished beyond others. Pindar saw victory in the games as a grace given by god to those who had developed their talents in the right way. It was an experience that transfigured the victor into a world of light that the poet made permanent in his ode. Pindar was not interested in the details of the contest, but in a realm of the spirit where the divine, the heroic, and the creative met.

Most of his odes are triadic in structure, i.e. consist of a series of triads, each of which consists of a strophe, an antistrophe, and an epode. Strophe and antistrophe are metrically identical not merely in the same triad but throughout the poem; the epode is in a different metrical pattern, but all epodes in a poem are exactly alike. Pindar not only mastered this structure but also invented a new metrical pattern for every poem. Sometimes, however, he wrote in a simpler monostrophic structure, where every strophe in an ode is metrically the same as every other. For some centuries after the Renaissance the principles of Pindaric composition were misunderstood, but we may now feel reasonably sure of his rhythms, though always within the limits discussed at the beginning of this chapter.

His language is a poetic fusion of dialects (Ionic, Doric, Aeolic); his style an extraordinary creation that moves from the simple to the difficult, the concentrated to the elaborate, with a swift abruptness of transition between subjects that seems to have been intended to give the effect of improvization. There is a tension between the strictness of form and the freedom of content. After an impressive opening he moves mysteriously from one part of his theme to another, as will or fancy dictates, and may end suddenly. The allusions are sometimes obscure. The imagery is always striking and often masterful. (Aristotle, in *Poetics*, 22, was to emphasize how essential the use of metaphor is to a poet: 'this is the one thing that cannot be learnt from anyone else, and it is the mark of great natural ability for the ability to use metaphor well implies a perception of resemblances.') Out of everything he creates a kaleidoscopic mixture.

His odes were made of traditional elements: myths, maxims, a praise of the victor, the glory of the gods (Pindar believed—Plato would have approved—that nothing but good should be spoken of them). He stresses the importance of the poet, who, like the victor, must exploit his talent and hope for the blessing of the gods in the form of inspiration. The poet was commissioned by the victor or his family to celebrate the triumph in an ode, which was performed by a choir to the flute and lyre, though perhaps sometimes by a single singer. Aspects of myth were selected to point a moral or relate the present to the past. It is not always easy to relate his ethical judgements one to another but we may say that Pindar believed in divinity, excellence, nobility, artistry, and the past. Man should strive to do his best but should never forget the gods.

In the ancient world, Greek and Roman, Pindar was famous and admired. Horace warned against trying to rival him, and, though he shows traces of his influence, created a different kind of ode. When Pindar was rediscovered in the Renaissance he exercised a dazzling attraction on some ambitious poets who tried to imitate him in the vernacular European languages—Chiabrera in Italy, Ronsard in France, Jonson in England. In important respects their poems are unlike Pindar's, though Jonson in the *Ode to Sir Lucius Cary and*

Sir Henry Morison reproduced the triadic structure of 'Turn, counter-turn, and stand' and achieved certain Pindaric effects, even if the over-all impression is more Horatian. The interplay of the influence of these two classical poets is an interesting feature of many modern odes.

Abraham Cowley, too, though his baroque verse is underestimated by modern taste, caught something of Pindar's manner in his translations and imitations and, despite his rejection of Pindaric structure, was an influence on poets—they included Dryden and Pope—for several decades. Cowley was impressed by Pindar's wildness, and asserted that if one were to translate Pindar word for word, it would be thought that one madman had translated another. Congreve took objection in his *Discourse on the Pindaric Ode* to the irregularity of Cowley's stanzas, but he admired 'the beauty of his verses, the force of his figures, and sublimity of his style and sentiments'. Congreve understood Pindar's structure though not the details of his metre; he offered his own Pindaric *Ode to the Queen* as an example. Gray wrote regular as well as irregular Pindaric odes (the two former, *The Progress of Poesy* and *The Bard*, more successful than the latter), and in one of them adapts two passages from Pindar's Fourth Pythian Ode. We may trace him in Shelley's Odes and in Hopkins's *The Wreck of the Deutschland* and elsewhere. In Germany, both Goethe and Schiller translated and imitated Pindar; so did Hölderlin, who felt so truly the relationship in Greek poetry between intensity and objectivity.

At Athens in the fifth century the poetry of the drama dominated, but there and elsewhere choral and other poetry continued to be written well into the fourth century. The dithyramb, converging with the *nomos*, now came to subordinate words to music and to adopt a mimetic approach in which changes of rhythm and sensuous effects were striking. Plato, in accord with his view that a change in musical modes is significant for the life of a nation, was unhappy about this new poetry, which was closely related to profound social, political, and economic developments. Our former ignorance has been enlightened by the discovery of a fourth-century papyrus (our oldest Greek manuscript) containing several hundred verses of a poem by Timotheus called *The Persians*. Its vivid pictorialism and dramatic expressiveness in a rich periphrastic style certainly point to a change in taste.

Appropriately, though unwittingly, Dryden in *Alexander's Feast* is in several respects less close to Pindar than to Timotheus, the relationship of whose art to that of Saint Cecilia is the subject of the poem.

As always there were epigrams—for inscriptions, as a form of literary art, and for polemic. Aeschylus wrote his own epitaph, alluding to his courage at the battle of Marathon but not to his plays; Aristotle praised the virtue of a friend and patron; Plato was the author of several poems. In a pair of linked elegiac couplets he may be referring to someone called Aster (which in Greek means 'a star').

> Thou gazest on the stars:
>   Would I might be,
> O star of mine, the skies
> With myriad eyes
>   To gaze on thee.
>
> (Translator unknown.)

and

> Thou wert the morning-star among the living
>   Ere thy fair light had fled.
> Now, having died, thou art as Hesperus giving
>   New splendour to the dead.
>
> (Translated by Shelley.)

The last full flowering of ancient Greek poetry was at Alexandria in the third century B.C., though some fine poems continued to be written for centuries afterwards. After Alexander the civilization of the small city-state gave way throughout the Greek world to large military kingdoms. A standardization of the Greek language went along with a pressure towards uniformity from which the individual might take refuge in writing or reading about the extraordinary or unexpected. At the cosmopolitan oriental city of Alexandria, in a scholarly and scientific circle under the patronage of the Ptolemies, learned poets, cut off from that sense of belonging to a whole society which had marked most classical poetry, wrote for one another poetry that carefully combines the rare and remote word or fact with a sophisticated feeling for romance. (The same era saw the birth of romantic fiction in prose.) For many readers of succeeding ages the work of the Alexandrians has been the most congenial kind of Greek poetry.

The extensive and influential work of Callimachus included: hymns (some of them to be admirably translated into English by Prior in the seventeenth century) that made use of mythology without subscribing to it; a lost work in four books of elegiac verse, the *Aetia*, about festivals, names, and customs; *The Lock of Berenice*, which told how that queen's hair became a constellation (the translation by Catullus has been the usual source for later uses of the story, as for example by Pope in *The Rape of the Lock*); satirical iambic poems which may have helped to shape early Latin satire; and a number of epigrams whose miniature scale and telling detail is appropriate to a poet famous for his saying that a big book is a big bore. The well-known version by Cory of Callimachus' epigram on his friend Heraclitus is affecting, but in its expansions, repetitions, and cadences is subtly false to the art of a poet who even in a romantic period retained a brevity, crispness, and poise more common in Greek than in English literature.

The two other famous poets of Alexandria were Theocritus and Apollonius of Rhodes, who, being a writer of epic, is discussed in Chapter 3. Theocritus is said to have been the author of various kinds of poetry, but he is known to us for his thirty *Idylls* together with a few epigrams and fragments. The word 'idyll' was applied later and seems to have meant 'a small poem'; the idea that it meant 'a small picture' is incorrect and has been misleading; the present meaning of 'idyllic' has come by association. They differ from one another in form, being more or less dramatic narrative or lyric, but all are coloured by the idea of pastoral. (As various forms have been used over the centuries to express a diversity of content, the idea of pastoral has become a complex of many aspects.) Theocritus was the creator of pastoral poetry, although its distant origins were ascribed to Linus, whose song is mentioned by Homer, and although it is Virgil who, through his creative imitations of Theocritus in the *Eclogues*, has had more influence on later European literature.

Theocritus was born in Sicily and put his shepherds in a Sicilian setting; he made them speak a Doric dialect of a kind associated with rustics, though in Syracuse, for example, it was actually spoken. Virgil changed the setting to Arcadia, a mountainous region of southern Greece, whose shepherds were said to be musical, but adding to this bare and primitive place the groves and meadows of Sicily transformed it into a spiritual landscape of beauty, music, and love, appropriate to a golden age in the past which may, as Virgil prophesies in his Fourth Eclogue, come again. In Virgil the ideal quality is paramount, but in Theocritus there are many realistic elements. In a poetry of refined and detailed technique but tender and fresh vision, there is a conscious simplicity that he exemplifies in the life of his shepherds and fishermen. In some of the *Idylls* they sing of love and death, work and nature, in monologue or in dialogue. Others are short mythological narratives, and it is from this kind that Tennyson derived his *Idylls of the King*. (Tennyson was an admirer of Theocritus, as can be seen in *Oenone* and elsewhere.) The second *Idyll* presents the moving picture of a girl trying to bring back her lover by magical spells. The fifteenth shows Sicilian women of Alexandria taking part in the worship of Adonis: it is a lively and amusing poetic mime. Perhaps the most influential *Idyll* has been the first: a lament for the dead shepherd Daphnis (who was perhaps originally a god); the beginnings of pastoral elegy. Another such elegy was written by Bion, an immediate successor of Theocritus, for the dying god Adonis, and the mode was developed further in a lament for Bion that was formerly ascribed to Moschus. In the last poem the author represented the dead poet as himself a shepherd—an idea that was to become a convention of pastoral elegy, as for example in Milton's *Lycidas*, Shelley's *Adonais*, and Arnold's *Thyrsis*. These titles merely recall one aspect of the immensely rich and various legacy that has flowed from pastoral poetry. Sannazzaro's *Arcadia*, Montemayor's *Diana*, Tasso's *Aminta*, and Guarini's *Il Pastor Fido* were the major works which made a new creation of pastoral for Europe in the sixteenth century, and Spenser showed himself a true heir of Theocritus, not least in the rustic language he gave his shepherds in *The Shepherds Calendar*—which earned him the rebuke of Sidney, himself the author of an *Arcadia* in poetic prose. We could linger for ever in a pastoral world where, in the words of Shakespeare in the play, *As You Like It*, where he most fully explores the idea, 'they fleet the time carelessly as they did in the golden age'. But it is as well to remember that from the time of Theocritus the more or less consistent aim of pastoral writing, however various the forms it has taken, has been to explore the relationships of romance to reality.

The epigram was revived in Hellenistic times and continued to be written through the years of the Roman Empire into the age of Byzantium. The four thousand poems of *The Greek Anthology*, which grew over the centuries from the *Garland* of Meleager in the first century B.C. and the *Garland* of Philip in the first century A.D. into a comprehensive selection of Greek poems late and early, show a range of subject and tone that are remarkable, even if few poets stand out as exceptional and many of the poems are mediocre or bad. Those parts of the *Anthology* that were known had a considerable influence in France and Italy during the Renaissance (though they were often read in Latin translation), and in England too we can find traces of this influence, although the Latin epigram, with its preference for point, has had more effect. But in some of the short poems of Tennyson and Landor, and occasionally elsewhere, there is a feeling akin to and perhaps influenced by the *Greek Anthology*. Many of its poems have been translated during the present century, which has in general been notable for the quality of its English and American translations of Greek poetry.

An anonymous poet of the fourth century seems to sound a farewell to pagan poetry at a time when the rising power of Christianity was beginning to be felt in literature:

Tell this to the king: the decorated court has fallen to the ground,
Phoebus no longer has a cell, nor laurel of prophecy, nor babbling
fountain; even the chattering water has dried up.

It is true that much Greek poetry has been lost, and that its direct influence on modern European literature has been small, but indirectly this influence has been substantial, and what remains of Greek poetry is a legacy in itself.

Translations

The translations of the Homeric *Hymn* and of Archilochus are my own.

Mimnermus (p. 101): from the *Oxford Book of Greek Verse in Translation* (Oxford, 1938).

Alcman (pp. 102–3): from Lattimore's *Greek Lyrics* (Chicago, 1949).

Alcman (p. 103): (1) from *Oxford Book of Greek Verse*; (2) from Bowra, *Greek Lyric Poetry* (Oxford, 1961).

Sappho (p. 104): from Bowra, *Greek Lyric Poetry*.

Sappho (p. 105): (1) from Barnstone's translation (New York, 1965); (2) from Lattimore, *Greek Lyrics*; (3) from Bowra, *Greek Lyric Poetry*.

Anacreon (pp. 107–8): (1) by Higham, from *Oxford Book of Greek Verse*;
 (2) from Bowra, *Greek Lyric Poetry*.
Epitaph on p. 109: from Lattimore, *Greek Lyrics*.
Yeats (p. 109): from Yeats, *Collected Poems* (Macmillan, 1950).
Poem on p. 117: from the *Penguin Book of Greek Verse*, ed. Trypanis (1971), p.
 356.

Further Reading

1. *English translations of Greek poetry*
There is a wide selection in *The Oxford Book of Greek Verse in Translation*
(Oxford, 1938). In the *Penguin Book of Greek Verse* (Penguin, 1971), running
from Homer to the present day, the Greek texts are accompanied by a
translation. *Greek Literature* (Penguin, 1973) is an anthology that includes
many Greek poems in translation. *Greek Pastoral Poetry* (Penguin, 1974) has
an interesting introduction by Anthony Holden, who also did the trans-
lation. Penguin Books are soon to publish a volume of translations of early
Greek poems by Peter Jay, who edited *The Greek Anthology* (London, 1973).
Willis Barnstone translated *Greek Lyric Poetry* (New York, 1962); F. L. Lucas
Greek Poetry for Everyman (London, 1953); and Richmond Lattimore *Greek
Lyrics* (Chicago, 1949). Dudley Fitts translated a volume of *Poems from the
Greek Anthology* (New York, 1938) and so did Kenneth Rexroth, *Poems from
the Greek Anthology* (Ann Arbor, 1962).

Translations of individual authors include Archilochus, *Carmina Archilochi*
by Guy Davenport (Berkeley and Los Angeles, 1964); Sappho by Willis
Barnstone (New York, 1965) and by Mary Barnard (Berkeley and Los
Angeles, 1958); Semonides by Hugh Lloyd-Jones in *Females of the Species*
(London, 1975), which also includes an important new fragment of
Archilochus; Pindar by C. M. Bowra (Penguin, 1969), by Richmond
Lattimore (Chicago, 1947), and by G. S. Conway (London, 1972);
Bacchylides by R. Fagles (New Haven, 1961). In his *Sappho and Alcaeus*
(Oxford, 1955) Denys Page translated twelve poems by Sappho, and A. S.
F. Gow translated Theocritus as part of his edition of the poet (Cambridge,
1953), the translation being also published as *The Greek Bucolic Poets*
(Cambridge, 1953).

The Loeb Library has translations (with Greek text) of all the major
Greek poets and most of the minor, either in volumes devoted to individual
authors or in its various anthologies: *Lyra Graeca, Elegy and Iambus, The Greek
Bucolic Poets*, and *The Greek Anthology*.

2. *Books about Greek Poetry and Its Influence*
Albin Lesky's *A History of Greek Literature* (London, 1966), C. M. Bowra's
Ancient Greek Literature (London, 1933), and H. J. Rose's *A Handbook of Greek
Literature* (London, 1934) offer a great deal of basic information. The
relevant chapters of *Fifty Years (and Twelve) of Classical Scholarship* (Oxford,
1968) provide detailed accounts of books and articles.

As a broad and often detailed survey of classical influences on European
civilization, Gilbert Highet's *The Classical Tradition* (London, 1949) remains
invaluable both in its text and in its references to useful studies. The various

works of J. A. K. Thomson, *The Classical Background of English Literature* (London, 1948) and *Classical Influences on English Poetry* (London, 1951) offer rather general but sometimes helpful comments. Thomson's *Shakespeare and the Classics* (London, 1952) has been superseded in many respects by J. W. Velz's encyclopaedic *Shakespeare and the Classical Tradition* (Minneapolis, 1968).

T. G. Rosenmeyer's *The Green Cabinet* (Berkeley, 1969) ranges over the entire field of the European pastoral lyric; P. V. Marinelli's *Pastoral* (London, 1971) is brief but suggestive. Bruno Snell in *The Discovery of the Mind* (Oxford, 1953) has some fascinating essays on Greek poetry and thought. J. Hutton's *The Greek Anthology in France* and *The Greek Anthology in Italy* (Ithaca, 1946 and 1935) are detailed studies.

On the pronunciation of Greek and the sound of Greek poetry there are two interesting books by W. S. Allen: *Accent and Rhythm* (Cambridge, 1973) and *Vox Graeca* (Cambridge, 1968), and one by W. B. Stanford (including a record) *The Sound of Greek* (Berkeley, 1967).

5

DRAMA

T. G. ROSENMEYER

In *Averroes' Quest*, Jorge Luis Borges (*A Personal Anthology*, ed. Kerrigan (1967), pp. 101–10) tells the story of an Arab traveller, just home from a long journey, who attempts to explain to his friends what it is like to attend a performance in the imperial opera house in Canton. The explanation is woefully inadequate because neither he nor his friends have had any experience of staged drama. The tale points up the truth that the art of the theatre is not a universal possession, available to all men as part of their cultural birthright. And even where a dramatic tradition exists, as in the ancient Near Eastern ritual performances, that tradition is not automatically identified with what Europe and America have come to regard as their theatre. European drama, Georg Lukács and others have shown, is almost entirely descended from Greek tragedy and comedy. Some, including Lukács himself, think that the twentieth-century innovations have succeeded in weakening the ancient hold. But it can also be argued that Strindberg, Wedekind, Beckett, and Pinter have, each in his way, forsaken the naturalist impasse of the nineteenth century and returned to forms and insights anticipated on the ancient stage. In spite of the manifestos of Artaud and Gordon Craig, and the directorial effects of Piscator and Vilar, modern playwriting continues in a vein that has more in common with the Greeks than with Japanese No drama or ancient Egyptian coronation texts.

For two thousand years, beginning with the Roman developers of Greek drama, and again with the Humanists of the Renaissance, the Greek models exercised a dominant role. The dominance could be oppressive; Jonson, and Addison, and the lesser spirits in France and their German emulators, were hostages to the tradition. It could also, with the same Jonson, and with Shakespeare and Calderón and Racine and Goethe, stimulate the native energies and shape the native lore into the creation of great masterpieces. In details, the conventions usually proved stifling. In France, no murder was shown on stage until Gresset's *Edouard III* (1740). But the products of the popular tradition which flourished everywhere in Europe in the shadow of the Humanists' prestige art—the passion plays and shepherds' dramas and the farces—were themselves indebted to usages which owed their being to the ancients.

The Legacy

At the risk of repeating what is said elsewhere in this book, I must stress that 'legacy' is a concept bedevilled with snares. Twentieth-century literary critics have grown acutely uncomfortable with the task of tracing and measuring the impact that earlier writers had on their immediate and distant successors. In many cases, it would seem, an elective affinity, with direct influence at a low ebb, produces more striking parallels than learned appropriation. Again, studied imitation can, given the right mentality and the right circumstances, lead to fruitful change, a process that must surely be included under the heading of 'legacy'. Shakespeare, with his allegedly 'small Latine', and his reliance on translations of Plutarch and Italian novelle, is as much a beneficiary of the ancient dramatic models as Racine and Schiller. For both Plutarch and the novellists are unthinkable without the critical tradition codified in Horace's *Art of Poetry*. A passionate innovator, a Büchner, or an Artaud, can be said to owe his vision to a scrutiny of the tradition he rejects. Moreover, his work may, in the end, own to an ironic kinship with essentials of the scorned past. The psychological and sociological intricacies of literary dependence are such that no strict construction will do.

One further caveat: in a summary statement it is impossible to do justice to the telling differences which, properly, make any two plays incomparable. A purist delicacy could reasonably rebel against the roughshod riding proposed in this chapter. But syntheses have their uses, and Dio Chrysostom, who left us a contrastive analysis of the Philoctetes plays by Aeschylus, Sophocles, and Euripides, is still read. In what follows I shall often slight the finer points of workmanship and design, and stress what Maynard Mack has called the 'vertebrate characteristics' shared by the plays (*Othello*, ed. Kernan (1963), p. 211, note).

The classical tradition that was reborn in the Renaissance was a tissue of many strands, none of them contributed directly by the Greeks. Among the strands we count the recovery of the plays of Terence and Seneca, their performance, their translation (first into Italian, and then, from the Latin or the Italian, into other languages), the creation of Italian works in the spirit of the ancient masters, the translation of these works into other languages, and the composition of similar dramas in other languages, including Latin. There was also the translation of Aristotle and Horace on poetry, and commentaries on their works. Finally, perhaps most important for later movements of independence, there was the amalgamation of ancient narrative material with medieval and Renaissance dramatic forms which issued in the pastoral play. It is an index of the vitality of the Greek sources that during the crucial centuries their impact upon European drama was indirect and manifold, through Roman adaptations of tragedy and comedy, and through the progressive assimilation of a critical literature which, at its start with Aristotle, was already at a spiritual remove from the bulk of the original experience.

Aristotle's *Poetics*, which had been inaccessible during the Middle Ages, re-emerged in the fifteenth century. But Aristotle's real influence, as distinguished from the reverent invocation of his name, continued to be slight. J. C. Scaliger's *Poetice* (1561) and Castelvetro's *Poetica* (1570), and the Italian and French elaborations of it, exercised a greater authority, down to the eighteenth century when the fever of sentimental middle-class tragedy caused sensible critics to look for tougher principles of appreciation. Meanwhile, some had undertaken to challenge Aristotle's gospel. Saint-Evrémond, in the *Réflexions sur la tragédie ancienne et moderne* written while he was an exile in England (1672), contrasts what is required in Aristotelian tragedy with the demands of the Christian faith. Twenty years later Charles Perrault opens the debate of the ancients and the moderns by subjecting the conventions identified with Aristotle and the Greeks to cheerful scorn (*Parallèle des anciens et des modernes* (1692), pp. 189–220). His Abbé insists that there has been progress on the stage, and that Garnier and Hardy, the French Sophocles and Euripides, were now replaced by Mairet, superior to both of them. Perrault might have added that Hardy's works, including his

tragicomedies and pastorals, were thought to constitute a
significant advance over Garnier's, and that Mairet's *Sylvie*
(1626) and *Sophonisbe* (1634) are not only in the ancient
mould themselves, but, in their elegant way, closer to what
Horace and Scaliger sanction than Hardy's angular exercises
in Senecan rhetoric.

The modern reluctance to play classical drama straight is a
sign that the Abbé's shortsightedness is still with us. Euripides
is jazzed up, Marlowe is acted in modern dress, Shakespeare
is put on with an all-male cast (almost correct, historically
speaking, but aesthetically skewed), Corneille is whispered,
and the *Phaedra* that is shown on the Paris stage is one by
Euripides *and* Racine. The modern director is impatient with
the conventions. From Strindberg's *théatre intime* to Weiss's
dramatized 'collapse of fictions', the aim is to overcome the
inhibitions imposed by the Humanist canons and the requirements of a stage that is no longer ours. There are mutterings
about the death of tragedy, and Beckett's eidetic lyricism
appears to lay to rest the hope for 'meaningful', 'serious'
drama in our time. But perhaps the mutterings have been
premature. Beckett himself gives us a drama that is remarkably Sophoclean: the tensed economy of the stage
action, the impossibility of defining precisely questions of guilt
and responsibility, the bitter-sweet combination of cruelty
and gentleness, and, above all, the ritual power of ordinary
language are features which cannot be found in precisely this
way outside the Western theatre, and which were put there by
the Greek ancestors of the line.

Meaning

Hebbel comments wistfully that the break-up of the world can
be shown dramatically only through the fragmentation of
particulars; an earthquake can be visualized only through the
collapse of churches and homes and the flooding tide of the
sea (Preface to *Maria Magdalena* (1844)). The modern dramatist, like his ancient colleague, wants the several dislocations
engineered on the stage to endorse a larger sense of disorder.
When Antigone undertakes the second burial of her brother,
and when Vladimir refuses to abandon his waiting-game, the
motion, or the lack of motion, is small by comparison with
what is felt to be its intention. Of all the principal genres—

lyric, epic, narrative fiction, drama—the drama presses most urgently for an answer to the question: what is the meaning of it? Generations of hard-headed critics have wrestled with the difficulty of formulating a listener's response to the experience of watching a play. The need for a positive answer, but also the virtual impossibility of reaching one, are painfully apparent in I. A. Richards, who tells us that tragedy does not say that 'all's right with the world' or that 'somewhere, somehow, there is Justice', but rather that all is right here and now in the nervous system (*Principles of Literary Criticism* (1928), p. 246). Earlier he had remarked, shrewdly, that tragedy forces us to live for a moment without suppressions or sublimations.

The commonly expressed expectation is that a tragedy, and in its way also a comedy, should throw light on the workings of justice. Kenneth Tynan does not speak as a socialist only when he objects to Ionesco that his plays fail to touch upon the significant social issues (in E. Ionesco, *Notes and Counter Notes* (1964), p. 94). It is useful to remember, however, that Aristotle stayed away from questions of this sort. He would, one imagines, have felt perfectly comfortable with a play like Ionesco's *Rhinoceros*, which does not open up to deliver a paraphrasable philosophical or moral insight. The neo-classical tragedians who argued, as Pope does in his prologue to Addison's *Cato*, that tragedy should convey a message, preferably a patriotic one, go against the very spirit of Aeschylean and Sophoclean tragedy, from which no such message can be learned. The notion of the fifth-century dramatist as a teacher is a Sophistic fiction. The history of modern drama may be written as a dialogue between the 'messagers' and the 'non-messagers': between Zola and Ibsen, Sartre and Giraudoux, Brecht and Wedekind. Aristotle's silence on the subject of a lesson, useful though the idea should have been to him in his implied rebuttal of Plato's attack on drama, is a realistic evaluation of what Greek tragedy (though not comedy) claimed to do.

Classification of Genres

Where Aristotle might have had some difficulty is with the classification of *Rhinoceros*, which Ionesco calls a *pièce*. In a rare critical mood, Ionesco refers to it as a tragedy, and complains that in America it was played as a comedy (*Notes and Counter Notes*, p. 208). There are moments when the play sounds like Terence or Menander, especially in the scene between Berenger and the Old Man and Jean's neighbour. This is so not only because of a certain light-headed humanity, and a circumscription of domestic space by means of locked doors and hints at nearby bedrooms, but especially because the characters, most of them too decent for high tragedy, tend to communicate glancingly. They engage in a sort of shadow-boxing; half of what they say passes by the addressee and goes to waste. Menander's and Terence's dialogue—less so that of Plautus—is built up of units of speech which go in every possible direction: into the audience, into the wings, upwards, sideways, and also towards the presumptive recipient, who may or may not rise up to the engagement. Ancient drama is, in any case, a drama of recitation rather than communication. An Oedipus or a Pentheus, like the comic Socrates, formulates ideas rather than attempting to enter into a partnership of meshing speech. But in New Comedy this tradition is, perhaps because of the greater appearance of art mirroring life, especially striking. Some of the most recent drama, from Pinter to Beckett to Israel Horovitz—*The Indian Wants the Bronx* (1968) is an extreme case—is once again committed to the art of glancing speech. Chekhov led the way. His auto-analyses, monologues disguised as dialogue, are, as Peter Szondi has shown, not designed for communication, but border on the 'lyric of solitude'.[1] The reasons for this are certainly different, but the result can be strikingly similar to what happens in Menander, and quite different from the nineteenth-century norm of maximal and adequate intercourse, disrupted only, as in *Hedda Gabler*, for special effect.

But *Rhinoceros* is also in the stream of high tragedy. The analogies between the play and, say, the *Bacchae* are instructive. The same juxtaposition of two worlds, political and animal; the same fussy old men whose impoverished vitality prevents them from entering into the conflict; the same exposition of the inadequacies of reason and science. With the beasts breathing down their necks, Jean and the Logician seek salvation in dressing decently and counting cats' paws.

[1] *Theorie des modernen Dramas* (1956), pp. 30–3.

Pentheus and Cadmus and Tiresias are all in the same camp with them, cleaving to the niceties of a civilized world which is in a state of collapse around them. The crash of Hebbel's building may have been difficult to engineer on the Greek podium stage. But its symbolic value is unmistakable, and an important part of the verbal structure of the *Bacchae*. So in Ionesco's play, the animals, first little more than a distant threat, at a certain point emerge into symbolic prominence, though their dramaturgic visibility remains minimal. A congeries of random exchanges gives way to a pitched solitary confrontation. Passion, and disaster, take over where careful plotting and small anxieties had been the rule. The demands, flowing from a source shrouded in mystery, prove overpowering. Daisy and Berenger walk their several ways. The ending is incomplete, and anticlimactic. But if we had Euripides' epilogue in full, the same anticlimactic ordering would be in evidence. In spite of the substitution of the bourgeois milieu for the Dionysiac setting, a play like *Rhinoceros* seems to be closer in spirit to the ancient mystery drama than a more obvious imitation, like Kleist's *Penthesileia* (1808), with its Agave-slaughter at the end.

In the ancient repertory, the classification of a drama was in part functional—the circumstances and requirements of the festival or occasion on which it was performed—and in part structural and stylistic. Aeschylus' *Agamemnon* and Euripides' *Iphigenia among the Taurians* share a basic vocabulary, a way of exploiting figures of speech, a reluctance to surrender the dramatic illusion, and an employment of certain metrical patterns, which make them quite distinct from Aristophanic comedy, with its licence of speech, its cartoon-like imagery, its sliding back and forth between character and actor, and its own, more relaxed, metrical regularities. New Comedy is, on these scores, closer to tragedy. Since much of European drama, including tragedy, looks back to Menander and Terence as well as to Seneca, the fusion of the genres may be thought to have begun in antiquity. But the fifth century must be exempted from this. It is true that the Menelaus of the *Helen* has little to distinguish him, as a character, from the bumbling husbands of the Hellenistic stage, and that the Hercules of the *Alcestis* anticipates the Roister Doisters of later comedy. This is perhaps one of the reasons why Euripides was, in his own time, regarded with a jaundiced eye. The fact remains that even in these venturesome plays Euripides observes an integrity of style and structure which classical scholars have found to be measurably tragic.

Within this classification, Aeschylus and Euripides represent two opposed conceptions of the kind of language tragedy demands. From Seneca to Ibsen, and from Corneille to Dürrenmatt, the successors can be separated into two camps: those who seek to underline the weight of the drama by means of massed words and tangled phrases, and those who prefer an appeal that is unadorned, or polished rather than dense. Aristophanes' emblematic duel between monstrous armour and whittled shavings pointed the way. Somewhere in Aeschylus somebody that is hardpressed is compared to both an anvil and a tunnyfish (fr. 307 N.²), and at *Agamemnon*, 795–8 we read about 'eyes that wag their tails', though it must be confessed that at this point the text may not be entirely sound. The Aeschylean mode of imagery and compression is an extreme which few have dared to emulate. But the contest between Aeschylus and Euripides seems to come back to life in Racine's decision, in the biblical plays, to use a richness of imagery which he had shunned in the secular pieces.

The critical sense that the tragic and the comic are distinct and, to a large degree, mutually exclusive continued long beyond the Renaissance. Fontenelle's laborious inquiry (*Réflexions sur la Poétique* (publ. 1742), in *Oeuvres*, ed. Depping (1818), iii. 438 ff.) into whether it is legitimate for comedy to produce tears or for tragedy to edge in laughter builds on the strictures of Cicero (*De optimo genere oratorum*, 1.1) and Horace (*Art of Poetry*, 89), but flies in the face of centuries of practical efforts to do precisely both. His *échelle dramatique*, ranging all the way from *terrible*, via *grand*, *pitoyable*, *tendre*, *plaisant*, to *ridicule*, is a not untypically mechanical stratagem to bridge the gap. He settles on the two middle terms, *pitoyable* and *tendre*, for a dramatic experience that is not hamstrung by the ancient separations. He also admits that the English have been following this recipe for years; there is a special reference to Nicholas Rowe's *The Fair Penitent* (1703). But the agony of gears grinding to legitimize the combination proves how compelling the old distinctions, reinforced by Scaliger and his successors, remained. The odd German dilemma whether to label a particular play a *Tragödie* or a *Trauerspiel*[2] was a further extension of the same classificatory scruple.

Chekhov, Giraudoux, Brecht, and Dürrenmatt continue to grapple with the problem of classification, perhaps because they suspect that audiences will want to be told whether to laugh or to cry. Chekhov's ironies, and Brecht's disengagement, are scarcely calculated to reassure the spectator that he has the right answer. It is useful to remember Jeremy Collier's remark about Shakespeare, quoted by Lamb (from *The Examiner* 1813, in *Works*, ed. Lucas, vol. i (1903), p. 158): 'though his genius generally was jocular, and inclining to festivity, yet he could when he pleased be as serious as any body.' Only an insidiously entrenched way of thinking about tragedy and comedy could have prompted an intelligent man to make so silly a comment. And it is not a long step from here to Dürrenmatt's notion that our age cannot afford tragedy, because tragedy assumes the reality of guilt, need, proportion, clearsightedness, and responsibility. 'In the topsy-turvy farce of our century, in the swill of the white race, nobody is guilty, and nobody is responsible' (*Theaterprobleme* (1955), pp. 47–8). As if fifth-century Athens or Jacobean England were oppressed with a special sense of guilt, or graced with a privileged feeling of responsibility. In fact, where such feelings prevail, in Puritan England or in Calvinistic Geneva, tragedy is the last thing to succeed. Modern thinkers have cast grim doubt on the epistemological justification for generic categories. But recent playwrights and directors and actors have, it appears, been unable to escape from the ancient spell.

Mixing of Genres

This was not always so. The history of European drama is full of unselfconscious combinations of what the ancients had kept apart: of the tragic rhythm of passionate involvement and eventual disaster, of the comic flourish of animal vitality, and of the domestic decencies first glimpsed dramatically in the fourth century B.C. Richard Edwarde's *Damon and Pythias* (1565) is entitled a 'tragical comedy'. The mixing of the genres started long before the anti-establishmentarians of the seventeenth century called for it. The sentimental bourgeois

---

[2] Though the distinction is by no means clearcut, German dramatists have tended to attach the Greek term to plays evoking the classical tradition, and have used the German term to designate plays of a more indigenous stamp.

drama of the eighteenth century, effortlessly carved out of the shambles of the old critical separations, flows into a current represented, at one end, by the anonymous *Arden of Feversham* (1592), which Goethe called 'untheatrical', perhaps because it defied the tragic call for grandeur; and, at the other, by the shocking distortions of Genêt. Pirandello's obsessive dovetailing of levels of reality and consciousness could not, any more than Büchner's break-up of the causal flux or Beaumont's impacting of audience response, have proceeded without a tacit understanding that the tragic and the comic belong together. Better yet, that the high and the low style, and high and low personages, are best conflated. For the purity of the genres had come to be defined in terms of the language used and through the characters.

When Guarini defends tragicomedy in his *Compendio della Poesia Tragicomica* (1599), the mingling of styles is a principal concern. Successful amalgamations, in which the high and the low are perfectly fused, are rare. Kleist's *Prinz von Homburg* (publ. 1821) may be one. The language absorbs, without apparent suture, echoes of the spirit of war, and of the warmth, even gentleness of the soldiers towards each other, and of their longing for the girl back home. The note of intimacy is, if one wishes to press the point, an heirloom of New Comedy, calmly asserting its rights in the face of the Aeschylean trumpet-calls, and merging its energies with them.

Menander's triumph is apparent also in the bud and beauteous flower of Love. Neither Aeschylus nor Sophocles nor, certainly, Aristophanes were much concerned with the feeling of men and women for one another, except on a very abstract level, in choral songs, or in divine apologetics. Perhaps, if we had some of the lost plays, our judgement would be different. A few of the fragments hint at an openness to eroticism, which the Byzantine compilers succeeded in keeping out of the school editions they arranged. In Aeschylus' *Myrmidonians*, for instance, Achilles chides the corpse of Patroclus with a lover's passion, in language unexpectedly precious (fr. 135 N.[2]):

> You did not reverence the chaste purity of your thighs,
> You did not show gratitude for our many kisses.

Euripides introduces the subject of love into the centre of the action. But his love is, more often than not, a point of departure rather than a sustained theme. It is but one of the courses designed to show up the asymmetry of human relations, and the imperfection of the social compact. The tale of love generated, threatened, and victorious was the invention of New Comedy, or rather it was the transfer to the stage of popular material which prior to the fourth century B.C. had not been granted the sanction of high art.

Tragedy

In many ways, therefore, in form, substance, and tone, Menander could be said to have won the day. It is tragedy, however, which is commonly thought of as the most significant dramatic legacy of the Greeks. Precisely what is meant by the term 'tragic' is not always clear. The romantic, and especially Hegelian, view that tragedy involves a tension of duality, or a clash between unity and multiplicity, goes back not so much to Greek tragic texts as to Plato. Jaspers remarks (*Von der Wahrheit* (1947), p. 960) that 'because the One is shipwrecked in the actuality (*Dasein*) of time, it emerges in the shape of the tragic'. Neither this nor many other formulations purporting to define the tragic have much to do with Greek dramatic realities. The Platonic victory over tragedy in the form of modern, especially continental, dramatic criticism using Platonic language is one of the curiosities of the history of thought.

Again, the thought that a tragedy must necessarily terminate in the destruction of a hero goes beyond ancient precedent. Grillparzer's tragedies—*Die Ahnfrau* (1817), *Sappho* (1818)—tend to end with the word 'dead' (*tot*), and Maeterlinck's early *drame statique* features man, Menandrian man, waiting to be caught up by death. The death focus has been encouraged by ritualist critics (Bodkin, Tillyard, Fergusson), for whom renewal through destruction forms the essence of the tragic experience. At the same time, the old Renaissance injunction against the presentation of death on stage made the enactment of the heroic undoing troublesome. Silius' suicide in Jonson's determinedly classical *Sejanus* (1603) was felt to be a daring breach of the conventions, in spite of the example of Sophocles' *Ajax*, and even though the proliferation of violent death in contemporary revenge tragedy must have insulated Jonson's audience against the shock. As

Dryden's Lisideius observed (*Of Dramatick Poesie*, ed. Boulton
(1964), p. 70), 'in all our Tragedies the Audience cannot
forbear laughing when the Actors are to die; 'tis the most
Comick part of the whole Play.' His warning went unheeded;
in the next century David Hume (*Four Dissertations* (1757), pp.
198–9) protested against a performance of Rowe's *The
Ambitious Stepmother* (1700), 'where a venerable old man,
raised to the height of fury and despair, rushes against a
pillar, and striking his head upon it, besmears it all over with
mingled brains and gore'. One envies the director his illusionist inventiveness. In our day Peter Brook has Goneril die in
the same fashion, but without the physiological exactitude.

Dryden, and Jonson, commended the ancient messenger-
speech, in the belief that a death told, rather than shown, is
more affecting. It is by no means clear whether Shakespeare's
'What's Hecuba to him' bears out the proposition. In most
nineteenth- and twentieth-century drama, death, whether on
stage or off, has turned even more intractable, because of our
growing insensitivity to mechanized slaughter, and also because of an enlarged sense of what death is, and in how many
shapes it comes. Burdened with too much knowledge, death
has taken on a primitive cast; it savours of emblems, and of
cheap choreography. Thus suffering, in modern drama, once
again manages to do without the 'sting of death, precisely as in
the *Prometheus* and the *Oedipus*.

Simplicity

In the matter of the economy of dramaturgy, also, the modern
stage has recaptured the ancient simplicities, after centuries
during which the rules were swept aside in favour of variety
and entanglement. Strindberg's *théatre intime*, with its recom-
mendation against intermissions, and Beckett's dramatized
silence recover some of the starkness for which Racine's
Bérénice (1670) was condemned. Both the neo-classical theorists of the seventeenth century, and later the naturalist
insistence on the rich texture of life, called for Aristotle's
complexity rather than for the spareness exhibited by the bulk
of the extant Greek repertory. Note Dryden's nostalgic
comment, in the preface to his and Lee's *Oedipus* (1678):

The *Athenian* Theater (whether more perfect than ours, is not now
disputed) had a Perfection differing from ours. You see there in every

Act a single Scene, (or two at most) which manage the Business of the Play, and after that succeeds the *Chorus*, which commonly takes up more Time in Singing, than there has been employ'd in Speaking. The principal Person appears almost constantly through the Play; but the inferiour Parts seldom above once in the whole Tragedy. The Conduct of our Stage is much more difficult, where we are oblig'd never to lose any considerable Character which we have once presented. Custom likewise has obtain'd, that we must form an Under-plot of second Persons, which must be depending on the first, and their By-walks must be like those in a Labyrinth, which all of 'em lead into the great Parterre: Or like so many several lodging Chambers, which have their Outlets into the same Gallery. Perhaps, after all if we could think so, the ancient Method, as 'tis the easiest, is also the most Natural, and the Best. For Variety, as 'tis manag'd, is too often subject to breed Distraction.

The disclaimer is unconvincing. For in the epilogue to the same play the authors argue that it took two English poets to emulate the Greek. The implication, suppressed out of veneration for the original, is that Sophocles had not given enough. And the first stage direction,

The Curtain rises to a plaintive Tune, representing the present Condition of Thebes; dead bodies appear at a Distance in the Street; some faintly go over the stage; others drop,

leaves all thoughts of simplicity behind. This is a play in which Creon, Eurydice, and a newly introduced Adrastus kill each other, and Oedipus flings himself out of a window, after discovering Jocasta dead, 'held by her Women, and stabb'd in many places of her Bosom, her Hair dishevel'd, her Children slain upon the Bed'.

There are Greek plays, such as the *Orestes* and the *Phoenician Women*, which veer away from the norm of simplicity by packing whole anthologies of legend and experience into the confines of the drama, and by exhibiting inflations and catastrophes worthy of Crébillon père. But the majority of the plays, from the *Persians* to *Iphigenia in Aulis* and beyond to Menander's *Dyskolos* (*The Grouch*) and *Aspis* (*The Shield*), satisfy our expectations of a structure which, in Aristotle's word, can be taken in at one glance. What happened later was, in a sense, inevitable. Imitation engenders enrichment though not necessarily improvement. The classical learning professed by the playwrights who worked in the Humanist tradition was bound to cramp simplicity. The voice of experience, Jaspers says, was replaced by the voice of culture (quoted by K. Ziegler in H. Kreuzer, ed., *Hebbel in neuer Sicht* (1963), p. 12). Greek drama, especially Aeschylean and Aristophanic drama, is uneducated. Its premisses of knowledge are available to all, and its information is native. This is true also, though perhaps less compellingly, of Sophocles and Euripides, and of the Greek originals of Terentian comedy. It is no longer true of Seneca, whose Medea, Wilamowitz once observed, acts as it she has read Euripides' *Medea*. In Jonson's *Sejanus*, Tiberius speaks a line of Greek which comes from Dionysius' *Roman History*. In Greek tragedy there is no awareness of foreign languages. That is reserved for comedy, in which everything foreign is villainous or funny. The Doric-speaking physician in the *Aspis* proves that on this score, New Comedy perpetuates an Aristophanic slant. The Senecan learning was something new. It is not until the late nineteenth century, the days of Antoine and Strindberg, that serious drama begins once again to do without recourse to learning and culture. This being so, it is interesting to note that with the rejection of erudition and polite taste comes a return to simplicity, and a repudiation of the canons of intrigue, of reversal, and of the criss-crossings of fate and retribution. In this instance the legacy of the Greeks appears to have succeeded in defiance of a critical tradition, beginning with Aristotle, that prized learning and piled canon upon rule.

The Unities

A word or two must be said about the unities, in spite of the nagging suspicion that the subject proved, in the course of its long history of discussion, something of a red herring. In the famous prologue to *Every Man in His Humour*, Jonson protests against the 'ill customs of the age', clearly with Shakespeare's Histories in mind. He does not want

> a child, now swaddled, to proceed
> Man, and then shoot up, in one beard and weed,
> Past threescore years; or, with three rusty swords
> And help of some few foot-and-half-foot words
> Fight over York and Lancaster's long jars
> And in the trying-house bring wounds to scars.

Instead he will provide plays

> Where neither chorus wafts you o'er the seas
> Nor creaking throne comes down the boys to please,
> Nor nimble squib is seen, to make afeard
> The gentlewomen, nor rolled bullet heard
> To say, it thunders, nor tempestuous drum
> Rumbles to tell you when the storm doth come.

This exemplary mixture of comic and tragic concerns echoes Aristophanes' mock-protests against his competitors' tricks and his loving persiflage of Aeschylean bombast. But chiefly it draws attention to the author's commitment (relaxed in his own tragedies) to the unities of time and place, and to keeping the action as plain as the style. Similar things are found in Voltaire's wistful attacks on Shakespeare.

The unity of place crops up also in the exchange between Orazio, the director, and Lelio, the starveling playwright, in Goldoni's *The Comic Theatre* (1750; ed. Sampietro, vol. vi (1967), Act II, Scene iii, p. 123).

Lelio: I think I have observed all the rules ... I am certain I have observed the most important, the unity of place.
Orazio: Who has told you that the unity of place is an important rule?
Lelio: Aristotle.
Orazio: You have read Aristotle?
Lelio: To tell the truth, I have not read him, but I have heard people say this.

As Orazio explains, 'the ancients did not have our facilities for changing scenes, and for this reason they observed the unity.' François d'Aubignac *had* read Aristotle. In his subtle analysis of Sophocles' *Ajax* (*La pratique du théatre* (1657), pp. 471ff.) he holds to the observance of all three unities, which had been elaborated in the course of ancient and Renaissance criticism, but which went far beyond Aristotle's unity of *mythos*. It is fascinating to see Strindberg caught in the strict constructionist scheme. In commenting on *Thérèse Raquin*, he praises Zola's attention to the unity of place, and finds fault with his neglect of the unity of time (*Werke*, tr. Schering, vol. i. 4 (1910), pp. 327ff.): Zola has an unnecessary year between Acts I and II, presumably in order not to offend against the social exigencies, in this case against the year of waiting imposed by widowhood. Thus verisimilitude wins out against a conflicting canon, and Strindberg would like to have the predominance reversed.

Verisimilitude

Verisimilitude, in the various narrow senses in which the Renaissance theorists and the naturalists understood it, has few ancient roots. Aristotle's scattered remarks about the requirements for a convincing and impressive character have little to do with the demands of a psychological or social realism. His stress on the probable impossible is sufficient proof of this. On the stage, nobody blushes, or coughs, or says he is embarrassed. Nor does Euripides attempt to moderate the stiffness of his prologues by the infusion of vignettes from life, as Kleist does in his *Penthesileia*, where Ulysses interrupts his progress report to ask for water—in a helmet!—and, 126 long lines later, gets it and thanks the bearer. As Hebbel puts it, speaking of Sophocles' *Ajax* which he admires almost as much as the *Antigone* (W. von Scholz, *Hebbels Dramaturgie* (1907), p. 92, from notes sketched in 1841): 'Modern criticism with its silly demands for naturalness considers it a capital fault that Teucer fails to provide his brother with artificial respiration, and merely looks to his burial.'

On the scale of the ancient canon, *Ajax* is a tolerably realistic play. Sophocles, as he came to show in the *Philoctetes*, has a genuine propensity towards physical and psychological realism. In that tragedy the unity of time is perfect, with play-time and clock-time identical and continuous, and the chorus is built into the action with due regard for social probability. The subject of the recluse resisting overtures that he should return to the bosom of society makes for a type of complexity, even fussiness, which is rare on the Greek stage, and which conjures up the rugged querulousness of Timon of Athens or the truculence of Molière's Alceste. And yet, the ultimate effect of the *Philoctetes*, like that of *Timon* (1604–5) and unlike that of *Le Misanthrope* (1666), is that of a drama acted out on the level of myth. What matters about it are the figural realities of the legendary action. We are not, in any important sense, supposed to get a 'feel' for the living texture and the significant insignificancies of a social transaction.

Verse and Prose

The indifference with which the ancients looked at verisimilitude is at once apparent in how the characters converse. One of the prominent features of Greek tragedy and comedy is the alternation of speech and song, more especially, the 'epic prose' of the hero and the ritual singing of the chorus. 'Prose' is, in this case, to be taken loosely, for the speech, like the singing, is in verse. Ancient drama does not recognize prose, except for the extrametrical cries of pain or despair, and comic quotations or imitations of bureaucratic decrees, which, it is felt, deserve to stand by themselves, separate from the continuities of the verse. The dramatic uses of unmetrical speech were a discovery of the later European stage. The old tradition was continued in the Humanist efforts to find equivalents for Greek and Latin verse-forms. And long after the first prose plays had appeared, Dryden was able to hesitate between blank verse and rhyme, without even considering prose as a likely option. The reason is obvious from what he says in favour of rhyme in the dedicatory epistle to *The Rival-Ladies* (1664): 'Imagination in a Poet is a Faculty so wild and lawless, that, like a high-ranging Spaniel, it must have Clogs tied to it, lest it out-run the Judgment. The great easiness of Blanck Verse, renders the Poet too luxuriant.' The Greeks, however, if any one had asked them, would more likely have agreed with Bernard Shaw, who wrote one of his plays in verse because, he said, he did not have the time to write it in prose. Plato's prose dialogue came into being at a moment when two generations of prose writers had finally made the new instrument sufficiently supple and varied to answer artistic demands. But the dramatists of Plato's own time and in the subsequent centuries preferred to work in the proven medium of the founders of the tradition.

The Chorus

Still, the alternation between speech and song which constitutes the inner tension of the ancient dramatic form comes close to satisfying a desire for contrasting mediums. The principal agent of the song is the chorus. But the music was not the only contribution expected of the citizen-choristers. Perrault has his Chevalier guess that the chorus was invented

only because the authors needed a vehicle for the commonplaces they carried in their attaché cases: on the inevitability of death, on the instability of human affairs, on the
inconveniences of kingship, the happiness of innocence, and so
forth. Thus, the Chevalier concludes, the ancient playwrights
and their imitators proceed like quacks who put on farces to
sell their nostrums and their lotions.

The chorus has always been recognized as an identifying
trait of the 'artificiality' of the ancient dramatic tradition, in
spite of the fact that Plautus and Terence, and their Hellenistic
models, had long discredited or abandoned this vestige of
communal involvement. When Addison writes his *Cato*
(1713), and Milton his *Samson* (1671), and Schiller his *Braut
von Messina* (1803), the classical experiment advertises itself in
the use of the chorus. Success in such a venture is precarious,
as T. S. Eliot found out in at least one play, *The Family
Reunion*. Jonson put it, defensively, in the prologue to *Sejanus*:
it is better not to use a chorus,

> whose habit and moods are such and so difficult, as not any, whom I
> have seen, since the ancients, no not they who have most presently
> affected laws, have yet come in the way of. Nor is it needful, or
> almost possible in these our times, and to such auditors as commonly
> things are presented, to observe the old state and splendour of
> dramatic poems, with preservation of any popular delight.

Eight years later, in *Catiline*, he disregards his own advice.

Thomas Hardy's *Dynasts*, though intended as a summoning
of more indigenous, Druidic traditions, and in the end
effective only as camera-eye reading, cannot, with its grand
choral apparatus, deny its Aeschylean stance. Even Perrault's
nostrums, the choral formulations of tribal wisdom, have
survived the ridicule. Such maxims are common in the
ancient plays, in the dialogue but especially in chorus songs.
Their function is to warn, or to comfort, or simply to voice the
reflected stabilities of the people's lives, of middle Athens,
cushioning the steep rise and fall of the heroic temperament.
These commonplaces can be vulgar; they often are in
Euripides, because vulgarity is part of his artistic scheme.
They can also be among the soaring beauties of the ancient
poems. Brecht, and Sartre, and Weiss have chosen to stress the
triteness of the maxims. Others have exploited their consolatory force. When Sonya, at the end of Chekhov's *Uncle*

Vanya, terminates the play with her surprising coda of patter and jubilation: 'We shall rejoice and look back at these troubles of ours with tenderness, with a smile—and we shall rest. ... We shall rest! We shall hear the angels. ... We shall rest!' (tr. Garnett); or when Mr. and Mrs. A. recite their mordant rhymes in Auden's and Isherwood's *The Ascent of F-6*, the commonplaces are choral. We respond to them as citizens, as fellow-sufferers.

The Music

But let it be remembered that the maxims, like most of the utterances of the ancient chorus, were sung, which cushioned their potential for banality. Actually, the distinction between speech and song was not a simple one. In all probability the tragedians wrote for a sliding scale of delivery, from near-conversational speech, bald and unaccompanied, through accompanied recitative, and choral chanting of a rudimentary kind, to solo arias and full-fledged choral systems of elaborate rhythmic and melodic structure. There is no agreement about the details of this scale. Of the actual music we have only pitiful fragments, and what we have has been variously interpreted. The writers of comedy were capable of providing for the same rich scale, especially during the scenes when tragedy is the butt. Later this musical variety was partly lost. New Comedy, besides abandoning choral singing as an integral part of the plot, generally downgraded the musical component (a process temporarily reversed by Plautus), thus completing a development which began when Dionysiac drama grew free of its ritual origins, prior to the advent of Aeschylus. For centuries it was felt that Greek drama was an art of the spoken word, of abstract ideas brought into articulate collision. Aristotle and Horace, with their attention to structure and diction, helped to confirm the impression. Meanwhile, native folk traditions and the musical obligato of the Catholic mass exerted their influence on medieval drama. Music, it appears, played a role in Tudor moralities. But like the music in Shakespeare or Dryden it seems to have been an occasional condiment rather than a fundamental constituent of the art. Racine's alexandrines, and the provincial speech-patterns of Yeats and Synge have their own music, which would be spoiled if it were joined with an instrumental or vocal line. This inner music is, historically speaking, a discovery of the Hellenistic poets, contemporaries of Menander and his generation, who disavowed the old overt musicality in order to emphasize the melodiousness of speech itself.

The nineteenth century rediscovered the elemental force of a combination of music and speech. Nietzsche's lament in his *Birth of Tragedy* upon the disjunction of Dionysus and Apollo prepared the ground for Wagner's synthesis and for the co-operation between dramatic poets—Maeterlinck, Hofmannsthal—and composers—Dukas, Debussy, Strauss. Thus the neo-classical attempts to revive the ancient chorus, as in Racine's *Athalie* (1691), or the necromantic ode, for three voices and chorus, in Dryden's *Oedipus*, Act III, were abandoned in favour of a two-track development, one perfecting modern opera, with its symbiosis of poetic text and music, and the other sustaining the rule of the spoken word. The Marxist, and Brechtian, use of unison speech is a different departure, as is Brecht's reliance, and that of his followers, upon music hall choruses and folk ditties to enliven the texture of the revolutionary play. The true heir of ancient tragedy is opera, in spite of the entirely different conceptions of the two art forms. For when all is said and done, it must be stressed that, in spite of the singing and the dancing on the Athenian stage, the Greeks themselves thought of their plays, and especially of their tragedies, as achieving their ends primarily through the agency of speech. It was the fullness of Aeschylus' language, more than the special quality of his airs, which struck the imagination of his contemporaries.

Speech

It is difficult, at this late date, to speculate about the power of the word in Greek drama, whether that word was recited or chanted or sung. But we may safely assume that the verbal signals were so authoritative that they absorbed much of what we would look for under the heading of 'action'. It may or may not be significant that the texts, or librettos, that have reached us lack stage directions or comments on the action, with a very few exceptions. Since our texts are, in fact, distant copies of manuscripts from which the dramatists directed their rehearsals, the absence of instructions to the actors should not surprise us. More important, it is inconceivable that a Greek play should be set going by a box on the ears, as is Corneille's *The Cid* (1637), and also *Sejanus*. Similarly, glances and facial expressions are ruled out. Racine, with his fine attention to what eyes can do, is on that score counter-classical, though he, too, puts everything into what the actors say. The only significant movements on the Greek stage are those of hands and feet, associated with the dance. Agamemnon's slow progress across the scarlet stuffs, and the broken movements of the dying Heracles, in the *Trachinian Women*, will have been thrilling sights. There is much room, especially in Aeschylus, for the ingenuity, of the director. When Electra recognizes Orestes, are they to embrace? How is Ajax' suicide to be enacted?

On the whole, however, these questions are marginal; they pertain to incidentals, however large the incidentals may loom in the whole. They do not pertain to what we understand by the plot, or the action. These are determined exclusively by the words. The model is that which is found also in Thucydides; it is that of political deliberation, of the analysis of general truths, and of the planning of specific enterprises, and of the response to success and failure. It is as if what mattered about the action in the *Iliad* were not the duels to the death, but the speeches, inflationary and deflationary, that precede and follow them. On the Greek stage the speeches, and the verbal confrontations and the laments, have encroached upon the action proper. This is what distinguishes classical drama from the kind of theatre on which Stanislavsky lavished his skills. And it could be argued that the illusionist theatre was never more than an interlude, and that the classical tradition of speech dominance continues unchallenged today.

Plots

For the theatre-going public, the continuity of the ancient tradition is most obvious in the survival of the archetypal plots, especially those taken from the heroic legends. Hofmannsthal, Claudel, O'Neill, Eliot, and the French 'existentialists' of the '40s and '50s have now themselves become part of the great reservoir of 'the classics'. But it will be remembered that they went back to the old myths *after* the rebels of the late nineteenth century had seemingly shut the door on that route for good. Apollinaire, a founding father of Surrealism, cannot by any stretch of the imagination be said to have been a spokesman for the ancients. But his *Les mamelles de Tirésias* (1917) owes much of its charm to the old Ovidian tale being employed as a whipping-post. The modern themes of fragmentation and of rootless passion are given elegant shape by a marriage with establishment material. The result is an instructive distancing which comes close to satisfying Brecht's call for an 'alienation effect'.

Greek drama goes to three kinds of sources for its plots. For tragedy and the satyr play, it goes to the legendary or historical past. For Old Comedy, it goes to the immediate, civic present. And for New Comedy, to the generic and domesticated present. The Aristophanic plot had few imitators. Its fearless exploitation of the fixations and animosities of a jostling community would have been difficult to duplicate in another political setting. Jonson at his most energetic comes close to it; the passionate drives of *Bartholomew Fair* generate a stampede all their own. The demolition of rank and order in Jarry, and the more exuberant critiques of intellectualism and culture in Ibsen and Shaw, show partial affinities. For a genuine analogue of Old Comedy one has to forget about drama and turn to prose satire, to Swift and Orwell and *Catch 22*. Of the other two kinds of plot, the dramatization of legend (or of the historical past) continued to attract notably those playwrights who thought of themselves as working in the Humanist line of succession, from Monchrestien's *L'Ecossaise* (1601) and Corneille's *Rodogune* (1645) to Dryden's *The Conquest of Granada* (1670–1) and *Aureng-Zebe* (1675). As on the Greek stage, the historical subject, however recent, was refashioned into legend, and the legendary material was given concrete, quasi-historical shape. What mattered was the orientation towards the past, and the revitalizing of familiar or exotic figures for present enjoyment and instruction.

The third type of plot, the Menandrian, was the one that remained in possession of the field while the others came and went. The dramatization of a social issue, through the agency of seemingly modern but essentially timeless persons, proved completely and devastatingly victorious, both in its Terentian, comic form, and in its tragic or melodramatic form, from the author of *George Barnwell* through Ibsen to Arthur Miller and Tennessee Williams. Even the Italianate

novelty of pastoral drama, which permitted Tasso and
Shakespeare and Daniel to mingle the tragic and the comic in
transparent and predictable ways, feeds on the conciliatory
social forces of New Comedy, with the prose romance, another
Greek invention, as a collateral source.

Justice

The neo-classical dramatists tend to favour a design in which
the virtuous win out and the wicked fall: a cheerful combination which is best achieved by means of a double plot and a
complex reversal. But ancient tragic practice disdains the
tidily reasonable. More often than not the evil is found to be
endemic among the virtuous, in a political nexus which defies
a separation of the deserving from the undeserving. Corneille
objects to Sophocles' *Electra* on the grounds that he made his
heroes guilty of a crime in order to bring about the punishment of the villain (K. E. Wheatley, *Racine and English
Classicism* (1956), p. 290). In his own *Rodogune* he has the
villain Cleopatre killed, not by her son, but by an impersonal
object. Blinded by the moral criteria of the Renaissance
canons, Corneille failed to appreciate the magnitude of the
Sophoclean conception, in which hero and villain are one, or,
rather, in which neither term is appropriate to the understanding of human wrongdoing. There is, in fact, no word for
either in classical Greek.[3]

The city as the relevant setting for tragic wrongdoing and
suffering is one of the lasting contributions of the ancient
playwrights. Brecht understood the need, and so did Hebbel,
whose Agnes Bernauer (1851), a latter-day Antigone, has to
be removed so that the commonwealth may once again
prosper. Dürrenmatt's Claire Zachanassian (1956) owes much
of her frightening power to the social setting in which she
moves; Hochhuth's dramatic art is nothing if not political.
Those dramatists who have attempted to restrict the am-
bience and explore evil solely within the eccentric confines of
the nuclear family, or of the drawing-room, have abandoned
the resonance and the distance which help to make suffering
into tragedy. This is, in part at least, what Aristotle must have
meant when, complaining about the dramatists of his own

[3] The Greek word *heros* designates a Homeric warrior-chieftain or a blessed
ancestor.

time, he said that the ancients had made their characters speak *politikos*, but that the authors of his own time made them speak *rhetorikos*.

Jacobean revenge tragedy (and its Spanish models) presents a scheme of poetic justice which deceives with its apparent moral balance. In fact, this type of drama is one of the least moral, for it derives pleasure from a suffering that is far in excess of what is deserved, and from a wrongdoing that is self-authenticating (*Sejanus*, Act II, Scene ii):

> A race of wicked acts
> Shall flow out of my anger, and o'erspread
> The world's wide face, which no posterity
> Shall e'er approve. . . .

Pleasure to be got out of suffering is the prime paradox which Aristotle's theory of *mimesis* and *katharsis* was supposed to clarify. The paradox is with us from the beginning of tragedy. The revenge plays, from Euripides' *Trojan Women* and *Hecuba* through Seneca's *Thyestes* to Kyd and Tourneur, merely point up the paradox in an unusually painful fashion. The villains of the Senecan succession are un-Greek in that their delight in evil amounts to self-indulgence. The horror felt by the audience, in their role as Stoic neophytes, is made more acute when the characters of legend or foreign climes are dropped in favour of Menandrian next-door neighbours. The discovery of evil, and of the necessity of evil, which gives *Othello* its deadly strength, comes from a showing that it flourishes in familiar and amiable surroundings. Desdemona's innocence argues the melodramatic dimension of the play.

Greek tragedy may be said to exhibit man oscillating uncertainly between the poles of animality and angelhood. The same is true, along different lines, in Aristophanic comedy, with this difference: that the comic peasant hero suffers no doubt about his capacities for vulgarity and beatitude. In tragedy there is no such assurance. The chorus from the *Antigone*, on man's fearsome powers:

> There is no task he faces
> Without resource. Death alone
> He does not control,

glances across grimly at the choral portrait, in the *Bacchae*, of the human animal hunting and being hunted. Oedipus the

solver of riddles and Oedipus the whelp of Cithaeron: these
are the limiting terms of a dialectic, between humane pride
and beastly terror, between orderly accomplishment and
coarse vulnerability, which defines much of the tradition.
Aristotle's 'compassion' and 'terror' were designed to characterize the response to the dialectic. The Stoic dramatists
tended to emphasize the terror, and its usefulness as a warning
against moral lapse.

Even where moral intelligibility is surrendered, terror
remains. *Inorridir*, 'to shiver with terror', is one of Alfieri's
favourite words. Science fiction drama exploits the same
frisson. But the companion appeal of compassion has, perhaps,
played an even more important role. The very protests of
Strindberg and Brecht, with their epic theatre and their
renunciation of empathy, confirm the tenacity with which
European drama for centuries enlisted, and continues to
enlist, the sympathies of the audience. Whatever the precise
meaning of Aristotle's *katharsis* may have been to begin with,
in the history of criticism it has been associated with those
feelings which cause spectators to shed tears of complicity or
compassion.

Gods and Man

What about the divinities whose dictates and quarrels shape
the classical plots? At first blush it might be thought that they
are so much ballast, to be dropped as the dramatic tradition
reaches the modern age. But those modern playwrights who
have adopted the gods along with the legends with which they
are linked have found them useful as a graphic code for the
constraints which render a human life worthy of dramatic
treatment. Marxist or Freudian formulas have shown themselves less serviceable than the figurative reign of the old
divinities. Like the epic, drama turned out to be an instrument of secularization. The fear of raw divine power, a
constant in the ritual realities of the day, was put aside in
favour of the belief that the gods stood for a pattern and
a regularity which gave meaning to life. The clash between
divine and human authority, dramatized in the *Suppliants* of
Aeschylus and in Sophocles' *Antigone*, and a pervasive theme
in much of ancient drama, retains its power today.
Mariamne, in Hebbel's play (1848), distinguishes between the

human judges, whose authority she rejects, and the higher court,

> Shades that fix their solemn glance upon me (V. v. 2822).

From Hamlet's ghost to Montherlant's *La reine morte* (1942), there is a readiness to acknowledge a court of appeal above or beyond man. This should not be confused with the anti-Humanist religious tradition of the miracle play, which develops the theme of God's power to the point of reducing the significance of the human outline. Greek drama too offers the occasional intimation of the cry that all is vanity. Aeschylus is not averse to citing the lyric, 'man, the shadow of smoke' (fr. 399 N.²). But more typically the awareness of an outer law—of the gods, or Fate or Necessity—leaves the human initiative intact, and human suffering meaningful. Conversely, where the playwright seeks to exhibit human action without reference to the traditional constraints, the lack is strongly felt.

Human initiative should not necessarily be understood in the sense of deliberate choice. Agamemnon, Pelasgus, Antigone, Admetus do not choose; they recognize alternatives, and proceed to do what an inner voice—or the legend—commands them to do. The playwright shows little interest in an agonizing, tensed duelling between options. What he gives us, after a recital of the horns of the dilemma, is an unmediated lapse from knowledge into action and commitment. Agamemnon, the chorus tells us, articulates the grievous options, and voices his despair in the face of them, only to

> bow his neck under the yoke of Fate,
> His spirit blown and changed to evil,
> Impure, unholy. . . .

Elsewhere on the Greek stage decisions are enacted without quite the same touch of ominous decline. But nowhere do we find an emphasis on the sense of freedom, of unenforced choice, beloved by the romantics and the Kierkegaardians. The celebrated utterance of Schiller's Marquis von Posa (1787), and Sartre's glorification of liberty in the face of coercion have nothing in common with the ancient dramatic view, according to which free choice is a contradiction in tragic terms. Once again it looks as if the Greek way of looking at the springs of action is gaining ground. Post-romantic drama has reverted to the Greek emphasis on constraint and obsession. Brecht's Galileo (1943) does not choose; he acts as society and the needs of his body demand. And in the best of modern drama the characters are driven by inner forces which make the libertarian principles of an earlier dramatic psychology look very thin indeed.

Character and Action

In his *Discours*, Corneille remarks that some people have taken it amiss that he does not conclude *The Cid* with the marriage of 'the first actors'. That is to say, Corneille neglects to distinguish neatly between actor and character. Much earlier Castelvetro translated Aristotle's *ta ethe* as 'costumi' (habits), on the valid assumption that the *Poetics* talks about behaviour patterns and not about character traits, which are in the eye of the beholder rather than in the play. The *Poetics*, though mindful of the kinds of agents with which drama should concern itself, is, on the whole, more concerned with the particulars of the action than with the idiosyncrasies of the agent. In spite of a certain amount of wavering, Aristotle defines the agents in terms of the actions they perform, and not the other way round. This way of looking at what motivates a dramatic plot is, perhaps, more appropriate to an appreciation of Aeschylus than to a reading of Euripides. The inner battles, the pangs of conscience, the second thoughts dramatized in Euripides get us closer to the experience of complex individuals than the more summary or the more sustained reflections in Aeschylus. The sudden, unexplained turnaround of Iphigenia in *Iphigenia in Aulis*—first she wants to live, then she elects death—is difficult to parallel in Aeschylus or Sophocles, and conflicts, it seems, with Aristotle's call for consistency, unless his alibi of the 'consistently inconsistent' can be made to apply, which is doubtful. But even in Euripides, and in Seneca, vacillation and reversal and other stirrings of the irrational soul are, one might say, scenic or, to use Wilson Knight's term, 'spatial', rather than organic. The violent changes take place because they are stipulated by the dramaturgy or the philosophy of the author, and not because the author is bent upon acquainting us with an unusually volatile or schizoid personality.

These distinctions are awkward, and not very rewarding.

But it has often been observed that romantic and naturalistic tragedy, with its high regard for the unusual man or woman, calls for a very special approach. It builds its plot around the logging and testing of a character. The specificity, and, often, the growth and transformation of the character shape the plot. Soliloquy, a dramatic mechanism which Euripides is the first to explore, grows in power and usefulness as characters come face to face with the mazes of their souls and destinies, and struggle to renew themselves. The prince of Homburg, with his proneness to dreaming, his disregard of tactical niceties, and, in the end, his crash as a man of honour, accounts for the argument in a way which is crucially different from the ancient scheme, or, for that matter, from the well-made play of the type associated with Scribe and still greatly favoured today. Ibsen's best plays are built around individuals whose ambitions or imagined roles create havoc in the world around them. But unlike their Greek prototypes, they do so with pride in their separateness and originality. The Greek convention of a legendary or historical plot, of, that is, a given authoritative series of events, reduces the scope for an autonomous personality kindling the dramatic explosion.

True, some of the ancient characters have themselves assumed the dimensions of originals. Eric Bentley's view (*The Life of the Drama* (1964), pp. 62ff.) that the drama, all through the centuries, has done much less with separate persons than with relationships is not completely true of the Greeks. But a Prometheus, an Oedipus, a Medea stand out as centres of action. We sense their speeches as structures of linked events, or rather of units symbolizing the events, and not as appraisals or vindications of heroic individuality. An Aeschylean character is not given a chance to exercise his peculiar power. He spends most of the play defining his position and his role in the action, or having other agents define it for him. The play ends when the role has been defined in such a way that a nexus with other role-definitions has been established. What matters, always, is the progress of the action in speech, not the progressive development of a character. Significantly, many of the ancient plays are named after the chorus, as if to remove the temptation to look too closely at the principals and explain what happens by pointing to their needs or attributes.

Now it is obvious that modern playwriting, for reasons of its own, has overcome the romantic preoccupation with the minutely inspected, idiosyncratic character, and that it has rewoven the tissue which binds together dramatic action and human agency as warp and woof. In the preface to *Miss Julie*, Strindberg despairs of catching the multiplicity of human motives, and proposes to keep his characters flat. Mme de Staël had earlier (*De la littérature* (1800), Part 1, ch. 2; ed. van Tieghem (1959), pp. 64–76) contrasted Racine's subtly complexioned heroes and heroines with the undifferentiated simplicity of their Greek forebears. In fact, the drama of character may be said at all times to have been a rare thing. In Shakespeare, few characters dominate and shape the action as toweringly as do Hamlet and Richard III and, perhaps, Lear. Most of the Tragedies and Histories, and certainly the Comedies and Romances, impress us with the panoramic variety of speech and action. They are poems, designed so movingly and so richly that they leave little room for a close focus on heroic completeness.

Marlowe's giants come closer to determining the events of their plays. They are, as is generally agreed, projections of the poet's personal dream. Ibsen's Brand, and Solness, are of the same sort. The twentieth century has sacrificed the heroic stature along with the psychological mode. Marx, and social psychology, and the consciousness of nameless terror have snapped the thread of human greatness and human completeness. Theophrastus, and New Comedy, had, with their tender types and their parodistic excesses, helped to kill the heroic instinct. Theophrastus and Menander remain alive in some of the more sharply and disaffectingly delineated personages on the modern stage. But there is no longer any room for the comprehensive authenticity of an Othello, or of a Peer Gynt. Strindberg replaced characters with 'souls'; Hauptmann's *Weber* (1892) abolished individuals.

Kings

The question of the hero can also be discussed in a more technical fashion.

> The tragic Muse, sublime, delights to show
> Princes distrest, and Scenes of Royal Woe.

Thus Cibber's prologue to George Lillo's *The London Merchant*, *or The History of George Barnwell* (1731). He follows this up with the plea that 'A London Prentice ruin'd' is as good a theme as a king undone. Looking back we can now say that he was wrong; what works for kings and queens does not work for apprentices. The Greeks had put princes at the centre of the tragic stage, though Euripides, in his *Electra* and elsewhere, came close to bridging the gulf between princes and commoners. It was felt that rulers, representing not only themselves but also their realms and everybody under their jurisdiction, were thereby more effective in the tragic detonation. The fall of a king, entailing the fall of a whole people, could touch the emotions more compactly than the discomfiture of the man in the street.

This had nothing to do with class distinctions. The Athens of the tragedians knew no kings. The kings on the stage are literary fictions, symbols of power and responsibility. Add to this that, beginning with Sophocles, the vitality of a prince was felt to border on *hubris*. An Oedipus or an Antigone, and especially a Heracles, is given to daemonic wrath because he is, in part, a personification of unlimited force. The Athenian political experience, jealously watchful for signs of tyrannical leanings in their leading men, also helped to shape the contours of the royal figure. Seneca and the Stoic ethic accentuated the tyrannic aspects of the Sophoclean hero. In Christian and Baroque drama, Herod is the archetype. But tyrant and sufferer—or, in Christian terms, persecutor and martyr—tend to be one and the same. Oedipus, Pentheus, even Herod are not only violent despots striving to assert their power over others, but also victims. They suffer more for the very reason that their capacity for experience is greater, and their suffering becomes a lightning-conductor for the suffering of others.

Sophocles made no distinction between men and women. The vital energies of the queen, and her inclination to powerful anger, fully match those of the king. Euripides was the first to strike dramatic capital from the defencelessness, the precarious social position of women. The innovation sat badly with his audience, and was soon misunderstood, so that Fulke Greville (*Life of Sidney* (1652), p. 222) could say that Sophocles' women are all virtuous, whereas Euripides' women are all vicious.[1] Brieux's and Ibsen's preoccupation with

[1] The text has the names in reverse.

women's rights, Shaw's secularization of the earth mother, and O'Neill's re-ritualization of the same figure all take their origin from Euripides' daring step in the direction of social realism. The figure of the confidante—nurse, servant, friend—, perhaps the single most predictable character in the history of drama, is similarly indebted to Euripides, whose delicate or endangered queens needed the aid of trusted secondaries, not only to bring comfort to them in their distress, but more especially to counsel and undertake actions which the ladies themselves, in their helplessness, could not afford to broach on their own.

To return to the kings: the English Renaissance concern, from *Gorboduc* (1565) on, with dynastic succession and legitimacy is historically conditioned. For obvious reasons the Athenian stage showed no interest in the question of legitimacy. But Prometheus and Andromache express an aversion to tyranny, to the irresponsible exercise of governance. Many Athenian plays, both tragedies and political comedies, regard the question of power in a philosophical light, rather than in the light of the practical politics or the law of the day. That means that the crimes a tyrant might commit are not as easily motivated as they are on the Elizabethan stage, where reasons of state, coinciding with the ruler's own aggressive nature, lead him to wrongdoing. The Elizabethan mode was widely imitated. Grillparzer's Ottokar (1822) is modelled on the Shakespearean dynast. But the play is weak; it lacks the urgency which comes with a particular historical situation. In Greek tragedy, only the lesser personages, a Lycus or a Menelaus, prove tyrants in that sense. The primary figures are usually in the opposite camp; their greatness is one of power that has nothing to do with jockeying for position.

Neo-classical tragedy, and all tragedy written in the grand style, continued to mark the difference between princes and commoners. The prince may be a prince of the church, or a business tycoon. What matters is the dependence of the many upon the decisions and the fate of the few. *Murder in the Cathedral* (1935) is the tragedy of the private needs and desires of the great man who is isolated from the little people but watchful for them, and who is shipwrecked in the tensions. The prince may also be, in the romantic way, the isolated visionary. Fielding, as Scriblerus Secundus (*His Preface*: to *The Tragedy of Tragedies* (1731)), finds that Tom Thumb makes a fine hero, and that if people wonder 'what greatness can be in a fellow whom history relateth to have been no higher than a span', they are mistaken about the relation between body and soul. This is the comic answer to Cibber and Lillo. In our century, the succession of Shelley and Hugo has exhausted itself. The prince, the great individual, has surrendered his sceptre, and the commoners, weak and undistinguished, have had the action thrust upon them. Two thousand years of millenarian preaching have taken their toll. The London Prentice, confused and abashed, has joined forces with Everyman and Harlequin to unnerve the heroic tension.

Tragic Enormity

One feature, however, continues to distinguish serious drama, and that is the test-tube nature of its concentration upon what is not caught in ordinary experience. Even Freud's speculations about repression and sublimation do not quite plumb the extraordinariness of what is found on the tragic stage, and, for that matter, on the comic, if we include the Aristophanic plots of utopia, of obstacles lightly brushed aside, and of animal man victorious. The tragedian ruthlessly discards what might conflict with the hallucinatory fixities of the imagination: the older woman falling in love with her stepson and killing herself to punish him; brothers fighting each other for the kingdom and killing one another in the process; a man murdering his father and sleeping with his mother; a woman murdering her husband to revenge her daughter. The special qualities and designs of the plays in which these events are set before us must be appreciated. But the central understanding, of the precariousness of social relations, and especially of the family bond, is obvious. Ancient taboos are dovetailed with modern frustrations; the social compact is unravelled, and man stands vulnerable and alone. His hopeless pilgrimage uncovers the latent horror and the perilous dignity of civilized life.

It is the enormity of the ancient plots, the obsessive dilemmas and the monstrous solutions, which pointed the way, and which have been abandoned only intermittently, and at great loss. Because the neo-classicists sought verisimilitude they tried to compensate for the lost improbabilities in other ways, with usually mawkish results. The social drama of Ibsen and Chekhov succeeded in achieving its own sense of fear. But by abandoning the extreme propositions of the old tragedians, the nineteenth-century realists produced a horror that goes a certain distance but often does not touch the heart. The parochial realism of Arthur Miller and of Albee registers its effects, but without the large tonality that makes the ancient works powerful. There are some modern plays, including Albee's own *A Delicate Balance*, in which the old enormities are darkly glimpsed. Such plays are our guarantee that tragedy has not yet died the death that has been predicted for it.

Roland Barthes (*Essais critiques* (1964), p. 78) has stated that the message of the *Oresteia* is anachronistic. Its gods have been displaced; it can appeal to us only as a piece of history. Hence a performance must insist on clarity and on historical veracity. Barthes's call for clarity of production can only be welcomed. The notion that the trilogy is out of date must, however, be chalked up to a wilful narrowness of the historical imagination. It is gainsaid by so modernist a critic as Georg Lukács, who finds the Greek drama, as compared with the drama of his own time, strangely satisfying (*Schriften zur Literatursoziologie*, ed. Ludz (2nd edn., 1963), p. 82; from *Die Theorie des Romans* (1920)). It is difficult to go along completely with his further reasoning· 'The Greek recognizes only answers, not questions; only solutions (which may be enigmatic), not riddles, only forms, not chaos.' 'The Greek' is, like all such shorthand cyphers, an implausible generalization. Still, Lukács's formula hits on an important truth. Viewed by hindsight, the Greek theatre seems to have been able, in one gigantic step, to bring to perfection insights and structures and 'conventions' which are, by and large, still valid. And it did so with an assurance that takes the breath away. The immediacy of the triumph was such that later generations could not escape its authority. Unlike the epic, and the lyric, the drama is still, essentially, in spite of so many innovations, what it was during those two or three generations in the fifth century B.C., and towards the end of the fourth, when the forms of Greek drama were established. August Comte considered dramatic performances a vestige of primitive silliness, and forbade the theatre in his ideal city (H. Gouhier, *L'essence du théâtre* (1943), p. 91). But in the positivist calendar prepared by him, Aeschylus, Calderón, Corneille, and Molière each have a Sunday named after them. We are at liberty to add further names to the list. But it will always have to start with Aeschylus.

Further Reading

1. *Translations of Ancient Texts*

For the tragedians, the most convenient collection is D. Grene and R. Lattimore, *Greek Tragedies* (1953-9, 3 vols.). The usable Aeschylean fragments are found in H. Lloyd-Jones's re-edition of H. W. Smyth's Loeb *Aeschylus*, vol. ii (1963). The most enjoyable translations of Aristophanes are the various fascicles of *The Mentor Greek Comedy*, ed. W. Arrowsmith. The most complete collection of Menander is that by L. Casson (1971). For Plautus, the two volumes of *Selected Plays*, tr. E. F. Watling (1964-5), furnish a generous sampling. Robert Graves has brought out *The Comedies of Terence* (1963), and Th. Newton *Seneca: His Tenne Tragedies* (1966). G. M. A. Grube's *Aristotle: On poetry and Style* (1958) presents the relevant texts; G. F. Else, *Aristotle: Poetics* (1967) adds a brief commentary. For Horace's *Art of Poetry*, see Palmer Bovie, *Horace: Satires and Epistles* (1959).

2. *Books on Ancient Drama*

H. C. Baldry, *The Greek Tragic Theatre* (1971) is a brief summary; A. Lesky, *Greek Tragedy* (1965) a more extended treatment. K. Lever, *The Art of Greek Comedy* (1956) and T. B. L. Webster, *Studies in Later Greek Comedy* (1970) deal with Old and New Comedy respectively. See now also F. H. Sandbach, *The Comic Theatre of Greece and Rome* (1977). R. Lattimore, *Story Patterns in Greek Tragedy* (1964) tactfully canvasses the plots. A. D. Trendall and T. B. L. Webster, *Illustrations of Greek Drama* (1971) lavishly presents the pictorial evidence. For the staging, see P. Arnott, *Greek Scenic Conventions in the Fifth Century B.C.* (1962).

3. *Books on Ancient Authors*

A. Lebeck, *The Oresteia* (1971) is chiefly on uses of imagery. There is no satisfactory general book on Aeschylus in English. K. Reinhardt, *Aischylos als Regisseur und Theologe* (1949) is probably the best concise book on the first tragedian. For Sophocles, see G. Kirkwood, *A Study of Sophoclean Drama* (1958) and B. Knox, *The Heroic Temper* (1964); for Euripides, D. J. Conacher, *Euripidean Drama* (1967) and S. Barlow, *The Imagery of Euripides*. For Aristophanes, see K. Dover, *Aristophanic Comedy* (1972). Humphry House, *Aristotle's Poetics* (1956) is brief and perceptive. John Jones, *On Aristotle and Greek Tragedy* (1962) seeks to dispel misconceptions about character and action. For interesting discussions of *katharsis* see H. D. F. Kitto in *Studies for Harry Caplan* (1966), pp. 133-47, and A. Koestler, *The Act of Creation* (1970), pp. 309ff.

4. *Books on Drama*

There are excellent brief introductions, with good bibliographies, in the series *The Critical Idiom*, ed. J. D. Jump: C. Leech, *Tragedy* (1969); S. Dawson, *Drama and the Dramatic* (1970); E. Dipple, *Plot* (1970); M. Merchant, *Comedy* (1972); and J. L. Smith, *Melodrama* (1973). Allardyce

154 *Drama*

Nicoll, *The Theatre and Dramatic Theory* (1962) is thoughtful and comprehensive. Th. R. Henn, *The Harvest of Tragedy* (1956) and Albert Cook, *Enactment* (1971) apply different critical approaches to basic issues. Northrop Frye, *A Natural Perspective* (1965) and L. J. Potts, *Comedy* (1948) are two adventurous discussions of comedy; Elder Olson, *The Theory of Comedy* (1968) is a more sober one. J. L. Styan, *The Dark Comedy* (2nd edn., 1968) and R. B. Heilman, *Tragedy and Melodrama* (1968) explore the mixed genre.

5. *The Study of Literature*

G. Watson, *The Study of Literature* (1969) is conservative and provocative. P. Goodman, *The Study of Literature* (1954) pays special attention to drama. S. S. Prawer, *Comparative Literary Studies* (1973) is the sanest introduction to the special problems of comparative literature, including the problem of literary dependence.

6. *Ancient and Modern*

R. R. Bolgar, *The Classical Heritage and its Beneficiaries* (1954) and G. Highet, *The Classical Tradition* (1949) are panoramic surveys. A. Belli, *Ancient Greek Myths and Modern Drama* (1969) explores the uses of myth in thirteen modern plays. The two best studies of the subject are in German: K. von Fritz, *Antike und Moderne Tragödie* (1962) and W. H. Friedrich, *Vorbild und Neugestaltung* (1967), as is K. Hamburger's more impressionistic *Von Sophokles zu Sartre* (1962).

For particular authors see J. A. K. Thomson, *Shakespeare and the Classics* (1952); M. H. Shackford, *Shakespeare and Sophocles* (1960); L. G. Salingar, *Shakespeare and the Traditions of Comedy* (1974); R. Trousson, *Le thème de Prométhée dans la littérature européenne* (1964); J. A. Stone, *Sophocles and Racine* (1964); R. C. Knight, *Racine et la Grèce* (1950); Fl. Prader, *Schiller und Sophokles* (1954); F. L. Lucas, *Euripides and His Influence* (1928); W. Suess, *Aristophanes und die Nachwelt* (1911); Coburn Gum, *The Aristophanic Comedies of Ben Jonson* (1969); G. François, 'Aristophane et le théatre moderne', *Antiquité Classique* xl (1971), 38–79; R. G. Tanner, 'The Dramas of T. S. Eliot and their Greek Models', *Greece and Rome* xvii (1970), 123–34.

6

HISTORY AND BIOGRAPHY

ARNALDO MOMIGLIANO

I.

Like the ancient Romans, we are conscious of having in-herited 'history' (*historia*) from the Greeks. Herodotus is to us the 'father of history', as he was to Cicero. We are also conscious that history has come to us as part of a greater legacy which includes the most important intellectual ac-tivities (philosophy, mathematics, astronomy, natural history, figurative arts, etc.) in which we are still involved—and, more particularly, the most prestigious literary genres (epic, lyric, eloquence, tragedy, comedy, novel, idyll), by which we still satisfy our needs for verbal expression.

However, we know that, properly speaking, we ought not to use the word 'inheritance' in the case of history or indeed for any other aspect of Greek culture. Since the humanists of the fourteenth and fifteenth centuries made it their business to restore the validity of the ancient models after medieval deviations, it has been a question not so much of legacy as of conscious choice. Modern history-writing has been by choice a continuous confrontation with the Greek originals and with what the Romans made of their models. Consequently there was in the Renaissance a revival and further elaboration of the theories (sketched rather than developed) which in ancient Greece defined the characteristics of history and its legitimate forms: the sophistic invention of 'antiquities', the Isocratean-Ciceronian notion of history as a rhetorical genre, the Polybian attribution of strictly utilitarian purposes to historiography, and finally the separation between biography and history, which is stated for instance by Plutarch (*Alexander*, 1. 2).

Fundamental questions are involved in the reception of Greek historiography. Of these we are perhaps more aware than the historians of previous generations. We may ask how far Greek historiography is compatible with the Biblical vision of the world; and how far it can express our modern views of the world. The former question had already been recognized by those Fathers of the Church who created ecclesiastical history (and perhaps even more radically by those rabbis who simply did not write history). The second question is at least implicit in the recent creation of the social sciences, for which there is no clear precedent even in the most 'modern' of Greek writers, Thucydides and Aristotle.

2.

A new branch of intellectual activity always poses problems of origins: it would be a true paradox if we had been spared the problems of the historical genesis of Greek historical writing.

As the Greeks had a long tradition of epic poetry before they began to write historical prose, it is tempting to take Homer as a predecessor of the historians and to add the poets of the 'cycle' and the writers of poems on the foundations of Greek cities (Semonides, Xenophanes). Herodotus may seem to encourage us in this direction. But the Greeks themselves, and the Romans, knew that there were two differences between history and epic poetry: history was written in prose, and was meant to separate facts from fancies about the past. Homer was too much of an authority not to be used by historians as evidence for specific facts. The use of a text as evidence was precisely one of the characteristic operations which distinguished Greek history-writing from epic poetry.

More attention has to be given to a statement by Dionysius of Halicarnassus (*On Thucydides*, 5) which seems to reflect the opinion of previous Hellenistic scholars but would not lose its interest if it had been inspired by Dionysius' acquaintance with Roman historiography. Dionysius thought that Greek historical writing had begun in the form of histories of cities or regions based on local evidence—whether sacred or profane. *A priori* this sounds likely enough, because city and temple chronicles existed not only in Rome but in some of those Eastern civilizations with which the Greeks had contacts. It is very doubtful, however, whether Dionysius knew of any history earlier than the fifth century B.C. Herodotus and Thucydides do not show any awareness of such archaic histories, though they were by no means disinclined to quarrel with their predecessors. Thucydides does not tell us in 1.13 where he found his information about naval history. After 500 B.C.

local chroniclers were just one—and not the most important—group among the writers who created the new climate of historical research. We hear of writers of biographical and autobiographical accounts (Scylax of Caryanda, Ion of Chios), of students of chronology (Hippias of Elis), of researchers in literary history (Theagenes of Rhegium, Damastes of Sigeum), and, of course, of local and regional historians (Charon of Lampsacus, Antiochus of Syracuse). Above all there were writers who, like Herodotus and in some cases probably before him, tried to inform the Greeks about the Persian Empire or some of its parts. The oldest (*c.* 460 B.C.?) is apparently the shadowy Dionysius of Miletus who is said to have composed both a book on 'Persian affairs' (*Persika*) and a book on 'after Darius'. More famous was Xanthus, the author of a history of Lydia, a hellenized native who tried to combine some of his national traditions with Greek stories for the benefit of the Greeks— a phenomenon which was to become characteristic of later, Hellenistic historiography. Two works on 'Greek affairs' (*Hellenika*) by Charon of Lampsacus and Damastes of Sigeum may already have been inspired by Thucydides. It is significant that the majority of the earliest writers in Greek on historical subjects, including Herodotus, came from Asia or from the Aegean islands. This does not necessarily support the opinion of Dionysius of Halicarnassus on the original types of Greek historical works but raises the more general question, easier to ask than to answer, whether contacts with Oriental nations and life under the Persian rulers gave an impulse to Greek historiography.

Herodotus (who wrote *c.* 445–425 B.C.) clearly treats Hecataeus of Miletus as his only authoritative predecessor. Hecataeus, a principal figure in the Ionian rebellion of *c.* 500 B.C., had tried to put order and 'rationality' into the mythical genealogies of the Greeks (whom he considered capable of transmitting 'many and ridiculous stories'), and had written a model travelogue (*periodos*) in which geography and ethnography were mixed. In his turn Thucydides intimated disapproval of two contemporaries. One was Herodotus himself; the other was Hellanicus, a learned man from the island of Lesbos who wrote many books of local history, mythography, and geography, among them a chronicle of Attica made public after 406 B.C.

The novelty of Herodotus, in comparison with his pre-decessors and contemporaries, seems to have been twofold. He appears to have been the first to produce an analytical description of a war, the Persian War. Furthermore, he was probably the first to use ethnographical and constitutional studies in order to explain the war itself and to account for its outcome. The very word *historia* in the sense in which we are using it is a tribute to Herodotus as the inventor or perfector of a new literary genre. Herodotus used *historia* in his ethnographic sections as a generic name for 'enquiry', but in the fourth century B.C. *historia* was taken to mean what Herodotus had done—namely, specific research on past events.

The three components of the Herodotean enquiry— ethnography, constitutional research, and war history—did not remain indissolubly united. The combination was most usually restricted to two elements: either ethnography and constitutions, or ethnography and wars, or constitutions and wars. Thucydides is the most obvious example of the almost total elimination of ethnography, though he preserved the close integration of war with constitutional history. Constitutional problems were indeed discussed independently, without reference to historical research, as we can see in the *Constitution of Athens*, attributed to Xenophon, but written *c.* 440–420 B.C. Yet the reciprocal relevance of customs, insti-tutions, and wars which Herodotus had discovered remained inherent in historical research—with the consequence that one series of facts was implicitly or explicitly treated as the explanation of another series (a better constitution explained a victory, but a defeat might result in changes of customs and institutions). To go one step further, it was Herodotus who made it a rule for historians to explain the events they told.

Explanation took the form of search for causes, especially of wars and revolutions. At least since Thucydides, a distinction had been made between immediate and remote causes—or between causes and pretexts. The causal analysis of consti-tutional changes often went deeper than the analysis of causes of wars because the Greeks took the existence of hostility between independent states for granted, whereas they did not regard internal political conflicts as inevitable. Greek his-torians therefore gave the impression of being more mature in their descriptions of revolutions than in their phenomenology of war. Even Thucydides and Polybius are no exceptions.

The search for causes, understandably enough, was less prominent or at least took more devious forms in the case of ethnographic research. Occasionally geographic factors were adduced as causes of somatic and psychic peculiarities: love of liberty was connected with a temperate climate. But the most famous of these explanations is to be found, not in a historian, but in the author of the Hippocratic treatise, *Airs, Waters, and Places*. Ethnography was based on the consciousness of the distinction between Greeks and Barbarians, and this distinction seemed to be in itself sufficient explanation. Research was further limited by the disinclination of the Greeks to learn foreign languages. Greek ethnographic research contributed extremely little to the knowledge of non-Hellenic tongues. Whatever acquaintance it had with foreign texts was second-hand and garbled. Thus Greek ethnography was fed by the peculiarities of Greek national consciousness, and in turn fed them. From this point of view there was little inducement to do ethnographic research on individual regions of Greece. What curiosity existed about Greek regions was better satisfied by research on specific topics, such as cults and monuments and, indeed, dialects. It was naturally connected with local political history. Particularly in the Hellenistic period, authors of local chronicles are also local antiquarians. Greece as a whole became of ethnographical interest to the Greeks only in the Hellenistic and Roman periods—and even then not very often.

3.

From Herodotus came the example of a near-contemporary subject (the Persian Wars) as the most suitable for a historian. This involved a specific perception of the structure of historical research as founded upon evidence which had to be tested. As the simplest way of knowing the facts is to see them, it is not surprising that Herodotus rated direct visual observation best, and next to it the collection of reports from reliable witnesses. In the Greece of the fifth century B.C., written evidence was not abundant, and the documents which had been transmitted from previous centuries raised problems of interpretation and reliability which were beyond Herodotus' powers. Thus a subject near in time became preferable, though the exploration of more remote events was not excluded, as Herodotus himself made clear. Thucydides basically did nothing more than reinforce the strictness and coherence of Herodotus' criteria by preferring contemporary to near-contemporary history and by refusing to tell anything which he did not consider absolutely reliable, whereas Herodotus had considered it legitimate to report with a warning what he could not vouch for directly. Thucydides was able to transcribe some written evidence (letters, inscriptions, and treaties) which came within his criteria of reliability, but it is remarkable that he did not depart from the Herodotean rule of preferring oral to written evidence. He definitely left his successors with the impression that direct observation and oral reports by witnesses were altogether preferable to written evidence. In so far as he suppressed what he did not consider trustworthy, there was a dangerous implication in his rigour. But he introduced a note of austerity which became part of the historian's ethos (if not of the historian's praxis). And though he did not consider possible a reconstruction in detail of the remote past, he produced a memorable sample of how one could reach *some* conclusions about archaic Greece.

With Herodotus and even more with Thucydides, the historian established himself as a witness and a recorder of changes—especially of recent changes—which in his judgement were important enough to be transmitted to posterity. In his choice he took into account, and even reflected, the prevailing interests of the community to which he belonged. Military and political events emerged as the main themes of Greek historiography.

It was also the example of Herodotus, and after him of Thucydides, that made the Greeks unwilling to accord the full dignity of history to mere narrations of local events. The Athenian local chronicle (Atthidography), though involving leading personalities and important constitutional changes, was never put on the same level as the history of the Peloponnesian War with its panhellenic horizon. The canon of the Great Greek historians constructed in the Hellenistic age reflects this opinion in its exclusion of local historians. The community about which and for which the 'good' historians spoke was not that of the individual city. Greece as a whole was their most obvious term of reference. Granted the difference between Greece and any barbarian land (as Herodotus had exemplarily shown), the historian had of course to recognize the conflicts between Greek States and inside Greek States (as Thucydides had exemplarily shown).

In the same perspective, it was difficult to attribute the quality of full history to the study of genealogies, foundations of cities, festivals, rituals, laws, customs, words, chronological systems, and the like. Research on such topics remained in a limbo to which Hippias apparently gave the name of 'archae-ology' (Plato, *The Greater Hippias*, 285D). According to the same Hippias, anything 'archaeological' had a special appeal for the Spartans. This denomination, however, was not generally accepted in the Graeco-Roman world. It was left to the Renaissance to collect under the name of 'antiquities', inherited from Varro, all the historical subjects which did not correspond to the Herodotean-Thucydidean notion of history centred on politics and war. For the same reason, bio-graphical accounts were not history, though proper history could contain short biographical sketches. Xenophon wrote twice on Agesilaus, once from a biographical and once from a historical point of view. That biography first appeared in the form of eulogy of an individual contributed to its separation from history. It was another implicit feature of the Herodotean-Thucydidean approach that history, aiming as it did at truth, should refrain from excesses of praise and blame. It is probable that local history, too, suffered from this suspicion of bias. The Greeks knew themselves: they ap-preciated the power of their local loyalties. 'Real' history was above local feuds.

4.

Herodotus' creation and the Thucydidean developments are rooted in the intellectual revolution of the fifth century, and derive their full significance from it. This was the time in which tragedy, comedy, medicine, philosophy, and eloquence were either created or transformed. Even if we did not know that Sophocles was a friend of Herodotus, we would perceive the latter's connections with the former in moral, religious, and political feelings. Thucydides, Hippocrates, and Euripides recall each other irresistibly. One of the inventions of Thucydides—the use of fictitious speeches to report currents of public opinion and to reconstruct the motivations of political leaders—is unthinkable without the formalization of public eloquence which happened in the late fifth century in and outside Athens. In other civilizations written accounts of events were inspired by contemporary figurative arts, or at least can easily be illustrated by contemporary figurative arts. Ancient oriental historiography has been said (not without exaggeration) to have its origins in narrative paintings and reliefs. Medieval historical accounts call to mind contemporary painting and, as a matter of fact, were often illustrated by illuminations. Greek historical accounts were hardly influenced by contemporary art. The 'pedimental style' attributed to Herodotus is not very convincing, even as a metaphor. The style of Greek history was essentially regulated by rules of prose writing and by its differentiation from other literary genres.

History in the Herodotean and Thucydidean form not only learns from other branches of knowledge and contributes to them (the reciprocal influence is especially evident in the case of philosophy), but presupposes them. It is not for history to give the ultimate sense of things or to measure in full the relevance of gods to men, or indeed to explore systematically the nature (*physis*) of man: for this there are other sciences. The direction given by Herodotus and even more by Thucydides to history-writing certainly presupposes—and helps to reinforce—the assumption that the intervention of gods in human affairs is neither constant nor too patent. But this is an implicit acceptance, or exploitation, of the general trend of Greek thought in the fifth century rather than a programmatic aim. Even in later centuries the marginal importance of gods in historical narrative presupposes, rather than expresses, Greek lack of interest in theological speculations. History had a limited purpose with a varied and by no means scholastically rigorous culture. It was meant to preserve a reliable record of past events and therefore had to establish criteria of reliability. It was meant to pay special attention to wars and political revolutions, because they produced consequential changes. It was bound to give an explanation of the events in so far as this was compatible with the use of evidence. Metaphysical explanations were, as a rule, either avoided or only briefly hinted at. Later in the

Hellenistic period some historians (the most important of whom was Polybius) used with special relish the notion of *Tyche* (fortune) which represented an elegant way of avoiding any serious religious or philosophical commitment.

Though historians seemed to be prepared to pay homage to philosophy, and some philosophers (such as Plato in the *Laws* and Aristotle) derived much instruction from research on historical facts, Greek philosophy as a whole was not kind to history. History seemed to philosophers to be rooted in that transient world of ambitions and passions from which philosophy was supposed to liberate man. A philosopher directly involved in history-writing and obviously enjoying it, like Posidonius in the first century B.C., is sufficiently exceptional as to become mysterious. The pressure of philosophy on historians induced some of them to turn historical books into philosophical novels. Xenophon supplied in the *Cyropaedia* the model of the pedagogic pseudo-biography. Two generations later Onesicritus turned the life of Alexander into a quasi-Cynic novel. His contemporaries Hecataeus of Abdera and even more Euhemerus presented their own speculations in the form of ethnography.

Since historians were free to introduce into their accounts any philosophical or religious reflection they fancied, it is possible to ascribe specific philosophical or religious opinions to individual historians. But it remains to be proved that any of them based their accounts on philosophic or religious notions. Many tedious discussions on the circularity of time in Greek historiography could have been spared if it had been observed that the span of time with which Greek historians normally operate is too short to be defined either as linear or as circular. Characteristically, Polybius theorized the cycle of constitutional forms, but reported ordinary military and political events without reference to any such circularity. It has been possible for later civilizations (notably the Arabic) to absorb Greek philosophic and scientific thought without being deeply affected by Greek historical thought.

5.

The historian's account was supposed to give some sort of pleasure to his readers. At the same time it could hardly justify its existence if it were not also useful. But the precise relation between pleasure and usefulness, and the form both of pleasure and use, had been matters of dispute and of personal preference at least since Thucydides accused Herodotus of putting delectation before instruction. The care with which Thucydides wrote his prose shows, however, that even he did not overlook the pleasurable side of his exposition. We must of course distinguish between the techniques actually adopted by individual historians to produce pleasure and the theories about the proper forms of giving pleasure. In the fourth century B.C., Ephorus and Theopompus used the rhetorical techniques they had learnt in Isocrates' school to enliven their expositions. Clitarchus and other historians of Alexander the Great became notorious for their propensity to amuse the reader. In the third and second centuries B.C. a technique of 'pathetic' over-dramatizations of events was in favour with some historians, such as Phylarchus (whom we know mainly through his critic Polybius) and the author of 2 Maccabees. What remains unclear is the relation between this 'pathetic' technique and the theory of historiography as 'imitation' (*mimesis*) which seems to have been propounded or supported by Duris in order to save political historiography from the strictures of Aristotle. Polybius reacted by condemning any appeal to emotions, and by emphasizing the importance of sober political experience and of geographical knowledge for the historian.

The most visible weakness of the Greek historians was their approach to the evidence (that is, their criteria for establishing the facts). The lack of precise rules about collecting and choosing data created confusion in the minds both of the authors and their readers. Herodotus could be treated by turn as the father of history and as a liar, because nobody was in a position to check the stories he had told. His younger rival Ctesias was believed when he accused Herodotus of lying, though he too was known as a liar. Only modern Orientalist research has been able to show that Herodotus was a truthful reporter (within the limits of his information), whereas Ctesias was unscrupulous. Rhetorical rules of composition further complicated matters by offering reasons or excuses for departing from the truth even when it was unmistakably known. The selection of topics for history corresponded so closely to the primary interests of Greek political life as to be imprisoned by them. Both spiritual and economic life remained marginal

(and hardly identified) themes for historians. This in turn
conditioned the principles of explanation. Other limitations in
the analysis and therefore in the explanation were inherent in
the absolute preference given to the narrative form for
political history, whereas biography and antiquarian research
frequently took a descriptive form which permitted better
analytical work. Some remedy was found in digressions and
excursuses in which Greek historians often said what mattered
most to them, but digressions leave the main line of the
interpretation unaffected (as is obvious, for instance, to the
readers of Thucydides' chapters on the fifty years before the
Peloponnesian War and of Polybius' theory on the cycle of
constitutions).

To the Greeks, therefore, history was not one of the sciences
with clear methods which create a body of undisputed
knowledge. As it was not included in ordinary education,
except as a provider of rhetorical examples, it was also a
basically non-professional activity. Though it was in the
nature of things that a good historian should find a continuator, the continuator could come from anywhere, without
any implication of a school. We do not know why Xenophon,
Theopompus, and the author (sometimes identified with
Cratippus) of the historical fragment known as *Hellenica
Oxyrhynchia* chose to continue Thucydides—or why Posidonius
and Strabo connected their histories with those of Polybius.
The work done in Aristotle's school on constitutional antiquities, and perhaps on biography, is the major exception to
the individual, unscholastic character of Greek historiography
as a whole; this work was not done on ordinary political
history and was intended to prepare the ground for philosophical theory.

It has repeatedly been noticed that historians were often
voluntarily or compulsorily exiles from their own city. The list
of distinguished historians who wrote abroad includes
Herodotus, Thucydides, Xenophon, Ctesias, Theopompus,
Philistus, Timaeus, Polybius, Dionysius of Halicarnassus, and,
in a sense, Posidonius, who wrote as a Rhodian citizen but was
born in Syria. This may even suggest that historiography,
unless it was local history written to satisfy local patriotism,
had an ambiguous status in Greek society. It was certainly
easier to get proper information for a large subject and to be
impartial if one had the mobility of an exile.

If the historian, as a rule, operated alone, he was not necessarily left alone after he had operated. The temptation to please and flatter was constant, especially when historiography was centred on recent events. States knew how to reward popular historians; even Herodotus got a big prize from Athens, according to a story which seems to have a documentary basis. Alexander the Great made the experiment of having a historian on his staff, Callisthenes—and killed him. Later, Hellenistic kings and Roman emperors had the power both to honour and to persecute historians. Not being supported by institutions (and therefore never exactly speaking on behalf of institutions), the historians had to rely on their personal inspiration and integrity.

Notwithstanding all these difficulties, the Greek historians after Thucydides showed great capacity for experiment and adaptation to new circumstances. Their vitality can be measured in two ways: by considering how many new forms of historical writing they created and transmitted to us, and by observing how after Alexander Greek historiography spread among non-Greeks and became an international form of communication. The point of departure of all these developments is of course represented by Herodotus and Thucydides. But their successors reshaped and simplified the highly individual Herodotean and Thucydidean models—or created new types. Even in the Renaissance and later, Herodotus and Thucydides were seldom closely imitated. They provided a stimulus rather than a rigid model. The idealization in the nineteenth century of Thucydides as the perfect historian marks the point at which modern historiography really began to create types of historical research unknown to the classical world (such as economic history, history of religions, and, beyond certain limits, cultural history).

6.

Greek culture was fiercely introvert in the fourth century B.C., and the continuation of Herodotus' work in ethnography was confined to cheap information on Persia (Ctesias and, for the little that is known of him, Dinon). The Thucydidean monograph on war and politics suited the age. It provided the model not only for accounts of individual wars, but for books on 'Hellenic affairs' (*Hellenika*), one of which, written by Xenophon, has come down to us. The main external divergence from Thucydides was the abandonment (gradual in Xenophon) of the annalistic scheme. Theopompus, who in his youth had competed with Xenophon by writing *Hellenika* of his own, realized that the intervention of Philip of Macedon in Greek affairs introduced a strong personal element into Greek politics. He transformed the *Hellenika* into *Philippika*, 'Philip's affairs'. The change would not have been possible without contemporary developments in the art of biography, but the essential elements of the Thucydidean monograph were preserved. On the other hand Philistus, a Sicilian historian, applied Thucydidean methods to the history of his island which had been treated in a Herodotean way by his predecessor Antiochus of Syracuse.

The Thucydidean model was never forgotten by Hellenistic, Roman, and Byzantine historians. Sometimes only its style and its liberal use of speeches were imitated, but normally the co-ordination of political and military analysis survived the changes. It proved to be a satisfactory instrument for recording a limited period of wars complicated by internal agitations or revolutions: Sallust, for all his personal traits, shows this. But already in the fourth century B.C. there is a tendency to turn the Thucydidean monograph into a comprehensive Greek history from the earliest times. Ephorus of Cyme (followed by Anaximenes of Lampsacus?) conceived this extension. Thucydides had of course pointed this way by his introductory chapters on archaic Greek history; and local histories started from the beginnings of a city or of a regional unit. Ephorus' ambition was to produce, not antiquarian details, but a full account of past political and military events for the whole of Greece. A history of this scope had to define its own limits in relation to the mythical age, and was bound to involve an account of foreign nations (or 'barbarians') in their political conflicts and cultural contrasts with the Greeks. Polybius considered Ephorus his predecessor in writing universal history, but one has to add that Polybius himself had a narrow view of universal history. Ephorus was rather the founder of national history, and already displayed (if we can trust what survives of him in later sources, such as Diodorus) that fatal characteristic of national history, patriotic prejudice. When Plutarch condemned Herodotus as philobarbarian, he accepted the set of values introduced by Ephorus. In Ephorus universality existed only in the form of excursuses subordinated to Greek history. Roman annalists substantially accepted the type of Greek national history with some accommodation to local habits of registering events (a legacy of the old pontifical chronicle, though Roman historians did not care much for it). In the Ephorean (and Roman) type of narration the exploitation of pre-existing historical work was conspicuous, and perhaps inevitable. Ephorus therefore started the fashion which has lasted into our day of 'books made of books', that is, of compilation. Not by chance does the genre of historical epitome—or summary—make its first appearance with Ephorus' contemporary Theopompus, who abbreviated Herodotus to two books. Compilations did not require much *historia* in the Herodotean sense. Polybius, for instance, was conscious of this; nevertheless, with Ephorus compilation had become an accepted practice in historiography.

Meanwhile Xenophon, who played so large a part in transmitting the Thucydidean model, created or contributed to the creation of new models by his personal memoir as a general in the retreat of the Ten Thousand (*Anabasis*) and by the encomiastic biography of King Agesilaus (in which he was preceded by Isocrates' encomium of King Euagoras). His 'Recollections' (*Memorabilia*) of Socrates and his *Education of Cyrus* were also potentially historiographical types, and operated as such in later times, though it is unlikely that Xenophon himself attributed any value to them as factual records.

Books on the education (or on the youth) of great men existed in ancient times and came into favour again with the Renaissance; their status between history and novel remained ambiguous. Collections of sayings of great men multiplied after Xenophon and have been used ever since to fill up the biographies of philosophers, saints, and even kings. The personal memoir of a general became a popular genre when, after Alexander, generals controlled the known world; it is still in our repertoire. The memoirs of two generals, Ptolemy (King Ptolemy I of Egypt) and Hieronymus of Cardia, were the principal sources for the history of Alexander and his successors. Caesar contributed his prestige and his stylistic skill to the genre. In the second century A.D. the Roman provincial governor and Greek historian Arrian used the memoirs of Ptolemy together with those of a minor companion of Alexander, Aristobulus, to compile what the chance of survival has made for us the most authoritative account of Alexander's campaigns. He also wrote a memoir of his own campaign against the Alans. It would be pedantry to try to separate in such memoirs—in which the author normally speaks in the third person, even if he is a protagonist—the biographical, the autobiographical, and the 'historical' elements. Polybius knew very well that a biography of a general is something different from a history of the events in which a general was involved, but how the distinction was preserved in practice is another matter. With the collapse of the city-state and the rise of monarchies, first in the Hellenistic East and then in Rome, the period of the rule of a sovereign became the natural unit for political history: history became increasingly biographical.

Altogether biography flourished in the Hellenistic and Roman periods, when writers extended biographical treatment to all sorts of people as representatives of certain forms of life (theoretical, practical, voluptuous, etc.). Biography of intellectuals produced its own problems of method: often very little was known about their lives, except what could be inferred from their works. Even for authors of the fourth century B.C. and later, for whom some biographical tradition existed, the question of how far the works reflected the character of the man remained. The ease and arbitrariness with which biographers inferred from the life the works and vice versa seem to us appalling. There was certainly a marked inability to appreciate the jokes of old comedy: they were often converted into facts. Little survives of Hellenistic biography in its original form (we had to wait for a papyrus to give us Satyrus' life of Euripides), but the masters of Greek and Latin biography of the imperial age worked on Hellenistic models and in their turn became the models for later ages. The Latin Cornelius Nepos and more conspicuously the Greek Plutarch idealized the Greek and Roman past and compared Greek 'heroes' with Roman 'heroes'. In the third and fourth centuries A.D., from Philostratus to Eunapius, biography was used to defend paganism, while the Christians also produced their exemplary lives of bishops, monks, and martyrs.

The pagan biographical models of the early second century A.D., Plutarch and Suetonius, survived into the Middle Ages, notwithstanding the introduction of new Christian themes and modes. The chronologically organized account of a life (such as we have it in Plutarch) is to be distinguished from the systematic description of an individual as we have it in the 'Caesars' of Suetonius and in the lives of philosophers by Diogenes Laertius (third century A.D.?). Both types have their roots in Hellenistic biography and ultimately go back to the two sections (on 'life' and 'virtues') of Xenophon's *Agesilaus*. After having variously found favour in post-classical times, the two types of biography are even now reflected in the distinction between the 'life' and the 'character sketch' or 'profile'.

Since the fourth century B.C. there have also been biographical or autobiographical letters, one of the most ancient and famous of which comes from or is attributed to the pen of Plato. Autobiography, whether in the form of letters or otherwise, contained possibilities of development towards the genres of soliloquy and confessions. The models for us are Marcus Aurelius' *Meditations* and St. Augustine's *Confessions*, but the origins of both genres are obscure.

7.

Alexander's conquests gave new scope to Herodotean ethnography. As the regions described by Herodotus were now for the greater part under Greco-Macedonian control, one could expect better information—and to a certain extent it was forthcoming. Some names of ethnographers became famous in the third and second centuries B.C.: Hecataeus of Abdera for Egypt, Megasthenes for India, and Agatharchides in general for Asia and Europe. The little we know of them is mainly second-hand. Agatharchides still appears to have been a very humane observer of ordinary life. More typical was Hecataeus of Abdera, the author of a philosophic Utopia rather than an authentic historian of Egypt. It is difficult to escape the conclusion that the Greek intellectuals of the early Hellenistic period took more interest in problems of physical geography and in astronomy (Eratosthenes) than in knowledge about the nations among whom they moved as masters. They did not learn the languages of the natives. Menander of Ephesus was the exception, if he was a Greek and really studied Phoenician and other foreign records, as Flavius Josephus states (*Against Apion*, 1. 116). The greatest work done by an early Hellenistic historian concerns not the East, but the unconquered West. It was the individual effort of a Sicilian exile in Athens, Timaeus, and reflected his isolation in contemporary society. As he was the first to include Rome in the horizon of Greek history, the Romans repaid him by much attention and probably learnt a great deal from him in their first attempts to absorb the Greek art of historiography. Polybius, therefore, attacked him as his most dangerous rival.

Isolated in his own day, Timaeus pointed to the future when the Romans began to conquer East and West. Greek students of ethnography—such as Polybius, Artemidorus of Ephesus, Apollodorus of Artemita, and Posidonius—hastened to describe Spain, Gaul, and Parthia. One great savant, who was imported into Rome as a slave, Alexander Polyhistor (*c*. 70 B.C.), specialized in providing his masters with the ethnographical knowledge they needed to rule, or at least to enjoy the world they ruled. One of his books, on the Jews, was sufficiently good to provide the Fathers of the Church with some of their most recondite quotations from Jewish writers. It is this late Hellenistic learning under Roman hegemony rather than early Hellenistic doctrine which is summarized in the geography of Strabo—itself a product of Greek erudition inspired by the ideals and interests of Roman imperialism. Chance made Strabo (first cent. A.D.) the main transmitter of ancient ethnography to later times: we have inherited from him our notion of 'historical geography'.

Also Hellenistic is our notion of a historico-geographical guide for visiting places of interest, in one's own country or outside it. Polemon of Ilium, who in the second century B.C. wrote on his own city, on the acropolis of Athens, on 'inscriptions city by city', on Samothrace, and even on Carthage, is a good early example of a mixture of Greek and non-Greek tourist interests. But Pausanias, who in the second century A.D. confined himself to Greece, became the prototype of this genre for Renaissance scholars—through the mere fact of having survived.

Though the transformation of Greek erudition from a local to a national one is especially noticeable in the Roman period, Dicaearchus had already written under the Macedonians in the third century B.C. an antiquarian and nostalgic 'life of

Greece' (a remarkable title). He does not seem to have had many followers in this comprehensive and exacting genre, but he inspired Varro to do the same for Rome. Besides writing a 'life of the Roman people' on the lines provided by Dicaearchus, Varro went beyond his model in the gigantic *Roman Antiquities* (divided into 'divine' and 'human') which dominated Roman erudition until St. Augustine. Varro's work did not survive the early Middle Ages, but what St. Augustine said about it moved Flavio Biondo to attempt a revival of the genre and ultimately to create the type of Renaissance and modern 'Antiquities'.

The Greeks did more than provide the Romans with materials for mapping their empire and with models of erudition. They tried to understand and recount Roman history in a way which might satisfy both Romans and Greeks. Some may even have tried to oppose the Greek to the Roman point of view in writing Roman history. The evidence is not clear. The famous debate, still echoed by Livy, Justin, Plutarch, and even Ammianus, on the part played by mere luck in the Roman successes seems to have originated in the heat of war propaganda before penetrating into historical works. Questions of erudition about Roman origins offered opportunities for pin-pricking Roman vanity which were less dangerous and required less thought. Dionysius of Halicarnassus refers with disapproval to some of these criticisms of Roman traditions. 'Real' historians, who had read their Thucydides and Ephorus, tried to explain the Roman Empire in forms acceptable to both nations. It is always difficult to produce consistent opposition history when there is no hope of shaking off foreign rule.

Polybius remains the unique expression of the moment in which the Greeks for the first time in their history recognized their complete loss of independence. The Macedonian-Greek symbiosis of previous centuries had not compelled, or even prepared them for, such a catastrophic admission. Polybius was a time-server of genius. He adapted Thucydidean historiography to the new situation by writing a history of the contemporary world with the scrupulous regard for factual truth, the political and military competence, the direct observation, and the care for speeches which Thucydides had prescribed. In the organization of a universal history, though limited to the last fifty years, Polybius was helped by the example of Ephorus, whom he respected, and of Timaeus, whom he affected to despise. But the plan of his exposition was his own. His own, too, was the emphasis on the practical use of history with which the skilful presentation of Roman victory as inevitable and lasting was connected. Polybius inspired Posidonius, guided Livy (as far as Livy was guidable), and in later days moved the pagan Zosimus (early sixth century) to tackle the decline of Rome as he, Polybius, had tackled her rise. Anthologized and therefore mutilated in Byzantium to provide examples for military operations and diplomatic missions, Polybius returned to western Europe in the early fifteenth century. First admired in Florence (by Machiavelli among others), by the middle of the sixteenth century Polybius had risen to the position of the master of military and diplomatic history for the whole of Europe. He remained the most authoritative Greek historian until the French Revolution, when he was replaced by Thucydides.

After Polybius the question of how Roman history stood in relation to universal history was always present. Posidonius saw deeply into the social unrest of the period between 145 and *c*. 63 B.C. He painted both the degeneration of the Hellenistic monarchies and the rapacity of the Roman capitalists. When he lovingly described the tribal life of Gaul and Spain, he was probably aware that the Romans were bound to transform it. The influence of Oriental, especially Jewish, speculations on the succession of empires combined with research by Greek historians. In the universal histories written in Greek in the first century B.C. by Diodorus and Nicolas of Damascus (the latter preserved only in fragments), Hellenic presuppositions prevail. Diodorus has in fact great difficulty in connecting Roman and Greek history. The mixture of Hellenic and Oriental elements is more deeply embedded in the structure of the universal history written in Latin by the Gallo-Roman Trogus Pompeius which belongs to the same period and has been transmitted to us only in the summary by Justin (second century A.D.). It is an open question whether Trogus was guided by a Greek source. Whoever first mixed Oriental speculations with Greek-Latin historiography prepared the way for the late-antique summaries of universal history, of which the one compiled in Latin by Orosius (early fifth century) was read in the Middle Ages even in an Arabic translation.

By modifying Greek forms to write Roman history other Greek historians created influential prototypes. Dionysius of Halicarnassus used the basic ingredients of local Greek history to construct a monumental Roman archaic history or 'Roman Antiquities'. He read both Roman antiquarians and Roman annalists. The result was imitated by Flavius Josephus in his *Jewish Antiquities* (where 'antiquities' is used again in the sense of ancient or archaic history). Too much is lost of the historiography of the Roman Empire to allow safe guesses as to the origins of the historiography of Barbarian nations which emerged in the sixth and seventh centuries. Where Cassiodorus, Gregory of Tours, and Bede found their models is not yet clear. But Dionysius' and Josephus' *Antiquities* belong to this story.

In the second century A.D., Appian used Greek regional history and Greek ethnography to encompass the expansion of the Romans. He divided their wars according to regions, with the consequence that he had to create a special section outside this geographic order for 'civil wars'. Appian (from Egypt) was expressing the new second-century feeling about the Roman Empire as an association of various regions. The feeling did not last long, and therefore Appian did not find immediate imitators, but his notion of the 'history of the civil wars' and his example of parallel histories of regional wars regained prestige in the Renaissance and after. Not only in Davila and Clarendon, but also in Ranke there is still more than a touch of Appian. In the third century A.D. the fusion of Greek and Roman historical traditions was such that the Greek historian and Roman senator Dio Cassius compiled a Roman history in 80 books according to the Roman annalistic scheme, yet in a style inspired mainly by Thucydides. Dio taught the Byzantines (through the summaries of his work rather than in the original text) most of what they knew about Roman history. But as a model the Byzantines preferred Herodian, who wrote *c.* A.D. 240 about events from the death of Marcus Aurelius to A.D. 238. They transmitted him to the early humanists, who shared their admiration. Both took seriously Herodian's professions of truthfulness which more rigorous tests have shown to be nearly empty. Dexippus, who really tried hard to follow Thucydides' example in his *Scythian Histories*, a story of the Gothic wars of the third century, was allowed to disappear.

8.

One of the technical factors which made universal history possible in the Hellenistic period was the development of chronological studies. The results were ultimately tabulated, and we have some of these tabulations in Christian chronographers (Eusebius). But the jump from the creators of scientific chronology in the third century B.C. (Eratosthenes) to the Christian canons is a wide one. We know the latter better than the former; and it was from the latter that Scaliger took his start in the late Renaissance. Yet we have enough of the original Hellenic texts—such as the fragments of the 'Marmor Parium' (a chronicle engraved in an inscription found at Paros) and of Apollodorus' Chronicle—to know what books of Hellenistic chronography looked like: one wonders whether Apollodorus wrote in verse in order to be memorized.

For the other types of Hellenistic antiquarian research we are in a worse position. Only seldom do we get a taste of the genuine product. A few good fragments have been recovered in papyri (for instance, a fragment of Didymus' notes on Demosthenes). A work by Dionysius of Halicarnassus on Dinarchus deals with the chronology and authenticity of texts in the best manner of Alexandrian philology. The same Dionysius and later Plutarch and Lucian present samples of literary discussions affecting historiography: they deal with both form and contents. The outlines of the interesting theory on history by Asclepiades of Myrleia (first century B.C.) are preserved by Sextus Empiricus. But the great works of Alexandrian and Pergamene philology—beginning with Callimachus' bio-bibliographical repertory or 'tablets' (*pinakes*)—are lost, and their results are known only from later scholia, epitomes, lexica, and similar compilations. We have none of the Hellenistic criticial editions, commentaries on texts, collections of inscriptions, examinations of customs and rituals, or treatises on 'discoveries' and 'inventions' (one of the earliest of which was by Ephorus). Nor have we any of the local chronicles, with the exception of the temple chronicle of Lindus (99 B.C.) discovered in an inscription and a partial summary of the chronicle of Heraclea Pontica by Memnon preserved in Photius' *Bibliotheca*. We would have quite a different notion of the variety and intensity of Greek historical research if works of Hellenistic erudition and of local history had been representatively preserved.

Renaissance antiquarian erudition, except for chronography and lexicography, had few Greek models to use. It had to depend mainly on the Roman equivalents; and there is a real question in many cases how far these Roman models reflected Greek prototypes. We do not know, for instance, the Greek predecessor of the *Attic Nights* by Aulus Gellius (second century A.D.), a book which was read in the Middle Ages and which through the mediation of Politian's *Miscellanea* became the model for short discussions of texts and antiquarian questions. No doubt the Hellenistic antiquarians were as original as the Greek political historians in relation to Eastern predecessors. They corrected, though they did not eliminate, the unilateralism of the Herodotean-Thucydidean historiography. This is not to underrate the stark fact that such research was seldom recognized and classified as history.

9.

The other criterion we suggested for an evaluation of Greek historiography, its spread among non-Greeks, can be dealt with more briefly because it is partly implicit in what was said about the reception of Greek historiographical forms in Rome. Greek historiography was accepted in several countries during the third and second centuries B.C., as a way in which native intellectuals could explain in Greek to the Greeks and to themselves what their local traditions were. The ambition to look Hellenized can hardly be separated from the effort to defend ethnic tradition against the inroads of Hellenization. The Egyptian Manetho, the Babylonian Berossus, the Jew Demetrius, and the Roman Fabius Pictor, who in the third century B.C. wrote in Greek about their own countries, did not all write under the same conditions and with the same purpose. A Babylonian or Egyptian historiography of the Greek type in the vernacular seems never to have developed. The Romans soon passed from writing history in Greek to writing history in Latin. They branched out from Greek forms with variations of their own. We know of no exact Greek parallel to Cato's *Origines*, the first historical work written in Latin under Greek influence. If it was inspired by Greek books on 'foundations of cities', it soon became something else which corresponded to the realities of second-century Italy.

Even Cicero's scattered theoretical opinions about historiography are not necessarily simple adaptations from the Greek.

The Jews were in a peculiar position in so far as they had powerful historiographical models of their own in the Bible. On the other hand, the majority of the Jews who migrated to Egypt, Asia Minor, and Italy lost the knowledge of Hebrew and Aramaic and replaced it by Greek. They had to have the Bible translated into Greek. Thus the challenge of Greek historiography produced among Jews various results which the First and the Second Book of the Maccabees can exemplify. Book 1 was originally written in Hebrew and was later translated into Greek. It is a dynastic history of the Biblical type in Biblical language, but with many technical details (including the semi-ethnographical chapter on Rome) suggested by Greek historiography. Book 2 is, characteristically, an epitome of a larger history in Greek written by the Jew Jason of Cyrene. The techniques of this book are very much those of the more popular Greek historiography with its abuse of miracles and of pathetic episodes. At the same time either the epitomist or Jason himself was acquainted with the Biblical Book of Judges, and presents Judas Maccabaeus in the splendid isolation of the Judges of old. The episodes of martyrdom indicate a new religious outlook which is of Jewish rather than Greek origin. Furthermore, the historical account serves to recommend to the Egyptian Jews the celebration of a new festival. The Greeks gave historical explanations of festivals (Callimachus, followed by Ovid), but do not seem ever to have written historical books to recommend the celebration of festivals. The Jewish author tries to improve on the Book of Esther which was the prototype of the Jewish festal book. By comparison, Flavius Josephus stands much more in the direct line of pure Greek historiography, notwithstanding his extensive use of the Bible and his early attempt to write history in Aramaic (about which we know almost nothing). Besides modelling his *Jewish Antiquities* on Dionysius of Halicarnassus, he wrote three other works in the Greek style—a history of a war (the Jewish War of A.D. 66–70), an erudite polemical work (*Against Apion*), and an autobiography.

The style of Greek historians affected their native imitators even in their use of evidence in the vernacular. The wealth of official chronicles and documents in the Near East had already been emphasized by Greek historians such as Ctesias, and became an occasion for the nationalistic boasts of Manetho, Berossus, and Josephus. But they never made extensive searches for documents. In the main they followed the Greek practice of reporting readily accessible traditions, whether written or oral.

The ease with which foreigners could use the Greek models for a variety of purposes goes together with the ease with which Greeks became historians of foreign nations and potentates. Greeks wrote on behalf of Hannibal, almost as his official historians; and Polybius was fortunate enough to discover that not only the Roman version of the first Punic war (by Fabius Pictor) but also the Carthaginian one (by the Sicilian Philinus) had been written in Greek. There probably were Carthaginian (and Etruscan?) histories in the Greek style but in the vernacular, which we shall never read. One of these may be mentioned in Sallust (*Jugurthine War*, 17). The national history which the Greeks wrote only partially and spasmodically for themselves, they managed to write easily enough for other nations. The type of national history the Italian humanists conceived for the benefit of the new national states of Europe (from England and France to Hungary and Poland) was a mixture of Livy and of late antique models. Humanistic national historiography corresponds in form, function, and ethos to the work done by Greeks (and later by Romans) in writing the history of other nations. This was always a history which, after paying due homage to legends of origins, gave pride of place to wars. It particularly suited the Romans, but even the Jews used Greek historiography mainly to narrate their own wars.

10.

The Greek historians were clearly not prepared for the Christian message either in the form communicated by Jesus and his immediate disciples or in the form which was elaborated by the Church of the first two centuries. The History of Salvation was not a Greek type of historiography in pagan days. Nor were the historical books of the Bible of much use as models to the Christians, because they told the story of an existing nation in its obedience or disobedience to God during its periods of organized political life. No Jew apparently ever thought of chronicling the Babylonian exile (or the period after the destruction of the Second Temple). The Christians were a new nation, and Jesus was the beginning of a new history. The nation was created by baptism, that is by individual choice. Yet it was also a nation *ab aeterno*, and destined to dissolve the other nations.

The historical works which expressed this new view, with its implication of eternity, had to be new creations. Even for Luke and Acts, written by men familiar with Greek historians and anxious to follow their tradition, it is impossible to find a parallel in the extant Greek historians: in fact, Luke had Mark as his main model. What the Gospels—either canonical or apocryphal—and Acts presented was the beginning of a new earth and a new heaven: no continuation of the story was expected (except perhaps in apocalyptic terms). For about two centuries there was no further Christian historiography concerned with Christendom as a whole. The Acts of the Martyrs can be compared with some chapters of 2 and 4 Maccabees and with the Greek and Roman literature on the death of illustrious men. Behind all there is the account of Socrates' death, though the Jewish texts are perhaps independent of it.

When Constantine made Christianity socially acceptable, a historical subject emerged which was amenable to at least some of the traditional practices of Greek historiography: the spreading of the true Apostolic Church and its consolidation against heresies and persecutions, culminating in its recognition and official toleration by the Roman State. The Gospels tell how the message of salvation had been revealed and spread. The new 'ecclesiastical' history as invented by Eusebius is the account of the development of the Church within definite limits of time and space, in its victorious struggles against heretics and persecutors. The new history was provided with documentation which would have been inconceivable in ordinary political history, but was not unheard of in antiquarian, polemical, and biographical works. The example of Alexander Polyhistor, famous as a diligent excerptor of texts about the Jews, was probably of special relevance to Eusebius. In Eusebius' continuators in the next two centuries (from Socrates, Sozomenus, Theodoretus, and Philostorgius to Euagrius) ecclesiastical history became the story of dogmatic controversies and of the relations between Emperors and Church. For reasons which we can perceive only faintly, ecclesiastical history lost its ecumenical meaning at the beginning of the seventh century. In the West the fragmentation of the Roman Empire worked against a literary genre which presupposed one State facing one Church and many heresies. In the East, where the Roman Empire survived, it became perhaps difficult to separate the affairs of the Church from the affairs of the State. There were attempts in the West to produce regional ecclesiastical histories, but, as the example of Bede is enough to show, it was impossible even within restricted boundaries to separate what was sacred from what was secular. An independent history of the Universal Church did not make sense again until the Reformation and the Counter-Reformation. Ecclesiastical history thrived in times of dogmatic controversies.

Ecclesiastical history was never meant to be and never was a substitute for political history. The Christians Procopius and Agathias wrote Thucydidean histories of wars long after Eusebius had produced his new type of history. The dualism between sacred and profane history, between history of the State and history of the Church—which for opposite reasons neither the Greeks nor the Jews had ever known—was born with Eusebius. This dualism was hard to defend against the complications of ordinary life. After Eusebius, ecclesiastical history proved to be an unstable compromise. It was written with a considerable contribution from Hellenic expertise. But it was very different from all the previous histories the Greeks had ever written. It presupposed Revelation and judged history according to Revelation.

II.

Before Christianity, Greek historians never offered more than interpretations of limited human transactions. They operated according to evidence, and graded evidence according to probability. From this point of view the main question to ask is the one we have already asked: how competent were the Greek historians in their evaluation of evidence? The question, if rigorously asked, involves the interference of rhetoric with historical research.

But the value which we are now prepared to attribute to

Greek historiography largely depends on what we expect from historical research. It is certain that historiography is more important to us than it was to the Greeks. This is mainly due to four factors. As Judaism, Christianity, and Islam are religions whose validity depends on the authenticity of certain traditions, historical research has a decisive importance in evaluating their claims (which was not the case with classical paganism). Secondly, the increasing rapidity and dimension of social and intellectual changes provoked a corresponding increase in the demand for historical research to explain and evaluate the changes. Thirdly, in the last two centuries history has been asked to provide community identity for the nations which have established themselves at a rate unknown in previous centuries. Finally, the physical and biological sciences have themselves developed a historical side, especially in theories about the evolution of the cosmos and of the species, and have encouraged the notion or the hope of an all-embracing historical explanation of reality.

Hellenic pre-Christian historiography was not meant to reveal the destiny of man. It is therefore also alien to any notion of development of the Hegelian variety, in which the events are both the progressive self-revelation of truth and the criterion of value. But the notion of a historical continuum from the beginning of the world, which is characteristic of the Old Testament in comparison with the New, does not seem to be ultimately incompatible with the empirical methods of Greek historiography: it becomes a question of evidence. Hints of a general evolution of human society are of course to be found in Greek thought, and the similarity continues in so far as both Greeks and Jews shared the illusion of an initial Golden Age. Nor does there seem to be logical incompatibility between the methods of Herodotus and Thucydides and the creation of a general empirical science of society. Aristotle, after all, operated with the data collected by previous historians or by his own school in order to create the sciences of politics and ethics. The limitations of historical research among the Greeks would turn out to be fatal only if we were satisfied that there is no way of unifying what the Greeks treated as real history and what they classified as biography, philology, antiquities, and so forth. But the unification of political history with other branches of research on the past is now a reality; and if anything is desirable, it is to avoid the delusion that there was never good reason for making some distinction between the different branches.

The most serious objection against the Greek approach to history would seem to be that it can never assess achievement except by reference to success, and therefore can never teach more than prudence. The objection cannot be answered merely by mentioning those cases in which Greek historians show appreciation of generosity or forgiveness or sacrifice. One would have to show that there was a real place for such values in Greek historiography. The demonstration would not be easy. Hence the devaluation of history not only in ancient, but in modern moral theories, even in Kant; hence the nostalgia for the Hebrew prophets who knew little history, but at least knew what was right. The fact is that Greek historiography never replaced philosophy or religion and was never wholeheartedly accepted by either. The status of historiography was never clearly settled among the Greeks. Choosing Greek historiographical models, even in modernized versions, therefore implies involvement in the difficulties of the use of such models when they are confronted by religion or philosophy.

Further Reading

There are innumerable studies on individual historians and their sources, but a true understanding of the nature and problems of Greek historiography is to be found in comparatively few authors, not necessarily the most recent. Modern studies begin with F. Creuzer, *Die historische Kunst der Griechen* (1803, 2nd edn. 1845), and H. Ulrici, *Charakteristik der antiken Historiographie* (1833), who judged from the points of view of Romantic historiography.

L. Ranke's admiration for Thucydides was of decisive importance for the historical outlook of the nineteenth century. Late in the century Eduard Meyer wrote with profound knowledge on Herodotus and Thucydides (*Forschungen zur alten Geschichte*, ii (Halle, 1899)) and based on them his theory which was the starting-point for his controversy with Max Weber. I. Bruns dealt with questions of social psychology, partly raised by J. Burckhardt, in *Das literarische Porträt der Griechen* (Berlin, 1896) and *Die Persönlichkeit in der Geschichtsschreibung der Alten* (Berlin, 1898). G. Misch, *Geschichte der Autobiographie*, i (1907, 3rd edn. translated into English as *A History of Autobiography in Antiquity*, London, 1950) was inspired by W. Dilthey.

The study of Greek historiography in the present century has been dominated by the school of U. von Wilamowitz-Moellendorff. He and his pupils combined fine perception of the basic peculiarities of Greek historiography—in comparison with Oriental and modern historiographies—with penetrating analytical work. The articles by E. Schwartz on Greek historians in Pauly-Wissowa, *Real-Encyclopädie*, include masterpieces on Arrian, Diodorus, Diogenes Laertius, Duris, and Eusebius and are now collected in a volume, *Griechische Geschichtsschreiber* (Leipzig, 1957). His other essays on Greek historiography in general are collected in *Gesammelte Schriften* (2 vols., Berlin, 1938, 1956) and *Charakterköpfe aus der antiken Literatur*, i, 4th edn. (Leipzig, 1912). F. Jacoby succeeded Schwartz as contributor to Pauly-Wissowa, and wrote for it his great monographs on Hecataeus, Hellanicus, Herodotus, and Ctesias (collected with other articles in *Griechische Historiker* (Stuttgart, 1956)). See also his *Abhandlungen zur griechischen Geschichtschreibung* (Leiden, 1956); *Apollodors Chronik* (Berlin, 1902); *Das Marmor Parium* (Berlin, 1904); *Atthis. The Local Chronicles of Ancient Athens* (Oxford, 1949). But the work which makes Jacoby the greatest student of Greek historiography of any time is his collection, with commentary, of *Die Fragmente der griechischen Historiker* (Berlin–Leiden, 1923–58), which, though unfinished, includes 856 historians and comments on 607 of them. As far as it goes, this replaces for scientific purposes, but not always for practical purposes, the previous collection by C. Müller, *Fragmenta Historicorum Graecorum* (5 vols., Paris, 1841–73). (Among later articles in Pauly-Wissowa, the following may be singled out: R. Laqueur on 'Lokalchronik', O. Regenbogen on Pausanias, and K. Reinhardt on Posidonius as original contributions; K. Ziegler on Polybius, O. Luschnat on Thucydides, and H. R. Breitenbach on Xenophon as *summae* of recent knowledge.)

The most original German researcher of recent years is H. Strasburger, who has presented a challenging reinterpretation of the whole of Greek historiography in *Die Wesensbestimmung der Geschichte durch die antike Geschichtsschreibung* (Wiesbaden, 1966); cf., among his other contributions, 'Die Entdeckung der politischen Geschichte durch Thukydides' (1954), reprinted in H. Herter (ed.), *Thukydides* (Darmstadt, 1968); and 'Poseidonios on the Problems of Roman Empire', *Journ. Rom. Studies*, lv (1965), 40–53. K. von Fritz has started a new and thorough *Griechische Geschichtsschreibung*, i. 1–2 (Berlin, 1967), on which see my review in *Gnomon* (1972), pp. 205–7. For his method it is important to compare his chapter in the collective Fondation Hardt volume, *Histoire et historiens dans l'antiquité* (Vandoeuvres, 1956).

In Italy, G. De Sanctis, and indirectly B. Croce, inspired the younger generation; cf. especially De Sanctis, *Studi di storia della storiografia greca* (Firenze, 1951). The most comprehensive treatise is S. Mazzarino's extravagant, but very learned and stimulating *Il Pensiero storico classico* (3 vols., Bari, 1966–7); cf. my discussion in *Quarto Contributo* (1969), pp. 59–76. My own notion of Greek historiography has been slowly developing since my dissertation on Thucydides (published in *Memorie Accademia Torino*, ii. 67 (1930)) and my *Prime linee di storia della tradizione maccabaica* (Torino, 1931; 2nd edn. Amsterdam, 1968). The majority of my essays are collected in *Contributo alla storia degli studi classici*, i–v in 7 vols. (Rome, 1956–75; vi forthcoming), selections of which are offered in *Studies in Historiography* (London, 1966) and *Essays in Ancient and Modern Historiography* (Oxford, 1977). See also *The Development of Greek Biography* (Cambridge, Mass., 1971).

In the French and Anglo-Saxon worlds the strong interest in theory of history and in the notion of historical explanation has not yet been reflected in many words of radical reinterpretation of Greek historiography, though H.-I. Marrou has given many hints, and R. G. Collingwood made more than a start in *The Idea of History* (Oxford, 1946). The main exception is M. I. Finley, who has firmly defined the position of Greek historiography in relation to myth (*History and Theory*, iv (1965), 281–302) and to traditionalism (*The Ancestral Constitution* (Cambridge, 1971)), both now in *The Use and Abuse of History* (London, 1975): see also his anthology of *The Greek Historians* (London, 1959). The question of myth is made acute by French research, especially in J.-P. Vernant's school (*Mythe et pensée chez les Grecs* (Paris, 1965); *Mythe et société en Grèce ancienne* (Paris, 1974)), while traditionalism is an issue raised by J. G. A. Pocock, 'The Origins of Study of the Past, a Comparative Approach', *Comparative Studies in Society and History*, iv (1962), 209–46, and *Politics, Language, and Time* (London, 1971); cf. also J. H. Plumb, *The Death of the Past* (London, 1969), and for analogous preoccupations, E. Voegelin, *Anamnesis* (München, 1966).

Important interpretations either of Greek historiography in general or of its origins can be found in the following: B. A. van Groningen, *In the Grip of the Past* (Leiden, 1953); F. Chatelet, *La Naissance de l'histoire: la formation de la pensée historienne en Grèce* (Paris, 1962); Ch. Starr, *The Awakening of the Greek Historical Spirit* (New York, 1968); R. Drews, *The Greek Accounts of Eastern History* (Cambridge, Mass., 1973); B. Gentili and G. Cerri, *Le teorie del discorso storico nel pensiero greco* (Rome, 1975).

For the history of the word *historia*, B. Snell, *Die Ausdrücke für den Begriff des Wissens in der vorplatonischen Philosophie* (Berlin, 1924); G. A. Press, 'History and the Development of the Idea of History in Antiquity', *History and Theory*, xvi (1977), 280–96. On the theory of history in Greece, F. Wehrli, 'Die Geschichtsschreibung im Lichte der antiken Theorie' (1947), now in *Theoria und Humanitas* (Zurich, 1972), pp. 132–44; G. Avenarius, *Lukians Schrift zur Geschichtsschreibung* (Meisenheim a.G., 1956); F. W. Walbank, 'History and Tragedy', *Historia*, ix (1960), 216–34; L. Canfora, *Teorie e tecnica della storiografia classica* (Bari, 1974). For the relation between style and contents, E. Norden, *Die antike Kunstprosa*, i (Leipzig, 1898), 79–155. On the social background of historiography, A. Momigliano, 'The Historians of the Classical World and their Audiences', *Annali Scuola Normale Pisa*, viii (1978), 59–75. On cyclical thought, G. W. Trompf, *The Idea of Historical Recurrence in Western Thought from Antiquity to the Reformation* (Berkeley, 1979).

7

EDUCATION AND RHETORIC[1]

H.-I. MARROU

The sphere of education is among those in which the importance of the legacy of Greece is most clearly apparent in the history of western civilization. The system of education that slowly took shape among the Greeks from the archaic period to the beginning of Roman rule was to be adopted in its entirety by the Romans, with a few minor modifications, and thereby incorporated in the legacy of Rome; through the latter, it would profoundly influence educational institutions and practices in Europe, an influence reinforced by the return to the antique that characterized the successive renaissances, the Carolingian of the twelfth century and the humanist in the fifteenth and sixteenth.

The long history of Greek education does not go back to the Mycenaean age. The decipherment of Linear B by Michael Ventris and John Chadwick has revealed a 'scribal' culture (and so necessarily an appropriate education) analogous to that developed in the ancient Near East to meet the administrative needs of the oriental monarchies. After the 'dark age' of the eleventh to ninth centuries, the Homeric poems introduce us to a radically transformed Greek world. What education may have been like in the 'heroic' age is difficult to discern through the idealized picture given by the epic. As the latter remained for centuries at the root of the cultural tradition and of the upbringing of Greek youth, certain values of that remote period exercised a permanent influence on the psychology and training of the Greeks. Nevertheless, the type of education characteristic of classical Greece, which would persist throughout the Hellenistic and then the Roman and Byzantine periods, only began to take its proper shape from the time when the ideal of the noble warrior, as he appears in Homer, was replaced by that of the citizen of the city-state.

[1] Professor Marrou died early in 1977 and was unable to review the English version. With the permission of his daughter, Mme Françoise Flamant, I have assumed full editorial responsibility for the final text, the translation, and the bibliography (Ed.).

Greek education always sought to foster a civic spirit, pride in belonging to a free city, loyalty to the political community. This psychology permeated the whole classical tradition so deeply that its influence must be assessed on a par with that of Rome as an important element in moulding the ideal of the citizen in modern democratic Europe.

At first the emphasis was on military training: the citizen must be capable of bearing arms. This archaic feature would always remain very marked in Sparta, where a highly elaborate system of institutions took charge of the child through his adolescence, and from the age of 7 to 20 subjected him to a rigorous training, moral as well as physical, within a series of age-classes—a system that recalls the organizations designed to regiment the young in modern totalitarian states, such as the *Gioventù fascista* and the *Hitlerjugend*. In the latter case, in particular, we should not rule out a direct borrowing: the 'Spartan mirage' seduced not only nostalgic spirits resistant to the triumphant progress towards democracy in ancient Athens, but also men of anti-liberal tendencies in nineteenth- and early-twentieth-century Europe, notably in Germany, who rejected the parallel evolution of our own societies.

But from the sixth century, at first in Athens, then in the rest of Greece—always excepting Sparta and conservative Crete—military preoccupations took second place in education as in life (*hoplomachia*, 'armed combat', is now merely the word for the sport of fencing). Nevertheless, education, now more civilian than military, was still primarily physical education. In our day, it is the school, letters, that we automatically associate with the word 'education'; for the Greek, it was first, and long remained, the palaestra and the gymnasium, where the child and the adolescent were trained in sports. When the Hellenic world was vastly extended following the conquests of Alexander, the Greek migrants who settled in the Orient, eager to prevent their children from abandoning the Greek way of life, founded gymnasia everywhere. One was recently discovered in the depths of Bactria, at Aï Khanum on the Amu Darya river (the ancient Oxus) on the northern frontier of Afghanistan. In Roman Egypt, the title of 'former pupil of the gymnasium' served to establish legal status as a Hellene, distinguishing him from the despised native, the 'Egyptian'.

At first restricted to an aristocratic élite, the athletic

training of the gymnasium was gradually opened to other social classes among the citizenry, in line with the evolution of society towards a 'democratic' levelling. Women were of course excluded—we must never forget that the Greek city was a men's club—though there was eventually some development of education, and so of sports, for women in certain places, Sparta and the Lesbos of Sappho, for example, and more widely in the Hellenistic period.

The first of the specialist teachers was the *paidotribes* ('coach for boys'), whose training was concentrated on sports: the expensive equestrian sports, riding on horseback and chariot racing (always reserved for an elegant minority), foot racing (the standard course was a stade in length, about 200 metres), the long jump, throwing the discus and javelin, wrestling, boxing, and the pankration (a violent form of wrestling, something like our catch-as-catch-can, in which few holds were barred). And by sport we mean competitive sport, for that was the context in which the 'agonistic' ideal inherited from the heroic age—to be the best, to be first, to overcome equals in one's class—was perpetuated in Greek civilization. Hence in the games, *agones* in Greek, competitions for the different age-classes of boys and adolescents were introduced, at first on a city basis and later on an international scale (at Olympia in 632 B.C.).

Though modern sport (and so also physical education) arose out of the rustic games of peasants, and, in the case of equestrian events and fencing, out of medieval chivalry, the importance assumed by the revival of the Olympic Games in 1896 is familiar to everyone. The desire to imitate the Greek model has even led to the re-invention of such forgotten sports as throwing the discus and the javelin (though the first is lighter, and the second heavier, than the ancient Greek equivalents). And this revival soon confronted us with the old conflicts: chauvinism or disinterested idealism, professionalism or amateurism, spectator sport or truly participatory, and therefore educative, sport.

Not only was Greek education more physical than intellectual, it was also artistic, specifically musical, before it was literary. The music master appeared immediately after the gymnasium master, both in date and in order of importance. Singing, especially choral singing in unison, dancing, and playing the lyre (or the aulos, a kind of oboe) became an integral part of the training of the young Greek in the archaic and classical periods. Indeed, a literary component entered the programme by the roundabout route of singing, which was normally accompanied by the lyre (hence the term 'lyric poetry'). Thereafter poetry was to play a role of the first importance in Greek culture, and therefore in education.

The use of writing, which had disappeared in the eleventh century with the collapse of Mycenaean civilization, was restored when the phonetic alphabet of Phoenician origin was adopted at the beginning of the eighth century. The diffusion of the alphabet stimulated the introduction of a third type of teaching, and the appearance of the school as we know it today, where the child, under the supervision of a master with a distinctive name, *grammatistes* or *grammatodidaskalos* ('one who teaches letters'), learnt to read and write. (Arithmetic would always remain peripheral, confined in practice to learning to count.) Here the legacy of ancient Greece, through her Roman 'descendants', was to weigh heavily on the history of European pedagogy almost to our own generation.

Like all ancient peoples, the Greeks completely ignored the existence of child psychology. Hence physical punishment was their only recourse against a child's resistance to learning to read, which they found incomprehensible. Furthermore, the rational—shall we say too naïvely rational?—Greeks spaced out the steps of instruction, proceeding from the simple to the complex, studying successively the different elements that had been analytically distinguished in the structure of the written language: first the alphabet, then syllables (working from the simplest, composed of two letters, then those of three, and on to the more complex), then words (from the shortest to the longest and most difficult), and last of all sentences. Only after the pupil had fully mastered each stage did he proceed to the next. Progress was therefore slow: it took three to four years to learn to read, thanks to the mechanical technique, still practised as late as the eighteenth century in Greek schools under Turkish domination, and long-lived in the west, too. There is no need to dwell on the modern difficulties in trying to replace this routine of passive reception by active, more effective, and less irksome methods.

Such is the picture of education established in Athens by the end of the sixth century B.C. It was to endure for more than a millennium, though obviously not without undergoing a gradual evolution. An increasingly important place was given to the study of literature and to a corresponding reduction in the role of sport and music. The latter were still highly regarded, but they were victims of their own technical progress: no longer practised in fact except by a minority, professional or amateur, they became a mere spectacle for the vast majority. The evolution was not completed until the later Roman Empire: thenceforth, the culture of antiquity was a literate culture, and triumphant Christianity, a religion of the book, could only confirm the transformation.

Until the final stage, however, Greek education remained less scholastic than our own has been since the early Middle Ages. We have to wait for such revolutionary critics as Ivan Illich to reclaim this particular Greek legacy, in which schooling and education were more sharply distinguished, if not even opposed, than they are with us. Among the Greeks, the masters, the technicians who transmitted the secrets of their arts to the child, were not educators in the strict sense: the schoolmaster was less important than the *paidagogos*. Originally a very humble person, often a slave, charged simply with taking the child to school, the *paidagogos* eventually became his true master, teaching him etiquette, good manners, how to conduct himself in life, in short, the moral ideal to which he should conform. With adolescence, another factor intervened, namely, pederasty, which, despite the opposition it was to meet from the Christian Church, is also part of the legacy. Quite apart from any sexual component in the physical sense, which is difficult to determine, pederasty played a capital role in the education of the adolescent. Through frequent association, especially in the gymnasium, with a loved and admired older man, the object of a fervent attachment on whom the young partner modelled himself, the adolescent was gradually initiated into adult life and learned to become in his turn a 'complete gentleman', a *kalokagathos* (literally 'beautiful and good (or valiant)').

We have so far discussed nothing but elementary education, the only kind available as late as the great generation of Pericles, Sophocles, and Phidias, who grew up in the first part of the fifth century. But the progress of Hellenic civilization and culture now required higher education: the revolution in pedagogy initiated by the Sophists, in the second half of the century, culminated in the work of two great educators, Isocrates, whose teaching career extended from 393 to 338 B.C., and Plato, who taught from 387 to 348. The competition between their rival schools eventually structured the two forms which Greek high culture would henceforward assume—the one oratorical, the other philosophical. It was a fruitful rivalry. The opposition between the two schools should not be overstated or seen as radical: there were reciprocal influences and mutual concessions between them. In the *Phaedrus*, Plato expressly acknowledged the legitimacy of the art of literature, and throughout his dialogues his practice contradicted his theory: every page reveals the fruitful effects of his knowledge of the poets. Isocrates, for his part, recognized that a limited study of mathematics and philosophy, which he called 'gymnastics of the mind', was useful preparation for eloquence.

Their successors drew the lesson from such convergences. From the beginning of the Hellenistic era, in the generation after Aristotle, we seem to see emerging the notion of a basic curriculum, of a general training, of a foundation common to the different forms of high culture. (There were also schools for the training of physicians, who could aspire to advance beyond the level of the mere technician to that of high culture.) This preparatory training, following upon the elementary education we have already examined, was a necessary prerequisite for attaining the higher level, and a synthesis was created between the two fundamental demands of the Isocratean and Platonic schools: it was at once literary and scientific. The programme of scientific studies was the one laid down by the Old Pythagoreans, namely, the four branches of mathematics—arithmetic, geometry, music (i.e. acoustics, the mathematical theory of intervals and of rhythm, not the practice of music as an art), and astronomy (also less directed towards empirical observation than inspired by the desire to 'save the phenomena', to account for the apparent movements of the heavenly bodies by the elaboration of a geometric structure). In the sixth century A.D., Boethius named this programme of studies the *quadrivium*, a favourite term in the Middle Ages. As for literary studies, they comprised the three subjects of grammar, rhetoric, and dialectic. (Not until the Carolingian period were they given the name *trivium*, to match *quadrivium*.)

Grammar was taught by a specialist, the *grammatikos*, quite distinct from his humble colleague the *grammatistes*. His basic function is most clearly revealed in periods of decadence, when the theoretical programme tended to be reduced to bare essentials, as in the west during the early Middle Ages. Even today our vocabulary bears witness to this irreducible nucleus; for example, we still have 'grammar schools'. The grammatical discipline was originally, and would always remain, principally a thorough study of the great writers, and especially of the poets. To be a cultivated Greek was, first and foremost, to be deeply versed in Homer. A legacy of the archaic period, knowledge of Homer would characterize Greek education throughout its history. For example, in the Byzantine period, Michael Psellus took pride in having learnt the whole of the *Iliad* by heart as a child just like a character in Xenophon fourteen centuries earlier. Similarly, the author of the most detailed Greek commentary on Homer, regularly consulted by philologists today, was Archbishop Eustathius of Thessalonica in the twelfth century.

This same fundamental technique, transmitted through the Romans—the reading, recitation, and full exegesis of the great authors of our literature—has remained the basis of all literary culture down the centuries, from the medieval renaissances to our own day. It is a legacy of this technique that a cultivated Italian will quote or evoke Dante when he puts pen to paper, and an Englishman Shakespeare, as spontaneously, and perhaps as appositely, as Plato alluded to Homer at every turn in a dialogue. In addition to the principal poet, the curriculum of the Hellenistic schools (like our own) included the study of a number of selected works by other great poets, such as Hesiod, Menander, and Euripides, and by prose writers, historians like Thucydides, and finally orators, Demosthenes above all! Again as today, some works and authors were represented only by anthologies; we note with some astonishment that minor authors such as the comic poet Straton were sometimes represented by the same purple passages in collections made five centuries apart.

At a later date the *grammatikos* also offered a theoretical study of the structure of the language. The first manual, still very elementary and sketchy, of this *techne grammatike* was written by Dionysius Thrax, who taught in Rhodes in the mid-first century B.C. His short treatise had an extraordinary success; endlessly copied, completed, and annotated, it remained the basis of Greek grammatical teaching well into the Byzantine era; it was even translated into Syriac and Armenian, and through Latin grammar and the grammarians of the Renaissance it was to have a lasting influence on modern teaching. It was not, however, one of the notable triumphs of the Greek genius: it is markedly inferior to Sanskrit grammar, the discovery of which by Europeans early in the nineteenth century was a decisive contribution to the birth of modern linguistic science. The grammar of Dionysius Thrax consists of a entirely formal analysis of the elements that had already been distinguished in the structure of the Greek language. Its main component is the study of the parts of speech—noun, verb, participle, pronoun, preposition, adverb, conjunction—essentially by way of definitions leading to a minute classification. The noun, for example, is examined, in turn, according to its three genders, its two types, its three forms, and finally it is divided into twenty-four classes. Obviously there was nothing very practical there: for the Greeks, grammar was a theoretical science with no end in view other than the intellectual satisfaction of seeing the complex phenomenon of language broken down into its constituent elements. Finally, the teaching of the *grammatikos* was completed by very elementary exercises in composition, preparatory to the more complex exercises which would be the special province of the *rhetor*. In these exercises, too, free rein was given to the taste for analysis and classification. The surviving manuals, from the Roman period, astonish us by the remarkable complexity of the rules they apply to these skilfully graded exercises.

Grammar was followed by rhetoric and dialectic, but, at the level of general culture we are now describing, there could be no question of more than a brief introduction to the theory and practice of the art of oratory, on the one hand, and to the elementary principles of logic and the art of discussion, on the other. We shall find rhetoric and dialectic carried to a higher level in the specialized studies we have yet to discuss.

Trivium and *quadrivium*, this was the curriculum of liberal arts that late antiquity would pass on to the Middle Ages. The term 'liberal' arts is more Roman than Hellenic: the Greeks preferred to speak of the 'rational/noble/learned' arts, synonymous adjectives which contrasted these disinterested studies with the mechanical arts of the manual worker, so despised by this aristocratic civilization. In the Roman period, the programme of general culture would also be given the Greek name *enkuklios paideia*, which in Hellenistic Greek meant no more than 'ordinary, common education'. We must not invest *enkuklios* with the modern value, 'encyclopaedic', a creation of sixteenth-century humanism (that appeared simultaneously in English—Elyot, 1531, and French—Rabelais, 1532). The ancients, of course, had the notion of 'universal knowledge', but they expressed it by *polymathia*, a word as often as not charged with a pejorative connotation. Greek humanism feared excess above all else, and always strove to retain for human culture the dimensions, and therefore the limitations, of the human individual. By the Hellenistic period, this humanism was at grips with a civilization which, though not so highly complex as our own, had acquired a wealth and a range beyond comparison with the culture of a sixth-century Ionian *physikos* or of Hippias in the fifth century, who could still aspire to know everything known to mankind.

If, then, the liberal arts seem to have been clearly defined early in the fourth century B.C., in the general sense of a common culture based on literature and mathematics, the unalterable list of seven subjects could not have been fixed until after the initiative of Dionysius Thrax and the promotion of grammar to the status of a *techne*. In fact, the list is not attested before the final decades of the pre-Christian era, in Varro and Cicero among the Latins, in Philo Judaeus in Greek. It is then important to stress the fact that this theoretical curriculum, accepted in principle by all (or nearly so, for we must except those *enfants terribles*, the Cynics, Epicureans, and Sceptics), seems often to have remained an ideal rather far removed from practice. The *grammatikos* very commonly took precedence over the *geometres*, and, apart from a few specialized vocations, such as architecture, Greek culture of the Hellenistic and Roman periods was predominantly literary at the expense of study of the sciences. Only with the relatively late return to Plato in Middle Platonism and especially Neoplatonism did a serious study of mathematics reappear, and then in restricted philosophical circles which regarded mathematics as an indispensable preliminary to philosophy proper.

Hellenistic Greece also developed a more advanced, and so

more specialized, form of education, in addition to the special case of medicine, which from the beginning had always had its own schools. At this higher level we again find the choice between the two major directions, the two rival callings, philosphy and oratory. To opt for the former meant a genuine conversion, comparable to what we call a religious conversion. It involved the adoption of an ascetic way of life and consequently a certain break with social ambition, luxury, the world in general. It also involved doctrinal instruction: in Athens, at least, the philosophical school paralleled a type of institution organized, juridically speaking, in the form of a religious fraternity dedicated to the cult of the Muses and of the heroized founder of the school. Plato's Academy, the Lyceum of Aristotle, the Stoa, and the Garden of Epicurus were all established on these lines (as well as minor foundations). The master at the head of each school, co-opted by his predecessor, ensured the continuity of succession and of doctrinal affiliation. From the time of the emperor Marcus Aurelius, the four heads were recognized more or less officially and endowed with stipends paid by the imperial treasury. Similar professorships seem to have been established in other great cities, such as Alexandria, by the municipalities themselves.

In their teaching, these schools of course resumed dialectic, at first in the sense employed by the fifth-century Sophists and retained by Aristotle, that of 'eristic', the art of discussion, mastery of the techniques of persuasion, of winning over the opponent, the art of convincing and confounding. Greek philosophy developed in an atmosphere of rivalry among sects, of disputes, of aggressive and heated discussions (most clearly seen among the so-called 'minor Socratic' schools). Hence the major part played at this level by dialectic.

But with Plato the term acquired a deeper meaning, namely, the method of the search for, and discovery of, truth. In this pre-eminent form, it became the principle itself of philosophical teaching: to retrace the path of discovery was deemed the best conceivable method of expounding a doctrine, for it alone made it possible to form the disciple and not merely to inform him. We all know to what degree of perfection and effectiveness the genius of Plato brought this method within the framework of the dialogue, a literary genre which was adopted by all the other disciples and intellectual heirs of Socrates, but which he alone was able to raise to such heights of dignity. Plato had many imitators, and the dialogue long enjoyed popularity among the Greeks, then among the Latins, from Cicero to St. Augustine and Macrobius. However, the imitation was often clumsy, for it was much more difficult to recapture the inimitable qualities of the model than to reproduce its procedures mechanically, such as the dialogue once removed, in which one questions a witness who relates a dialogue that was supposed to have taken place. The genre could be debased into a very artificial way of presenting a dogmatic exposition, or even into a scholastic catechism, proceeding by question and answer. But the fact remains that the formula was to enjoy an amazing success, beyond antiquity through the Middle Ages and into modern times, from the Platonizing humanists of the Renaissance, such as Leone Ebreo (Judah Abarbanel) with his fine *Dialoghi d'Amore*, to Spinoza, Malebranche, and Berkeley.

From the time of Aristotle, philosophical teaching also included a more technical side, having thenceforth at its disposal, in the *Organon*, a complete corpus of formal logic. In the Roman imperial period, all schools accepted instruction in Aristotelian logic—studied both in the original text and in the commentaries that soon abounded—as an obligatory starting-point for the study of philosophy proper. In late antiquity, this initiation began with a study of Aristotle's *Categories*, or rather with Porphyry's introduction (*Isagoge*) to the treatise. On the other hand, the prestige of the founders or first great masters of the various schools, Plato, Aristotle, Epicurus, Zeno, and Chrysippus, led to increasing stress in the teaching on 'reading', exegesis of the texts of major works by these great thinkers of the past, thus returning to the characteristic technique of literary study. Philosophy was becoming the pupil of philology, Seneca already complained: *quae philosophia fuit, facta philologia est* (*Epistles*, 108. 23). This technique of the commentary, of original reflection on the margins of a revered text, was to impose itself down the centuries; it lay at the base of medieval scholasticism, and still influences the practice of our universities and of the most innovatory of contemporary philosophers.

But philosophy never recruited more than a tiny minority of the élite minds; statistically, so to speak, Isocrates decisively defeated Plato. Throughout the Hellenistic and Roman periods, the normal form taken by Greek culture at its highest level was that of eloquence, the art of speaking, which was also that of writing. The common practice of reading aloud (whenever possible using the services of a 'reader', *anagnostes*) meant that there was no clear dividing-line between the two; a term such as *logos* signified both an oration to be spoken and a treatise intended to be read. This characteristic feature of ancient culture is paradoxically becoming topical in our own day. As audio-visual techniques (sound broadcasting, television, tape-recording) are gradually breaking us away from the 'Gutenberg galaxy', from the primacy of the printed text, which stamped modern culture so deeply since the Renaissance, the living, winged word is slowly regaining the pre-eminence it enjoyed in antiquity. Has this not already happened in politics? A televised speech by a political leader now plays the part of a pamphlet or a newspaper article a century or two ago.

In the Greek world, this oratorical art was taught by the highly elaborate technique of rhetoric. Its first important theoretician was Gorgias of Leontini, one of the major Sophists, and the technique came to maturity between his generation and that of Aristotle. At the start rhetoric was a positive science based on observation. Experience had shown that some orators succeeded in exerting the desired influence, while others did not, and rhetoric arose as a systematic formulation of the methods and techniques employed by the successful. But the speculative spirit and rational brilliance of the Greeks, their taste for definition, classification, and systematization, went to work in this field as in geometry or grammar. Although Isocrates, with much good sense, sought to reduce the importance attached to theory in favour of practice (advocating the study and imitation of the great models provided by famous orators, and exercises in composition), manuals proliferated from the outset until long after Aristotle, *technai* of ever-increasing complexity, using a terminology of daunting precision.[2]

How can one convey an idea of this teaching in a few words? A complete treatise of rhetoric had five parts: invention, arrangement, elocution, mnemonics, action. What was invention? It meant finding ideas to develop. The orator did

---

[2] The texts are assembled in the collection called *Rhetores Graeci*.

not have to create these ideas; they already existed, and the problem was to know *where* to find them—hence the theory of 'places', intrinsic and extrinsic. Within these rich seams there was a mass of general, all-purpose ideas which it was easy to re-use for almost anything and everything. These were the famous 'commonplaces' (*koinoi topoi*), those grand general ideas of generous scope that recur endlessly in classical literature, giving it both its monotony and its permanent human value. Invention was the most highly developed part of the system, often the subject of separate treatises. But the other parts were equally objects of the most refined analysis: proper arrangement of the oration (in principle in six parts, from the exordium to the peroration); elocution, or the theory of style, distinguishing the plain, middle, and grand genres, the figures of thought (periphrasis, antithesis, hyperbole, and so forth) and the figures of speech, and concerned with the rhythm of a sentence;[3] mnemonics, utilizing spatial guide-marks; and action, concerned with the rules of pronunciation and delivery, and the movements and gestures of the orator. An Anglo-Saxon reader would once have smiled to hear mention of these last items—the Greeks, after all, were voluble, gesticulating Mediterraneans. But television has now taught our politicians the importance of the speaker's posture and bearing. Yet a difference remains: we are still improvising in this recently rediscovered field, whereas the ancient Greeks had had the time to codify here as everywhere else. The carriage of the head, facial expression, movement of the hands, each had its own rules and a conventional ter-minology, reminiscent of the way in which historians of Indian art have learnt to decipher the equally stylized gestures found in graphic representations of the Buddha.

The acquisition and mastery of so complex and elaborate a technique called for prolonged effort. Isocrates was already insisting on three or four years of study, and in the Hellenistic and Roman periods the time was extended up to eight years. Indeed, the ancient orator never stopped practising; in a way he spent his life 'declaiming', just as a pianist never ceases to keep his hand in.

---

[3] Gorgias was credited with the three devices known as the 'Gorgianic figures', e.g. the *isokolon*, a parallelism between elements of the sentence of identical length and rhythm.

There was something more: because a reasonably thorough initiation into the art of oratory was the normal apex of a liberal education, a kind of complicity based on prior agreement arose between author and public, a little like that between composers and informed music-lovers in modern classical music. Just as a late-eighteenth-century composer knew that his audience understood the rules of harmony, of the fugue or the sonata, so all literate men in antiquity knew the rules of the art of oratory. They knew, for example, that the *enkomion* or 'eulogy' of a person, living or dead, could exploit thirty-six themes, beginning with external attributes (origin, milieu, personal advantages), passing on to physical, and then to spiritual, attributes; they knew it all the better because the *enkomion* was one of the exercises most regularly practised in the school of the *rhetor*, and was the subject of scholastic competitions corresponding to our examinations. Fortified with this knowledge, one lay in wait, as it were, for the author, and he was the more easily able to give proof of his originality, perhaps by developing an expected *topos* in a piquant way, or by deliberately omitting it, confident that the omission would be noticed and appreciated. In time classical rhetoric gave way to what might be called a baroque rhetoric, which systematically sought to surprise, for example by changing the balance of a sentence and destroying an expected symmetry—the equivalent, in effect, of that expressive distortion to which modern painters, from the Cubists on, have accustomed us.

It has been necessary to dwell on this technique, which reigned so tyrannically over classical education and so over classical literature, because most modern readers, unless initiated into it, can neither grasp nor appreciate the subtlety of the ancient art. Furthermore, rhetoric exercised a profound influence down the centuries. Its study and practice flourished in the east throughout the Byzantine era, and in the west from the time the Romans were civilized by contact with Hellenistic Greece. The *ars rhetorica* was transposed into Latin by the rhetors of the time of Marius, then by Cicero and Quintilian, but it remained wholly Greek in inspiration and often in vocabulary. Stricken by the sclerosis of decadence, it was forgotten during the Dark Ages. The Carolingian renaissance, putting first things first, initially concentrated on the revival of grammar, but Greek rhetoric (known through

Cicero) reappeared in the eleventh century with Anselm of Besate, for example, and was then diffused in the flourishing literature of the twelfth century. Subsequently obscured by the dialectical hypertrophy of scholasticism and the prosaically utilitarian technique of the *ars dictaminis*, rhetoric resurfaced with the Humanists. Together with purism of language, it was the main demand of the Humanists in the face of what had become medieval barbarism. It again became one of the foundations of western culture, in education and in practice, even when that culture abandoned the primacy of Latin for the living national languages. In French, the word *rhétorique* was eventually to designate the last year of secondary education before pupils were introduced to philosophy, and all over Europe the teaching of rhetoric remained faithful to the principles formulated by Gorgias, Isocrates, and Aristotle. It did not disappear from the schools until a relatively recent date, in France in 1885.

This lasting influence is therefore an important historical fact by any standards. Was it beneficial or disastrous? Today the epithet 'rhetorical' is most often used with a pejorative connotation, the equivalent of bombastic, pompous, artificial. This is because our literary taste has been completely transformed by the romantic revolution, which ranked originality as the most important quality of an artistic or literary work; perhaps also because we have again become barbarians, ignorant and contemptuous of what we no longer understand. We must react against this denigration of everything that may appear to be formal; what we term 'artificial' was for the Greeks *entechnos*, composed according to the rules of art, artistic. Once one accepts its rules and techniques, classical rhetoric defines an aesthetic of prose similar to that of formal verse and equally endowed with authentic values. Above all, we must not judge rhetoric in isolation. Already with Isocrates it was only the crown of a complete system of training the mind and spirit, of education, of culture, and that system must be examined as a totality.

Isocrates triumphed over Plato, as we have said: succeeding generations overwhelmingly followed his precepts, and not in antiquity alone. Burnet called Isocrates the 'father of humanism', with good reason: his ideal, recovered by the West in the Renaissance, has dominated the tradition of classical humanism almost to our day. In place of the perhaps excessive ambition of the philosopher, who dared to aspire to rational knowledge, Isocrates substituted the more reasonable, more truly attainable, and finally more fruitful ideal of the *honnête homme*. This humanism, as the word indicates, sought to equip man, every man, for life: it was a type of training common to all, capable of suiting everyone, no matter what particular direction he would later take. Hence the predominantly literary culture, reserving for the future specialist the advanced study of mathematics or philosophy. It was based, as we have seen, on familiarity with the great writers, admired and acknowledged, above all with the poets. For poetry was the marvellous instrument that enabled everyone, child and adult alike, to acquire an intuitive knowledge of man and of life. How much wisdom might be found encapsulated in a chorus-ending of Euripides!

This was the kind of wisdom that the whole programme of classical studies sought to develop. Faced with the concrete problems posed by life, problems always so complex that it would never be possible to solve them rationally by logical processes, the important thing for man is to be able to 'hit on' (*epitunchanein*) the right solution, or at any rate the least wrong one, the solution best suited to the circumstances, the concrete situation, the moment in time. It was such mental dexterity— a matter of shrewd subtlety rather than mathematical calculation—that this type of education sought to foster. Not surprisingly the emphasis was on verbal expression, the *logos*, for speech, language, is not only the privileged means of contact and communication between men, but is also, for each individual, the instrument that enables thought to be formulated with precision and clarity; as Isocrates himself was fond of saying, 'appropriate speech is the surest sign of sound understanding' (3. 7; 15. 255).

Isocrates' ideas and the system of education which put them into practice reigned virtually unchallenged in western Europe almost to our own generation. Now it finds itself under attack. It is threatened first by the increasing democratization of western society, whereas classical culture, like the whole of ancient civilization from which it sprang, was fundamentally aristocratic in spirit, the culture of an intellectual élite resting on the tradition and customs of a social élite. Still more radical is the challenge from the 'technological explosion', which demands that education should above all produce the trained managers, engineers, and technicians it requires.

Does this mean that the classical tradition no longer has any part to play? It should be realized that its survival and the persistence of its influence do not depend on the continued teaching of Greek, Latin, and classical literature, as some gloomy prophets suppose. We have already seen that the influence of the classical educational tradition continued in many ways even after the vernacular languages had pushed Greek and Latin to the background. Educational techniques can be radically changed by the progress of the human sciences, especially psychology; it is the spirit of classical education that played a fruitful role, and still can. Its fundamental inspiration retains a permanent value, that of an education, a culture, which has as its goal the training of man, of man as such, of the whole man, and not of a mere producer-consumer, a mere cog in the industrial economy.

Further Reading

The outstanding account is H.-I. Marrou, *Histoire de l'éducation dans l'antiquité* (6th edn. Paris, 1965). The English translation (New York and London, 1956) is wholly unreliable.

For Greece, the old book by K. J. Freeman, *Schools of Hellas, an Essay on the Practice and Theory of Ancient Greek Education from 600 to 300 B.C.* (3rd edn. London, 1932), retains its value. See also F. A. G. Beck, *Greek Education 450–350 B.C.* (London, 1964), chiefly on the theorists; M. L. Clarke, *Higher Education in the Ancient World* (London, 1971), important on the teaching of philosophy.

On Rome, the basic work remains A. Gwynn, *Roman Education from Cicero to Quintilian* (Oxford, 1926; paperback in *Classics in Education*, no. 29, New York, n.d.).

On rhetoric: George Kennedy, *The Art of Persuasion in Greece* (Princeton and London, 1963); M. L. Clarke, *Rhetoric at Rome, a Historical Survey* (London, 1953); Josef Martin, *Antike Rhetorik: Technik und Methode* (Munich, 1974), a detailed technical study, with full documentation.

On late antiquity and the early Middle Ages: Pierre Riché, *Education and Culture in the Barbarian West, Sixth through Eighth Centuries*, trans. by J. J. Contreni from the 3rd French edn. (Columbia, S.C., 1976); T. J. Haarhoff, *Schools of Gaul, A Study of Pagan and Christian Education in the Last Century of the Western Empire* (2nd edn. Johannesburg, 1958); M. L. W. Laistner, *Thought and Letters in Western Europe, A.D. 500–900* (2nd edn. London, 1957), chs. 2, 7–10.

8

PHILOSOPHY

BERNARD WILLIAMS

The Greeks and the History of Philosophy

The legacy of Greece to Western philosophy is Western philosophy. Here it is not merely a matter, as in science, of the Greeks having set out on certain paths in which modern developments have left their achievements far behind. Nor is it just a matter, as in the arts, of the Greeks having produced certain forms, and certain works in those forms, which succeeding times would—some more, some very much less—look back to as paradigms of achievement. In philosophy, the Greeks initiated almost all its major fields—metaphysics, logic, the philosophy of language, the theory of knowledge; ethics, political philosophy, and (though to a much more restricted degree) the philosophy of art. Not only did they start these areas of enquiry, but they progressively distinguished what would still be recognized as many of the most basic questions in those areas. In addition, among those who brought about these developments there were two, Plato and Aristotle, who have always, where philosophy has been known and studied in the Western world, been counted as supreme in philosophical genius and breadth of achievement, and whose influence, directly or indirectly, more or less consciously, under widely varying kinds of interpretation, has been a constant presence in the development of the Western philosophical tradition ever since.

Of course philosophy, except at its most scholastic and run down, does not consist of the endless reworking of ancient problems, and the idea that Western philosophy was given almost its entire content by the Greeks is sound only if that content is identified in the most vague and general way—at the level of such questions as 'what is knowledge?' or 'what is time?' or 'does sense-perception tell us about things as they really are?' Philosophical problems are posed not just by earlier philosophy, but by developments in all areas of human life and knowledge; and all aspects of Western history have affected the subject-matter of philosophy—the development of the nation-state as much as the rise and fall of Christianity or the progress of the sciences. Yet even with issues created by such later developments, it is often possible to trace contemporary differences in philosophical view to some general contrast of outlooks which had its first expression in the Greek world.

Granted the size of the Greek achievement in philosophy, and the depth of its influence, it would be quite impossible to attempt anything except a drastically selective account of either. Some very important and influential aspects of Greek philosophy I shall leave out entirely: these include political philosophy (which is the concern of another chapter), and also Greek contributions to the science of logic, which were very important but demand separate, and moderately technical, treatment.[1] Moreover, in the matter of influences, I shall not attempt to say anything about what is certainly the most evident and concentratedly important influence of Greek philosophy on subsequent thought, the influence of Aristotle on the thought of the Middle Ages. Aristotle, who was for Thomas Aquinas 'The Philosopher', for Dante *il maestro di color che sanno*, 'the master of those who know', did much to form, through his various and diverse interpreters, the philosophical, scientific, and cosmological outlook of an entire culture, and the subject of Aristotelianism would inevitably be too much for any essay which wanted to discuss anything else as well. Aristotle's representation in what follows has suffered from his own importance.

After saying something in general about the Greeks and the history of philosophy, and about the special positions of Plato and Aristotle, I shall try to convey some idea of the variety of Greek philosophical interests; but, more particularly, I shall pursue two or three subjects in greater detail than any attempt at a general survey would have allowed, in the belief that no catalogue of persons and doctrines is of much interest in philosophy, and that a feel for what certain thinkers were about can be conveyed only through some enactment of the type of reasons and arguments that weighed with them: of not just what, but how, they thought. In this spirit, if still very

---

[1] For an accessible and informative treatment, see William and Martha Kneale, *The Development of Logic* (Oxford, 1962), chs. i–iii.

sketchily, I shall take up some arguments of Greek philosophers about two groups of questions—on the one hand, about being, appearance, and reality, on the other about knowledge and scepticism. In both, the depth of the Greek achievement is matched by the persistence of similar questions in later philosophy. In another matter, ethical enquiry, I shall lay the emphasis rather more on the contrasts between Greek thought and most modern outlooks, contrasts which seem to me very important to an understanding of our own outlooks and of how problematical they are.

I have said that the Greeks initiated most fields of enquiry in philosophy, and many of its major questions. It may be, by contrast, that there are just two important kinds of speculation in the later history of philosophy which are so radically different in spirit from anything in Greek thought as to escape from this generalization. Greek philosophy was deeply concerned, and particularly at its beginnings, with issues involved in the contrast between *monism* and *pluralism*. It is not always easy to capture what was at issue in these discussions: in some of the earlier Greek disputes, the question seems to be whether there is in reality only one thing or more than one thing, but—as we shall see later—it is not easy to make clear what exactly was believed by someone who believed that there was, literally, only one thing. In later philosophy, and already in some Greek philosophy, questions of monism and pluralism are questions rather of whether the world contains one or more than one fundamental or irreducible *kind* of thing. One sort of monism in this sense which has been known both to the ancient and to the modern world is *materialism*, the view that everything that exists is material, and that other things, in particular mental experiences, are in some sense reducible to this material basis. Besides *dualism*, the outlook that accepts that there are both matter and mind, not reducible to one another, philosophy since the Renaissance has also found room for another kind of monism, *idealism*, the monism of mind, which holds that nothing ultimately exists except minds and their experiences. It is this kind of view, with its numerous variations, descendants, and modifications, which we do not find in the ancient world. Largely speculative though Greek philosophy could be, and interested as it was in many of the same kinds of issues as those which generated idealism, it did not form that particular set of ideas, so important in much modern philosophy, according to which the entire world consists of the contents of mind: as opposed, of course, to the idea of a material world formed and governed by mind, a theistic conception which the Greeks most certainly had.

The other principal element in modern philosophy which is independent of the Greeks is something that first established itself at the beginning of the nineteenth century—that type of philosophical thought (of which Marxism is now the leading example) which places fundamental emphasis on historical categories and on explanation in terms of the historical process. The Greeks had, or rather, gradually developed, a sense of historical time and the place of one's own period in it; and their thought also made use of various structures, more mythological than genuinely tied to any historical time, of the successive ages of mankind, which standardly pictured man as in a state of decline from a golden age (though an opposing view, in terms of progress, is also to be found). Some of the more radical thinkers, moreover, regarded standards of conduct and the value of political arrangements as relative to particular societies, and that conception had an application to societies distant in time. But the Greeks did not evolve any theoretical conception of men's categories of thought being conditioned by the material or social circumstances of their time, nor did they look for systematic explanations of them in terms of history. This type of historical consciousness is indeed not present in all philosophical thought of the present day, but its absence from Greek philosophy is certainly one thing that marks off that philosophy from much modern thought.

It may be that these two, idealism and the historical consciousness, are the only two really substantial respects in which later philosophy is quite removed from Greek philosophy, as opposed to its pursuing what are recognizably the same types of preoccupation as Greek philosophy pursued, but pursuing them, of course, in the context of a vastly changed, extended, and enriched subject-matter compared with that available to the Greeks.

This is not to say that the Greeks possessed our concept of 'philosophy': or, rather, that they possessed any one of the various concepts of philosophy which are used in different philosophical circles in the modern world. Classical Greek applies the word *philosophia* to a wide range of enquiries;

wider certainly than the range of enquiries called 'philosophy' now, which are distinguished from scientific, mathematical, and historical enquiries. But we should bear in mind that it is not only Greek practice that differs from modern practice in this way: for centuries 'philosophy' covered a wide range of enquiries, including those into nature, as is witnessed by the old use of the phrase 'natural philosophy' to mean natural science—*The Mathematical Principles of Natural Philosophy* is what Newton, at the end of the seventeenth century, called his great work on the foundations of mechanics. It does not follow, however, that these ages did not have *some* distinction between scientific and what would now be called philosophical enquiries—enquiries which, however they are precisely to be delimited, are concerned with the general presuppositions of knowledge, action, and values, and proceed by way of reflection on our concepts and ideas, not by way of observation and experiment. Earlier ages often did make, in one way or another, distinctions between such enquiries and others—it is merely that until comparatively recently the word 'philosophy' was not reserved to marking them.

It is important to bear this point in mind when dealing with the philosophy of the past, in particular ancient philosophy. It defines, so to speak, two grades of anachronism. The more superficial and fairly harmless grade of anachronism is displayed when we use some contemporary term to identify a class of enquiries which the past writers did themselves separate from other enquiries, though not by quite the same criteria or on the same principles as are suggested by the modern term. An example of this is offered by the branch of philosophy now called 'metaphysics'. This covers a range of very basic philosophical issues, including reality, existence, what it is for things to have qualities, and (in the more abstract and less religious aspects of the matter) God. There is a set of writings devoted to such subjects in the canon of Aristotle's works, and it is called the *Metaphysics*; and it is indeed from that title that the subject got its name. But the work was probably so called only from its position in the edition of Aristotle's works prepared by Andronicus of Rhodes in the first century B.C.—these treatises were *ta meta ta phusika*, the books that came 'after the books on nature'. Aristotle's own name for most of these metaphysical enquiries was 'first philosophy'. Nor is it just the name that was different, but so were the principles of classification, both in the rationale given of them and hence in what is included and excluded. Thus Aristotle has an account of his enquiries into 'being in general' which relates the themes of 'first philosophy' in a distinctively Aristotelian way to the rest of knowledge (roughly, he supposed that it was distinguished by having a subject-matter which was much more general than that of other enquiries); and it excludes some enquiries which might now be included in metaphysics, such as *a priori* reflections on the nature of space and time. These latter Aristotle takes up in the books now called the *Physics*, which were included among the books 'about nature'; the name *Physics* itself being misleading, since what their contents mostly resemble is parts of metaphysics, and also what we would now call the philosophy of science, rather than what we now call *physics*.

These various differences do not stop us identifying Aristotle's enquiries as belonging to various branches of philosophy as we now understand them: this level of anachronism can, with scholarship and a sense of what is philosophically relevant, be handled—as it must be, if we are going to be able to reconstitute from our present point of view something which it would not be too arbitrary to call the history *of philosophy*. But there is a second and deeper level of anachronism which we touch when we deal with writings to which modern conceptions of what is and what is not philosophy scarcely apply at all. With those writers who did not themselves possess some such distinctions, to insist on claiming them for the history of philosophy as opposed to, say, the history of science, constitutes an unhelpful and distorting form of anachronism. So it is with the earliest of Greek 'philosophers', the earlier *Presocratics* (a label which as a matter of fact is used not only for thinkers earlier than Socrates, but for some late-fifth-century contemporaries of his as well).

With regard to the earliest of Greek speculative thinkers, Thales, Anaximander, and Anaximenes, who lived in Miletus on the Greek seaboard of Asia Minor in the first seventy years of the sixth century b.c., it is impossible to give in any straightforward modern terms a classification of the kinds of question they were asking. This is not just because virtually nothing remains of their work (Thales, the oldest, in any case wrote nothing) and we have to rely on disputable reports;

even if we had all their writings we could not assign them, in modern terms, to philosophy or to science. They are usually represented as asking questions such as 'what is the world made of?', but it is one achievement of intellectual progress that that question now has no determinate meaning; if a child asks it, we do not give him one or many answers to it, but rather lead him to the point where he sees why it should be replaced with a range of different questions. Of course, there is a sense in which modern particle theory is a descendant of enquiries started by the Milesians, but that descent has so modified the questions that it would be wrong to say that there is one unambiguous question to which we give the answer 'electrons, protons, etc.' and Thales (perhaps) gave the answer 'water'.

We can say something—and we shall touch on this later—about the features of these speculations which make them more like *rational enquiries* than were the religious and mythological cosmologies of the East, which may have influenced them. And this is in fact a more important and interesting question than any about their classification as 'philosophy', something which in the case of these earliest thinkers is largely an empty issue.

Classical Philosophy and the Philosophical Classic

The involvement of Greek philosophy in the Western philosophical tradition is not measured merely by the fact that ancient philosophy originated so many fields of enquiry which continue to the present day. It emerges also in the fact that in each age philosophers have looked back to ancient philosophy—overwhelmingly, of course, to Plato and Aristotle—in order to give authority to their own work, or to contrast it, or by reinterpretation of the classical philosophers to come to understand them, and themselves, in different ways. The Greek philosophers have been not just the fathers, but the companions, of Western philosophy. Different motives for this concern have predominated in different ages: the aim of legitimating one's own opinions was more prominent in the Middle Ages and the Renaissance (which, contrary to popular belief, did not so much lose the need for intellectual authority, as choose different authorities), while the aim of historical understanding and self-understanding is more important in the present day. But from whatever motive, these relations to the Greek past are a particularly important expression of that involvement in its own history which is characteristic of philosophy and not of the sciences.

It has been a characteristic also of literature, though the nature of the involvement in that case is very different. It has been suggested[2] that our conceptions of Western literature have room for the notions both of a 'relative classic'—a work which endures and has influence and stands at least for a period of time as an exemplar—and of the 'absolute classic', above all the *Aeneid*, which defines for ever the high 'classical' style. Adapting these notions to philosophy, we might say that the classical philosophers Plato and Aristotle are classics in the sense that it has been impossible, at least up to now, for philosophy not to want to make some living sense of these writers and relate its positions to theirs, if only by showing why they have to be rejected: this is a status which they have shared, in the last 200 years, only with Kant. But they might be said also to define a classical style of philosophy—meaning by that a philosophical, not a literary, style. They are both associated with a grand, imperial, synoptic style of philosophy; though beyond that very general description, they have been acknowledged from ancient times to define two different styles, Plato being associated with speculative ambitions for philosophy, seeking to establish that another world of intellectual objects, the Forms, accessible to reason and not to the senses, was ultimately real, while Aristotle renounced these extravagant other-worldly hypotheses in favour of a more down-to-earth, classificatory, and analytical spirit, more respectful of the ordinary opinions of men—but defining a grand style for all that, since the systematic impulse was directed to producing one unified, ordered, and hierarchical world-picture.

Oppositions of the Platonic and the Aristotelian spirits have been a commonplace. In our own century, Yeats wrote, in *Among School Children*:

> Plato thought nature but a spume that plays
> Upon a ghostly paradigm of things;
> Solider Aristotle played the taws
> Upon the bottom of a kind of kings ...

[2] See Frank Kermode, *The Classic* (London, 1975).

Most famously, the received contrast is expressed in Raphael's fresco in the Vatican called *The School of Athens*, which displays the two central figures of Plato and Aristotle, the one with his eyes turned towards heaven, the other downwards towards earth. In this connection one must remember the mystical elements which were associated with Platonic thought: not altogether falsely, so far as some of Plato's own writings are concerned, but very heavily selected for and modified by the neo-Platonist tradition. It is connected with this image of Plato that for a period in the early Middle Ages only the *Timaeus* (in Latin translation) was known, an untypical dialogue in which a theistic cosmogony is advanced.

Looked at more than superficially, the famed contrast is a very complex and ambiguous matter. The spirit of Plato has sometimes been associated with the religious impulse as such; but equally, and in fact more importantly, where the framework of thought is already religious, an expanded Aristotelianism has represented an ordered and stable understanding of the world in relation to God, while Platonism has been taken to represent variously humanism, magic, or individual rational speculation.

The old picture by which the Middle Ages built on Aristotle, but the Renaissance got its inspiration from Plato, has been much qualified by modern scholarship, but it retains enough truth,[3] and more than one important Renaissance thinker agreed with the words of Petrarch, that Plato 'in that group came closest to the goal that may be reached by those whom heaven favours'. Much of this Platonic influence flowed into humane studies and the betterment of the soul, rather than the study of nature; and where the study of nature is pursued in the Renaissance, outside the continuing traditions of Aristotelian science, there is deep uncertainty and disagreement about what kinds of procedure or lore may prove effective in uncoding the messages hidden in phenomena. It is rather later, and with a vision much closer to modern conceptions of mathematical physics, that Galileo expressed what is still a Platonic influence in saying:

[3] See P. O. Kristeller, 'Byzantine and Western Platonism in the Fifteenth Century', in *Renaissance Concepts of Man* (New York, 1972), and references. The quotation from Petrarch (*Trionfo della Fama*, 3. 4–6) is taken from this article.

(Natural) philosophy is written in that vast book which stands forever open before our eyes, I mean the universe; but it cannot be read until we have learnt the language and become familiar with the characters in which it is written. It is written in mathematical language, and the letters are triangles, circles, and other geometrical figures, without which means it is humanly impossible to understand a single word. (*Il Saggiatore*, Question 6.)

From this point on, the business of decipherment could be more readily detached from notions of an arcane mystery, which were present in the Renaissance, as they were originally in the early Pythagorean sects which influenced Plato; it could become the public task of critical scientific discussion.

Thus in one context Platonism may represent a mystical or cabbalistic interest, against which Aristotelianism stands for a cautious, observational approach, concerned to stick to the phenomena; in another, while a Platonic influence encourages rational enquiry into nature, Aristotelianism can be seen (as it was by Descartes, despite his occasional dissimulations) as an obscurantist attachment to mysterious essences and muddled vitalistic analogies. An opposition of the Platonic and Aristotelian spirits is indeed something real, which can be traced through very complex paths in the history of Western thought; but it defines not so much any one contrast, as rather a structure within which a large number of contrasts have in the course of that history found their place.

Various as these contrasts have been, what can be said is that the majority of them have been associated with interpretations of these philosophers' *views* and, in many cases, with what have been believed to be their systems. Under these various interpretations, they have still been seen as authors of large world-views, as classical system-builders. Modern scholarship, encouraged by a philosophical scepticism about system-building, has tended to reduce the extent to which these philosophers are seen as expressing systems. In both cases, their works are now more clearly seen as the product of development over time, with corresponding changes of outlook; while discussions which in the past were taken to be fundamentally expository can be seen to be more provisional, exploratory, and question-raising than was supposed. If this point of view is accepted, does it mean that the importance of Plato and Aristotle, as more than a purely historical recognition, will for the first time be radically reduced? Perhaps not: the power and depth of their particular arguments may come to be what command admiration and interest rather than the breadth and ambition of their systems. Yet it would be superficial to rest too easily on this idea. The interest that these two philosophers have always commanded in the past has been generated not merely by admiration for their undoubted acuity, insight, and imagination, but, very often, by a belief that they had vast and unitary systematic ambitions, of a kind which we now have rather less reason to ascribe to them.

Apart from these issues of how the work of Plato and of Aristotle is to be interpreted, there are in any case other, more general influences likely to affect their traditional standing. Those features of twentieth-century culture which have weakened the hold of the classic, and of the idea that past works can have any authority over the taste of the present, apply in some degree to philosophy. Past geniuses of philosophy, as of the arts, look different under the influence of our idea, deeply felt and largely correct, that twentieth-century experience is drastically unprecedented. Again, in more technical areas of contemporary philosophy, there have been developments from which some of it has attained the research pattern of a science, and in any such area its interest in any of its past, let alone its Greek past, becomes necessarily more external and ultimately anecdotal. For both these reasons, the role of an absolute classic in philosophy, the role which Plato and Aristotle have peculiarly played, is one that quite conceivably may lose its importance. The question here is not whether philosophy might cease to be of interest—there is more than one dispiriting kind of reason why that might prove to be so—but whether, granted philosophy retains its interest, Plato and Aristotle might not do so, and might become finally historical objects, monumental paradigms of ancient styles. It is not impossible, but if it were to happen at all, there is one reason why it is less likely to happen to Plato than to his great companion: the fact that Plato's work includes as a vivid and independent presence the ambiguous figure of Socrates, whose aspect as ironical critic of organized philosophy can be turned also against the Platonic philosophies, which at other points he is presented as expounding.

What We Have

The pre-eminent status of Plato and Aristotle is both the cause and the effect of their work being quite exceptionally well preserved: though in the case of both, and particularly of Aristotle, there was some luck involved. Of Plato's works, we have everything that he is known to have published. Of Aristotle, we do not have his dialogues (for which he was most admired in antiquity), but we do have a large body of treatises which contain material prepared by him or in some cases by close associates or students.

Work later than Aristotle will not in general be touched on here except for some discussion of ancient scepticism; but we should not forget the large influence exercised on Western thought by the later schools, particularly the Stoics and Epicureans, quite apart from those influences on Christianity which are discussed in another chapter. The Presocratics will be of closer concern to us. They are known to us through fragments of their writings, and in many respects the situation is as described in the chapter on Greek science, that we have to rely on summaries and accounts by later writers, who may be remote in time, or stupid, or—as in the case of Aristotle, who was neither—have their own axe to grind. There does remain one very considerable and nearly continuous fragment of Presocratic writing, a substantial amount of the poem of Parmenides (who was born probably *c.* 515 B.C.): we owe this entirely to the Neoplatonist scholar Simplicius, who, in the commentary on Aristotle's *Physics* which he wrote in the sixth century A.D., copied out long extracts from the poem on the ground that Parmenides' book had at that time become very rare. Thanks to Simplicius, we have enough to reconstruct a continuous argument (which we shall turn to in the next section).

By contrast, another challenging figure, Heracleitus, who was almost certainly rather earlier than Parmenides and perhaps born *c.* 540 B.C., is known only from an assemblage of brief disconnected fragments, conflicting and obviously puzzled reports, and a number of unreliable anecdotes illustrating an original, pessimistic, and contemptuous personality. In his case, it is not clear what has been lost, either in terms of works, or, indeed, in possibility of understanding: it seems anyway that he wrote in the form of brief and dense epigrams, and he was famed already in antiquity for his obscurity. Plotinus said of him (*Enneads*, 4. 8), 'He seems to speak in similes, careless of making his meaning clear, perhaps because in his view we ought to seek within ourselves, as he himself had successfully sought.' The idea of searching within oneself was in Heracleitus, as it was in Socrates: 'I searched myself', Heracleitus said (fr. 101).[4] But he was almost certainly not *careless* of making himself clear: rather, his conception of truth was of something that essentially could not be expressed in a direct, discursive way. He probably thought of philosophical speech as he said of 'the king whose oracle is at Delphi: he does not say, and he does not conceal—he gives a sign' (fr. 93). In this, Socrates vitally differed from him.

Heracleitus' views, so far as they can be discovered, centre on the necessity to the cosmos of constant change and 'warfare' between opposing principles, though these are held in some kind of reciprocal relation and balance. They elicited, at some remove, the respect of Lenin, but it was undoubtedly Nietzsche's admiration that came closer to him—and not only because of his greater sympathy for Heracleitus' contempt for the masses. Heracleitus has seldom had followers, but his deliberate ambiguities and startling images (as in fr. 52: 'time is a child at play, playing draughts: the kingdom is a child's') have contributed to the deep resonances which he has occasionally evoked in later philosophy, most recently in Heidegger.

Of the later Presocratics, again no complete work survives; the most numerous fragments are of two contrasted writers. One is Democritus (roughly a contemporary of Socrates, being born *c.* 470 B.C.), who was concerned both with ethical questions and with the explanation of natural phenomena; he is most famous as one of the first theorists of physical atomism. The other is the riddling figure of Empedocles, who came from Acragas in Sicily, and was falsely represented by tradition as having died by throwing himself into Etna. He wrote not later than 450 B.C. two poems which later came to

---

[4] All references to the Presocratics are to the 6th edition of Diels-Kranz, *Die Fragmente der Vorsokratiker*, in each case to the 'B' section of the material on a given writer.

For an exegesis of these words of Heracleitus, see W. K. C. Guthrie, *A History of Greek Philosophy* (Cambridge, 1962——), i. 417-19.

be called *On Nature* and *Purifications*. As these titles suggest,
naturalistic elements, an interest in physical explanation,
coexisted in his thought with a religious strain, and it is still
disputed how they were combined, and whether his interest in
nature was subordinate to magical concerns rather than the
product of curiosity and free enquiry. Curiosity did to some
extent motivate the Milesian thinkers, and free enquiry was
consciously practised by Democritus and others of similar
temper, such as the ingenious thinker Anaxagoras (born *c.*
500 B.C.), who is said to have been prosecuted by the
Athenians for holding an impiously naturalistic view of the
heavenly bodies.

There is one further group among the predecessors and
contemporaries of Socrates, whom we should mention at this
point; the so-called 'Sophists', whose interests were neither
cosmological nor religious, but more practically orientated,
largely towards the training of pupils in techniques for
political and forensic success, a training for which they
received money. These activities earned them an extremely
bad reputation from Plato, whose attitude to them, expressed
in all modes from the glittering mockery of the *Protagoras* to
the contempt and disgust of the *Gorgias* and *Republic*, has not
only left the Sophists in low esteem, but has helped to make
the word 'sophist' useless for any historical purpose. This is
particularly because Plato tended to conflate four different
charges against them: that their teaching had a practical
rather than a purely theoretical bent; that they took money;
that they produced bad arguments, designed to puzzle and
impress rather than to get at the truth; and that they
advanced cynical, sceptical, amoral, and generally undesir-
able opinions.

It is not at all easy to disentangle these elements, nor to
establish how far the Sophists, or some of them, had what we
would now identify as genuine philosophical interests. They
were prone to confuse, as has been well said,[5] the force of
reason and the power of the spoken word, two things which
Socrates' method of question and answer gave a way of taking
apart. Gorgias of Leontini, a celebrated stylistic innovator
who influenced one of the greatest geniuses among Greek
writers, the historian Thucydides, was a teacher of rhetoric

---

[5] Edward Hussey, *The Presocratics* (London, 1972), p. 117.

whose excursion into metaphysics, a lost work called *On What is Not*, may well, to judge from later summaries of it, have been parodistic. But more serious claims can be made for Protagoras of Abdera (born *c.* 490 B.C.), who commanded enough interest and respect from Plato for him to construct in his *Theaetetus* a sensitive elaboration of a relativistic theory of knowledge starting explicitly from a Protagorean basis. It may be true, as a recent writer has said,[6] that 'he dominated the intellectual life of his time without being a truly original thinker', setting rather an intellectual tone, sceptical and irreverent; but it is possible that he articulated more searching and systematic thoughts about knowledge and society than this implies. It would be interesting to know more of his work than we do, both to learn about the radical strain in fifth-century thought, and to form a more detailed idea of developments, which certainly occurred, in the theory of knowledge and the philosophy of language before Plato. It would be interesting, too, as a matter of sheer curiosity, to know how he continued his book *On the Gods*, of which we have only the discouraging first sentence: 'About the gods I cannot know, whether they exist or not, nor what kind of beings they might be; there are many obstacles to knowledge, both the obscurity of the subject and the shortness of man's life.'

The Birth of Metaphysics

Greek philosophy started at the edges of the Greek world: on the off-shore islands and the western seaboard of Asia Minor—Ionia—and to the far west, in the Greek colonies of Southern Italy and Sicily. The latter were not in any case independent of Ionian influence. Many received new colonists from Ionia after it was annexed by the Persians in the sixth century, and, in particular, the city of Elea in Southern Italy, famous for the philosophy of Parmenides and his pupil Zeno (thus called the 'Eleatics'), was founded by the citizens of Phocaea, a city in Ionia, who had emigrated in large numbers.

The question has been much and inconclusively discussed, of why systematic cosmological thought, embodying an ele-

---

[6] Hussey, p. 116.

ment of rational criticism, should have arisen in Ionia at this time. The great empires of the East had acquired a good deal of empirical information about measurement, positional astronomy, and such matters, while the Babylonian tradition embodied considerable sophistication in mathematical computation, though with little impulse, it seems, to discover an *a priori* order in the mathematical subject-matter. These various techniques, moreover, coexisted with pictures of the origin and structure of the universe which were straightforwardly mythological. Knowledge of these beliefs, transmitted through the Persian empire, may have played a role in the formation of Ionian cosmology, but, if so, they were essentially modified in a more critical and less mythological direction. The relatively autonomous political life of the small Greek cities perhaps played a part in the growth of critical and reflective thought, as contrasted with those 'Asiatic vague immensities', in Yeats's phrase, of the great empires.

Open speculative enquiry was a necessary condition for the development of Greek philosophy, but it would be a mistake to think that everything which eventually fed into it was equally an example of that openness. The Milesians and Eleatics formed 'schools' only in the sense that these thinkers were connected by ties of intellectual influence and teaching; the Pythagorean school, on the other hand, which was founded in Croton in South Italy towards the end of the sixth century, was more like a religious brotherhood or secret society. The history of this school and its founder is wrapped in obscurity and legend, though we know that Pythagoras himself was another who emigrated from Ionia, having been born and having gained a reputation in Samos. The Pythagorean school played an important, if much disputed, role in the development of mathematics, though it is doubtful to what extent those studies figured in its earlier years. Its life was devoted, more certainly, to an ascetic religious discipline centring on concepts of the purification of the soul and reincarnation: ideas and practices perhaps influenced by shamanistic beliefs which would have reached Greece through the Thracians and Scythians.

Pythagorean ideas were to play an important part in the development of the idea of a rational, immaterial soul, separate from the body, an idea which was much developed by Plato; and which passed from him through Augustine to become the basis of Descartes' dualism—though it lost, in the context of seventeenth-century mechanical science, a basic feature which it shared with all Greek ideas of 'soul', namely the conception that it was the presence of soul which gave living things their life. (Descartes marked the difference when he said something which Pythagoreans, Plato, Aristotle, would all equally have been unable to understand: 'it is not that the body dies because the soul leaves it—the soul leaves it because the body has died.')

Whatever exactly the early Pythagoreans did and believed, they did it in secret, and the concept of being initiated into a mystery applies in their case better than that of making an intervention into an open rational debate. Their existence, contemporary with the later Milesians, reminds us also of something else: that from its beginnings two motives were brought to Western philosophy which have been active alongside one another ever since, the desire for salvation and the desire to find out how things work.

We have already suggested that while the question of how far Milesian thought was philosophical is an unhelpful one, the question of how far its enquiries were rational may be a better one. There are of course various criteria of rationality, but certainly one very important expression of it is to be found in reflection, guided by general principles, on what questions require an answer. There is a very striking example of such thought in a famous argument of Anaximander, who worked in the first half of the sixth century and, according to an ancient writer, was 'the first of the Greeks, to our knowledge, who was bold enough to publish a book on nature'.[7] The argument relates to a question which bothered other Presocratics: what keeps the earth in its place? Others were to appeal to material supports of various kinds: but Anaximander argued that the earth was symmetrically placed in the centre of the universe, and thus needed no support. This argument represents an early application of a purely rational principle, the Principle of Sufficient Reason. If the earth were to move in one direction rather than another, there would have to be a reason for this, in the form of some relevant asymmetry or difference: so, if there is no such asymmetry, the earth will not move in any direction rather

[7] Themistius Or. 26, p. 383, Dindorf.

than another, i.e. will stay where it is. This impressive argument brings out clearly how the application of rational principle, even if it is to basically primitive cosmological materials, marks out such thought from mythological picture-making.

A different exercise of rationality, however, and a much more purely abstract one is represented by the extraordinary work of Parmenides. Parmenides expressed his philosophy in verse, a choice less eccentric than it would be now, but still a choice (the Milesians wrote in prose). The effort to express abstract and logical considerations in epic hexameters gives an intense but also strained effect, and his style was poorly viewed in antiquity. His aim throughout seems to be to achieve as much clarity as possible, and the syntactical obscurities that remain are the unintended results of the language being drastically bent to his unprecedented subject-matter. His ambiguities are thus of a very different kind from the revelatory puns of Heracleitus. Even the very little we have of Heracleitus (compared with 154 lines of Parmenides) shows that he was the more controlled and sophisticated writer; but Parmenides was attempting something quite different from him or anyone else before,[8] which was to determine the basic nature of reality entirely by argument from premisses self-evident to reflection—just one premiss, in fact, though Parmenides (fr. 5) says that it makes no difference where one starts. Whatever exactly we say about the Milesians, in this undertaking we can certainly recognize the first example of pure metaphysical reasoning: it remains one of the most ambitious.

Parmenides' poem represents a goddess as revealing to him the true way of enquiry. What she gives as the key to the true way is this: 'it is, and it cannot be that it is not.' We must not try to think 'it is not': for 'you could not know what is not (that is not practicable), nor speak of it (fr. 2). The same thing is there to be thought, and to be (fr. 3). What is there to be spoken of and thought, must be; for it is there to be, but *nothing* is not (fr. 6).'

We will leave for the moment the question of what is meant

---

[8] In this emphasis, as also on some central questions of interpretation, I follow the important article of G. E. L. Owen, 'Eleatic Questions', reprinted in R. E. Allen and D. J. Furley ed., *Studies in Presocratic Philosophy*, vol. ii (London, 1975), pp. 48–81.

by 'it' in 'it is' and 'it is not' (in the Greek the verb 'is' stands by itself). Parmenides' first conclusion is that there is no coherent or possible enquiry into what is not, or which uses the thought 'it is not'; this is because 'the same thing is there to be thought, and to be', and what is not, *nothing*, is not available, so to speak, for thought. Parmenides' ultimate backing for this radical claim is hard to recapture with total precision, and is still the subject of controversy. Some believe that the basic argument (as given in fr. 6, 1–2, the last sentence quoted above) is this: with regard to what can be thought and spoken of, it is true (at least) that it *could* be—and this might be conceded even by those of us who suppose that some things which can be thought and spoken of do not, as a matter of fact, exist (unicorns, for instance). But now consider: of *nothing*, it is not true that it could be. So a thing which can be thought and spoken of cannot be identical with nothing. But then it must be something; and so, contrary to what you first thought, *must* actually be.

This is at least a clear fallacy. But in the strange phrase translated as 'is there to be', Parmenides has a more primitive conception than this version captures, a notion of language and thought having a content only because they touch or are in contact with what is—the touching and seeing models of thought and meaning operate more directly on Parmenides' ideas than is quite brought out by the excursion through what *could* be. But however exactly we are to reconstruct Parmenides' rejection of the thought 'it is not', his rejection of it is clear and total, and he proceeds to deduce from that rejection, in order, a series of surprising consequences. What is can have no beginning or end; if it had, then, before or after, it would *not be*, and that is excluded. He adds to this proof of 'its' having no beginning, another based on an elegant use of the Principle of Sufficient Reason: 'what necessity would force it, sooner or later, to come to be, if it started from nothing?' (fr. 8, 9–10).

'It neither was nor will be, since it is altogether now': here Parmenides gives the first expression to an idea of eternity. His conception is not of something outside time altogether, as some later conceptions of eternity have it, something to which no temporal notions apply at all. It is *now*. But, equally, it is not merely indefinitely old—it has no past, and no future. Its time, such as it is, is represented as a perpetual present. 'It' is uniform, unchanging, has no divisions, is the same under any aspect—for to deny any of this would involve thinking that there was some place, or some time, or some respect, with regard to which it *was not*, and this, once more, is excluded.

Above all, there is only one of it. For 'there is and will be nothing besides what is' (fr. 8, 36–7)—anything else would have to be something which *was not*; and 'what is', itself, cannot consist of two distinguishable things or be divided, 'since it all, equally, is; it is not more or less in any way . . . so it is all continuous, for what is sticks close to what is' (fr. 8, 22–5). Once the uniqueness of 'it' is seen to be a conclusion of Parmenides' argument, and not (as some earlier scholars supposed) a premiss, the question of what 'it' is lapses. It is just that thing, whatever it is, that we are thinking and speaking of, when we succeed in thinking and speaking of something—and Parmenides certainly supposes that we can think and speak of *something*, though very evidently it is not what, in our everyday error, we take ourselves to be thinking and speaking of.

The philosophical legacy of this remarkable argument is very extensive and various. The concept of eternal, unchanging, and uncreated being is one which Plato was to use in characterizing his Forms; his debt to Parmenides was explicit and acknowledged, though he had to differ from him, as he gravely concedes in the *Sophist*, by admitting into reality also principles of change. He differed from him already, however, about the world of unchanging being: Plato had held, from the earliest introduction of the Forms, that there were *many* of them, which could be intellectually distinguished. How this could be, however, is something he did not take up until in that same late dialogue, the *Sophist*, he directly faced the challenge of Parmenides' proof and sought to meet it by systematically distinguishing different senses of 'is not'.

That same attempt was also to provide the solution, as Plato hoped, to another problem which directly related to Parmenides' argument, the problem of falsehood. To think, surely, is to think *something*—to think nothing is not to think at all. So what is the 'something' that is thought by one who thinks falsely? Thought or speech which is false cannot be nonsensical: what relation to reality is possessed by speech which has a meaning, but is not true? This problem Plato made a powerfully original attempt to solve, in the course of which he developed a distinction essential to these issues, that between a name and a statement. What is in many ways the same set of questions has recurred in increasingly sophisticated forms to the present day; and Wittgenstein's *Tractatus*, a metaphysical work comparable in both boldness and abstractness to Parmenides', takes its start from a question which implies the converse of Parmenides' principle: 'how can we say what is not?'

Other strains of Parmenidean influence come from his denials of plurality and change. His pupil Zeno invented a series of famous paradoxes which apparently deduce contradictions from the suppositions that there is plurality, or that motion is possible; paradoxes such as that of the Arrow, which (in its shortest form) runs thus: an arrow in flight occupies at each instant a space which is just its own length; but any body which at any time occupies just such a space is, with regard to that time, at rest; so the arrow is at rest at each instant; so it is at rest at every instant, that is to say, it does not move. These paradoxes gave rise to a complex debate which belongs as much to the history of mathematics as to philosophy, from which there emerged eventually the concepts of the continuum and of a limit. But even after mathematical techniques had been established to characterize the phenomena which Zeno thought could not be coherently characterized, there have remained philosophical problems about the application of mathematics to physical space and time in which some of Zeno's arguments have still played a role; while the method which he invented, of generating from a set of assumptions an infinite regress (or progress)—a method which can be used either destructively, or constructively to determine some infinite set of items—has remained an essential resource of analytical thought.

Apart from difficulties for common sense from the Eleatic arguments, there were particular problems for the most advanced form of theoretical pluralism, atomism, which held that the world consisted of atoms moving in empty space—for how was totally empty space to be conceptualized to avoid the Eleatic argument (which impressed others, such as Anaxagoras) that it would have to be *nothing*, and hence could not exist? It seems that the first of the Atomists, Leucippus (born near the beginning of the fifth century) asserted the existence of the void against the Eleatics by saying that void is *not being*, yet *is*—a formulation which seems too much like a contradiction. Aristotle's treatment of this subject in the *Physics* represents a great advance in the conceptualization of empty space, and although he himself does not accept a void, he does not include the Eleatic type of argument among the several bad arguments he uses against it. It is all the more remarkable that Descartes, in the seventeenth century, when he denied a vacuum on the basic of his own physics (which involved a close assimilation of matter and space), was able to use a startlingly Eleatic type of argument: 'If it is asked what would be the case if God removed all the matter from a vessel and let nothing else take the place of what had been removed, then the answer must be, that the sides of the vessel would be contiguous. For if there is nothing between two bodies, they must be next to each other' (*Principles of Philosophy*, ii. 18).

Appearance and Reality

Parmenides' poem had a further part, mostly lost, in which the goddess expounded a pluralistic cosmological theory; which, however, she was committed to regarding as nonsense, and probably advanced only as a sophisticated example of the kind of thing she had warned against at the beginning of the poem, the way of ignorant mortals, who 'drift along, deaf and blind, amazed, in confused throngs: they think that to be and not to be are the same, and not the same' (fr. 6, 6–9)—that is to say, they think, confusedly, that it is possible for what *is* here and now, *not to be* at other times and places. There has been much discussion of what relation Parmenides supposed the opinions of men to bear to reality as he explained it. But if that discussion tries to rest anything on what it would be consistent for Parmenides to hold, it must recognize from the beginning the important fact that there is nothing which Parmenides could consistently hold on this subject. For the opinions of men certainly change, and are different from one another: so if everything is (literally) one and (literally) nothing changes, there are no such opinions.

This point applies just as much to the true thought of the instructed philosopher. Some interpreters have claimed that Parmenides believed being and thought to be one, that nothing existed except thought (Parmenides would thus be something like an idealist, in the sense in which it was claimed earlier that no ancient philosopher was an idealist). This view is based partly on highly resistible interpretations of two ambiguous lines (fr. 3; fr. 8, 34), but also on the argument that since Parmenides thought everything was one, and agreed that there was thought, he must have supposed, not being stupid, that thought was the one thing there was. But this type of argument ignores the obliquities of the metaphysical imagination. One might as well argue that since Parmenides thought everything was one, and conceded (since he refers to himself more than once) that *he* existed, he must have supposed that he was the only thing there was. It is clear[9] that Plato regarded himself, more than a century later, as forcing Parmenides to face the question of the existence of thought as part of reality. Let us call Parmenides' one thing 'It'. Then one of Plato's points was that Parmenides agreed that there was at least a name of It; but if there is only one thing, then It must be that name; and since It is a name, then Its name must be the name of a name; so Parmenides' theory comes out as the view that there is only one thing in reality, a name which is the name of a name.

This mildly jocular argument contains in fact both a narrower and a wider point. Since naming is, by both Parmenides and Plato, closely connected with thinking, it raises the question of thought being part of reality, a question which Plato goes on to pursue. But it raises also the general issue of what it is to take a thesis like Parmenides' seriously. Is it, for instance, to take it *literally*? An Eleatic might reply that of course it was never meant to be taken in the literal way in which Plato's argument takes it; but then the question can be pressed, as it was repeatedly pressed against metaphysical arguments by G. E. Moore in the present century, of how it is to be taken. Moore himself was burdened by a prejudice that to take something seriously was to take it literally; we do not have to agree with that, in order justifiably to demand some directions from the speculative metaphysician about how to take him seriously. One guide about how to take him seriously is provided by the direction of his arguments: but in Parmenides' case, this gets us no further on, since his argument either proves nothing at all, or proves just that literal absurdity which Plato objected to.

[9] As Owen showed, 'Eleatic Questions', n. 54.

Parmenides had a theory so simple and radical that, taken literally, it leaves no room even for what he regarded as *correct* thought. With regard to other, false, ideas, the deluded beliefs of men, and indeed the pluralistic world itself as it seems, he and his followers were disposed to relegate these to the category of 'appearance'.[10] This contrast between appearance and reality can be aligned, as it is by Parmenides (fr. 7), with a contrast between sense-perception and reason: sense-perception is deluded by mere appearance, it is the power of reason that grasps reality. But such a distinction, whatever else may be said about it, does not solve the problem that we have been pressing on Parmenides. For even if men are deluded by the senses, and appearances conceal rather than reveal reality, at least it is true *that there are appearances*, and any full account of what actually exists must include the actual existence of (misleading) appearances. As the English twentieth-century metaphysician F. H. Bradley insisted, appearance must itself be part of reality.

The point was seen, once more, by Plato in that late dialogue the *Sophist* to which we have already referred. But it was a truth which Plato himself had to learn to take as seriously as it needs to be taken. In his middle-period dialogues, above all the *Republic*, he had offered a picture of knowledge and reality which was itself open to this criticism, or at least was deeply ambiguous on the issue. On the one hand, there was the world of Forms, immaterial and unchanging objects of purely intellectual knowledge, which were supposed, in that simple and ambitious theory, to solve a lot of problems at once: to explain, for instance, what mathematical truths are truths about (for evidently they are not about such things as the inaccurate geometrical figures one sees on blackboards), and, at the same time, to be what give general terms a meaning. Over against these, were the objects of sense-perception and everyday belief, the things of the natural world which are mistaken for reality by the 'lovers of sense-experience', who are contrasted with the philosophers, the lovers of truth.

In the *Republic*, the distinction between these worlds is hammered home by a series of dichotomies: in the model of the Divided Line, which separates the realm of Forms from that of matter, and assigns reason to the one, the senses to the

[10] Cf. Parmenides, fr. 8, 37; and also a later monist, Melissus, fr. 8.

other; and in an image which has haunted European thought, which represents the philosopher's education as a journey into the sunlight from a cave, in which ordinary men, prisoners of their prejudices, raptly watch a flickering procession of shadow images. This distinction, and the ordering of value that goes with it, Plato sometimes represents as one between 'being' and 'becoming', where 'becoming', we are told, is constituted by some unsatisfactory and unstable combination of being and not being. Plato was to abandon these formulations, though certainly not his belief in eternal intellectual objects.

Interpreters have not found it easy to capture exactly what Plato meant when, in the *Republic* and other dialogues of his middle period, he claimed 'real being' for the Forms, and denied it to the everyday objects of sense-perception. There is, in fact, more than one level of difficulty. There is the very general philosophical problem, which we have just touched on in the confrontation of Parmenides and Moore, of giving a sense to metaphysical assertions which deny the reality of some large and evident dimension of experience. Problems of that general sort are still with us. But there is also an historical problem, of understanding those particular metaphysical formulations which belong to a time before the development of any systematic logical theory, and which we are particularly likely to misrepresent in the light of later conceptions. Beyond that again, there is a very specific historical problem of understanding Plato, who seems himself to have become dissatisfied with some of these formulations and to have become, in his later work, a critic of his earlier self. If Plato became dissatisfied with these formulations, there is really not much reason to suppose that they ever had some fully determinate sense which we could now recover: it is rather that Plato is one of those who helped to put us into a position from which these formulations may be seen to have no fully determinate sense at all.

His later dissatisfaction with what he had said in the *Republic* lay in some part in technical issues about the idea of *being*: certainly he came to a clearer understanding of that notion, and also to a more patient and analytical conception of the kind of philosophical enquiry that such an understanding demanded. Related developments away from a simple *Republic* image occurred, as we shall see, in Plato's conception of knowledge.

It may be also that, more broadly, he became less governed by images of the rational mind being clogged or imprisoned by the empirical world. Those images themselves, it must be said, always stood in an uneasy relationship to another kind of picture which at the same time he offered of the material world, equally unfavourable to it, but in a contrary direction—that it was evanescent, flimsy, only appearance. The world of matter had to be ultimately powerless but at the same time destructively powerful, two conflicting aspects which stand to one another as the shadows of the Cave stand to the fetters which bind its prisoners. Such tensions express something very real in Plato's outlook (notably, his own deep ambivalence towards political power, and towards art), but their theoretical costs, for so ambitious a theory, are high, and Plato seems to have become aware of them.

The *Republic* theory, however, refuses to go away; it is perhaps Plato's most famous doctrine, and besides its appearances in history and literature as 'the Platonic philosophy', it itself, or at least its terminology, has recurred in many forms. Its tensions themselves help to explain how it keeps a hold on the philosophical imagination; and here one factor to be mentioned—which particularly relates to the associated Platonic doctrine of love, expressed in the *Symposium*—is that there is a constant and vivid contrast, in these middle-period works, between Plato's world-denying theories and his literary presentation of them. The resonance of his images and the imaginative power of his style, the most beautiful ever devised for the expression of abstract thought, implicitly affirm the reality of the world of senses even when the content denies it.

A more general point is that it is only philosophers and historians of philosophy who worry much about what is entailed by a theory such as that of the *Republic* when it is taken strictly. Others—artists, scientists—get what they need out of it, and if Plato's theory is taken broadly enough, much more can be got from it than is strictly in it. That includes the rationalist spirit so important to the seventeenth-century scientific revolution, which we have already referred to in the person of Galileo, the spirit which sought an underlying mathematical structure under the flux of appearances. It is clear how this can be thought to be in the spirit of Plato's *Republic*; it is clear also how it contradicts what is actually said there, since Plato quite explicitly says that there is no hope at all of giving a scientific account of the material world. His message is, and quite clearly, not that physics should be mathematical, but that one should give up physics and pursue mathematics. If philosophers are going to be influential, it is as well that they should be misunderstood.

Knowledge and Scepticism

Not all philosophical thought that regards reality as different from appearances need be as drastically dismissive of appearances as Parmenides, or the *Republic* taken strictly. It may rather encourage, like the *Republic* taken loosely, some rationalistic, perhaps scientific method for uncovering the reality from the appearances. One important difference between these attitudes is that the rationalist programme which finds an intellectual order under appearances may also find it to be, to some extent, systematically related to appearances, so that discovery of the hidden order can lead to control of what happens even as it appears: all control of the environment which is grounded in physical theory is of this character.

The fact that the view of the *Republic* was not really of this kind presented a serious difficulty to Plato. He was not, of course, interested in physical technology; but he was concerned with social technology, and the dream of the *Republic* is that philosophers, who have seen the truth about reality, would return to the Cave and, after their intellectual sight had adjusted to the darkness of empirical life, would be able to order things better than those who had never left. But despite some hopeful references to the paradigm that they carry in their memory, he does not provide enough to bridge the disjunction between the two worlds, and, as we shall see rather later, the theory of knowledge which he offers is unable to help in the basic task of political education.

The search for a coherent theory of how scientific knowledge might be possible was a preoccupation of some late-fifth-century thinkers. Anaxagoras had said (fr. 21A) that appearances were 'a glimpse of the hidden', and for this he was praised by Democritus, who evidently struggled with these questions. Democritus took the point that while sense-perception could be misleading, and thought had in some sense to get behind appearances, nevertheless it was only with the help of other perceptions that this could be done: 'colour, sweetness, bitterness, these are matters of convention', he interestingly said (fr. 125), 'and what there is in truth are atoms and the void'; but he represented the senses as replying, 'Poor mind, are you going to overthrow us when you take your beliefs from us? If you throw us, you fall over.'

In trying to resolve the epistemological problems of atomism (and we do not know how far he got), Democritus was facing not only the Eleatics, who thought that they knew something incompatible with his atomism, but also a range of Sophists who thought that they had arguments against anyone's knowing anything at all—or at least, anything of a theoretical, general, or scientific character. The inconclusive speculations of the earlier Presocratics, and in particular the mind-numbing conclusions of Eleatic logic, served to encourage attitudes of scepticism.

A general sense that certainty, at least on any large or speculative issue, is impossible, is itself an early phenomenon. But the Sophists, or some of them, pursued a more aggressive line against philosophical theory of any kind and the use of dialectic to support it; wishing in this to advance their own claims to teach something useful, in the form of rhetoric and the all-important power to persuade in the courts and the political assembly—activities in which, as they agreed with their critics, scrupulous logical demonstration was not at a premium. The arguments used in these attacks on the possibility of knowledge seem now a mixture of almost childish muddles or tricks, and penetrating insights into real difficulties; a few arguments embody both at once, as some of those recorded in Plato's *Euthydemus*, or found in a rather rough and ready compilation of dialectical material called the *Dissoi Logoi* or 'Double Arguments', which is generally taken to date from this period. We do not know how far Protagoras himself developed the positions which Plato ascribes to him, offering a relativized view of truth and knowledge, by which what seems to each man is true *for him*: but we do know that Democritus used against him, and may have invented, a form of argument which was to be very important in the later history of scepticism and the theory of knowledge. This form of argument is called the *peritrope* or 'reversal', and consists in applying a philosopher's criterion of knowledge, truth, or meaningfulness to his own statements—in this case, asking

Protagoras whether his own thesis is supposed to be (non-relatively) true.

Some of the material which survives from these early excursions into scepticism seems naïve—naïve, that is, not just by some arbitrary standard of later logical theory, but by the contemporary standards of insight set by Herodotus or Thucydides or, differently, Sophocles—adult persons, compared (it seems) with clever children. The point is not about the individual psychological fact, of the talents or maturity of Sophists compared with those of historians or tragedians; the question is about the social fact, that these arguments were capable of genuinely impressing and bewildering the Sophists' contemporaries. The basic question is, as Nietzsche unforgettably said about Socrates, *how did they get away with it?* Here it is important to remember the gap that always exists between intelligent practice and the theoretical reflective understanding of that practice; and, more particularly, how utterly puzzling the theory of reasoning must have seemed at this point. On the one hand, there existed already startling intellectual achievements in mathematics, and some systematic thought about such subjects as medicine made sense; while, even more evidently, the practice of argument in everyday life could be seen to rest on some assumptions about the connexions between proof and truth—at the very least it was possible to show a person through dialectical refutation that he was contradicting himself and must be wrong somewhere. But at the same time, the Eleatic arguments—which were in fact deep and powerful—led to impossible results; it seemed that one could prove anything. Many other invalid arguments, neither deep nor powerful, could not be decisively shown up because no systematic vocabulary of logical criticism yet existed. The fundamental achievements of Plato and Aristotle in setting logic and the philosophy of language on their feet can conceal from us how random and unstructured reflective logical thought was before the fourth century.

Plato and Aristotle sought foundations for philosophical and (in Aristotle's case at least) scientific enquiry which would resist scepticism. Aristotle's theory of knowledge is complex, and no general account of it will be attempted here. It judiciously combined appeal to some intuitively or self-evidently known principles, with an important role for sense-experience. It also made a very characteristic appeal to the consensus of informed and thoughtful persons: Aristotle champions a programme which applies equally to metaphysics, ethics, and science, of considering and seeking to reconcile the views of the best authorities, and when he says that one's theory should accord with *ta phainomena*, 'the appearances', he includes in that not only data of observation, and what competent speakers would be disposed to say, but also, at least presumptively, existing well-entrenched theoretical opinions. The weight of proof, for Aristotle, is against those who would try to unseat such a consensus. Even granted that the strength of the presumption is not necessarily very strong, so that Aristotle can throw it over with some ease if he thinks he has a strong argument; granted, too, the element of pre-selection that Aristotle exercises in what is to count as a worthwhile opinion; nevertheless, the fact that he can hope to find any soil in which to ground such a method shows how far things have travelled by his time from the age of the Sophists.

For Aristotle, the advance of knowledge is a collective and on-going enterprise, to which earlier thinkers, unless too exotic, primitive, or capricious, can be seen as contributors. That idea exists powerfully today in the conception of a scientific community, whose practitioners are recruited through an apprenticeship in experimental and observational techniques, and again there is a presumption in favour of expert consensus. But in a world where there were few experimental techniques, the question of who was to be counted as part of the informed consensus was interpreted differently, and there was a strong pull towards intellectual activity coming to be seen (as it scarcely was by Aristotle, but was by many later) as the scholastic undertaking of harmonizing the contents of authoritative books.

This methodological respect for an informed consensus provides a contrast between Aristotle's outlook and Plato's, something which emerges in particularly stark terms with regard to ethics. But there is another set of beliefs about knowledge which they share, and which has been of the greatest importance for the history of philosophy: beliefs which represent knowledge as, in more than one way, quite special, and in particular very different from mere belief or opinion, even true opinion. One idea of this kind is that real knowledge, as opposed to random true belief, should form a system, should be theoretically organized in a way which itself corresponds revealingly to the structure of the subject-matter. This idea relates most directly to an ideal body of *scientific* knowledge, an ideal which Plato (in relation to philosophy and mathematics) did much to form, and Aristotle carried much further. It can be seen, however, also as a condition on what it is for a particular person to know anything. It represents a person's thought as real knowledge only insofar as that thought approximates to the system—the knower is the *savant*, one in whom some part of the ideal body of theoretical knowledge is realized.

This requirement leaves out, needless to say, a good deal of what in everyday acceptance would count as knowledge. This divergence is increased when there is added a further idea, that organized theoretical knowledge can be had only of an unchanging subject-matter, that contingent and particular and changeable matters of fact are no subject for science. Taken together, these ideas yield the conclusion that no person's thought can strictly and properly be said to be knowledge unless it relates to a necessary and unchanging subject-matter. This conclusion—and there are other routes to it besides this—exerted a notable fascination on both Plato and Aristotle, and has since recurred in philosophy more than once.

In Plato's thought, a development on this subject can very clearly be followed. In the *Meno*, a dialogue which marks a boundary between the early and the middle period of his work, his views are in a rich and unstable solution. Faced with a sophistic puzzle about how it is possible to learn anything at all, he introduces for the first time the doctrine of *anamnesis* or 'recollection', which represents the process of learning as the recovery of opinions already in the soul but forgotten. In the dialogue, this process (or, more strictly, its earlier steps) is illustrated by a scene in which Socrates elicits from a slave-boy, by questioning, assent to a geometrical truth of which the boy had no conscious idea before. A great deal could be said about this famous doctrine, and the Pythagorean ideas of pre-existence, reincarnation, and immortality which Plato attached to it, sketchily in the *Meno*, but more extensively in the *Phaedo*. The present point, however, concerns only one feature of it: that as an account of learning, it could not really look appropriate to anything except a necessary or *a priori* subject-matter, such as mathematics. There is indeed something which is striking and demands explanation in the fact that one can elicit from a pupil, by argument, mathematical conclusions which have never occurred to him before; but no amount of Socratic questioning could elicit from anyone a set of particular facts of geography or history which he had not already, in the mundane sense, learned. The reader of the *Meno*, however, finds that Socrates seems to hold also all of the following: that knowledge can be acquired only by such 'recollection'; that there is a distinction between knowledge and mere true belief; and that this last distinction can be applied not only to mathematics, but also to contingent matters—we can distinguish between a man who knows the way to Larissa and a man who merely has true beliefs about it. If we accept the obvious fact that 'recollection' does not apply to such matters (and it is not entirely clear whether the *Meno* accepts that point or not), these claims produce an inconsistency.

However it may be with the *Meno*, there is no such inconsistency in the *Republic*, where Plato makes it clear that for him the distinction between knowledge and belief is a difference of subject-matter: they relate to those two ontological worlds represented by the Divided Line. This neat co-ordination, however, leads to absurd conclusions, compounded by the fact that at this stage Plato has no adequate theory of error. The consequence that there is no empirical knowledge presents a problem, of which we have already seen the outline in discussing the Cave, of how the philosophers' knowledge can play any constructive role in this world at all; for to apply knowledge to this world requires propositions which are about this world, and if no such proposition can ever be more than believed, then it is incurably obscure how the philosopher kings' knowledge can, with regard to the empirical world (which is where, reluctantly, they rule), make them better off than others. Not only can there be no empirical knowledge—equally there can, strictly speaking, be no mathematical or other *a priori* belief, and the situation of apprentice or lucky mathematicians (let alone mistaken ones), which had been discussed in the *Meno*, becomes indescribable. Plato has, indeed, got a place in his classification for something roughly analogous to *a priori* belief, but that, interestingly, concerns not so much individual knowers or believers, as the status of a whole subject, the partially axiomatized mathematics of his day, which he believed to lack foundations.

In his later work Plato went back to the view that knowledge and belief could relate to the same subject-matter, and he may very well have accepted that there was empirical knowledge. The *Republic* represents the high-water mark for him of a theory of knowledge controlled by the categories of subject-matter, by the ideal of a body of *a priori* knowledge, rather than by questions about what has to be true of someone who knows something (as contrasted, for instance, with someone who merely believes that same thing). This emphasis in the *Republic* deeply defeats Plato's own purposes. Plato's anxious question, to which he repeatedly came back, and to which the *Republic* was supposed to give the great answer, was how moral knowledge could be institutionalized and effective in society, as opposed either to the rhetoric of the Sophists, or to the unreasoned and hence vulnerable perceptions of conservative tradition. Knowledge had to be present in society in the form of persons who knew, and who commanded an effective theory of education. Real knowledge, and the ability to impart it—or rather elicit it—went together.

This idea helped in the understanding of the life of Socrates, for it served to join something which Socrates admitted, that he had no knowledge, with something that had to be admitted about him, that his influence did not necessarily make his friends better: it was a fact, which contributed to Socrates' condemnation, that among his associates were such men as the brilliant deserter, Alcibiades, and Critias, prominent among the Thirty Tyrants. Plato's theory of effective moral education was meant to complete the work, and the apology, of Socrates. The *Republic*'s account of knowledge seems at first to yield just such a theory; but in fact it totally fails to do so. It says quite a lot about what it is for a body of propositions to be knowledge, and something about what it is for a person to acquire such knowledge, but it says ultimately nothing about the cognitive difference that that process is supposed to make to a person's handling of matters in the everyday world which, by ontological necessity, lie outside that body of knowledge altogether.

There is another way in which knowledge can seem to make quite special demands. This arises from considering the

standards which should govern personal or individual knowledge; whereas the last line of thought was more concerned
with the question of what constitutes an impersonal body of
scientific theory. More intimate to the concept of knowledge
itself, it was equally started in Greek reflection, and has
played an even more prominent part in subsequent theory of
knowledge. This is the idea that knowledge implies certainty;
that an individual cannot be said to know a thing unless he is
certain of it, where that implies not only that he feels utterly
sure of it, but that—in some sense which it has been a
repeated undertaking of philosophy to try to make clear—he
could not, granted the evidence he has, be wrong.

This is not, as some modern philosophers have implied, a
merely arbitrary condition on knowledge. It is a quite natural
suggestion to arise from reflection on knowledge; by more
than one route, perhaps, but one could be the following.
Obviously, there is a distinction between knowing a thing,
and being right about it by luck—even ordinary speech,
which is lax about ascriptions of knowledge, distinguishes
between knowing and guessing correctly (even where the
guesser actually believes his guess). But now consider the
condition of a man who believes on ample evidence that a
given thing is true, but whose evidence is such that he might
still be wrong. Then even if he is not wrong, that seems to be,
relative to his state of mind, *ultimately* luck. Here we can take
the case of two men, each of whom has, on two different
occasions, exactly the same kind and amount of evidential
basis for his belief in a certain kind of fact; but, as it happens,
one is right and the other is wrong. There is real pressure to
say that the one who, luckily, was right, did not really *know*,
and a natural English phrase marks this exactly, when it is
said of him that *for all he knew* he might have been wrong. By
this kind of argument, it can be plausibly claimed that so long
as one's evidence falls short in any way of conclusive certainty, one does not, even if one is right, really know.

It is just possible that this powerfully influential line of
argument was sketched out near the beginning of Greek
philosophy, by the poet Xenophanes of Colophon (born about
the middle of the sixth century), who wrote lines which can be
translated (fr. 34):

No man has discerned certain truth, nor will there be any who
knows about the gods and all the other things I say: for even if by

chance he says what is totally correct, yet he himself does not know it; appearance (*or* opinion) holds over all.

Plato in the *Meno* apparently refers to this as expressing the sceptical view that knowledge is unattainable because you would not know when you had attained it—which is another version of the demand for certainty. But Plato may have been wrong about Xenophanes' meaning; the sense is much disputed, but it is most probable[11] that he speaks only of a distinction, itself very important to Greek thought, between what one has seen for oneself or established at first hand, and what can only be the subject of inference, such as questions about the gods. But besides some good reasons for so taking it, one bad one has been advanced:[12] that on the view of the lines as expressing a general sceptical point, there is no way in which the second sentence could stand as a reason for the first—it would rather have to be a consequence. On the contrary, the second sentence might express a subtle and powerful reason for the first—'no-one knows about these things, because if he did know, it would have to be more than luck that he was right, which it cannot be.' The trouble about this as an interpretation of Xenophanes is not that it is too weak an argument, but rather that it is, by a century or so, too sophisticated.

But what Xenophanes probably did not say was eventually said. The requirement of strong certainty having been deduced from the concept of knowledge, a variety of thinkers took the step of claiming that strong certainty, and hence knowledge, were not to be had. Plato attempted to answer such a sceptical conclusion, while sharing the premiss that knowledge demanded strong certainty. But the negative view recurred, and it is interesting that it was, much later, members of the school that Plato founded, the Academy, who made some of the more interesting contributions to the rather episodic intellectual movement which is called Scepticism.

Our knowledge of ancient Scepticism comes in good part from the writings of an undistinguished medical writer of the second century A.D. called Sextus Empiricus. Sextus himself

---

[11] The case is argued by H. Fränkel, 'Xenophanes' Empiricism and his Critique of Knowledge', in A. P. D. Mourelatos ed., *The Presocratics* (New York, 1974), pp. 118–31; English translation of an article collected in his *Wege und Formen frügriechischen Denkens* (Munich, 1960).

[12] Fränkel, p. 124.

belongs not to the Academic school of scepticism, but to that called 'Pyrrhonian', after Pyrrho of Elis (*c*. 360–275 B.C.); Pyrrho himself is a shadowy figure, whose views came to Sextus as reported and amplified by his pupil Timon and other writers. Later Pyrrhonism inherited from the Academic Arcesilaus the technique of laying alongside any set of evidences or supposedly convincing argument another with contrary effect, in order to induce total suspension of assent— an attitude which was expressed in a phrase which already had an earlier history in philosophy: *ou mallon*, 'no more this than that'. The aim of this technique was practical, to achieve that state of mind which more than one ancient school made its aim, *ataraxia*, quietude of mind or freedom from disturbance.

The Pyrrhonists were careful to withhold assent even from the claim that there was no knowledge; they recognized that, expressed dogmatically, it would be open to the *peritrope* or charge of self-refutation, and this very reflection helped them to get rid of that dogma along with others. The sceptical proposition, they said, was like the purge which 'does not merely eliminate the humours from the body, but expels itself along with them'.[13] Correspondingly, the slogan 'no more . . .' was to be taken, not as a theoretical statement or the right answer to a theoretical question, but as an element in a practice which leads to the same state as having the right answer would lead to, if there were such a thing as having the right answer. *Ataraxia* followed, for the Pyrrhonists, not on answering fundamental questions, but on being induced to give up asking them. They illustrated the point with a story of the painter Apelles, who, despairing of being able to paint a horse's foam, flung his sponge at the canvas, which produced the effect of a horse's foam.

The later Pyrrhonists criticized the Academic school, of which the outstanding figure was Carneades (*c*. 213–129 B.C.), for being less prudent in withholding assent, and accused them of dogmatism, for asserting definitely that there was no knowledge. It is clear that Carneades worked very directly on the conception of knowledge as entailing certainty. His target, and the focus of his problems, was set for him by the theory of knowledge advanced by the Stoic school, which had been founded *c*. 305 B.C. by a gruff eccentric, Zeno of Citium. The

[13] Sextus Empiricus, *Outlines of Pyrrhonism*, 1. 206, 2. 188.

theory had been developed in the late third century by a figure important in the history of logic, Chrysippus. (A line of verse said of him that if he had not existed, neither would the Stoic school, and equally elegantly Carneades added, 'if Chrysippus had not existed, neither would I.') The Stoics' theory of knowledge cannot be discussed here, but it is notable for pursuing quite directly the requirements which follow from the argument set out earlier against 'luck': needing, as they believed, some certain criterion of truth, they had recourse to a supposedly self-validating state of mind, one which would eliminate the possibility that what was assented to could be false. They introduced the concept of a 'kataleptic impression'—a form of conviction which was supposedly both subjectively indubitable and objectively unerring. It was this that Carneades attacked, by trying to show that no impression which had the first of these characteristics could be guaranteed to have the second. This was the first enactment of a dispute which was to become central to much modern philosophy, above all through Descartes' appeal, in his notion of a 'clear and distinct perception', to what is, in effect, a kataleptic intellectual impression.

The views of ancient Sceptics are not altogether easy to reconstruct from the accounts, rambling and sometimes inconsistent, offered by second- or third-rate thinkers such as Sextus or Cicero. To some, and varying, degrees they were actually sceptics, denying the possibility of knowledge or indeed of truth, or Pyrrhonianly withholding assent even from these denials. But at the same time there were strains, particularly in Carneades, of what would in modern philosophy rather be called empiricism or positivism, which ascribes certainty only to statements about impressions of sense or subjective appearances, and emphasizes verifiability, the probabilistic character of all empirical inference, and the heuristic uselessness of deduction (J. S. Mill's criticism of syllogistic inference as circular was anticipated by ancient Scepticism). It may be that to Greek thinkers the two strains of scepticism and of radical empiricism seemed more closely associated than they do in modern philosophy, where radical empiricism has sometimes been invoked (as by Berkeley) precisely *against* scepticism. But to Greek thought the distinction between appearance and reality was so basic, and knowledge so associated with reality, that knowledge which was merely *of subjective appearances* perhaps did not count as genuine knowledge at all. This is a large subject,[14] but if this line of argument is correct, it illustrates once more a point made before, that subjective idealism was not a view which occurred to the Greeks.

What is certain is that both the empiricist and the more purely sceptical strains in ancient Scepticism were to be of great importance later. Sextus Empiricus was destined to be one of the most influential of Greek philosophical writers. The translation into Latin and printing of his works (1562, 1569) coincided with an intellectual crisis precipitated by the Reformation about the criterion of religious faith, and it has been shown[15] how sceptical arguments from Sextus became important instruments in subsequent controversies. The weapons of scepticism were used both against, and in defence of, traditional religious faith. One style of defence was expressed by Montaigne, who emphasized the inability of man to reach knowledge, and his pretensions in trying to do so; among the innumerable considerations assembled to support this outlook are the arguments of ancient scepticism. A fideistic, unfanatical attachment to traditional religious belief emerges as the basis of the life of *ataraxia*. As he winningly puts it in his celebrated *Apologie de Raymond Sebon*: 'La peste de l'homme, c'est l'opinion de sçavoir. Voilà pourquoy l'ignorance nous est tant recommandée par nostre religion comme piece propre à la créance et à l'obeïssance.'

In sharp contrast is the attitude of Descartes, whose use of the armoury of sceptical devices in his Method of Doubt was designed to be pre-emptive, and to enable him to arrive at certainties which, as he put it, 'the most extravagant hypotheses of the sceptics could not overthrow'. Descartes goes through doubt, not to give up philosophy, but to establish it. Finding certainties, as he supposes, first about himself as a rational soul, then about God, then about the structure of the physical world, he attempts a project which is, in effect, to reverse the relation of Carneades to the Stoics: he advances beyond doubt to a new form of kataleptic impression, and it is significant that among his first and basic certainties are those

---

[14] For this suggestion and discussion, see Charlotte L. Stough, *Greek Skepticism* (Berkeley and Los Angeles, 1969).

[15] By Richard H. Popkin, in his *History of Scepticism from Erasmus to Spinoza* (Berkeley and Los Angeles, 1979).

about subjective states of mind which, we have suggested, neither the Stoics nor the Sceptics regarded very highly as truths about reality. But both Descartes' conception of certainty, and still more some of the propositions which he regarded as certain and which were essential to his system, lacked kataleptic effect on his critics, and Descartes' fundamental achievement, contrary to his hopes, was to help to radicalize doubt, not to eliminate it.

When Montaigne said that Christianity should be taken on faith, because all arguments defeat one another, he almost certainly meant what he said; when Hume and Bayle, in the eighteenth century, spoke in similar terms, they did not. By that time, Pyrrhonian *ataraxia* was to be found not in Christianity, but in as little enthusiasm as possible for any religious issue. In cultivating that, as much against militant atheists as against zealots of the Church, Hume was a genuinely Pyrrhonian thinker, as also in his conservative social views; and besides the standard sceptical material which he used, a basic element in his epistemology, the theory of 'natural belief', can be found crudely prefigured in Sextus.

Hume and the ancient Pyrrhonians had something else in common. For all of them, the rejection of philosophy was the *eventual* rejection of philosophy, and *ataraxia* a state of mind achieved by working at sceptical considerations and then letting natural belief have its sway, so that one ends up living calmly by the customs of one's society (or, rather, by some critical liberalization of them). These thinkers would not have been impressed by the suggestion that it might have been simpler never to have started reflecting at all; or if they express envy for those innocent of reflection, this attitude is formed and expressed at a level of self-consciousness which does not invite the reader to take it simply as it stands. Some, and notably the ancients, believed that people who had never embarked on any reflection did not in general experience *ataraxia*, but were rent by passions and prejudice; but even those who were less sure of that would not have favoured an educational or psychological regime which produced the benefits of a passionless rationality by entirely unphilosophical means. Scepticism remained an *intellectual* posture, and for all these thinkers, the Pyrrhonian outlook was both a minority state and (what is not quite the same thing) an achievement. The Pyrrhonist had, in relation to the rest of society, the role of a sage: a very quiet one.

This is one of several reasons why this posture is no longer possible. There is in modern society no serious role of a sage, as opposed to those of the expert, the commentator, or the entertainer. There is also no serious point of view, or at least none which can be publicly sustained, by which wars, calamities, and social upheaval can be quite so distantly regarded as Scepticism suggested they should be. Again, outlooks shaped by Romanticism and by modern psychological theory demand a deeper view of the emotions than Pyrrhonism had, and a more sceptical view of *ataraxia* itself. These points are well, if negatively illustrated by the thought of Bertrand Russell, whose philosophical stance in the theory of knowledge was, broadly, that of a twentieth-century Humean, but who notably failed to reconcile his social and moral concerns with his theoretical scepticism about ethics, or the strength of his feelings with his understanding of the mind. A book about Russell was called *The Passionate Sceptic*; while there could still be some outlook to which that phrase applied, it is notable, and a significant comment on Russell's own difficulties, that in the terms of ancient or even Humean Pyrrhonism, it is a contradiction in terms.

Ethical Enquiry

'The discussion is not about any chance question,' Socrates says towards the end of Book I of the *Republic* (352D), 'but about what way one should live.' The discussion was with the sophist Thrasymachus, who had claimed that it was only ever a second-best situation in which a man had reason to act in accordance with the requirements of *dikaiosune*—'justice' as we necessarily translate it, though in the *Republic* it covers a wide ground, and relates to all aspects of being concerned for others' interests as well as one's own. One often does have, according to Thrasymachus, a reason, as things are, for acting in this way, but this is only because one's power is limited— typically, by the greater power of another; one whose power was not so limited would have no such reason, and would be a lunatic if he put others' interests before his own. This view Socrates sets out to refute. Discontented with what he offers against Thrasymachus, and confronted rather later with a more sophisticated version of this kind of thesis, he is represented by Plato as spending the rest of the *Republic* in giving the ultimate answer to it.

Although the speaker is Socrates, and although the question
of what exactly in the Platonic Socrates was Socratic is still
unanswered,[16] there would be much agreement that the
Republic's answer was Platonic, but the problem was Socratic.
It was a problem raised by Sophistic scepticism, a form of it
more genuinely alarming than scepticism about cosmological
speculation or logic, for in this case there existed recognizable
and possibly attractive alternatives to the considerations
displaced by sceptical criticism.

The nub of the sceptical attack was that there was no
inherent reason for anyone to promote or respect anyone else's
interests, and that the belief that there was such a reason was
the product of various kinds of illusion: in particular, it
stemmed from an innocent failure to see that the rules and
requirements on people's conduct which were found in
different societies obtained only 'by convention', a concept
which for the Sophistic critics meant that such rules were
social products, about which it could be asked whose interest
they served. There were, on the other hand, perfectly good
'natural' motives to self-interested conduct, and this was well
illustrated by the behaviour of agents where there was no such
framework of convention, notably by the behaviour of one
city-state to another—a set of considerations brilliantly and
grimly represented in the famous 'Melian dialogue' in Book 5
of Thucydides' *History*.

Part of the problem was set by this kind of use of the
concepts of 'nature' (*phusis*) and 'convention' (*nomos*),[17] and
the attendant question of what kind of life it was 'naturally'
rational to live; together with the suggestion that it was
'naturally' rational to pursue self-interest, the ideally satisfying forms of life being represented, in some of the more
uninhibited expositions, in terms of sheer gangsterism.
Thrasymachus offers this kind of picture; at this level what is
in question is not only an entirely egoistic conception of
practical rationality, but also a very simple schedule of

[16] The state of the question is set out in Guthrie, vol. iii, ch. 12.
[17] This was not the only use of this celebrated distinction. By some writers, *nomos*
was praised for saving us from *phusis*; by others, *phusis* was indeed used in criticism of
nomos, but in order to extend rather than contract the range of moral ideas, as in a
famous fragment of Alcidamas (quoted by the scholiast on Aristotle, *Rhetoric*, 1373b):
'God made all men free: *phusis* never made anyone a slave', and cf. similar opinions
referred to by Aristotle, *Politics*, 1253b20.

egoistic satisfactions, in terms of power, wealth, and sex.[18] This set of considerations just in itself yields the materials of fear and envy, rather than any on-going structure of social relations, and indeed Thrasymachus' view, reduced totally to these elements, turns out to be even descriptively quite inadequate for any account of society.

However, this picture was superimposed on, and derived some appeal from, something different: a picture of a certain kind of social morality, which does offer some impersonal criteria of who is to be admired and respected, but finds them particularly in certain kinds of competitive success and inherited position—an aristocratic or feudal morality. It was from the context of a such a social morality that the fifth and fourth centuries inherited the concept of *arete*, 'personal excellence' (the standard translation of this term as 'virtue' is only sometimes appropriate, and can be drastically misleading). This term carried with it certain associations which Plato, and probably Socrates, made strong efforts to detach from it: in particular, the notion of being well thought of and spoken of, cutting a good figure. Here a vital term is *kalos*, 'fine', 'noble', 'splendid', a word more strongly aesthetic than *agathos*, 'good', and an important term of commendation, but bearing with it implications of how one is regarded; as its opposite, *aischros*, 'base' or 'shameful', carries implications of being despised or shunned.

The deeds that made one admired if one was a Homeric hero were typically but not exclusively individual feats of arms, and one's *arete* was displayed in such. One could be shamed and lose repute not only by failing in such feats, but by being mistreated—such things led to the anger of Achilles and the suicide of Ajax. What happened to one mattered for one's esteem as well as what one did, and among things one did, competitive success ranked high: all this, of course, among those who themselves ranked high, for women and members of lower orders had other *aretai* and kinds of repute. In this area, there are two importantly different points, which discussion of this subject has often confused. One is that, for

---

[18] In the *Gorgias*, a dialogue probably a little earlier than the *Republic*, Plato offered, in the person of Callicles, a more striking, eloquent, and altogether more formidable expression of the egoistic alternative. Socrates' answers to him are less than satisfactory; in part, this is because Callicles is unconvincingly made to accept the idea that egoism must come down to a very crude form of hedonism.

such a morality, shame is a predominant notion, and a leading motive the fear of disgrace, ridicule, and the loss of prestige. A different point is that excellence is displayed in competitive and self-assertive exploits. While socially and psychologically these two things often go together, they are independent of each other: in particular, the occasion of shame and disgrace may be a failure to act in some expected self-sacrificing or co-operative manner. The confusion of these two things is encouraged by measuring Greek attitudes by the standard of a Christian, and more particularly of a Protestant, outlook. That outlook associates morality simultaneously with benevolence, self-denial, and inner-directedness or guilt (shame before God or oneself). It sees the development of moral thought to this point as progress, and it tends to run together a number of different ideas which have been discarded—or at least rendered less reputable—by that progress.

The ideas of *arete*, shame and reputation, were of course much older notions than the self-interest conceptions of the Sophists and the simply reductive social theory that went with those. Insofar as these Sophistic speakers (and, still more, conventional persons influenced by them, such as Meno) appeal to notions of *arete*, and offer for impersonal admiration the ideal of a man of power, they are in fact expressing ethical conceptions which have an aristocratic structure in itself old-fashioned by the end of the fifth century; but these conceptions have been given a new, opportunistic, content, and detached from the base in traditional society which had originally made them part of a working social morality.

This structure of ideas is thus more old-fashioned than another theory presented in the *Republic*, the theory offered by Glaucon and Adeimantus in Book 2. This represents the conventions of justice not as a device of the strong to exploit the weak (which was Thrasymachus' formulation), but as a contractual device of the weak to protect themselves against the strong. This theory, only sketched in the *Republic*, is the prototype of many which view public norms as the solution to a problem which would now be expressed in the language of games-theory. It reaches, in fact, outside the most characteristic terms of Greek ethical theory, concerned as that was with *arete*. In two important respects, it resembles modern Utilitarian and contractual theories. First, the notion of a rule or practice is more fundamental in this theory than notions of character or personal excellence. Second, the desires which are served by the institutions of justice and, generally, the practices of morality are in the first instance self-interested desires: morality is represented as a device for promoting egoistic satisfactions which could in principle occur without it, but which are as a matter of fact unlikely to do so because of everyone's weak position in an amoral state of nature.

This instrumental or contractual view of morality was rejected by Socrates, Plato, and Aristotle. It is in many ways different from the crude Thrasymachean outlook—indeed, in expression it is its opposite. Yet for Plato it shared a basic fault with that outlook: morality was represented by both as an instrument for the satisfaction of non-moral, selfish desires which existed naturally in independence of morality. This was not just a moralizing prejudice on Plato's part, a desire for the moral motivations to appear more dignified. Still less was it the expression of an idea, later insisted on by Kant, that there can be no reason for moral conduct at all, except that it is one's duty—that the very nature of morality requires it to consist in a completely autonomous demand which cannot be rationalized or explained by anything else. The point for Plato was precisely that there had to be a reason for moral conduct, but that no theory of the instrumental kind could provide it. A theory of morality, in his view, had to answer Sophistic scepticism by showing that it was rational for each person to want to be just, whatever his circumstances. The contractual theory failed in this respect: if one were powerful and intelligent and luckily-enough placed, it would cease to be rational for one to conform to the conventional require-ments of morality. This is readily admitted by Glaucon and Adeimantus in the dialogue; indeed, they basically agree with the Platonic Socrates in viewing the contractual theory, not as an answer to Sophistic scepticism about morality, but rather as a more sophisticated expression of that scepticism.

The contractual solution was particularly weak because it was unstable relative to a *superior* agent, one more intelligent, resourceful, and persuasive than the average. It was above all for that kind of agent that Plato thought that the sceptical demand had to be met, and the objectives of morality and justice shown to be rational. The life of Alcibiades had been scepticism in action, and the answer had to apply to a man of his superior powers. Here the first feature, too, of the contractual theory had to be rejected, the view that notions of character came second to the notions of a desirable or useful practice. The demand to show to *each* man that justice was rational *for him* meant that the answer had to be grounded first in an account of what sort of person it was rational for him to be. If anything outside the soul (as Socrates and Plato said) or outside the self (as we might put it) is what primarily has moral value—some rule, for instance, or institution—then we are left with a possible contingency, that there could be a man whose deepest needs and the state of whose soul were such that it would not be rational for him to act in accordance with that rule or institution; and so long as that contingency remains possible, the task that Socrates and Plato set themselves will not have been carried out.

It has been said by Kantian critics that Platonic morality is egoistic, in a sense incompatible with the real character of morality. This misses the point. It is formally egoistic, in the sense that it supposes that it has to show that each man has good reason to act morally, and that the good reason has to appeal to him in terms of something about himself, how and what he will be if he is a man of that sort of character. But it is not egoistic in the sense of trying to show that morality serves some set of individual satisfactions which are well defined antecedently to it. The aim was not, given already an account of the self and its satisfactions, to show how morality (luckily) fitted them; it was to give an account of the self into which morality fitted.

For Plato, as also for Aristotle, it was a trivial truth that if it is rational for one to pursue a certain course of life or to be a certain sort of person, then those things must make for a satisfactory state of oneself called *eudaimonia*—a term which can only be translated as 'happiness'. But not everyone now will regard it as a triviality, or even as true, that it is only rational to do what in the end makes for one's own happiness. Moreover, many people who do agree that that is true will not in fact be agreeing with the same thing as Plato and Aristotle meant. These facts are due not only to imperfections of that translation, but also to changes in views of life—changes which themselves have no doubt affected our understanding of the term 'happiness'. A proper charting of the complex relations of these words would involve a whole history of

Western ethical thought. What is certain is that *eudaimonia* did not necessarily imply the maximization of pleasure; and when Plato, supposedly having shown in the *Republic* that justice is the proper state of the soul, goes on to argue that the life of the just man is also a large number of times more pleasant than that of the unjust, this is meant to be an entirely additional consideration. It is in this respect much like Kant's assurance that virtue will be rewarded in an after-life, coming as that does after his insistence that it must be regarded as its own reward (a manoeuvre which Schopenhauer disobligingly compared to slipping a tip to a head-waiter who pretends to be above such things). The state of *eudaimonia* should be interpreted as that of living as a man best could, and when one finds some Greek thinkers suggesting that one can attain *eudaimonia* although one is the victim of torture, the linguistic strain that is undoubtedly set up expresses not just a semantic difficulty, but, under that, the substantial difficulty of supposing that being tortured is compatible with living as one best could.

The Platonic aim, then, can be seen as this, to give a picture of the self such that if one properly understands what one is, one will see that a life of justice is not external to the self, but an objective which it must be rational for one to pursue. That is the sense of Socrates' question with which we started, about the way 'one should live': the 'should' is formally that of egoistic rationality, but the task is to reach the right understanding of the ego.

Both Socrates and Plato gave that account in terms of reason and knowledge. Plato saw the fullest expression of these powers in the form of systematic theoretical understanding, something which led to the consequence that the philosopher was the happiest and most fully developed of human beings; it led also to the Utopian political system of the *Republic*. Socrates himself certainly never developed the latter ideas (though the view, popularized by Popper,[19] that Socrates himself was politically a democrat who was betrayed by the authoritarian Plato has no historical basis). The idea, however, that the real self, which is fully expressed in the life of justice, is the self of the discursive intellect, is only a development of Socratic conceptions. It may be that Socrates

[19] In his *Open Society and its Enemies* (London, 1957).

laid more weight than Plato on 'knowing how to act', and less on knowledge expressed in systematic theory, but certainly the notion that knowledge had to be reflective and rational was already there. An 'interest in definitions', as well as a concern with ethical questions, is what Aristotle plausibly tells us can be ascribed to the historical Socrates, and the interest in definitions with regard to ethical matters certainly took the form of trying to reach a reflective and articulate understanding of the criteria of virtuous action, which would make good practice more rationally lucid and self-critical.

If the essence of virtuous action lay in rational knowledge exercised by the soul, then there could be no separate motives represented by the various virtues, as conventionally distinguished: justice, self-control, courage, and the rest. All of them could only be expressions, in different spheres or aspects of conduct, of the same basic rational motivation. When Socrates taught the 'unity of the virtues' under rational prudence or intelligence, he did not mean that there were no ways of distinguishing one virtue from another. He meant rather that they were not basically different motivations: they were the same power of the soul, under different manifestations. Since, further, rationality must be displayed in balancing one kind of demand against another, and an exaggeration of, say, 'courageous' behaviour would not in fact be an expression of real rational understanding of what was required of one, it followed that it would not be an expression of the one underlying power of reason, and hence not of any virtue at all. So the unity of the virtues implied, as might be expected, that one does not properly display any virtue unless one displays all of them.

Virtue is the pursuit of one's interest, construed as a rational agent—the proper interest, as Socrates put it, of the soul, and this was probably already taken by Socrates in a way which implied that the interests of the soul were a separate matter from those of the body, an implication which Plato's drastically dualistic theory of soul and body was to pursue further in the direction of asceticism. Virtuous action is a matter of the calculation of what truly matters most to one, and what matters most to one is what matters most for one's soul: these are the demands of the virtuous life, of courage, honour, justice. Hence if one does not act in accordance with those demands, one acts to defeat what matters most to one;

no man can consciously act in such a way; so wrong action must involve a failure of knowledge and understanding, and be something which one could not possibly have chosen with open eyes. So all error is involuntary, and 'no-one willingly errs', as Socrates put it: a conclusion still discussed under the name of 'the Socratic paradox'.

The paradox raises in fact two different questions. The first is whether a person can voluntarily do one of two things, while fully and consciously holding that he has stronger reason to do the other. The second question is whether a person must, if clear-headed, admit that he always has stronger reason to do acts of justice, honour, and so forth, rather than acts of mean temporal self-interest. Most would now find it hard to give a simply Socratic answer to the second question, supported as that is by the ascetically dualistic view of the self. One difficulty that such a view inevitably raises, and which Plato himself treats uneasily, is the marked contrast between the spiritual view of one's own interests which is needed by the account of morality's motivations, and the less spiritual view of other people's interests which is needed by its subject-matter. Socrates thought that the good man cannot be harmed, for the only thing that could touch *him* would be something that could touch, not his body, but the good state of his soul, and that is inviolable. But— apart from other and perhaps deeper weaknesses of that picture—we must ask why, if bodily hurt is no real harm, bodily hurt is what virtue so strongly requires one not to inflict on others?

To the first of those two questions, however, the one in terms purely of conscious action and rationality, some philosophers would still give the Socratic answer. To those of us whose actions seem often very divergently related to what we take to be our reasons, that answer will still seem a remarkable paradox. It should be offered, if at all, not as a demure tautology about action and reason, but rather as conveying an ideal (a highly problematical one) of a state in which action becomes wholly transparent to the agent. That is still, itself, very much a Socratic ideal.

It is surprising how many elements in Socratic-Platonic morality are still to be found in the complex and very interesting ethical theory of Aristotle, different though it is in certain central respects. It is different, most importantly of all, because not all the weight is put on intellectual excellence and pure rationality. Aristotle distinguishes between 'intellectual excellences' and 'excellences of character', and emphasizes the importance to the latter of the correct formation of desire and motivation through training. Without correct upbringing nothing can be done: the hopes for the regenerative powers of philosophy itself which are implicit in the Socratic stance have gone, as has the sense of any combative scepticism against which morality has to be defended. A more settled order is in question. Aristotle, moreover, did not believe in a soul wholly separate from the body, and that denial goes with a rejection of Socratic asceticism, and with more worldly possibilities for *eudaimonia*. The old link of *arete* and public approval, which Plato sought to cut altogether, cautiously reasserts itself in the Aristotelian account, though his theory of the motivation of the virtues is much more sophisticated than anything that had been achieved at an earlier time, or indeed by Plato himself.

Yet, granted these differences, Aristotle still ends by regarding the life of theoretical reason as the highest form of human life, a conclusion which does not follow as directly, or even as coherently, from his premises as it did from Plato's. He preserves also something like the Socratic paradox about action and reason. He even preserves, in effect, the Socratic conclusion about the unity of the virtues, since he thinks that one cannot genuinely have any one excellence of character without the presence of *phronesis*, 'practical reason' (itself one of the intellectual excellences), but if one has *phronesis*, then one must have all excellences of character. This emphasis on the rational integration of character, as also on the integration of a good life over time, its retrospective rational shapeliness, is indeed a central feature of Aristotle's outlook. In the matter of the ultimate unity of virtuous traits of character, certainly this is one issue on which the Greek view seems far from ours: nothing is more commonplace to us than that particular virtues not only coexist with, but carry with them, typical faults. But this is one of the many differences with the Greeks where the contrast itself points to an illuminating area of discussion: what divergences in the understanding of human nature underlie these different conceptions of a rationally desirable life.

It is worth bringing together several features of Greek

ethical thought which mark it off in many ways from current concerns and from the moral inheritance of the Christian world. It has, and needs, no God: though references to God or gods occur in these writers, they play no important role. It takes as central and primary questions of character, and of how moral considerations are grounded in human nature: it asks what life it is rational for the individual to live. It makes no use of a blank categorical moral imperative. In fact— though we have used the word 'moral' quite often for the sake of convenience—this system of ideas basically lacks the concept of *morality* altogether, in the sense of a class of reasons or demands which are vitally different from other kinds of reason or demand. The sharp line that Kantianism, in particular, draws between the 'moral' and the 'non-moral' is very partially paralleled by another sharp line, Plato's line between soul and body; but the parallelism is far from total, the distinctions are drawn on quite different principles, and the discussion of the merits and failings of each will be a quite different sort of discussion. Relatedly, there is not a rift between a world of public 'moral rules' and of private personal ideals: the questions of how one's relations to others are to be regulated, both in the context of society at large and more privately, are not detached from questions about the kind of life it is worth living, and of what is worth having or caring for.

In all these respects the ethical thought of the Greeks was not only different from most modern thought, particularly modern thought influenced by Christianity, but was also in much better shape. There are of course respects in which its outlook could not be recaptured now, and some in which we could not want to recapture it. Some of its thoughts express a certain integration of life which perhaps existed for a short while in the city-state, but which, as Hegel emphasized, would have to be recovered, if at all, only in some totally changed form. Other features of its perceptions, its substantive attitudes to slavery, for instance, and to the role of women, we must hope will never be recovered at all.

At a more theoretical level, it is important that Greek ethical thought rested on an objective teleology of human nature, believing that there were facts about man and his place in the world which determined, in a way discoverable to reason, that he was meant to lead a co-operative and ordered life. Some version of this belief has been held by most ethical outlooks subsequently; we are perhaps more conscious now of having to do without it than anyone has been since some fifth-century Sophists first doubted it. But when all that has been said, it is true that Greek ethical thought, in many of its basic structures and, above all, in its inability to separate questions of how one should relate to others and to society from questions of what life it is worth one's leading and of what one basically wants, represents one of the very few sets of ideas which can help now to put moral thought into honest touch with reality.

In these last remarks I have mentioned 'Greek ethical thought', and that principally refers, of course, to the philosophical ideas of Socrates, Plato, and Aristotle which, very sketchily, I have discussed. But there is a question which I should like to raise in closing, which reaches behind them, and behind some other aspects of Greek philosophy which have been touched on in this chapter.

I have mentioned already Socrates' saying, that the good man cannot be harmed: it expresses an ideal of rational self-sufficiency, of freedom from the damage of contingency. There is an analogy, not merely superficial, between this type of assertion of rationality, and that cognitive demand for the elimination of luck, which appeared in the discussion of knowledge, certainty, and scepticism. The ideal of self-control, always high among Greek aspirations, turned into the aim that, in both cognition and action, what is of highest value, what matters most, should be entirely under the self's control. In later schools, this theme reappeared in various forms: in the Cynic exaggeration of Socratism, that virtue was sufficient for *eudaimonia* and that the good man really could be happy on the rack; in that hope for a state of *ataraxia* which the Sceptics were not alone in cultivating. Aristotle expressly discussed the question of how far *eudaimonia*, the ultimately desirable state, could be subject to risk, and replied that to a small but ineliminable degree it had to be. This represented, however, not so much any large or perilous aspiration, as rather the entirely sensible thought that it is unreasonable to leave out of account the apparatus of social life within which men live and express themselves, and which is subject to fortune. Very notably, a dimension of life which to us is one of the most significant precisely because of its reaching outside the defended self, friendship, is discussed by Aristotle in a way which now seems bizarre in its determination to reconcile the need for friendship with the aim of self-sufficiency.

A deeper sense of exposure to fortune is expressed elsewhere in Greek literature, above all in tragedy. There the repeated references to the insecurity of happiness get their force from the fact that the characters are displayed as having responsibilities, or pride, or obsessions, or needs, on a scale which lays them open to disaster in corresponding measure, and that they encounter those disasters in full consciousness. A sense of such significances, that what is great is fragile and that what is necessary may be destructive, which is present in the literature of the fifth century and earlier, has disappeared from the ethics of the philosophers, and perhaps altogether from their minds. Nietzsche found Socrates to blame for this, with his excessive distrust of what cannot be discursively explained, his faith in the 'fathomability' of nature, and his 'Alexandrian cheerfulness'.[20] Those remarks belong, in fact, to the first period of Nietzsche's long and ambivalent relations to the figure of Socrates, and it was a period in which Nietzsche thought that the 'metaphysical solace' of tragedy could be understood only through a fundamentally aesthetic attitude to life, an attitude which we have even greater reason to reject than Nietzsche eventually had. But however much he or we may qualify his account of Greek tragedy and Greek thought, what he pointed to is truly there: Greek philosophy, in its sustained pursuit of rational self-sufficiency, does turn its back on kinds of human experience and human necessity of which Greek literature itself offers the purest, if not the richest, expression.

If there are features of the ethical experience of the Greek world which can not only make sense to us now, but make better sense than many things we find nearer to hand, they are not all to be found in its philosophy. Granted the range, the power, the imagination and inventiveness of the Greek foundation of Western philosophy, it is yet more striking that we can take seriously, as we should, Nietzsche's remark: 'Among the greatest characteristics of the Hellenes is their inability to turn the best into reflection.'[21]

---

[20] *The Birth of Tragedy*, particularly sec. 17. On the question of Nietzsche's attitudes to Socrates, see Werner J. Dannhauser, *Nietzsche's View of Socrates* (Ithaca N.Y., 1974).

[21] In his lectures on Greek philosophy: *Gesammelte Werke*, Musarion ed. (Munich, 1920–9), ii. 364–9. Quoted by Dannhauser, p. 109.

Further Reading

This is a list of some translations of the Greek writers themselves, and a few books about them; it does not try to include any of the innumerable works about their later influence.

Details of works marked '(N)' will be found in the notes.

The Presocratics and Socrates

Guthrie, vols. i–iii (N) provides much useful information, but is not very searching in philosophical interpretation. All *translations* of the Presocratics involve vexed questions of interpretation: those offered by G. S. Kirk and J. E. Raven in *The Presocratic Philosophers* (Cambridge, 1957), with commentary, are no exception. Less ambitious is *Ancilla to the Presocratic Philosophers* by Kathleen Freeman (Oxford, 1948).

Hussey (N) is interesting and firmly argued. Allen and Furley (N), and its companion volume Furley and Allen (London, 1970), are useful collections of essays, as is Mourelatos (N). A similar collection on Socrates is edited by G. Vlastos, *The Philosophy of Socrates* (New York, 1971).

Plato

A *complete translation*, by various hands, is offered in one volume edited by E. Hamilton and H. Cairns (New York, 1961); some of the translations come from the well-known complete translation by Benjamin Jowett (4th edn., revised by D. J. Allan and others, 4 vols, Oxford, 1953).

There are many general accounts of Plato's philosophy, but most suffer from outdated assumptions, and some are very fanciful. *An Examination of Plato's Doctrines* by I. M. Crombie (2 vols., London, 1962, 1963) offers a sober study of the arguments.

A useful series of new commentaries on important dialogues, with translation, is offered by the Clarendon Plato Series (Oxford), general editor M. J. Woods.

A collection of essays parallel to that on Socrates is edited by G. Vlastos (2 vols., New York, 1970).

Aristotle

The standard *translation* is the Oxford Version, in 11 vols., general editor W. D. Ross; extensive selections from this are in *The Basic Works of Aristotle* (New York, 1941). A useful series of commentaries with translation is in the Clarendon Aristotle Series (Oxford), general editor J. L. Ackrill.

General works on Aristotle include: W. D. Ross, *Aristotle* (London, 1923); D. J. Allan, *The Philosophy of Aristotle* (Oxford, 1952); G. E. R. Lloyd, *Aristotle: the Growth and Structure of his Thought* (Cambridge, 1968).

Useful collections of essays include one by J. M. E. Moravcsik (New York, 1967); and *Articles on Aristotle*, ed. J. Barnes, M. Schofield, and R. Sorabji (2 vols. published so far, London, 1975, 1977).

Other

On *scepticism*, see Stough (N), and for a more general survey of post-Aristotelian philosophy, A. A. Long, *Hellenistic Philosophy* (London, 1974). The works of *Sextus Empiricus* are translated (facing the Greek text) by R. G. Bury in the Loeb Classical Library (4 vols., London, 1933). An important collection of articles is *Doubt and Dogmatism: Studies in Hellenistic Epistemology*, ed. M. Schofield, M. Burnyeat, and J. Barnes (Oxford, 1980).

The everyday moral ideas which underlie, and differ from, the ethical philosophies of Socrates, Plato, and Aristotle are valuably considered in K. J. Dover, *Greek Popular Morality in the time of Plato and Aristotle* (Oxford, 1974).

Finally, in the context of this chapter it is specially important to mention E. R. Dodds' great book, *The Greeks and the Irrational* (Berkeley and Los Angeles, 1951).

SCIENCE AND MATHEMATICS

G. E. R. LLOYD

In many areas of scientific enquiry it is only comparatively recently that practising scientists have not needed to turn to the Greeks, whether for part of their basic scientific education or as a source of ideas. From the revival of learning in the twelfth century right down, in some cases, to the nineteenth, first one and then another strand of Greek scientific thought, as it was understood by each successive generation, was a focus of scientific debate. From the twelfth to the fifteenth century Aristotle was the Philosopher—and that meant also the Natural Scientist—*par excellence*. Although the notion that Aristotelianism remained largely unchallenged throughout that period is a myth of nineteenth-century historians of science, it is true that initially critics of Aristotelian positions generally worked within the framework of ideas and problems provided by Aristotle. Much of the work of such thirteenth-century writers as Albertus Magnus takes the form of commentaries on Aristotle's treatises, and so too does Oresme's most important cosmological work, his *Livre du Ciel et du Monde* (1377). Yet a close reading of Aristotle himself was enough to reveal something of the heterogeneity of Greek cosmology, and the phenomenon of Greek authorities being cited on both sides of scientific controversies is a recurrent one at least from the fourteenth century.

When the battle between the Ancients and the Moderns was joined in earnest, many of those who were most vociferous in advocating a break with the past were themselves steeped in it. Even that great anti-Aristotelian polemicist and propagandist for the conception of the practical utility of science, Francis Bacon, represented some of the pre-Platonic philosophers as having approximated to the true (that is, his own) method of study of natural science. When, beginning in the sixteenth century, Aristotelian physics and cosmology came to be not merely criticized in detail, but rejected as a whole, this was done in part in the name of a revival of Platonism, conceived as a tradition that embraced such diverse thinkers as Pythagoras on the one hand and Archimedes on the other. Later still, Greek ideas remained influential in biology and medicine long after they had been largely superseded in astronomy and physics. There was a revival of interest in Greek biological theories in the debates on generation that were renewed in the seventeenth century; the Hippocratic Corpus and Galen continued to figure prominently in medical education well into the eighteenth; and Aristotle's descriptive zoology continued to be studied profitably right down to the nineteenth.

In dealing with the history of scientific ideas, especially, we cannot afford to ignore that ideas as such have no history. We may find theories taken up, even equivalent propositions repeated word for word, but their significance depends, on each occasion, upon the whole context of discussion as it presented itself to the ancient or modern author concerned. Obviously the pagan debate for and against heliocentricity was set in a totally different framework from that which obtained in the sixteenth and seventeenth centuries, not least because the Church's teaching was then felt to be implicated. Throughout we are dealing with what passed for Greek science in each successive age. As one ancient author after another was rediscovered, he was reinterpreted, and in many cases what he came to stand for owed more to the interpreters than to the ancient writer himself. The doctrines associated with the names of Plato and Aristotle, especially, are sometimes the end-products of intricate intellectual developments with a barely recognizable origin in Plato and Aristotle themselves, so that at points we have the impression of studying not so much the history of ideas that originated in the ancient world, as their mythology.

But apart from the problems that are common to any enquiry concerning the transmission of ideas, the study of the influences of Greek science faces its own particular difficulties. In many cases there is a severe shortage of evidence, and in many others the evidence has yet to be subjected to a thorough critical examination.

Already, so far as Greek science itself is concerned, the fragmentary nature of our information for many important writers is an embarrassment. Much work of the highest quality is lost, and the patterns of those losses are revealing. It is clearly not the case that what survived represented what was judged the finest scientific work at any given period in antiquity, even according to the very varying views that were taken at different times of what the finest was. Time and again a major synthesizing treatise eclipsed earlier work, including work of far greater originality. The success of Euclid's *Elements*—in large part due to its systematic nature—led to the loss of most pre-Euclidean mathematics, which now has to be reconstructed mainly from accounts in late commentaries on Euclid. The comprehensive astronomical and biological syntheses of Ptolemy and Galen in the second century A.D. ousted the important Hellenistic contributions to those fields. Both Ptolemy and Galen are in parts abstruse and technical, and in late antiquity we can trace a growing disinclination to study, let alone to 'edit', any difficult or complex scientific work. While several elementary introductions to mathematics survived, advanced mathematics was far more vulnerable. The influential *Mathematical Collection* of Pappus in the early fourth century A.D. contains extensive reports of Archimedes and Apollonius, but we would have little of either mathematician in the original but for the revival of interest in them led by their sixth-century editor Eutocius of Ascalon. We have a rule of the survival of the fittest, but 'the fittest' so often meant not what was most advanced, but what was easiest to understand, the popular not the specialized work. Again, although we should not exaggerate the extent to which there was a scientific orthodoxy in the ancient world, those who argued against such commonly accepted theses as the purposiveness of nature are much less well represented in what is extant than those who maintained the usual view—that is, in many cases, the view that had the backing of Plato or Aristotle or both. The meagre remains of the earliest ancient atomists illustrate this; and so too may the fact that our knowledge of Aristarchus' heliocentric theory comes not from his own exposition but from the reports of Archimedes and others.

Moreover, if the picture we have of Greek science itself is necessarily fragmentary and in parts conjectural, so too is that of its influences. Here too much has been lost, and the critical appraisal of the existing material has, in many cases, only just begun. Much fundamental work has, to be sure, been done on such topics as the manuscript tradition of ancient texts and the production of translations, both Latin and vernacular, from the original Greek or from intermediate, usually Arabic, versions. Thus the main phases of the recovery of the works of Archimedes have been established, beginning with the translations of Gerard of Cremona and others in the twelfth century, through those of Moerbeke in 1269 and of James of Cremona in about 1450. It was Moerbeke's and James's versions that formed the basis of several of the important and influential editions of the sixteenth century, by which time, thanks to the printing press, books could reach a much wider audience far more rapidly than had been possible hitherto.

Yet even when we have fairly firm evidence concerning the availability of the relevant texts and translations, the problems of evaluating influences are formidable. The first obvious point is that the extent to which ancient authorities are named varies both between periods and between individuals at the same period, and can be a misleading index to the degree to which ancient authors were actually studied. The lists of ancient authorities that are common not only in medieval but also in some Renaissance writers may, as is well known, signify little. Conversely, although the high value set on originality is generally thought of as a modern phenomenon, it is far from unknown for medieval and Renaissance scientists to suppress mention of ancient writers whose ideas they used.

Secondly a distinction must be observed between what was known and what was common knowledge, between the ancient authors studied by exceptional individuals and those whose ideas won general or even popular acceptance. The study of such problems as the actual use of remedies derived from ancient pharmacological writers such as Dioscorides is still, in most cases, in its infancy. Even if we confine ourselves (as we must here) to the influences of ideas, rather than of practices, the concentration of scholarly attention on those medieval and Renaissance works that happen to have been particularly influential themselves can be a distorting factor. What are now represented as decisive turning-points in the advance of science were seldom recognized as such at the time, as the history of the unfavourable reception of Copernicanism shows. It is all too easy to assume that after Galileo's work in kinetics, Aristotle's ideas in that field must have soon lapsed into oblivion. Yet this was certainly not the case. In his *Two Treatises*, written in 1644 and often reprinted, Kenelm Digby defends Aristotle's positions on motion through the void and on the role of the medium in sustaining the motion of projectiles against Galileo's arguments, and it is clear from the conclusion of his first treatise that Digby's worry is that he will seem insufficiently orthodox to contemporary Aristotelians. Again, while Galileo and Kepler were looking back to Archimedes and Plato, other seventeenth-century writers who were prominent at the time, such as Robert Fludd, drew ideas from a range of ancient texts that included Iamblichus, Porphyry, and, especially, the Hermetic writings.

Given both the vastness of our subject, and the fact that detailed analyses of many aspects of it have yet to be undertaken, only the broadest account can be attempted here, and this, in many respects, only a provisional one. We must begin with points of terminology that relate to substantial questions concerning the way the Greeks viewed the enquiries they engaged in. Although most of our own terms for the various branches of science have Greek origins, or at least Greek etymologies, Greek ideas concerning the boundaries between different intellectual disciplines differ in important ways from our own. Thus the Greek terms from which our own 'mathematics' and 'physics' come are both very general ones. The term *ta mathemata*, derived from *manthanein*, which simply means to learn, is applied not only to what we should call mathematical studies, but also generally to any branch of learning. In the fourth century B.C. we find it used by Plato, for instance, of dialectic as well as of arithmetic (or more strictly calculation, *logistike*), plane and solid geometry, and astronomy. Greek *physike* too was far wider than our 'physics', as it covered the whole of the enquiry into nature, and differing views were taken in the ancient world on the relations between it and *mathematike*. Thus, in Aristotle, who was the first to attempt systematic distinctions between different domains of enquiry, *mathematike* differs from *physike* in that, although physical bodies contain volumes, surfaces, lines, and points (which are the subject-matter of *mathematike*), the mathematician studies them in abstraction from physical bodies. Aristotle calls optics, harmonics, and astronomy 'the more physical of the *mathemata*', in that optics, for example, studies mathematical lines *qua* physical. *Physike* itself is the study of natural objects as such, nature being defined in terms of a capacity for movement and change. The work we know as his *Physics* contains a general discussion of causes and deals with time, place, the continuum, and infinity as well as with motion in general. He considers the ultimate constituents of matter, their compounds and modes of mixture, roughly the areas now covered by our 'physics' and 'chemistry', in such works as *On Generation and Corruption* and *On the Heavens*. Nor is there a separate term in Aristotle or any other ancient writer to correspond to our 'biology'. Aristotle's zoological treatises, for example the *Enquiry concerning Animals* and *On the Generation of Animals*, belong, in his view, to *physike*.

The Greeks had no term that precisely corresponds to our 'science' as such. The subject-matter of the natural sciences is covered by the term *peri physeos historia*, the enquiry concerning nature. In other contexts the Greek term often translated 'science' is *episteme*, literally 'knowledge'. For most ancient writers the enquiry concerning nature formed part of *philosophia*, philosophy, the love of wisdom, and most ancient scientists thought of themselves first and foremost as philosophers. They saw their enquiries as contributing to the good life, either for negative reasons, because, as the Stoics and Epicureans argued, some understanding of nature is necessary to achieve peace of mind and freedom from superstitious fears, or for positive ones, because of the value attached to understanding for its own sake. Both Plato and Aristotle (and many other ancient authors) considered wisdom the highest goal for man, although they differed on what wisdom comprised and on the extent to which it involved the detailed study of nature. But others who engaged in what we should term scientific investigations saw themselves not as philosophers but as *mathematikoi*, or as doctors, or as 'architects' or engineers. Thus much of the important work in the biological sciences was done by medical practitioners, and while some of these tended to minimize the difference between the true physician and the philosopher (as Galen did when he wrote a treatise on the theme that 'the best doctor is also a philosopher'), others emphasized the contrast between the speculative nature of the philosophers' theories and what they represented as the tried and tested skills of the doctors.

The economic, social, and ideological framework of ancient science differs profoundly from the modern situation: there was, indeed, no place in ancient society for science or the scientist as such. Although there were foundations, such as

Aristotle's Lyceum and the Museum at Alexandria, where programmes of research were planned and undertaken on a joint basis, most ancient scientists worked in isolation and without support from either individual patrons or institutions. To be sure, such points also apply, in varying degrees, to the Middle Ages and early Renaissance. But the rapid growth of science in the last two hundred years has reflected a transformation in beliefs concerning its role, and in particular the increasing importance of the idea that science holds the key to material progress. Whilst the notion of applying theoretical knowledge to practical purposes was certainly not unknown in antiquity, it was less prominent than the conception that knowledge is an end in itself, and the idea of material progress was of negligible importance. Yet the influence of some ancient scientific ideas persisted long after major changes had occurred in some of the aims or expectations with which scientific work was conducted.

If, for convenience of exposition, we discuss first mathematics, then physics and cosmology, and finally the life sciences, under those broad heads, it must therefore not be assumed that these modern categories correspond precisely to ancient ones. Rather each writer's work must be judged first and foremost in relation to his own conception of the nature of the enquiry he was engaged on.

When in his private correspondence Galileo remarks that he assumes his readers to be well grounded in geometry, he puts it that he expects them to have made a thorough study of Euclid, Archimedes, Apollonius, and Ptolemy. The first three are indeed the outstanding names in what has survived of Greek mathematics. The nature of their several contributions is, however, rather different. Euclid's chief work, the *Elements*, composed *c.* 300 B.C., represents a synthesis of earlier geometry, the work of a series of mathematicians some of whom, such as Eudoxus of Cnidos, a contemporary and associate of Plato, were evidently more original than Euclid himself. As already noted, the very success of the *Elements* as a systematization of elementary geometry ensured that earlier works did not survive, and many aspects of pre-Euclidean mathematics and of its relations with philosophy remain obscure. We can, however, reconstruct some of its features from the information in Plato, Aristotle, and later writers, especially the ancient commentators on the *Elements* itself.

What distinguishes Greek from Egyptian or Babylonian mathematics is, above all, the use of rigorous demonstration. Our evidence for pre-Euclidean geometry makes it clear first that a body of demonstrations was built up in the fifth and fourth centuries and secondly that some progress was made towards their systematization. Although in many cases, as for example in that of the theorem named after Pythagoras, it is not certain which of several possible methods was the one by which the theorem was first proved or who was responsible, in other instances some specific information is available on such points. Thus we know from Archimedes that the theorems setting out the relations between the volumes of the cone and the cylinder and those of the prism and the pyramid were discovered by Democritus but first demonstrated by Eudoxus. It is clear that elsewhere Eudoxus used, and he may indeed have invented, the method of exhaustion, based on the proposition we find stated in Euclid, 10.1 and one of the most powerful techniques used in Greek mathematics. Eudoxus was also responsible for the general theory of proportions in Euclid, Book 5, usually recognized as one of the finest parts of the *Elements* and the subject of frequent commentaries both in antiquity and subsequently. Whilst an interest in proportion goes back to the very beginnings of Greek mathematics, the great merit of Eudoxus' theory is that it applies to incommensurable as well as to commensurable magnitudes.

Euclid's was certainly not the first attempt to compose a book of *Elements*. Aristotle tells us how the term 'elements' itself was used in fourth-century mathematics when he indicates that the elements are the primary propositions from which other propositions may be derived. Proclus, the most important of the ancient commentators on Euclid, reports that the first person to compose a book of *Elements* was Hippocrates of Chios (late fifth century) and that such men as Archytas and Theaetetus (in the fourth century) 'increased the number of theorems and progressed towards a more scientific arrangement of them'. Describing Euclid's relationship to this earlier work, Proclus says that he 'brought together the elements, collecting many of Eudoxus' theorems, perfecting many of those of Theaetetus and providing with incontrovertible demonstration propositions that had been proved less rigorously by his predecessors'. Not many of the theorems and demonstrations in the *Elements* are likely to have been Euclid's own discoveries. His own chief contribution relates, rather, to the systematic ordering of the material. This had no doubt been the aim of earlier writers of *Elements* also, but it was one that was achieved to a quite remarkable degree in Euclid's book. Beginning with certain fundamental assumptions, and proceeding to the demonstration of propositions and to the resolution of problems of construction in increasingly complex cases in orderly sequence, the whole is a highly methodical and coherent presentation of a considerable body of theorems.

The immediate, and the long-term, impact of the *Elements* was twofold. First it served as a textbook of elementary geometry, and has justly been called the most successful textbook ever written. Right down to the nineteenth century, school textbooks of geometry followed Euclid's exposition, and in many cases his proofs, closely.

Secondly, the *Elements* was important as a model of method. More than any earlier Greek scientific work, it exemplified the notion of an axiomatic, deductive system. While the *use* of demonstration was, we said, characteristic of Greek mathematics, our main evidence concerning the development of the *concept* of proof comes from the philosophers. Both Plato and more especially Aristotle had investigated the nature and conditions of proof. In particular Aristotle insisted (against Plato) that not all true propositions can be demonstrated and that the starting-points of demonstrations are principles that are themselves indemonstrable but known to be true, and he distinguished three sorts of such principles, namely, definitions, axioms, and hypotheses. Euclid too distinguishes three types of first principles, two of which correspond closely to Aristotle's, that is, definitions and 'common opinions' (equivalent to Aristotle's axioms: one of Aristotle's examples of an axiom reappears in Euclid as the third of his common opinions, namely, 'if equals be subtracted from equals, equals remain'). His third kind of first principle, the 'postulates', differ from Aristotle's hypotheses, which were distinguished from definitions as the assumptions of the existence (or non-existence) of the objects defined. The first three of Euclid's five postulates are assumptions concerning the possibility of carrying out certain geometrical constructions (for example, 'to draw a straight line from any point to any point') and the last two assume certain truths concerning geometrical constructions, namely, that all right angles are equal, and that non-parallel straight lines meet at a point. Thus, where the common opinions are self-evident principles that apply to the whole of mathematics, the postulates are the fundamental geometrical assumptions underlying Euclid's geometry.

Euclid's general conceptions concerning the form and foundations of an axiomatic system have obvious affinities with those that Aristotle formulated in the context of his study of reasoning in general, although we cannot be sure how far these similarities are due to direct influence, or how far Euclid was merely following and developing ideas that were already current among earlier mathematicians. Yet if Aristotle, especially, provided later writers with a clear account of the structure of an axiomatic system, it was Euclid who presented the chief early example of that conception applied in practice in the organization of a body of mathematical knowledge. Whether we turn to such ancient works as Aristarchus' treatise *On the Sizes and Distances of the Sun and Moon*, Archimedes' *On the Sphere and Cylinder* or *On the Equilibrium of Planes*, or Ptolemy's *Optics*, or again, among medieval and Renaissance works, to Jordanus' *De Ratione Ponderis* (*c.* 1250), Bradwardine's *Geometria Speculativa* (fourteenth century), Tartaglia's *Nova Scientia* (1537), or indeed to the *Principia* (1687) of Newton himself, among many other examples, the systematic presentation first of the postulates and (where necessary) definitions, then of the theorems to be demonstrated, follows an example originally set by Euclid.

In several of the particular definitions, common opinions, and postulates that he adopted, Euclid took a stand on what were already controversial issues. Thus his definitions of unit (that by virtue of which each of the things that exist is said to be one) and of number (a set composed of units) in Book 7 show that one was not treated as a number. The difference between Euclid and some post-Euclidean mathematics here is not merely one of convention. In Euclid, the one is by implication itself indivisible: in the arithmetic of Book 7 fractions are dealt with as ratios or proportions between numbers. To understand the background to this view, we must again turn to philosophy, to the problems concerning the one and the many raised by Parmenides and Zeno of Elea in the fifth century. Euclid, it seems, may have been influenced by arguments of the type reported by Plato when he says that certain mathematicians refused to allow the one to be divided, 'lest it should appear to be not one, but many parts'. If the one is allowed to be divisible, it becomes at the same time many: to avoid this apparent contradiction, it must be defined as indivisible, and the number series is, accordingly, viewed as constituted by indivisible units rather than as an infinitely divisible continuum.

The background to the famous fifth postulate, about parallel lines, is more complex. A passage in Aristotle shows that fourth-century mathematical theory on the topic of parallels was thought open to the charge of circularity, for he remarks that mathematicians who 'think they can construct parallels unconsciously assume such things as cannot be demonstrated if parallels do not exist'. Euclid's position is quite different, in that, having defined 'parallel' in Definition 23 of Book 1, he adopts as a postulate the proposition that non-parallel straight lines meet at a point. Already in antiquity several writers, including Ptolemy and Proclus, attempted to prove this postulate, and it was an attack on this problem that eventually led to the development of non-Euclidean geometries such as those of Lobachevsky and Riemann in the nineteenth century. Whilst there is no evidence that Euclid or any other Greek geometer envisaged the possibility of such geometries, it should be noted that Euclid's *Elements* are not merely an axiomatic, but also an explicitly hypothetical, system, in this sense, at least, that it was one based on postulates and common opinions which include propositions that he must have known to have been questioned or denied by other Greek thinkers. Moreover, whilst in late antiquity and again in the Renaissance it was a stock criticism of Euclid that he had not *proved* the parallel postulate, more recently—thanks to the exploration of non-Euclidean geometries—the wisdom of his treating it as a *postulate*, in the context of the geometry that he constructed on its basis, has been acknowledged.

Greek pure mathematics after Euclid comprises two original geniuses of the highest order, Archimedes and Apollonius, together with a galaxy of lesser talents, unevenly represented in our sources, such as Hipparchus, Hero, Menelaus, Ptolemy, Diophantus, Pappus, and Proclus. Archimedes' extant mathematical treatises include both arithmetical works (such as the *Sand-Reckoner*, which sets out, among other things, a notation to express numbers up to the number we should represent as $10^{8 \cdot 10^{16}}$), and geometrical ones, ranging from the comparatively elementary *On the Measurement of the Circle* to the more advanced treatises such as *On Spirals* and *On the Quadrature of the Parabola*. As we have remarked, the style of presentation in these works is, in the main, Euclidean. Archimedes begins with a statement of the relevant assumptions and proceeds to the orderly demonstration of a sequence of theorems, although, unlike Euclid and thanks largely to his work, Archimedes can take the proof of many elementary theorems in geometry for granted.

His methods of argument, too, follow and build on those of Euclid, both in the general use of *reductio ad absurdum* (which assumes the contradictory of the proposition to be proved and shows that this leads to a contradiction) and in that of the method of exhaustion in particular. Whereas Euclid had confined his use, in determining an area for example, to inscribing successively larger regular polygons, Archimedes used both inscribed and circumscribed figures, compressing them, as it were, on the curved figure to be measured. The principle, however, is the same: the figure whose area is to be found can be 'exhausted' in the sense that the difference between it and the inscribed, or circumscribed, figure can be made as small as desired. A more strikingly original aspect of Archimedes' methods is the application of mechanical concepts, such as the law of the lever, to geometrical problems. Thus by thinking of a plane figure as composed of a set of parallel lines indefinitely close together, and then thinking of these lines as *balanced* by corresponding lines of the same magnitude in a figure of known area, he finds the desired area in terms of the known one. Yet with a characteristic Greek insistence on rigour, he remarks in his *Method* that this is not a method of proof (no doubt because it depends on infinitesimals), only one of discovery, and he gives a strict geometrical demonstration, using *reductio* and the method of exhaustion, of the theorems concerning the area of a segment of a parabola that he had discovered by mechanical methods. Although he found the theorem for the area by these methods, he proved it by showing that the area is neither greater, nor less, than $\frac{4}{3}$ of the triangle with the same base and height.

In two respects Archimedes' procedures have been hailed as anticipating the integral calculus, first in his use of infinitesimals in the *Method* (where areas and volumes are treated as composed of their line and plane elements respectively), and secondly in certain applications of exhaustion in determining areas or volumes. Thus in *On the Quadrature of the Parabola* the theorem for the area of a parabolic segment is obtained by taking the sum of an infinite series, that is, of a series of n terms plus a remainder than can be made as small as desired. Strictly speaking, no Greek mathematician used the integral calculus, since this depends on the rigorous definition of the concept of a limit of an infinite series, an idea foreign to Greek mathematics.[1] Yet Archimedes' procedures, while not based on a general theory of integrability, are *practically* equivalent to integration, in that they yield, case by case, results that would now be obtained by that process. The *Method* was not known until the beginning of this century, but his other geometrical treatises exercised a great, and increasing, influence from the Middle Ages right down to the seventeenth century, with the focus of attention gradually shifting from the elementary works (*On the Measurement of the Circle* was already much studied in the thirteenth century) to the more advanced ones. Galileo, for instance, who as a student made detailed notes on *On the Sphere and Cylinder*, made frequent use of such works as *On Spirals* and *On the Quadrature of the Parabola*, and among those who were responsible for important mathematical developments leading up to the invention of the calculus by Newton and Leibniz, both Cavalieri and Torricelli took the starting-point for their studies of the geometry of indivisibles from Archimedes.

The work of Archimedes and others on conic sections was carried further by Apollonius of Perge (*c.* 210 B.C.), whose *Conics*, though less well known than the geometrical treatises of Archimedes, was recognized in the Renaissance as one of the masterpieces of Greek mathematics. The ellipse, hyperbola, and parabola, which had originally been thought of as sections of acute-, obtuse-, and right-angled cones respectively, were known to be generable from a single cone before Apollonius, but he was responsible for their standard Greek names, derived from the application of areas, and in the *Conics* gave a detailed and in many respects definitive analysis of

---

[1] Indeed the method of exhaustion, in which the difference between two magnitudes is made as small as desired, is, in general, a way of *avoiding* integration.

their properties. Of the eight original books, only the first four survive in Greek, the next three in an Arabic version, whilst the eighth is lost. Commandino's Latin translation of Books 1–4 in 1566 was particularly influential. Books 5–7 were meanwhile mainly known from the summary in Pappus' *Mathematical Collection*: several writers, including for example Santini in correspondence with Galileo in 1614, lament the lack of a Latin version of these books, though one was eventually done in 1661. The importance of Apollonius in the seventeenth century can be judged from the fact that both Vieta and Fermat attempted reconstructions of lost works, Vieta of the *Tangencies* (in his *Apollonius Gallus*, 1600) and Fermat of the *Plane Loci*. Later he was still studied by Newton and by Edmund Halley (who produced the first Greek edition in 1710), and although Descartes' algebraization of the geometry of curves—which facilitated, among other things, the attack on curves of third and higher degrees—led to a decline in interest in Apollonius, this was revived by nineteenth-century mathematicians and commentators on his work such as Poncelet and Zeuthen.

Although it was mainly through Archimedes and Apollonius that Greek mathematics won the reputation it had in the fifteenth to seventeenth centuries, other work too was known and studied. Thus the history of Greek trigonometry (included in 'sphaeric') goes back at least as far as Hipparchus in the second century B.C. (though his mathematical works have not survived) and continues with Menelaus (whose *Sphaerics*, composed at the end of the first century A.D., is extant in an Arabic version), but it was largely known from either Ptolemy's *Syntaxis* or the late Greek commentators. As so often, there is a difference in approach in that the Greeks worked not with sines, cosines, etc., but with chords and arcs, but the techniques they developed for handling these had important practical applications in astronomy. Finally some knowledge of one of our chief sources for Greek algebra, the *Arithmetic* of Diophantus (mid-third century A.D.), can be traced in the West from the fifteenth century. His analysis of equations provides the chief example of the introduction of symbolism into Greek mathematics: in general the Greeks made more use of symbols in logic than in mathematics. In the sixteenth century Simon Stevin made a Latin paraphrase of the first four books of Diophantus, which forms a continuation of his own *Arithmetic*, and he claimed Diophantus as support for his own idea of number as a continuous quantity.

Whilst pure mathematics is acknowledged as an area of outstanding Greek achievement, another lies in the application of mathematics to physical problems, where again, as in pure mathematics, rigorous demonstration was the goal. There are no less than five main fields in which such applications were attempted at various periods in antiquity, namely acoustics, optics, geography, statics, and astronomy. The last-named provides our most important single case-study, but before we turn to it, some comments are necessary on our other examples.

The three points that demand particular notice are: (1) the richness of the original Greek material, (2) the evidence of methodological controversy within several of these fields, and (3) the extent of Greek influence on later writers. Thus the history of acoustics goes back to early Pythagorean investigations of the ratios of the simple harmonies, and apart from several introductory treatises, such as the *Sectio Canonis* ascribed to Euclid, and the important collections of material in the *Elements of Harmonics* of Aristoxenus and Boethius' *De Institutione Musica*, we have major treatises in Ptolemy's *Harmonics* and Porphyry's commentary on that work. In optics and catoptrics (the theory of mirrors), the extant sources are, if anything, even richer: apart from numerous isolated passages in other writers, we have several specialized treatises by, among others, Euclid, Hero of Alexandria, Ptolemy, and Theon of Alexandria. Mathematical, as opposed to descriptive, geography begins with the debate on the shape of the earth in the pre-Platonic period, includes the series of attempts, starting with that recorded by Aristotle, to determine the size of the earth, and is later represented, for example, by Ptolemy's *Geography* which, drawing heavily on such earlier writers as Eratosthenes and Hipparchus, begins with a systematic account of such topics as the division of the earth by parallels of latitude and meridians of longitude and the principles of map-making. Finally, although certain areas of mechanics, especially kinetics, may be cited as examples where the Greeks failed to advance to a quantitative, mathematical analysis of the phenomena, in others, such as statics and hydrostatics, they achieved notable successes in doing so. Elementary statics begins with the treatise *On Mechanics* attributed to Aristotle but probably by one of his pupils, and is represented not only by one of Archimedes' masterpieces, *On the Equilibrium of Planes* (which, in contrast to the kinetic approach in *On Mechanics*, gives a purely geometrical demonstration of the law of the lever), but also by later works by Hero and Pappus; and in hydrostatics, another of Archimedes' works, *On Floating Bodies*, is a further superb example of the rigorous geometrical demonstration of a set of theorems relating to complex physical phenomena.

In several cases the ancient texts provide direct or indirect evidence of a fundamental methodological dispute between empiricists and rationalists on the relation between theory and observation. Thus in acoustics Plato makes Socrates insist, in a well-known passage in the *Republic*, that, contrary to what some of his predecessors and contemporaries had held, the study is one of numerical relations. Socrates speaks contemptuously of those who 'measure the harmonies and sounds they hear against one another' and who 'look for numbers in these heard harmonies', instead, that is, of studying the ratios in themselves. These contrasting methodologies are referred to again in, for example, Aristoxenus' and Ptolemy's *Harmonics*, Aristoxenus putting it that one group of his predecessors 'rejected the senses as inaccurate' and 'fabricated rational principles', while he himself maintained that 'for the student of musical science accuracy of sense-perception is a fundamental requirement', whereas Ptolemy in turn criticized the Aristoxeneans for a misplaced empirical bias.

In general, ancient theorists were sharply divided into two camps, those who insisted that harmonics, optics, and so on are the study of ideal, mathematical relations to which the phenomena are necessarily unreliable guides, and their opponents, who maintained the priority of the sensible data and saw the mathematically expressible laws merely as abstractions from them. Both sides could and did claim to 'save the phenomena', but that slogan masks the different views taken on the status and validity of those phenomena. A striking instance of the greater trust in mathematically determinable relations than in empirical data is provided by Ptolemy's *Optics*. His treatise (extant only in a Latin translation of an Arabic version) is remarkable, among other things, for the experiments it describes both to confirm the elementary principles of reflection and to investigate refraction in different media. Yet while there is no reason to doubt that Ptolemy conducted the investigations he records, it is clear that in stating his results he has adjusted them to tally with the general law of refraction which he assumes, but does not state, namely, $r = ai - bi^2$, where r is the angle of refraction, i is the angle of incidence, and a and b are constants that depend on the specific media between which refraction occurs.[2]

The impact of the works we have mentioned on medieval and Renaissance science is a complex one, but each of these areas of Greek science had an important, and in some cases a long-lasting influence. This applies even to what might appear to be some of their least promising aspects. For example, Kepler adapted to a heliocentric system the ancient idea that the intervals between the planets may be explained in terms of musical intervals—a doctrine that is found in, for instance, Ptolemy's *Harmonics*, to which Kepler devoted a critical appendix in his own *Harmonice Mundi*.

As is clear from the extant manuscripts, a considerable body of Greek work in optics, statics, and so on was available, though not necessarily widely known, either in the original or in Latin versions, from the eleventh century. Sometimes ancient texts were directly imitated. Some medieval treatises, especially in statics or 'the science of weights', not only followed ancient models closely, but actually purported to be by an ancient author such as Euclid or Archimedes, and in some cases the question of whether or not what we have in an eleventh- or twelfth-century manuscript is an authentic Greek work is still a matter of dispute. More often, we are dealing not with imitations so much as with the extensive assimilation of ancient ideas. This is the case, for instance, with the great series of medieval treatises on optics, dealing with the principles of reflection, the explanation of the rainbow, and many other topics, by such men as Grosseteste in the twelfth century, Roger Bacon, Pecham, Witelo, and Theodoric of Fribourg in the thirteenth, all of whom drew heavily on Greek work either directly or indirectly through such Arabic writers

[2] This is more accurate than the assumption that i/r is a constant, but less so than the modern sine law, according to which the ratio of the sines of the angles of incidence and refraction is a constant for refraction between any two media, which stems from the work of Snell and others in the seventeenth century.

as Alhazen. Thus Grosseteste, Bacon, and Pecham all cite the *Catoptrics* of pseudo-Euclid (now thought to be a compilation by Theon of Alexandria) under the title *De Speculis*, and Ptolemy's *Optics* is quoted at some length by Bacon, while Ptolemy's tables of refraction are reproduced, with additions but without acknowledgement, in Witelo's *Perspectiva*. Some parts of medieval work in kinematics and dynamics owe less to Greek ideas;[3] yet here too an initial stimulus was provided by passages in Aristotle's *Physics* and *On the Heavens*, where already in the thirteenth century Aquinas dissented from some of Aristotle's positions which in the next century were subjected to an increasingly searching critique, notably by Oresme.

As more original work came to be done in the physical sciences,[4] the influence of some elementary ancient treatises was replaced by that of more advanced works. The importance of Archimedes' statics and hydrostatics in the sixteenth century is an obvious example. In hydrostatics, for instance, there is no real advance, indeed no systematic discussion, between Archimedes himself and Stevin, who explicitly takes Archimedes as his model in his *Elements of Hydrostatics* (1586). In statics and kinetics Aristotle, who was generally assumed to be the author of *On Mechanics*, comes to be attacked increasingly extensively by Tartaglia (in the *Nova Scientia*), by Benedetti (in his *Demonstratio proportionum motuum localium contra Aristotelem et omnes philosophos*, 1554), and by Galileo, although Galileo especially saw himself as an adherent of the 'Platonic' tradition of Archimedes.

The principal general lesson that was to be learned from the ancients in these areas was one that was still of cardinal importance throughout the sixteenth and seventeenth centuries, namely, the pursuit of an ideal, mathematical analysis of physical phenomena. As is clear, above all, from the writings of Galileo, the validity of this approach was as controversial in his day as it had been in antiquity, and to justify his own methods he appeals frequently to the example

[3] None of the ancient proponents of an impetus theory, Strato, Hipparchus, and Philoponus, was available to Buridan, although some of their arguments were known indirectly through the Arabic tradition.

[4] In some, comparatively rare, cases enquiries were initiated in the Middle Ages that owe little or nothing to Greek science, one notable instance being the studies of magnetism that began with Petrus Peregrinus' short treatise (1390) and culminated in Gilbert's *De Magnete* (1600).

of Archimedes. Thus already in his early work, the *De Motu* (*c.* 1590), when defending his own methods against the charge of postulating things that are impossible in nature, he cites the precedent set by the 'superhuman' Archimedes, and late in his life he again invokes Archimedes on this issue in his correspondence with Baliani (1639).

The most important early example of the successful application of mathematical methods to explain complex physical phenomena in the ancient world is astronomy. Speculation concerning such problems as the relative distances and the constitution of the heavenly bodies, the causes of eclipses and so on, goes back to the very beginnings of the enquiry into nature in Miletus in the sixth century B.C. We know from Aristotle's discussion of the position and shape of the earth that already before Plato some of the Pythagoreans had removed the earth from the centre of the universe, which they held to be occupied by an imaginary central fire; but it is apparent that neither they nor any other fifth- or early fourth-century theorists attempted a precise mathematical account of the movements of the heavenly bodies.

The credit for the first such account goes to Eudoxus (whose work in mathematics has already been mentioned). By postulating that each of the planets, sun, and moon is moved by a number of concentric spheres, he was able not only to explain the phenomena that we should say are caused by the daily rotation of the earth about its axis and by the yearly movement of the earth round the sun, but also to give some account of the stations and retrogradations of the planets and of their movement in latitude. The combined movement of the lowest two spheres of each of the planets produces a geometrical figure (the hippopede, or spherical lemniscate, a sort of figure of eight) which, when added to the movement of the second sphere carrying the planet along the ecliptic, can be made to yield a tolerable approximation to the looping motions described by the planets. Although by Eudoxus' time fairly accurate estimates of the periods of revolution of the sun and moon had been made, the extent to which he had access to, or had himself made, detailed observations of the courses of the planets is a matter of conjecture. Yet it appears that he assigned specific values both to the periods of revolution of his various spheres and to the angles of inclination of their axes to one another, and thus formulated a comprehensive, and exact, theory. Its importance at the time would be hard to exaggerate: this was, as we said, the first outstanding example in which some highly complex phenomena were explained by a simple geometrical model, and from this moment astronomy was seen as the prime instance of a demonstrative science. Yet the subsequent influence of Eudoxus' particular theories (as opposed to his method of approach) on later Greek astronomy was short-lived. Although his doctrine of concentric spheres was modified by Callippus to take certain recalcitrant data into account, and this mathematical model was then translated into physical terms by Aristotle, it was subsequently replaced by other geometrical solutions. Eudoxus' own work was lost: it is now known only from Aristotle and some late commentators, and indeed Eudoxus' system was only reconstructed in detail in the nineteenth century.

Third- and second-century B.C. Greek astronomy produced two notable developments, Aristarchus' heliocentric theory and—what was to the ancients far more important—Apollonius' model of epicycles and eccentrics. To understand the background of Aristarchus' theory we must refer to some of his predecessors. As already noted, Aristotle reported a Pythagorean theory which removed the earth from the centre of the universe and treated it as one of the planets. But although not geocentric, this was not a heliocentric theory either, since the sun too circled the invisible central fire. Nor was the theory worked out as a detailed explanation of the movements of the several heavenly bodies. Then Plato, in an obscure passage in the *Timaeus*, spoke of the 'winding round' of the earth, and this was often taken, both in antiquity and subsequently, to imply that the earth rotated on its axis. The issue is still controversial, but it is clear that Plato continued to assume that the circle of the fixed stars moves. The notion of the daily rotation of the earth about its axis is, however, attested in the fourth century B.C., since the Aristotelian commentator Simplicius ascribes to Heraclides of Pontus the view that 'the earth is in the centre and rotates while the heaven is at rest.' But as that testimony makes clear, Heraclides still assumed geocentricity, and the extent to which he, too, attempted a detailed astronomical theory is doubtful.

Thus, although in the sixteenth and seventeenth centuries the heliocentrists often claimed that their view had been anticipated by several ancient astronomers, the combination of daily axial rotation and heliocentricity is not found before Aristarchus himself, a slightly older contemporary of Archimedes, who is indeed our chief source for his theory. The only original work of Aristarchus that is extant is his treatise *On the Sizes and Distances of the Sun and Moon*: this is incidentally interesting for its purely geometrical treatment of those problems—Aristarchus adopts a wildly inaccurate value for the angular diameter of the moon and is evidently not interested in giving actual estimates of distances—but it does not mention the heliocentric theory. Yet despite our not having Aristarchus' own statement, we can be certain from Archimedes' reference to the doctrine that the fundamental hypotheses were (1) that the sun is at the centre, (2) that sun and fixed stars remain unmoved, and (3) that the earth is borne round the sun, to which must be added (4) that the earth rotates daily on its axis. Where there is some room for doubt, however, is on the extent to which Aristarchus gave detailed accounts of the movements of the individual planets on the basis of his general hypothesis.

But whether or not the heliocentric theory was worked out in detail, it was rejected all but unanimously in the ancient world. Indeed we hear of only one other ancient astronomer, Seleucus (second century B.C.), who adopted it. The reasons for its rejection were complex, and outside astronomical circles they included religious considerations, although these played a far smaller role in antiquity than they were to do when the established Christian Church came to reject heliocentricity in the sixteenth century. But so far as the ancient astronomers were concerned, the theory was considered open to three main physical and astronomical objections, each of which was to be discussed again by Copernicus. First there was the argument from the Aristotelian doctrine of natural places, much emphasized, for example, by Ptolemy: since all heavy objects naturally travel towards the centre of the earth, it must be assumed that the centre of the earth is the centre of gravity of all the heavy constituents in the universe. Secondly, it was recognized that if the earth is subject to daily axial rotation, the speed of a point on its surface must be very great, and it was argued that this should have a marked effect on the movements of objects through the air, whereas no such effect was observed. Thirdly, the main astronomical objection was the apparent absence of stellar parallax, that is of any change in the positions of the stars viewed from different points in the earth's orbit. Possible answers to both the second and third objections had certainly occurred to ancient astronomers. To (2) an initial response was that the atmosphere moves with the earth, although Ptolemy for one argued that this counter was inadequate. Against (3) Aristarchus himself had included as one of his postulates that the ratio of the circle of the earth's orbit round the sun to the circle of the fixed stars is that of the centre of a sphere to its surface, that is, that the fixed stars are infinitely distant, when, of course, there would be no stellar parallax. Nevertheless, the cumulative effect of these objections was enough to undermine the theory as a whole.

From the late third century B.C. onwards one other major factor that contributed to the unfavourable reception of the heliocentric theory was the availability of an alternative model that appeared to offer the basis of a comprehensive account of all the movements of the heavenly bodies. This was the twin model of epicycles and eccentrics, developed initially by Apollonius and later applied in both major ancient astronomical syntheses, those of Hipparchus in the second century B.C. and of Ptolemy in the second century A.D. In these models it was assumed both that the earth is at rest in the centre of the universe, and (as in Eudoxus' theory) that the complex apparent paths of the heavenly bodies are to be explained in terms of combinations of simple, uniform, circular motions. Either the heavenly body was imagined as moving in a circle (the 'epicycle') whose centre itself moves along the circumference of a second circle (the 'deferent') whose centre is the earth. Or the heavenly body was assumed to move along the circumference of an eccentric circle, that is, one whose centre does not coincide with the centre of the earth. Moreover it is probable that Apollonius himself recognized, and indeed had demonstrated, the geometrical equivalence of these two models, that is, he had shown that, if the appropriate parameters are taken, then for every eccentric system one can construct an epicyclic one that will yield exactly equivalent results. This being so, the choice between an eccentric and an epicyclic model depended, in any particular case, on which of the two models provided the simpler solution, that is, the one that is mathematically easier to handle.

These models enabled a wide range of astronomical phenomena to be explained quite economically. One simple case is
that of the inequality of the seasons, that is, the inequality of
the sun's apparent movement along the ecliptic. Fairly
accurate estimates of the lengths of the four seasons had
already been made in the fourth century B.C. But if one
assumes that the sun moves round the circumference of a
circle whose centre is some distance from the earth, the
doctrine of uniform circular motion can be retained and the
data accounted for far more simply than on any theory based,
like Eudoxus', on concentric spheres. Here was a case where
the issue of heliocentricity versus geocentricity was irrelevant.
The fact that, both here and in lunar theory, eccentrics or
epicycles had apparently to be postulated, undoubtedly
strengthened the view that these were the models to be
applied also to the planets, where indeed an approximate
solution to the problem posed by the phenomena of stations
and retrogradations can easily be obtained by a simple
epicycle model.

The dominance and success of the models of epicycles and
eccentrics in ancient astronomy should not surprise us. It is
true that adjustments were found to be needed and the
applications of the model became increasingly elaborate. The
extent to which Hipparchus modified the theory is hard to
determine, since his major astronomical treatises (like those of
Apollonius) are lost and his contributions have to be reconstructed mainly from Ptolemy, whose *Syntaxis* eclipsed
almost all earlier work with the exception of some specialized
treatises and general introductions to astronomy. Ptolemy
himself, however, introduced several new conceptions into
astronomical theory, notably the doctrines of 'direction' and
of what later came to be known as the 'equant'. In assessing
Ptolemy's astronomy (often represented as intolerably complex) we must first give full weight to the complexity of some
of the data he set out to explain. This applies particularly to
his lunar theory, where he employs both an equant and the
doctrine of direction and where, of course, his rejection of
heliocentricity is irrelevant. Secondly, in judging the ancient
adherence to the basic models of epicycles and eccentrics, we
should recognize the flexibility that these models provide in
the number of parameters to be chosen, for example, the
angle between the plane of the epicycle and that of the

deferent, or the relation between the dimensions of those circles.[5] Nor, finally, should we forget that Ptolemy himself was well aware that problems, some of them serious, remain unsolved and that, like Aristotle, he was less of a dogmatist than many of those who later claimed to follow him. Although much of the credit belongs to his predecessors, the detailed application of the models of epicycles and eccentrics to astronomical problems in the *Syntaxis* must rank as one of the greatest achievements of Greek science.

The overthrow of the Ptolemaic system has long been taken as the case-history *par excellence* of the 'scientific revolution'. While the attention devoted to this one topic has sometimes been disproportionate, there is, at least, no longer any excuse for over-simplifications of the type implicit in the common use of the epithet 'Copernican' to indicate a total break with a tradition. The *Syntaxis* (or *Almagest* as it became generally known from its Arabic title) began to be translated in the late twelfth century, notably by Gerard of Cremona in 1175. If in the thirteenth Ptolemy came to be acknowledged as the supreme authority in astronomy, this was partly thanks to the reputation of his astrological treatise, the *Tetrabiblos* or *Quadripartitum*, translated earlier than, and as often as, the *Syntaxis*. Yet by then astronomers, at least, generally recognized that the model of epicycles and eccentrics is superior to that of concentric spheres found in Aristotle. Thus in his *Theorica Planetarum*, written *c.* 1262, Campanus of Novara followed Ptolemy closely, defending his own work by claiming that anyone who wants to attack it must first attack Ptolemy, and that his own astronomical models (ymaginationes: i.e. picturings of the arrangements of things) are 'solidly based on the irrefragable demonstrations of Ptolemy'.

Yet although Ptolemy's system came to be accepted in the

---

[5] Although, as we noted, physical arguments play an important part in Ptolemy's denial that the earth has any movement, elsewhere he notably ignores the physical difficulties presented by the parameters he adopted for the sizes of the epicycle and deferent of the moon, for example, that the difference between the moon's apparent diameter at apogee and at perigee should, on his theory, vary by a factor of nearly two. At this point, as in general in the *Syntaxis*, Ptolemy's *chief* concern is to give a mathematical account (a model by which the motions of the heavenly bodies can be computed). Yet that his ultimate goal was an account that was not only mathematically exact but also physically true is clear, above all, from his *Hypotheses of the Planets*, where he represents the circles of the heavenly bodies as strips of spheres and explains their motions as due to their possessing a vital force.

main, doubts were expressed about aspects of it, for example about the phenomenon of the precession of the equinoxes, where several writers believed it to be necessary to correct Ptolemy's theory by invoking the doctrine of trepidation attributed to Thabit ben Qurra. In the late fourteenth century, Oresme even developed arguments to show that 'it is impossible to demonstrate by experience that the heavens have circular motion and that the earth does not have the same', even though he himself concluded: 'However, everyone maintains, and I think myself, that the heavens do move and not the earth. . . . What I have said by way of diversion or intellectual exercise can in this manner serve as a valuable means of refuting and checking those who would like to impugn our faith by argument.'

So far as Copernicus himself goes, the closeness of his relation to Ptolemy is now fully recognized. First, the *De Revolutionibus* is directly modelled on the *Syntaxis* in the order in which the material is presented. Secondly, while Copernicus cited new astronomical observations, he generally accepted those recorded by Ptolemy even when he himself had doubts about them (for which he was later sharply reprimanded by Kepler). Thirdly, and most importantly, the basic geometrical models that Copernicus used, namely, epicycles and eccentrics, were, of course, precisely those that Ptolemy had employed in his geocentric system. Indeed on this point Copernicus sought to return to a purer version of these models. His objections to Ptolemy were directed not only to his adherence to geocentricity, but also to his departure from the assumption of uniform motion. For Copernicus, both the doctrine of the equant and that of direction were breaches of the fundamental principle according to which the movements of the heavenly bodies are to be explained in terms of combinations of regular, circular motions. Thus he attacked Ptolemy's lunar theory on the grounds that it makes the apparent regular movement of the epicycle to be 'in fact irregular' and to take place 'contrary to the principle set up and assumed'. Nor, on the key issue of the earth's motion, did Copernicus fail to invoke ancient authorities, in the shape of Heraclides, Ecphantus, Hicetas, and Philolaus, on his side of the argument. Indeed it is now known that—like Melanchthon when he attempted to refute the *De Revolutionibus* six years after it appeared, in 1549—Copernicus was also aware of Aristarchus' theory, though for reasons we can only conjecture he did not refer to him.

This is not to deny the importance of Copernicus' work both in its own right, as providing a clear statement of the heliocentric theory and thereby initiating the debate that was to remain in the centre of astronomical enquiry for over a century, and as a symbol of a new and more critical attitude towards the authority of the ancients. Nevertheless there is an essential continuity in astronomical theory from the Greeks, through the Arabs, to the *De Revolutionibus*. After Copernicus, the decline in that tradition was eventually accelerated both by the amassing of new data (the first important work to cite observations obtained with the telescope was Galileo's *Sidereus Nuncius* in 1610, but even before that Tycho Brahe's detailed records were to provide the essential data for Kepler), and, more especially, by the devising of new astronomical models: here Kepler's demonstration, in 1609, of the elliptical orbits of the planets marked the decisive break with the assumption of circular motion that had pervaded astronomical speculation ever since the fourth century B.C.

Yet if Kepler stands outside the ancient astronomical tradition, he still saw himself as an adherent of that other strand in ancient thought, the mathematical philosophies of Plato and Pythagoras. He is chiefly known, today, for the three laws of planetary motion named after him, (1) that the planetary orbits are ellipses with the sun as one focus, (2) that the line joining a planet to the sun sweeps out equal areas in equal times, and (3) that the squares of the periods of the planets are as the cubes of their mean distances from the sun. Yet if he described the *Syntaxis* as outmoded, we have noted that he studied Ptolemy's *Harmonics* carefully, and he maintained, throughout his life, that the numbers of, and distances between, the planets follow the geometry of the five regular 'Platonic' bodies. The intervals between the six planetary spheres (Saturn, Jupiter, Mars, Earth and Moon, Venus, Mercury) correspond to the ratios of the spheres inscribing or circumscribing the cube, tetrahedron, dodecahedron, icosahedron, and octahedron respectively, and, in his eyes, these ratios, just as much as the laws of planetary motion, are illustrations and proofs of the dictum he attributed to Plato that 'god always does geometry.'

Greek astronomical theories influenced, and were them-

selves influenced by, cosmological and general physical doctrines on such topics as the elements. Having considered some of
the areas of physical science where the Greeks attempted
rigorous mathematical accounts, we must now turn to some
others where their approach owed more to philosophy than to
mathematics. From the very beginnings of the enquiry concerning nature the Greeks produced an amazing variety of
cosmological theories. We have already mentioned the problems created by the fragmentary nature of our sources for the
Presocratics, whose views have largely to be reconstructed
from the reports in later Greek writers, especially Aristotle
and the Aristotelian commentators. Yet since Aristotle often
discusses his predecessors at length, anyone who read his
Aristotle carefully was thereby introduced to a wide range of
earlier thinkers, and it was principally through this source
that something of the richness of Greek cosmologies was
known from the thirteenth century onwards. Scanty though
our evidence is, it is clear that already in the Presocratic
period both sides of such questions as whether the world is
eternal or created, and whether there is one world or many,
had been upheld, whilst on the problem of the elements
various monistic and pluralistic doctrines were advanced,
such as that all things arise from water, or air, or earth, water,
air, and fire, or from such natural substances as flesh, wood,
and gold.

The philosophy of Parmenides, who was the first thinker to
insist on trusting reason rather than the senses and who
denied plurality and change, was a major influence on all
subsequent fifth-century cosmological speculation, and in
particular on the most famous late-fifth-century physical
theory, atomism. The earliest Greek atomists, Leucippus and
Democritus, postulated that atoms and the void alone exist.
The differences between physical objects are all ultimately to
be explained in terms of modifications in the shapes, arrangements, and positions of the atoms that compose them. The
atoms are infinite in number and they are dispersed through
an infinite void: the void is that which separates the atoms
and through which they move. Although each individual
atom is—like Parmenides' One Being—ungenerated, inde-
structible, unalterable, homogeneous, and indivisible, the
assumption of the existence of the void enabled the atomists to
reinstate both plurality, and movement and change (the last

understood in terms of the combinations and separations of atoms).

Such a theory is, in the main, the outcome of reflection on the problems left by Parmenides, not one that was based on, or even supported by, empirical data. Although Democritus put forward a detailed account of sensible qualities (explaining sharp or acid tastes, for instance, in terms of sharp, angular atoms), the debate between the various versions of atomism and continuum theory, both in the fifth century and later, turned on the arguments that could be adduced for and against the infinite divisibility of matter. Thus Aristotle reports what may well be an original argument of Leucippus or Democritus in the form of a dilemma. If we assume a body is divisible throughout, let us further assume it to be so divided. What then is left? We cannot say a magnitude, since a magnitude can be further divided. Yet if not a magnitude, the body will consist either of points or of nothing at all, which again, in both cases, is impossible. We must, then, conclude that bodies are not infinitely divisible. Although Aristotle himself rejected this conclusion, maintaining that bodies are only *potentially* infinitely divisible, not actually so, atomism was again upheld by Epicurus in the late fourth century B.C., although, unlike Leucippus and Democritus, Epicurus' own chief interest was in ethics, and physical enquiry was undertaken solely to secure peace of mind. In two other respects also the ancient atomists adopted positions antithetical to those of Plato and Aristotle and thereby acted, both in the ancient world and later, as a focus of opposition to the dominant strand in ancient cosmology. First they provided the clearest ancient statement of the possibility and the existence of innumerable worlds. Democritus' pupil, Metrodorus, is reported to have said that it is as unlikely for only one world to be produced in the boundless void as for one ear of corn in a great plain. Secondly, both Leucippus and Democritus implicitly, and then Epicurus and Lucretius explicitly, rejected the view that the world is the product of purpose and design.

Although some atomistic conceptions are to be found already in Galileo, for example, the first major revival of atomism came in the mid-seventeenth century with Gassendi, a contemporary and opponent of Descartes. Gassendi was careful to dissociate himself from Epicurus' theology and to reaffirm that god governs the universe, but otherwise advocated a return to Epicureanism to which he devoted extensive commentaries. But whether or not they adopted an atomic view of matter, a number of seventeenth-century writers saw the ancient atomists as the chief ancient proponents of the fundamental principle that all natural change is ultimately to be explained in terms of matter and motion. This principle was common ground to a series of otherwise quite widely diverging mechanical or corpuscular philosophies, such as those of Descartes himself, Boyle, and Hobbes. The ascendancy that the mechanical philosophy had gained by the end of the seventeenth century can be judged from the scandal that was caused, in some quarters at least, by Newton's advocacy of the principle of action at a distance in his gravitational theory.

In the seventeenth century atomism was generally understood in its ancient sense: for the Greeks the atom is by definition indivisible. But later 'atomic' theories sometimes have little in common with ancient atomism bar the name, since they depart from one or other of the fundamental tenets of Greek atomism whether in its fifth- or its fourth-century B.C. form. Thus Dalton's atomism admitted different elemental substances, and since the atom has been split both in theory and in practice, modern atomic theory is not an atomic theory at all in the Greek acceptance of the term. Leucippus' doctrine was the first clear formulation of the view that matter exists in the form of discrete particles, and as such it may legitimately be considered the prototype of all subsequent theories of the discontinuous structure of matter. Yet otherwise those theories evidently differ profoundly in their content, in the problems they were designed to resolve, and, especially, in the methods used to establish them. Similarly, although the most sophisticated ancient proponents of a continuum theory, the Stoics, proposed doctrines that have been hailed as forerunners of the nineteenth-century notion of a field of force, the difference in context is again fundamental: Stoic physics was based on philosophical arguments, a qualitative theory not formulable in mathematical terms, and not related to experimental evidence.

Plato's influence has been mentioned several times already. Although his cosmological dialogue, the *Timaeus*, is today less highly regarded than many of his other works, it was for long periods both in antiquity and in the Middle Ages the chief composition by which he was known. It contains theories on the constitution of matter (where Plato adopts a version of atomism), on human anatomy and physiology, even on the causes of diseases. But more important than these particular theories is the framework in which they are set, the three main elements in which are the divine Craftsman (Demiurge), the eternal Forms, and the sensible phenomena modelled on them. Although the Demiurge does not make matter itself, he is the divine, benevolent, purposive agent who creates the world in the sense of bringing order into disorder.

The *Timaeus* thus provided a powerful, if picturesque statement of a teleological interpretation of nature—and one which was easily accommodated to Christian beliefs—and it incorporated certain fundamental ontological and epistemological doctrines. The Forms are the eternal, unchanging, immaterial models of which the changing world of becoming is necessarily an imperfect copy. The Forms alone can be known: sensible phenomena are, at best, the objects of true opinion. Some of the applications of this epistemology to the physical sciences have already been noted. In acoustics and astronomy, for instance, Plato distinguished, in the *Republic*, between the study of the sensible phenomena which are necessarily only rough approximations to the intelligible, in this case mathematically expressible, relations, and the study of those relations themselves. Plato left no doubt that in his view it is the latter study that is valuable. Indeed at times he wrote in a way that could be, and was, taken to suggest that observation is not merely inferior to reason, but completely worthless.

Platonism has, of course, stood at different times for a bewildering variety of beliefs, some far removed from anything in Plato himself. Thus the metaphysics of light developed by Grosseteste and others in late medieval philosophy, and often connected with a special interest in optics, is distantly derivative, through many intermediaries, from Platonism. Plato's most important influence came, however, in the sixteenth and seventeenth centuries when such men as Galileo invoked his name in their reaction against Aristotelianism. What Plato was then taken to represent was the ideal of the mathematization of physics, which had some justification, at least, in his advocacy of the mathematical approach to astronomy and acoustics. Yet at other points those who had aligned themselves with Plato on the importance of mathematics diverged sharply from theses he had maintained. Thus, whereas for Plato sensible phenomena are at best the objects of true opinion, Galileo insisted on the possibility of necessary and certain demonstrations in physics, in this adopting a position that *we* should say is antithetical to that of Plato and has more in common with that of Aristotle.

While Plato generally stood, above all, for a particular philosophy of science, Aristotle's influence, both in antiquity and subsequently, was both more pervasive and more diffuse. First his epistemology and methodology contrast, in certain respects, with Plato's. Whilst he agrees with Plato that knowledge is of forms, these, for Aristotle, are not transcendent entities that exist independently of the particulars. Attention is now turned back to the particulars, the individual substances, themselves, though not from the point of view of their particularity, but from that of the forms they possess. In the logical treatises, where he analyses the conditions of proof and shows that it proceeds by deductive, that is syllogistic, argument from indemonstrable primary premisses, his model is often mathematics. But he draws an important distinction between the method of demonstration, where the starting-point is the universal or what is better known 'absolutely', and the method of discovery or learning, where the starting-point is what is more familiar 'to us'—the nature of which will differ in different contexts but which includes the immediate data of experience. Moreover, he contrasts mathematics (and first philosophy or theology) with physics in point of exactness. Whereas the subject-matter of mathematics is abstract, sensible substances (the domain of physics) possess matter as well as form; while mathematics deals essentially with what is true without qualification, physics is concerned with what is true 'always *or for the most part*'.

His doctrine of the four causes, material, formal, efficient, and final, identifies the types of question to be investigated concerning any object or event, whether natural or artificial. Thus the four causes correspond, in the case of a natural object, to the answers to questions about what it is made of, what its essential character is, what instituted the change that produced it, and what end or function it serves. The method of procedure adopted in the physical treatises is a complex one, generally beginning with the definition of the subject-matter and a statement of the difficulties, *aporiai*, to be resolved. In resolving them he employs broad distinctions between appeals to arguments, *logoi*, and appeals to facts, *erga*, or to 'appearances', *phainomena*, but what this last term, especially, includes varies according to the subject-matter. In the dialectical discussions of such topics as time and place in the *Physics*, the 'appearances' are generally a matter of common beliefs, *endoxa*, not observational data. Elsewhere, especially in the zoological works, the latter figure more prominently. He certainly both recommended in theory and himself practised a method that paid much greater attention to observation, indeed to deliberate empirical research, than Plato had allowed, but to exaggerate his inductivist tendencies is quite mistaken.

The range of investigations he undertook is vast. After discussing the nature of physics itself as well as such topics as infinity, the void, and motion in general in the *Physics*, he proposes doctrines concerning the elements, their modes of mixture, and the compounds they form, in *On the Heavens*, *On Generation and Corruption*, and the *Meteorologica*. His element theory is linked in turn to a doctrine of natural motion, since two of the four simple bodies, earth and water, naturally move downwards, and two, air and fire, upwards, 'down' and 'up' being defined in terms of movement towards or away from the centre of the earth, conceived as the point to which all heavy objects tend. He contrasts natural with forced motion—where an external agent is involved—and occasionally remarks on certain proportionalities between time, distance, force, and weight. Influential as these statements were, they were not intended as a fully-fledged kinetic theory: in each case the context in which they are made is not any systematic enquiry into the laws of motion (there is no such enquiry in Aristotle), but the dialectical discussion of such specific issues as the existence of the void.

Aristotle did, however, link the doctrine of natural motion with one of natural places. In *On the Heavens* he offers proofs to show both that the earth is spherical and that it is at rest in the centre of the universe. His conception of natural motion is also a major consideration leading him to conclude that the heavenly bodies cannot be composed of any of the four 'sublunary' elements either singly or in combination. Their movements are rectilinear, whereas the heavenly bodies move eternally (and therefore naturally) in circles. They must, therefore, consist of a fifth element, *aither*, that has the property of natural circular motion. His extensive zoological enquiries are connected to the rest of his physical investigations by his doctrine of soul. All living beings are differentiated according to the vital faculties they possess, and they belong to a single hierarchy of being that extends from the gods to the inanimate elements.

Many of his particular doctrines build on those of earlier theorists, whose ideas he often reviews systematically when he outlines the 'common beliefs' on the various problems he discusses. Thus the doctrine that other physical objects consist of earth, water, air, and fire was first clearly stated by Empedocles in the fifth century B.C. Here, as often, Aristotle systematized and modified earlier views. He suggested that each of the simple bodies can itself be analysed in terms of a pair of primary opposites, hot or cold, and dry or wet, and he explained the transformations between them (which Empedocles had ruled out) by the substitution of one opposite for another, as for example of hot for cold when water (cold and wet) is turned to steam (conceived as 'air', hot and wet). Elsewhere, especially in his zoology, Aristotle appeared more often as a pioneer, both in the solutions he proposed to such problems as generation and reproduction, and in the scope and methods of his investigations. He gave far more detailed descriptions of a much greater number of animal species than had ever been attempted before, and although he was certainly not the first Greek to use dissection, he was the first to do so at all extensively.

These wide-ranging enquiries are linked not only by a common methodology, but also by key doctrines, especially the priority of form to matter and the role of final causes in nature. As was recognized in the ancient world and later, his physics and cosmology provide a remarkably consistent and comprehensive whole. It is not for nothing that in Boyle's *Sceptical Chymist* (1661), Themistius, the representative of Aristotelianism, is made to compare Aristotle's ideas with an arch where 'each single stone ... is sufficiently secured by the solidity and entireness of the whole fabric of which it is a part'.

But although a synthesizer and a systematizer, Aristotle is

not the dogmatist he was sometimes later made out to be. Statements of remaining difficulties, and of the need for more research, are common, especially though not exclusively in his zoology. Moreover, his ideas were far from being unchallenged both in the period immediately following his death and later. Both Theophrastus and Strato, the next two heads of the school he founded—both of them original scientists of considerable calibre—criticized him on fundamental points. Again, in the late fourth and third centuries B.C., both Epicureanism and Stoicism offered rival physical systems which survived, with admittedly fluctuating fortunes, until the second century A.D. Later still the sixth-century Aristotelian commentators were sometimes sharply divided, Simplicius generally supporting what he represented as Aristotle's position, but Philoponus occasionally attacking it bitterly, notably on such issues as the permanence of the universe and the doctrine of natural and forced motion. In the latter case, Philoponus anticipated some of the arguments used in the sixteenth century in his refutation of the general laws that he took Aristotle's statements to imply. In particular he gave both rational and experimental grounds for rejecting the notion that the speed of a freely falling body is proportional to its weight, adducing, for instance, some 1,000 years before Galileo, what actually happens when two weights that differ greatly are let fall from the same height.

Yet it was one thing to attack and even refute individual theories: it was another to overthrow the whole. Despite the criticisms of some of his ideas, and the counter-attractions of other systems, Aristotle's physics dominated speculative thought intermittently throughout antiquity. In the second century A.D., for example, his four-element theory was adopted both by Galen (who believed, however, that it went back to Hippocrates) and by Ptolemy, whose astronomy incorporated, as we saw, certain fundamental Aristotelian physical assumptions, especially the doctrine of natural places. Nor is this dominance hard to explain, when we reflect that Aristotle's was not only the most comprehensive physical system, but also the one that in many cases appeared to have the strongest arguments and evidence in its support. Thus on the major question of qualitative versus quantitative theories of matter, whereas the atomists' explanations of physical properties in terms of geometrical shapes seemed quite arbitrary, Aristotle's account, in terms of hot, cold, dry, and wet, had one immediate, if superficial, advantage, in staying closer to what can actually be observed.

Aristotle's physics, mediated first by the Arabs, rapidly achieved a dominant position in European thought, once most of his works had become available in Latin versions. The interest in his ideas in the thirteenth century was in no way weakened, and may even have been stimulated, by the Church's proscriptions of some of his doctrines in a series of condemnations from 1210 to 1277. Although criticisms and doubts were, as we noted, expressed already in that century, it took over 300 years effectively to undermine his system as a whole. The attack on such weak areas as his kinetic state-ments, the overthrow of geocentric astronomy, the raising of fundamental questions concerning the distinction between elements and compounds, all contributed to this. But even after Aristotelianism as a whole was no longer an important force, his ideas in some areas, especially biology, continued to be influential. In the debates between preformation and epigenesis in the seventeenth and eighteenth centuries, the epigenesist C. F. Wolff claimed in his *Theoria Generationis* (1759) that experiments had vindicated Aristotle's view (that there is a true formation of new structures in the embryo), and some of Aristotle's detailed zoological descriptions, such as the famous account of the placenta-like formation in the 'smooth shark', *Mustelus Laevis*, had to wait until the mid-nineteenth century to be verified.

So far we have been dealing with the work of men who considered themselves either mathematicians or (more usually) philosophers. In the life sciences, however, much of the important work was done by men who earned their living primarily as doctors. There are, to be sure, exceptions, notably Aristotle's researches in zoology and Theophrastus' in botany; and in the ancient debate on generation and heredity one of the main theories (apart from Aristotle's), the so-called pangenesis doctrine, according to which every part of the body is represented in the seed, was probably first suggested by the atomist philosopher Democritus. But the great majority of the anonymous authors represented in the Hippocratic collection, and most of the chief names in biology both in the Hellenistic period and later, such as Herophilus, Erasistratus, Rufus, Soranus, and Galen, were, first and foremost, medical practitioners. Medical men were far from unanimous in their attitudes towards philosophy. But early on, one group of doctors chose to contrast medicine with philosophy both in their aims and in their methods. Thus in the fourth century B.C. the author of the Hippocratic treatise *On Ancient Medicine* attacked what he saw as the intrusion of philosophical methods into medicine, claiming that the latter is a practical art with an established method founded on experience, that has no need of the type of arbitrary assumptions on which cosmological speculation must be based.

The medical writers provide a rich source of information concerning many aspects of Greek science, but from the point of view of later influences we may concentrate on two groups of texts, the treatises of the Hippocratic Corpus and the works of Galen. The story of the influence of 'Hippocrates' is extraordinary. What we know as the Hippocratic Corpus consists of some sixty treatises, all anonymous, that vary widely in subject-matter, style, and date. They deal not only with pathology, diagnosis and prognosis, and methods of treatment, but also with physiology (the constitution of man), embryology, gynaecology, surgery, and medical ethics. A few are clearly-defined wholes, for example lectures addressed to a medical (or a lay) audience. But many are composite productions, manuals or notebooks, in some cases the work of several hands. While most were written betwen *c.* 430 and 330 B.C., some are later works; although the bulk of the Corpus as we have it was probably put together by scholars in Alexandria in the third century B.C., other anonymous treatises were added later.

The collection is the work of a large number of medical writers belonging to different groups or schools and often representing opposed viewpoints not only on aetiology and treatment but also on the aims and methods of medicine itself. The question of what works, if any, are by Hippocrates himself already exercised the ancient commentators in the late third century B.C., and is still disputed. The evidence available to us is tenuous and at points conflicting, and no single treatise can now be shown definitely, or even with a fair degree of probability, to be by him. Yet in the absence of firm evidence, modern scholars, like their ancient, medieval, and Renaissance counterparts, still sometimes tend to ascribe to Hippocrates those works that they themselves happen to value most highly.

The heterogeneity of the collection is such that few

meaningful generalizations about 'Hippocratic medicine' can be made. From the point of view of Greek science in general, apart from the methodological debate already mentioned, the ideas on causation expressed in some treatises are important: they include the insistence that every phenomenon has a cause, the implicit recognition of the distinction between cause and coincidence, and the clear rejection of the idea of supernatural intervention in disease. We find, too, a mass of physiological and pathological doctrines, notably those based on a view of the importance of humours in the body. Thus the treatise *On the Nature of Man* proposed an elaborate schema of correlated tetrads of primary opposites, seasons, ages of man, and humours, while other works advanced other doctrines, and the number, identity, and origin of the humours were all disputed questions. Above all there is the recognition, in many works, of the importance of observation in medical practice, particularly in diagnosis. The treatise *On Prognosis* explains in detail how to examine patients' symptoms, and sustained and minute observations were made and recorded in the collections of case-histories known as the *Epidemics*. These last, indeed, provide some of our best extant examples of the practice of observation in early Greek science.

Although the doctrines found in the Hippocratic writings were often criticized in the third century B.C. and later, the veneration of Hippocrates continued to grow, and reached a peak with Galen in the second century A.D. Galen was, to be sure, aware of the 'Hippocratic question'; yet he held that most of the treatises are genuine and that several of those that are not were, nevertheless, by pupils or associates of Hippocrates who could be taken as reliable guides to his teaching. Thus he assumed that the schemata of *On the Nature of Man* represented Hippocrates' views correctly, and he incorporated many ideas from this and other treatises in his own doctrines.

For Galen, Hippocrates was supreme not only as a medical practitioner, but also as a physiologist, and this view was enormously influential. Thus when later Greek, Arabic, and medieval writers bracketed Galen and Hippocrates as models and authorities, Hippocrates was often seen through Galen's eyes. Yet when, as we shall be discussing shortly, Galen's own reputation in anatomy and physiology came under attack, that of Hippocrates survived, though now for different reasons. In the sixteenth century, de Baillou, who was one of those responsible for the revival of detailed clinical histories, took the *Epidemics* as his model, and in the seventeenth, Sydenham and Boerhaave advocated a return to Hippocrates. For Sydenham, for example, Hippocrates had 'founded the art of medicine on a solid and unshakeable basis', namely, the principle that 'our natures are the physicians of diseases' and the method of 'the exact description of nature'. What these men admired in Hippocrates was not the anatomy or physiology, so much as first the exact observation of the patient's whole condition, and second, the ideal of the doctor's unselfinterested devotion to his patients. Here, indeed, an influence continues today, for there are still medical writers who call for a return to Hippocrates on just these two grounds, even while acknowledging that much of what is found in the Hippocratic Corpus has been superseded by the progress of medical science.

The century after the founding of Alexandria saw great advances in both medicine and biology, the work of such men as Praxagoras (the discoverer of the diagnostic value of the pulse), Herophilus, and Erasistratus. The last two were the first investigators to dissect, and perhaps also to vivisect, human subjects. They were also the first to investigate the nervous system, indeed to identify the nerves as such and to distinguish between sensory and motor nerves, and to Erasistratus goes the credit of discovering the valves of the heart and of inferring the presence of connections between veins and arteries. But just as most of Hellenistic astronomy was supplanted by Ptolemy, so Hellenistic biology was even more completely eclipsed by later writers, especially Galen. Not a single complete treatise of any of the great Alexandrian biologists is extant. It is largely through Galen (who cites his predecessors at length) that their work has been known since Galen's own time, and their influence in the history of biology has, accordingly, not matched their evident originality.

Although a handful of works have survived from the period immediately preceding Galen, including Rufus' elementary *Anatomy*, Dioscorides' *Materia Medica*, and Soranus' *Gynaecology*, the other chief ancient authority on medicine and biology, apart from 'Hippocrates', was Galen himself. One of the great polymaths of antiquity, Galen wrote voluminously on a wide range of subjects including logic, ethics, and philology, although little of his work outside medicine has survived. Even so the treatises extant in Greek run to nearly 20,000 pages in Kühn's edition, to which must be added other works that exist only in Arabic versions.

His medical works cover every aspect of the study of health and disease and of the nature of the human body. Some are introductory works; others are devoted to examining other writers' views, the extensive commentaries on Hippocrates being a special case, given the particular respect that Galen had for his authority. Although Galen's physical theory owed much to what he found in the Hippocratic treatises and to Aristotle, and his psychology is indebted to Plato, especially, the originality of other aspects of his work should not be underestimated. He developed a complex, if in parts obscure, physiology, distinguishing the liver, heart, and brain as the sources of the venous, arterial, and nervous systems respectively. He conclusively refuted the common Greek view (upheld by Erasistratus) that the arteries normally contain only air. Yet holding that the liver manufactures the blood, which it then sends into the veins and right heart, he had to explain how the blood reaches the left heart and arteries, and he inferred (partly on the basis of the analogy of the capillaries between veins and arteries) that it must pass through invisible pores in the interventricular septum. This is clear, if mistaken, but elsewhere the unresolved difficulties in his general physiology show up in, for example, the special pleading he needed to explain the character of the pulmonary arteries (the 'artery-like veins') and veins (the 'vein-like arteries'), and in the vacillations and ambiguities in his accounts of the origins of the different kinds of *pneuma* (air or spirit) that he held to be responsible for vital functions. Nevertheless, in more particular physiological contexts his achievements include, for instance, the demonstration—by means of experimental vivisections on animals—of the peristalsis of the alimentary canal and the contraction of the stomach in digestion.

But if in theoretical physiology some of his work is unclear or speculative or both, as an anatomist he is often superb, even though, unlike Herophilus and Erasistratus, he had to work mainly with animal subjects. In his comprehensive anatomical masterpiece, *On Anatomical Procedures*, we find him insisting on practice in dissection, explaining how the difficulties of complex operations may be overcome, warning his students not to delegate work to assistants, and repeatedly emphasizing the need for care and precision. His own skill as a dissector is apparent in, for example, the vivisections he performed to investigate the nervous system, where he conducted a series of tests making incisions either right through, or through one half of, the spinal cord at various points on the spinal column in order to discover what effect each operation had on the animal's vital faculties. Yet it was not primarily for such investigations that Galen was later to become so influential, as for his schematic physiology, his humoral pathology, and, in anatomy itself, for his championship of teleological explanations in such works as *On the Natural Faculties* and *On the Use of Parts*. Indeed the latter, which Galen in a famous and often quoted passage calls a 'sacred book which I compose as a true hymn to him who created us', is explicitly devoted to showing the useful function of each part of the body in turn.

Although later Greek biology produced no one to compare with Galen, the extensive extant medical writings of such men as Oribasius (mid-fourth century), Aetius of Amida, Alexander of Tralles (both sixth century), and Paul of Aegina (seventh century) show that they maintained a high level of knowledge. But whilst research did not die out completely, the efforts of these writers were increasingly devoted to systematizing and summarizing medical knowledge (particularly that contained in Galen), as opposed to adding to it. Original medical treatises give place to digests, commentaries, and medical encyclopedias, and the encyclopedias become more concise as time goes on. Appeals to authority, already extensively used by Galen, eventually take precedence over and supplant evidence and argument.

As with other branches of ancient science, the decline of medicine, whilst occasionally arrested in the Greek East, was more precipitate in the Latin West where medicine was, in one respect, worse placed than mathematics or astronomy. Elementary arithmetic, geometry, astronomy, and music formed the quadrivium which, with the trivium (grammar, logic, and rhetoric), had constituted the basic curriculum of Roman education and continued to do so in the early Middle Ages. But medicine was not one of these seven 'liberal arts', and it was particularly poorly represented in the popular

Latin authors, such as Macrobius, Martianus Capella, and Cassiodorus, through whom a smattering of Greek learning was preserved. Yet doctors were always needed: medicine of some sort was always practised and medical education began to be revived in the West with the founding of the school of Salerno, renowned for its doctors already in the tenth century. This was also one of the first centres at which Greek and Arabic medical texts were translated, notably by Constantine the African in the eleventh century. From the twelfth century the pace of translation increased, and from the thirteenth such works as the Hippocratic *Aphorisms*, and Galen's *On the Medical Art* and *On the Method of Healing*—usually known as the *Tegni* and *Megategni* respectively—occupied an important place in the curricula of the medical faculties of the universities. At the same time many spurious works, including books of 'Secrets' and astrological treatises, also passed as by Hippocrates or Galen.

By about the middle of the fourteenth century Galen had once again achieved the position of ascendancy, as the outstanding authority on anatomy, physiology, and pathology, that he had enjoyed in late antiquity. Yet it was not long before pro- and anti-Galenical factions were locked in rivalry and dispute. Paracelsus' burning of the texts of Galen in the sixteenth century was dramatic, but less effective than the criticisms of his theories by, for example, Vesalius. His attack—directed, to be sure, against contemporary Galenists as much as against Galen himself—explicitly raised the question of principle, of the relative value of Galen's authority and first-hand observation. He insisted on the importance of dissection (as indeed Galen had done, although now Vesalius stressed that human subjects must be used for human anatomy), and he accused the medical profession of being slow to trust 'their own not ineffectual sight and powers of reason' rather than what Galen had written. Yet, as is well known, Vesalius had to struggle to free himself of Galenical assumptions, as his successive positions on the doctrine that blood passes through pores in the septum of the heart illustrate. In the first edition of the *De Humani Corporis Fabrica* (1543) he accepted Galen's doctrine, though remarking that 'we are compelled to admire the industry of the Creator of things' in achieving this effect through pores 'that escape the sight', and it is not until the second edition (1555) that he expressed disagreement with the theory.

Galen's physiology was further undermined by Harvey's demonstration of the circulation of the blood; yet Harvey too was ambivalent in his attitude towards ancient authorities. If in the *De Motu Cordis* (1628) he often cited, and declared his admiration for, Hippocrates, Aristotle, and, especially, Galen, this was not purely from a desire to avoid antagonizing contemporary Galenists, but, among other reasons, because he believed those authors provided a model of scientific method and he shared their teleological approach to biology. Moreover, it took long for the full implications of Harvey's work for Galen's physiology to be generally realized. Galen's influence was still immense in the late seventeenth century (when Galenical medicine was satirized by Molière), his texts were still used to teach medicine in most European universities in the eighteenth, even in some cases in the nineteenth, century,[6] and, like Hippocratism, though admittedly less frequently, Galenism—understood as a theory of the importance of constitution-types in medicine—has been the subject of revivals right down to the present century.

Our sketch of the impact of Greek science must be understood as subject to the reservations we have mentioned: we can attempt no more than a very general, and at many points only a provisional, account. If, in the broadest terms, the revival of Western science depended first on the re-discovery of ancient texts, and then on their criticism, the recovery of ancient science was, in one important respect, only completed in the second phase. The medieval attitude towards the authority of ancient texts is comparable with that of late antiquity; the critical examination of them, especially in the sixteenth and seventeenth centuries, is closer to the original spirit in which the chief ancient scientists had conducted their investigations.

---

[6] Thus in 1713 the Statutes of the medical faculty at Wurzburg laid it down that the second examination for medical graduands was to take the form of questions on passages from Hippocrates' *Aphorisms* and Galen's *On the Method of Healing, to Glaucon*, to be selected by the candidate inserting a knife into each book. In a Statute of Oxford of 1636, not repealed until 1833, the exercises prescribed for those proceeding to the degree of Doctor of Medicine were either six solemn lectures on any part of Galen, chosen by the candidate, or at least three expositions on one of four selected books of Galen, and even the new Statutes of 1833 stipulated that in the examination of Bachelors of Medicine, 'the ancient writers, Hippocrates, Aretaeus, Galen, and Celsus, two of whom at fewest are always to be made use of at every examination, must in all cases be added'.

In most fields of enquiry there is a very real continuity between Greek, Arabic, medieval, and Renaissance science. From a modern point of view it can be argued that the major weakness of Greek science was neither a matter of the subjects they investigated, nor of the ways they investigated them, but lay in the social and ideological framework within which scientific work was done, in particular in the failure to create the conditions necessary for the continuous growth of science. It is here that fundamental changes began in the seventeenth and eighteenth centuries and it is this that chiefly differentiates the modern period. Yet, as so often, what may now seem a failure of ancient science was one of its essential features. Ancient science, we might say, never fully emancipated itself from philosophy: yet if it had not been seen as part of philosophy it would scarcely have been pursued at all.

In due course, most of the particular scientific theories that had dominated ancient thought were inevitably superseded. But the most durable legacy of ancient science lies in the methodological ideas it both formulated and exemplified, and especially in three such ideas, (1) the notion of an axiomatic, deductive system, (2) the application of mathematics to natural science, and (3) the conception of detailed empirical research. Each of these ideas has been implemented in ways, and on a scale, that would have astonished the Greeks, and we now take them so much for granted that it is easy to forget that each was the product of a specific intellectual development in the ancient world. But long after the particular theories of the Hippocratic writers, Plato, Aristotle, Euclid, Archimedes, Ptolemy, and Galen had ceased to be in the centre of scientific debate, science owed, and in some respects still owes, them a debt for their conceptions of the nature and methods of scientific enquiry itself and for their first explorations of its potentialities.

Further Reading

Greek Science
Good editions and translations of most of the major extant works of Greek science are readily available, for example, T. L. Heath's *The Thirteen Books of Euclid's Elements* (3 vols., Cambridge, 1908; Dover Books, 1956), *Aristarchus of Samos* (Oxford, 1913), *The Works of Archimedes* (Cambridge, 1912; Dover Books, n.d.), and *Apollonius of Perga* (Cambridge, 1896; Heffer, 1961), the translations in the Loeb edn. of Plato (Cambridge, Mass., and

London), and *The Works of Aristotle translated into English*, ed. W. D. Ross (Oxford). Greek medicine and late Greek science are, however, less well served. The best translation of the most important Hippocratic treatises is *The Medical Works of Hippocrates*, by J. Chadwick and W. N. Mann (Oxford, 1950; Penguin edn., *Hippocratic Writings*, 1978) which can be supplemented by the four-volume Loeb edn. (ed. W. H. S. Jones). There are up-to-date translations of only a handful of Galen's works, for example *Galen, On Anatomical Procedures, The Later Books*, trans. W. L. H. Duckworth, ed. M. C. Lyons and B. Towers (Cambridge, 1962); Ptolemy's *Syntaxis* has been translated by R. Catesby Taliaferro (Chicago, 1952), and there is an extended commentary by G. Pedersen, *A Survey of the Almagest* (Odense, 1974); his *Optics* have been edited by A. Lejeune, *L'Optique de Claude Ptolémée* (Louvain, 1956).

A Source Book in Greek Science, ed. M. R. Cohen and I. E. Drabkin (2nd edn. Cambridge, Mass., 1958) contains a good selection of passages (though not on cosmology) in generally reliable translations, and has an adequate bibliography for the available texts and translations up to 1958.

The classic work on Greek mathematics is still T. L. Heath, *A History of Greek Mathematics* (2 vols., Oxford, 1921), that on Greek astronomy is O. Neugebauer, *A History of Ancient Mathematical Astronomy* (3 vols., Berlin, 1975).

The most important general discussions of Greek science are S. Sambursky, *The Physical World of the Greeks* (trans. M. Dagut, London, 1956), O. Neugebauer, *The Exact Sciences in Antiquity* (2nd edn., Providence R.I., 1957, Harper, 1962), M. Clagett, *Greek Science in Antiquity* (London, 1957), B. Farrington, *Greek Science* (revised one vol. edn., Penguin, 1961) and G. Sarton, *A History of Science* (2 vols., London, 1953–9). Most of the useful introductory books and some articles are mentioned in the brief bibliographies in my *Early Greek Science, Thales to Aristotle* (London, 1970) and *Greek Science after Aristotle* (London, 1973), and there are useful collections of articles on Greek and later science in *The Roots of Scientific Thought*, ed. P. P. Wiener and A. Noland (New York, 1957) and *Scientific Change*, ed. A. C. Crombie (London, 1963).

Medieval, Renaissance, and Modern Debts to Greek Science

On the medieval period, modern scholarship may be said to date from P. Duhem's *Le Système du monde* (10 vols., Paris, 1914–59) (see also his *Les Origines de la statique*, 2 vols., Paris, 1905–6), although many of Duhem's views are now contested. G. Sarton's *Introduction to the History of Science* (3 vols., Baltimore, 1927–48) provides indispensable biographical and bibliographical information, which can be supplemented by referring to the articles in the *Dictionary of Scientific Biography*, ed. C. C. Gillespie (New York, 1970–8).

The following works provide excellent introductions to the subjects with which they deal (those with particularly extensive bibliographies are marked *): M. Clagett, *The Science of Mechanics in the Middle Ages* (Madison, 1959)*; M. Clagett, *Archimedes in the Middle Ages, vol. 1, The Arabo-Latin Tradition* (Madison, 1964); A. C. Crombie, *Augustine to Galileo* (2 vols., rev. edn. London, 1959)*; E. J. Dijksterhuis, *The Mechanization of the World Picture* (trans. C. Dikshoorn, Oxford, 1961)*; E. Grant, *Physical Science in the*

Middle Ages (New York, 1971)*; A. R. Hall, *The Scientific Revolution* 1500–1800 (2nd edn. London, 1962)*; C. H. Haskins, *Studies in the History of Mediaeval Science* (new edn. London, 1960); M. Hesse, *Forces and Fields* (London, 1961); T. S. Kuhn, *The Copernican Revolution* (Cambridge, Mass., 1957)*; A. G. M. van Melsen, *From Atomos to Atom* (2nd edn. New York, 1960); E. A. Moody and M. Clagett, *The Medieval Science of Weights* (Madison, 1952); J. Needham, *A History of Embryology* (2nd edn. Cambridge, 1959)*; O. Pedersen and M. Pihl, *Early Physics and Astronomy* (London, 1974); H. Rashdall, *The Universities of Europe in the Middle Ages* (new edn., ed. F. M. Powicke and A. B. Emden, Oxford, 1936); G. Sarton, *The Appreciation of Ancient and Medieval Science during the Renaissance* (Philadelphia, 1955).

10

MYTH

S. G. PEMBROKE

Perseus and Andromeda, Heracles and the Nemean lion, Leda and the swan—there is no great difficulty in giving an instance of a Greek myth, but to give a definition or point to the distinctive characteristics common to these examples is more of an undertaking, and may even prove a mistaken one. It is a recurrent phenomenon in language that when two words derived from the same stem are observed to have taken different forms, one of these becomes available to have a new meaning attached to it and is accordingly displaced in sense. In English, for example, 'story' and 'history' both have the same pedigree, starting with the Greek *historia* which was the title of Herodotus' work, an 'inquiry', though not at that time necessarily or by definition one concerned with the past or even with specifically human affairs. The restriction in sense came later in antiquity, but the term was never pejorative, whereas in our own language the unhelpful label of story-teller so often attached to the father of history is clearly derogatory, placing emphasis on the element of discontinuity in his narrative—an emphasis belied by the extremely careful selection and organization of subject-matter which a less superficial reading reveals—yet the label is ultimately derived from his own title. Etymology, as Aquinas observed, is not the same as meaning. With the word myth, itself Greek (*mythos*), we can to some extent observe the process of transformation taking place. In the earliest Greek literature, it means no more than speech or utterance, and is already contrasted with action in much the same way that *logos* (which came to replace it in this sense) was in the time of Thucydides placed in opposition to fact, the pair standing respectively for theory and practice. It is perhaps worth noticing that *logos* itself was by no means restricted to a single usage, since the term enjoyed a spectacular subsequent career, firstly as the Stoic principle permeating the entire universe and finally as that co-existent with God in the Gospel according to St John.

In the specific sense of speech, *mythos* was gradually ousted by the new term. Herodotus' predecessor Hecataeus of Miletus began his work by contrasting the version of things he was to set out (the verbal form *mytheitai* is used) with the accounts (*logoi*) given by other Greeks, the distinction lying not in the greater degree of rationality of the latter but rather (as he explicitly tells us) in that his own version is what he believes to be the truth, whereas other accounts are many and ridiculous. In Pindar, on the other hand, *mythoi* are associated with falsehood and contrasted with the true *logos*, and although some skill is required for their elaboration, he is explicit that this can deceive and may even be a force for wrongdoing. Herodotus alternates between representing his work as a single discourse (*logos*) and as one sub-divided into a plurality of separate *logoi*, yet he rejects as *mythos* the traditional picture of the River Ocean encircling the world and the story of the Egyptians attempting to submit Heracles to a human sacrifice. In the former case he adds that this picture is beyond the bounds of proper inquiry, but 'story' in the sense suggested earlier is probably a close equivalent. Ironically, this anticipates the famous claim made by Thucydides for the superiority of his own account of the Greek past over earlier versions in both verse and prose, and for the permanent value of his description of the Peloponnesian War: the prevalent traditions used by the writers of prose could not be subjected to rigorous criticism but had in the process of time 'won out' towards 'the mythical', and he was aware that the absence of this element of story-telling (*to mythodes*) might appear unattractive to the less assiduous of his own readers. With Plato, the polarity between *mythos* and *logos* is virtually complete: the stories we tell children are false in the sense that they are not literally accurate (the adjective *pseudes* does not distinguish fiction from lying, as Augustine was able to do in contrasting *ficta* with *mendacia*), yet they contain an element of truth—a formulation which points to the need for stories to be interpreted but gives no indication as to how this should be set about.

This brief and far from comprehensive survey of usage may well seem laboured, but should suffice to indicate that the usage prevalent in the past two hundred years whereby myth—which becomes a universal abstraction when reduced to the singular—is represented as the expression of a mode of thinking, one peculiar to a certain stage of psychological development or characteristic of the prehistoric beginnings of human society, is an extension of the term which was not anticipated in antiquity, though it is of course not invalidated on this score alone.

One further caveat is needed before the equation of *mythos* with story can be accepted. If story-telling can be contrasted with more serious pursuits this is in terms of the arbitrary and discontinuous nature of the subjects chosen: a succession of stories connected neither by their themes nor their characters has little more claim to being an art-form than the bottomless dream of Shakespeare's Bottom. The subject-matter of Greek myths, however, was far from arbitrary, being strictly and even (at a stage which it is not easy to pinpoint) chronologically delimited, and so far from being a mere conglomeration of isolated anecdotes, like the animal scenarios of Aesop, which form a *corpus* quite distinct from myths proper, they were linked in an extraordinarily coherent form which is at least internally continuous and remained until late antiquity a vital aspect of Greek consciousness of the past.

How far this was in turn continuous with the contemporary world is a larger question. The *Iliad* of Homer repeatedly emphasizes that its characters are not like his contemporaries and are vastly superior to them: one man could single-handed lift a stone so large it would defeat two men today. Homer does not however claim to give an account of the Trojan War as such: the anger of Achilles is an isolated incident in the tenth year of the war, and the homecoming of Odysseus to Ithaca gives no more than glimpses of the Greek world as a whole in the decades that followed. With Herodotus, a decisive step is taken when, after briefly rehearsing a so-called 'Persian' account of the origins of the conflict between Greeks and barbarians—one which traced the Persian Wars of the fifth century directly back to the abduction of Io, Europa, and Helen—he rejects this in favour of a historical space which has no antecedents prior to the King of Lydia who initiated aggression against the Greeks in the first half of the sixth century B.C.

It was this affirmation of discontinuity between myth and history which made historical investigation in our sense possible. The Stoics, despite the decisively unhistorical character of their world-picture, gave a higher status to causality than had been accepted by any previous philosophers, stating that every single event had a cause, that each cause was 'enslaved' to its predecessor in an unbroken chain, and that a single event without a cause would be sufficient to destroy the universe. Though in one sense a necessary prerequisite to a scientific view of the world, this would, if applied literally to human affairs, rule out the possibility of a new departure of any kind and lend credibility to the absurd claim, fashionable in fifteenth-century Rome, that the destruction of Constantinople by the Turks in 1453 redressed the imbalance caused by the Greeks destroying the city of the Trojans. In antiquity, the demarcation implied by Herodotus between myth and history was later made explicit and indeed duplicated. The Roman antiquarian Varro adopted a Greek division of the past into three main periods: the uncertain (from the beginning of mankind to the first Flood), the 'mythical' (from the Flood to the first Olympiad), and the historical, which began in 776 B.C. This is less schematic and artificial than it may seem and is broadly correct in its location of Greek myths, at least heroic ones. Accounts of the births of the gods could not be brought into relation with the generations of heroes and belonged to an altogether different time-scale (the generation being the only means available for computing dates prior to the first Olympiad), except in such unusual cases as that of Dionysus, whose mother Semele was mortal and indeed predeceased him.

According to Herodotus, it was Hesiod and Homer who composed the Greek account of the birth of the gods, gave them their titles, distinguished the honours appropriate to each and their respective specialities, and even indicated what they looked like. This statement, which sounds less controversial today than was probably intended, is accurate to the extent that no earlier account is known from Greek literature, but clearly calls for some qualification in the case of the Homeric poems, which have little to say of divine births except by way of parenthesis. (It is worth noticing in this context that Homer's allusions to events prior to the Trojan War are in the case of human beings confined, with few exceptions, to the previous two generations). The *Theogony* of Hesiod is a more systematic treatment and unique among other such accounts in having survived intact. It should be emphasized, however, that its author had no kind of official status. The poem may or may not be the hymn for which he tells us in the *Works and Days* he was awarded a prize at the funeral games of Amphidamas at Chalcis in Euboea, but this detail neatly symbolizes his actual locus in Greek literature, that of a successful competitor: rival versions, such as that of the later Epimenides of Crete, did not in Thucydides' term 'win out', and though priority came later to be a factor in this process, the poem's initial success would hardly be explicable if it had not been at least broadly compatible with received ideas. (The legitimation he claims explicitly is that of the Muses who appeared to him on Mount Helicon and placed a sceptre in his hand, but there is clearly a limit to the degree of blasphemous innovation which could be countenanced on this score.) Neither Hesiod's account nor that which can be pieced together from Homer was so far canonical as to exclude any subsequent additions to the pantheon or indeed to rule out in perpetuity the construction of different versions, and in both cases what Herodotus represents as being laid down by the two poets is on the contrary more presupposed than stipulated.

Much the same is true of the earliest known versions of the heroic myths which belong to the second of Varro's three periods. The broad distinction between gods and heroes is occasionally blurred, as when Apollo is condemned by Zeus to a period of service in the house of the unheroic mortal Admetus, or when together with the sea-god Poseidon he stoops to casual labour, building a wall for King Laomedon of Troy and failing to elicit the pay due to him. More often the relation was a more formal one. Many heroes were demi-gods in the literal sense of having one divine parent. In a minority of cases, this favour was granted by a divine mother to a mortal father, the best-known instance being probably that of Aeneas' father Anchises, who was so honoured by Aphrodite herself, although a number of the more obscure nymphs also displayed a weakness for mankind. They are however sufficiently few to constitute an exception to the pattern of divine father and mortal mother which is the rule. And just as in the Homeric poems, divine intervention often appears to add no more than an extra dimension to what could have been expressed in purely human terms (for instance when Athena breathes strength and daring into Diomedes), so in the genealogies intervention by a divine begetter did not normally result in single-parent families or prevent the girl from obtaining a mortal husband to act as the social father of her child. Thus, while Zeus was the *genitor* of Heracles, Amphitryon was his *pater* and indeed in this case already married to the hero's future mother Alcmene, leaving Zeus with no more convincing disguise to adopt than actual impersonation. Herodotus was sufficiently struck by the absence of a mortal father for Perseus corresponding to the shower of gold in the form of which Zeus gained access to the hero's mother Danae as to make this generation the turning-point in the Hellenization of the family tree, himself taking the highly unorthodox view that Danae's father Acrisius was an Egyptian.

In extant classical texts, myths are preserved largely by brief allusions, which need to be collated carefully if the development and changing treatment of a particular theme is to be traced. It is despite this a not uncommon experience for students of the literature to be asked a question about Greek myths by an interested non-specialist and to find not merely that they do not know the answer but that they have never thought of the question themselves. In antiquity, the Emperor Tiberius regularly catechized the grammarians precisely in order to create the same embarrassment: who was Hecuba's mother (or Nestor's wife), what was the song sung by the Sirens? For routine queries, a provisional reply, though one often liable to over-simplification, is usually to be found in a handbook of mythology—an ambiguous term, since the suffix *-ology* can mean not only 'science of' (as in psychology), but also 'collection of' (as in anthology), and one whose use does not make for clarity. Many such handbooks were already circulating in antiquity, and of the few which have come down to us, far and away the most valuable is the work of Apollodorus known as the *Library*, which dates from the Imperial period. What gives this work its special importance is not only its comprehensive character or the fact that in the case of variant traditions it frequently cites by name very much earlier sources, but also the way in which it is arranged, starting with the births of the gods and then setting out the generations of heroes in a strictly genealogical sequence: first the descendants of Deucalion, the survivor of the Greek flood, among whom those of his grandson Aeolus have a special prominence, then the descendants of Io, and finally the third great family tree of the Atlantids. A separate section is devoted to the kings of Athens and finally, in an epitome which is of less unique value but was not identified as such until 1885, the exploits of the Athenian Theseus are set out, followed by the events of the Trojan War down to the ill-fated return of the Greeks after the city's destruction.

Handbooks are seldom easy reading, and though the main exploits in the repertoire of Greek myths—the voyage of the Argonauts, the labours of Heracles, the Calydonian boar-hunt, and the Theban cycle—are duly set out in their place, the *Library* is for consultation rather than continuous reading, since the grand total of deeds summarized is far more than can be absorbed at a single sitting, nor do the genealogical threads provide a modern reader with much guidance through this labyrinth of narrative. They are however quite certainly an early feature. It has long been known that essentially the same format was adopted by some of the earliest writers of Greek prose, such as Pherecydes of Athens and Hellanicus of Lesbos. More recently, it has become unquestionable that the earliest prose writers had a poetic antecedent in the *Catalogue of Women* now known from over 400 fragments and compiled, probably in the sixth century B.C., as an extension to the brief list of heroes with divine mothers which is placed at the end of Hesiod's *Theogony*. The *Catalogue* is not brilliant as verse but is a significant achievement in that it is quite certainly conceived on a unitary plan and is apparently successful in reducing the entire corpus of Greek myths to an orderly structure consisting of three main families spanning no more than seven generations prior to the Trojan War. These three families are further mutually linked by intermarriage and individual migrations from one part of the Greek world to another. It is also remarkable in that so far from excluding non-Greeks, the *Catalogue* is at pains to incorporate the individual ancestors of all neighbouring peoples that can be located: the descendants of Io include not only Cretans but the eponymous Phoenix, Arabus, and Aegyptus, who have counterparts on both the Northern and Southern coasts of Anatolia. A rather similar inclusiveness is reflected in the family tree of the Kings of Lydia, where Candaules is represented as a descendant of Heracles, and still more strikingly in the pedigree which makes the eponymous ancestor of the Persians into the son of the Greek Perseus by Andromeda—both pedigrees, surprisingly, recorded by the writer who made his subject-matter the conflict between Greeks and barbarians, Herodotus.

This aspect of Greek myths is not, of course, one which has most fired the imaginations of successive generations, but it is one which raises important questions regarding their origin: a genealogical background may or may not appear minimally necessary for beings of a hybrid nature, like Centaurs and Silens, but is not easy to discard from the story of the flight of the Danaids from their amorous cousins. It is also an aspect which throws light on Greek attitudes to their heroic past. In a famous passage of one of the Platonic dialogues, Socrates asks the sophist Hippias which of the latter's various specialities are most in demand at Sparta. On hearing that the Spartans have no interest in astronomy and are insufficiently numerate to spend any time on mathematics, he tries the suggestion that rhetoric and the study of language may be more popular, but these too are, it seems, a closed book to the Spartans: the only thing they do want to hear about is 'the families of heroes and mankind, and how cities were founded in the old days—they like any kind of account of the old times (*archaeologia*)', and Hippias admits to having gained expertise in this field for the sole reason that it was at such a premium in Sparta (Plato, *The Greater Hippias*, 285D).

There is good evidence that Spartan tastes were widely shared throughout the Greek world, while the linking of heroes with ordinary mankind points to the role played by the mythical past in validating new foundations as the Greeks spread overseas. A persistent tradition which goes back at least to the sixth century B.C. represents the Greek cities of Asia Minor as founded about the time of the Trojan War by Messenian exiles from Pylos, usually represented as having first put in a brief stay at Athens. This is sometimes regarded as containing an element of historical truth, but is probably more in the nature of propaganda: we know from an inscription that leading citizens of fifth-century Miletus bore such distinctively 'Messenian' personal names as Cresphontes, and by this time Messenia had long since been taken over by the Spartans.[1] To anyone in need of ancestors, Nestor and his sons, last heard of sacrificing to Poseidon in the *Odyssey*, had

---

[1] R. Meiggs and D. M. Lewis, *A Selection of Greek Historical Inscriptions* (Oxford, 1969), No. 43.

much to recommend themselves. Propaganda of this kind continues well into the Hellenistic period, with learned pedigrees transforming the Cypriot king Cinyras—a marginal figure in the *Iliad* and not himself a participant in the Trojan expedition—into a descendant of the Athenian Cecrops, and hence a half-way stage towards establishing the antiquity and authentically Greek character of cities in Cilicia and of even more recent foundations in Syria. In Southern Italy, the gradual Hellenization of a non-Greek people is reflected in their claim to Spartan descent, and at a probably still later date, the Nasamones of Libya are turned into a Greek colony from Naryca in Locris. The traditional framework of genealogy was open-ended to the extent that it remained permanently susceptible to additions as well as to revisions. Ideologically, a mythical pedigree expressed and validated the Greek character of a city wherever this was not otherwise firmly rooted in the heroic past. As late as the second century A.D., the Hellenized cities of Asia Minor are to be seen not only constructing new genealogies for themselves but visibly embodying them in the public imagery of their coins.

The race of heroes is defined by Hesiod as those who were killed fighting at Thebes and those who took part in the Trojan expedition and met with a similar fate, a definition which is far too restrictive and by no means corresponds to the highly complex reality of hero-cults in religious practice. If the prevailing image of a hero was that of an exceptional human being who had lived and died—a status intermediate between that of gods and men and comparable with that of saints, with the important qualification that saintliness was not a requirement—many cults are known in which the hero or heroine seems to have no biography and some in which they have no name either, merely a local habitation. Commentators of late antiquity, developing a somewhat revisionist suggestion made in the *Laws* (717A) of Plato, tried to make out that the cult of gods and that of heroes were symmetrically opposed, and that it was the norm to sacrifice white animals to the gods in the morning and black ones to heroes in the afternoon or even at night. This is undoubtedly far too schematic, since daytime was the norm for all offerings but those of an unusually sinister character, such as the one made to the dead by Odysseus (in strict accordance with the detailed instructions of Circe) at the entrance to the under-

world. Heroes were looked on as the protectors of a city no less
than were its gods, and they were often more easy to locate: in
the sixth century, Spartan morale was sufficiently boosted by
the 'discovery' (prompted by an oracle) of the bones of
Orestes to achieve a long-delayed victory over Tegea in
Arcadia, and while (as can be seen from Pausanias) the
prestige of relics underwent something of a decline in the
period of Imperial tourism, it was still a significant feather in
the cap of the Athenian Cimon that he was able to bring back
to Athens the bones of Theseus which had conveniently
turned up on the island of Scyros in 476 B.C.

In literature, as is well known, Greek myths were subject to
constant modification and readaptation, from the palinode of
Stesichorus (supposedly smitten with blindness as a punishment for what he had said about Helen) to Pindar's refusal to
state the fate of Bellerophon or represent Demeter as so greedy
in her mourning for the loss of Persephone as absent-mindedly
to consume the shoulder of Pelops served up to the gods by his
father Tantalus, or Euripides' unorthodox if not unprecedented representation of Medea as the murderess of her own
children (they are elsewhere said to have been killed by the
people of Corinth).[2] It is not easy to assess the statement in the
Poetics (1451b25) of Aristotle that of the two kinds of plot,
familiar and invented, even the first will be familiar only to a
minority of the audience, since we have little more evidence
with which to control this than we do for the extent of literacy
in the age of the tragedians.

It is however disconcerting to hear of still more drastic
revisions made at a popular level and affecting actual religious practice. Thucydides (5.11) tells us of the systematic
decision of the people of Amphipolis to eradicate all traces of
their founder Hagnon in favour of the Spartan commander
Brasidas shortly after the latter's death, marking his services
to the city in the first decade of the Peloponnesian War by
recognizing him as their founder and holding funeral games
and annual sacrifices in his honour. In the following century,
heroic status undergoes a radical extension almost comparable
to the spread of the horseless carriage in modern times. From
about 300 B.C. onwards, inscriptions reveal men and women
endowing cult foundations for the perpetuation of their own

[2] Stesichorus: Plato, *Phaedrus*, 243A; Pindar, *Olympian*, 1. 52.

memory as heroes or heroines. So also, surprisingly, does the last will and testament of the philosopher Epicurus, who despite his highly unorthodox view of the nature of the gods is known to have advocated fairly strict observance of conventional religion. His will provides for monthly commemoration as well as annual heroic offerings on his birthday.[3] With these endowments, heroic status enters the age of the common man.

The date of this transition is not without significance, in that it was only after the death of Alexander and the subsequent carving-up of his empire into three that the first systematic attempt was made, in Ptolemaic Alexandria, to establish a library on a 'copyright' scale with at least one text of every significant work of classical literature. The scholars associated with this huge project were all Greek, and despite the multi-racial (though highly stratified) nature of their environment, present themselves as more Greek, and considerably more learned, than were their predecessors on the mainland. In their creative writing (as distinct from works of scholarship), they concentrated not on the hackneyed main thoroughfares of Greek myth but on the untrodden paths which Callimachus (*Aetia*, fr. 1, 21–8) tells us were recommended to him by Apollo when the poet first placed a writing-tablet on his knees. At its worst, this tendency could result in almost impenetrable obscurity, like that of Lycophron's appalling messenger-speech known as the *Alexandra*, some 1,500 lines placed in the mouth of a Cassandra no less hideously erudite than she is gloomy, and predicting every conceivable disaster in language so recherché that we could hardly begin to understand it without the aid of a Byzantine commentary many times longer than the original. A more positive aspect is to be seen in the transformation by Theocritus of the Cyclops Polyphemus from the inhuman cannibal of the *Odyssey*, who overturns the rules of hospitality by eating his guests, into the charmingly naïve and self-conscious admirer of Galatea; in the substitution by Eratosthenes of entertainment (*psychagogia*) for instruction as the primary aim of poetry; and in the throw-away urbanity of Callimachus, a poet early admired and edited by the great Renaissance scholar Angelo Poliziano, but one whose direct influence on European literature thereafter is not easy to trace

[3] Diogenes Laertius, 10. 18.

apart from one sentimental translation of an epigram.[4] The Hellenistic legacy also includes the earliest surviving treatment on a full scale, by Callimachus' younger contemporary Apollonius of Rhodes, of the story of the Argonauts, previously known only from Pindar's Fourth Pythian Ode, which takes a 'short cut' at the precise moment when the full narrative seems to be forthcoming, thereby baulking the reader of the anticipated details in favour of a plea to his patron about a deserving exile.

The sophistication of these writers is a fact of vital importance in European literature, since the captive Greece which Horace was to represent as itself taking Rome captive with its cultural tradition was not the Greece of Homer or even of Sophocles, but the highly learned, literary Greece of the Alexandrians. It is partly for this reason that mythical allusions in Latin poets such as Propertius so often take what seems a needlessly indirect form, and it is most unlikely that the *Metamorphoses* of Ovid—probably the single most important source for the transmission of Greek myths to Western Europe, and one by no means eclipsed in the Renaissance with the recovery of earlier sources—would have been cast in so contrived a format if the groundwork and selection of themes had not at least in part been carried out in earlier works such as the lost *Transformations* of Nicander of Colophon.[5]

Greek myths were known to the Etruscans long before the time of Callimachus, and quite a number (particularly the story of the Trojan exile who was to be the central figure of Virgil's *Aeneid*) were circulating in the Italian peninsula at a surprisingly early date. It is worth emphasizing, however, that by the time of the late Republic, when the full impact of Greek culture was being felt at Rome, there came with it a long tradition of conscious interpretation of myths in accordance with a number of firmly established criteria. It is not easy to pinpoint the beginnings of this sort of speculation. In the *Phaedrus* of Plato, Socrates is asked (229C) if he believes the story of Boreas (the North Wind) abducting Oreithyia to

---

[4] Theocritus, *Idyll* 11; Eratosthenes in Strabo, *Geography*, 1. 1, 10. Callimachus' epigram to Heraclitus (No. 2) is widely known in the version of William Cory (1845).

[5] For reasons of space, what follows is concentrated largely on the study of myths as such and in their relation to prehistory and religion, at the expense of literature and art. See further the list of Further Reading.

be true, and replies that he could try and be clever by saying that what really happened was that she was blown off a rock by a gust of wind, but then he would have to go on and deal with composite beings like Centaurs, Gorgons, and Chimaeras, and that he does not have the time for this kind of rather boorish ingenuity. Elsewhere, we hear of individuals who went in for extricating the 'hidden meanings' (*hyponoiai*) of Homer, and there is some evidence that rhapsodes themselves were expected to give an account of the poems in addition to reciting them. There is undoubtedly much in Homer to suggest the validity of an allegorical approach, since the poet presents not only dreams but rivers and even prayers in a personal form, these last being at one point termed daughters of Zeus (*Iliad*, 9. 502). Other commentators, notably the Stoics, took this a stage further, making the various deities involved no more than personifications of natural forces such as air, fire, and water, that is to say, making Homer out to be himself an exponent of their own philosophical system. The number of deities to be interpreted exceeded that of the explanatory notions available, and hence there are some surprising identifications: both Apollo and Dionysus are said to represent the sun, but this can now be paralleled in a papyrus commentary on verses attributed to Orpheus which was found in a tomb at Derveni in Thessalonica in 1962 and probably dates from the early third century B.C., where Zeus is identified not only with the air, which is also said to be represented by the Ocean, but with Aphrodite and Harmonia.[6]

A third approach is associated with the name of Euhemerus of Messene, whom Callimachus labelled a criminal scribbler. Euhemerus claimed to have visited an island in the Ocean where he found an inscribed monument which revealed that all the gods had really been simply human beings, kings and rulers whose real position during their lifetimes had subsequently been misunderstood. Euhemerus was translated by the early Roman poet Ennius, fragments of whose work are preserved in the polemical writing of the Christian Lactantius. They were therefore still circulating at the close of antiquity, and both the physical and the Euhemerist interpretations found their way into the various mythological com-

---

[6] S. G. Kapsomenos, *Arch. Deltion*, xix (1964), 17–25.

pendia by which the stories themselves were precariously transmitted from late antiquity to the Carolingian revival of learning. The Greek word allegory is itself not attested until the time of Cicero, but its subsequent career was more than enough to make up for this late start.

In a period when cultural activity is generally inhibited, allegory may at first sight appear to be one area in which there is still scope for originality, particularly when the gap between the outward semblances of the figure undergoing interpretation and its supposed real meaning is sufficiently breath-taking, for example when Odysseus' wife Penelope is said to be the spirit of philosophy, combining propositions in the web of syllogism, then undoing it by analytical means. There is also a physical interpretation: Penelope is a manifestation of Nature, weaving the transient bodies of mankind on the marble loom of our bones. Interpretations of this kind, however, are ultimately more arbitrary than original, and the comparison is most often purely adventitious, not selected against the background of an accumulation of previous interpretations but simply plucked out of the air. In late antiquity, the situation was complicated by pagan and Christian polemic: the pagans, on the defensive against onslaughts on the cruder aspects of traditional myths and religion—not a particulary difficult target, since both had been the object of an ongoing critique which can be traced back via Plato to the rhapsode Xenophanes—resorted to claiming a hidden moral content for the outwardly often embarrassingly down-to-earth ritual prescriptions of Pythagoras, and to hinting at a secret doctrine imparted to those initiated in the mysteries.

The Christians had a wider repertoire of explanatory notions at their command, and could attribute such success as was enjoyed by pagan cults prior to their overthrow by Constantine to the presence of evil demons actually inhabiting the statues of the gods (a number of the neo-Platonists are known to have dabbled in 'theurgic' procedures to bring statues to life which have distant Mesopotamian antecedents in nocturnal ceremonies by means of which the eyes and mouths of the statues were opened). Later, after the triumph of Christianity and when pagan literature was found to be irreplaceable as a vehicle of education, it could also be used to point either to an advance revelation of the incarnation or to the distortion of the gospel by other demons, which like the Almighty were regarded as capable of direct intervention in both deed and word.

Against this background, it could hardly be expected that much progress was to be made in the study of Greek and Roman myths. The Middle Ages brought new personifications, such as the Vices and Virtues, but Dante's *bella menzogna* is no significant theoretical advance on Plato and Augustine, and the range of interpretations in Boccaccio's *Genealogia* is wholly prefigured by those of antiquity. No real progress in the study of myths was to be made in Western Europe until the vast quantity of ancient texts recovered in the half-century preceding the fall of Constantinople (1453) became available, and for a considerable time thereafter their readers were largely at the mercy of the substantial quantity of works purporting to be what they were not, such as the Judaeo-Christian Greek hexameters presented in the form of Sibylline oracles, or the Hermetic treatises which are now dated to the second and third centuries A.D. but which on the authority of the Church fathers were of immense antiquity, indeed older than Moses. Plato himself was supposed to have visited Egypt and there associated with Egyptian priests who revealed to him the truth of monotheism which they had learned from Moses, a doctrine he was only restrained from propagating by the contemplation of the fate of his master Socrates. A further impetus in this direction was probably given by the earliest Greek immigrants to Italy: Gemistus Plethon (d. 1452) drew up a long list of early prophets of the truth, of whom far-and-away the earliest was Zoroaster, whom he dated to over 5,000 years before the coming of the descendants of Heracles. It is well known, and understandable, how long Virgil's Fourth Eclogue was thought to herald the birth of Christ, but it is perhaps more startling to find that the immensely influential Latin translation of Plato by Marsilio Ficino which was commissioned by Cosimo de' Medici was in 1463 actually postponed, on his orders, so that priority could be given to the wisdom of Thrice-Great Hermes.

Another teacher of secret doctrines was the legendary Thracian poet Orpheus, under whose name a vast quantity of hexameter verse was circulating in antiquity (including an epic poem about the Argonauts, the late date of which was not established until the early nineteenth century). The authenticity of the Hermetic treatises and the Sibylline oracles was finally rebutted by the great scholar Isaac Casaubon in the year of his death (1614), but Orpheus had a lengthier career: as late as 1738, Bishop Warburton could advance the view (subsequently endorsed by Voltaire) that the secret doctrine imparted at the Eleusis mysteries was Orpheus' doctrine of the one true God, and that the mutilation of the Herms during the Peloponnesian War was a spontaneous expression of protest against polytheism by the revellers to whom the secret was illicitly revealed by Alcibiades.

A further source of confusion was the number of ancient traditions about foreign immigrants to Greece. In Book 2 of the *Iliad* Pelops, the son of Tantalus appears as an ancestor of Agamemnon. Thucydides, because the southern peninsula of Greece was known as Pelops' island and because Pelops' father was thought to have lived in Asia Minor, concluded that the house of Atreus was an invading dynasty, thereby lending their arrival an importance comparable to that of the Norman conquest of Britain. Many other such traditions were similarly interpreted in antiquity, such as the 'Thracians' associated with Orpheus at Eleusis and above all the 'Phoenician' Cadmus of Thebes.

The reconstruction of prehistory on a still more ambitious scale was a widespread preoccupation from the Renaissance onwards. In antiquity, allegory was frequently reinforced by the use of highly shaky etymologies. From the sixteenth century onwards, the Hebrew language was also brought to bear on the problem of Greek prehistory, which it was at the same time sought to reconcile with Biblical tradition. This was achieved by such drastic means as identifying Agamemnon's daughter Iphigeneia with the daughter of Jephthah, supposing Deucalion to be identical with Noah, and, in general, giving to the Phoenicians a role as intermediaries which went far beyond anything directly reported in ancient sources. The attempt to reconcile sacred and secular tradition reached its height in the seventeenth century, yet despite the quantity and diversity of ancient evidence scholars such as G. J. Voss were able to bring to bear on the problem, or perhaps rather precisely because this was virtually unmanageable, the result was if anything a retrograde step in terms of method. The use made of the material becomes little more than eclectic, Noah being identified with the Roman gods Janus and Saturn, and the Egyptian Apis-calf described by Herodotus turned into a symbol of the patriarch Joseph. The *Demonstratio Evangelica* of P. D. Huet (1679) is at least more systematic in representing virtually every Greek deity from Apollo to Priapus, together with a throng of mythical figures such as Teiresias and Orpheus, as each being no more than a distortion of Moses (of whom the Greeks had learned from Cadmus). In the same way, the story of the Argonauts was later seen as derived from the crossing of the Israelites from Egypt into Palestine. Lord Herbert of Cherbury went further than Voss in supposing all mankind to have an innate knowledge of the one true God, its corruption from a purely symbolical adoration of the manifestations of His glory to an idolatrous one being due to manipulation by a race of crafty priests—a view which came dangerously close to rendering the Christian religion superfluous, but which also anticipates the anti-clericalism which is evident between the lines of much written about ancient myths and religion in the eighteenth century. A turning-point is marked by Fontenelle, not so much with his paper on the origin of fables, which is original in seeing myths as a kind of primitive explanation but superficial in its treatment of detail, as with the *History of Oracles* (1687), which is admittedly derivative but which is very much more readable than the two Latin dissertations of his immediate source, and which effectively put paid to the use of evil demons as a means of explaining the oracles' working, substituting for them the purely human agency of priestly deception.

In the following century, the priority of monotheism was reversed in David Hume's *Natural History of Religion* (1757), which argued that this had everywhere been preceded by idolatry or polytheism. In France, this sequence was given wider circulation by Charles de Brosses, who lifted whole passages from Hume but also prefaced polytheism with a still earlier stage, the cult of 'fetishes' reported from West Africa by Willem Bosman in 1704, to which, once it was seen as having a universal character, ancient descriptions of animal-worship in Egypt and the aniconic cult objects listed in Pausanias also seemed to refer. For the interpretation of myths, a more significant development was the new emphasis apparent in Germany in the second half of the century on their collective or rather national character: Herder rejects

the view of entire peoples being the dupes of their priests or
shamans with the observation that the shamans themselves
live among and are influenced by the imaginations of their
people. In 1795 F. A. Wolf, developing a suggestion of the
English traveller Robert Wood (1767), challenged the view
that Homer was a real individual (a view already rejected in
the brilliant *New Science* of Giambattista Vico, the final version
of which was published in Naples in 1744 but which remained
largely unknown outside Italy until the following century),
and this led to a quite new perspective of the 'mythical age'.
In the next generation, Karl Otfried Müller, in his *Prolegomena
to a Scientific Mythology* (1825, Engl. tr. 1844) actually rejects
the question whether myths are a collective creation or that of
individuals as wrongly posed, since their unconscious and
inevitable nature is such that the individual becomes no more
than the voice through which the people speaks.

Also apparent in the first half of the nineteenth century is a
new respect for the phenomenon of personification, not at the
superficial level at which the Greeks invented eponymous
heroes but as a characteristic of human perception, early man
being in the slightly later formulation of Auguste Comte
virtually limited to transferring the sense of existence he felt
within himself to the outside. That this tendency could be
observed by his readers in themselves also is suggested by the
example of a clock stopping, to which, he observes, the
natural immediate reaction is to view it as misbehaviour on
the part of a capricious being. It is a far cry from these
insights to the rigidly inflexible notion of primitive mentality
advanced in the first volume of Sir James Frazer's *Golden
Bough* and later associated with the name of Lucien Lévy-
Bruhl.

The collective nature of myths seemed in the first half of the
nineteenth century to be borne out by the children's tales
preserved by oral tradition and recorded by the brothers
Grimm. Despite this, the allegorical tradition was by no
means as yet extinct, being successively revived in England by
Richard Payne Knight, and in Germany by Friedrich
Creuzer. Finally, as an indirect result of the discovery of the
Indo-European family of languages, Adalbert Kuhn and Max
Müller attached such prominence to the sky-god prototype of
Zeus and Jupiter that they saw the real subject-matter of all
myths as meteorological events such as the sun being obscured

by clouds—a late reversion to the 'physical' allegories of
antiquity which made the chief factors in the formation of
myths no more than misunderstanding and forgetfulness. In
the second half of the century, a new interest in the evolution
of human society was prompted by a succession of works of
which the earliest was that of J. J. Bachofen on 'mother-right'
(1861), and Greek myths came to be scanned for indications
of early social conditions and family structure, though the
period for which antiquity retained its classic status in this
debate was relatively short-lived, and a growing preoccupation with the problem of 'totemism' came to suggest that
evidence of more direct value was to be found among
contemporary peoples, particularly when (as Andrew Lang
put it) Heaven, to punish the sins of the learned, allowed the
northern tribes of Central Australia to be discovered.

Another significant development of this time is a renewed
interest in the nature of ritual and its relation to myths, to
which fresh impetus was given by W. Robertson Smith's work
on early Semitic religion. In this connection it had already
been made clear by K. O. Müller that the part-time nature of
priesthoods in the Greek world, the absence of any kind of
hierarchical organization corresponding to a clergy, and
above all the lack of contact between the cult personnel of
different cities ruled out the picture of waves of immigrant
preachers from the East so often advanced in the previous
century. A one-to-one correspondence between myth and
ritual is not to be found in Greece, and the aetiological stories
told to explain the institution of particular rites and festivals
are clearly a secondary derivation from the main corpus of
Greek myths which has no light to throw on their origin. At
the same time, detailed study has revealed the presence in
Greek myths of some recurrent themes which do have ritual
aspects, such as the supernatural means of rendering children
immortal by plunging them in a cauldron, and the exchange
of clothes between the sexes which is not only a feature of the
mythical adolescence of Achilles and Dionysus but is also
known as a characteristic of wedding-ceremonies in many
different parts of the Greek world.

The new approaches made to the study of myths in the
present century cannot be fully indicated here. In the sphere
of psychology, few reinterpretations have been more dramatic
than the theme identified by Sigmund Freud in the story of

Oedipus of the fulfilment of suppressed incestuous desires, though this is not directly applicable to the more normal pattern whereby the exiled hero is successful in escaping his origins, and the primal act of parricide envisaged in Freud's *Totem and Taboo* is more in the nature of a modern myth than an interpretation of ancient ones. In comparative studies, use has often been made of the Jungian notion of the collective unconscious, although the equivocation of this term, sometimes represented as an inherent predisposition to certain modes of perception, corresponding to the notion of instinct in the sphere of behaviour, sometimes in terms of latent psychological contents, was never fully resolved by Jung. Anthropological fieldwork has created a clearer picture of the function, location, and typology of myths in existing societies, and in the study of folk-tales, the compilation of thematic indices such as those produced by Stith Thompson and his associates has made it possible to establish with greater precision the extent to which Greek myths conform to patterns known from other societies. If they emerge as less distinctive than was previously thought and therefore less classic in status, this brings with it the converse advantage of reducing in scope the questions they should prompt, although the structural study of myths developed by Claude Lévi-Strauss over the past quarter of a century has proved no less fruitful in analysing motifs and patterns in Greek myths than in those of other societies, particularly since the opposition between nature and culture, derived by Lévi-Strauss from Rousseau, was one of which the Greeks themselves were highly conscious. Indeed, they are to be seen keenly debating the nature of morality in precisely these terms in the fifth century B.C.

That the questions prompted by Greek myths should be seen as virtually universal in scope was natural at a time when the early history of Greece appeared (as it did to the Greeks themselves) the most appropriate point at which to study the early history of mankind. In the century since the excavation of Troy, Mycenae, and Tiryns, the picture of classical Greece as a civilization effectively devoid of precedents has gradually been replaced by that of a society best explained in terms of re-emergence after the collapse of a more elaborate structure which, though it bore points of resemblance to the contemporary state societies of Anatolia and Mesopotamia, was undoubtedly Greek. The names of Greek gods found on the Linear B tablets deciphered since 1953 have perhaps yet to be squared satisfactorily with the archaeological record, and here as elsewhere, it must be borne in mind that the tablets themselves were not intended to convey to us a picture of the society in which they were written. Countless documents allocating rations are known from Mesopotamia and have more recently been found in smaller numbers at Persepolis, the latter dating from the general vicinity of the Persian Wars, yet they throw little light on the nature of the economy of these societies and none whatsoever on their literatures; and the complete absence to date of literary texts from Mycenae, Cnossus, or Thebes suggests that there are definite limits to what can be expected from the decipherment of the Linear A tablets if ever this is achieved.

Knowledge of Mesopotamian and Anatolian myths, on the other hand, has been increasing at a growing rate, and the whole question of Oriental influence was reopened with the discovery of a Hittite (Hurrian) myth of succession, in which one dynasty of gods after another is displaced by violent means. This is now widely regarded as having provided the model for the dynasties preceding Zeus in the *Theogony* of Hesiod. The Hittite story has even been used to restore credit to a document long suspect as evidence for early relations between East and West, the Phoenician history of Sanchuniathon (himself described as antedating the Trojan War), supposedly based on temple records written in an unknown script and then translated into Greek by Philo of Byblus in the second century A.D. It should however be emphasized that in the quotations which survive, whatever the ultimate date of the non-Greek data (there is some equivocation between Phoenicia and Egypt, and the *dramatis personae* include the highly suspect Hermes Trismegistus acting as scribe to Cronus in the home town of Philo), this text has many features which suggest Hellenistic influence, such as 'inventors' of boats and of the use of salt, and extreme caution is called for in its handling. However, cuneiform texts survive written as late as 75 A.D., and the interplay between East and West is a subject which will continue to receive attention in this and other fields.

That Greek myths as a whole date from the second millennium B.C. was maintained long before the decipherment of Linear B in M. P. Nilsson's *The Mycenaean Origin of Greek Mythology* (1931), on the grounds that their geographical setting consistently takes the form of areas which were of little or no importance in classical times but which are known to have been significant centres of population in the previous millennium. This has been widely accepted, but there remain many problems regarding the strictly local basis of these myths. If it was possible for an Ionian poet or poets in the eighth century to devote an entire epic to the hero whose home was a small island off the west coast of the mainland, it may seem questionable whether in Mycenaean times stories of Thessalian heroes like Jason should necessarily be thought of as originating on the spot in Thessaly itself, particularly since travel is almost a *sine qua non* for heroic exploits, which almost by definition take place abroad and not at home.

What has greatly increased our knowledge of the location of Greek myths in the classical world (in a way which literature cannot do) is the recovery and classification of the enormous number of painted earthenware vases on which mythical scenes are represented, mostly dating from the sixth and fifth centuries B.C. In the absence of a comparable corpus from the previous millennium, the question of origins is likely in many cases to remain an open one. Greek myths do not in any case present themselves in the classical period as mere survivals from a different era. They are on the contrary subject to a continual process of growth and adaptation, and for this reason provide a natural focus for the masterpieces of Greek literature and art. And while the rise of early Greek philosophy is often seen as representing a break with traditional modes of thinking, no such conflict is apparent in a letter from Aristotle which gives us a glimpse of the philosopher relaxing: 'the more time I spend on my own,' he writes, 'the fonder I have become of myths.'[7] The sense of wonder which Aristotle saw as the starting-point of philosophy, both for his predecessors and in his own time, is not so much abandoned here as revealed in another facet when, in the intervals of his own discourse, Aristotle exchanges the role of the speaker for that of the fascinated listener.

[7] Demetrius, *On Elocution*, 144 = Aristotle, fr. 15, Plezia; cf. *Metaphysics*, 982b18.

Further Reading

Of the ancient sources, the *Library* of Apollodorus is available in a Loeb translation by J. G. Frazer (1921), with copious documentation of variant accounts. Peter Levi's Penguin translation of Pausanias' *Guide to Greece* (1971) contains a wealth of local traditions recorded by a learned visitor in the second century A.D. Translators of Ovid's *Metamorphoses* have included Dryden, Congreve, and Pope, while the rhyming version of Arthur Golding (1567, reissued 1965) is known to have been used by Shakespeare. A prose translation by Mary M. Innes (1955) is available in Penguin.

Of the many modern accounts, C. Kerényi's *The Gods of the Greeks* (1951) and *The Heroes of the Greeks* (1959), both illustrated from ancient vases and now in paperback (Thames and Hudson), take the form of straightforward narratives which adhere closely to ancient sources and are well documented. An excellent general introduction is G. S. Kirk, *The Nature of Greek Myths* (Penguin, 1974). Many theoretical questions and some ancient Near Eastern material are also discussed in his *Myth: its Meaning and Functions* (Cambridge, 1970; also in paperback); on the former see, more briefly, P. S. Cohen, 'Theories of Myth', *Man* n.s. iv (1969), 337–53.

For the interpretation of myths in antiquity and the Middle Ages a useful outline is provided by Jean Seznec, *The Survival of the Pagan Gods* (New York, 1953; paperback, Harper Torchbooks, 1961). A detailed survey of the earliest allegorical treatments is made by N. J. Richardson, 'Homeric professors in the age of the sophists', *Proceedings of the Cambridge Philological Society*, n.s. xxi (1975), 65–81. For the history of the study of myths from late antiquity to the beginning of the twentieth century, Otto Gruppe's *Geschichte der klassischen Mythologie und Religionsgeschichte* (1921), originally issued as a supplement to W. H. Roscher's lexicon of Greek and Roman mythology, is the standard work of reference with an exhaustive bibliography and has since been reissued in paperback (Olms, Hildesheim, 1965). For the long history of the misconception of the antiquity of the doctrines of Hermes Trismegistus, Orpheus, and Zoroaster, D. P. Walker, *The Ancient Theology* (London, 1972; also in paperback) is an excellent, carefully documented account from the Church Fathers to the late seventeenth century and beyond; see further Frances A. Yates, *Giordano Bruno and the Hermetic Tradition* (London, 1964), esp. chs. i–iii, xxi. A useful source-book is Burton Feldman and Robert D. Richardson (ed.), *The Rise of Modern Mythology 1680–1860* (paperback, Indiana University Press, 1972), with extensive quotation and bibliography. Frank E. Manuel, *The Eighteenth Century Confronts the Gods* (Princeton, 1959) is an excellent account of primitive religion as seen during the Enlightenment, particularly in France. Two writers discussed briefly by Manuel are given a more substantive treatment by Sir Isaiah Berlin, *Vico and Herder* (London, 1976). David Hume's *Natural History of Religion* is now available in a meticulous edition by A. Wayne Colver (Oxford, 1976).

A balanced critique of anthropological theories of the nineteenth and early twentieth centuries is given by E. Evans-Pritchard, *Theories of Primitive Religion* (Oxford, 1965; also available in paperback). A classic study of the typology of myths in a non-literate society is Bronislaw Malinowski's *Myth in Primitive Psychology* (1926), reissued in his *Magic, Science, and Religion* (London, 1974; also in paperback), pp. 93–148. For Stith Thompson's

Motif-Index of Folk-Literature the revised and enlarged edition (6 vols., Copenhagen, 1955–8) should be consulted.

Claude Lévi-Strauss, *Totemism* (London, 1964; Pelican Books, 1969) reduces this notion to its proper size. His own substantive work on myths has largely concentrated on the South American Indians, but in addition to his early article 'The Structural Study of Myth' (1955), reissued in the first volume of his *Structural Anthropology* (London, 1968; Penguin Books 1972, 1977), pp. 206–31, a representative selection of studies is now collected in *Structural Anthropology II* (London, 1977), pp. 115–268.

On the relationship between myths and the rise of philosophical thinking, particular mention may be made of F. M. Cornford's posthumous *Principium Sapientiae* (Cambridge, 1952), and J.-P. Vernant, *Mythe et pensée chez les grecs* (Paris, 1966). A representative selection (in English) of the work of Vernant, P. Vidal-Naquet, and M. Detienne on Greek myths is forthcoming from Cambridge. H. and H. A. Frankfort (ed.), *The Intellectual Adventure of Ancient Man* (Chicago, 1948; later issued in Penguin under the title *Before Philosophy*) discusses the Eastern background, but the chapter on Greece is unduly influenced by the philosophy of Ernst Cassirer. Oriental precursors of Hesiod are strongly emphasized in the editions of M. L. West (Oxford, 1966, 1978).

E. R. Dodds, 'The religion of the ordinary man in classical Greece', in his *The Ancient Concept of Progress and other Essays* (Oxford, 1973), pp. 140–55, is a masterly short account, while H. W. Parke, *Festivals of the Athenians* (London, 1977) is a concise survey of State religion in the city where this is best known. A useful repertoire of early visual representations is Karl Schefold, *Myth and Legend in Early Greek Art* (London, 1966). For the classical period, Jane Henle, *Greek Myths: a Vase Painter's Notebook* (paperback, Indiana University Press, 1973) is a good introduction.

11

GREEK CULTURE AND THE JEWS

A. D. MOMIGLIANO

1.

Greek and Hebrew texts and archaeological evidence show that at least from the tenth century B.C. onwards (not to speak of the Mycenaean age), Greeks went into Palestine as sailors, merchants, and mercenaries. King David would appear to have employed Cretan mercenaries. At Samaria, Greek pottery is earlier than the destruction of the city in 722. At Tall Sukas south of Latakia in western Syria a Greek settlement (including a temple) apparently lasted with interruptions for more than one century until *c*. 500 B.C. In Askalon, Greek pottery appears at the end of the seventh century when the city was probably controlled by Egypt. When Egyptian armies penetrated into Palestine in the seventh and sixth centuries, they were partly made up of Greek mercenaries. It has even been suggested that a sort of fortress of the late seventh century (Mesad Hashavyahu) north of Ashdod was occupied by Greek mercenaries of a king of Judah. When the Jews returned from the Babylonian exile in the fifth century, traffic with the Greeks was re-established. Ashdod, the Philistine capital, has yielded abundant Athenian pottery of the late sixth and early fifth centuries. In the fourth century some Greeks lived in Acco, and the earliest coins of Judaea imitate Athenian coins. As Jews shared with the Greeks the reputation of being good mercenary soldiers there were other occasions for acquaintance in the armies of Babylonian, Egyptian, and Persian kings.

Yet there is no sign that before Alexander the Great the Greeks knew the Jews by name or had any information about their political and religious peculiarities. Herodotus went to Tyre, not to Jerusalem. For him, as for the Greeks of his own and earlier times, the Phoenicians were a recognizable entity to whom, among other things, the discovery of the alphabet was due. The existence of the Jews seems to have remained concealed under the notion of Palestine (Herodotus, 2. 104; 7. 89). Jewish writers of the Hellenistic and Roman periods did their best to discover indirect allusions to the Jews in Greek classical texts, but were themselves surprised by the poverty of their harvest.

To judge from the Bible, the Jews before Alexander knew a little more about the Greeks, but not much. They had a name for them (which was the current one in the whole Near East): Yawan, that is, Ionia. They also had a special name for the inhabitants of Cyprus, Kittim (from the city of Kition). The name does not seem to have been limited to the Phoenician section of Cyprus. In the table of the nations of Genesis, chapter 10, Kittim is a son of Yawan. In the prophecy of Balaam (Num. 24: 24), the Kittim coming by sea clash to no avail with the Assyrians, which may be an echo of the fighting between Greeks and Assyrians in the late eighth and seventh centuries B.C. In the Hellenistic age, Kittim came to indicate the Greeks in general, the Seleucids in particular, and even the Romans. Furthermore, Ezechiel and Joel—in passages variously dated in the sixth or fifth century, or even later— know the Greeks (Yawan) as slave-traders who buy the children of Judah and Jerusalem. There is a glimpse of a higher world when Yawan is mentioned in the last chapter of Isaiah (late sixth century?) as one of the nations to whom God will declare his glory. We have no evidence that the Jews knew of Sparta and Athens before Alexander the Great penetrated into Palestine in 332 B.C.

2.

Under the Persians, Judaea was a semi-autonomous province of the fifth satrapy ('beyond the river', that is beyond the Euphrates, looking from Persia). It was 1,000 square miles large and centred on the temple city of Jerusalem. The High Priest and his Council, who ran the country under the control of the Persian governor, had to reckon with the influential Jewish community left behind in Mesopotamia, with the hostility of the Samaritans, and with the powerful Jewish sheiks of Ammanitis, the Tobiads. The quality of Persian rule was never questioned in the Jewish tradition. The Biblical legends connected with it (in the Books of Esther, Judith, and Daniel) are so unreal as to defy explanation. But they are consistently favourable to Media and Persia: in the Book of Daniel King Darius deprives himself of food and sleep when he is compelled to throw his Jewish servant into the lions' den. If Jerusalem and Jericho rebelled and were punished by the Persians *c.* 350 B.C., as later classical sources hint (Solinus, 35. 4; Hieronymus, *Chron.* 2. 113, ed. Schoene), the Jews forgot this event. Under Persian rule the Jews had in fact created the theocracy which was later to remain their ideal point of reference. Nehemiah, the master-mind behind it (*c.* 450 B.C.), established a new social equilibrium by cancelling debts, elevating the conditions of the Levites, opening Jerusalem to Jewish immigrants, and reducing the influence of his enemies, the Tobiads. Furthermore, by prohibiting marriage with non-Jews he reinforced religious uniformity (and perhaps hit at the landed aristocracy) in a way which proved to be acceptable to many, but was perhaps indirectly criticized in the Book of Ruth. In the new society the cult of Yahweh excluded any other cult, the study of the Holy Law became a mark of social distinction outside the priestly class, and piety was no longer confined to temple ceremonies. The figure of the scribe—the predecessor of the rabbi—and the building of the Synagogue became characteristic features of this association of study, private worship, and exclusiveness in post-exilic Judaism. Though the Greek word synagogue is not to be found with this meaning until the first century B.C. (its synonym *proseuche*, however, occurs already in texts of the third century B.C.), the institution certainly antedates the diffusion of the Jews in the Mediterranean World (the so-called diaspora) which started at the end of the fourth century B.C. In Judaea the new education of the laity forcibly contributed to keeping Hebrew as the main literary and liturgical language, though Aramaic was not only the main spoken language of Judaea but penetrated even into the Bible (Ezra, Daniel).

Exclusiveness has never prevented unconscious or surreptitious assimilation of foreign ideas. In the Persian period, contacts between Persian magi and ordinary Jews existed even at the personal level, as an Aramaic papyrus from Elephantine in Egypt has shown.[1] The devil Asmodeus who plays a nasty part in the Book of Tobit is clearly of Iranian origin, though the Book of Tobit seems to have been written in Mesopotamia in the Hellenistic period by a very pious Jew. The sharp dualism of the so-called Manual of Discipline, one

[1] E. G. Kraeling, *Brooklyn Museum Aramaic Papyri* (1953), p. 175.

of the Dead Sea Scrolls (second century B.C.?), may owe something to Zoroastrian influence. The word *raz* for mystery in the Book of Daniel is Iranian. The Iranian influence in Judaism and early Christianity has undoubtedly been exaggerated by some scholars, but it was not negligible, though it is difficult to date. It may go back to the Persian rule over Palestine; or it may be a concomitant of the widespread prestige of the Magi in the Hellenistic world.

3.

During the 120 years after Alexander's death in which the Ptolemies of Egypt ruled Palestine, the Jewish society fashioned under the Persians seemed to be able to absorb the shocks of the new situation and to adapt itself without revolutionary changes. The Ptolemaic administration was far more interfering and exacting than the Persian. Its tax-collectors were ubiquitous, and tax-collecting provided the Tobiads with an excellent opportunity for regaining power in Jerusalem. Greek armies frequently marched through the country. The higher priests and the landed gentry fared better than the Levites and the lower classes. Many Jews were taken away as slaves, others became soldiers or military colonists of Hellenistic kings (especially, of course, of the Ptolemies). Voluntary emigration became attractive—and postponed acute social conflicts. Jews became one of the most important ethnic groups of Alexandria, though as a rule they were not admitted to the full rights of Alexandrian citizenship. They spread throughout Egypt and formed conspicuous communities all along the Mediterranean and the Black Sea. In Asia Minor their settlement was favoured by the Seleucids. By 150 B.C. there must have been Jews in Rome. The diaspora was mainly urban, with a variety of employments, but in Egypt, where we know it best, we find peasants, too.

A Greek education became desirable even in Judaea, both for its intrinsic merits and for its usefulness in daily contacts with the rulers. The Tobiads were among the first to have Greek tutors. Greek-speaking centres multiplied around the tiny territory of Judaea through colonization and assimilation of local upper classes. The Greek gymnasium began to cast its shadow on the Jewish school (*yeshiva*) connected with the synagogue. Outside Judaea, the Mesopotamian Jews retained an Aramaic dialect as their main spoken language. Elsewhere the Jews adopted Greek. Special study by some Jews and recent emigration from ˙Judaea by others maintained a measure of acquaintance with the Hebrew and Aramaic religious literature of Judaea and Mesopotamia, but the great majority were unable to recite the simplest prayers in the original language. Even Philo the philosopher was apparently unable to understand Hebrew. No wonder that later rabbis thought that the Jews had deserved the exodus under Moses because they had stuck to their language in captivity.

Impromptu translators into Greek of the relevant passages of the Bible were perhaps used in the synagogues of Greek-speaking Jews, just as translators into Aramaic served the needs of the uncultivated in Judaea and Mesopotamia. But as early as the third century B.C. a written translation of at least part of the Bible became available in Egypt. A legend which gained favour in the second century B.C. and inspired the 'Letter of Aristeas' attributed the translation of the Five Books of Moses to seventy or seventy-two Palestinian Jews sent by the High Priest at the invitation of King Ptolemy II. No other Greek or Hellenistic government is known ever to have been involved in the translation of books (while at least one case is known in Rome, where translation from foreign languages became more frequent). The translation into Greek of the so-called demotic legal code of Hermopolis, which has been revealed by Oxyrhynchus Papyrus xlvii. 3285 (published in 1978), belongs to a different order of enterprises. The legend to explain the Septuagint translation seems to have no factual basis whatsoever, and can be compared with Philo's later statement that God himself approved the translation (*Mos.* 2. 36). In the course of about two centuries the whole Bible became available in Greek: the last book to be translated was perhaps *Esther* in *c.* 77 B.C. This translation of the whole Bible (which we call Septuagint by an arbitrary extension of the term) was not the only translation into Greek—we know of at least three others, by Aquila, Symmachus, and Theodotion; but it was always the most famous. The Alexandrian Jews felt proud of it at least until it was adopted by the Christians, and celebrated the achievement by a yearly festival which in its motivation must have been unparalleled in the Hellenistic world. The achievement itself was probably unique; traditions stating that bulky

Zoroastrian texts were translated into Greek are subject to caution.

Emigration from Judaea and change of language arguably presented favourable conditions for apostasy. The lapse of Dositheus son of Drimylus, a third-century B.C. individual known from papyri, is mentioned in 3 Maccabees, 1 : 3. But apostasy seems to have been rare and more than compensated for by proselytism. In the first century A.D., even a dynasty of Adiabene in Northern Mesopotamia embraced Judaism. Nor was there any spectacular decline in piety. Pilgrimages to Jerusalem maintained religious ties and, at least in a dedicated minority, some linguistic competence in liturgical Hebrew. Annual offerings of money were sent to the Temple. The habit of living together in what became Jewish quarters favoured the retention of ancestral habits and beliefs. There was adaptation to Greek customs. The 'first Greek Jew' is characteristically a slave of the beginning of the third century B.C., who sought help to regain freedom by incubation in the oracle-temple of Amphiaraus in Boeotia.[2] Jews very often took or were given Greek names not only in the Diaspora, but in Judaea. In the early second century B.C. one of the High Priests was called Menelaus and one of the most popular rabbis Antigonus (of Socho). Often a Jew received two personal names, a Hebrew one for use within the community and a Greek one for external contacts (and possibly domestic life). This habit of double names seems to have been learnt by the Jews from the Phoenicians. The gymnasium and the theatre attracted Jews. Philo was a theatre-goer. It is curious to note that in Miletus, at least in Roman times, special places in the theatre were reserved for Jews. We owe to Clement of Alexandria and to Eusebius of Caesarea the preservation of large fragments of a tragedy on the Exodus written by a Jew called Ezechiel. As the tragedy was already quoted by Alexander Polyhistor (on whom see above, p. 171), it cannot be later than the first century B.C. It is clearly influenced by Euripides, but cleverly uses the device of the dream to present the figure of Moses according to Jewish post-biblical notions. Similarly, Jews wrote epic poems in Greek about Jewish history. 'Synagogal Greek' must have occasionally provoked smiles, if Cleomedes, a vulgarizer of Posidonius' cosmology (first century A.D.?), decried Epicurus' arguments by comparing them to what one hears in and around synagogues. Yet what we have of Jewish writing in Greek normally shows command of Greek rhetoric, not to speak of Greek syntax.

4.

In Judaea, as elsewhere, Greek culture had two aspects. It challenged alien ways of life and it invited dialogue and reciprocal knowledge. The most obvious limit of Greek curiosity was linguistic. The Greeks were seldom prepared to make the effort to learn a foreign language. They maintained this attitude even in the face of the Romans, when they passed from the role of the conquerors to that of the conquered. We have no evidence that any Greek ever mastered Hebrew or any other oriental language in order to study the sacred books of the East in the original. Even when the books were available in translation, which was the case with the Bible, they did not circulate outside the circles of the believers. Most of the indirect allusions to biblical passages which modern scholars have spotted in Hellenistic writers are patently imaginary. We are left with a probable allusion to Deuteronomy, 29: 1 in Hecataeus of Abdera—which implies acquaintance with Jews rather than with the text of the Bible—and with a very uncertain reference to the account of the Creation in Genesis in the treatise on the Nature of the World attributed to the Pythagorean Ocellus Lucanus (second or first century B.C.). The first certain quotation of a biblical passage, the reference to Genesis, chapter 1 in the *Sublime* attributed to Cassius Longinus, is not earlier than the first century A.D. Acquaintance with the Bible by the cynic Oenomaus of Gadara, a friend of Rabbi Meir (early second century A.D.) is vaguely attested in the Talmud. The allusions in Galen and in the Neoplatonic Numenius of Apamea of the late second century belong to the very different world of the religious controversy accompanying the diffusion of Christianity. The quotation in the *Sublime* is certainly remarkable: it attributes literary value to the Bible, that is, to something non-Greek. But the author of the *Sublime* shows close acquaintance with the ideas of the rhetorician Caecilius of Calacte (early first century A.D.), who was a Jew: Caecilius may have provided the quotation. Before Christianity gave new readers to the Old Testament, the Bible remained essentially the patrimony of full Jews.

It would be interesting to know whether anyone ever became a Jewish proselyte *because* he read the Bible. Though Juvenal presupposes acquaintance with Moses' book in his picture of the Jewish proselyte, it is very uncertain what a proselyte was supposed to know. We hear very little about the instruction of Jewish proselytes, not to speak of those sympathizers who did not intend to become full Jews and were known as 'God-revering' (Lat. *metuentes*), indeed we have an incomplete picture even of the initiation of Christian catechumens to the Bible. The general impression provided by the evidence is that whatever acquaintance Gentiles made with the people of the Book was not made through the Book. Proselytism was initially a matter of attraction towards a certain style of life, definite religious ceremonies and taboos, and, among the most educated, a specific notion of God and creation such as was indicated by the whole Jewish rejection of pagan cults. Proselytes could become sufficiently proficient in the study of the Bible to translate it into Greek, as Aquila did in the time of Hadrian. Proselytes or sons of proselytes could in fact become respected rabbis, such as Rabbi Meir, to whom legend attributes descent from the emperor Nero (Bal. Talmud, *Gittin*, 56a). But this indicates the deep involvement which conversion to Judaism, when perfected, might imply.

Greek writers who speak about Jews and Judaism rely on personal observation and guesses—or on hearsay. The utmost we can expect is a presentation of Judaism according to the categories of Greek ethnography. Plato and his pupils had prepared the Greeks to appreciate Oriental wisdom. When the Jews were discovered at the end of the fourth century B.C., they naturally appeared as a new variety of Brahmans or Magi. Theophrastus, the pupil of Aristotle, saw them as the first nation to abolish human sacrifices (he may have heard indirect reports of the story of Isaac)—philosophic people who contemplate the stars and invoke them in their prayers, and who fast frequently. Another peripatetic philosopher, Clearchus of Soli, in a dialogue on *Sleep* makes his teacher Aristotle tell about his (probably fictitious) meeting with a Jew 'who was Greek not only by language but in soul': this Jew no doubt had something very interesting to say about sleep, that is, about the behaviour of the human soul during sleep, but the indirect quotation ends too early to satisfy our curiosity. According to Clearchus, Aristotle took the Jews to be descendants of the Indian philosophers called Kalanoi. The comparison between Jews and Indian philosophers was also made by the great authority on India, Megasthenes (early third century B.C.). The reputation of Jews as philosophers is still presupposed by Hermippus (late third century), when he declares Pythagoras to be a pupil of Jewish thinkers. Posidonius, probably writing after Pompey's intervention in Judaea, is perhaps the last to stress the philosophic value of the teaching of Moses as a religious and political leader. By his time the interpretation had lost whatever function it might have had when it was presented two centuries and a half before, and it now served only as a foil to the contemporary situation.

Even in the climate of idealization of the late fourth century B.C., Hecataeus of Abdera had to elaborate a more complicated account when he decided to introduce the Jews into his picture of Egyptian history and society. The Jews were again a force to be reckoned with in the contemporary Egypt of Ptolemy I. Their national legend had given a central place to the rise of Joseph to power in Egypt and to the subsequent exodus of the descendants of Jacob from the country. We do not know whether before Hecataeus the Egyptians had already reacted to these traditions; nor whether it was their idea to associate the Exodus with the overthrow of the Hyksos. Hecataeus knows of the Exodus and presents it as the elimination of foreigners from Egypt. He sympathizes with the foreigners, among whom he includes Danaus and Cadmus. The Jews led by Moses stopped in Palestine, while Danaus and Cadmus reached Greece. Moses was in the great tradition of philosophic leaders; he founded the Temple of Jerusalem, gave laws, divided the land into equal portions and made them inalienable. If there were hard and misanthropic features in his legislation, the experience of exile was sufficient explanation. Hecataeus himself admitted that his picture of Judaea no longer corresponded to contemporary realities. What remained relevant was the projection into the past of the frictions which the settlement of the Jews in Alexandria and elsewhere under the auspices of the conquering Macedonians created between Jews and Egyptians.

Flavius Josephus devotes large sections of his *Contra Apionem* to exposing the hostile account of the Exodus which the Egyptian priest Manetho had allegedly given in his history of Egypt written in Greek *c.* 270 B.C. The identification of the Jews with the Hyksos had been made more unpalatable by a further identification of the Jews with lepers. No other ancient source attributes these stories to Manetho, and there are various internal difficulties in the report of Josephus. One wonders whether he did not use an interpolated text of Manetho (as he and other Jewish apologists used an inter-polated text of Hecataeus of Abdera). Be that as it may, there existed hostile versions of the Exodus coming from Egyptian sources. As long as the Jews got on reasonably well with the Greek population of Alexandria and had the support of the Ptolemies, Egyptian hostility was not of decisive importance. The Egyptian Jews faced dangers rather by getting too involved in the factions which rent the Macedonian mon-archy in Egypt in the second and first centuries B.C.

5.

The evidence as a whole seems to indicate that the Jews of Egypt maintained prestige, gained prosperity, and developed an intellectual physiognomy of their own at least until A.D. 50. In the third century B.C. a historian, Demetrius prepared for Greek readers one of those accounts which non-Greeks were supposed to give to the Greeks about their own past. Later, in the second century (?) B.C., Artapanus wrote a biography of Moses in which he appeared as a teacher of Orpheus and a legislator to the Egyptians before becoming the leader of the Exodus. According to Artapanus, Moses would have intro-duced the cult of animals for the benefit of the Egyptians. Rivalry was assumed between the King of Egypt and Moses, but of course Moses would have been popular with ordinary Egyptians and Ethiopians. In the same century the *Letter of Aristeas* not only spread the legend that Ptolemy Philadelphus had organized the translation of the Septuagint, but presented the King in friendly disputations with the Jewish sages. If the story of *Joseph and Aseneth* (difficult to date) belongs to this period, it idealizes paradigmatically the love between the biblical upstart Joseph and Aseneth, the daughter of the High Priest of Heliopolis, who becomes a Jewish proselyte. About 160 B.C., Aristobulus applied the allegorical method of the

Greeks to the interpretation of the Bible, and dedicated an explanation of the Books of Moses to Ptolemy VI. 2 Maccabees therefore treats Aristobulus as a teacher of Ptolemy VI. Aristobulus believed that Pythagoras, Plato, and some 'ancient' poets—such as Homer, Hesiod, Orpheus, and Aratus —learned from Moses' books, naturally in pre-Alexandrian translation. The existence of a pre-Septuagint is also implied in the *Letter of Aristeas*, when it asserts that the historian Theopompus (fourth century B.C.) became insane when he tried to use it. Aristobulus in his extant fragments shows that forged or modified lines of Greek poets circulated to prove their acquaintance with Judaism. It is therefore probable that other specimens of such forgeries which we have (for instance, a moral poem by Phocylides) were produced in Egypt.

The uncertainties about the origins and the chronology of Jewish-Hellenistic texts prevent us from following the development of thought which led to the philosophy of Philo in the first half of the first century A.D. Philo himself vaguely recognizes predecessors. There must have been innumerable occasions in the synagogues and Jewish schools of Alexandria for reinterpreting Jewish religion in terms of Greek philosophy. One obvious candidate as a predecessor of Philo is the unknown author of the *Wisdom of Solomon*, which addresses the kings of the earth and invites them to heed Wisdom, the intermediary between God and Man. But the book is not necessarily the product of one author only, and the final onslaught on the Egyptians (chs. 16ff.) may be too much for an Egyptian Jew. More generally it must be observed that there is no reason to confine to Egyptian Jews those philosophical activities which culminate in Philo.

6.

Jerusalem, not Alexandria, was the place where the future of Judaism was played out.

Until the eve of the persecution by Antiochus IV (170 B.C.), Hellenism might have seemed to have created far fewer problems in Judaea than among the Jews of Egypt. Yet even if we confine ourselves to the interpretation of the two texts which are most likely to belong to the period of the peaceful penetration of Greek culture into Judaea—*Ecclesiastes* or *Kohelet* (late third century B.C.?) and the *Ecclesiasticus* by Ben

Sira (early second century, the first Hebrew text to have a certain author)—we discover reactions to Hellenism which are the more profound because the Greeks are never mentioned. Ecclesiastes has no doubts about the omnipotence of God—who is the God of the Fathers. But he has lost the sense of history or, rather, the sense of direction in events which characterizes all the other biblical texts, including perhaps even Job. He wanders in the maze of reflections and interpretations to which it is only too easy to attach the labels of Epicureanism and Scepticism. If the obscure word *Kohelet* means 'speaker, assembler' it may allude to the street-speakers of the Hellenistic world. The man who edited Kohelet's work and appears to have known him personally described him as a sage 'who taught the people knowledge, weighing and searching and fashioning many proverbs' (12: 9). But Kohelet did not teach the rules of a different and better life, like a Greek philosopher; for man 'cannot discover the meaning of God's work which is done under the sun'.

Ben Sira, who had meditated on Ecclesiastes, reacted to all the temptations of the foreign world by putting himself to school under the wise men of the Hebrew tradition from Enoch to the recently dead High Priest Simon. The praise of the Fathers by Ben Sira may well be formally influenced by Hellenistic biography: it certainly reminds us of the Roman *elogia* and of Book 6 of Virgil's *Aeneid*, though Ben Sira would be surprised. The purpose of the praise is a neat rejection of Hellenic wisdom. The central figure is Aaron, the High Priest; his advice is oriented towards harmonious collaboration between Temple and Synagogue. A few years after Ben Sira had written, King Antiochus IV with the help of Jewish High Priests and of a considerable section of the Jewish upper class of Jerusalem, including the Tobiads, transformed the temple-city into a Greek *polis*, with the naked young men of the gymnasium as its prominent feature. Ben Sira's worries had not been vain. By further steps the cult of Yahve was Hellenized and turned into that of Zeus Olympius; the Sabbath and circumcision were prohibited and books of the Torah were burnt.

The transition from the Ptolemaic to the Seleucid rule was a decisive factor in this crisis in Judaea. The Ptolemies never pursued Hellenization as a policy; indeed, they were glad to use Jews in the administration of Egypt. The Seleucids always relied (not very successfully) on urban settlements of the Greek type and on Greek loyalties to keep together their enormous multi-national state. After the disastrous peace with the Romans in 188 B.C., the Seleucids were ever more afraid of disloyalty and in need of the wealth of the sanctuaries. But the alternative between traditional Judaism (as established by Nehemiah) and Hellenization was a real dilemma for many Jews—not only in Judaea. We know very little of the process of settlement of Jews in Asia Minor and in Europe. But when Flavius Josephus provides us with evidence we find Jews in difficulty with local authorities and public opinion because of their non-conformism. The Hellenizers among the Jews of the Diaspora and the Hellenizers of Judaea must have encouraged each other. We have an inscription from Iasus in Asia Minor which tells us that Niketas son of Jason the Jerusalemite donated a sum of 100 drachmas for the festival of the god Dionysus (*Corp. Inscr. Jud.* 749). In Judaea Hellenization was clearly an upper-class attitude, while social conflicts and group rivalries were rampant: what are hints in Ecclesiastes and Ecclesiasticus become definite statements in later sources, such as the Book of Enoch, 94–105 (late second century ?). The ultimate victory of the brothers Maccabee against what the contemporary Daniel calls the abomination of desolation was equivalent to a partial social revolution, in which lower priests replaced higher ones, a part of the aristocracy had to flee to Egypt or elsewhere, and the Syrian inhabitants of Palestine were ruthlessly attacked with obvious consequences in the transfer of wealth and territory.

Civil war could not be combined for too long with an aggressive policy towards Transjordan, Idumaea, Galilee, and the Greek towns of the coast. As political independence was obtained by degrees with the help of the Romans, reactions in Rome had to be watched. The mere formation of new political ties implied a certain acceptance of Greek forms of life. Some pre-existent legend about the common origins of Spartans and Jews was exploited. The Eupolemus who went to Rome to negotiate the alliance on behalf of Judas Maccabaeus is probably the author of a book in Greek on the kings of Judah, in which Moses invents the alphabet and Solomon pursues the expansionist policy of the Hasmoneans. Even the earliest account of the Maccabean revolution, written in five books by Jason of Cyrene (*c.* 160 B.C.) and summarized in the extant 2 Maccabees (*c.* 124 B.C.?), is evidence of Hellenization; the tale is told in Greek in the style of popular pathetic historiography. There is no end to the story of the penetration of Greek words, customs, and intellectual habits into Judaea during the rule of the Hasmoneans and the subsequent reign of Herod. The contradictory statements in Talmudic literature about the value and legitimacy of knowledge of Greek are based on the reality of the power and influence of Greek culture in Palestine. Hermeneutic rules derived from the Greek tradition were adopted by rabbis; Greek legal terminology was borrowed; Greek was used in inscriptions on ritual objects of the Temple; a synagogue in Caesarea used Greek in the liturgy. A famous Talmudic passage (Bab. *Sotah,* 49f.) speaks of 500 students of Greek wisdom and 500 of Hebrew wisdom in the school of Gamaliel II (*c.* A.D. 100)—which is a symbolic indication of the penetration of Greek culture into rabbinic schools. Yet the results of the Maccabean movement did not go against the anti-Hellenic premisses of the movement itself. Below the surface of Judaic society of the two centuries 150 B.C.—*c.* A.D. 50 there prevail two forces which, whether in combination or in contrast, remove Judaism from Hellenism.

One force is apocalyptic. Prophecy in the ordinary biblical sense was over: no prophet appeared to warn and guide the Jews during and after the Maccabaean revolt. The nostalgia for prophecy may indeed have contributed to the popularity of substitutes of an equivocal nature like the Sibylline oracles. Prophecy died because the new expectations were far more radical and dramatic and extended to the territory of the after-Life which had not existed for the biblical prophets. The apocalyptic writers, significantly, attributed their teachings to men of the past, from Adam to Daniel. There is of course no uniformity in the visions of the future contained in Daniel, Enoch (itself a composite work), Jubilees, the Testaments of the Twelve Patriarchs, and the various texts known as the Dead Sea scrolls. But they approximately agreed in dividing history between 'this world' where Belial rules and the 'next world' which belongs to the sun of righteousness. The notion of the Messiah became for them associated with the end of days, when the dead will rise to receive their final award. For this apocalyptic literature the end of days is often a return to the events of creation. The great contribution of the discovery of the Dead Sea scrolls to our knowledge of apocalyptics is that it revealed one of the centres of diffusion of such beliefs. This was a monastic community characterized by a strong hostility towards the ruling class of Jerusalem, by a precise code of daily conduct, and by a dualistic scheme of things. It matters very little whether or not we identify this community with the Essenes known from Flavius Josephus and other sources.

The other force leading away from Hellenism was Pharisaism, which was nearer to the main stream of Jewish life after Ezra and Nemehiah. First the Hasidim (pious) and then their successors the Pharisees developed as an opposition to the aristocracy, which, with the slowing down of the Maccabean revolution, had formed again round the Temple and taken the name of Sadducees. Unlike the Sadducees, the Pharisees believed in the immortality of the soul and in the resurrection of the dead. They were far from being insensitive to apocalyptic expectations. But they practised _ante litteram_ the rule of Hillel (late first century B.C.) not to separate themselves from the community. It is characteristic that when they came to control Jewish religious life from about the time of the destruction of the second Temple they kept all the apocalyptic books except Daniel outside the Canon of Holy Scripture. Their main aim was to use the synagogue and the school to regulate by multiplication of rules the sanctification of daily life. By insisting on the value of oral tradition, study, and work they differentiated themselves from the Sadducees who controlled the Temple, kept up the literal interpretation of the written law, and were reluctant to accept the increase in commandments or _mitzvot_. On the other hand, the Pharisees looked down with contempt at the 'people of the land', the Jews who did not care for study, ritual purity, and punctilious payment of the sacred tithes. The Pharisees trusted God and felt they were trusted by God in a direct way without any other intermediary than the Law (Torah). They were prepared to live and die for the Law. Martyrdom was elevated—for the first time in history—to an ideal: and the ideal was put to the test of reality.

Though there is no exclusive connection between Pharisees and 'sages'—that is, the teachers and scholars who gained

authority individually or as schools from the second century
B.C. to the end of the second century A.D. (and beyond it)—
the sages were often Pharisees, and the ethos of the sage
became progressively indistinguishable from the Pharisaic
ethos. The sages seldom underrated the power and attraction
of Greek civilization. Altogether they were not even too harsh
against those who succumbed to it. The great Rabbi Elisha
ben Avuyah who became an apostate under the influence of
Greek thought in the early second century A.D. is treated more
in sorrow than contempt by the Talmudic tradition. It is
explicitly said that his pupil Rabbi Meir never broke his
friendship with him. But what the sages taught about God,
the Law, the 'relations between Jews and Jews and the
relations between Jews and Gentiles, amounted as a whole to
a repudiation of Greek culture. The test was the Torah, for
'even a Gentile, if he practises the Law, is equal to the High
Priest' (*Sifra*, 86A, ed. Weiss).

Whether one turned to apocalyptic seers or to humane
rabbis (two groups which, we emphasize again, were not
easily separable), it was a different world from that of the
neighbouring Gentiles. There was no serious economic conflict between Jews and Gentiles. The Jews were to be found in
too many occupations to be obnoxious in any. In all the
papyri there is just one specific complaint about Jewish
moneylenders (*Corp. Papyr. Jud.* 152), and this belongs to the
first century A.D. The dividing line was exactly between Jews
and Gentiles. Given the Greek laziness about foreign
languages and traditions, it is perhaps not surprising that
derogatory reports about the Jewish cult were heard with
increasing frequency. Certainly the initial sympathy of the
Greek intellectuals at the end of the fourth century B.C. was
replaced by undercurrents of hostility or, at least, of irony.
Mnaseas in the second century B.C. is the first author known
to us to talk about the cult of the Ass in the Temple of
Jerusalem. About the same time we find the first rumours
about ritual sacrifices of aliens. Both insinuations were of
course extended later to the Christians. The accusation
against Jews of ritual homicide seems to have gained little
hearing, but the curious idea that the Jewish God was
iconographically comparable with the figure of Typhon-Seth
found some credit even with an admirer of Moses like
Posidonius, and is still repeated by Tacitus.

7.

Very little is heard about the Babylonian Jews now under Parthian rule in the two centuries before and after Christ. From the little we know we can assume that they largely followed the religious leadership of the Palestinian Jews and became increasingly imbued with Pharisaic principles. What is more remarkable—and decisive for our story—is the acquiescence of the Jews of the Greek Diaspora and particularly of Egypt.

We know that the Palestinian leaders took care to have the approval and following of the Egyptian Jews. For a long time they needed the support—or at least the neutrality—of the Ptolemies in their struggles against the Seleucids. When one of the members of the family of the Oniads—the previous High Priests—founded a Hebrew temple at Leontopolis in Egypt and made it a centre for the recruitment of Jewish mercenaries in the service of Egypt, it became imperative for the men in Jerusalem to silence the competition of Leontopolis without offending the Ptolemies. In this they were remarkably successful. The introductory letters of 2 Maccabees show the repeated attempts of the Jerusalem authorities to persuade the Egyptian Jews to join the Palestinian ones in the celebration of the festival (Hanukkah) for the reconsecration of the Jerusalem Temple after its profanation by Antiochus IV. Such propaganda for new festivals was a familiar feature in the Hellenistic world at large. The Palestinian sages accepted Greek as a language into which the Bible could be translated; at least one sage was convinced that it was the only language (*Mishnah, Megillah*, 1. 8). About 132 B.C. a Palestinian Jew who had moved to Egypt translated Ecclesiasticus into Greek to make the conservative thought of Jerusalem available to the Diaspora. Translation from Hebrew (or Aramaic) into Greek was a frequent event: another example is the translation of 1 Maccabees, a very pious account of the Maccabean revolt written in biblical style about the end of the second century B.C.

The Jews of Egypt seem to have been only too glad to follow the Palestinian leadership. The *Letter of Aristeas* emphasizes Jerusalem's approval of the Septuagint translation: the translators themselves had been chosen by the High Priest of Jerusalem. 3 Maccabees (first century B.C.?) imitates 2 Maccabees and purports to show that the Egyptian Jews, like the Palestinian Jews, suffered persecution under Ptolemy IV Philopator. There seems to be no historical foundation for the story, which is a document of the solidarity between the Jews of Egypt and the Jews of Palestine. The Third Book of the *Sibylline Oracles*—a Jewish-Egyptian composition, the oldest section of which goes back to the Maccabean revolt and the most recent to the time of Augustus—backs the Palestinian Jews in their struggles against the Seleucids and, later, the Romans. Nothing in it can be interpreted as favourable to the schismatic temple of Leontopolis. The Sibyl, in so far as she was persuaded to speak on behalf of the Jews, was certainly no champion of Alexandrian Judaism.

8.

It has in fact become very difficult to give any precise meaning to the notion of Alexandrian ('Hellenistic') Judaism, which nineteenth-century scholars used to oppose to Palestinian ('normative') Judaism, with its implied consequences for the development of Christianity.

Given the loose organization of the Jewish Diaspora, we must assume a wide range (personal, sectional, and local) of Jewish attitudes to the surrounding, and by no means uniform, world. We happen to hear, precisely from Alexandria, that two rival Jewish factions sent two different legations to Rome (*Corp. Papyr. Jud.* 153). Different kinds of evidence are bound to tell different stories. It is difficult to decide whether the epitaphs of the cemetery of Leontopolis in Egypt indicate deeper Hellenization than the Jewish manumission documents for which Panticapacum in the Crimea is famous. Who can say how typical (typical of what?) was the Greek sermon on martyrdom which goes under the name of 4 Maccabees (first century A.D.)? If many Jews indulged in magic and enjoyed a reputation for it among Gentiles, it would be foolish to suggest that they were unorthodox Jews. E. R. Goodenough tried to give to this notion of Alexandrian Judaism the massive support of the archaeological evidence which he so meritoriously collected in twelve volumes of *Jewish Symbols in the Greco-Roman Period*. The utmost he could prove was that the Jews did not systematically avoid objects with pagan symbols: that is, that they lived in a pagan world.

Philo of Alexandria (first century A.D.) presents a different problem which does not lend itself to generalizations. He accepted the Law, the Torah, as he knew it and recommended its observance. Though himself a practitioner of the allegorical interpretation, he did not approve of Jews who made the symbolism of the Law an excuse for dispensing with literal observance (*Migrat. Abrah.* 88–93). He did not, however, seriously contribute to Jewish jurisprudence. He read the Pentateuch as a chart for a journey towards God. He really loved God and felt that everything good was a gracious gift from Heaven. He based knowledge on revelation, and personally experienced revelation in the ascent of his soul towards God through the mediation of the Word—the Logos (*Somn.* 1. 65ff.) What he contemplated he gladly described in the language of the Greek philosophers (Plato, the Stoics) he admired; he was reassured by this coincidence. There was little in his approach to commend itself to those Jews who read the Bible in order to learn God's orders or to pray to God. Characteristically Philo did not care much for the Psalms and the Prophets. Nor was there much in Philo to attract the sympathies of the Gentiles. Those among them who wanted philosophy had a better one nearer home. Those who needed salvation would not have found it in his message. Philo's form of exposition—a commentary on biblical texts— would in most cases be unintelligible to readers unfamiliar with the Bible. If the anti-Christian Celsus (late second century A.D.) read some Philo, he did it to polemize against the Christians. Thus Philo, who wrote with both the Jews and the Greeks in mind (but mostly perhaps for the Jews), was of no great interest to either. He found his readers mainly among Christians, beginning perhaps with the author of the Epistle to the Hebrews. Hellenizing Christians recognized in him their predecessor in the attempt to buttress Revelation with Greek philosophy. Clement of Alexandria and Origen were keen students of Philo. In the fourth century, Eusebius (*Hist. Eccles.* 2. 17. 1) knew of the legend that Philo had met St. Peter in Rome and had been converted (cf. Photius, *Bibl.* 105). The Jews forgot Philo even before they forgot Greek. Philo was rediscovered for the Jews in a Latin translation by the Italian Jew Azariah de' Rossi in the sixteenth century, and even after rediscovery he never counted much in Hebrew thought.

We come therefore to the conclusion that among the Greek-speaking Jews known to us only very few can qualify as real

Hellenizers. One was perhaps Jason of Cyrene, the source of 2 Maccabees. The other was—not unexpectedly—another historian, Flavius Josephus (first century A.D.).

Flavius Josephus was a Palestinian Jew of priestly descent who started to write history in Aramaic and never mastered the Greek language well enough to dispense with helpers. He used Jewish sources—biblical and extra-biblical—and brought to his task considerable knowledge of Jewish oral tradition. But as his task was to write the history of the Jews for the pagans (the Romans), he could fulfil it only by adopting Greek models. Furthermore, he chose to write his autobiography and to refute the theories of some pagan writers about the Jews: this again implied Greek models. Like Philo, Josephus was appropriated by the Christians, but unlike Philo he enjoyed some reputation among pagans (Porphyry in the third century, perhaps Vegetius *c.* A.D. 400). He also had some indirect readers among Jews in the Middle Ages. Part of his work was utilized in the compilation by an anonymous Jew of Southern Italy in the tenth century (the so-called *Josippon*).

However, the fate of Greek philosophy and of Greek historiography among the Jews was to a great extent similar. With the development of the interpretation of the Torah as the foundation of communal and private life—and as the source of joy and holiness—neither philosophy nor historiography, as the Greeks understood it, could appeal to the Jews. As for historiography, there were other factors to render it unnecessary even in its biblical form which 1 Maccabees had preserved, though with modifications. Comparison with other cultures shows that there is not much stimulus for history-writing when one's own national and religious centre is destroyed—which is what happened to the Jews in A.D. 70. More specifically, the triumph of Rabbinism meant the virtual disappearance of that sense of providential direction from the remotest past to the present, and beyond it, which is so characteristic of biblical history. The Rabbis (unlike Ecclesiastes) replaced it by exclusive emphasis on the annual re-enactment of select events of the past which the Jews had always performed. The Jews remained in contact with select episodes from their past through Passover, the Festival of the Covenant, the four fasts connected with the first destruction of the Temple, Hanukkah, etc. But the continuum of history was lost. It was a substitution, in difficult times, of an optimistic and contemplative outlook for the puzzling and often tragic vision of the biblical historians and prophets. It will be enough to observe that Greek philosophy came back to the Jews via the Arabs in the tenth century, but Greek historiography had to wait until the nineteenth century.

Further Reading

The texts on Judaism by non-Jewish Greek and Roman writers are collected and translated by Th. Reinach, *Textes d'auteurs grecs et romains relatife au Judaïsme* (Paris, 1895; reprint Hildesheim, 1963), and now, with masterly introductions and commentary, by M. Stern, *Greek and Latin Authors on Jews and Judaism*, vol. i (Jerusalem, 1974; vol. ii forthcoming). Fragments of Jewish pseudepigrapha and of historical works in Greek are available in A.-M. Denis, *Fragmenta pseudepigraphicorum quae supersunt Graeca* (Leiden, 1970, together with *Apocalypsis Henochi Graece*, ed. M. Black). Greek fragments of historians of Judaism, whether Jewish or not, are collected, and partly commented on, in F. Jacoby, *Die Fragmente der griechischen Historiker* (Berlin-Leiden, 1923–58); of special importance is section III C, xii, nos. 722–37.

J. B. Frey, *Corpus Inscriptionum Iudaicarum* (2 vols., Rome, 1936–52), must be used with caution (cf. L. Robert, in *Hellenica*, v (1946), 90–108). V. A. Tcherikover, A. Fuks, and M. Stern, *Corpus Papyrorum Judaicarum* (3 vols., Cambridge, Mass., 1957–64), is masterly. For apocrypha and pseudepigrapha of the Old Testament, the best collection is edited by R. H. Charles (2 vols., Oxford, 1913; reprint 1963). The best edition of the *Oracula Sibyllina* (without commentary) is by J. Geffcken (Leipzig, 1902). The most easily available English translation of the Dead Sea scrolls is by G. Vermes (2nd edn., Harmondsworth, 1975); cf. G. Vermes, *The Dead Sea Scrolls. Qumran in Perspective* (London, 1977). The *Mishnah* is translated by H. Danby (Oxford, 1933); the *Babylonian Talmud* by I. Epstein and others (London, 1935–48). Among the anthologies of Talmudic texts, often misleading, the most useful is J. Bonsirven, *Textes rabbiniques des deux premiers siècles chrétiens* (Rome, 1955). Archaeological evidence will be found in E. R. Goodonough, *Jewish Symbols in the Greco-Roman Period* (12 vols., New York, 1953–65).

Essential guides to the evidence are E. Schürer, *Geschichte des jüdischen Volkes im Zeitalter Jesu Christi* (Leipzig, 1901–9), of which a much-revised version of vols. i–ii has been published in English by G. Vermes and F. Millar, *The History of the Jewish People* (Edinburgh, 1973–9); *The Jewish People in the First Century*, by various authors (2 vols., Assen, 1974–6); V. Tcherikover, *Hellenistic Civilization and the Jews* (2nd edn., Philadelphia, 1961); Morton Smith, *Palestinian Parties and Politics* (New York, 1971), very original and excellently documented; M. Hengel, *Judaism and Hellenism* (2 vols., London, 1974), with an admirable bibliography; E. P. Sanders, *Paul and Palestinian Judaism* (London, 1977).

An excellent choice of modern studies with a bibliographical guide is H. A. Fischel, ed., *Essays in Greco-Roman and Related Talmudic Literature* (New

York, 1977). Fundamental are the works of J. Bernays (see his *Gesammelte Abhandlungen* (2 vols., Berlin, 1885) for further bibliography); E. Bickerman (for instance, *Der Gott der Makkabäer* (Berlin, 1937), and the *Collected Papers*, forthcoming); D. Flusser (partial bibliography in his *Jesus* (Reinbeck, 1968)); I. Heinemann (for instance, *Philons griechische und jüdische Bildung* (Breslau, 1932; reprint Darmstadt, 1962)); S. Lieberman (for instance, *Greek in Jewish Palestine* (New York, 1942)); A. D. Nock (see *Essays on Religion and the Ancient World* (2 vols., Oxford, 1972)); G. Vermes (see *Post-Biblical Jewish Studies* (Leiden, 1975)).

On Jewish apocalyptic, D. S. Russell, *The Method and Message of Jewish Apocalyptic* (London, 1964); K. Koch, *The Rediscovery of Apocalyptic* (London, 1972); on Pharisaism, G. F. Moore, *Judaism* (3 vols., Cambridge, Mass., 1927–30), J. Neusner, *The Rabbinic Traditions about the Pharisees before 70* (3 vols., Leiden, 1971), E. E. Urbach, *The Sages* (Jerusalem, 1975); on antisemitism, J. N. Sevenster, *The Roots of Pagan Antisemitism in the Ancient World* (Leiden, 1975); on education, C. H. Dodd, *The Bible and the Greeks* (London, 1935; reprint 1964); J. N. Sevenster, *Do you know Greek?* (Leiden, 1968), B. Th. Viviano, *Study as Worship* (Leiden, 1978); on messianism, L. Landmann (ed.), *Messianism in the Talmudic Era* (New York, 1979).

12

GREEK PHILOSOPHY AND CHRISTIANITY

A. H. ARMSTRONG

If we are to understand the encounter of Greek philosophy and Christianity, we need to know something about the religious cults and beliefs traditional in the Hellenic world and the attitudes of philosophers towards them; and we need to appreciate what an unprecedentedly odd and original phenomenon the Christian Church was when looked at from the point of view of traditional Hellenic religious observance and piety. It is a commonplace to say that ancient Hellenic religion was a matter of cult, not of creed. What really mattered was the due performance of the sacrifices and other sacred rites according to what was believed to be immemorial tradition: this was as true of the worship of newly introduced deities from Egypt or the East as of those rites which centred round the old Greek gods and heroes: the newly arrived deities were either worshipped according to the traditions of their homelands or in the traditional Greek manner.

The stories told about the gods, especially those closely connected with particular ritual acts, were not of course unimportant in Hellenic piety (for a full discussion of the myths see Chapter 10). They coloured people's religious imaginations, and were quite possibly more widely believed down to the end of paganism than our familiarity with the writings of the tiny educated minority might lead us to think (how the philosophers dealt with the myths will be discussed shortly). But even the most authoritative tellings of the myths by poets generally considered to be venerable and inspired, like Homer and Hesiod, did not have the authority of sacred scripture till a very late period indeed in the history of Hellenic religion. And one very important reason for this was that there was no body of professional clergy who were authorized guardians and interpreters of the sacred stories and official teachers of doctrine and morality. A priest in the ancient world was a person who had inherited or had had conferred upon him by public authority (or, sometimes, had bought from his city) the right and duty of performing certain specific sacrifices and ceremonies: and there his right and duty ended. Doctrinal teaching and moral instruction were none of his business. Even the full-time clergy of the great Egyptian or Eastern temples were concerned with ritual, not with teaching.

There were, besides the priests, the *manteis*, soothsayers or diviners, religious professionals who were held to possess a special technical skill in interpreting the signs and omens which indicated the intentions and attitudes of the gods on particular occasions. There were also oracles of the gods, probably regarded by most people as genuine divine messages, and officials whose duty it was to interpret them, the 'prophets' and 'exegetes'. But, though the *manteis* were consulted and required to read the signs on all important occasions (e.g. before a battle), their technical advice could be accepted or disregarded by the responsible general or states-man, and neither they nor the interpreters of oracles exercised any real continuing doctrinal or moral authority.

There were also small sectarian groups, the Orphics, who claimed to possess sacred books of vast antiquity which gave divinely inspired information about myths generally unknown and prescriptions for a life of austere ritual purity and for rituals specially effective for purification. But though the Orphics had distinctive religious and moral ideas, they do not ever seem to have formed anything like a church with a coherent body of doctrine, and though some of their ideas became widely diffused, their books and teachers were never generally considered authoritative in matters of religion: the later Neoplatonists did regard the Orphic poems, and an extraordinary farrago of popular religious philosophy in obscure and inflated language, the *Chaldaean Oracles* (probably dating from the second century A.D.), as sacred scriptures which were the ultimate authority for their religious doctrines and practices, but this was not till the fourth century A.D.

Even if one gives the fullest weight to such authority as soothsayers, oracles and their interpreters, or Orphics and their books possessed, one cannot discover in the ancient Hellenic religious world anything like a teaching Church. Consequently anyone, as long as he did not grossly neglect his ritual duties and refrained from sacrilegiously irreverent behaviour, could believe, and even say, what he liked about the gods within rather unpredictable limits set by the state of public opinion at various times and places. (The extreme religious nervousness and irritability of the Athenians of the later fifth century B.C. was probably not altogether typical; but it is likely that it would always have been excessively imprudent to say anything rude or incredulous about Demeter and Persephone at Eleusis, especially around the time of the celebration of the Mysteries.)

The contrast with the Christian Church is obvious. Here cult developed rather casually and only reached a high degree of elaboration comparatively late: and ritual practices, though they became matters of venerable tradition, sometimes with remarkable speed, and could be appealed to as evidence of the faith of the fathers, were never sacrosanct in themselves in the same way in which they were in paganism. Liturgical innovation and liturgical reform have always been easier in the Christian Churches than they would have been in Hellenic paganism, though the 'Old Believer' attitude of extreme cultic conservatism is one which recurs regularly in particular groups when major liturgical changes are introduced. Sacraments and public worship have always been central in Christian life; but what is taught, in church and out of it, about that worship and the god to whom it is directed and the way in which his true worshippers ought to live has always mattered to Christians in a way which cannot be paralleled in the old Hellenic world. This is because Christian piety is normally based on what is claimed to be a special revelation, contained in a body of sacred writings with a doctrinal and moral content, interpreted according to the traditions of a community by the clerical leaders of that community whose business it is to preach doctrine and to give moral instruction and exhortation as well as to celebrate the liturgy. Any preaching and teaching of religion or morals which was done in the ancient world was done by philosophers, who had no more to do with cult-celebrations than anybody else and never held anything remotely resembling the position of the authoritative teachers of a church-type community. A philosopher had no more authority than his personality and intelligence could give him; and this remained true even if he held a salaried chair or was head of a venerable philosophical institution like the Academy at

Athens (positions of this sort seem to have made very little difference to the influence or reputation of philosophers).

We now need to enquire why philosophers in the period which chiefly concerns us (roughly from the second to the sixth century A.D.) had, unlike most philosophers of modern times, a great deal of very positive religious teaching and practical moral instruction to give, and why many educated Christians from the second century onwards, including a considerable number of the increasingly authoritarian chief teachers of the Christian communities, the bishops, were prepared to accept, with momentous consequences for the future of Christianity, a very great deal from these independent Hellenic pagan religious teachers, in spite of their fanatical hostility to Hellenic cult and mythology and their confidence in the superiority of their own 'barbarian' revelation. Philosophy by our period was generally regarded as a way of life based on a comprehensive understanding of reality. It made considerable moral as well as intellectual demands on those who took it seriously. A philosopher was expected to be (of course the expectation was sometimes disappointed) a man of austere goodness leading a life of reasonable and moderate asceticism, and philosophic wisdom was not supposed to be attainable without virtue and detachment from worldly concerns. And in the second and third centuries A.D. the goal of the philosophic life and the content of philosophic wisdom became more and more explicitly religious. This was no revolutionary development, but an intensification of tendencies which had been apparent among some (though by no means all) Greek philosophers since well before Socrates, and which are particularly apparent in the immensely influential later writings of Plato. The *Timaeus* and the *Laws* set the tone for a great deal of later philosophy. As a result of this development the philosophers, who had long been expected to give practical moral guidance (not just to speculate about ethical concepts) were more and more thought of as spiritual guides, helping men to find the way to the divine, and their thought about divinity became a more and more central and important part of their philosophic teaching.

This was true of most, but not of all philosophers. An important feature of the intellectual life of the early part of our period was the vigorous survival of the Hellenistic sceptical tradition down to at least the second half of the second century A.D., when it found its most extensive and important surviving expression in the works of Sextus Empiricus. But the sceptical attitude to religion should not be misunderstood. The ancient sceptic did not hold that any positive or certainly true conclusions could be arrived at about the divine, any more than about moral principles or anything else. But the practical conclusion he drew from this was that, since certainty in these matters is impossible, one should follow inherited beliefs and customs, of course undogmatically and with due suspension of judgement (Sextus Empiricus, *Outlines of Pyrrhonism*, 1.24, 3.2). Scepticism in the ancient world was a conservative, not a revolutionary force.

Apart, then, from the Sceptics, philosophers in our period gave a great deal of positive religious teaching, founded upon what seemed to them a rational belief in the demonstrable existence of divine reality. Their theologies were independent in the sense that they did not derive their religious ideas from cult and myth, though they were increasingly inclined to read their own ideas into the old stories and practices and to regard them as allegorical or symbolic expressions of philosophical truth. The fierce and radical criticism of the poets' tales about the gods by Xenophanes and Plato, the rationalistic explanations of traditional beliefs of the sort which had been given by Prodicus, Democritus, or Euhemerus, and the casual contempt for the old stories apparent in Aristotle's occasional references to them, had generally given place in our period to the belief that the myths could be made to yield a religious sense satisfactory to the philosophers by the fatally easy method of allegorical interpretation, which Jews and Christians applied with equal enthusiasm to extract reasonable and edifying sense from the Bible where this was not very obvious. But the older, more critical attitudes to myth and the rationalistic explanations of pagan religion remained on record, and both provided excellent material for Christian controversialists and helped to make Christians feel that Hellenic philosophy as such was not totally committed to the paganism whose rites and stories they so vehemently detested.

As regards cult-practices the attitude of the philosophers varied considerably. Not even the fiercest critics of the myths had ever put forward any practical proposals for abolishing the traditional sacrifices and ceremonies and replacing them with a ritual more conformable to their own theologies. Even

Plato is quite content that the old rituals should continue unchanged in his ideal states (though of course the poems used on public religious occasions are to be drastically censored). And in our period we can see within the most important philosophic school, the Platonic, a change of attitude from the respectful indifference of Plotinus in the third century, for whom true religion was purely inward and spiritual, and external rites did not matter very much, to the passionate pagan sacramentalism of Iamblichus and his successors from the fourth to the sixth century. The Christians of course much preferred the former attitude, and the more philosophically inclined among them were curiously inclined to talk, sometimes at least, as if their own religion was purely inward and spiritual and they had no sacraments or liturgy at all: this is particularly characteristic of the period before the official triumph of Christianity in the fourth century and the rapid development of the liturgy, but something of it persists in later Christian tradition.

What has been said about the relationship of philosophy to cult and myth applies just as much to the 'mystery-religions' as to the public cults. (A mystery in the ancient world was simply a cult conducted in strict privacy, admission to which was by initiation and from which non-initiates were rigorously excluded.) The mysteries had no philosophical or theological ideas of their own. Any ideas which their devotees may have had in their heads in our period were more probably derived from popular philosophy than the other way round. And the use of the mystery-language of initiation, illumination, and vision, by philosophers like Plotinus (and by Jews and Christians like Philo and Clement of Alexandria) to express symbolically the progress of the soul to knowledge of the divine probably owes at least as much to literary reminiscence, above all of Plato's use of it in the *Symposium*, as to any actual experience of particular mystery-cults.

As for any general influence of the mystery-cults on Christianity,[1] it cannot have been doctrinal, because the

---

[1] The best introductions to this voluminously debated subject available in English are probably still A. D. Nock's two essays, 'Early Gentile Christianity and Its Hellenistic Background' and 'Hellenistic Mysteries and Christian Sacraments', reprinted in his *Essays on Religion and the Ancient World* (2 vols., Oxford, 1972), i. 49–133, ii. 791–820.

mysteries did not have doctrines. Nor is there good evidence for any important influence of mystery-rituals on the development of the Christian liturgy. From the fourth century A.D. onwards, especially in the East, a certain 'mysteric' attitude of mind becomes apparent in the conduct of the Eucharist, a growing sense of fearful awe expressed particularly in a tendency to conceal the most sacred acts from public view (the drawing of curtains before the altar and the screen which later developed into the iconostasis). And, naturally enough, as Christianity developed in the Mediterranean world and attracted the sort of people to whom the mystery-cults appealed, the Christian piety which centred round the paschal mystery of the death and resurrection of God incarnate had some resemblances in feeling and devotional expression to the piety of the dying vegetation-gods who were the central figures of most mystery-cults. These resemblances continued to increase long after the end of paganism, and some of the Holy Week and Easter ceremonies and customs which suggest most forcibly to the modern observer the rites (public or private) of Adonis, Attis, or Osiris are in their present form medieval, sometimes quite late medieval.

Two particular philosophical interpretations of pagan cult should be briefly mentioned here, as they are relevant to our main theme of the encounter of Greek philosophy and Christianity. The first is the theory, which seems to go back to Xenocrates the pupil of Plato (Plutarch, *Isis and Osiris*, 361B) and which is expounded by the Neoplatonist Porphyry in his treatise on vegetarianism (*De Abstinentia*, 2. 40–3) that those traditional stories and ceremonies which philosophers found offensive should be referred to the lower, evil class of spirits (*daemones*) rather than to the gods. This in the period of pagan-Christian controversy proved a most apogetically unfortunate device, which so far from doing anything to save the reputation of the pagan gods was taken by Christians to show that even in the opinion of the more intelligent pagans these gods were really nothing but demons in the Christian sense. The other, which was more important and has had a positive influence on Christian doctrine and practice, was the defence of the veneration of images of the gods in human form against, probably, Stoic critics of the practice, which can be traced back to the end of the first century A.D., was later used by Celsus, Porphyry, and others in response to Christian accusations of idolatry, and was eventually, about the end of the sixth century A.D., taken over by the Christians who were then abandoning their traditional Judaic aversion to the veneration of sacred images.[2]

The Greek philosophers of past and present might seem to the Christians of our period to have a good deal of religious and moral teaching to offer which was not inextricably bound up with pagan cult and myth and could be useful for Christian purposes. It remains to consider what the Christians who took over Greek philosophical ideas were trying to do, which ideas most commended themselves to them or unconsciously influenced them, and how these ideas developed in their new Christian context. (There seems little solid evidence for any reciprocal influence of Christianity on later pagan Greek philosophy, though Ammonius 'Saccas', the master of Plotinus in the third century is said to have been a lapsed Christian, and some Christian influence here and there on the very late pagan Neoplatonism of the fifth and sixth centuries cannot be absolutely ruled out.) The Christians who used Greek philosophy to help them to understand their religious beliefs, to commend them to others, or to define them in opposition to other Christian doctrinal positions were engaged in essentially the same kind of activity as their great Jewish predecessor, Philo of Alexandria (an older contemporary of St. Paul), whose influence, direct and indirect, on Christian thinkers was very great, though he had little or no influence on Jewish thought. They were trying, that is, to translate the religious revelation given in the Jewish Scriptures, to which they added their own New Testament, into terms intelligible and acceptable to people educated (more or less) in Greek philosophy.

The revelation was paramount for them. The Bible was the criterion of truth, and, as we shall see, any Greek ideas which they consciously recognized as incompatible with Biblical truth were vigorously rejected. But none the less it was important to those educated Christians who were not fero-

[2] On this philosophical defence of images and its taking over by the Christians and subsequent employment in the Iconoclast Controversy see P. J. Alexander, *The Patriarch Nicephorus* (Oxford, 1958), ch. ii and A. H. Armstrong, 'Some Comments on the Development of the Theology of Images' (*Studia Patristica*, ix (Berlin, 1966), 117–26).

ciously fideist and anti-rational, in the manner of Tatian and Tertullian, to express their faith in such a way that it could be seen to be not a mere barbarian obscurantism, but the true 'philosophy' in the ancient sense, the true way of life and way to God. This meant, inevitably, the use of Greek philosophical language, and, equally inevitably, with the language came some Greek philosophical ideas, which can be seen to affect the minds even of the most violently anti-philosophical articulate Christians when they try to argue intelligibly and convincingly against pagan or Christian opponents.

The Christians' task of translating their religion into Greek was particularly difficult and particularly urgent for two reasons. One was that the revelation with which they started was not, of course, one given in 'universal' philosophical terms, but an account of God's dealings in history with a particular people, the Jews, and their spiritual heirs, the Christians, the 'new Israel' with whom God in the Christian view had made a new covenant which superseded the old covenant. The other was their sense of a universal missionary vocation, an obligation to convert the whole of mankind to their religion, which made it necessary for them to express this particular and peculiar revelation in the most universal terms which seemed to them at all suitable.

That the Christian thinkers of the early centuries accomplished their task as successfully as they did was probably due to a great extent to some mental limitations which they shared with other thinkers of their age. Like nearly everyone else in their period (and long after) they completely lacked any critical historical sense, and their method of dealing with the sacred texts which they interpreted was anything but scholarly. If the Fathers had dealt with the Bible and early Christian tradition like modern scholars, Christianity in the form in which it became the religion of Europe could never have developed: this of course means that, when considered from the point of view of modern critical scholarhip, there are certain weaknesses in the foundations of its development. Following Philo, the Christians applied to the Bible the methods of allegorical interpretation which the pagan philosophers used to explain the inner meaning of poetry and myth. In addition they had their own distinctive method of typology (based to some extent on earlier Jewish exegesis) in which the lives and actions of Old Testament characters were understood as prefiguring Christ.[3] These methods, and a general lack of any sense of anachronism and of the improbability of discovering the ideas of their own age in the writers of the past, made it a good deal easier to find in the Scriptures what minds trained in Greek philosophy could regard as universal wisdom.

There was also another limitation which made it easier for the Greek- and Latin-speaking Christians of the Roman Empire to give universal expression to their particular revelation. (We should not of course forget the existence of the large body of Syriac Christians who extended beyond the frontiers of the Empire to the East, and whose outlook was very different: but, in our period at least, they were not very interested in Greek philosophy and do not come into consideration here.) This was that the 'universality' which they sought was a very limited one. They did not, any more than other thinkers of their time, make any serious attempt to study the great religious and philosophical traditions outside the Graeco-Roman world, or realize how different they were from Greek religious and philosophical traditions. Many Greek philosophers, of course, believed in ancient Oriental wisdom which had been the source of Greek thought (Christians, as we shall see, made apologetic use of this belief), but they thought of this wisdom as much the same as Greek philosophy, and interpreted such knowledge as they had of Persian and Indian beliefs and practices in Greek terms—Brahmins as a sort of Pythagoreans, or Zoroastrian dualism as a variety of Pythagorean-Platonic philosophical dualism. So the universality the Christians sought was a way of expressing Christian belief which would be intelligible and credible to educated men of the *oecumene*, the *orbis terrarum*, the Graeco-Roman civilized world. This limitation, looked at from a modern point of view, throws doubt on the claims of Christianity to be a genuinely universal religion, but was probably a necessary condition for the successful development of European Christianity. The wider outlook and more limited achieve-

---

[3] On allegory and typology see W. den Boer, 'Allegory and History', in *Romanitas et Christianitas* (Amsterdam, 1973), pp. 15–27. Much has been written recently on typology. A good introduction is to be found in A. D. Nock, 'Hellenistic Mysteries and Christian Sacraments', pp. 805ff.

ment of Mani in the third-century Persian Empire may be contrasted.[4]

We now have to consider the particular forms of Greek philosophy which appealed to and influenced Christians. The predominant Greek philosophical influence on Christianity, not only in the early centuries but down to our own time, has always been Platonism. Stoic influence on the moral thinking of the early Church was considerable, but there was a large Stoic element in Platonic ethical theory from the first century B.C. onwards, and much of the Stoicism apparent in Christian thinking could have come from Stoicized Platonism as much as from Stoicism proper. Most philosophically inclined Christians were repelled by the corporealism of Stoic theology, the doctrine that God is an 'intelligent fiery breath' (the word for 'breath' is *pneuma* in Greek and *spiritus* in Latin) of which our souls are material parts; though the anti-philosophical Tertullian is quite happy to believe that God and human souls are *spiritus* in the Stoic corporeal sense (*Against Praxeas*, ch. 7; *On The Soul*, chs. 7–9)—not, of course, that souls are parts of God—and there is some Stoic influence on the forms of the Trinitarian heresy called Monarchianism which regard the three divine persons as modes or manifestations of the one divine being, conceived as expanding and contracting into himself in the manner of the dynamic corporeal Stoic God. Later, too, in the fifth century there was an interesting group in Gaul of which the principal member was Faustus of Riez[5] who, while insisting that God is incorporeal, maintained the corporeality of the human soul and of angels in order to preserve the sharp distinction between the Creator and his creatures on which orthodox Christians, especially in the West, have always laid great stress. But in general Christians influenced by Greek philosophy followed the Platonists in believing God and created spirits to be wholly incorporeal (though they often thought that angels had some sort of aethereal bodies like those of Platonic *daemones*) and rejected Stoic corporealism along with Stoic pantheism.

---

[4] For some interesting remarks on Mani's self-conscious universalism see Wilfred C. Smith, *The Meaning and End of Religion* (New York, 1962), pp. 86–90.

[5] See E. L. Fortin, *Christianisme et culture philosophique au cinquième siècle* (Paris, 1959).

The influence of Aristotelian philosophy on Christian thought in our period was modest and secondary. Much of it came through Platonism, for the Platonic schools of the Roman Imperial period had absorbed a good deal of Aristotelianism (though there was also a strong anti-Aristotelian tendency, manifest in Atticus in the second century and to some extent in Plotinus in the third). From Porphyry onwards the study of Aristotle's logic was regarded as an indispensable preliminary to the study of Platonic philosophy, and by the fifth century the study of the whole of Aristotle's philosophy was part of the Neoplatonic curriculum. Christians like pagans studied and used Aristotle's logic (which was often thought to be 'safe' and neutral, in contrast to the dangerous and aggressive paganism of Platonic metaphysics in its last phase). Augustine may have made some use of it in his Trinitarian theology, and there was an important Aristotelian element in Greek Christian thought from the sixth century onwards. But there is no sign of any un-Platonized or anti-Platonic Aristotelianism among Christian thinkers in our period or for centuries afterwards. The evidence for a particularly strong influence of Aristotelian ideas on particular groups of Christians in the fourth century, the 'school of Antioch', or the Arians, is not at all convincing.

The Sceptics provided Christian controversialists with an arsenal of arguments which they used for attacking particular philosophical doctrines or philosophy in general, but could not, naturally, make any positive contribution to Christian thought. Christian theologians were decidedly hostile to any sort of Academic or Sceptical agnosticism or suspense of judgement. So in considering the history of the interaction of Christian belief and Greek thought in the first centuries of our era it is predominantly, though not exclusively, the interaction of Christianity and Platonism which we have to consider. This does not of course make the story altogether a simple one. Both traditions were already at their beginning somewhat complex and ambiguous, admitting a variety of differing emphases and attitudes. On the Christian side these often go back to differences already apparent in the New Testament literature itself. Some of these may be due to the varying influence of ideas derived from popular Greek philosophy in the Hellenistic-Jewish religious speculation which is the background of many of the New Testament writers.

Some of the varieties and tensions of Platonism will appear in what follows. But it may be helpful here to try to say something (inevitably rather personal and subjective) about the unity which underlies the varieties. Perhaps the safest description of 'Platonism' is that it is any philosophy which is inspired by a reading, generally rather selective, of the *Dialogues* of Plato, or at least by ideas which are derived, through however many intermediaries, from such a reading. Anyone who has read the *Dialogues* knows their bewildering variety and frequent inconclusiveness. But it is perhaps worth trying to give one man's version of the underlying unity of thought and purpose which may be detected in the writings of Plato and of most Platonists, including those of our period.

What follow are not articles of any sort of Platonic creed: but it is difficult to see why it would be useful to call anyone a Platonist who did not believe something like this. (i) There is a transcendent immaterial reality in some sense other than and independent of (though not necessarily separate from) the empirical world which we know through sense-perception, which gives this empirical world such reality and value as it has, and is generally thought of as culminating in or derived from the ultimate source of reality and value, the Good. (ii) Knowledge of this is an immediate insight, difficult to attain and requiring a wholehearted commitment to the philosophical quest and a lifelong intellectual and moral discipline. It is not identical with the empirical, deductive, or analytic processes which we generally describe as 'reason', though they may contribute to its attainment. (iii) Man's capacity for this knowledge is generally taken by Platonists to be evidence that he can live a life transcending that of the body and continuing after bodily death (and, in pagan and very occasionally in Christian Platonism, not beginning with bodily birth). But any fuller life hereafter depends for Platonists on how we live here and now, and the primary reason for seeking knowledge of the transcendent is to discover norms and standards and attain an insight into reality which will enable us to live our present life as well as possible. Platonism is eminently a practical philosophy: and this applies to those late Platonists who for historical reasons did not share Plato's concern with social and political reform as well as to others who have done so.

The Platonism of the Roman Imperial period which influenced early Christian thought conformed to this very general description of Platonism. It had however lost a great deal which is to be found in Plato's own writings, and those aspects of his thought which were not part of the mental furniture of these later Platonists were not generally adverted to by and did not influence the minds of Christians in our period, even when they read the works of Plato himself. In the Platonism of the Roman Empire and the Christian Platonisms which originated from its interaction with Christian belief, only one range of the possibilities inherent in Plato's own thought was actualized. To begin with, this later Platonism had limited itself by becoming dogmatic and systematic. When Plato's thought was presented as a dogmatic system its character was by that very presentation radically changed: the aporematic, Socratic, side of it, the way of seeing philosophy as always unfinished business, the vivid sense of the inadequacy of language, the element which could legitimately give rise to the Scepticism of the Middle and New Academy, was submerged, though perhaps never completely lost: it seems to contribute something to the Neoplatonic conviction of the unknowability of God. This increased dogmatism, of course, made Platonism, on the whole, all the more acceptable to the Christian theologians of our period. Again, the whole political and social side of Plato's philosophy was nearly lost. For the Platonists of the Roman Empire, unlike Plato, it was no longer the philosopher's primary task to try to reform society, though some later Platonists saw that, if opportunity offered, it would be part of his task.

The Platonists of our period called themselves simply 'Platonists'. But modern scholars have found it convenient to make a division, and to refer to Platonic philosophy from the first century B.C. to the third century A.D. as 'Middle Platonism'; this covers everything from the resumption of dogmatic teaching in the Academy by Antiochus of Ascalon in the age of Cicero to the new start given to Platonic philosophy by the great philosophical and religious thinker Plotinus (205–70). Some thinkers with ideas closely related to those of the Middle Platonists preferred to call themselves Pythagoreans (the Pythagorean–Platonic tradition was thought of in late antiquity, with some justification, as one tradition). These are referred to by modern scholars as 'Neo-Pythagoreans', a term which also covers some not very philosophical occultists, wonder-workers, and vegetarians like

Apollonius of Tyana. From the point of view of our consideration of Greek philosophical influence on Christian thought
they do not need to be clearly distinguished here. The
philosophy of Plotinus and of the successors who critically
developed his thought, with a good deal of reference back to
earlier forms of Platonism, down to the end of the teaching of
philosophy by pagans in the sixth century A.D. is generally
referred to as Neoplatonism.

Middle Platonism was the first kind of Platonism to
influence Christian thought (an early form of it had already
influenced Philo). This influence is clearly apparent from the
second century A.D. onwards. Middle Platonist philosophers
varied a good deal in their opinions and their intellectual
attainments. Alongside the serious philosophy taught by
professed philosophers there was a good deal of popular or
'vulgar' Platonism, based on handbooks for the general reader
and disseminated by philosophically inclined rhetoricians like
Maximus of Tyre (late second century), the influence of
which was widespread and can be detected in pagan and
Christian Gnosticism as well as in orthodox Christianity. But
the variations of Middle Platonism (and serious Neo-
Pythagoreanism) are within narrow limits and a rough
general account which is not too inaccurate can be given as
follows, from the point of view (that of religious and moral
teaching) which interests us here. This form of Platonism is
much more explicitly theistic than Plato's own thought ever
is, at least according to most modern interpreters: though the
Middle Platonists may well only be bringing out more clearly
something which is really there in Plato.[6]

At the head of the system stands a supreme eternal reality
and first principle to whom the Greek word *theos* is applied
almost as a proper name—it can often be legitimately
translated 'God' with a capital G; of course the word *theos*
continues to be used of other subordinate divinities. The
transcendence of this God is often very much stressed (especially by thinkers of Pythagorean inclination). The language
of 'negative' or 'apophatic' theology, which stresses that God's
reality exceeds our thought and imagination by denying every
predicate which can be applied to him, is already being used

---

[6] See J. B. Skemp, 'Plato's Concept of Deity', in *Zetesis* (Antwerp–Utrecht, 1973),
pp. 115–21.

in a way which points forward to Neoplatonism. But it is not yet quite clear (as it is in Neoplatonism) that God is something more than some sort of supreme Mind and Being: and a rather simple pious theism, in which God's good will and loving care for the world is stressed, is often found in Middle Platonists, notably in Plutarch (who combines it with a good deal of very transcendentalist language) in the first century and Atticus in the second. The Platonic Forms or Ideas are generally represented by the Middle Platonists as the 'thoughts of God', a view of them which cannot be traced back with certainty beyond the first century B.C., but is of the greatest importance in later Platonic thought, both pagan and Christian. God is usually thought of as forming and directing the world through intermediaries, subordinate gods and spirits (daemones) in the more popular versions of the philosophy and by a Second Mind or God in the more philosophical versions (as in Alcinous and Numenius in the second century).

The Middle Platonists retain Plato's conviction that the physical universe is good as a whole, but the problem of evil worries them, and they tend to attribute its origin to some sort of evil, irrational soul independent of God at work in the world, an idea for which they find Platonic authority in the *Timaeus* and the tenth book of the *Laws*. Their conception of man is marked by a sharp body-soul dualism in the manner of the *Phaedo*, though the asceticism they preach is notably humane and moderate for their period. Their moral teaching often shows strong Stoic influence. They generally hold vigorously to the strict Stoic doctrine that virtue alone is sufficient for human well-being, and that external goods are irrelevant. (It should be noted that the Stoics professed a body-soul dualism at least as sharp as that of any Platonist: their belief in the corporeality of the soul made it very easy for them to think of it as something quite distinct from the body, a pure fiery rationality which could only be contaminated by association with inferior substance and whose good, virtue, was quite distinct from the goods of the body.)

This relatively simple theism, with its high and austere moral tone, was easy for Christians to assimilate, and probably left the deepest mark of any kind of Platonism on Christian thought. The reasons by which educated Christians justified the use which they made of this pagan philosophy were of two kinds. They maintained that the Greek philosophers had stolen their best ideas from the Jewish Scriptures, regarded as immeasurably more ancient than any Greek writings, and reproduced them with various pagan distortions and additions. This is a variant of the belief in ancient Oriental wisdom already noticed (p. 356), and could of course be used to denigrate Greek philosophy as well as to justify its use. But the Christians most sympathetic to Greek thought, notably Justin and Clement of Alexandria in the second century, also put forward another idea which has lasted better and which has frequently helped Christians to regard other ways of thinking than their own as at least of some value. This was the idea that Christ the eternal *Logos* who was incarnate in Jesus of Nazareth had been active in human history from the beginning as God's living word, teaching and inspiring wise and good men everywhere, Gentiles as well as Jews, including the great Greek philosophers, so that philosophy could be seen as it was by Clement and many later thinkers, as the divinely ordained preparation of the Gentiles for the Gospel.

For some time, probably, before any Christians began to think seriously about Greek philosophy, the Christian body had been disturbed and deeply divided by a variety of interpretations of Christianity which belong to that powerful and distinctive contemporary religious movement which we call pessimistic Gnosticism. This was a religion of deep alienation from this world. For the Gnostic believer the whole material universe was an evil place, a prison and a trap, produced as the result of an incursion of the powers of darkness into the world of light, or made by some hopelessly second-rate and inferior being (identified with the God of the Jews) who was the product of some pre-cosmic fall and utterly distinct from the true God of the transcendent world of light. The Gnostic Redeemer, identified by Christian Gnostics with Christ, came into this evil and alien world to give Gnostics that saving knowledge or *gnosis* which would lead them back to the true God and their true home in the world of light. Mainstream Christians and second-century Platonic philosophers, though they may sometimes have been influenced by this Gnostic way of thinking more deeply than they knew, in the last resort agreed in rejecting it. For both of them this world, though there was much evil in it, was a good world made by a good creator.

This common opposition to Gnosticism may have helped Christians to look more favourably on Middle Platonism (though some of them, notably Hippolytus (third century A.D.) were inclined to regard all heresies as due to the influence of various Greek philosophies), and the developed theology of the good God, the Creator, and his good creation which they stated in opposition to Gnosticism, owed a good deal to the Middle Platonists. But there were certain important differences. The Christians emphasized more than most of the pagans the disjunction between God and his creation, the transcendent otherness and separateness of the Creator from the world which he had made. And they insisted that this sharply separate God was solely responsible for the existence of everything in the created world. They rejected, that is, the idea, which commended itself to some Middle Platonists, of an independent principle of evil or irrational disorder closely connected with the everlastingly pre-existing matter on which God in making the world had to work. In rejecting this explanation of the problem of evil, the Christians were probably to some extent influenced by their intense hostility to Gnosticism, as the philosophers who accepted it were sometimes (notably in the case of Plutarch) influenced by the Iranian conflict-dualism which is the background of one form of Gnosticism, and which has profoundly influenced Christian attitudes to the world, though never admitted as formal Christian doctrine.

The Christians of course passionately rejected what they regarded as the idolatrous side of Platonism, its acceptance of the existence and cult of subordinate divinities and spirits through whom God works in the world and communicates with men. This is not (as the Christians represented it to be) a conflict between polytheism and monotheism, but between two forms of monotheism, one, the Biblical, rigorous and exclusive, believing in a God who stands utterly apart from the world which he has made and is only accessible to mankind through such revelation of himself as he may condescend to give, and the other, the Greek, in which God communicates his divinity as far as possible to the world and all its parts and the rich variety of subordinate divinities therein, and is at least mediately accessible to each and every man through his native, local religious traditions. And we should note that the Christian tradition later underwent a good deal of modification which brought it nearer to the Hellenic type of monotheism.

The Christians generally (with the exceptions already noted on p. 357) wholeheartedly accepted the Platonist doctrines of the absolute incorporeality and changeless eternity of God (however difficult the latter might be to reconcile with a good deal in the Bible literally interpreted). 'God is a spirit' soon came to mean 'God is incorporeal', and all statements of doctrine which seemed to imply change in God were vigorously rejected by orthodox theologians. They generally found the mixture of positive and negative statements about God characteristic of Middle Platonism congenial, as orthodox Christian theologians have tended to do ever since. There was already a strong tendency in Jewish thought to believe in the unknowability of God, which reinforced the 'apophatic' or negative tendency in Middle Platonism. (The belief in God's unknowable transcendence is also clearly marked in early Gnosticism from at least the time of Basilides in the early second century.) On the other hand Scripture, Church tradition, and, increasingly, the pressure of theological controversy compelled theologians to make a great many positive statements about God and to deal with his self-revelation as that of an intelligible and definable being. This positive (or 'kataphatic') tendency was reinforced by one of the most influential Christian borrowings from Middle Platonism, the doctrine that the Platonic Forms, the eternal archetypes or models of all created things, were thoughts in the mind of God. Though Christians often associated these eternal and unchanging thoughts closely with the Logos-Christ, they were not generally prepared (even when they accepted some degree of subordination of the Logos) to make the sharp distinction made by the Neoplatonists (see below, p. 368) between the transcendent unknowable One and the first divine reality derived from him, the Divine Intellect which is also the World of Forms. The tension, and at times contradiction, between the two ways of thinking was never fully resolved. (A little more will be said about this when considering the influence of Neoplatonism.)

The Christian theologians down to the third century generally found the Middle Platonist idea of the Second Mind or Second God congruous with the New Testament data, and represented Christ the *Logos* as the Father's subordinate and intermediary in creation and revelation, though sharing fully in his divinity. It was through his *Logos* (inadequately translated 'Word'—it conveys the idea of expressed thought as a living power) that God the Father made the world, and only in the *Logos* that he revealed himself and became to some extent knowable to men. The position of the Holy Spirit in this system was of course rather difficult to determine. Christians could not simply identify him with the Platonic Third God, the immanent World-Soul, and his nature and status remained rather indefinite till after the Council of Nicaea in 325. (The profound change in Trinitarian theology which took place in the fourth century will be briefly considered later.) Middle Platonist influence is particularly marked in the great speculative system of the most powerful thinker among Christians before Nicaea, Origen (*c.* 185–255), who probably studied under Plotinus' master Ammonius 'Saccas'. In spite of his sharply critical and independent attitude to Greek philosophy, there is much that is genuinely Platonic, as well as deeply Christian, about his vision of how the Father, through his subordinate but divine and eternal *Logos*, created a community of free and intelligent spirits on whose free choices and God's response to them the rest of world history depends: they fall in varying degrees from their first love and purity and are incarnated in bodies appropriate to their demerits, and move up and down the scale of existence, like Plato's reincarnating souls, according to their successive choices: but all may be brought back in the end to their first perfection (though not perhaps, without the possibility of another fall) by the continuing redemptive love of the *Logos* through whom they were made, who was incarnate in Jesus of Nazareth: no creature ever falls outside the hope of redemption in him.[7]

In their practical teaching about man and how he ought to live, the Christian thinkers of our period generally agreed better with the Platonists than might be expected in the adherents of a religion which lays so much stress on the body as an integral part of man in its doctrines of the Incarnation and Resurrection. When speaking and thinking 'theologically' about these doctrines and others closely connected with them,

---

[7] For Origen's system see especially his treatise *On First Principles*, most easily accessible in the annotated translation by H. Butterworth (London, 1936; reprinted 1967).

of the sacraments and of men's final bliss or damnation, they
vigorously defended the unity of body and soul and the
goodness of the body against Platonists and others. But when
it came to moral theory and moral practice they were quite
happy to adopt a very sharp body-soul dualism as a working
principle and found the asceticism of Stoic-Platonist morality
very congenial. The relatively humane and moderate austerity of the philosophers, in fact, generally tempered the
extremism of Christian hatred of the body among those
educated Christians whom it influenced. The practical dualism of the Christians was justified theologically by appealing
to the doctrine of the fall of man and the corruption and
disorder which it had introduced into human nature (as that
of the pagan Platonists was by their belief that the soul had
descended into this lower world from the higher regions where
it was rightfully at home). It should be noted that both
pagans and Christians tended to regard their own bodies with
much more dislike and suspicion than the material world as a
whole. The goodness of the visible universe as the beautiful
and well-ordered work of the perfectly good and wise Creator
was vigorously upheld by both Christians and pagans, especially against their common enemies the Gnostics, though
with a certain difference of emphasis. For the pagans, the
material cosmos was the one supreme perceptible self-
revelation of divinity, and the way back to God at least began
with its contemplation. For the Christians, the religious centre
of interest here below was not the cosmos but the incarnate
Christ and his Church.

From the later fourth century onwards Christian thinkers
were influenced by the form of Platonism which modern
scholars call Neoplatonism. It is impossible here to describe in
any way adequately the richness and power of this very
widely influential development of Middle Platonism, which is
due first and foremost to the genius of the greatest of Greek
religious philosophers, Plotinus (A.D. 205–70). The most
striking difference between Middle Platonism and
Neoplatonism is to be found in the account of the First
Principle. Plotinus, clarifying and developing ideas which
were already present in Middle Platonism and Neo-
Pythagoreanism (see pp. 361–2), and following a line of interpretation of Plato's *Parmenides* and *Republic*, 6. 508–9 which
was already well established in the Platonic school, taught that

the source of reality was not a Supreme Being or Supreme Intellect but the One or Good beyond being and intellect. For him and his successors, that is, there stands before intelligence and formed, determinate reality an infinite creative goodness and freedom, inaccessible to thought because in him (the masculine pronoun is in accordance with Plotinus' own usage) thought finds no determinate object—he is not a 'this' or 'that', and reachable only in the mystical union to which the love which he gives leads us back.

From this One eternally proceed the successive levels of the great hierarchically ordered universe of the Neoplatonists, in diminishing degrees of unity and so of reality and goodness, but never falling outside unity and goodness altogether, each in its degree, down to and including the material universe, mirroring and expressing on its own level the higher realities on which it depends, and each in its degree turning back in contemplation and aspiring to return to the One. In Plotinus, and to a considerable extent still in the stiffer, much more sharply demarcated and elaborate hierarchies of his suc- cessors, the levels of reality correspond closely to states of man's inner experience. Intellect or Real Being, the living world of forms (the Platonic Ideas) into which the life springing from the One eternally structures itself in its return, is the world in which we find ourselves at home when we wake up and understand who we truly are: and we are one, though not in a way which destroys our own individuality, with the universal Soul which descends through the material universe, forming, ordering, and vivifying it as a whole and in every part, and can and should experience that unity. Neoplatonism is very much a philosophy of experience, the experience of mystical union with the One, the experience of being awake and alive in the world of Intellect, and the experience of unity with the universal principle of life and rational order of our universe, all experiences attainable (by the few) here and now in our life on earth: and even some who have little use for Neoplatonism as a metaphysical system find it rings re- markably true psychologically. Though older dualistic atti- tudes persist, Neoplatonism is often very positive in its attitude to the material universe, seeing it as a theophany or divine manifestation, the glorious image of its intelligible archetype to which it stands very close.

In considering the influence of this last great form of Greek philosophy on Christian thought, we have first to remember that it was a considerable time after the death of Plotinus before Neoplatonism became at all widely influential. The edition of the writings of Plotinus edited and arranged by his disciple Porphyry which we know as the *Enneads* did not appear till the beginning of the fourth century: there had been an earlier edition by another close friend and disciple, Eustochius, but there is no evidence that it was widely read, though the fourth-century Christian writer Eusebius of Caesarea may have used it. And the great Platonic school of Athens did not become definitely Neoplatonist till towards the end of the fourth century, and that of Alexandria perhaps not till somewhat later. The great Athenian and Alexandrian Neoplatonic teachers and writers belong to the fifth and sixth centuries. Consequently any formal philosophical education which any fourth-century Christians received is likely to have been Middle Platonist rather than Neoplatonist, though it is certain that in the Greek-speaking East the Cappadocian Fathers, Basil of Caesarea, Gregory Nazianzen, and Gregory of Nyssa read Plotinus and Porphyry and perhaps also the great early-fourth-century Neoplatonist Iamblichus: and in the Latin-speaking West the influence of Plotinus (who taught at Rome) and, particularly, of Porphyry, who both popularized and developed the thought of his master, was strong well before the time of Augustine (354–430).

A particular difficulty in assessing the influence of Neoplatonism properly so-called (that is, the Platonism of Plotinus and his successors) is that ideas which appear first in Middle Platonism persisted in later pagan as well as in Christian Platonism: there was a great deal of common ground between the different forms of Platonism in our period, earlier and later, Christian and pagan. Neoplatonic influence should not be confidently asserted, even when there is clear evidence of the use of Neoplatonic writings, except where there is some acceptance of the distinctive ideas of Plotinus and his successors. This is particularly hard to show clearly when we are dealing with the most distinctive and original of Neoplatonic doctrines, that the first principle and source of reality, the One or Good, transcends being and thought and is therefore by his very nature unknowable, a doctrine which the pagan successors of Plotinus maintained with even greater emphasis than Plotinus himself. Christian thought, generally speaking, tended in the fourth and fifth centuries and often later to remain, as has already been noted (p. 365), in the Middle Platonist position, combining the strongest assertions of the unknowability of God with very positive assertions about him as an apparently in some way intelligible Supreme Being.

Thus the Cappadocian Fathers in the East, especially Gregory of Nyssa, assert the infinite unknowability of God in the strongest terms, and use the assertion as a weapon against their extreme Arian (Anomoean) opponents, whom they accuse of Hellenic rationalism, and who certainly believed that God's nature was knowable and definable. But at the same time the requirements of orthodox Trinitarian theology after the Council of Nicaea compel them to make very positive (and at times logically curious) assertions about Substance and Persons in the Godhead. Augustine in the West also knows much too much about the precise relations to each other of the Persons in the Trinity for one who asserts the unknowability of God in the strong terms which he sometimes uses.

Later, however, in the Greek East, there does appear a very influential writer who takes the Neoplatonic insistence on God's transcendent unknowability really seriously. This is the unknown person (perhaps a Greek-speaking Syrian) who at some time between the end of the fourth and the early sixth century produced a body of writings to which he gave practically apostolic authority by passing them off as the works of St. Paul's Athenian convert Dionysius the Areopagite. His works show clearly the influence of the type of late Neoplatonism which we know best from the writings of Proclus (410–85) the Platonic Successor—i.e. head of the Platonic school, the Academy—at Athens. Notable among the signs of this influence is a very clear and strong insistence on the doctrine of the unknowability of God, which is combined in an intentionally paradoxical way with the positive assertions about God as Trinity and Creator made necessary by Christian belief. This deliberate maintenance of affirmative and negative statements about God in tension and contrast has remained characteristic of Eastern Christian thought. The Christian Neoplatonism of 'Dionysius', developed and to some extent corrected in a more positive, world-accepting, and incarnational direction by one of the greatest of Greek

Christian theologians, Maximus the Confessor (580–662), continued to exercise great influence in the Christian East: and the tradition of Dionysius and Maximus was introduced and boldly developed in the West by Johannes Scottus Eriugena (*c.* 810–77), the influence of whose thought has been persistent and powerful, though generally somewhat restricted.

There is an interesting parallelism between two developments of thought, Christian and pagan Neoplatonist, in the fourth century, though there does not seem to be evidence of any widespread or decisive influence of one on the other. As is well known, orthodox Christians in the fourth century, after much bitter argument and conflict, decisively rejected the older 'subordinationist' type of Trinitarian theology described above (p. 366), of which Arianism, on one side at least, can be regarded as an extreme development, in favour of the theology of the Trinity-in-unity of co-equal persons, in which Father, Son, and Holy Spirit are on the same level and not arranged in descending order of subordination one to the other: this is the theology expressed in what we call the Nicene Creed. In the fourth century also there appears in pagan Platonism a way of thinking about the One and Intellect (see p. 368) in which the unknowable and infinite One eternally determines itself in the triad Being, Life, and Intellect, of which the first member is identical with itself. This has some roots in the thought of Plotinus, but departs from him radically in the way in which it sees the One and Intellect as different aspects or phases or modes of the same reality. It is probably due to his pupil Porphyry, and is certainly deeply influenced by Porphyry's way of interpreting his master.[8] It influenced the fourth-century Christian philosophical theologian Marius Victorinus, who adapted it to his purpose of defending the Nicene doctrine of the Trinity, and perhaps through him Augustine. But there seems to be no evidence that the major architects and defenders of orthodox Trinitarianism in the East, from Athanasius onwards, were aware of it. Iamblichus and later pagan Neoplatonists

---

[8] The doctrine is found fully expressed in an anonymous commentary on the *Parmenides* of Plato edited by P. Hadot in the second volume of *Porphyre et Victorinus* (Paris, 1968), a book which is the most complete and authoritative discussion of this whole development. Later Neoplatonists criticize Porphyry by name for holding what appears to be essentially the same view.

strongly rejected the identification of the first member of the intelligible triad with the transcendent One, though the triad itself became an important part of their system.

However difficult it may be to determine precise points at which distinctively Neoplatonic ideas influenced Christian doctrine, and the precise extent of their influence, there can be no doubt that many of the great Christian thinkers from the middle fourth century onwards read the Neoplatonists and were deeply affected by what they read. This is particularly clear in Augustine (354–430), who freely and generously acknowledges his debt to Plotinus and Porphyry. They liberated his mind from Manichaean corporealism and convinced him of the spirituality of God and the soul, and they helped to form his introspective way of thinking, the way in which for him the journey to God is a journey to the interior, in which he finds God within and transcending his own soul. Of course there is very much in Augustine's thought which does not come from the Platonists. His later doctrine of predestination is all too Biblical, and the remarkably original ideas about human history and society which he expounds in his *City of God* do not seem to have any Greek philosophical source. Augustine is altogether too powerfully individual a figure to be regarded as the typical Christian Neoplatonist. Though there is little that is distinctively Neoplatonist about it, the simple and noble theism, with its confidence in the goodness of God and his world, which the last great philosopher-statesman of Rome, Boethius (480–524) expounds in his *Consolation of Philosophy*, is perhaps nearer to the Christian Platonist norm—if there is one. Christian Platonism, in the centuries with which we have been dealing and later, has generally been a force working against fanaticisms (including the fanaticism of insane logicality), helping to promote a sense of the mystery of God, and reinforcing belief in the goodness of the world as an image of divine beauty.

Our account of the influence of Greek philosophy on Christianity must end here. But it is important to emphasize that this influence did not end with the sixth century. The study of Plato and the Neoplatonists, of Aristotle, and (to a very much lesser extent) of the Stoics, has often in later centuries stimulated new developments in Christian thought. And, just as pagan Neoplatonism not only influenced

Christian thought but provided a centre of intellectual resistance to Christianity down to the sixth century,[9] so the persistence of independent Hellenic ways of religious thinking as part of our traditional inheritance has often led to criticism of and resistance to what are generally taken as distinctively Christian attitudes, especially those which make sharp distinctions and oppositions between God and creation, or faith and reason, or church and world.

Further Reading

(Bibliographies relevant to earlier Greek Philosophy and religion will be found in Chapters 8 and 10.)

Editions and Translations
(i) *Middle Platonists.* Few serious Middle Platonist or Neo-Pythagorean works survive. The most important is the *Epitome* (or *Didaskalikos*) of Alcinous (or Albinus), which is to be found together with his *Isagoge* in vol. vi of C. F. Hermann's Teubner edition of Plato (*Platonis Dialogi* (Leipzig, 1921–36)) and has been edited separately by P. Louis (Paris, 1945). Many of the essays of Plutarch collected under the title *Moralia* have a serious philosophical content. There is an edition with English translation in the Loeb Classical Library (London, 1927 onwards: in progress). The surviving fragments of Atticus are to be found in Eusebius, *Praeparatio Evangelica*, 11. 1–2; 15. 4–12: they have been separately edited by E. des Places (Paris, 1977). The fragments of Numenius have been edited by E. des Places (Bris, 1973).

(ii) *Neoplatonists*
 (a) *Plotinus.* The great critical edition by P. Henry and H. R. Schwyzer is now complete (*Plotini Enneades* (3 vols., Paris and Brussels, 1951–73)). An extensively revised *editio minor* is appearing in the Oxford Classical Texts: vols. i and ii have been published, containing *Enneads*, 1–5 (Oxford, 1964 and 1977). The revised Henry–Schwyzer text (with slight modifications) is being published in the Loeb series with an English translation and notes by A. H. Armstrong. Vols. i–v (*Enneads*, 1–5) have so far appeared (London, 1966———). There is an excellent edition of the text with German translation by R. Harder, R. Beutler, and W. Theiler (Hamburg, 1956–67: index volume with general survey of Plotinus' philosophy, Hamburg, 1971). There is a complete English translation by S. MacKenna revised by B. S. Page (latest edn. London, 1969). Selections in English translation by A. H. Armstrong (*Plotinus, Religious Classics of East and West* (London, 1953; New York, 1962)).

---

[9] There has been no space to discuss this in this chapter: it is not strictly relevant to the main subject. A good account will be found in R. T. Wallis, *Neoplatonism*, chs. 4 and 5.

(b) *Later Neoplatonists*. The best introduction to the thought of the later Neoplatonists is still the edition of Proclus, *Elements of Theology* by E. R. Dodds, with English translation and commentary (2nd edn. Oxford, 1963). There is an excellent edition of the *Platonic Theology* of Proclus by H. D. Saffrey and L. G. Westerink in the Budé series, with a French translation and a long and valuable introduction (Paris, Book 1, 1968; Book 2, 1974; Book 3, 1978; in progress). For editions and translations of others of the voluminous works of the later Neoplatonists (mostly commentaries on Plato and Aristotle), reference should be made to the bibliographies of the *Cambridge History of Later Greek and Early Mediaeval Philosophy* and R. T. Wallis, *Neoplatonism* (see below).

(iii) *Jewish and Christian Writers*. The best and most easily accessible edition of Philo is that in the Loeb Classical Library by F. H. Colson, G. H. Whitaker, and R. Marcus, with English translation (12 vols., London, 1929–62). The Christian writers of our period are numerous and there are too many good editions and translations of their works to be listed here. Reference should be made to the bibliographies in the *Cambridge History* and Daniélou (see below) and to the Patrologies of R. Altaner (Eng. tr. Freiburg, Edinburgh, London, 1960) and J. Quasten (Utrecht, Antwerp, 1966). The principal series of Christian texts are J. P. Migne, *Patrologia Latina* (221 vols., Paris, 1844–55) and *Patrologia Graeca* (161 vols., Paris, 1857–66), containing editions of very varying quality and appallingly produced but reasonably complete; *Die Griechischen Christlichen Schriftsteller* (Berlin, 1897 onwards); *Corpus Scriptorum Ecclesiasticorum Latinorum* (Vienna, 1866 onwards); *Sources Chrétiennes*, an excellent series, all with French translations and often very valuable introductions and commentaries (Paris, 1941 onwards): *Oxford Early Christian Texts*, a new series with English translations, introductions, and notes which promises very well (Oxford, 1971 onwards).

The principal series of English translations are *The Ante-Nicene Christian Library* (24 vols., Edinburgh, 1866–72, supplementary vol. 1897: reprinted as *The Ante Nicene Fathers*, 10 vols., Buffalo, 1884–6); *A Select Library of Nicene and Post-Nicene Fathers*, 28 vols. (Buffalo and New York, 1886–1900); *Ancient Christian Writers*, tolerable translations, often with good introductions and commentaries (Westminster, Maryland, 1946 onwards); *The Fathers of the Church*, originally of poor quality and without adequate introductions and notes, but much improved lately (New York, 1947 onwards).

Modern Works
The *Cambridge History of Later Greek and Early Mediaeval Philosophy*, ed. A. H. Armstrong (Cambridge, 1967; reprinted with corrections and additional bibliography 1970) covers the subject-matter of this chapter fairly thoroughly in its first six parts, and has moderately extensive bibliographies. John Dillon, *The Middle Platonists* (London, 1977), is a very thorough survey of Middle Platonism with a good short bibliography. The best introduction to Neoplatonism is R. T. Wallis, *Neoplatonism* (London, 1972), which has good, though brief remarks on Middle Platonism in the first chapter and on the influence of Neoplatonism on Christian thought in its last, and an excellent short bibliography. Very much has been written on Greek philosophy and early Christian thought. A. Harnack's *History of Dogma* is

still interesting (4th edn. of German original, Tübingen, 1909–10: English translation of 3rd edition, 2nd edn. New York, 1958). Good recent books are G. L. Prestige, *God in Patristic Thought*, (3rd edn. London, 1952): J. Daniélou, *Gospel Message and Hellenistic Culture* (English translation extensively revised by the author, London, 1972); R. A. Markus *Christianity in the Roman World* (London, 1974). A. H. Armstrong and R. A. Markus, *Christian Faith and Greek Philosophy* (London, 1960) is still perhaps worth looking at, though the authors have changed and developed many of their opinions since the book was written. Maurice Wiles, *The Making of Christian Doctrine* (Cambridge, 1967) gives a new and important view of Christian doctrinal development in the period considered in this chapter. There is much that is illuminating in A. D. Nock, *Conversion* (Oxford 1933; paperback edn. 1961) and *Essays on Religion and the Ancient World* (2 vols., Oxford, 1972); Peter Brown, *Augustine of Hippo* (London, 1967) and *The World of Late Antiquity* (London, 1972); and E. R. Dodds, *Pagan and Christian in an Age of Anxiety* (Cambridge, 1965).

13

ARCHITECTURE AND CITY PLANNING

PETER KIDSON

During the last hundred years, thanks largely to the incessant activity of archaeologists, the number of Greek buildings of which we can claim to have some knowledge has increased almost beyond number. Yet at the same time it has been the fate of Greek architecture, as with so many other manifestations of Greek genius, to lose much of the inflated prestige which it once enjoyed. The Greek orders no longer play even a token part in the education of a modern British architect. If the Parthenon has not yet lost its status as one of the world's great buildings, this is largely due to the enterprise of a tourist industry that thrives on masterpieces, but which prudently allows its clients little time to think about what they see. Among those who do still think seriously about such things, however, it is by no means self-evident either that the Parthenon deserves to be ranked with, say, the Pantheon, or the Hagia Sophia, or Bourges Cathedral; or that there is any point in trying to measure the comparative quality of such buildings. Advanced opinion is even prepared to dismiss the Parthenon as the sacred cow of a discredited past. Not everyone as yet subscribes to such views; but the times are hardly auspicious for defence or counter-attack; and even if they were, it may be doubted whether anything more than a modest rehabilitation could be expected.

The implications of this paradox are various but not necessarily inconsistent. We may now claim to have a broader, more varied, and better balanced basis than ever before on which to form an estimate of what Greek architects actually achieved. The alleged perfection of Greek architecture was simply part of a wider myth, and no more than the rest could survive the cooling of enthusiasm. Attempts to substantiate the claim on the part of nineteenth-century interpreters gave rise to some of the most curious special pleading in the literature of the arts. The number of aesthetic

The Hephaestion, Athens

The Maidens' Porch, Erechtheion, Athens

tope No. 29. From the Parthenon. British Museum, London

Part of the Parthenon Frieze, British Museum, London

Part of the Parthenon Frieze, British Museum, London

Cleobis, Delphi Museum

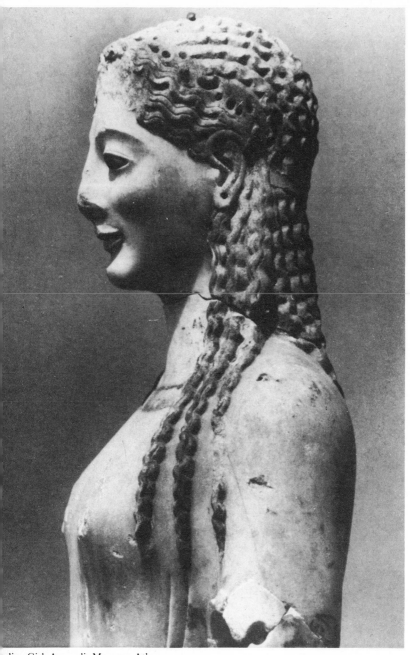

nding Girl, Acropolis Museum, Athens

Head of Aphrodite, Petworth House

souls that were genuinely ravished by the subtlety of Greek mouldings can never have been large; and one may suspect that the esoteric zeal affected by earlier generations of cultivated travellers for the unerring excellence of Greek taste always included a fair measure of cant.

The modern processed tourist, though perhaps less well grounded in the classics than his predecessors, is also less likely to resort to affectation; and despite his hurried progress he is in some respects better placed to exercise judgement. The prospect of the sun setting behind the broken columns of the temples at Agrigento may move him to take a photograph, but he will seldom pretend that the experience has opened his eyes to the delicate mysteries of modules and intercolumniations. What he will quickly grasp, however, when he has taken several tours and many photographs, is that before they were ruined, one Greek temple would have looked remarkably like another, and Greek theatres even more so. He may then come to suspect that the same applied to all the sorts of building that have disappeared without leaving substantial traces—and even to entire cities. If so, he will have put himself in a position to appreciate in essence what the archaeologists have demonstrated in detail, namely, that Greek architecture was far more concerned with functional types than with individual designs; and that the artistry which has been so much admired, was at all times firmly rooted in the conventions of an extremely cautious and conservative building industry.

This does not mean that the refinements are now considered to be of no account; merely that in a wider perspective their importance is less likely to be measured by their self-evident beauty than for what they tell us about the peculiar way in which Greeks thought that beauty could be achieved in architecture, and their sense of the sort of occasion when such efforts were considered appropriate. The purely formal qualities of Greek architecture have always been obvious, and rightly emphasized. In the past this led to an almost excessive preoccupation with temples—not merely on the pragmatic grounds that hardly anything else has survived in sufficient detail for us to study intensively, but from the conviction that temples alone offered scope for formal design; so that even if we knew a great deal more than we do about Greek secular or military buildings, it would do little or nothing to enhance our ideas about what the Greeks themselves understood by architecture. We can now see that if ever this was the whole truth, it applied only to the early, i.e. archaic period of Greek history. It was certainly not the case during the Hellenistic centuries; and in all probability the shift of emphasis was one of the consequences of the great debates which we may imagine architects conducting among themselves during the classical age of the city-states. No doubt the formal impulse first made itself apparent in the design of temples, and in any case the condition of the evidence makes it impossible for us to study its origins and development in any other context. But individual temples were seldom conceived in isolation. From the earliest times Greeks seem to have been acutely aware of the mutual restraints which adjacent buildings ought to impose upon one another, both in sanctuaries and in cities. Perhaps the greatest achievement of the archaeologists has been to open our eyes to the conscious planning of these larger, complex unities, which was in a sense the ultimate preoccupation of Greek designers. We can now see how the stock of formal ideas worked out for the embellishment of temples was modified and extended to the end of transforming the city itself into a work of art. Thanks to their labours and the help of aerial photography, several Greek sites are now prepared to disclose something of their ancient dispositions. But great efforts of imagination, historical as well as visual, are still required if we are to appreciate this most elusive of Greek architectural achievements.

The circumstances under which the Greeks first took to building on a large scale are almost totally obscure. For centuries after their arrival in Greece, they appear to have made do with structures whose character was modest and ephemeral enough to have left no trace. Then, quite suddenly, in the middle of the second millenium B.C., some of their aspiring chieftains discovered a taste for styles of life that eventually required large halls, permanent defences, and ambitious tombs. The position of Greece at the edge of outer darkness from the point of view of the really civilized parts of the world at the time makes it reasonably certain that the social and political impetus behind the first Greek attempts at serious architecture came from the eastern Mediterranean. The nearest and most obvious source was Crete; and it may well be that Mycenaean Greeks borrowed their ideas about gracious living mostly from Crete and Egypt. But the mature fortifications of Tiryns and Mycenae were quite clearly inspired by those of Hittite Boghazkoy, even though they were on a smaller scale. This goes both for their approach to military engineering, and the kind of masonry which they used—the huge, roughly trimmed cyclopean stones, which in the course of time gradually approached the regular shapes of ashlar. The great halls around which these fortifications were deployed also had their models in Anatolia. The megara of Troy anticipated by almost a thousand years those of Mycenae. It is all the more remarkable, therefore, that the tholos tombs which were the most spectacular novelties of Mycenaean architecture seem to have no obvious prototypes in that direction, or indeed, any other.

The problem which these tombs present is a fascinating one, and its ramifications are almost endless. For on one side, they seem to link up with the prehistoric barrow tombs of western Europe, while on another they anticipate one of the most persistent and widespread traditions of later funeral monuments: that of honouring the illustrious dead by erecting a dome or vault over their mortal remains. The scale and quality of the Mycenaean tholoi imply dynastic megalomania, and it is easy enough for us to associate them with the names of heroes. Yet the picture which emerges remains equivocal. On the one hand we can plausibly postulate ambitious rulers eager to adopt the architectural trappings, along with other manifestations of oriental divine monarchy; but on the other, the performance seems to have fallen rather short of any known oriental model. Only the fortifications and the tombs were first-class of their kind. For the rest, we have only to compare the accommodation at Pylos or Mycenae with the palaces of Crete, Anatolia, and Mesopotamia, to realize that life must have been lived at a somewhat different level of complexity. To do them justice the Mycenaeans seem to have borrowed from their sources only the kind of architecture for which they had any use. If they showed no interest in vast palaces but were impressed by great halls, this was a matter of choice: a preference that perhaps reflects the heroic style of life in Homer, better than the meticulous details of the Pylos tablets. Their traditional rituals of burial seem to have remained intact. All that a masonry vault added to their more primitive graves was monumental dignity. Agamemnon may have yearned to be numbered among the great kings of the east but there was also some fairly stiff resistance at home, and a limit beyond which in fact no progress was made. One may suspect that this successful resistance ultimately centred on the peculiarities of Greek religion, and the tenacity with which they were preserved.

Here we come to the question of temples. One of the unexpected features of Mycenaean archaeology is that although it has produced evidence of religious sanctuaries in full operation, remarkably few buildings have been uncovered to which the name 'temple' can be applied with unqualified confidence. This is not to say that there were no temples in Mycenaean Greece, but they can never have been the conspicuous feature of the landscape that they were to become in the classical period; and we must therefore draw the conclusion that they were not considered necessary to the proper conduct of religious ceremonies. In this respect Mycenae seems to have resembled Crete, and both offered stark contrast to Egypt and western Asia.

Like most primitive peoples, the Greeks first recognized the epiphanies of their gods in the powers and high places of nature. It is still not difficult for us to understand why they thought the gods lived on Olympus; or why they felt there was something uncanny about Delphi, or dangerous about Sounion; or equally, why there was something miraculous and holy about every spring of water. A drought at the wrong time of year or a bumper harvest betokened the active intervention of some malign or beneficent god; and by extension almost every event, whether normal or exceptional in a man's life, could be construed in the same terms. But whatever form the encounter took the appropriate human response was to offer a sacrifice. All that was required was an altar in the open air. A temple was a gratuitous extra. The idea of tethering a god to an altar by providing a permanent home for him in the form of a temple seems to have occurred first to the Sumerians, for whom it presupposed a relationship between men and gods that was at once too intimate, well regulated, and all embracing for Greek taste. It also required a highly organized priesthood in exclusive charge of what was known about the gods, and this, too, the Greeks managed to avoid. In fact, on reflection it would seem that hardly any of the practical needs which determined the development of temple architecture in the Middle East applied in Greece; and the absence of these factors goes a long way to explain the totally different character of Greek religious architecture, and in particular its preoccupation with the purely formal aspects of design.

Exactly when and under what circumstances the Greeks began to build temples remains a mystery. It is often said that temples evolved out of the Mycenaean megaron, *pace* Homer, where Athena took up her abode in the house of Erechtheus. In a sense this may well be true, but just how such a basic change of function could take place remains the subject of a profound silence. One may hazard a guess that the experience of going to live overseas had something to do with it— especially the emigrations which led to the settlement of Ionia, movements which brought Greeks into contact with people who habitually built temples. Periclean Athens apart, colonial Greece was at almost all times ahead of the homeland in the scale and standards of its temple architecture. As for the megaron theory, it may be conceded that from the moment we are in a position to observe what the Greeks thought a temple should look like, it appears to have had something akin to a megaron as its nucleus. This remained true for as long as the Greeks continued to build temples. Whatever innovations they were prepared to introduce, they never repudiated this venerable starting-point. Invention was always a matter of improving, adding, or refining. Such intensely conservative respect for a traditional form was not merely a matter of national character. It suggests that the megaron had always been regarded as inherently suited for its purpose. As this can hardly have been on the grounds of how it was used, we may presume that it was a matter of appearance. So it could follow that temple building went back to the Mycenaean period when the megaron was the most splendid kind of building the Greeks knew. But it is equally possible that they borrowed the form a second time during the Dark Age, from western Asia where the Phoenicians, like King Solomon, had considered it appropriate for their own temples.

Whatever the explanation of its origins, the subsequent history of Greek temple building resolves itself into a prolonged inquest into the right form for the house of a god. Certain fundamental assumptions remained constant throughout. The interior of the temple belonged more or less exclusively to the god. As the domestic needs of gods were deemed simple and unchanging this part hardly altered over centuries except in scale. It is here that the contrast with Asiatic or Egyptian temples must have been most extreme. Greek temples were little more than conspicuous objects of decoration in sanctuaries where human attention was concentrated on altars. What mattered was their shape, their size, their colour—in short, their ability to create a suitably grand and solemn setting for a religious ceremony. All that the Greeks needed to borrow from their eastern neighbours were details: fluted columns and the hawkshead moulding from the Egyptians, or the volute capital from western Asia. However, the effect of these self-imposed limits was in no way inhibiting. The transformation of the megaron into the classical temple was achieved in fits and starts over a period of perhaps 500 years, but in retrospect the process has something of the inevitability of a biological evolution. The chamber of the god was raised up on a high platform. Its dignity was further enhanced by the addition of a porch or porches at the ends, and the lateral walls were protected by colonnades to which the roof was extended. The most conspicuous effect of these developments was to call into special prominence the column as a unit of decoration; and this evidently touched off a whole new line of investigation into the right form for columns: how they should be placed in relation to one another, to the walls from which they were projected, and to the roofs which they supported. Even more important was the aspiration to build temples entirely of stone. This raised questions of statics to which the timber constructions of previous generations offered no answers, and so another field of trial and error was opened.

In the most general sense this series of experiments, which extended well into the fifth century, resulted in the proliferation of alternatives, most of them of a purely aesthetic nature; and this in turn created the need for decisions about what would go with what. It was characteristic of the Greeks that whereas everyone before them seems to have made do with columns as such, they should eventually have produced two major categories: tall and thin (Ionic) or short and fat (Doric), and that they should have worried themselves as to whether these should be fluted, and about the right number of flutes that was appropriate to each. Ultimately it was decided that the flutes on one should be separated by a sharp edge, whereas the other should have fillets; that one required a capital and a base while the other did not; and that while both should taper upwards, one should sometimes perceptibly bulge, whereas the other should retain a more or less straight profile. Similar preoccupations extended to the entablatures which the columns carried. In its principles, Greek temple architecture was very simple: a matter of walls and trusses, posts and lintels. It has always been supposed that the triglyph-metope sequence, the mutules and guttae of the Doric entablature, which certainly resemble woodwork, survived as visual features from the early days when columns and entablatures as well as roofs were made of timber. On this analogy triglyphs would represent the beam ends of timber trusses, and Doric entablatures would derive from the side elevation of a timber building. By a similar analogy, the façade of such a building could produce something approximating to the Ionic entablature. But if there ever was a stage when both sorts of entablature were present in the same building, all trace of it has been lost. By the time there is evidence to consult, i.e. by the sixth century, timber models had already been left far behind, and the two kinds of entablature had more or less sorted themselves out into visually consistent and mutually exclusive systems, in which the logic of construction was entirely subordinate to the logic of decoration.

More important than the actual elements of which entablatures were composed, however, was the question of their size and weight in relation to the colonnades. Here the critical moment was the decision to replace timber by stone. So far as we can tell, the period when this happened was the beginning of the sixth century. But again the circumstances are obscure. It is tempting to connect the change with the arrival of the tyrants, their policies of conspicuous public works, and the annexation of certain cults by the cities. Corinth may well have given the lead, but the earliest evidence, such as it is, comes from Corinthian colonies: Syracuse and Corcyra, with Selinus and Paestum not far behind. Ionia seems to have followed soon after. Whatever the circumstances, this must have been the occasion when Doric and Ionic began seriously to diverge, and devote themselves to the pursuit of contrasted aesthetic impressions. For no obvious reason, the earliest-

known stone Doric entablature (Apollo, Syracuse) was conceived on a colossal scale that must have completely reversed
all previous thinking on the subject of the ratio between
columns and entablatures. Almost in a chain reaction, the
heavy entablature called into being the massive Doric columns
with which we are familiar from the surviving monuments;
and this was soon followed by the bulge, or entasis, which,
far more effectively than capitals or bases, offset the rigid
lifelessness which threatened to qualify their monotonous
bulk. Then one curve led to another, so that in the end,
hardly a straight line was to be found in a really sophisticated
Doric temple like the Parthenon.

All this no doubt imparted a sense of heroic energy to the
monumental dignity of classical Doric. But success was not
achieved at a stroke. The heavy entablature presented its own
internal problems. Everyone seems to have agreed that the
earliest examples were too heavy; and throughout the sixth
century they were progressively reduced. Yet equally clearly,
the effect of monumentality was felt to be bound up with the
entablatures, and there was no going back to the simple
contrast between vertical and horizontal elements which
presumably had once sufficed in timber temples and which
continued to suffice in the context of Ionic. It was this
situation rather than the innate conservatism of some mainland architects that explains why the triglyph-metope
sequence was retained for some stone temples and not others.
What made the heavy entablature bearable was the presence
of subordinate verticals, the triglyphs at regular intervals. It
was the same sort of calculated contrast which required
concave flutes to offset the convex surfaces of columns.

By contrast, Ionic architects felt no such need for con-
trapuntal features in their own entablatures. This must have
something to do with the fact that they successfully resisted
the fascination of heavy superstructures, an attitude which
perhaps represented a preference for the more slender proportions of archaic columns. These they proceeded to embellish
with exquisite variations on the Asiatic volute capital, and
with elaborate bases, both of which have their own way of
conveying a hint of elasticity after the manner of springs and
bearings. Although the Ionians were the first to explore the
possibilities of truly gigantic dimensions, they seem to have
done so without making any serious concessions to the

monumental ideals of Doric; and in this they were almost certainly repudiating one aesthetic paradigm in favour of another.

The persistent care with which Greek architects devoted themselves to such minute questions of visual effect is almost without parallel in the history of their profession. Perhaps the masons who invented Gothic in northern France during the twelfth and thirteenth centuries of our era shared something of this concern for the relation of part to part. But medieval masons on the whole lacked the fastidious self-imposed discipline of the Greeks; and if comparisons are needed, they must be sought outside architecture altogether. The analogy that comes perhaps most readily to mind is that of Bach's Art of the fugue, in which similar magnificent abstractions emerge from the manipulation of equally rigorous mathematical rules.

Ever since the Renaissance it has been a commonplace that the architecture of the ancients was grounded in formulas of proportion, and for many eighteenth- and nineteenth-century admirers the aesthetic excellence of Greek buildings has been closely identified with this feature. The extent to which the Greeks themselves held this view is obviously a matter of great importance. Unfortunately the whole subject has been profoundly infected by generations of cant and nonsense which have centred around two of the most persistent of Renaissance myths; one being that the mathematical principles of classical architecture had been lost during the barbarian invasions and remained unknown through the Middle Ages; the other, that these elusive principles were recovered by certain virtuous Italians who made it their business to purge architecture of its medieval solecisms during the fifteenth and sixteenth centuries. It has now been shown beyond reasonable doubt that the whole range of medieval architecture was as deeply impregnated with ratios and proportions as that of either antiquity or the Renaissance. More to the point, there is every reason to suppose that the architectural mathematics of the Middle Ages were far closer to those of Greece and Rome than were those of Renaissance Italy; in fact, that there was a straight line of descent—a continuous tradition which, ironically, was to some extent disrupted by the very zealots who thought they were restoring it. At the heart of this misunderstanding is to be found the equivocal figure of Vitruvius.

Vitruvius enjoys the distinction of being the only ancient author whose views on the subject of architecture have survived in the form of a systematic treatise. Plenty of random remarks are to be found in other sources, such as Strabo or Pausanias, and these are immensely valuable. But the sort of professional know-how supplied by Vitruvius is not to be found elsewhere, and this has tended to give the status of a primary source to everything his book contains. It may seem ungrateful to cast doubt on the value of our only substantial ancient authority, and to do so will no doubt arouse the sort of suspicions which often greet the efforts of art historians to sidestep documents which fail to fit their theories. In the case of Vitruvius, however, we are on fairly firm ground. We may read with respect what he has to tell us about contemporary Roman building practice, but his efforts to present himself as a master of Greek aesthetic theory do not stand scrutiny. Vitruvius lived at a time when Augustus and Agrippa were rebuilding Rome, and his book was dedicated to the Emperor in the transparent hope of landing one of the plum commissions for himself. But it is clear that the best jobs were going to Greeks. So, in order to show that Roman architects were in no way inferior to Greek, he went in for an impressive display of Greek name-dropping. However, it is doubtful whether Vitruvius had read any but a few of their learned works; or if he had, then he made no use of them. Not only are his views on Doric, and its alleged shortcomings, manifestly those of a narrow Hellenistic pedant; but his entire classification of temples into types based on arrangements of modules betrays a similar background of brisk summaries and articles in encyclopedias. While this may tell us something about the way Hellenistic architects thought about their profession in the last two centuries before Christ, to read it back into the formative period of Greek architecture is both gratuitous and wrong. Early temples were simply not designed in the ways Vitruvius describes. The module method, i.e. making all the dimensions of a building multiples of a small unit, was itself almost certainly the result of a process of simplification and tidying up. In all probability the men responsible for it were fourth-century Ionian architects, such as Pytheos, whose works supplied models for the Hellenistic temples which proliferated across the Middle East in the wake of the Macedonian conquest.

What happened before has to be inferred from the sites. This is seldom a simple matter. It is one thing to prove that Vitruvius's classification does not work, quite another to elucidate a more satisfactory alternative. We have two clues. In the first place there is the evidence of imperial Roman architecture, a good deal of which paid no attention to Vitruvius, and secondly there is the testimony of Greek mathematics. Roman methods of setting out a building had a lot in common with the technique of mensuration used by the *agrimensores*. They shared a repertory of calculations, and were interested in the same lengths, shapes, and ratios. For instance, the *actus* of 120 ft, or the *clima* of 60 ft, both of them used for measuring land, are liable to turn up among the dimensions of Roman buildings, often in conjunction with the diagonals of squares with sides of these lengths. The ratio between the side and the diagonal of a square was only one, if the most readily detectable, of a range of such devices, the practical purpose of which seems to have been to enable any number of dimensions to be calculated quickly and easily from one another. All that was needed to get things going was a general specification, and one major dimension—usually a width.

It was this stock of ideas that was handed down to the Middle Ages. But there are no strong grounds for supposing that they were invented by the Romans, whose contributions to mathematics were slight. In any case, these have an unmistakably Pythagorean flavour. At the heart of the tradition there was a constant preoccupation with certain irrational numbers: the square roots of 2, 3, and 5, and the ratio of mean and extreme proportion, which is perhaps better known to us as the Golden Section. The ground which these notions have in common is provided by the construction of the regular solids. However, in architecture we nearly always meet them in the form of standard arithmetical approximations, e.g. 12:17 for root 2; 15:26 for root 3; 5:8 for the Golden Section, and these, or at least some of them, take us all the way back to Babylon. If we put the question, at what moment in history were the regular solids, surds, and naïve attempts to fathom their mysteries by playing games with numbers, likely to have entered the realm of architecture, the answer must surely be: when mathematics was still at a rudimentary stage, i.e. early rather than late. And if we ask why architects should have been fascinated by such things at all it seems difficult to avoid the conclusion that they felt them to be inherently relevant to what they were doing. We know that high claims were made for the cosmic significance of the regular solids in Pythagorean circles; and if the gods in whose honour temples were built were taken at all seriously by the men who built them, what better way of matching the building to its purpose then to incorporate into its design the celestial mathematics of the gods themselves?

Until we start looking, of course, this is nothing but speculation. But when the question is put to the ruins, always subject to the proviso that the archaeologists have got the measurements right, there appears to be a fairly impressive quantity of corroboration. Where the corners of the naos and the stylobate can be fixed with some confidence, it is nearly always possible to find simple numerical expressions which relate one rectangle to the other. The same is true for colonnades and entablatures. No two temples are ever found to be exactly the same, but insofar as we are in a position to compare a series of designs over a long period of time, the process of visual refinement can be expressed as the replacement of one arrangement of ratios by another. In other words, the mathematical ingredients required to make a temple formally perfect seem to have been recognized long before it was agreed that visual perfection had been achieved; and they remained fairly constant.

Exactly when all this began it is impossible to say. It is obviously tempting, and to some extent plausible, to see a connection between the use of certain favoured ratios by Greek architects on the one hand, and the interest of Pythagorean philosophers in mathematics on the other. In this respect the sixth-century Heraion on Samos is an especially fascinating monument. Its remains are scanty, but they have been measured with more than usual care and accuracy by members of the German Archaeological Institute, from whose publication we may deduce that both its detailed and its over-all dimensions were chosen by someone with an inordinate attachment to the square root of 2. This happened during the lifetime of Pythagoras himself, within a few years of his departure from the island. The architect must almost certainly have known the philosopher.

However, it does not follow that the architects took their

inspiration from the philosophers or that they confined themselves to the particular ratios which preoccupied the philosophers. Historians of Greek mathematics have committed themselves to a wide range of opinions as to how and when the problem of surds was recognized and solved; and it would be impertinent of a mere historian of architecture to do anything more than draw their attention to the substantial body of ostensibly relevant evidence that can be extracted from the ruins of temples. The Heraion was by no means a special case, and there is no reason why it should have been the first design of its kind. Nor were such designs in any sense confined to Ionia. On the contrary, there is every reason to suppose that in Greece itself the tradition went back at least to the beginnings of the all-stone temple. It may even have been one of the items for which the Greeks were indebted to their predecessors in Egypt and Mesopotamia. However they came by it, the architects' experience of applied geometry may well have supplied the philosophers with the raw material of their theorems. Furthermore, the Pythagorean notion of form as number makes better sense in terms of the arts, and especially architecture, than in any other context; and some of the most persistent philosophical terminology of later times (e.g. the form/matter antithesis) was clearly derived from the arts.

So far as Doric was concerned, the sixth century was an age of experiment. But by the beginning of the fifth century, the differences between one temple and another had become less striking, and if this means anything, it was surely that architects felt the ideal norm to be within their grasp. During a period of about fifty years, on the mainland and throughout the western Greek world, a fairly large number of Doric temples were built, among which there was an impressive degree of uniformity. The first of which we have any precise knowledge was on Aigina, but the one which made the type fashionable was undoubtedly the great temple of Zeus at Olympia (c. 470). Here if anywhere some sort of consummation was achieved and acknowledged. It is a point that needs to be emphasized if only because the title of the most perfect example of Doric has almost invariably been bestowed upon the Parthenon.

While it is perhaps no misfortune that we know more about Athenian Doric than any other kind, accidents of survival have tended to distort our estimate of its importance. This is particularly true of the Parthenon itself. If every other Doric temple had survived intact we should probably still be disposed to say that the Parthenon was the best of them all. But we should be less tempted to do so in terms of its place within the development of the Doric order. The reputation of the Parthenon turns on three features: the excellence of its materials; the subtlety of its refinements; and the amount and quality of its sculpture. Of these, only the second has strictly to do with architectural form. But if anything, the refinements tend to make it a maverick among Doric temples. Everything about the Parthenon suggests that it was conceived to incorporate a series of Ionic compromises. We have become accustomed to compare it with the Ionic Erechtheion; but tend to forget that when it was started (447), the Erechtheion was not there, and there is no reason to suppose that the intention to build it was as yet in anyone's mind. Indeed, the frieze of the Parthenon is incomprehensible unless it was originally meant to house a cult which was later transferred to the Erechtheion. From this point of view, the significance of the Parthenon lies not in its claim to represent the quintessence of Doric, but rather in its being the first major monument to combine elements of both orders. Ionic at Athens in the fifth century must have conveyed rather special political overtones; and while no doubt the contrast between Doric and Ionic had its conventional aspect there as elsewhere, the Athenians alone of the mainland Greeks are likely to have seen virtue in Ionic, and felt the need to bring the two orders together.

There was another, more technical reason why they should have done so. Given their peculiar sensitivity to the appropriateness of proportion, it was evidently repugnant to orthodox Greek architects that internal columns should be larger than those which formed external colonnades. But a situation calling for such columns regularly occurred inside the naos of any large temple where supports were required for the roof trusses. The normal way round this difficulty was to superimpose one row of small Doric columns on top of another. In the rear chamber of the Parthenon, however, this expedient was not practical, and there the problem was solved by resorting to Ionic columns which had a different ratio of height to radius, and which could therefore be made taller than the external colonnades without becoming more massive.

These columns in the Parthenon have not survived; but in the Propylaia, where a similar problem arose, an Ionic column can still be seen among the Doric, flanking the approach to the main gate.

The Propylaia of the Acropolis at Athens were remarkable in another respect. It needs no more than a moment's reflection to realize that the elements of temple architecture did not readily lend themselves to use in buildings that were not themselves freestanding, rectangular blocks. Colonnades required more or less horizontal platforms, and more or less uniform columns. Roofs could have only parallel pediments. Changes of level, contiguous colonnades of different heights, roofs which met at right angles would present almost insuperable difficulties. Yet the Propylaia went out of the way to confront them all; and the success of Mnesicles' design in effect liberated Greek architecture once and for all from its hitherto self-imposed limitation to isolated compositions. The exuberance of emancipation soon showed itself again on the Acropolis, when in 421 the architect of the Erechtheion accepted the challenge of two different levels in the same building. This meant giving up the continuous symmetrical colonnade. In its place we find no less than four essays in porch or façade composition, all different and disposed around the building in places the choice of which, though no doubt justified by function, strikes us as arbitrary, not to say mannered.

In their several ways, the three great buildings which came to adorn the Acropolis during the second half of the fifth century broke decisively with precedent. This must have been even more apparent in the impression which they made collectively. It was not just a question of mixing the orders, or exploiting levels. One senses a new aesthetic purpose, a different kind of appeal to the imagination than formal symmetry alone could make. At Selinus, the temples were simply grouped in rows. At Akragas they were strung out like divine sentinels around the perimeter of an incomparable site, but too far apart to enter into visual relations with one another. The buildings on the Acropolis were sufficiently close together, yet sufficiently different in shape, scale, level, and detail, to suggest a coherence that was both dramatic and picturesque. It is perhaps not too fanciful to see their intended relation to the rest of the city in terms analogous to that between a temple and its altar. Without losing any of the atmosphere of a traditional sanctuary, the Acropolis contrived to evoke overtones that were as much political as religious. Whether the citizens of Athens were transacting their commercial business in the Agora or debating affairs of state on the Pnyx, the beautiful buildings on the Acropolis, while not exactly obtruding on their attention, were always in sight, to remind them of the higher aspirations to which their city was dedicated. Part sanctuary, part war-memorial, the Acropolis also in a sense offered a vision of an ideal Athens. It was ironical that the final effect was achieved only as the empire crumbled. Even so the consequences were far-reaching. Here for the first time, so far as we are in a position to say, an architect's task was conceived in large measure as the embellishment of a city. Temples were designed as much to edify the pride of citizens as to serve the gods. Only one further step was needed: that civic amenities should be considered worthy to be treated in the same way as temples, and the way would be opened to the conception of the city itself as an object of beauty.

It would be a mistake to suppose that fifth-century Athenians committed themselves consciously and whole-heartedly to the idea of transforming their city into a setting worthy of the good life. But the remodelling of the Agora had already begun, and when the Piraeus was laid out, they took the trouble to consult Hippodamus of Miletus the great exponent of 'gridiron planning'. Their south Italian colony at Thurii also received the benefit of his wisdom. For much of the Greek world, the fundamental conditions were established by Alexander and his successors, who, in depriving public-spirited citizens of the traditional delights of an independent foreign policy, deflected their attention from the pursuit of glory to the more solid advantages of living in a well-planned town. The Ionians, understandably not much given to heroics after the failure of their revolt against the Persians at the beginning of the fifth century, may have been the first to find themselves in this position, and it is perhaps no accident that fifth-century Miletus should have enjoyed the status of an archetype.

But there was more to the problem of producing a well-planned town than setting all the streets at right angles to one another. In any case, the gridiron was no novelty in the fifth century. The idea was already familiar in both Middle and New Kingdom Egypt, where it had been considered suitable for labourers' cantonments; while Old Smyrna at one end of the Greek world, and Selinus at the other, show it to have been commonplace among the early colonial settlements. What recommended the gridiron to the planners of the fourth century and their Hellenistic successors was the ease and convenience with which it could be combined with rectangular public buildings, and with urban houses in which rectangular rooms were arranged around a rectangular court. Where we are in a position to measure the plots formed by the grid, as for instance at Priene, it is clear that the streets were laid out with almost Roman precision—a feat which implies considerable mastery of the techniques of surveying. Yet there is no reason to suppose that the effect was unduly monotonous. On an absolutely level site, like that of Paestum, perhaps it would have been. But few Greek cities were built entirely on flat ground, and irregularities were often skilfully exploited. In this respect the site to which Priene was removed in the fourth century seems to have been particularly well chosen. The city occupied a broad bevelled spur, sloping down from the precipitous face of a mountain, which made a superb natural acropolis, towards what then must have been the estuary of the Maeander. The streets which in plan look as though they made no concessions at all to the landscape, running almost exactly north to south and east to west, in fact rose gradually on three sides to a natural eminence near the centre where the more important public buildings of the city could be grouped; while the fourth side presented a somewhat sharper slope towards the acropolis, and this provided ideal conditions for a theatre. In the central area, the fall of the land was turned into terraces, and these again were put to good effect—the commercial area around the market place being appropriately less elevated than the council chamber, the theatre, and the principal temple. The temple itself, though not large, was clearly intended from the outset to be the most conspicuous and beautiful building in the city. To this end the grid was interrupted so that several streets terminated against it; one of them, perhaps the main street, pointing directly towards the temple's façade.

At Priene, and perhaps generally in western Asia, new twists were given to the Athenian mingling of the orders. Here

Ionic seems to have been reserved for temples and certain other religious buildings; while a species of Doric, now suitably emasculated, was considered fit for secular structures. The orders were also contrasted in other ways. Where two rows of columns were required, Doric would be assigned to the outer row, Ionic to the inner. And where there were two storeys, the lower would be Doric, the upper Ionic. One senses a much more ambitious if still carefully graded hierarchy of ornament, which not only diversified but also linked together the architectural forms to which it was applied. Everything below the temple was in some degree muted. But everything led up to the temple. In the widest sense of the term, the unity of style must have been complete. What made city centres like that of Priene immediately and overwhelmingly impressive, however, was the wholesale use of colonnades. There must have been places in Priene from which in whatever direction one looked, the prospect was almost entirely circumscribed by rows of columns of various sizes, on different levels and at assorted angles. Porticoes and stoas, much more than temples, contributed to this all-embracing effect, the like of which can hardly ever have been experienced by earlier Greeks, except perhaps on a limited scale in some of the more ambitious sanctuaries.

What was it like to conduct one's affairs, indeed to live the greater part of one's life in the presence of such architecture? For it has to be remembered that there were scarcely any activities in which the full citizens of a Hellenistic city engaged that did not have buildings specially designed to accommodate them. It would be ridiculous to make exaggerated claims for these designs on the grounds of their beauty or splendour. When we can contemplate their ruins, what is striking, even touching, about most of them is their functional simplicity and small scale, the parochial quality of the life which they presuppose. The great exception to this rule is of course the theatre. The size of audience which designers of Greek and Roman theatres appear to have envisaged seldom fails to amaze modern travellers. It may be doubted, however, whether all the seats were always taken, and if they were, whether the occasions were always theatrical. To judge from what Vitruvius has to say on the matter, the designing of classical theatres was a recondite affair involving acoustics, and it may well be that theory played an even greater part in the process than estimates of the likely number of customers. Theatres apart, however, there is good reason to suppose that the scale of buildings in ordinary daily use was kept roughly commensurate with the men who used them. This recognition of a limit beyond which size merely diminished human dignity has often been hailed as the special virtue of Greek civic architecture, as though it reflected an instinct for the kind of moderation that was enjoined upon Greece by the Delphic oracle. And perhaps rightly so.

Apart from a handful of colossal temples on the colonial fringes, and visionary schemes such as Deinocrates put before Alexander, there are few symptoms among the Greeks of the architectural megalomania practised by Egyptians and Babylonians before them, and by Romans after them. But it would be naïve to postulate a straight antithesis between Greek decorum and barbarian bad taste. There is simply not enough evidence to establish whether lapses into vulgarity were frequent, or who was responsible for them. Conspicuous ostentation on the part of local worthies eager to provide their cities with public amenities could easily be construed as more than local patriotism; while on the other hand, there may well have been an element of prudence as well as aesthetic discretion in the commendable modesty of most Hellenistic public monuments. Moreover, in practice the money that was normally available to pay for these things was seldom enough to encourage aspirations much above the level of what was decently functional. In any case, it was not just the intimate scale of their buildings that made Hellenistic cities attractive places in which to live; but the achievement within these limits of a genuine monumentality in miniature. Provided there were sufficient columns, carved entablatures, and fine mouldings, size did not matter. The illusion of grandeur depended on the completeness and coherence, not the magnitude of the experience.

It is one thing to visualize such a setting, and quite another to grasp how it must have seemed to the people for whom it was a part of everyday life. That they found it agreeable and that it catered for their self-esteem may be taken for granted, if only because the same features tended to repeat themselves in city after city, and to have changed remarkably little over hundreds of years. To some extent this stagnant quality may be explained by the extravagant use of stone and marble, the durability of which tended to reduce the number of occasions when designs could be improved. Generally, if this happened at all, it had to wait until imperial Roman times. This was particularly the case with installations supplying running water to public fountains and baths, the *sine qua non* of city life, and perhaps its most highly prized luxury. Roman prodigies apart, however, there can be little doubt that there was a widely accepted norm of what a Hellenistic city centre should look like, and this must in some measure have represented what the citizens themselves wanted.

It is also tempting to resort once more to the concept of theatricality, which so often comes to mind when Greek architecture is discussed. One must be careful not to press this too far. Greeks were not necessarily more given to self-conscious attitudinizing than other people; and splendid colonnades are not likely to have made them feel bigger and better men than they really were. But this is not to say that the tone of their lives was not affected. Columns did not embarrass them, as they undoubtedly would embarrass a great many modern Europeans for whom the experience of town life has grown out of something rather different from the Mediterranean tradition. The distinction turns on how people use their cities and the extent to which their mode of life generates the appropriate sentiment of civic pride. For Hellenistic Greeks, one may suspect that this attunement achieved a kind of perfection. Not only did they pass most of their time in public places; but what went on there made life really worth living—above all, endless talking. Greek cities must have provided marvellous settings for rhetoric.

This was a man's world. Nothing is more striking, even in ruins, than the contrast between civic monuments and private houses in a Hellenistic city: on the one hand, extrovert aspirations to splendour, on the other, the inward-turned seclusion of domestic privacy. Greek men oscillated between the two; but the place for Greek women was emphatically at home, even if they were not exactly kept under lock and key. Houses belonged to the family. It is sometimes supposed that there are links between the status of women and the level of private social life, and between private social life and domestic architecture. However, it would be unwise to use these tenuous connections in order to draw exciting inferences from the few houses that can be reconstructed. Nothing so far uncovered encourages suspicions of extravagance. The best-known house at Priene had for its principal room something oddly reminiscent of an ancient megaron; but we simply do not know enough to be able to decide whether this was sheer coincidence, deliberate antiquarianism, or the manifestation of a continuous tradition. As yet, few generalizations can be sustained on the subject of Greek domestic architecture. One such is that as and when private life became more enterprising, the peristyle house found the starting-point for a series of elaborations; i.e. adjacent houses were knocked together, more rooms were added, and paintings and mosaics occurred more frequently. Nearly all this could be done, however, without seriously altering the relation between house and city in the estimation of its owner. At all times, so far as we can tell, domestic buildings remained a foil to the public amenities.

Small cities like Priene are interesting precisely because they were unexceptional. There, if anywhere, we can grasp the pattern of urban life which eventually imposed itself from one end of the Mediterranean to the other, by sheer self-evident merit. Even Rome under the emperors felt obliged to turn itself into a sort of Hellenistic city.

It is hardly likely that Romans took much notice of places like Priene. Their attentions would naturally turn to the great Hellenistic capitals: Pergamum, Antioch, and, above all, Alexandria. One of the great gaps in our knowledge of Greek architecture centres on Ptolemaic Alexandria, and the effect of this is compounded by the paucity of what is left of Seleucid Antioch. These two cities, together perhaps with Seleucia-on-the-Tigris, might have been expected to disclose what, if anything, Hellenistic Greeks condescended to learn from Egyptian and Mesopotamian architecture, in particular when they mastered the art of constructing masonry vaults about which Hero of Alexandria wrote his tantalizing treatise, sadly lost long ago.

Compared with such possibilities Pergamum had less to offer. But if the Attalids ever competed with their greater neighbours, they did so entirely on their own terms. In seeking to present themselves as the guardians of Athenian culture, they probably ensured that the pure Greek element in the Hellenistic amalgam was not swamped. The hill on which the upper city of Pergamum once stood is now almost denuded of masonry; but thanks to the German archaeologists who explored the site in the nineteenth century, and their great model, which is not least among the attractions of the Pergamon Museum at Berlin, we can still imagine some of the effects achieved by the buildings that once festooned its summit. In this case there was no room for a grid of streets—merely a single narrow lane winding along the crest which, rising slightly, curled around a shallow concavity. Here was the theatre, which formed the focal point of the whole design. Above and behind the theatre were four colonnaded courts with temples, libraries, and the altar; each court on its own terrace and a different axis, but together more or less concentric with the cavea of the theatre. These were the conspicuous features. Beyond the courts was the lane, and beyond the lane the unobtrusive palace of the kings, the offices of their administration, and the barracks of their guards. The whole area could be sealed off from the world below, was difficult of access and easily defended: a veritable Kremlin no doubt, but one which also contrived to present to the world a vision of an ideal city, on the lines of the Acropolis at Athens. In an obvious sense such effects were propaganda. But it was all done with conviction and apparently accepted at its face value, which is surely one of the tests of successful architecture.

The last word on this subject, however, should be one of caution. We may recognize that the Greeks were among the first to see it as the business of architects to design whole cities as opposed to individual buildings, and that this was the most ambitious of all their demands upon architecture. Beyond that, however, and with the exception of a few privileged sites, it is still impossible for us to form a precise and comprehensive estimate of what they accomplished. The ruins make it easier for us to reconstruct their intentions than their achievements. We know nothing of the experiments they conducted, or of the awful mistakes they may have made; and we can hardly begin to assess how partial were their successes. In such circumstances it would be easy for the myth of Greek superiority to reform around an idea of town-planning which is seductive in proportion to its vagueness. This should be resisted.

To think of such a vast assortment of efforts and experiences as a legacy at once raises an ambiguity. It could mean everything the Greeks were in a position to bequeath, or whatever posterity was able to receive. The two do not necessarily coincide. The bequest can be regarded under two headings. On the one hand it comprised what might be called visible models. These included in the first place a vocabulary of ornament, a collection of mouldings, and the orders, which were transmitted more or less whole. They have been intermittently used or ignored ever since. At the moment they are out of favour, but it would be rash to claim that they have disappeared for ever from the repertory of western architects. In a somewhat more restricted sense the same could be said of building types, which come under the same heading. The extraordinary feat of those neo-classical architects of the early nineteenth century who managed to convince churchmen of almost every persuasion that the Greek temple was the right form for a Christian church gives one to pause lest some further improbable use be found for it.

Manifest imitations however are not the only proof of sympathy or interest. The second term of the bequest covers Greek views about the nature of architecture. Unlike the tangible items, which have nearly always been received with a kind of passive reverence, these only disclose themselves in active attitudes, and they are not always to be found in the obvious places. During the European Middle Ages for instance, when it might be supposed that no one knew or cared anything about Greek ideas on the subject, methods of design were in common use, the basic principles of which had been handed down, in what seems to have been an unbroken line of descent, from the earliest period of Greek monumental architecture. It is quite certain that no one knew this at the time, but that is irrelevant. The important thing was the assumption that for a building to be properly designed its dimensions ought to conform to a limited range of mathematical ratios. This attitude was Greek, both in its essence, and in the choice of ratios considered suitable. So also, and more obviously, was the belief, taken up again for a time during the Renaissance, and occasionally since, that formal perfection in building consisted in the regular repetition of certain favoured shapes. This idea of symmetry however has been the subject of much subsequent equivocation. Lip service has been plentiful but few of their admirers have ever been able to persevere with it, as the Greeks themselves did for centuries, without getting bored.

Finally, there is the idea of architecture as a consciously

arranged environment. This is not to be confused with planning as such. New York does not become a Greek city merely because its streets are laid out at right angles. No doubt certain Greek themes were filtered down to later ages, chiefly through Roman mediators. But it would be idle to suppose that what passed as a fine city in Greek eyes would have made a similar impression in the European Middle Ages, or on the people who developed America, any more than it could conceivably be relevant to the problems of the inflated populations of modern industrial cities. Insofar as town planning has any real achievements to its credit since Greek times, these owe little or nothing to Greek precept or example except in the very general sense that some Greeks were put to a great deal of trouble and expense to get the kind of city they wanted; and that everyone else who has thought it worthwhile to surround themselves by buildings of quality has found it necessary to do the same. From this we may go on to draw the elementary but chilling conclusion that cities accurately reflect the aesthetic standards of the people who live in them. In the last resort most of us do not think that architecture matters; and this is what separates us from most Greeks, who did. One suspects that the average Greek citizen actively liked Greek architecture.

Further Reading

H. Berve, G. Gruben, and M. Hirmer, *Greek Temples, Theatres, and Shrines* (London, 1963). A splendid collection of reproductions.

J. J. Coulton, *Greek Architects at Work* (London, 1977).

W. B. Dinsmoor, *The Architecture of Ancient Greece* (3rd edn. London, 1950). Still the standard handbook, if a trifle austere.

T. Fyfe, *Hellenistic Architecture* (Cambridge, 1936).

R. J. Hopper, *The Acropolis* (London, 1974).

R. Martin, *Manuel d'architecture Grecque*, vol. i (Paris, 1965).

R. Martin, *L'Uurbanisme dans la Grèce antique* (2nd edn. Paris, 1975).

F. C. Penrose, *Principles of Athenian Architecture* (2nd edn. London, 1888). The most complete exposition of the famous refinements.

R. V. Schoder, *Ancient Greece from the Air* (London, 1974). A comprehensive set of photographs of major archaeological sites.

V. Scully, *The Earth, the Temple, and the Gods* (New Haven and London, 1962). An idiosyncratic study of the relation between temples and landscapes.

H. A. Thompson and R. E. Wycherley, *The Agora of Athens* (Princeton, 1972).

F. E. Winter, *Greek Fortifications* (Toronto and London, 1971).

14

THE FIGURAL ARTS

PETER KIDSON

A considerable effort of historical imagination is now required for an educated European of the last quarter of the twentieth century to realize that Greek art was once more or less synonymous with art as such. Until not so very long ago it was generally agreed that all art worthy of the name conformed to a single set of universal and unchanging standards. These had been discovered by the Greeks, transmitted to the Romans, destroyed or rejected by the barbarians, and slowly brought to light again by the Italians of the Renaissance. The two closely related notions: that ancient art had matured gradually in the course of time and then declined; and that 'modern' art had a special relationship with the art of antiquity, that it was in some sense a repetition of it at least to the extent of being concerned with the same formal problems, and subject to the same criterion of excellence, were perhaps first widely put about by Vasari.[1] But it was not until the eighteenth century that serious efforts were made to disentangle the specifically Greek contribution to the joint heritage of Greece and Rome.

Two tasks were recognized. One was to identify the masterpieces mentioned in the literature among the fragments and copies that had survived; the other, to grasp the development which the ancients themselves claimed to have detected in the history of Greek art. The great names had never been forgotten: Myron, Pheidias, Polykleitos, Skopas, Praxiteles, and Lysippos in sculpture; Polygnotos, Apollodoros, Zeuxis, Parrhasios, and Apelles in painting. Even though not one of their works was known for certain, anecdotes and opinions to be found in the pages of Pliny the Elder or Quintilian proclaimed them as men who had brought their respective arts to a state of perfection beyond which no further advance could be imagined. All had lived during the century and a half which separated the Persian wars from the career of

[1] *Le vite de più eccellente architetti, pittori e scultori italiani de Cimabue insino a tempi nostri* (2nd edn. 1568. ed. by G. Milanesi, Florence, 1878–85), esp. the preface and introductions.

Alexander. Clearly this had been a golden age. By implication, the imperfect art which had appeared before that time
could be judged as works of apprenticeship. The shedding of
ineptitudes provided a yardstick of appreciation. On the other
hand, what cannot be improved upon may only be imitated,
and more often than not falls prey to mannerisms. Thus, by
what might seem an accident of chronology, all the art of the
Hellenistic world was irredeemably infected with incipient
decline, a condition which became critical under the Romans
and terminal at the onset of the barbarians.

The man who took it upon himself to give substance to
these ideas, and who imposed them firmly upon the attention
of the learned world, was J. J. Winckelmann (1717–68).
Winckelmann's book on ancient art appeared in 1764, that is,
before hardly any of the considerable number of Greek
originals now well known to us had found their way into
accessible collections. Nevertheless, for over a hundred years
its structure and critical attitudes exercised a singular fascination over his successors in the field of classical archaeology.
When Adolf Fürtwängler wrote his *Masterpieces of Greek
Sculpture* in 1893, he had at his disposal a far greater number
of authentic pieces than Winckelmann; yet the distribution of
his approval fell more or less in the same places. This was not
just because Winckelmann matched his position to the aesthetics of antiquity. To an extent that he perhaps did not
realize, the message he addressed to posterity was one to
which its sympathies were peculiarly attuned. In the short
term, he anticipated a generation of readers especially in
Germany who were actively engaged in creating for their own
use a myth of Greece, and for whom his exalted vision of
Greek art was both apposite and timely. But this was of less
importance than the way in which he wrote about art.
Winckelmann saw the evolution of style in genetic terms.
Whether or not he owed anything to Vico, the Neapolitan
philosopher would almost certainly have approved of his
approach. Vico's views about the ways in which societies
evolve and cultural patterns repeat themselves were taken up
by the German Romantics and developed by their nineteenth-
century successors, until they culminated in the concept of the
cultural cycle as a kind of historical unit, with its features
frankly conceived on the model of living organisms. This way
of thinking about history abounded with terms like birth and

death, growth, maturity, and decay, all borrowed from the dominant nineteenth-century science of biology and applied to human cultures and societies if not literally, at least with scant respect for the proper limits of metaphor. The study of the history of art during much of the nineteenth century was conducted against the background and under the influence of this outlook, for in the diagnosis of a cultural condition art was liable to be one of the most telling symptoms. Winckelmann's views about Greek art fitted easily into this context. They flourished so long as the biological analogy flourished, but have passed into disrepute as that analogy itself has been criticized and found wanting.

The circumstances under which this happened are too complicated to be gone into in much detail here. In a purely pragmatic sense, the process began soon after Winckelmann wrote his book. For the curiosity which was already taking Europeans off in search of genuine Greek art, also took them elsewhere, and soon brought them face to face with works of imagination to which their inherited stock of critical ideas simply did not apply. Not only was Egyptian art not Greek; it never developed, at least not in any way that could be interpreted in biological terms. The same was true of Mesopotamian art. Then in the course of the nineteenth century the more adventurous among European artists found themselves less and less enamoured of the classical tradition, and sought to escape from it in all manner of exotic directions.

This shift of allegiance was matched by a steady change in speculations about what art is or is not, and its place in the spectrum of human experience. Until the eighteenth century, aritistic theory had concerned itself more or less exclusively with the notion of the ideal, which was in some sense to be construed as a claim to knowledge about the world. As the venerable—ultimately Greek—presuppositions which sustained this view were steadily eroded by the natural sciences, there grew up alongside it alternative theories which were all in some measure concerned with the subjective element in aesthetic experience. The first dents were made in the name of the Sublime, to which 'Longinus'' treatise lent the convenient classical authority of its title. These were followed by the antithesis between classical and Romantic art, the separation of the beauty of art from the beauty of nature; the claim that the essence of art was creative expression, with music as its

paradigm; and finally, the affirmation of the complete autonomy of art.

Perhaps the most insidious formulation of these pretensions
is to be found in Riegl's doctrine of *Kunstwollen* which was
launched upon the world in the same year as Fürtwängler's
book—1893. The concept is untranslatable; but what Riegl
seems to have had in mind was a sense of styles being forced to
disclose themselves through the efforts of artists who struggled
to apprehend their possibilities; almost as though the artist
was the servant of his style, even if his situation could
sometimes resemble that of the hero of Kafka's *Castle*. The
inferences to be drawn from this somewhat metaphysical view
of art were many and far reaching. Among other things, it
presupposed a radically different view of style; and this in
turn led to a drastic reduction in the amount of bad art that
was about in the world. What had once been called early or
late phases need no longer be regarded as maladroit versions
of something else. The way was thus opened for them to
qualify as styles in their own right. Received opinion about
Greek art quickly felt the force of these ideas. Only a few
years previously, Kavvadias had unearthed on the Acropolis
at Athens some charming sixth-century marble statues of girls.
In no time at all, these were being hailed with enthusiasm,
and any doubts there may have been as to the artistic quality
and stylistic independence of archaic Greek art soon
evaporated.

The rehabilitation of Hellenistic art took place at much the
same time. During the 1870s, German archaeologists began to
interest themselves in the ruins of Pergamum; and slabs from
the frieze around the great altar gradually found their way
back to Berlin. As a museum piece the Pergamum frieze was
every bit as impressive as the Elgin Marbles; and if theory
declared it to be late and degenerate, so much the worse for
theory. At the end of the nineteenth century, Germans were
acutely sensitive about late styles. Their own art included a
great deal of late Gothic and Baroque, and not much from the
'best periods'. This was not at all consistent with the virile
stance adopted by the newly established Empire; and much
thought was duly given to the task of putting matters right.
The upshot was that by the beginning of the present century
all three late styles were being treated with unprecedented
sympathy and insight.

A preliminary assessment of these adjustments of taste may be disposed to attribute little importance to them, insofar as it was only a question of liking what was once disliked. However, much more was involved than personal preferences. In the first place they entailed the recognition that masterpieces could occur at random in any or every period. This concession releases us from the obligation to suppose that the incidence or fulfilment of artistic genius is in some obscure way connected with certain propitious moments in the evolution of a style, and that certain ages are therefore bound to be blessed with an undue share of the world's great works of art. It was this that wrecked the biological analogy; and with it went that convenient system of prefabricated value-judgements which was one of the great attractions of the Vasari–Winckelmann kind of art history. A further consequence was that transitions from one period to another ceased to appear as normal, natural, and inevitable, like growing up or growing old. Such things could no longer be glossed over or taken for granted, but turned into genuine historical problems, which soon proceeded to displace the pinnacles of stylistic maturity as focal points of critical attention.

Even more profound were the results of exposing Greek art to comparison on equal terms with art of totally different kinds. Not only did this have the effect of reducing the more outrageous claims to perfection made on its behalf; but it led to its being pushed back, so to speak, firmly into the context of Greek civilization. We are now in a position to see clearly that what the Greeks did was not so much to discover something essential about the nature of the figural arts, as to give them a highly idiosyncratic twist. They entertained certain attitudes towards the arts which were peculiar to themselves, and which changed only as and when their experience of the world at large changed. Except perhaps at the very outset they identified their preferences among alternatives presented to them by their own artists; and they made sense of art entirely in terms of their own ideas. The 'special relationship' with the Renaissance was a one-sided affair, and although it may tell us something about Renaissance art, it does not help us to understand Greek art. Indeed, the fact that classical studies have largely dropped out of modern education may be helping to obscure the extent to which the modern world is

essentially out of sympathy with Greek art, and the intellectual difficulties that are likely to beset any attempt to come
to terms with it. Whether or not Greek art still has anything
to offer the modern world is another matter. But that is a
question best left until the whole topic has been given up to
closer scrutiny.

It is remarkable that the Greeks, who were destined to
transform monumental sculpture and painting out of all
recognition, seem to have managed to do without these arts
until the seventh century B.C. To the question: what was
being produced in the figural arts of Homer's time, the answer
is almost certainly: nothing of importance. No large objects
have survived, and it is extremely unlikely that if there had
been anything, every single piece would have been destroyed.
It is true that Homer devotes one whole book of the *Iliad*
(Book 18) to the description of a piece of metal work in which
figure subjects of an extremely subtle and complicated kind
were ostensibly depicted. But if anything like the shield of
Achilles ever existed, it must have been made long before
Homer, in fact in Mycenean times, by men who rivalled the
virtuosity of the goldsmiths who produced the Vaphio gold
cups. Mycenean art died with the Myceneans. In Homer's
own time the arts which really mattered to the Greeks were
those presided over by Apollo and the Muses—poetry, song,
music, and dancing—which contributed largely to the content
and character of their religious festivals. There were no muses
of the visual arts. Craftsmen had their own god: Hephaestus,
who was married to Charis or Aphrodite, thereby signifying
the union of skill and beauty; but he was never the social
equal of Apollo. By the same token, though smiths had a
similar kind of craft organization to that of the poets, and
shared some of their privileges when they travelled abroad, in
general the prestige enjoyed by poetry was far beyond their
reach. The distinction with its pejorative overtones persisted
into Hellenistic times and beyond, in the classification of the
arts into manual or liberal.

The only considerable works of art that have come down to
us from the so-called Dark Age of Greece are pots, mostly
covered with bands of intricate abstract ornament to which
the appropriate designation—geometric—has been assigned.
These pots testify that two of the abiding characteristics of all
Greek art were present from the start: a highly developed

sense of pattern, and an instinct for mathematical form. But some of them also provide us with our first indication as to how the Greeks conceived the human figure: tiny, schematic shapes with triangular torsos, wasp waists, and massive thighs. Solid bronze votive offerings from Olympia and Delphi share the same form and presumably similar dates. Despite the diminutive scale of these objects, recollections of their mode of stylization evidently survived the introduction of monumental statues during the seventh century. Traces of it can be detected in male nudes right down to the invention of the classical style. This alone should warn us against too hastily assuming that the Greeks took over monumental sculpture as they found it among the Egyptians when they established their trading-port at Naukratis in the Nile delta.

It is of course true that the Greeks were particularly receptive to influences from the eastern and southern shores of the Mediterranean at that time. The most obvious of their acquisitions from those parts was their alphabet, which they adapted from that of the Phoenicians. But they were also eager to receive new kinds of ornament like the palmette; and all manner of exotic monsters such as griffins, harpies, sphinxes, gorgons, not to mention lions or panthers. The large-scale male nude fits fairly easily into this context of wholesale borrowing. The colossal scale on which the earliest Greek figures were conceived, the methods used in their design, their postures, some of their hair-styles, all these indicate debts to Egyptian precedents. Yet there is not a single statue that any competent judge is likely to mistake for an Egyptian figure. If the Greeks owed their general concept of the *kouros* to Egypt, they were highly selective about the ingedients which they put into it, many of which were Greek. This almost certainly had something to do with the wishes of those for whom the statues were made, and the purposes which they were intended to serve.

When the Greeks emerged from the shadows of their Dark Age, they had shed almost all the political and religious institutions that might have linked them with Egypt. Any tendencies there might have been in the direction of divine monarchies on the oriental model seem to have disappeared with the fall of Mycenae. By 700 they were firmly committed to the *polis*; and their society was aristocratic. The governing classes at least had largely emancipated themselves from the stifling impact of overwhelming deities. Instead of obsequious religiosity, well-to-do Greeks, so to speak, affected to share the world with the Olympians, who were themselves aristocrats as the poets knew, and from whom favoured dynasties could still claim descent through the Homeric heroes.

It is perhaps no accident that the first *kouroi* were made for a social class obsessed wtih Homer's world and the larger-than-life characters who inhabited it. Always consciously striving to emulate this magnificent past, Greek aristocrats needed little prompting to visualize their own great men as well as their literary heroes in monumental terms; and as soon as their attention was drawn to the statues of the Egyptians, which were both colossal and ancient, these no doubt recommended themselves as perfect models for such an enterprise. Some of the *kouroi* are known to celebrate men who performed deeds that found favour with the gods, like Cleobis and Biton; or to have died in battle, like the Croesus whose statue was found at Anavysos in Attica. Perhaps the whole series represented latter-day heroes, though of this we cannot be certain. What is certain is that right from the start, literature supplied not only much of the subject-matter used by the figural arts, in the form of myth, but also certain fundamental attitudes about style.

The series of archaic *kouroi* which has come down to us reflects with curious accuracy an ambivalence in the heroic ideal of Greek aristocrats. In their knowledge of being set apart from the rest of mankind, their conservative sense of the past, their pride of blood, their wealth and power, such men might seem to qualify for a sort of image, long familiar to the ancient East, in which physical features were somewhat stylized to suggest the transfiguring privilege of intimacy with the gods. Egyptian pharoahs and Mesopotamian conquerors are never presented as mere men. The whole point of the exercise was to suggest the extent to which they were more than mortal. But the Greeks for whom Homer wrote did not quite share this point of view. Their heroes were no doubt also men whom the gods loved; but unlike Gilgamesh, Achilles and Odysseus were prepared to accept the destiny of death, were even prepared to choose it. The mortality of heroes divided them sharply from the gods; and this became the starting-point of Greek humanism. It gave them an independent sense of the moral dignity of man by which to judge both the inhuman and the ungodlike aspects of their gods; who not only lost their power to deform men by their presence, but became in effect the yardsticks of human excellence. It also gave Greeks room to manoeuvre, to conduct their lives in terms of purely secular purposes. Every Greek in a position to do so subscribed to the view that to be foremost was what made life worthwhile. It is therefore not surprising that they became a race of inveterate competitors. They saw their cities as projections of themselves, and warfare between them was endemic. Not content with real hostilities, they invented the artificial conflicts of the games. Even the musical and dramatic events at their festivals were made competitive. But success was ephemeral unless it was suitably commemorated. Given their preoccupation with fame, it is easy to understand how Greeks came to mobilize the resources of the visual arts to add some sort of permanence to their achievements; and why the young, vigorous bodies of athletes and warriors should seem the most satisfactory symbols of what mattered most to them.

From all this there emerged elements of artistic discord, which turned on the question of stylization. When the Greeks began to make statues on a large scale they took it for granted that what gave the figure its value was the form which it embodied. Forms were in fact formulas; and they were handed down from generation to generation in much the same way as the verbal formulas which, as Milman Parry showed, were preserved and transmitted to Homer by the epic poets who preceded him. Capricious invention for its own sake was not encouraged. When changes were made, they were introduced reluctantly, and with good reason. The conviction that everything that was really important and decisive in human affairs had happened long ago was as prevalent in this as in other spheres of Greek life; and if anyone was ignorant or bold enough to want to know what made traditional forms sacrosanct, he would no doubt be told that in the beginning they had been revealed by the gods themselves. In the case of the figural arts the first to whom the secrets of form were divulged would be legendary demi-gods like the Egyptian Imhotep or the Greek Daedalus.

But over against this disposition to preserve intact the initial stylized form, there developed an equally strong conviction that the purposes of Greek art did not really lend themselves to such treatment. There were no invisible meanings to be conveyed, no intrusions from another level of reality to be symbolized. The heroic qualities of warriors and athletes were entirely temporal and physical. The only way these could be expressed was through postures, gestures, and muscular stress. Accordingly, Greek sculptors of the sixth century devoted themselves to the study of human anatomy, and their figures became more and more correct in the sense of being accurate likenesses. Yet these improvements modified the *kouros* form far less than might have been expected; and to say that the Greeks spent the whole of the sixth century learning how to make their *kouroi* resemble real men, though perhaps in one sense true, would be quite misleading. Clearly if they had committed themselves wholeheartedly to artistic naturalism, they would have mastered the appropriate techniques in far less time. It was not a question of progress being slow, but of a conflict between aesthetic allegiances.

The dilemma remained unresolved throughout the archaic period. Although any account of it is liable to give an impression that the situation was at all times volatile, this is not necessarily how it must have seemed at the time. Only those with the advantages of hindsight are in a position to know where the tendency towards representational art was leading. In any given work the contradictory elements were likely to achieve a satisfactory equilibrium. There were two good reasons why archaic art lasted as long as it did. One was the monopoly of patronage enjoyed by conservative aristocracies, which evidently continued to control taste even when in political terms they were displaced by tyrants. The other was the absence of what might be called an alternative sanction. As long as some acknowledgement of the traditional formulas was felt to be obligatory in order to establish the credentials of a work of art, there was something invidious or disturbing about too great a preoccupation with the correct rendering of physical detail. Naturalistic art was a contradiction in terms. For the situation to change, attitudes about art which had been taken for granted more or less universally and for thousands of years had to be questioned, repudiated, and replaced, not just to the satisfaction of artists themselves, but with the consent and understanding of the society within which and for which they worked.

In due course, this was done; and when it happened, Greek

art was transformed with a speed and thoroughness that remains astonishing to contemplate. Someone born when democracy was first established at Athens may well have received his first impression of the figural arts from men whose notions of style were not fundamentally different from those of the Assyrians who made the hunting reliefs for the palace of Assur-bani-pal at Nineveh. Such a man could have lived to see the pediments of the Parthenon. Yet although this revolution was in a sense the most far-reaching achievement which may be accredited to the Greeks in the field of art, they have left us hardly any account of it, other than a few retrospective platitudes concerning the principal protagonists. For the rest, all we have to go on are some of the works themselves, together with what we can deduce about them. These are not very substantial grounds on which to build an imposing structure of interpretation. However it does not follow that the origins of classical art are entirely mysterious. Greek artists may have been unusually inarticulate, but their views on the subject are not the only ones that we might wish to hear. Indeed it can be argued that the decisive elements in the case were utterly beyond the control of practising artists, who merely caught the prevailing mood of their time. This may be going too far the other way. Ephemeral styles often spring up like weeds after rain in response to contemporary social and political innovations. But styles which meet serious spiritual needs over long periods of time invariably require the active imagination of men of genius to get them going. The classical style was certainly one of these; and if on the subject of its genesis we seem able to say more about factors that were brought to bear on artists from outside their profession than from within, this is no more than a reflection of the capricious way in which the evidence has come down to us.

The first point to be made does in fact concern a technical matter. The invention of hollow bronze casting in the seventh decade of the sixth century made it possible for metal-workers to produce figures on the same scale as stone-carvers. From this time onward the prestige of bronze stood consistently higher than that of marble. Until some early bronze *kouroi* were discovered in the Piraeus in 1958 there were no means of judging how this reputation was acquired, but we can now see that almost at once the designers of figures in bronze set about exploiting the material, to introduce movements and gestures which were not easy to achieve in marble. These novelties were combined with perhaps more sensitive modulations of surface which, if common, may explain why bronze could seem even better suited than marble for the rendering of flesh. More important, however, was the method of working. The actual modelling was done in clay, and the figure built up by the addition of part to part. This was the exact antithesis of the procedure used in the making of a marble *kouros*, where the sculptor started with outlines drawn on the surfaces of the block, which was then cut away to reveal the figure. It was almost certainly the drawings which enshrined the traditional element in archaic Greek art; and precisely because bronze casters did not depend on such drawings, they were from the start in a position to emancipate themselves from the tyranny of the stone-carvers' canon.

The implications of this are easy to appreciate, but they may also be exaggerated. We can begin to understand how the reputation of bronze statues was bound up with the search for a totally different kind of canon, and how the technique of modelling in clay would require this to be expressed in terms of observed ratios between the components of the human body, as opposed to a preconceived over-all shape. Moreover, we can see that a canon of this type could apply to a figure in any attitude or posture, and thus the way would be opened for a whole range of possibilities never contemplated in archaic art. But although hollow bronze casting may have provided the occasion for a new canon, it was not itself the cause which brought such a thing into being. For that, we have to turn elsewhere.

If we could ask the guests of Plato's *Symposium* what it was that made the works of Polykleitos superior to the archaic statues of the previous century, their replies would probably have included reference to the physical beauty, which aroused the Eros that was the subject of their famous conversation. Archaic statues may have been beautiful statues; but classical statues were beautiful in the way that young men could be beautiful, and this was not quite the same thing. What for want of a better term may be called the homosexual features of aristocratic life in Greece seem to have extended as far back as there is evidence to consult; and it was quite certainly within this context that Greeks encountered the problem of

what to make of physical beauty. Not only did they experience beauty intensely, as no doubt everyone does at some
time or other; but they attached overwhelming importance to
the experience, and in this respect they went far beyond what
has been usual among civilized peoples. For a long time the
cultivation of beauty was an upper-class prerogative; and
while this remained the case, it does not seem to have been
recognized that there was any special connection between art
and physical beauty. At a crucial moment towards the end of
the sixth century, however, emphasis seems to have shifted. It
was then conceded that over and above the special kinship of
birth that linked certain privileged families with the gods,
there was a more general kinship which may be described as
one of form. The beauty that excited Eros was something that
men possessed not by virtue of their social class, but by being
human, or at any rate Greek; and this was all of a piece with
the beauty of the gods. No doubt among men it was transient;
but to be beautiful, even if only for a moment, was to be
touched with divinity. This exalted sense of the holiness of
beauty was essentially Greek. Pindar was its spokesman; but
poetry was not the only channel through which it found
expression. The seductive power of these experiences and
attitudes eventually dissolved the residues of archaic art, and
brought to birth the classical style. The ultimate artistic
sanction was no longer an appeal to precedent, but to some
timeless notion of ideal perfection; and henceforth the proper
business of art was seen to be with aspects of form which art
could share with nature, and the gods.

The concept of form is now perhaps most familiar to us in
the context of Greek philosophy, where it figures prominently
in theories associated with the names of Pythagoras, Plato,
and Aristotle. However, it is beyond doubt that the term, like
others, was borrowed by philosophers from the practice of the
arts. When Greeks wished to speak of art they used the word
techne. The meaning is not quite the same as that usually
conveyed by the English 'art', despite the fact that the latter is
derived from the Latin *ars* which was the equivalent of *techne*.
The sense of the Greek and Latin comes closer to English
words like technical or artfulness, than to what we understand
by fine art. At the centre of the antique meaning lies the
notion of skill, craft, or even cunning; and any field of activity
which called forth displays of ingenuity worthy of admiration

was liable to be called an art. Thus there was an art of healing, and an art of war. For Ovid there was an art of love. Plato seriously discussed the question whether there could be an art of statesmanship. What all these activities had in common was the power to bring about certain foreseen ends by the operation of suitable skills. But the primary instances were provided by the activities of craftsmen. In the making of a work of art Greeks recognized two constituent elements. On the one hand, there were given materials such as bronze, marble, or colours. Pliny's remarks about the figural arts, on which we depend for much of our detailed information, were prompted by his interest in the different kinds of natural substances that were used in their making.[2] A man was an artist in Greek or Roman eyes only if he had complete mastery over his material; and his talent was bounded by its limitations. But although this attitude persisted throughout antiquity, and provided a practical basis for the social distinction between manual and liberal arts, the division was not rigid. Horace's dictum: '*ut pictura poesis*', which was really as old as Simonides, suggests that under certain circumstances figural artists could be assimilated into the ranks of men whose skill was with words.

Insofar as this was done, it turned on the second factor in the case, which was the form that artists imposed on their material. Every art had its appropriate stock of forms. This was no doubt augmented and altered from time to time as the scope of the art in question widened. But so long as the visual arts kept within the conventions of an inherited tradition, their forms were in no essential respect different from those used by other craftsmen. In particular they were subject to no external criterion. All this must have changed abruptly, however, once it was acknowledged that the forms with which artists operated were so to speak prescribed to them from outside. Henceforth the defining characteristic was to be *mimesis*. The precise meaning of this elastic term is not easy to establish. The usual English translation is 'imitation'; and this implies the notion of one thing being in some sense a copy of another. Up to a point this works well enough. A statue and a

---

[2] *Natural History*, 34–6, published separately with English translation and appendices by K. Jex-Blake and E. Sellers under the title, *The Elder Pliny's Chapters on the History of Art* (1896).

human being may share a common form. But essentially the form belongs to the human being, not the statue. The statue merely 'borrows' certain visual aspects of the form for artistic purposes. This was almost certainly how *mimesis* was first used. But its meaning was gradually stretched to include painting, poetry, and music as well; and writers from Plato onward evidently regarded the concept of *mimesis* as a device for separating what we would call the fine arts from the rest.

For some Greeks, however, the situation was complicated by a view of the world which took ordinary mortal human beings to be themselves copies of ideal archetypes. This at once raises the question whether artists copied archetypes or copies. The issue is perhaps best known to us through Plato's censorious attitude towards the arts, though it is perhaps worth pointing out that later Platonists, like Plotinus, did not follow Plato in this respect, and in fact contradicted him. Plato's position is not entirely unambiguous. The arts which presented the greatest threat to the peace of his city were poetry and music; but his derisory argument about the bed in the *Republic* (10. 596A–598B) was directed against painting. Granted that all copies lose something of their originals the argument works well enough in this limited context: but it is by no means obvious that the extended notion of *mimesis* would allow it to be transferred with equal rigour to his principal targets. Be that as it may, Plato was quite clear that figural artists made copies of copies, and had no direct access to ideal archetypes. What he had in mind seems to have been the sort of dubious reasoning that is illustrated in a well-known anecdote about the painter Zeuxis. In one version of the story (Cicero, *De inventione*, 2. 1), the citizens of Kroton had commissioned a picture of Helen of Troy; in another (Pliny, *Natural History*, 35. 61), the city was Akragas and the subject the goddess Hera. For such legendary subjects, no adequate model could be found. The artist therefore assembled five of the most beautiful girls in the city and compounded his image from the best features of each. From Plato's point of view it made not the slightest difference that Zeuxis elected to copy bits of several girls rather than one complete girl. For Zeuxis, however, the difference was crucial. The whole point of the story is that by eliminating the manifest blemishes of particular instances he convinced himself that he was raising his art to the higher ontological plane of the archetype. That some artists at some time had claimed privileged access to the realm of ideal forms is the presupposition of Plato's criticisms.

How this came about is a matter for speculation. The eclectic method of uncovering archetypes, which Zeuxis was in effect demonstrating, was certainly not invented by him. Archetypes came into prominence as archaic formulas fell into disrepute. The problem was: how to recognize them. No doubt the gods knew, and in moments of exuberance sculptors and painters who wished to make beautiful images of beautiful men may have thought of themselves as aspiring to the perceptions of the gods. In practice, however, they regarded the gods as craftsmen like themselves, and living men as examples of their handiwork. It was therefore really quite sensible to take statistical samples of what the gods could do, and try to separate, in Aristotelian language, the accidents from the essence of the form. There was of course no question of their seeking to understand essences in an Aristotelian sense. They were concerned with shapes, and in their experience shapes had always been defined in mathematical terms. Their quest thus resolved itself into something closely akin to that of Pythagorean philosophers, who sought to identify forms with numbers. It is perhaps not going too far to suggest that the research which lay behind arcane Pythagorean doctrines such as 'ten being the number of man' was conducted by sculptors. On slightly less obscure ground, the men to whom credit is given for the invention of hollow bronze casting, Theodoros and Rhoikos, were contemporaries of Pythagoras on Samos. This may of course be nothing more than coincidence. What is certain, however, is that the men who habitually thought of forms as numbers were artists. Like the archaic formulas of their predecessors, this knowledge was codified in canons. Unfortunately we are woefully ill-informed about these indispensable devices. The only one much discussed in ancient literature is that of Polykleitos, which was embodied in a famous statue called 'The Canon'.[3] But beyond the general principle that the component members of the human body were related to one another by mathematical ratios, the rest is guesswork. Unlike temples, statues seldom leave clear traces of the co-ordinates which

[3] The statue was so named because it was made to illustrate the theory formulated by Polykleitos in a treatise called *The Canon*. The Doryphoros, known through Roman copies, is often assumed to embody the 'canon'.

ratios may have fixed; and it is doubtful whether anyone will ever succeed in reconstituting the canon of Polykleitos, or any other.

In a sense, however, this does not matter. It is enough for us to know that there were such things as canons; and as soon as they are linked with the speculations of philosophers we begin to realize that the metaphysical pretensions of the arts were perhaps no figments of Plato's imagination. By Plato's time the progress of mathematics had shifted the serious discussion of forms to the level of logic; and he could afford to take a condescending view of sensible forms. But for earlier generations the emphasis must have been the other way. The fact that mathematics seemed to explain sensible forms represented a considerable insight, and provided just the encouragement that was required to launch classical art on its career.

The classical style rested on the identification of beauty with archetypes and archetypes with canons. In a manner peculiar to themselves, the Greeks were thus able to resolve the paradox of how art could be both naturalistic and religious. This encouraged them, indeed it laid upon them the obligation, to re-fashion the images of their gods. In their classical form, the immortals became a collection of ideal human types: larger than life; beautiful in youth, dignified in age; sometimes models of deportment, or else affecting splendid rhetorical gestures. As transfigured consummations of mortal performance they functioned as a kind of Aristotelian final cause; and Aristotle's description of god as the unmoved mover comes readily to mind when we are confronted by the bored indifference of the waiting Olympians on the Parthenon frieze.

In a wider context, the subject-matter of classical art was taken as it had always been, from the myths. The difference was that myths could now be re-enacted in art with far greater verisimilitude. It was no accident that the invention of the classical style coincided with the beginnings of the other great mimetic art—drama. Analogies between painting or sculpture on the one hand, and tragedy on the other were frequently drawn. For Aristotle in the *Poetics* it was self-evident that tragedy was the most complete and overwhelming of all the manifestations of *mimesis*; and from this it was only a short step to the view that the figural arts should present character studies or 'stills' from dramatic action. Around these notions we can reconstruct the fortunes and mutations of the classical style.

In principle there is no limit to what may be required of mimetic art. In practice, however, the Greeks seem to have stopped well short of total illusion; and they tended to deal with problems one at a time.

The first task was to master form in its literal, physical sense. What is known as the 'severe style', of the first half of the fifth century, was clearly preoccupied with problems of anatomy and movement, often to the exclusion of everything else. The results were sometimes ludicrous, as for instance on the west pediment at Olympia, where scenes of extreme violence are performed by figures with totally blank expressions. For this reason many sculptors preferred to treat their themes indirectly, and chose moments of repose, before or after exertions. But it was impossible to postpone the problems of emotions indefinitely. The first Greek artist to achieve fame for the emotional violence and pathos of his subjects was the sculptor Skopas, who lived in the middle years of the fourth century. But this does not mean that he was the first to try. The same may well be true of attempts to convey character. The crux of the matter is the shift of interest away from the formal perfection of the gods to the details of human psychology. Gods do not have feelings and characters in the way that men do; and so long as the primary business of artists was to make the gods visible to men, the purely human aspects of humanity could be safely neglected. Pheidias was perhaps the supreme master of this kind of art. He may also have been one of the last. During the second half of the fifth century the cultural revolution at Athens passed into the hands of playwrights, sophists, and philosophers who gave it an impious twist. Advanced opinion ceased to take the conventional gods seriously. If the tragedies of Euripides put humanity firmly at the centre of attention, it is unlikely that painters and sculptors waited for the best part of a century before they began to take notice of what was going on around them. The point is of some importance for the beginnings of what it generally called Hellenistic art.

The convenience of supposing that Alexander's career put an end to one complete state of affairs in the Greek world, and replaced it by another, is no doubt great. However, there is little evidence to suggest that the arts were much affected. The transition from classical to Hellenistic is not of the same order as that from archaic to classical. If there is any justification for the distinction, it lies within the classical tradition; and if it has to be explained by any external event, this was not the advent of Alexander but the decline of the Olympians.

Any change in a religion as visually orientated as the Greek was bound to have repercussions on the arts. The value of mimetic art depended entirely on the value of its subject-matter. Once the credibility of the myths, and the cults that were bound up with them, was questioned, the arts faced the predicament of having their traditional subject-matter reduced to the status of fictions. When Plato added his charges of fraud shortly afterwards, the situation must have seemed critical. The whole problem was obviously much discussed throughout the fourth century in Academic and Aristotelian circles. The only substantial document that has survived is Aristotle's *Poetics*; and this only rarely touches on the visual arts. However, one of the things Aristotle set out to do was to vindicate mimetic art in a changed world, and to some extent what he says about poetry would apply to painting and sculpture as well. Aristotle made poetry respectable on the grounds that the subject-matter with which it dealt was typical, and therefore of universal significance. From this point of view myths could be regarded as archetypes of human situations. But emphasis had shifted. Aristotle simply took it for granted that poetry mattered because it was concerned with the substance of human life. The primary objects of artistic *mimesis* are human beings in action, men performing or undergoing something.

The doctrine that man, not some formal abstraction but man in the concrete richness of his experience, was the proper subject of *mimesis*, opened the door to all manner of innovations. Perhaps the first sign of what was to come was a compromise about beauty itself. Toward the end of the fifth century there appeared a new kind of prettiness, certainly not countenanced by austere metaphysical theories, but frankly designed to be seductive. This persisted right down to Roman times. In the fourth century some artists were prepared to tamper with the classical canons, not because they had better statistics to work on, but because they discovered that calculated distortions could sometimes express the effect they wished to convey better than the orthodox forms. They also began to explore character. Here training and experience probably came by way of portraiture. By the fourth century Greek obsession with young athletes and warriors began to abate. Physical prowess was no longer the exclusive measure of a man's worth. Aristotle could even entertain reservations about the excessive cult of gymnastics (*Politics*, 1338b9–1339a10). In return, there grew up a demand for portaits of great men, such as orators, poets, politicians, and sages. The notion of portraits was in a sense incompatible with the principles of ideal art; but it was justified by exceptional merit. Apart from the question of getting an accurate likeness, this kind of work often entailed taking liberties like putting wrinkles into faces and setting eyes deeper into the skull than had previously been allowed. In practice, there was much compromise. The generalized image of the 'noble old man' from the gallery of ideal types was often blended with an actual likeness to suggest both the greatness and the individuality of the subject. Portraits were even invented for men such as Homer who lived long before likenesses were recorded. Lesser men were treated in other ways. Aristotle knew of painters who specialized in depicting men of average and even subnormal talents (*Poetics*, 1448a6). It seems likely that if idealization was the mark of distinction, caricature was reserved for its antithesis.

At a more ambitious level, statues could be combined into groups. The first serious essays in this direction were made for the pediments of temples. Pediment sculpture as such goes back to the sixth century, but like everything else ideas on the subject were completely transformed during the fifth to bring them into line with the precepts of mimetic art. In more ways than one the exigencies of elongated triangular frames proved highly refractory. In particular there was the difficulty of linking extremities to the centre in a coherent design. There was also a potential inconsistency between the function of pediments which required that images should be projected outward at audiences assembled in front of them, and the internal logic of dramatic situations which could only be effective if figures addressed themselves to one another.

In the course of the fifth century sculptors like those of Aegina, Olympia, and the Parthenon successively devoted their energies to the solution of these problems. They began to exploit the recumbent postures of river gods and fallen warriors to fill corners, and the convenient anatomy of creatures with long backs and high heads like horses and centaurs for middle zones. They learnt how to modulate the intensity of their dramas, concentrating action at the centre and dissipating it gradually at a distance. They discovered the value of oblique attitudes, and how to direct attention by turning movements, gestures, and glances, sometimes with sudden emphasis, some-times gradually through a succession of adjacent figures. They explored the possibilities of intertwined limbs and drapery as devices for binding figures together or creating accents. At the end of these intense researches, Greek sculpture had mastered most of the fundamental rules of large-scale figure com-position, and in this respect it is fascinating to compare Carrey's drawings of the Parthenon pediments with, say, Leonardo's *Last Supper* or Raphael's *Disputà*.

But pediments did not exhaust the possibilities of groups. Confined within their frames, they remained fundamentally two-dimensional. In the fourth century however groups were made which were independent of architecture. Some were entirely free-standing; others set up apparently with great skill in settings that were themselves carefully designed to show the sculpture to advantage. None have survived except in isolated fragments; but descriptions suggest that they were conceived by men whose talents included a fair measure of theatrical instinct. They were as much stage directors as sculptors.

The loss of these ambitious works makes it particularly difficult to form a clear impression of what Greeks expected of the figural arts after the classical period. But, if, as seems likely, the sense of context was highly developed, it is perhaps legitimate to sense a link between the direction in which the arts were moving and contemporary trends in town-planning, even to suppose that they were mutually complimentary. The space in which free-standing groups were set up was in one sense imaginary, in another real. To blur the sharp edges of such distinctions, to extend the theatrical reality of statues on public display so that it merged with the architecturally contrived setting in which citizens conducted their affairs, thereby suggesting that the good life of the city was all of a piece with the world of myth and history, seems to have been

one of the persistent if seldom fulfilled visions of those Greek
architects who were called upon to design or redesign whole
cities.

This was just about as far as it was possible to go with
mimetic sculpture. But on its own terms painting could
perhaps be taken even further. Not much has been said on the
subject of Greek painting, for the good reason that none of its
acknowledged masterpieces have survived. The only considerable body of painting about which we are in a position to
form an opinion is on pots. Here, however, the industrial
nature of the operation, the limitations imposed by the
material, the miniature scale, not to mention the oddity of
working on convex or concave surfaces, gave the whole
activity a somewhat specialized aspect. Pot painters must
have been about as far removed from the principal masters of
their art as, say, medieval enamellers were from the illumi-
nators of manuscripts. This is not to say that they were not
often very good. At their best, as for instance in the work of
the sixth-century black-figure artist Exekias, they bring us
about as close as we are ever likely to get to a proper
appreciation of all those qualities of archaic art with which
free-standing sculpture was not concerned. In any case they
are extremely useful. It is only on pots that we can grasp how
myths were treated before art became mimetic; and the
changes of style that can be detected in their decoration
assume greater interest if they are taken to reflect issues and
fashions that were agitating the attention of more august
practitioners.

Nevertheless, the conspiracy of silence which surrounds
them in Greek sources implies that the Greeks themselves did
not share the high esteem in which we hold their pot painters.
They were agreed that the first painter whose merits entitled
his name to be remembered was Polygnotos. Theophrastus
went so far as to claim that Polygnotos introduced painting
into Greece (Pliny, *Natural History*, 7. 205). As Polygnotos was
active during the first half of the fifth century, Theophrastus
must have meant mimetic painting. Exactly what was novel
in the work of Polygnotos is not clear. We are told more about
the artist than his art. He is said to have enjoyed the favours
of Cimon's sister, and to have painted the Stoa Poekile at
Athens without fee. If such tales were true, then he comes
perhaps closer to our notion of the self-appointed genius than

that of the common craftsman. Pausanius (10. 25–31) gives an unusually full account of his paintings for the Cnidians at Delphi; and while Pausanias could never resist a digression into iconography, it is hard to avoid a suspicion that these deserved a fuss, and that they occupied a place in Greek art akin to that of Giotto's Paduan frescoes in the European tradition.

The one precise piece of information about his style that has come down to us is that he was the first to paint women in diaphanous draperies, a remark which tends to evoke instant impressions of some of the Parthenon pediment groups. On the whole, Greek and Roman writers about art are consistent in suggesting that sculptors led the way, and that progress in painting was measured by the invention of techniques which allowed similar effects to be achieved in two dimensions. But there is no reason why, on occasion, the relation should not have been reversed; and it is not impossible that Polygnotos was responsible for those qualities in the work of Pheidias which distinguish him from the exponents of the severe style.

Whatever the achievement of Polygnotos, the subsequent landmarks of Greek painting, as recorded by Pliny, are all steps in the direction of illusionistic art. *Trompe l'oeil* may not have been the only aim of Greek painters, but it was high on the list of what got them talked about. For Romans like Pliny the only test of a successful illusion was that someone should be taken in; and the anecdotes which he used to illustrate the genius of painters were often about virtuoso performances in the art of deception. Some of them are still quite funny, as for instance one (*Natural History*, 35. 61) which describes a competition between Zeuxis and Parrhasios, in which Zeuxis deceived the birds, whereas Parrhasios deceived Zeuxis. The value of these tall stories may have been confined to the ancient equivalent of after-dinner speeches at the Royal Academy; but they leave us in no doubt as to what impressed the public at large, if not the connoisseurs.

By common consent the climax was reached in the career of Apelles. 'He surpassed not only those who came before, but also those who came after him' (Pliny, *Natural History*, 35. 79). It is never easy to make sense of this sort of sweeping judgement. Apelles' pictures seem to have had a peculiar charm which no one could emulate; and to some extent his success may have been personal. On the other hand it is unlikely that charm alone would have made such an impact if it had not been supported by less elusive qualities. We may therefore suppose that his works included every conceivable ingredient of mimetic art, and left critics with the feeling that there was little left to be done. Pliny's list of Apelles' subjects, beyond showing a predictable preference for the human form in its various heroic, mythological, and divine guises, gives little indication as to treatment and setting. What one would like to know is whether these paintings offered a total equivalent to the realities of ordinary experience, which is what the artists of the Renaissance set out to do. Renaissance pictures were veritable re-creations in the sense that spectators could look through the frame into a world as coherent and as completely visualized as their own, and be present, so to speak, at what was going on there. The two principal instruments by which this was achieved were modelling and perspective. The art of drawing outlines in such a way as to suggest corporeality of form was certainly familiar to the Greeks. It was an accomplishment for which Parrhasios was particularly distinguished. On the other hand, the extent to which Greek painters ever bothered to master the theory of perspective is less certain. Up to a point any successful rendering of a solid figure creates its own perspective; and the preoccupation with human form may have rendered further research into the subject redundant. It may even have been thought to detract from the 'tragic feeling and weight of style' in which Zeuxis and Apelles excelled. Until late in their history Greek painters were never much interested in landscape for its own sake; and even when they were, it was the atmospheric effects of aerial perspective rather than linear constructions that seem to have caught their attention. Later still, in Roman times, the practical mathematicians of Alexandria who studied optics and applied their knowledge to the construction of miniature automatic theatres must have been aware of the principle of the vanishing point; but it remains an open question whether their theories were based on the experience of painters.

Apelles was court painter to Alexander the Great. In other words, everything that was thought to matter in painting had been achieved before the Hellenistic period began. Are we therefore to draw the conclusion that nothing of importance happened to Greek art during the next three hundred years?

If the question is taken to mean: were there no great artists and were no great works of art made?—then the answer is simple. There was clearly no dearth of talent and no lack of occasion for it to be demonstrated. Nor is it necessary to suppose that art became repetitious. If the Laokoon is typical, then groups became not merely bigger but more intricate. The bronze colossus at Rhodes, well over a hundred feet high, was more than a technical masterpiece; it must have created an entirely new relation between a city and a monument. One has the impression of incessant probing in search of new tricks and new effects. Piraeicus made a name for himself by specializing in scenes of low life. Landscape, as an independent genre, was credited to a contemporary of Augustus. The whole range of this profusion, from copies of old masters down to Priapic titillations, is well represented in the paintings and mosaics that were preserved at Pompeii, Herculaneum, and Boscoreale.

One has only to consult such an anthology, however, for it to become evident that in spite of all the diversification, Hellenistic artists were reluctant to depart too far from the rubrics that had been laid down in the fourth century. No one really questioned the theoretical structure on which mimetic art was based. They simply applied themselves to squeezing the concept for its last nuances. So there is perhaps a sense in which it is legitimate to regard Hellenistic art as the working out of a series of deductions from premises stated by the artists of previous generations.

More is to be gained by considering the matter from the point of view of patronage. If there is any definite characteristic of the Hellenistic age which separates it from the preceding age of the city-states, it is to be found in the number and variety of people who considered themselves to have use for the arts. Far from becoming redundant, their conventional religious and commemorative functions can only have multiplied with the foundation of new cities; and the divine status claimed by Hellenistic rulers must have provided a special impetus to the development of ideal portraiture. But these were more or less traditional roles. An entirely new phenomenon appeared in the person of the private patron and collector, who cared little or nothing for the occasions which works of art were made to celebrate, but a great deal for the qualities which made them interesting and beautiful objects.

Art became a commodity and entered the market-place. It did so in two contrasted, but related ways. On the one hand there were collectors whose taste had been educated by critics and historians. The end products of this process were the notions of the masterpiece and the old master, the development of the reproduction industry, and ultimately the one-way traffic by which the best of what could be transported came to rest at Rome. On the other hand, there was the 'customer calls the tune' aspect of the situation. Few tired Hellenistic or Roman businessmen who were in a position to buy statues or have their houses painted would have had much use for high-minded mythologies. What they are likely to have wanted, and what they often got, was pornography. In a somewhat different way, one can imagine private religious confraternities taking equivalent liberties with the subject-matter and perhaps even the style of time-honoured mythological themes. So also with Rome. Art did not really change when the Empire was established. The Roman state merely took its place among the patrons of Hellenistic art; and made sure that it got what it wanted.

In becoming all things to all men, it is small wonder that Hellenistic art should seem full of paradoxes. But one of these calls for particular comment. Though the arts flourished as perhaps never before, vitality was not indiscriminate. The ideal element, from which it all began, was disposed to atrophy. Images which, when they were first fashioned, must have seemed profound religious or metaphysical intuitions were in danger of being reduced to the status of empty husks for official propaganda. Insight into forms conceived as public and universal gradually became the esoteric affectation of a few learned connoisseurs with a taste for the past. How much antiquarianism was involved in Hellenistic aesthetics is difficult to ascertain. But whenever taste is in the hands of scholars, as was the case at Alexandria, it is likely to be prominent; and it was certainly instrumental in resurrecting archaic styles for the Roman market.

At a more poetic level, however, we may perhaps detect the presence of antiquarianism in a grandiose conceit like the imperial villa at Tivoli, which Hadrian had built for himself *c.* 130 A.D. To extend the limits of Hellenistic art so as to include Hadrian is to take undoubted liberties with established terminology. It may well be that in his attitude towards the past, Hadrian already had more in common with the cultivated princes of the Renaissance than with antiquity itself. Nevertheless, the idea of calling upon all the visual arts: architecture, sculpture, painting, perhaps even landscape gardening, to create a single, vast, all-embracing experience, in which 'real' and illusionistic elements merged inextricably one with another, was not only in the spirit of Hellenistic art, but a worthy consummation of centuries of effort devoted to the pursuit of *mimesis*. Tivoli must have been the ultimate in make-believe. But it was wholly personal and private, the retrospective fantasy of an educated, sensitive, and isolated individual. Posterity seems to have viewed it with indifference. The only known use to which it was subsequently put was as a prison for Zenobia. A similar fate of incomprehension eventually overtook the entire tradition to which Tivoli belonged.

The conviction which gradually took possession of the ancient world: that ultimate reality was not accessible to the rational intelligence of man, had consequences for the figural arts as far reaching as those which had once grown out of the opposite conviction. To make visible what cannot be known, the resources of mimetic were useless. If it could be done at all, it required a return to the language of symbols and stylization; and when artists seriously committed themselves to this task, the classical view of art was to all intents and purposes dead.

In the early nineteenth century, Hegel found it necessary to warn the enthusiastic Hellenists of his generation that however beguiling they found classical art, there was no going back to it. The admonition is no longer necessary. If Greek attitudes toward mimetic art have left any trace at all on the arts of our own time, we need not look for them in anything more elevated than the Hollywood notion of cinema, where ideal beauty has been equated with sex-appeal, and illusion put to the service of escapism. Entertainments of this kind are no more than animated versions of certain conspicuous strands of Hellenistic art, and need be judged by no other standards. On the other hand the best Greek art, though no longer taken into account by serious artists, is probably more admired now than it has ever been. This apparent paradox is not hard to explain. There is a tendency for the great religious and humanist art of the past to be taken as a prophylactic against unacceptable aspects of the modern world. Whether this habit is legitimate; or whether it is confined to the elderly, who have not quite forgotten what the world was like before metaphysics had been finally eliminated, and prefer narcotis to the truth; it is perhaps still too early to decide.

Further Reading

S. Adam, *The Technique of Greek Sculpture* (London, 1966).

P. Arias and M. Hirmer, *A History of Greek Vase Painting* (London, 1962). Good reproductions.

M. Bieber, *The Sculpture of the Hellenistic Age* (revised edn. New York, 1961).

A. Burford, *Craftsmen in Greek and Roman Society* (London, 1972).

A. Furtwängler, *Masterpieces of Greek Sculpture* (London, 1895).

R. Lullies and M. Hirmer, *Greek Sculpture* (revised edn. London, 1960). Good reproductions.

H. Payne and G. Mackworth Young, *Archaic Marble Sculpture from the Acropolis* (2nd edn. London, 1960).

J. J. Pollitt, *The Ancient View of Greek Art* (New Haven and London, 1974).

J. J. Pollitt, *The Art of Greece 1400–31 B.C.* (Englewood Cliffs, 1965). Sources and documents.

G. Richter, *Korai* (London, 1968).

G. Richter, *Kouroi* (London, 1960).

G. Richter, *The Portraits of the Greeks* (London, 1965).

M. Robertson, *A History of Greek Art* (Cambridge, 1975). By far the best comprehensive account currently available.

15

THE GREEK LEGACY

R. R. BOLGAR

Rome

Rome was not the first beneficiary of Greek influence. Egypt, Asia Minor, and Syria had preceded her in that role. But she was the first to learn substantially from the Greeks and to establish at the same time an independent culture active not only in art and technology, but also in literature and thought.

The nature of the attraction exercised by a sophisticated culture on its simpler neighbours is not easy to define. Utilitarian considerations play some part in it. Men have always hankered after convenient or pleasing artifacts that they did not possess and have wanted to enjoy the benefits of other people's practical skills. But the context is one in which irrational longings can also exercise an important influence. We see the unsophisticated led on by hopes of enlightenment, as if the sophisticated had somehow the power of revealing the mystery of life; led on too by expectations of refined pleasure which they think will come with a greater luxury and licence. And if the motives for cultural borrowing are often complex, so are the methods by which the borrowing occurs. Initially, the borrower will acquire the objects and hire the skills he wants. But one cannot surround oneself with the products of an alien culture without coming insensibly to adopt the manner of life which that culture favours; and this leads in its turn to the final, the really important stage in the borrowing process, when imitation takes over from borrowing and the unsophisticated make the objects and practise the skills of the sophisticated for themselves.

The Romans began to take an interest in Greek culture during the middle years of the third century B.C. They imported goods and services from Greece, and after a while their writers began to copy Greek models. A work of literature is the one product that a foreign public cannot appreciate in its original form. If the New Comedy was to be enjoyed, Rome had to have Plautus, and so it is not surprising to find that the imitation of Greek achievements started first in the literary field. Then, early in the second century, the Romans were tempted by the idea of studying Greek rhetorical techniques, which had an obvious use in a society dominated by its deliberative assemblies and law courts. This meant setting up schools similar to those in Greece; and in Greece, as in most advanced countries, the school course served as introduction to the cultural traditions of the day. The fact that it was organized round rhetoric made no difference to this. Orators who wanted to be persuasive had to appeal to generally accepted ethical and political principles. They had to speak on a variety of topics, and in Greek practice, it was usual for them to invoke historical and literary parallels. When they decided to study rhetoric, the Romans opened the door to a flood of Greek culture. That was why the elder Cato urged the banishment of Greek teachers from Rome. But matters had already gone too far for a reversal to be possible; and by the time Cicero was a young man, studying under Greek teachers in Rome and going abroad to complete one's education in Athens or Rhodes had become a common practice.

Once Rome had committed herself to the overlordship of the East, which she did between 200 and 133 B.C., a situation that left her with a monopoly of political and military power, while Greece enjoyed a monopoly of cultural achievement, could not be allowed to endure. It was injurious to Roman pride, and pride was not the only issue. Not only were the Greeks more expert in fields like medicine, architecture, and astronomy, but their skill in persuasion, their capacity for lucid statement, their more subtle understanding of complex problems also had a utilitarian value. The education given to the young in the Hellenistic Empires was not in any systematic way a training for administrators, but a man who had attended schools of grammar and rhetoric does seem to have had certain advantages when it came to the routine conduct of affairs. At least he was accustomed to handling words and ideas. If the Romans rejected Greek education while keeping their contacts with the Greek world, there was a real danger that they would come to rely so much on Greek subordinates that the reality of power would slip from their grasp.

Rome had to assimilate Greek culture, if it was to rule the Greek world efficiently; and the forces which pulled the two halves of the Mediterranean basin apart were deliberately resisted. These divisive forces had looked threatening during the second Triumvirate, but Actium had sealed their doom. Augustus encouraged contacts between West and East, welcomed the settlement of Greeks in Italy, and at the same time pressed forward the development of a Latin culture to match the Greek. This policy, which most of his successors also adopted, was pursued against a background of Greek infiltration at a humbler level. Freeborn immigrants, freedmen, and slaves who had received a Greek education were prominent in the learned professions, arts, and luxury trades. They served as secretaries, tutors, actors, and courtesans. It is not surprising therefore that eventually, under the Flavians and Antonines, we find on the one hand men of Greek origin alongside the Romans in all social categories, and on the other hand, a Latin literature and a Latin educational system which have come to mirror the Greek with substantial success.

The emergence of this new version of Greek culture based on another language was perhaps the most important result of Rome's attempt to unify the Mediterranean world. Roman imitative effort had covered a wide area, comprising in the main literature, thought, scientific knowledge, and the fine arts. From the lifetime of Livius Andronicus to the Silver Age, Latin writers had been primarily concerned to reproduce and adapt Greek models. They took over the literary genres invented by the Greeks, a multitude of themes used in Greek literature, and a poetic world derived partly from the actualities of Greek life, partly from myths and other fictions. They blended these borrowings with Latin elements and produced, as we know, an amalgam that was recognizably in the Greek tradition and yet recognizably new. They also took over many of the categories the Greeks had used to interpret human nature and the physical universe; and from the first century B.C. they endeavoured to make Greek learning available in Latin. Here Varro and Cicero played outstanding roles, covering in the main grammar, rhetoric, and philosophy. Science, which they touched upon marginally, was then given fuller treatment by the elder Pliny. In the technological field, Columella, Frontinus, Vitruvius actually improved on the material they reproduced. In medicine, Celsus translated an unidentified Greek work of considerable merit. Later, Apuleius found it profitable to turn Greek textbooks into Latin; and later still, when no one troubled any longer to imitate works of Greek literature, writers like Martianus Capella, Cassiodorus, and Isidore went on producing compendia of existing (largely Greek) knowledge, which were to transmit that knowledge to the Middle Ages.

In learning, Rome added little to its inheritance except in law, where its masterful conceptions evolved more or less independently of the Greek example. But when we come to the fine arts, we see a development that parallels the one we have observed in literature. Here the Graeco-Roman world was the natural heir of the Hellenistic empires, and the tradition it inherited altered in its keeping. The problem of assessing the significance of the changes that occurred has inevitably caused some trouble. Were they due to the impact of a specifically Roman taste for realism and architectonic effects? Or were the transformations we see simply transformations in the Hellenic tradition due to the passage of time? No set of artistic conventions has ever survived unchanged in a vigorous society. But in the present context, the answer hardly matters. It is plain anyway that Roman art owed an enormous debt to the Greek, and that its products, which until the last century were better known than those of early Greece, did much to transmit Greek techniques to future generations.

When we consider the survival of the Greek tradition, interest must centre on Rome as one of the principal avenues through which that tradition reached modern Europe. To assess the full extent of the Roman debt to Greece would take many volumes. Even the epitaphs chosen by ordinary Romans in the imperial era followed Greek models! The task is certainly too great to be attempted within the compass of a brief essay. The assertion that the debt was an enormous one must in general suffice. There are however some considerations affecting the nature of the debt that it is useful to mention. There are first of all the obvious facts that Latin literature and learning did not at any time cover the whole of what was available in Greek, and that the Latin works which have come down to us certainly fail to do this. Secondly, it is well to remember that the Romans did not just copy. They were concerned to create something new in the tradition they were adapting. Plautus' plots are drawn from the New Comedy, but the society he depicts has as many Roman as it has Greek characteristics. Ovid may have taken his legends from Boeus, Parthenius, and Nicander. He imitated Callimachus' variety of tone. But the *Metamorphoses* is nevertheless original in the breadth of its conception, in combining elements from different sources, and in the very speed of its narrative. Thirdly, if the Romans were selective in their borrowing from individual works, they were also selective in what they took from Greek culture as a whole. Latin writers have a good deal to teach us about Greek literature, rhetoric, and philosophy. In other fields, in historiography, in medicine, science, and technology, they hand on only fragments of what they had at their disposal. Livy is no Thucydides, and Pliny the Elder gives us a poor idea of the thousands of books he read and excerpted.

Finally—and this is a consideration we must set against the three mentioned earlier—we must not forget that a substantial amount of Greek learning has reached us through Latin that has not survived in the original. Many of the philosophers whose doctrines Cicero transmits are lost to us, and so are many of the Hellenistic poets imitated by the writers of the Augustan age. If Petronius had a Greek model for his *Satyricon*, we cannot guess at its nature, any more than we can reconstruct the Milesian tales that Apuleius used. The Greece we get from Rome is a Greece truncated, a Greece subtly supplemented and often misrepresented; but at times it is a Greece that no other source has preserved.

The Early Christian Tradition

The absence of the stimulus provided in earlier times by communal dangers, and the feeling of helplessness induced by the size of the Empire (there were obvious problems, but no one could see how they were to be solved) led more and more people during the first three centuries A.D. to turn to philosophies and religions that offered to subordinate life to some supernatural purpose. We have Apuleius recommending the worship of Isis. The legend of Apollonius of Tyana vaunts the virtues of a Neo-Pythagorean asceticism. The cult of the Sun God flourished in the third century and found expression in the *Aethiopica* of Heliodorus. Plotinus wanted to bring back the divine in man to the divine in the All.

Christianity considered as a social phenomenon presents itself in its first beginnings as one of these several systems of supernaturalist belief that offered relief from an aimless and comfortless world. Its promise of salvation was validated by an historical event (or series of events), the life and death of Jesus, which, interpreted within the a-philosophical, theocratic system of Judaism, gave men the Gospel story as a powerful focus for their religious experience. But in a society such as the one that existed under the early Empire, where educated men were obsessively habituated to philosophical speculation, a religious belief could not survive without a theology, and it had to be a theology adequate to the critical needs of the time. Christians had to defend their faith against Stoics, Epicureans, Platonists, and Peripatetics, and had to do so in the categories these thinkers employed, for no others would have served their purpose. A succession of Christian apologists from Justin Martyr to Augustine formulated a theology that owed a mounting debt to pagan thought.

The point must be made, however, that only one current in Greek philosophy, its rationalism (in the sense that Descartes and Hegel are rationalists) was fully represented in the Christian synthesis. Arguments worked out by Plato, by Aristotle, by the later Stoics, the New Academy, and the Neoplatonists were reproduced; but teachings with an Epicurean or Sceptical bias were kept alive only in the refutations composed to disprove them. It is this highly selective character of Christian theology that will serve to explain the real nature of that later movement which we call the Renaissance. What we see then is not the recovery of classical culture in its entirety, for much of this had never been lost; it is more precisely the recovery of those parts of classical culture that the Christian tradition had in the beginning preferred to exclude.

Outside the theological field, the Christians' attitude to their pagan heritage remained notably ambivalent. All patristic writers, even those who are generally in favour of reading ancient literature, display a lively distrust of the pagan tradition and habitually enlarge on the dangers of corruption and disbelief. When you study their diatribes, you wonder why pagan texts were not banned from the schools immediately the Christians came into power. But they were not banned, although the reorganization of the schools after the death of Julian (363) and the failure of his effort to exclude Christian teachers would seem to have afforded an excellent opportunity for this; and half a century later, when we have Augustine drawing up his plan for a Christian education, he too refrains from recommending a wholehearted reform.

The motives behind this policy (or lack of policy) are puzzling. Patristic writers on education justify the retention in the curriculum of the pagan material that they describe as dangerous and harmful, by claiming that this material is indispensable for the teaching of grammar, comprehension, and rhetoric. But by Augustine's day this was not a very convincing argument. Augustine himself informs us that the Bible contains all that a man needs to get an adequate mastery of grammar and rhetoric; and even if it did not, Christians had a substantial literature of their own by the fifth century. The hymns of Synesius (praised by Elizabeth Barrett Browning), the letters and sermons of Basil, John Chrysostom, and Gregory Nazianzen, or, in Latin, Prudentius' poetry and Lactantius' prose did not perhaps reach the same high level of literary excellence as their pagan models; but it is plain that they would have provided good reading matter for school use. From a crudely utilitarian point of view, the pagan classics were not indispensable.

One suspects that the early Christians may have valued the pagan classics for reasons they would not or perhaps could not put into words. Driven to be precise, they talked of the usefulness of having efficient models when one was learning to write. But Basil, in the tract which the Renaissance called *Ad adolescentes* and read with great enthusiasm, does remark in general terms that pagan literature has much to teach Christian youth;[1] and Augustine, when he puts forward his famous theory that Christians should take from the pagans whatever they find useful, remains significantly vague as to the elements that may be regarded as falling within that category. A literature that offered glimpses of a different civilization that had not dismissed the everyday world as unimportant was after all too precious to be irretrievably discarded.

It is not surprising therefore that when paganism finally collapsed in the fifth century, the independent Christian culture that emerged should have been deeply indebted to its

[1] Luzi Schucan, *Das Nachleben von Basilius Magnus 'ad Adolescentes'*, Travaux d'Humanisme et Renaissance 133 (Geneva, 1973).

predecessor. Much had been admittedly neglected, forgotten,
was perhaps lost for ever: the writings of the hedonists and
sceptics, an unknown amount of poetry, drama, and fiction,
and in the West at any rate a mass of scientific and
technological learning that a war-torn civilization had no
longer the means to utilize. But the rationalist philosophers
had fared very well. Their concepts and arguments were
embedded in the new theology. Important elements of ancient
political thought survived in Augustine's *City of God*, and the
traditional methods of the classical historians were applied by
Eusebius and his imitators to the events of a new era.
Established prose genres—autobiography, dialogue, the semi-
formal letter—were employed for religious purposes. Nonnus
drew on the skills he had acquired composing the last pagan
epic to compile a verse commentary on St. John's gospel. In
Latin, the New Testament story was related in hexameters
that borrowed substantially from classical sources, while
Prudentius, whom Bentley was to call 'the Horace and Virgil
of the Christians', produced a *Psychomachia* whose personified
virtues and vices engaged in Homeric hand-to-hand combats.
And more important still, in both Greek and Latin, the hymn
writers, even where they employed new accentual metres,
depended to a greater extent than is commonly realized on
the poetic diction and rhetorical techniques of the classical
period.

Greek influence also operated at a more popular level.
Research into Christian epitaphs has shown death attributed
there to Fate, malign Fortune, the envy of the gods, and even
the greed of Charon! The Christian soul is pictured escaping
from a body that is abandoned for ever and finding a home
among the stars. Comfort is sought not from hopes of the
soul's survival, but from the fact that the tomb or the dead
man's fame would endure. Such epitaphs were probably
composed by professionals who worked within a long-
established convention; but a similar dependence on pagan
motifs shows itself in the legends told about the Christian
saints. The stock of anecdotes that had circulated orally in
Greece since Ionian times, growing from generation to generation, and had been used by the authors of New Comedy and
the love romances, now came to provide hagiography with
incidents and themes. The figure of St. Thekla for example in
the New Testament Apocrypha has traits in common with the

heroines of Heliodorus and Xenophon of Ephesus, and we find a variant of the Menaechmi story enlivening the theology of the pseudo-Clementine *Recognitiones*.

We can see therefore that, even if the study of the classical literatures had been abandoned after the fifth century, Christian culture would have transmitted a massive inheritance of ancient Greek origin. As it turned out, however, the elements mentioned above were reinforced for each generation by a direct acquaintance in school or elsewhere with some at least of the ancient classics, so that the amount transmitted was even greater. What was excluded consisted in the main of ideas and ideals that clashed with the supernaturalist values of the Christian faith, and of knowledge that a materially backward world could no longer use.

The Early Medieval West

The sixth century was a watershed. It was then that the two halves of the Roman Empire split irremediably apart, so that we have from that time a Christian Latin West and a Christian Greek East, divided not only by language and the rivalries of power, but also by their level of civilization. Their histories were to be very different, and they must be considered separately.

The West crumbled rapidly under the hammer-blows of barbarian conquest. Disruptions caused by war and invasion were aggravated by the incompetence of unpractised rulers, who neither knew how to preserve the civilization they had overwhelmed, nor cared particularly to do so. The countryside was depopulated. Land went out of cultivation. Towns dwindled to villages. Commerce and industry declined. Italy alone retained a small measure of secular education. Elsewhere, by the middle of the seventh century, the monasteries were the sole custodians of learning in a society lately emerged from a tribal state.

Latin remained the official language of the Western Church. Its Eastern counterpart, firmly based on a large Greek-speaking population, could allow its missionaries to use Old Slavonic in their services and instruction, since there was no danger that the new Church would be tempted to break away from the old. But in the West, the daughter Churches in the barbarian kingdoms vastly outnumbered the Roman faithful. Had each used its own language, the ties between them would have been easily loosened. So Roman Christianity clung to the language of its imperial past. Knowledge of Latin remained essential for an understanding of its traditions; and when the general level of that knowledge was seen to be insufficient, as was the case during the seventh and eighth centuries, deliberate and vigorous efforts were made to improve it. The need to learn Latin led to a study of the classical grammarians, which were still the best available; and that in turn led to an increased interest in the classical authors whom they recommended. The ordered revival of learning in the Carolingian age, when Latin manuscripts were copied in great numbers and poets imitated Virgil and Ovid, was the natural culmination of this process.

But how much did these learned and partly learned monks know about Greek culture? The reputation of Greek stood high during the period of darkest ignorance. It was looked upon as the key to a superior wisdom. The garbled language of that strangest of books, the *Hisperica Famina*, produced probably during the sixth or seventh century in the west of Britain, contains numerous Greek terms, or terms that seem intended as Greek, and the suggestion has been made that lists of imperfectly recorded Greek words, treasured in Celtic monasteries, were used in its composition.[2] But neither the Irish scholars, who liked to boast of their knowledge, nor their successors up to the twelfth century had many opportunities to learn a Greek they could really use.

During this period, contacts with the Eastern Empire that had any hope of being intellectually fruitful were confined to Italy, where the two civilizations had a common frontier till the fall of Bari in 1071. Theodore of Tarsus (d. 690), the only immigrant of intellectual eminence to arrive from the East at this early stage, settled in Rome before being sent to be Archbishop of Canterbury. His companion, the Abbot Hadrian, who also knew Greek, was a native of Southern Italy; and there was a colony of Greek-speaking, probably South Italian, monks in Rome as late as the ninth century, whose members were probably responsible for the few papal letters we find written in that language. It is true that by that time there were also traders from Italian ports who visited the

[2] Francis John Henry Jenkinson, *The Hisperica Famina* (Cambridge, 1908).

Levant. The pilgrims who crossed Byzantine territories on their way to the Holy Land must have used interpreters. And the German Empire had diplomatic relations with the Byzantine court, which culminated in the marriage in 972 of Otto II to the princess Theophano. But none of these casual exchanges yielded much fruit. The Byzantines who met their Western neighbours were not the ones most conscious of their country's intellectual heritage, nor were the Latins who had dealings with them ready as yet to benefit from an alien culture.

A few scholars of the calibre of Aldhelm, Notker, or Gerbert seem to have had a smattering of Greek, derived from the teaching of Hadrian or culled from books. But only one man, John the Scot (*c.* 810–*c.* 875) can be shown to have read the language with full understanding, and where he learnt to do this remains a mystery. Moreover, western libraries had very few Greek manuscripts at this time: some copies of the Psalms, some (usually incomplete) of the New Testament. That was all. The knowledge of Greek culture that came directly from Greek sources was negligible.

But when we turn to possible Latin sources, we have a different picture. Some Greek books were available in translation. There were Latin versions of the New Testament Apocrypha, notably the gospel of Nicodemus, of the *Visions* of the Shepherd of Hermas, the pseudo-Clementine *Recognitiones*, Josephus, Eusebius, and the *Historia tripartita*; and also (though in fewer copies) of works by Basil of Caesarea, Cyril of Alexandria, Gregory Nazianzen, John Chrysostom, Origen, and Palladius. And pagan learning was also represented. Chalcidius's translation of the *Timaeus*, some of the old Boethian versions of the *Organon*, and Porphyry's *Introduction to the Categories* in the version by Victorinus were widely known.

Admittedly no single scholar, however well endowed, is likely to have studied every one of these works. There were not enough copies. But a great many writers, pagan and Christian, who had known, plundered, and imitated Greek literature were also to hand. Augustine above all, but also Jerome, Gregory I, the *Institutiones* of Cassiodorus, the *Etymologiae* of Isidore served to transmit such Greek ideas as the Christian tradition had absorbed, while those it had not absorbed came through pagan sources, which were also available. There was Cicero's *De inventione* with its rhetorical precepts; his *De amicitia*, which exercised considerable influence on Aelred of Rievaulx (d. 1167); and his *Tusculanae disputationes*, the philosophical teachings of which were supplemented by Boethius' *De consolatione*. Scholars who failed to read translations of the Greek historians could learn about ancient historiography from the more vigorous examples of Sallust and Suetonius. The epic tradition was represented by the *Aeneid* and the *Pharsalia*, the pastoral by Virgil's Eclogues, New Comedy by Terence, whom the nun Hroswitha felt impelled to copy. In these authors, all of whom owed a debt to Greece, the men of the early Middle Ages were brought into contact with a substantial sector of Greek culture, even though they were not in a position to recognize the fact.

The intellectual achievements of the early Middle Ages that we admire all had a traditional character. They depended on the past. The classical verses of the Carolingian poets, Einhard's life of Charlemagne, the *Waltharius*, the complexities of the debate on Predestination, John the Scot's Neoplatonism, and finally the growing interest in logic during the eleventh century would not have come into being if the Graeco-Roman heritage had not been there to supply models and material; and that heritage, both in its pagan and Christian modes drew its inspiration originally from Greece.

The Latin culture of this period had as strong roots in the Greek past as the culture of Byzantium or the Renaissance. It differed from these however in one important respect. It did not so much build *on* its inheritance as build *from* it. Hampered by unfavourable social and economic conditions, the best it could achieve was a rearrangement of the material that had been transmitted to it.

Byzantium

The influence of Greek culture can be traced in the Latin world. It can be traced, as we shall see, among the Arabs. But in the main, its preservation and transmission were the work of the Byzantines. The East escaped the worst of the disasters that overwhelmed the West, so that the Byzantine Empire grew out of the Roman without a catastrophic break. It managed to retain the ancient Greek language at least for formal and literary use. It kept safe, and to some extent renewed by regular copying, a huge store of ancient books;

and what was most important, it maintained among its upper and middle classes a level of education which allowed substantial numbers access to this learned heritage, so that the past remained a living force.

The original division of the Roman Empire dates back to Diocletian. But it was in the fifth century that the links between the two halves began to weaken with an alarming rapidity, until in the sixth we can regard them as effectively severed. The period of transition, during which the new order took shape, was characterized by efforts to save something of the legacy of the past, but whereas in the West these were confined to a few gifted individuals like Boethius, Cassiodorus, and later Isidore, in the East the movement had a much wider scope.

Historians of classical scholarship have drawn attention in this context to the long survival of paganism. Neoplatonist philosophy had some distinguished fifth- and sixth-century representatives in Proclus, Ammonius, and Simplicius, the last of whom emigrated to Persia, while the poetic traditions of the past enjoyed an Indian summer with the school of Nonnus. But the persistence of such overtly pagan modes of thought and expression was a symptom rather than a primary cause of the major role that ancient learning was to play in the development of the Eastern Empire. What counted for more was the energy with which the Christians of the time set themselves to learn from their predecessors. They seem to have been prepared to make their own everything except direct incitements to pagan worship and ideas in obvious conflict with their theological beliefs.

As one would expect, the greatest efforts were made in the field of practical knowledge. There the task was one of careful systematization. Material scattered in a multitude of books had to be brought together in a form in which it could be handily consulted and preserved. This was achieved spec-tacularly in law by the Justinian Code; in medicine by the compendia of Oribasius, Aëtius, and Alexander of Tralles; in veterinary science by a fifth-century Hippocrates; in zoology by Timotheus of Gaza; in agriculture by Didymus in the fourth or fifth century, and Bassus in the tenth; in grammar by John Philoponus and John Charax in the sixth century.

Philosophy presented special problems. The questions which interested a Christian society were those which had theological implications, so that the relevant classical theories had to be handled with imaginative tact. The foundations of this enterprise had been laid by the Cappadocians, Basil of Caesarea and his friends, who had undertaken to expound Christianity in terms Platonists could understand. They were followed, probably in the fifth century, by the mysterious Dionysius the Areopagite whose beliefs inclined to the Neoplatonism of Proclus, and in the seventh by Maximus the Confessor, who combined ideas from Aristotle and Porphyry with Christianity. A further reconciliation between Aristotle and Christian theology was effected a hundred years later by John of Damascus. In each of these cases, one observes a careful process of selection at work; some theories are elaborately developed, others are disregarded. The developments, where they occur, do however show these Byzantine thinkers to have possessed philosophical powers of a very high order. In this field at any rate, which caught their deepest interest, they were capable of making an original contribution.

Their literary achievements were less distinguished. But in three genres, history, oratory, and the epigram, their avowed aim to produce a literature purified of pagan values and beliefs was substantially achieved. The sixth-century historians, Procopius, Agathias, the Theophylactus Simocattes, writing on the political and military events of their time, modelled their work on Thucydides and Polybius, making a fetish of accuracy, analysing the causes of events, the motives for men's actions, and summing these up every so often in an invented speech. Here was the beginning of a Christian historiography that did not fall far below the standards set by the classical tradition.

In oratory, the eloquence of Chrysostom (344/7-409) provided speakers on sacred subjects with models which were thought to stand comparison with Demosthenes or Isocrates. The Byzantines excelled in writing celebratory sermons, panegyrics, and funeral orations; and letter-writing, also based on fourth-century models, was a successfully practised minor art.

In verse, attempts to revive the epic proved a failure. But Justinian's chamberlain, Paul the Silentiary, and the historian Agathias composed epigrams that rank with the best Greece has produced.

It would be wrong however to regard these imitations of

particular genres as more than the tips of an iceberg. The literary influence of antiquity had at the same time some broad, pervasive, and deep-seated effects on Byzantine culture whose importance far outweighed these localized triumphs. Two examples, drawn from very different fields, will perhaps suffice as evidence of this. Saints' lives continued to draw on antiquity's stock of popular stories, delighting their Christian readers with the same hairbreadth escapes from rape or shipwreck, the same miraculous resuscitations and savage animals suddenly tamed that had delighted the readers of Heliodorus. Young boys continued to attend rhetorical schools on the ancient model, practising the exercises that Hermogenes and Aphthonius had framed; and what they learnt affected all forms of verbal communication. Brilliance was inhibited, but competence was universally guaranteed.

The Graeco-Roman foundations of Byzantine culture were firmly laid during this initial period of the Empire's existence. Then after 650 there followed a period which historians have equated with the Dark Ages in the West. There was a sudden decline in intellectual activity, which can be explained to some extent by the Arab conquest of Syria and Egypt, the heartland of the old Roman East, by the dangers that pressed on Byzantium itself, and by civil disorder. The hostility of the iconoclast emperors towards Greek culture, which they identi- fied with the orthodox cause, and the closure of the patriar- chal school by Leo III (717–41) were contributory factors of some importance.

But even so, the darkness of this supposed dark age should not be exaggerated. There was a good deal of theological writing; and in the composition of hymns and saints' lives the period ranks with the best. The monasteries, all rigidly orthodox, held on to their special fields of learning. It was just the secular world that turned philistine; and there one cannot be quite sure how philistine it was. Long before higher studies were re-established by Bardas (c. 850), we find patriarchs distinguished in various branches of secular learning, chroni- clers like George Syncellus, grammarians, and even poets. Photius, who was born c. 810 and must have been educated under the iconoclast emperors, was a man of amazing erudition and the centre of a group devoted to the study of the classics. When they turned once again to the past, the Byzantines did not need to start from scratch.

The period of the Macedonian dynasty (867–1057), which followed the settlement of the iconoclast controversy, represents the high-water mark of Byzantine power; but in literature and learning it was still a time of consolidation, of imitative achievement. Its monuments are the *Lexicon* and *Bibliotheca* of Photius, the *Anthology* of Cephalas, the handbooks written or commissioned by Constantine VII, Porphyrogenitus (912–59), the hagiographical collection of Metaphrastes, and the 'Suda' encyclopedia. Works of creative merit were rare. The libraries of Byzantium, stuffed with books, offered a store of past knowledge that no man, however industrious, could hope to master in its existing unorganized state. Photius' approach to the problem posed by this situation was that of an amateur. His volume of critical notices, the *Bibliotheca*, was not intended to do more than communicate to his brother the fruits of some months' reading. Its value for us derives from the fact that many of its notices concern works we have now lost. The enterprise initiated by Constantine VII was of a more serious order. The treatises produced under his aegis were intended to replace their sources. But if Photius had been amateurish, Constantine's collaborators were incompetent. They simplified rashly; and some of their summaries of ancient knowledge have little practical value. The anthologists did better, for our purposes at any rate. Cephalas' collection of epigrams and Metaphrastes' collection of saints' lives have preserved a great deal of material that would have been lost otherwise. But for the most interesting feature of this work of consolidation we must turn to the labours of Photius and others on lexicography and literary history. They provided the basis for that strangest of Byzantine achievements and the one which was to prove most important for the future of Western culture: the successful maintenance, in a relatively correct state, of a classical language and classical modes of writing.

After the Macedonian period, the middle years of the eleventh century saw what has been often described as a 'renaissance', and the credit for this is given to Michael Psellus (1018–78). The parallel with fifteenth-century Italy is not entirely convincing; for it would not be easy to demonstrate that scholars after 1050 knew more about antiquity than their immediate predecessors. They did not give the ball of learning a first decisive push. They just helped to roll it a little further. Nevertheless, there was a change, and one that mattered. A useful, pedestrian interest in the classical past was replaced by enthusiasm. Platonism gained ground as a study worth undertaking for its own sake. Psellus, himself an indifferent stylist, laid great stress on the deliberate imitation of ancient authors; and his propagandist fervour, coming at a point when the labours of lexicographers and grammarians had prepared the ground for a more exact knowledge of Attic usage, had a decisive effect on education. Employing a variety of techniques, among which the exercises of the *progymnasmata*, parsing, and the study of ancient authors predominated, the schools of Byzantium evolved a course that imparted an ability to write an accurate classical Greek.

After Psellus came the age of the Comneni. The century of their rule (1081–1185) was politically a period of retrenchment and decline, but for Byzantine Humanism it was a golden age. In its historians (among whom the princess, Anna Comnena, is the most widely read), in rhetoricians like Doxoprates and Michael Acominatus, in the iambic poet, Christopher of Mytilene, in Prodromos, the witty imitator of Lucian, we have the Greek counterparts of those learned Latinists who were to dominate the intellectual life of the Italian Renaissance.

When Eustathius, who has preserved for us a greater volume of ancient learning than any other Byzantine commentator, died *c.* 1192, his panegyrist called him 'the last survivor of the golden age'; and for once a hyperbole was aptly chosen, since the next century opened with a catastrophe. The Frankish sack of Constantinople in 1204 was probably responsible for the loss of more learning and more art than any other disaster contrived by man; and the subsequent Latin kingdom remained barren of cultural achievement. Even the task of spreading Greek learning in the West, which it was well qualified to perform, remained unattempted.

The expulsion of the Latins in 1261 did not bring with it a recovery of Byzantine power. The Paleologue Empire was to last till 1453, but it tottered chronically on the brink of ruin. For that very reason however it was now prepared to welcome contacts with the West, and for the first time since the fourth century, the two great European cultures embarked on a serious interchange of ideas. Prompted by the enthusiasm Aristotle aroused in the West, the Greeks began to interest themselves in his philosophy. A certain Demetrius Cydones translated the *Summae* of Aquinas, and this led by a natural reaction to a revival of the Platonism that had coloured Byzantine thinking since the days of Psellus. The main champion of Plato was an eccentric, Gemistus Plethon (1355–1450), who openly professed a desire to bring back the old gods of Greece. Remarkably, his avowed paganism did him no harm. He actually accompanied the Byzantine delegation to the Council of Florence, where he discoursed on Beauty to admiring groups of Humanists; and his conversation did much to encourage the growth of Florentine Platonism.

The destruction of 1204 had also had the further effect of making the Byzantines aware of the need to preserve their literary heritage. The Paleologue scholars were zealous copyists; and it is their zeal we have to thank for the ease with which the collectors of the Renaissance were able to bring the treasures of Greek literature to the West. At the same time, the pens of Planudes, Moschopoulos, and Thomas Magister poured forth a multitude of word-lists, grammars, and easy readers designed to help students with what had become an unfamiliar language to users of demotic, and which were to serve later not only to teach Greek to the peoples of the West, but also as models for books on the teaching of Latin.

The role of Byzantium in the transmission of classical literature has come in for a fair amount of comment, not all of it favourable. Her scholars were 'pedantic, dull and blundering', if Frederic Harrison is to be believed: 'their very merit to us is that they were never either original or brilliant';[3] and notoriety attaches among textual critics to the *vitium Byzantinum*, a tendency to alter iambic lines to make them conform to a Byzantine norm. But the fact remains that if the Eastern Empire had not survived, most of what we know about ancient Greece would have perished. And surely it is not reasonable to look upon Byzantium merely as a transmitter of classical culture. She built on that culture a great power that held off its enemies for close on a thousand years, and a civilization that was the brightest jewel of a disturbed age. Achievements of this magnitude deserve attention. The problem of how Byzantium used the legacy of Greece is interesting in its own right. That she benefited from the practical

[3] In his 1900 Rede lecture, cited by John Edwin Sandys, *A History of Classical Scholarship*, vol. i (Cambridge, 1913), p. 427.

knowledge, the military and civil institutions that she inherited is a fact no one would question. But what of her inheritance in the field of ideas, language, and art? Was that of value to her? And if so, how? And in what ways was her use of it selective? What did she alter and what did she fruitfully develop? Most of these questions still wait for an answer.

Arab Culture in the Middle Ages

When the Arabs subjugated the Middle East and North Africa in the seventh century, they preferred where possible to retain the existing machinery of government, to draw tribute and use the civilized skills of their new subjects. This leniency had excellent results. Gradually, over the next two hundred years, the conquered adopted the faith and language of their masters. The learning at their command was made available in Arabic, while the Arabs on their side absorbed this alien knowledge, added to it (mostly now from Greek sources), and began the hard task of bringing it into line with Islamic theology.

Greek influence made itself felt first of all in military science and civil administration, where the Arabs were quick to copy Byzantine practices. Then it was the turn of religion. Islam did not yet possess a developed theology. Its adherents were prepared to engage in debate with Christian apologists, and categories such as substance and accident, concepts such as eternity and creation in time, which Christian theology had taken over from the Greek philosophers, found their way into the interpretations of the Qu'ran.

Other fields of study were not tapped till later, not until the end of the eighth century, and in these Greek learning came to the Arabs initially through Aramaic, which had been the language of the ruled in the Roman East. We hear of translations into Aramaic, mostly of theological works, as early as the fourth century. One assumes that the Syrian clergy were prompted to make Christian thought more easily accessible to their flocks. In 461 however the school at Edessa which had been responsible for this work was closed because of its Nestorian leanings, and its teachers fled to the Persian court, where they were joined by Neoplatonists from the school of Athens. Aramaic communities then lived on undisturbed in Persia after the Arab conquest and extended their work of translation to philosophy and science. Their academy at Gondeshapur was famous for its medical learning, so that, when in the ninth century the caliphs developed an interest in Greek culture, the earliest translations of Aristotle and Galen into Arabic were made from Aramaic versions. Later, however, the celebrated 'House of Wisdom' was set up (833), an institute of translators who worked from the original Greek and produced accurate Arabic and Aramaic translations of a great number of ancient scientific and philosophical writings.

Translation was followed by assimilation. The earliest of the Arab 'philosophers', al-Kindi, who died *c.* 850, was essentially a popularizer. He expounded the ideas of Aristotle and Galen. But his successors in the next century fall into a different category. Al-Razi was an empiricist, a believer in Reason, who was prepared to criticize every authority including Aristotle and the Qu'ran. His empirical approach showed to best advantage in medicine, where he moved from summarizing his sources to making his own observations. He was the first to distinguish smallpox and measles. His younger contemporary, al-Farabi, was more specifically a speculative thinker. He owed a debt to Plato, from whom he took the idea of the philosopher-king, while his physical doctrines were derived from Aristotle.

These two men established what were to become the distinguishing characteristics of Muslim thought: its sheer voluminousness, each writer producing a multitude of treatises; its polymathy, that covered all branches of philosophy and science; its familiarity with a number of ancient authors, Aristotle and sometimes Plato, Hippocrates, Galen, Euclid, and Ptolemy; and finally, its readiness to improve on this heritage. Their achievements in the tenth century prepared the ground for the greatest of Arab thinkers, Ibn Sina ('Avicenna') in the eleventh. He too was a physician as well as a philosopher, and compiled a vast textbook of medicine in which observation and experiment supplemented Greek teachings. In philosophy, he followed Aristotle, but maintained several doctrines that were not to be found in the late Greek Aristotelians whose treatises he knew: doctrines such as the immortality of the soul, that essence possesses being, and (foretelling Descartes) that man has an intrinsic awareness of his own ego.

The relationship of philosophy and religion held no particular interest for Ibn Sina. But it was to matter greatly to the philosophers who succeeded him. Al-Ghazali condemned a number of Ibn Sina's doctrines because they contradicted Islamic beliefs. Ibn Rushd ('Averroes' 1126–98), who wrote detailed commentaries on Aristotle, maintained that religion and philosophy would reach the same truth by different roads, but both he and his older contemporaries, Ibn Bajja (d. 1138) and Ibn Tufayl (d. 1185), drew a sharp distinction between the intellectually gifted and the common run of mankind. The former could speculate, but ought to keep their speculations to themselves; the latter were best left with their simple faith undisturbed.

Any attempt to estimate the Arab debt to Greece must take note of the fact that it was confined almost entirely to the fields of philosophy and science, the only exception to this rule being provided by fiction, where compilations like the *Thousand and One Nights* borrowed heavily from Greek sources. Arab interest in the past was narrower therefore than the Byzantine, but within its narrower scope it was more thorough; and it was not limited to simple imitation or repetition. The Arabs built on what they learnt. In philosophy, they raised issues unknown to antiquity, which were important for an age of religious faith. In mathematics and the natural sciences they made a host of small advances using the theoretical framework provided by the Greeks; and here the full extent of their achievement is not yet known.

The Late Medieval West

By the twelfth century, Western civilization had made great strides forward. Trade, wealth, and education had all increased. Cities were populous again, and civil order was guaranteed by firmer institutions. No longer confined in a universe of monasteries and war-racked villages, the people of Western Europe wanted to know more about medicine, mathematics, and technology, and about the works of Aristotle whom their passion for Logic had taught them to admire. They were hungry for information whose ultimate source was in nearly all cases Greek. And they were no longer as isolated as they had been. They had contacts with the Arab world and with Byzantium, cultures which had some knowledge of the Greek heritage. Arab learning survived in Sicily, now ruled by the Normans, and in parts of Spain regained by Castile and Leon. The loss of Anatolia to the Turks laid Byzantium open to Western infiltration. Italian merchants enjoyed extensive trading concessions. There were discussions on Church union, since the emperors hoped that this would win them military aid, until finally the Latin conquest of 1204 put Byzantium wholly at the mercy of the West. If there was a demand for Greek knowledge, the means for satisfying the demand were also at hand.

Byzantium had more to offer than the Arabs. It stood closer to antiquity; and yet by a curious chance most of what the age learnt about the ancient world came through Arabic. The earliest translator known to us was Constantine the African (d. 1087), who produced Latin versions of Hippocrates and Galen for the Salerno medical school. Then, during the following century, Gerard of Cremona and others, many of them Jews or converted Muslims working in the newly reconquered Spanish city of Toledo, put into Latin something like a hundred scientific and medical works: Greek texts that had been translated into Arabic and Arab manuals that summarized Greek knowledge; and these were further supplemented after 1200 by versions of Aristotle's treatises on natural history that were made at the Sicilian court and by some of Ibn Rushd's Aristotelian commentaries that had appeared in Spain. Enough became available to serve as a foundation for the Aristotelian renaissance of the thirteenth century and for the considerable advance in mathematical and medical knowledge that occurred during the same period. Meanwhile, at a different level, the Greek stories that had been absorbed into the fictional stock of the Arab world were finding their way back into Europe by devious ways which can no longer be traced. Most of what the Arab world assimilated, it transmitted in its turn to the West.

Contacts with Byzantium were less fruitful. Although these swelled in the twelfth century from a trickle to a flood, they did not contribute much to classical learning. The language situation was a complicated one. The demotic Greek, which was what merchants, soldiers, and missionaries generally learnt, served at most for the transmission of technological information. The language used in formal writing and discourse held the key to the heritage of the past, and that was mastered by only a handful. Moreover, the Latins who knew Greek, whether it was demotic Greek or classical, were not poets and scholars who would have welcomed information about Greek literature or science, but traders, soldiers, diplomats, and theologians, who had no immediate interest in ancient learning. Burgundio of Pisa, who in the twelfth century added the *Aphorisms* of Hippocrates and some treatises by Galen to his translations from the Greek Fathers, was an exception; and so was Aristippus, the Sicilian translator of the *Phaedo* and *Meno*. The gap between the erudite world of the universities and the adventurers who exploited the Levant remained however a substantial one, and persisted even after the Latin conquest and the establishment of Frankish principalities in Greece. Byzantine treasures were carried to the West. A great deal was learnt about Byzantine crafts and techniques. But the intellectual inheritance of the Greeks was neglected. Perhaps the most important gains in that field were the manuscripts of Archimedes and Aristotle which enabled Aquinas's contemporary, William of Moerbeke (fl. 1268–81), to complete his new corrected translations.

But when we consider not only Byzantium, but the Arab world as well and what was learnt from each of these, we can see that the charge of ignorance that the Humanists levelled against their predecessors cannot be sustained. The men of the later Middle Ages studied a substantial number of Greek authors, pagan as well as Christian. Directly or indirectly they learnt a great deal about the Greek past. They laid the foundations without which the Renaissance could not have flourished. Two points however call for attention before we can assess the nature of their indebtedness to the ancient world. A certain peculiarity attaches both to the character of their borrowings and to the manner in which these were assimilated.

Their borrowings were utilitarian in character, limited to what they thought would help to solve problems they regarded as being of importance; and their interests were restricted to certain fields: technology, science, medicine, logic, metaphysics, and theology where they were particularly concerned with issues relating to church union. They were practical men, and as such they made ruthless efforts to assimilate what they learnt. Laboriously over some eighty years Aristotle's metaphysics and cosmology were worked into that synthesis with Christian beliefs that appears in the writings of Aquinas. What did not fit was discarded. The teachings of Ptolemy and Galen were unquestioningly accepted, but no one grasped the importance of the attitudes— the lively curiosity, the habit of observation—that had amassed the facts on which these teachings rested. Scholars who worked in the scientific field added little to what they had inherited except by way of explanation; and their method of interpreting phenomena relied on a verbal framework of definition and deduction.

There were classical precedents for this. But the medieval scholars altered the classical balance between fact and theory, putting all emphasis on the latter. When one tries to work out how the thirteenth century used its heritage, one begins to feel a certain sympathy for the complaints of the Humanists. These men of the late Middle Ages saw the trees, not the wood; and for them a tree was just so much timber. They were selective; and literature, the truth of history, the more poetic forms of philosophy were excluded from the selection they made. They were in touch with the Byzantine civilization that owed much to the Greek literary heritage, but they disregarded its teachings. They grabbed at its artifacts, but they were contemptuous of its spirit.

The Renaissance

What distinguishes the Renaissance from the Middle Ages in the field of Greek studies is a shift of interest from scientific (or what was held to be scientific) knowledge to literature, morality, and politics.

Initially, the fourteenth century followed the pattern set by the thirteenth. Relations with Byzantium were dominated by commercial and ecclesiastical interests. Repeated demands were made for schools that would teach Greek, but these, like the often-cited eleventh canon of the Council of Vienne (1312), which provided chairs of Greek in five universities, merely reflected the missionary orders' need for men who could preach to Byzantine congregations. There was no question yet of anyone studying the classical language.

In the meantime, however, men were becoming interested once again in the achievements of antiquity. The first indications of this have been traced during the last quarter of the thirteenth century; and soon after that, Petrarch emerged as the triumphant propagandist of poetry and eloquence. The names of some Greek authors—notably Homer and Plato—had been long known in the West, and in an unreflective manner, their greatness had been acknowledged; but Petrarch was the first to envisage clearly the implications of the fact that they had been writers of genius. His longing to read their works made him try to learn Greek. His first teacher, Barlaam, was a distinguished scholar and theologian. He had written with equal felicity on Stoicism and algebra. But Petrarch did not find his lessons helpful. A second attempt twenty years later, when he employed the Byzantine, Leontius Pilatus, was also a fiasco. Petrarch's biographers have bemoaned his ill-luck in not finding better instructors; but the fault may have been his own. Perhaps he lacked patience. At all events, he finally solved his problem by setting Pilatus to work translating the *Iliad*.

Pilatus's word-for-word version disappointed Petrarch; and printed eventually alongside the Greek text as a crib, it was to prove similarly disappointing to later generations of scholars. The verse translations which Marsuppini (*c.* 1450) and Eobanus Hessus (1540) produced seemed not much better; and eventually the Humanists came to realize that the fault did not lie wholly with the translations. They had expected the *Iliad* to display the qualities of the *Aeneid* at a much higher level; but Homer's references to the commonplace events of daily life seemed vulgar by that criterion. His lack of a great political theme was deplored, and so were the morals of his heroes. These were neither chivalric nor Christian. Homer continued to be mentioned as a great poet. But he was little read, and when read, he was not liked or understood.

Other, less eminent writers proved more acceptable. Towards the end of the fourteenth century, a Byzantine theologian, Simon Atumano, fabricated a word-for-word translation of Plutarch's *De cohibenda ira*. The leading Humanist of the day, Salutati, condemned its language as *semigraeca*, but was sufficiently impressed by its content to state that he would rather have Plutarch in bad Latin than not at all. About the same time, eleven of the *Lives* were translated first into demotic Greek, then from demotic to Catalan; and they delighted John I of Aragon (1387–95). John deserves our attention. Here we see a powerful prince whose one wish was to learn 'about the glorious deeds of the Greeks'. He was no scholar. He preferred Catalan to Latin. But he showed an enthusiasm for antiquity that would have puzzled his medieval forebears.

Enthusiasm of this sort was a feature of the fourteenth century. How it first developed remains a mystery. But by 1396 Manuel Chrysoloras benefited from its existence. Like so many Byzantines, he arrived in Italy on a diplomatic mission; and the Florentines were by then so interested in Greek learning that two young nobles travelled to Venice specially to see him and persuaded the city fathers to invite him to lecture in Florence at the public expense, which he did successfully for three years.

For the next half century, Greek studies in Italy were dominated by the pupils of Chrysoloras and by the few adventurous scholars who had actually studied in Byzantium. Many of these men were collectors. They transferred to Greek that appetite for classical manuscripts which had been responsible for notable finds in the field of Latin. It is true that the situation in the two languages was not the same. When Poggio discovered his Petronius or his *Brutus*, these represented an immediate enlargement of contemporary knowledge. In Greek there was more to acquire: a whole literature, not just its missing parts; and the texts were harder to understand, so that many Greek manuscripts, one suspects, lay in their owners' libraries unread or partly read. However, to have laid up a store for future use was an achievement in itself; and the store was a great one. Aurispa alone is supposed to have brought back nearly 300 manuscripts from the East in 1417, most of them classical; others returned with thirty, forty, fifty. By the middle of the fifteenth century, most of the works of the better-known Greek authors had found their way to Italy. There were exceptions, notably in the scientific field, but for practical purposes the task of transplantation was complete.

The other achievements of the 'Chrysoloras generation' were less spectacular. They recognized the need to make Greek authors available in Latin; but their efforts at translation, though courageous and sustained, were confined almost entirely to prose works of no great length: essays, dialogues, speeches. Working on a larger scale, they preferred paraphrase, and only five full-length works appeared in Latin before the middle of the century. Their range too was limited. Except for an indifferent version of *Iliad*, 1–16, they did not touch the poets; and they made a poor job of the historians. Their real interest lay in moral philosophy and political thought. Most of these early Humanists held positions of importance in public life, and it is not surprising therefore that they should have looked to the classics for lessons on how a citizen ought to behave.

The period before 1450 was essentially one of preparation. Its Greek studies were not far enough advanced to produce impressive results; and the one thing the Humanists did learn through Greek that was to prove of lasting importance for their movement câme to them from Byzantium rather than the ancient world. Guarino, writing after the death of his master Chrysoloras, praises him for reviving *Latin* studies.[4] The unwary reader wonders if he has not by chance come across a misprint. But the statement is to be taken seriously. Chrysoloras introduced his pupils to Byzantine methods of imitation: the use of lexicons to check vocabulary, of grammars to check usage, the practice of choosing and then carefully following a specific literary model. He intended them to write Greek, but they applied his precepts to Latin. They had difficulties at first since they lacked the necessary aids. But then the aids were created. Lorenzo Valla's *Elegantiae* (printed 1471) provided a guide to classical Latin that made accurate imitation possible, and the basis was laid for Ciceronianism.

The situation that had existed in the first half of the fifteenth century changed radically during the next hundred years. A stream of exiled scholars arrived from Byzantium. Humanism spread to the North. The education it favoured was introduced all over Europe. Printing was invented. And the vernacular literatures, hitherto the poor relations of Latin, emerged as its supplanters. These developments, occurring independently but then interacting, transformed Greek studies as they transformed so much else in Western culture. What had promised to be a renaissance bred a revolution.

The new wave of Byzantine scholars arrived between 1430 and 1460. They were young men in their 20s and early 30s, not distinguished visitors like Chrysoloras, but immigrants

---

[4] Guarinus Veronensis, *Epistolario*, ed. R. Sabbadini (Venice, 1915–19), ii. 580–1, 583, 588.

who aimed to make their knowledge of Greek and Greek culture yield them a living. Unfortunately for them, they arrived at the very moment when the Church, which had been urging the study of spoken Greek for over a century, lost interest because the East was now closed to missionary enterprise. The newcomers had to build on the recently developed enthusiasm for their country's past, when they would have been better suited to forward an interest in its existing culture; and it is to their credit that they managed as well as they did. Except for one Michael Apostolios, who was noted for his inadaptibility, they did not base their courses on the language they normally spoke. They concentrated on the written idiom, which stood closer to Attic, and which Byzantine teaching methods were well framed to impart. They taught Greek as their Italian colleagues taught Latin, insisting merely on a correct pronunciation.

In another respect however they did make a novel contribution. They did not turn to Greek, like the early Humanists, because they hoped that it would shed light on problems with which they were otherwise concerned. Since their personal fortunes depended on the popularity of their subject, they looked on it as an end, not as a means; and this attitude, which their Italian colleagues also came to adopt, weakened the connection which had previously existed between Greek studies and the interests of the day. Scholarship opened its gates more widely to the past at the cost of becoming more remote from the present.

The work of communicating Greek knowledge to a more extensive readership made a great spurt forward during the pontificate of Nicholas V (1447–55). Employing all the notable Humanists of his day and setting them to work on long historical or philosophical texts, he broke the back of the translation problem. The next generation of scholars completed his enterprise, and by the end of the century the best of Greek prose was accessible to Latin readers.

In the meantime occurred the event which did more than any other to revolutionize academic studies. Printing was introduced into Italy in 1465. The publishing of Greek texts, which presented exceptional difficulties, was rather slow off the mark; but by 1535 all but a few of the important ancient writers could be found in print.

A work that was to appear in a large number of identical

copies was bound to have a status that no single manuscript could possess. There was a good chance of its coming to be regarded as the received text; and how scholars reacted to this challenge was obviously a matter of moment. When the fourteenth-century Byzantines had set out to multiply the manuscripts of their favourite authors in an effort to make good the losses caused by the Latin conquest, their main purpose had been to produce texts that their contemporaries could understand; and with readability as their main criterion, they had indulged in conjectures that there was often no evidence to support. The scholars who produced the *editiones principes* had this example before them, and many were influenced by it. Chalcondyles' highly praised Homer could, for example, have been compiled in Byzantium a hundred years before it actually appeared.

In the meantime, however, other influences were making themselves felt. Valla had studied Latin usage with the needs of literary imitation in mind. But the knowledge he gained showed him that textual conjecture was valueless if it did not take the rules of the language into account. He laid down this critical principle in his emendations to Livy, and half a century later we find it adopted by Politian (1454–94). Scholars came to realize that not all manuscripts were of equal value, and that doubtful readings called for a systematic appraisal of *all* the evidence. Gradually, the crude methods of the early editors gave place to a finer expertise, though the progress that could be made was limited. Musurus, for example, who edited texts for the Aldine Press, was a most competent scholar, but his emendations were based on his wide reading and precise knowledge of Greek. In the absence of accurate library catalogues and in a world where travel remained hazardous, not much more could be achieved.

If the invention of printing had a momentous effect on Humanism, so had the transplantation of learning from Italy to the North. Fifteenth-century Italians had wanted to write like the ancients, but in their attempts to do this, they had not looked beyond usage and style. The Northerners who took over their aims were more thorough-going. They realized that accurate imitation would involve content as well as form, that it would involve making one's own ancient categories of interpretation, ancient theories about the nature of the universe, and the facts the ancients had cited to support or illustrate their arguments. They added *copia rerum* to *copia verborum*, and its acquisition became the central feature of their drive to educate themselves.

Erasmus advised intending writers to read widely in the classics and to note down for themselves what they felt they could use in their own compositions. But simultaneously, he did more than anyone to render this painstaking, scholarly approach unnecessary. He published the fruits of his own note-taking in the *Adages*, a vast collection of moral sayings from Greek and Latin sources, which proved exorbitantly popular and was followed during the sixteenth century by an army of similar handbooks. They made the content of classical literature—or such elements in it as a Renaissance writer might need to use—readily accessible to all, and many writers, Rabelais, for example, and Gascoigne and Jonson, did come to owe them a substantial debt.

At this point, reference must be made to the rise of the vernaculars. The effort that the fifteenth century made to write like the ancients in Latin affected the intellectual development of a small, if important, educated class. Parallel efforts to write like the ancients in Italian, French, English, and Spanish were to have a more serious and lasting effect. That people should have wished to do so was a measure of what Humanist propaganda achieved. That they should have done so successfully, to the extent that they did, was due to the techniques that had been developed to facilitate imitation. There were the handbooks, and there was also the new educational system of the day. The curriculum of the Humanist schools that Protestant and Jesuit endeavour had spread all over Europe was dominated by the cult of imitation. Boys learnt to write like Cicero. As far as the handbooks allowed, they learnt to think like Cicero, or at any rate as the ancients did.

The spread of classical influence into the vernacular literatures occurred at a number of points. Greek and Latin words were given modern forms. Cicero's periods and Seneca's hopping style found imitators. Attempts were made to write Pindaric hymns, epigrams after the manner of Martial, classical tragedies and comedies, orations, and letters. English and French writers adopted an elevated diction that transformed their verse into poetry. But more important than these explicit borrowings was the insidious, but massive transformation of the literary content of vernacular writing by the inclusion of material from classical mythology, ancient history and fiction, philosophy and political thought. Thanks to this, European literature was given a new dimension. It was set on a new path that was to lead it to its finest triumphs.

In sketching out these developments, we have had to consider Greek and Latin together, for the two were not divided in men's minds; and much of what came through classical Latin was anyway Greek in origin. To estimate how much the Renaissance learnt directly from Greek or from translations of Greek works would be an impossible task. Knowledge of Greek did count for something. Alberti and Erasmus certainly read Lucian before composing their ironic satires. Ronsard read Pindar before composing his odes. Racine read Euripides in the original. Keen undergraduates like John Milton familiarized themselves with a number of Greek authors; but for their less able colleagues and for most schoolboys, Greek remained of marginal importance. Their studies embraced a few texts which they perused with the help of an interlinear Latin version to gather material for use in their own compositions. But this was a field in which self-education could replace education; and the energy of translators amply compensated for the shortcomings of the schools. The effort to make Greek literature accessible to readers of the vernaculars did not begin till after 1500, but was then pursued with such vigour that by the end of the century the more important Greek authors had all been translated into at least one or two of the major languages of Europe.

But it was not so much Greek in the broadest sense of the word as certain authors that can be seen to have exercised an influence. Platonism gained a wide following after Ficino's translation was published (1482). Presenting sexual attraction as a stage (eventually to be transcended) in one's quest for absolute beauty, it provided lust with a justification and fickleness with an alibi. Aristotle also continued to be read in spite of the Humanists' declared contempt for his scholastic disciples, and his reputation gained fresh support when the Council of Trent established Thomism as the official philosophy of the Roman Church. It gained support too from the sudden popularity of the *Poetics*. This work had been neglected until 1536, when the text and a Latin translation were published. By 1561 three more editions had appeared, and the elder Scaliger was describing Aristotle as 'bonarum artium dictator perpetuus'. The choice of noun is significant. The age saw the work as a normative treatise. His generalizations were treated as rules. Where Aristotle had written vaguely about the unity of time, the Italian critic Castelvetro (1505–71) propounded in all seriousness that the time of performance ought to equal the duration of the action represented. The parallel development of Ciceronianism—the fuss scholars made when someone used a word that did not appear in Nizzoli's Ciceronian lexicon (1535)—suggests that the sixteenth century was avid for prescriptive direction. But why it should have been so remains a problem.

The *Poetics* had the further effect of transforming men's attitude to the fictional. Up to this time, critics had treated fictions as next of kin to lies, and tolerated them only because of their power to amuse. It is true that they undermined the harshness of this judgement by claiming simultaneously that the fictions found in poetry were allegories, and by accepting as history much that was manifestly legend. But even so, they made it difficult for story-telling to rank as a respectable form of art. Aristotle's theory that fiction showed what might be expected to happen, and could therefore be regarded in a sense as more real than history, was eagerly embraced, and it was to make possible the rise of the novel.

Another Greek author whose influence deserves notice was Lucian. The brevity of his dialogues made him attractive to apprentice translators, but for some time his irony went undetected. It was Leon Battista Alberti, architect, scholar, and satirist, who discovered the real Lucian and imitated his ambiguity and his use of the fantastic. The Lucianic technique of satire became part of the European heritage. It was employed by Erasmus to notable effect in the *Praise of Folly*. It left its mark on Rabelais, on Ben Jonson, on Cervantes. One tale, the *Vera Historia*, with its travellers who visit the moon and the isles of the Blest, produced a great crop of imitations among which *Gulliver's Travels* has the most honoured place.

Plutarch, prosaic where Lucian is oblique, appealed to a different type of mind. The *Moralia* fortified Montaigne. The *Lives* fired Shakespeare. And mention must also be made of a work which has received little attention from professional scholars. The *Aethiopica* of Heliodorus had found its way with other Byzantine treasures into the Vatican Library, was printed in 1534, and thirteen years later was made famous by Amyot's French translation. It arrived at a moment when the fiction-reading public had grown weary of the knights, giants, and magicians that infested the popular literature of the late Middle Ages. They wanted the excitements of romance, but with some pretence of realism, and Heliodorus supplied this need. His influence can be traced in a long series of works from Sidney's *Arcadia* to Mlle de Scudéry's *Clélie* and *Le Grand Cyrus*.

But Greek learning also made a contribution to the progress of science, which was eventually to prove of great importance. The recovery of correct texts of Archimedes and Euclid by the labours of Italian scholars prepared the way for the discoveries of Galileo. There were new departures in mathematics which the study of Diophantus made possible. The botanists of the sixteenth century built their systems on foundations laid by Dioscorides; and in a more immediately practical field, the training of the Dutch armies, which other armies were later to copy, looked back to Byzantine manuals which had drawn their precepts from Roman and Hellenistic experience.

The Renaissance is the period in our history when antiquity mattered, when its study contributed to many separate strands of intellectual growth. If we look beneath the surface of contemporary enthusiasms, we see that the knowledge of Greek developed in fact at a slow and steady rate. The ancient authors were made available, grammars and lexicons were produced, the ancient language was learnt by more scholars, more effectively in each generation. But this gradual progress was complicated by enthusiasms for particular authors whose works, read in translation, came to exercise an influence out of all proportion to the actual state of Greek studies. By the time we reach the seventeenth century most of what Europe was to learn from Greece lay within men's grasp, though many of the finest achievements of classical scholarship were still in the future.

The Age of the Classical Education

For three hundred years Europe had sat at the feet of ancient Greece. She had learnt what could be learnt from a straightforward reading of the Greek thinkers and poets; and further progress along the well-tested lines of imitation and assimilation had become difficult. In the field of Greek studies, the eighteenth century marks the beginning of a new era. The discovery of fresh information in classical sources was now no longer an essential precondition of cultural advance. The philosophical and scientific concepts, the literary, mathematical, and technological procedures that Athens, Alexandria, and Byzantium could readily contribute, had been absorbed into the European tradition, and an impressive superstructure of new ideas and techniques was rising on the foundations antiquity had supplied. In this changed situation, Greece came to be seen as a world remote from ours, whose virtues constituted a challenge to the imperfections of the present.

This new approach to the past made its appearance towards the end of the seventeenth century in the famous controversy about the merits of Homer. As has been mentioned earlier, Homer had disappointed the scholars of the Renaissance. They had hoped for a greater Virgil; and when it became plain that this hope would remain unsatisfied, they had either lost interest in the Greek poet, or following the lead given by Hessus's translation, tried to make him as Virgilian as possible. Chapman (*c.* 1559–1634) admittedly made an effort to catch the tone of his original, but even with that example before him, Dryden almost a century later gave the Hector and Andromache episode a markedly Virgilian character. It was only during his second attempt at translation, when he began work on *Iliad*, Book 1, that he came to realize what Homer had to offer. And in reaching this insight, Dryden was not typical of his period. The popular view, exemplified by La Motte in France and Pope in England, represented the *Iliad* and *Odyssey* as products of an early stage in man's development, magnificent but crude, which had to be polished to suit a civilized taste. Homer was defended against La Motte by Mme Dacier. It is significant however that this eminent bluestocking agreed that the epics were primitive. Where she differed from La Motte was in holding that the primitive had some value.

Interest in primitive peoples had been growing ever since Columbus's discovery of America; and by the end of the seventeenth century the cult of the noble savage had a considerable vogue. Greek learning had made a contribution in this field at an earlier stage when the Spanish Humanist Sepúlveda had demonstrated in 1550 that the Indians were Aristotle's 'natural slaves';[5] and now it was Homer's turn. Bentley had suggested in 1713 that the *Iliad* had consisted originally of separate songs, and Vico in 1730 had carried the argument further with the theory that these songs had been by different writers. Five years later the Aberdeen professor, Thomas Blackwell, published a major study in which Homer's world was treated as an example of a primitive culture. Scholarship was working round to link the *Iliad* and *Odyssey* intimately with the society that had produced them. Its advance however was hampered by the distaste which the crudities of the primitive aroused in eighteenth-century minds, the polite distaste which had made La Motte and Pope feel that Homer needed rewriting in spite of his manifest excellence.

In the next generation this obstacle was removed thanks largely to a successful fake. One of Blackwell's pupils, James Macpherson, produced in 1762 what he claimed to be the translation of a Gaelic epic, and his 'Ossian' became one of the most popular books of the day. Its diction and incidental content, modelled largely on Homer, were what men had learnt to expect from an unsophisticated bard. But its heroes were morally admirable, unlike their Homeric counterparts, and the manners it depicted were suitably refined. It was a book in which the age could indulge its taste for the primitive without any qualms. Macpherson moreover was a militant patriot. His account of the Gaelic tribes was intended to glorify the historical origins of Scottish culture. He forged the link between primitivism and nationalist aspirations that was to characterize the Romantic period.

Critics who believed 'Ossian' to be authentic ended by maintaining that only a young and unsophisticated culture like the Gaelic or the Homeric could produce a really great poem. Herder told the world that as each race had its own language, so each had its own special form of poetry which was best exemplified in its popular ballads; and with the appearance of F. A. Wolf's *Prolegomena* (1795), which related the *Iliad* to a bardic tradition, the stage was set for the nineteenth-century study of folk art, of racial origins and early societies.

[5] Lewis Hanke, *Aristotle and the American Indians* (Bloomington and London, 1959).

The eighteenth century is not easy to bring into focus. Its scholars explored the Homeric world because they were fascinated by primitive cultures. Its writers and literary critics explored the possibilities of poetic fire and the sublime because they were impressed by the insights of the pseudo-Longinus. Montesquieu ransacked ancient history for materials on which to base his analysis of the nature of governments. The founding fathers of the United States studied the Greek leagues as possible models for a federal state. But these various enterprises, which had their own importance for the development of European culture, were then overshadowed by new kinds of interest in antiquity that emerged towards the end of the century.

The men of the Enlightenment accorded to the ancient world something of the respect that previous generations had given to the Bible. They liked to cite ancient precedents for aims that they had at heart. The American colonists rebelling against George III and later the French Jacobins both paraded a great admiration for Sparta. We find them holding up the simplicity and disciplined hardihood of the Spartans as the model that their contemporaries should follow.

Meanwhile, scholars with other interests were discovering a Greece that had an aesthetic message for mankind. Archeologists had laboured patiently since the fifteenth century assembling information about the surviving examples of ancient art; and then in the decades following the year 1700 the collectors took over. Men like Pope Clement XI (1700–21), his nephew Cardinal Albani, and the French Comte de Caylus bought lavishly, and they set up galleries where their treasures were displayed. Unfortunately these treasures were for the most part late Roman copies of Hellenistic works, so that when J. J. Winckelmann, the eccentric genius who was to popularize Greek art, settled in Rome (1755), his passion for antiquity was condemned to feed on the second-rate.

This man Winckelmann put forward the famous definition that the Greek genius was characterized by simplicity and a serene greatness, a half-truth that was to enjoy a tremendous vogue. He held that the Greeks were moved by strong passions, but controlled these and achieved a state of calm; and by what seems to us the oddest of choices, he suggested the Laocoon group as an example of this control. His views were attacked by the learned Lessing, who pointed out that they did not apply to literature, for the protagonists in Greek tragedies were often far from serene. But the charm of Winckelmann's conception was too strong for rational argument. Herder defended it, and Goethe, who was trying at this juncture to master the passions of his youth, followed Herder's lead. His *Iphigenia* (1783) transformed Euripides' unscrupulous heroine into a high-minded girl who was the perfect embodiment of spiritual control.

Goethe may have been the most eminent of Winckelmann's disciples, but he was not the only one. In France the cult of antiquity inspired a number of bad poets; at the same time, painters like Vien and J. L. David, the sculptor Canova and his English imitators, Nollekens and Flaxman, attempted to embody Winckelmann's ideals in works that aimed to be grand and simple. They created what the public of the nineteenth century was to think of as classical art: something chill, unrealistic, and grandiose. And in the case of David this art gained an additional element of unreality through its espousal of political aims. He was an eager partisan of the French Revolution, and many of his huge canvases depict ostentatious gestures in the cause of Liberty.

Surveying all this, one is tempted to dismiss Winckelmann's influence as generally harmful. But that would not be fair. What he said about Greece may have been misleading. But the enthusiasm he generated was not without value, and it laid the foundations of nineteenth-century Hellenism.

We have our first hint of this new Hellenism in a nostalgic poem about the gods of Greece that Goethe's contemporary, Schiller wrote in 1788. He mourns for an Arcadia, a Greek golden age when man's instincts and his love of beauty were fully satisfied; and this lyrical outburst was followed by a critical essay, *On naïve and sentimental poetry* (1794–5), in which Homer figured as the exemplar of the naïve, sensitive to nature, simple and direct. About the same time, the French poet, André Chénier, whose mother had been Greek, captured with remarkable success not only the clarity, but also the sensuousness and melancholy of the ancient poets. His conviction that pleasure however fleeting was the true purpose of life supplied that human element which the high-flown Hellenism of the Winckelmann period had lacked. Chénier's poems were not published till 1819, but in the meantime the implications of Schiller's theories for contemporary attitudes to ancient Greece were finding expression in the work of two writers whom he influenced: the poor madman, Hölderlin, and more unexpectedly, the later Goethe. They both nourished a vision of beauty that was not simply statuesque, but had a marked sensuous element, longed to see this beauty realized in the world around them, and admitted its realization to be impossible. Where the Goethe who had written *Iphigenia* had hoped to impose an ideal of Winckelmannian simplicity and serenity, the later Goethe linked a more sensuous awareness of what beauty had meant to the Greeks with a recognition of its fugitive character.

The struggles of these early Romantics laid the intellectual foundations for the Hellenism that their successors—men of smaller mental and emotional calibre—could then comfortably adopt. It centred on the dream of a Golden Age identified more or less certainly with the primitive beginnings of Greece, an age in touch with Nature, when human instincts found free satisfaction, and beauty was present on every side. Some thought of this Golden Age as attainable, if men were to return to a simpler manner of life. For others it was an ideal tinged with melancholy, for ever out of reach.

This picture was constructed of Greek elements, but it bears little resemblance to the one which a professional scholar derives from reading the classics and little resemblance to the Greece that Erasmus had contemplated. By the time we reach the nineteenth century, the classical education and the Hellenism of literary men had parted company. 'Greek', Dr. Johnson had said, 'is like fine lace. A man gets as much of it as he can.' Eighteenth-century schoolmasters like Joseph Warton had read Greek tragedies as a treat to their senior boys, and one Samuel Parr in his school at Stanmore had made his pupils act the *Trachiniae* and the *Oedipus Tyrannus*. But during the second half of the century this attitude, which made men cherish Greek as an elegant, but inessential accomplishment, gave way to a very different approach. The University of Cambridge had for some time followed the practice of awarding various medals and prizes for proficiency in classical studies, and now translation began to play an important part in the exercises set to the candidates. Ability to reproduce a passage from Burke in the style of Demosthenes, to make Hume write as Thucydides had written, emerged as the hallmark of scholarly achievement; and tests of that ability were adopted for the examinations held at Oxford under the new 1800 statutes and at Cambridge in the new Classical Tripos (1824). First in a few schools, such as Shrewsbury under Samuel Butler, but soon almost everywhere, the classical education of the day came to centre on what was called 'composition', that is, translation from English into Latin or Greek. Such exercises are easy to grade. Well done, they provide an almost infallible proof of intelligence, industry, and a boy's willingness to work along lines prescribed for him. The educational value of the effort expended in preparing for them could be questioned, but there is little doubt that they constituted a more effective instrument for picking out able youngsters than any previously devised. As the activities of the State expanded, the task of selecting competent persons for its service became increasingly important. A form of training which facilitated such selection was certain to flourish; and the classical education, which had been moribund for nearly a century after 1680, when Latin went out of use, took on a new character and a new lease of life.

It is enlightening to study the polemics in the debate between classics and science that was conducted in the nineteenth century. The champions on the classical side— Matthew Arnold is an obvious example—extol the merits of the ancient literatures, but have little to say on how these are taught. Their opponents concentrate on attacking the teaching, which they regard as useless and narrow. The two camps failed to find common ground, because they had not the same activity in mind. What the reading of Greek authors was able to give you at its best, and what it gave you under the auspices of a Benjamin Hall Kennedy, could not be usefully equated.

While the classical schools served a selection technique, literary Hellenism continued to propagate ideals which we see to have been desirable, but which their defenders pursued for the most part without considering their implications.

It is true that Matthew Arnold, writing in 1849, recognized natural beauty's inability to satisfy man's deepest needs and tried to solve the problems this produced. The hero of his *Empedocles on Etna* transcends the happiness Nature offers in the service of a higher purpose connected, it would appear, with creative energy. But Arnold was an exception. In the main, the current of ideas emanating from Schiller found expression in poems steeped in a nostalgic, sensuous longing, like Swinburne's imitations of Greek tragedy and Mallarmé's *L'après-midi d'un faune*: works intended to appeal to the emotions rather than the intellect. But then, as the end of the century approached, a new interest made itself felt.

Exploration had flourished during the Victorian Age; and by the 1870s there was enough information available about primitive societies to provide a basis for a new science—ethnography. Collected by amateurs, this information centred on the more picturesque aspects of primitive life. Religious practices had received particular notice; and that was an area where classical learning had a good deal to contribute. Soon ancient beliefs about the soul, the gods, the survival of the dead were being submitted to systematic analysis. J. G. Frazer related them to kindred material from other cultures. He brought a number of common motifs to light; and his *Golden Bough* (1890) caught the public imagination. Frazer's work in giving importance to myth was then carried further by Freud. In 1905, the latter advanced the hypothesis—familiar now to all of us—that infants are attracted to their mothers, jealous of their fathers, and that the neuroses of maturity often stem from this experience. He called the mechanism involved the 'Oedipus Complex', to emphasize that a universal and universally ostracized urge had found expression in a well-known ancient legend; and later he used the figure of Narcissus to exemplify yet another aberration of the sexual instinct. Simultaneously, his colleague and rival, Carl Jung, argued that the figures of mythology had their origins in a Collective Unconscious.

For Swinburne, myths had been pleasing traditional stories. For a writer in the first decades of the twentieth century, they wore a more serious face. They were thought to have expressed varieties of human experience that lay hidden from their creators' awareness. It became the fashion to base modern works on ancient stories. Some authors like Jean Cocteau in *La Machine infernale*, which he based on the Oedipus legend, kept the original characters and setting, but introduced a modern note and so lifted the legend out of time by references to night-clubs and the use of up-to-date slang. Others transferred the Greek story to a more recent setting. Eugene O'Neill's *Mourning becomes Electra* (1930) played out the drama of the *Oresteia* in a New England port at the close of the American Civil War. Anouilh located his Eurydice in present-day France. Jean Giraudoux in *La Guerre de Troie n'aura pas lieu* borrowed his characters from Homer, but then invented what was essentially a prelude to the *Iliad*; and, the strangest enterprise of all, James Joyce used the *Odyssey* to provide a shadowy framework for his novel, *Ulysses* (1922), establishing a series of uneasy parallels between the epic and the events of a Dublin day.

More important perhaps than the varied means by which the myths were introduced, were the varied purposes for which they were employed. The Oresteia story was used by O'Neill to illustrate Freud's Oedipus Complex, by T. S. Eliot to preach Christian repentance in *The Family Reunion* (1939), and by J.-P. Sartre to preach Existentialism in *Les Mouches*. The Frenchman, H. R. Lenormand (*Asie*, 1931), and the American, Sherwood Anderson (*The Wingless Victory*, 1936), transformed the Medea legend into attacks on racial prejudice. Giraudoux's *Guerre de Troie* was a lament over the imminence of the Second World War. In most of these works, the ancient legend and the modern aim failed to match with close exactitude. The products of our last classical revival are clever, often startling, but in the end they leave us uneasy. It is not surprising that after the 1950s this particular fashion should have drooped and died.

In the meantime, the twentieth century saw the decline of classical studies as an educational discipline. Up to the Second World War, this decline was slow. Interest shifted gradually to modern subjects and to science. Since 1945, it has been rapid. Of all forms of study, Latin and Greek benefited least from the vast post-war expansion of secondary education. The old ruling classes, selected on a basis of general ability, were being replaced by a meritocracy of

470 The Greek Legacy

experts, and the candidates for this meritocracy naturally
favoured subjects that opened the gates to some form of
expert knowledge: the sciences, mathematics, economics,
social and business studies.

Paradoxically however, this decline has come at a time
when our knowledge of the ancient world is more extensive
than ever before. Since the beginning of the nineteenth
century, scholarship has been making significant advances
and most particularly in those ancillary fields that have
so much to contribute to the study of Greek culture. Textual
critics, epigraphers, numismatists, archaeologists have perfected their techniques and assembled the vast works of
reference on which their success so much depends. Comparative philologists and art historians have opened up
new and fruitful fields of learning. Students of literature,
of history, and above all of the history of culture are
coming to realize how great a need they have for information
about the ancient languages and the ancient world. Greek
is no longer Dr. Johnson's fine lace, of which every man
wants as much as he can get. It is no longer an entrance
ticket to the upper layers of society. But there must be
a role for it in the educational system of the future; and
Greek literature will continue to exercise an influence over
those who come to read it.

When one considers our indebtedness to ancient Greece,
one is struck by the variety of the elements that were
borrowed. They include, for example, metaphysical and
ethical theories; mathematical procedures; literary, artistic,
and practical techniques; historical facts; and fictions which
range from the profoundly symbolic to the trivial. The
hypostases of Plotinus, the 'appropriate acts' of the Stoics,
Pythagoras' theorem, the dramatic unities, the three orders
of architecture, the words of command used on the barrack
square, the legend of Oedipus, and the story of the Ephesian
matron, all form part of the legacy of Greece. And one
is also struck by the way in which interest shifted over
the centuries from one set of these elements to another.
That the scientific and technical learning of the ancients
should have been neglected until Europe was ready to
use it appears natural enough. But the neglect of Scepticism
and Epicureanism until the fifteenth century, the relative
neglect of Homer until the seventeenth, the brief cult

of Heliodorus, the popularity of Plutarch and Lucian during the Renaissance and their subsequent disappearance from the canon of important authors are phenomena which are harder to explain. The reasons for a shift of interest are not always obvious, but the fact remains that for every generation Greece wore a different face, and there is no reason to suppose that we have come to the end of its potential metamorphoses.

Further Reading

F. B. Artz, *The Mind of the Middle Ages* (New York, 1954).

T. W. Baldwin, *Shakespere's small Latine and lesse Greeke* (2 vols., Urbana, 1944).

M. Boas, *The Scientific Renaissance* (London, 1962).

R. R. Bolgar, ed., *Classical Influences on European Culture 500–1500* (Cambridge, 1971).

R. R. Bolgar, *Classical Influences on European Culture 1500–1700* (Cambridge, 1976).

G. W. Bowersock, *Greek Sophists in the Roman Empire* (Oxford, 1969).

N. T. Burns and C. Reagan, eds., *Concepts of the Hero in the Middle Ages and the Renaissance* (Albany, 1975).

M. L. Clarke, *Classical Education in Britain 1500–1900* (Cambridge, 1959).

C. N. Cochrane, *Christianity and Classical Culture* (Oxford, 1940).

P. Courcelle, *Les Lettres grecques en Occident* (Paris, 1948).

D. Hay, *The Italian Renaissance* (Cambridge, 1970).

J. M. Hussey, *Church and Learning in the Byzantine Empire* (Oxford, 1957).

G. L. Laing, *Survivals of Roman Religion* (New York, 1931).

W. G. Langlois, ed., *The Persistent Voice: Essays on Hellenism in French Literature since the 18th Century* (Geneva, 1971).

P. O. Kristeller, *Renaissance Thought: the Classic, Scholastic, and Humanist Strains* (New York, 1961).

P. O. Kristeller, *Renaissance Concepts of Man* (New York, 1972).

K. Krumbacher, *Geschichte der byzantinischen Literatur* (2nd edn. Munich, 1897).

M. Manitius, *Geschichte der lateinischen Literatur des Mittelalters* (3 vols., Munich, 1911–31).

D. L. O'Leary, *How Greek Science passed to the Arabs* (London, 1949).

H. Peyre, *L'Influence des littératures antiques sur la littérature française moderne* (New Haven and Oxford, 1941).

F. J. E. Raby, *History of Christian Latin Poetry* (Oxford, 1937).

F. J. E. Raby, *History of Secular Latin Poetry in the Middle Ages* (Oxford, 1934).

L. D. Reynolds and N. C. Wilson, *Scribes and Scholars* (Oxford, 1968).

R. Sabbadini, *Le scoperte dei codici latini e greci ne' secoli XIV e XV* (2 vols., Florence, 1905, 1914).

J. E. Sandys, *A History of Classical Scholarship* (3 vols., Cambridge, 1908).

J. Seznec, *La Survivance des dieux antiques*, Warburg Inst. Studies xi (London, 1940; English trn. New York, 1953).

J. W. Thompson, *The Medieval Library* (Chicago, 1939).

H. Trevelyan, *Goethe and the Greeks* (Cambridge, 1941).

C. Vasoli, *La retorica e la dialettica del umanesimo* (Milan, 1968).

G. Voigt, *Die Wiederbelebung des classischen Altertums* (3rd edn. 2 vols., Berlin, 1893).

J. H. Whitfield, *Petrarch and the Renascence* (Oxford, 1943).

INDEX

OXFORD PAPERBACKS

THE GREEKS

KENNETH DOVER

In this lively, authoritative, and stimulating book one of our foremost Greek scholars shows what it meant and felt like to be Greek, and what the importance of the Greeks is to us today. He describes how they thought and lived, and examines their distinctive and rewarding approach to history, poetry, art, and philosophy. He makes clear how radically new and different Greek civilization was, and how, no matter how much we may have learned since their day, the way we think and organize our lives is still profoundly affected by Greek ideas.

OPUS

ANCIENT GREEK LITERATURE

KENNETH DOVER AND OTHERS

Kenneth Dover and three other classical scholars have collaborated in writing this new historical survey of Greek literature from 700 BC to AD 550. The book concentrates on the principal authors and quotes many passages from their work in translation. Attention is drawn both to the elements in Greek literature and attitudes to life which are unfamiliar to us, and to the elements which appeal most powerfully to succeeding generations. Although it is recognized that this appeal lies above all in the most creative and inventive period (700–300 BC), an account is given of the eight hundred years which followed, which saw the results of earlier inspirations. Poetry, tragedy, comedy, history, science, philosophy, and oratory are all examined through the available literature.

OXFORD PAPERBACKS

LORD ELGIN AND THE MARBLES

WILLIAM ST. CLAIR

The 7th Lord Elgin removed portions of the ancient sculptures from the Parthenon at the beginning of the last century, and sold them in 1816 to the British Museum where they still reside. *Lord Elgin and the Marbles* is the definitive historical account of the extraordinary circumstances in which the Marbles were acquired, of the tremendous impact which they made on modern appreciation of Greek art, and of the bitter reactions of Napoleon, Byron, and many others to their acquisition. In a new epilogue the author states the arguments for and against their return to Greece.

THE WORLD'S CLASSICS

THE NICOMACHEAN ETHICS

ARISTOTLE

Translated with an introduction by David Ross

In his best-known work on ethics, Aristotle sets out to discover the good life for man: the life of happiness or *eudaimonia*. He concludes that happiness is to be found in a virtuous life, that is, a life that follows the famous 'golden mean' between opposing extremes. The greatest happiness of all is to be found in a life of philosophical contemplation, though Aristotle allows that this is not for everyone.

PAST MASTERS

ARISTOTLE

JONATHAN BARNES

The influence of Aristotle, the prince of philosophers, on the intellectual history of the West is second to none. Jonathan Barnes has written a critical account of his fundamental teachings which places him in his historical context.

'With compressed verve, Jonathan Barnes displays the extraordinary versatility of Aristotle the great systematising empiricist.' *Sunday Times*

PAST MASTERS

PLATO

R. M. HARE

Even after twenty-three centuries, Plato's work remains the starting-point for the study of logic, metaphysics, and moral and political philosophy. But though his dialogues retain their freshness and immediacy, they can be difficult to follow. R. M. Hare has provided a short introduction to Plato's work that makes their meaning clear.

'in less than ninety pages [R. M. Hare] makes his monumental subject real, intelligible, and interesting'
Times Literary Supplement

PAST MASTERS

HOMER

JASPER GRIFFIN

The *Iliad* and the *Odyssey* stand at the very beginning of Greek literature. Much has been written about their origins and authorship, but Jasper Griffin, although he touches briefly on those questions, is here concerned with the ideas of the poems, which have had such an incalculable influence on the thought and literature of the West. He shows that each of the two epics has its own coherent and suggestive view of the world and of man's place within it.

'a brilliant little introduction' *The Times*

'Mr Griffin brings English scholarship up to date by bringing it firmly back to Homer.' *London Review of Books*

PUFFIN BOOKS

THE SEARCH FOR THE GOLDEN PUFFIN

In 1941, Merlin the magician saves a young man from a terrible fate. In return for his life, the young man has to promise to find the legendary Golden Puffin given to King Arthur by Merlin hundreds of years before. But his quest cannot begin for fifty years and by that time the young man is a grandfather!

When Anna and Ryan find Grandpa inventing a time-machine in his garden shed on New Year's Day 1991, they think he's crazy! But soon all three of them are off on the quest to find the Golden Puffin. To do this, they have to travel fifty years through time, stopping at each year to solve a puzzle set by Merlin. Each puzzle they solve correctly gives them a clue which will help them to find the Golden Puffin.

Now YOU can join Anna, Ryan and Grandpa and travel through time in your armchair time-machine. YOU can solve the puzzles and find out some amazing facts about the last fifty years at the same time. YOU will also have the chance of a lifetime to win an exact replica of the Golden Puffin itself.

Part story, part game, set in the real world of the last fifty years – 1941 to 1991 – fifty glorious Puffin years!

THE SEARCH FOR THE
GOLDEN PUFFIN

ILLUSTRATED BY STUART TROTTER

PUFFIN BOOKS

PUFFIN BOOKS

Published by the Penguin Group
Penguin Books Ltd, 27 Wrights Lane, London W8 5TZ, England
Penguin Books USA Inc., 375 Hudson Street, New York, New York 10014, USA
Penguin Books Australia Ltd, Ringwood, Victoria, Australia
Penguin Books Canada Ltd, 10 Alcorn Avenue, Toronto, Ontario, Canada M4V 3B2
Penguin Books (NZ) Ltd, 182–190 Wairau Road, Auckland 10, New Zealand

Penguin Books Ltd, Registered Offices: Harmondsworth, Middlesex, England

First published 1991
3 5 7 9 10 8 6 4

Text copyright © Complete Editions, 1991
Revised edition © Complete Editions, 1991
Illustrations copyright © Stuart Trotter, 1991
All rights reserved

Printed in England by Clays Ltd, St Ives plc